HANDBOOKS

D0292754

VIRGIN
ISLANDS

SUSANNA HENIGHAN POTTER

VIRGIN ISLANDS

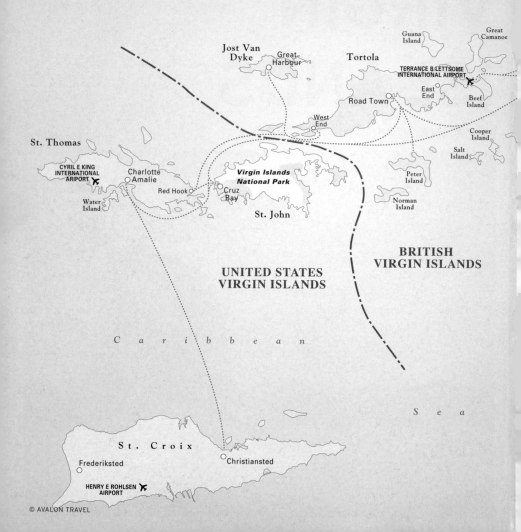

Jost Van Dyke
Great Harbour

Tortola

Guana Island
Great Camanoe

TERRANCE B LETTSOME INTERNATIONAL AIRPORT

East End

Beef Island

Road Town

West End

Cooper Island

Salt Island

St. Thomas

CYRIL E KING INTERNATIONAL AIRPORT

Charlotte Amalie

Virgin Islands National Park

Peter Island

Red Hook

Cruz Bay

Norman Island

Water Island

St. John

UNITED STATES VIRGIN ISLANDS

BRITISH VIRGIN ISLANDS

C a r i b b e a n

S e a

St. Croix

Frederiksted

Christiansted

HENRY E ROHLSEN AIRPORT

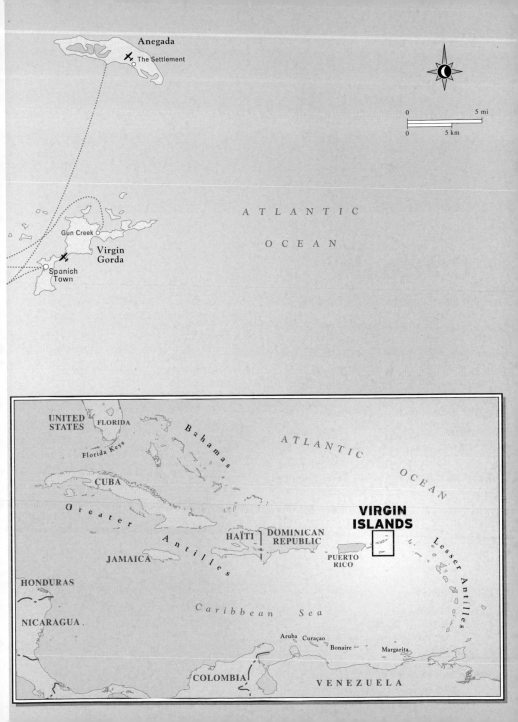

Contents

Discover
the Virgin Islands

The colors are the first things you notice in the Virgin Islands. The shimmering sea is a palette of blue, green, and purple. Bright white sand and green coconut palms create a picture so pleasing to the eye it is difficult to look away. When the sun shines brightly from above, the tropical colors intensify until they dance beneath the light.

At other times of day, color is more muted, but no less beautiful. At dawn, curls of orange and pink glow from behind the mountains. After the sun drops below the horizon in the evening, the sky turns a deep, dark blue so pure it could swallow you. At night, the sky is black—the perfect backdrop for the extravagance of stars above.

But the Virgin Islands are much more than beautiful. They are alive. Step off the plane and you are bombarded by the lyrical and seemingly indecipherable tongue of the islanders—an English awash with colorful phrases, colloquialisms, and a dialect that is part West African, part American, and part Caribbean. Study this language long enough and you have studied the Virgin Islands in their entirety.

One of the greatest things about the Virgin Islands is their sheer variety. Each island is distinct. You can immerse yourself in the pleasant bustle of St. Thomas's Charlotte Amalie, or choose to drop off the map on isolated Anegada. Pick your way through

St. Croix's numerous museums and historic attractions, or set sail from Tortola to one of the British Virgin Islands' remote cays.

Many visitors simply want respite and relaxation. And there is nothing wrong with that. Indeed, when the first travelers began "discovering" the Virgin Islands, emptiness and obscurity were their greatest attractions. Despite decades of growth, it is still possible to find the same quietude that so delighted the first visitors to the Virgin Islands. At the right places and the right times, there is a stillness so powerful it steadies your mind and heart. In the middle of the forest of St. John, on a quiet beach in St. Croix, or at the heart of a seaside village on Tortola the stillness surrounds you. Dust settles, no one moves, and the world pauses just long enough for you to notice.

Life exists in equal measure to this silence: comings and goings on the harbors; dancing under the stars; a delightful mélange of cultures; the exciting start of a regatta. The joy of the Virgin Islands is that you choose your proportions: two parts stillness, one part life, chill and serve. Yield: paradise.

Planning Your Trip

▶ WHERE TO GO

St. Thomas

Bustling, crowded, and commercial, St. Thomas is the hub of the Virgin Islands and the entry point for most travelers to the region. Historic Charlotte Amalie is the main attraction, although spectacular beaches like Magen's Bay and Smith Bay provide an escape from the city. Duty-free shopping for watches, jewelry, and crystal is a major draw for the millions of cruise ship passengers who visit here annually.

St. John

Rapid development has not spoiled St. John's natural beauty, protected—thankfully—by the Virgin Islands National Park. St. John has the best beaches in the U.S. Virgin Islands, and the best hiking in the whole archipelago. Accommodations range from beachfront campgrounds to high-end resorts. Laid-back Cruz Bay and even-more-laid-back Coral Bay provide an antidote to the outdoors with funky shops, hip restaurants, and buzzing bars.

St. Croix

The largest of the Virgin Islands, St. Croix offers an appealing balance of history, natural beauty, and culture. Christiansted and Frederiksted are classic West Indian harbor towns with exquisite Danish colonial architecture. Buck Island is an ideal place for hiking and snorkeling. A lush, damp rainforest is a perfect contrast to the sunny, sandy beaches, and divers come to explore the storied Wall off the island's north coast.

Tortola

Tortola is an island of steep hills, remarkable vistas, and quiet beaches. Delight in the exquisite white sand at Smuggler's Cove, hike through a tropical forest at Sage Mountain National Park, or admire tropical flowers and trees at the Joseph Reynold O'Neal Botanical Gardens. Nightlife is laid-back, except when full moon parties ignite the night with infectious Caribbean music and creative libations.

Virgin Gorda

At The Baths National Park giant boulders create grottos and pools that have delighted visitors for generations. On the other end of the island, North Sound is a sailor's paradise: a community without roads, where the fastest route between two points is over the water.

WHICH ISLAND IS FOR YOU?

If you're interested in...

- **a weekend getaway:** St. Thomas
- **beaches:** Virgin Gorda
- **nature:** St. John
- **authentic island culture:** St. Croix
- **an escape:** Anegada
- **sailing:** The Out Islands
- **beachside bars:** Jost Van Dyke
- **views:** Tortola
- **a family vacation:** St. John
- **romance:** Virgin Gorda
- **history:** St. Croix

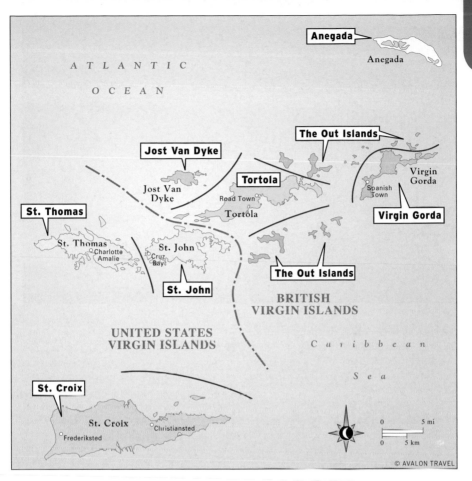

In between, find a series of unspoiled beaches and a quaint, neat, and friendly town. Gorda Peak National Park, home to the world's smallest lizard, is good for hiking.

Jost Van Dyke

This tiny island has more goats than people, and more visitors than year-round residents. Sailors especially delight in some of the best beach bars around. Great Harbour is picturesque—its main street is a sandy path lined by palm trees. White Bay is one of the

most beautiful beaches in the Virgin Islands. Offshore cays and little-known attractions, like Little Jost Van Dyke, Bubbly Pool, and Sandy Cay reward visitors who venture off the beaten path.

Anegada

The most unusual of the Virgin Islands, Anegada is a universe unto itself. Totally flat, very dry, and sparsely populated, Anegada is famous for its miles of sandy coastline, endangered iguanas, and the fresh lobsters fishers

Charlotte Amalie Harbor

harvest from reefs around the island. Anegada is also a sportfisher's mecca: Elusive bone-fish live in the shallows around the island, and wahoo, marlin, jack, and tuna patrol the nearby North Drop.

The Out Islands

A sailboat is the best way to explore the other islands of the BVI, including Norman Island, believed to be the inspiration for Robert Louis Stevenson's *Treasure Island*. Underwater ex-plorers can delight in the reef around the Dog Islands or the world-famous wreck of the RMS *Rhone*. World-class resorts on Peter Island, Guana Island, and Necker Island cater to visi-tors seeking peace, quiet, and exclusivity.

► WHEN TO GO

Prices, experiences, and weather vary consid-erably depending on the time of year you visit the Virgin Islands.

Winter (December–March) is the high sea-son, when North Americans and Europeans come to escape cold weather back home. This coincides with the dry season in the islands, and the season of the best sailing winds and coolest, most comfortable temperatures. If cost is no ob-ject, there is simply no better time to visit than when the weather is clear and sunny, the breezes blow, and there is a whole array of things to do.

During the summer (May–September), travelers will find bargains. Most hotels offer discounts of up to 40 percent during summer, and airfare tends to be less, too. It is hotter, and the winds tend to die down for sailing. Some establishments, including dive shops, museums, cultural centers, and stores, cut back their hours.

The so-called shoulder seasons (April, November) may be the best time of all to visit the islands, especially if you're on a budget. You'll typically enjoy pleasant weather (not

White Bay is one of the Virgin Islands' finest beaches.

too hot), lower prices (15–30 percent lower than winter rates), and fewer tourists (you'll have the beaches to yourself).

Also take into account the hurricane season (June–November). While you should not expressly avoid traveling to the Virgin Islands during the hurricane season, buy trip insurance if you do, especially for trips from August to October, the peak of the hurricane season. Flights are usually the first thing to be canceled when a storm approaches.

▶ BEFORE YOU GO

Passports

Citizens of the United States traveling to the U.S. Virgin Islands will not require a passport. Travelers to the British Virgin Islands do, however, need a passport with at least six months validity remaining.

Getting There and Around

Visitors to the Virgin Islands can fly directly to St. Thomas and St. Croix from several major American cities. You can also fly to San Juan, Puerto Rico, and catch a commuter flight to St. Thomas, St. Croix, Tortola (Beef Island), or Virgin Gorda. Visitors from Europe can also consider routing through Antigua, St. Maarten, or the Dominican Republic.

You should always make hotel (or charter boat) reservations ahead of time, and it's a good idea to reserve a car in advance, too, especially if you come in the high season. Other arrangements can be made once you get to the islands.

What to Take

When it comes to packing, light, loose-fitting clothes are best; pack a few long-sleeved shirts

A diver explores the Wreck of the RMS *Rhone*.

and light pants for the evenings, especially in the winter.

Nothing ruins a vacation faster than a ruined camera, so consider bringing a few disposable waterproof or underwater cameras for use near the water.

Be sure to prepare for the sun: Bring sunglasses, a wide-brimmed hat, lip balm with sun protection, and lots of reef-safe sunscreen. The chemical oxybenzone, commonly used in sunscreens, has been proven to negatively affect coral reefs, already under stress from disease, rising sea temperatures, pollution, and careless snorkelers and boaters. When you're stocking up, carefully check sunscreen labels and look for formulas whose active ingredients are zinc oxide or titanium dioxide instead.

Explore the Virgin Islands

▶ WEEKEND GETAWAY TO ST. THOMAS

Dip your toes into the Virgin Islands with a weekend getaway to St. Thomas. Sample the beaches, snorkeling, shopping, and dining, and return home revived and refreshed. Good air connections make this a practical choice for visitors from the eastern United States.

Day 1

Fly to Cyril E. King International Airport on St. Thomas. Check into your hotel near Charlotte Amalie. Get in sync with island living with a swim at Brewer's Bay Beach, and then ride a gondola up Havensight hill to take in the sunset from Paradise Point. Dine on creative cuisine at Craig and Sally's in Frenchtown and end the evening dancing to soca at The Green House on the waterfront.

Day 2

Begin this active day by swimming with sharks and touching sea turtles at Coral World Marine Park. Have a burger with your Funky Monkey at Duffy's Love Shack for lunch. Then head to Magen's Bay for an afternoon at the beach, where the sporty among you can try your hand at stand up paddleboarding. Mix it up with Latin-Asian fusion for dinner at Havana Blue.

Day 3

Stroll King's Quarter in historic Charlotte Amalie. Climb the narrow step streets to Blackbeard's Castle and tour historic townhouses. After a lunch of fried fish at Cuzzin's Caribbean Restaurant & Bar, go on a kayak and snorkel tour of the East End Marine

A kayaker explores East End Marine Sanctuary.

Sanctuary. End your day with a romantic dinner at the Old Stone Farmhouse.

Day 4

End your stay by relaxing over breakfast at Gladys' Cafe. Stroll Main Street and pick up a Virgin Islands hook bracelet as a souvenir before heading to the airport.

▶ FAMILY FUN ON ST. JOHN

St. John is a playground, and every child loves a playground. Beaches, hiking, snorkeling, and sailing provide diversions for all ages. Leave the iPad at home, but bring a camera to record your family's encounters with sea creatures like turtles, dolphins, rays, and conch. Eco-resorts and campgrounds are ideal for adventurous families; others may prefer the comforts of one of the island's two resorts.

Day 1

Fly to Cyril E. King International Airport on St. Thomas and take a ferry to St. John. Ride on the top deck for the views. Check into the campsite or hotel of your choice and go for a quick swim at the closest beach. Eat dinner at your hotel.

Day 2

Hit the beach. Make it an early start at Trunk Bay to beat the crowds. Follow the underwater snorkel trail and play in the sand. After lunch drive to Annaberg Plantation and tour the windmill ruins. Have dinner at Pavilion Restaurant at Maho Bay and watch the sunset.

Day 3

Hike or kayak. Take the National Park Service guided hike at Reef Bay, stopping at the petroglyphs on the way down, or take a

Salt Pond Bay on St. John's southeast tip is protected from waves and offers excellent snorkeling.

THE BEST BEACHES

Trunk Bay

What's a Virgin Islands vacation without a beach? There are hundreds of beaches in the Virgin Islands. There are small beaches and large beaches; pebbly beaches and fine-sand beaches; beaches with bars and restaurants and beaches with no human development at all. Some beaches have great snorkeling, others have great waves. Some are comfortable and easy, others awe-inspiring. Sometimes the best beach is the one closest to your hotel, but if you need more inspiration, check out these standouts.

U.S. VIRGIN ISLANDS

- **Trunk Bay, St. John:** Fluffy sand, picturesque coconut palms, and a charming offshore cay. This beach is as perfect as it gets.

- **Francis Bay, St. John:** Perfectly calm waters and magnificent sunsets are the rewards for those who seek out this off-the-beaten-track bay.

- **Magen's Bay, St. Thomas:** The finest beach on St. Thomas, this deep, heart-shaped bay is calm, expansive, and lined with a canopy of coconut palms.

- **Cane Bay, St. Croix:** A windmill ruin stands watch over this north coast beach with outstanding snorkeling and a fun-loving atmosphere.

- **Jack and Isaac Bays Preserve, St.** Croix: Protected and unspoiled, these twin beaches on St. Croix's east end are accessible only by foot and reward hikers with peace and solitude.

BRITISH VIRGIN ISLANDS

- **Long Bay, Beef Island:** An expansive half-moon bay is good for long walks, beach picnics, and watching the planes take off and land at the nearby airport.

- **Apple Bay, Tortola:** Hardly a beach, but it's where the surfers come for waves. Come here to watch them, plus the pelicans that dive for their dinner.

- **Spring Bay, Virgin Gorda:** This lesser known bay is littered with the same giant boulders as the Baths just down the road, but is far less crowded.

- **Loblolly Bay, Anegada:** Powder-white sand, excellent snorkeling, an endless horizon, cool hammocks, and an outstanding beachside restaurant. What more do you need?

- **White Bay, Jost Van Dyke:** So picturesque it seems unreal, this delectable bay has powdery sand, an offshore reef, and a handful of friendly beach bars. You can also camp under the palm trees.

Cinnamon Bay beach on St. John's North Shore

kayak-snorkel tour of the remote East End. Sample St. John–style barbecue at Uncle Joe's Bar-B-Q for dinner.

Day 4

Take a day sail to the Baths on Virgin Gorda. Keep a tally of all the fish you see while snorkeling, and learn the parts of a boat. Take a detour to southeast Asia at Rhumb Lines for dinner.

Day 5

Spend the day in Coral Bay. Take a morning trail ride through the forest at Carolina Corral. Bring a picnic to Salt Pond Bay. Snorkel the reef and take the short hike to

Drunk Bay for beachcombing. Have dinner at Cafe Concordia or, if it's pizza night, the M&M Donkey Diner.

Day 6

Spend the day at Cinnamon Bay. Hike the half-mile nature trail, visit the archaeology museum, and relax on the beach. The more active among you can try your hand at windsurfing or kayak out to Cinnamon Cay. Get dressed up for dinner at the Lime Inn.

Day 7

Go for a morning swim before catching the ferry back to St. Thomas for your flight home.

THE BEST SNORKELING

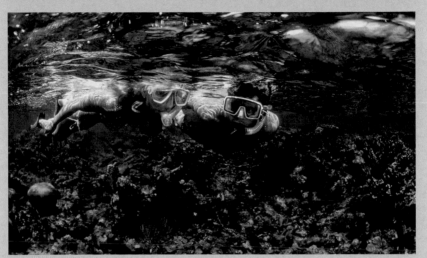

Snorkelers explore a reef in the U.S. Virgin Islands.

Good snorkeling is in the eye of the beholder, but most people gravitate to reefs. It's here, after all, where you will see the greatest diversity of fish, marine life, and coral. But sea grass and mangrove habitats are also fun to explore.

U.S. VIRGIN ISLANDS

- **East End Marine Sanctuary, St. Thomas:** A small human-made reef off Cas Cay attracts a wide variety of fish, and the mangroves are home to tiny juveniles of every shape and color.

- **Coki Beach, St. Thomas:** The reef here is easy to access and teems with colorful fish, from angels to doctors.

- **Waterlemon Cay, St. John:** The reef that encircles this small offshore cay is a cornucopia of marine life, from squid to parrot fish to the waterlemon shark that give this spot its name. Don't overlook the sea grass beds at nearby Leinster Bay, habitat for turtles, conch, and sea stars.

- **Salt Pond Bay:** Swim along the rocky edge to a magical underwater landscape populated by schools of tiny angelfish.

- **The Frederiksted Pier:** The old Frederiksted pier was destroyed in Hurricane Hugo in 1989, and now it's a fabulous reef.

BRITISH VIRGIN ISLANDS

- **Smuggler's Cove, Tortola:** An easy offshore reef near the western end of the beach is a good snorkel stop for beginners.

- **Around the Bight, Norman Island:** There are a half-dozen excellent snorkel spots near the Bight: Beginners will delight in the reef just off the beach, while the more adventurous explore **The Indians** and **The Caves.**

- **Loblolly Bay, Anegada:** Explore the inner edge of the **Horseshoe Reef** and find huge brain coral and sea fans.

- **Sandy Spit, Jost Van Dyke:** Schools of bright blue tang patrol this underwater garden, best visited on a calm day.

- **Dog Islands:** Head to this cluster of islands lying between Virgin Gorda and Tortola with a snorkel guide to explore some of the healthiest reefs in the Virgin Islands.

▶ CARIBBEAN LIFE: AUTHENTIC ST. CROIX

St. Croix is the largest and least-traveled of the Virgin Islands. It also offers the greatest variety to its visitors, including outstanding historical sites and untouched natural areas. But you may enjoy the St. Croix sensibility—which prizes authenticity—most of all.

Day 1

Fly to St. Croix and check into a hotel near Christiansted. Spend a few hours on Protestant Cay beach before dinner at Savant.

Day 2

Take a day trip to Buck Island. Snorkel the reef, hike the peak, and sun on the beach. Stroll the Christiansted boardwalk before dinner and down a few microbrews at the Fort Christian Brew Pub.

Day 3

Spend the morning sightseeing around Christiansted National Historic Site. Tour the fort and browse the shops. Choose between French cuisine at Cafe Christine or West Indian specialties at Harvey's for lunch. Eat an early dinner and then paddle the bioluminescent bay at Salt River just after sunset.

Day 4

Rent a car and hit the road. Head east to Point Udall and then pass through cattle country along the southern shore. Sample St. Croix–style barbecue at the La Reine Chicken Shack before heading west to Frederiksted. Go for an afternoon swim at Sprat Beach and watch the sunset.

Day 5

This is your history day: tour the great house at Whim Plantation Museum; learn about St. Croix's first family of cattle at the Lawaetz Family Museum; and study the history of

The Customs House is part of Christiansted National Historic Site.

SUNKEN SHIPS AND PLANTATIONS PAST

The Virgin Islands' astounding beauty has long overshadowed their unique history—at least in the eyes of most visitors. But for people interested in learning about the islands' fascinating past, there is plenty to see and do. St. Croix is the best base for historical and cultural exploration.

ST. THOMAS
Downtown Charlotte Amalie is a pleasant jumble of historic buildings, cobbled alleyways, and converted sugar warehouses. Explore **King's Quarter:** climb **99 Steps** to **Blackbeard's Castle.** Admire **Fort Christian,** a red-brick fortress on the St. Thomas waterfront, and visit the **St. Thomas Synagogue,** one of the oldest synagogues in the Western Hemisphere. Take a kayak tour to **Hassel Island** to tour old forts and the remains of a fascinating marine railroad.

ST. JOHN
Annaberg Plantation, deep within the Virgin Islands National Park, is a quiet reminder of St. John's plantation past. The **petroglyphs** in Reef Bay were carved by the hands of prehistoric residents of St. John; learn more about them at the archaeology lab at **Cinnamon Bay.**

ST. CROIX
Christiansted is an exquisite Danish colonial harbor town. Tour **Fort Christiansvaern,** a yellow fortress on the waterfront, and admire the lovely St. Croix Government House. Search for the place where U.S. Treasury Secretary Alexander Hamilton was raised, and learn about the pre-Columbian peoples at the **St. Croix Archaeology Museum.**

See **Salt River Bay,** where Christopher Columbus landed during his second voyage to the Caribbean, and then take a guided hike to **Maroon Ridge,** where escaped slaves lived in the remote hills before emancipation.

In the countryside, count the number of windmill ruins you can spot and tour an elegant restored great house at **Whim Plantation Museum.** Head to the foothills of the rainforest to see a St. Croix-style farmhouse at the **Lawaetz Family Museum.** Stand beneath a **baobab tree,** planted by slaves at Estate Butler Bay.

In St. Croix's second city, Frederiksted, you will find its most picturesque fort, the red-brick **Fort Frederik. Fort Frederik Museum** recounts the story of St. Croix's successful slave uprising, which culminated here.

TORTOLA
In Road Town, three museums tell of the BVI's history: **Old Government House Museum** is a monument to its colonial past, while the **Virgin Islands Folk Museum** and the **Lower Estate Sugar Works Museum** celebrate the culture and accomplishments of native Virgin Islanders.

On an island tour, drive past the **Fahie Hill Mural,** which depicts life on the island before widespread development.

Breathe the rum-soaked air at **Callwood Rum Distillery,** where little has changed in the manufacture of rum in more than 200 years. Take a picnic lunch to **Mount Healthy National Park,** the site of Tortola's only remaining windmill ruin.

VIRGIN GORDA
Drive out to **Coppermine Point** to see the ruins of a mining operation built by Cornish miners.

SALT ISLAND
Dive the **wreck of the RMS *Rhone*** off the coast of Salt Island. Come ashore at Salt Island to see what remains of a traditional island settlement and to visit the windswept burial ground of the *Rhone* victims.

ANEGADA
See a collection of coins, tools, crockery, and other remnants of ships wrecked on Anegada's treacherous reef at **Pomato Point Museum.**

slavery and freedom at Fort Frederik Museum. Your midday pit stop is Rastafarian-style vegetarian food at UCA Kitchen in Frederiksted.

outstanding views at Maroon Ridge, or exquisite beaches at Jack and Isaac Bay Preserve. Stroll along Cane Bay beach at sunset and then have dinner at eat @ cane bay.

Day 6
Go for a guided hike through St. Croix's wilderness with Ay-Ay Eco Hikes and Tours. Choose between the lush, tropical rainforest,

Day 7
Stop for a tour of the Cruzan Rum Distillery on your way to the airport for your flight home.

▶ TEN-DAY SAILING ADVENTURE

Renting your own sailboat, with or without a skipper, is the ultimate Virgin Islands vacation. You choose your own schedule, unfettered by ferry timetables. Quiet coves and empty beaches are yours. And the view from your deck is different each morning. Trade winds, mild weather, and generally calm conditions make the Virgin Islands favorable for sailing, and the British Virgin Islands are the epicenter of the charter yacht industry.

Types of Charter Vacations

Crewed charters come with a full crew, usually a captain, cook, and mate, who take care of all the work. Your only responsibility is to decide what you want to do each day—and even that can be delegated.

Bareboat charters are the most popular kind of charter vacation in the Virgin Islands. Bareboating simply means chartering without a crew, although it is common to hire a skipper for the peace of mind.

Sandy Spit, off Jost Van Dyke, is a popular stop for swimming and snorkeling.

Fishermen travel to the North Drop near Anegada to pursue wahoo, marlin, and other prized species of large fish.

The Baths National Park is one of the Virgin Islands' most popular destinations.

When to Charter

The best time for sailing in the Virgin Islands is winter (November–April), when winds average 15–20 knots from the northeast. In spring and summer the winds slack off to 10–18 knots, although this can still be a nice time to sail. Avoid chartering August–October, when the weather tends to be unsettled and the chances of a hurricane are greatest.

Costs

The high-season cost of a two-cabin bareboat (sleeping up to six people) begins at about $4,000 per week. Additional costs to consider are provisioning, insurance, and a skipper (from $180 per day).

Average prices for a week-long crewed yacht are $2,000 per person for a monohull; $2,500 per person for a catamaran; and $3,500 per person for a power yacht.

In summer, rates generally go down 20–30 percent.

Booking a Crewed Charter

Call the Charter Yacht Society of the BVI (284/494-6017, www.bvicrewedyachts.com) for help matching your party with the perfect boat. BVI Yacht Charters (Road Town, 284/494-4289 or 888/615-4006, www.caribbeancruisingvacation.com) represents a number of crewed BVI yachts. In the U.S. Virgin Islands, contact the Virgin Islands Charter Yacht League (340/774-3944, www.vicl.org).

You can also use a charter yacht broker such as Swift Yacht Charters (508/647-1554, www.swiftyachts.com) or Ed Hamilton and Co. (207/882-7855 or 800/621-7855, www.ed-hamilton.com).

Bareboat Charter Companies

BVI CHARTER COMPANIES

The largest charter yacht company on Tortola is The Moorings (Wickham's Cay II, 284/494-2331, 727/535-1446, or 888/952-8420, www.moorings.com). Its fleet features 32- to 52-foot

OFF THE WATER: FORESTS AND PARKS

hiking at Shark Bay National Park

Away from the water, the Virgin Islands are a fascinating and richly diverse landscape: rocky bluffs and wide plains; mountain peaks and dry seaside forests; salt ponds and rainforest. Within these habitats dwell yellow-breasted bananaquits and menacing chickenhawks, handsome white-tail deer and alien-looking iguanas, as well as a mind-boggling array of life forms uniquely adapted to the tropical climate: ancient trees, knobby cactus, fast-growing fungi. Pack a pair of walking shoes, a water bottle, and a sense of adventure to get up close to the natural world away from the ocean.

U.S. VIRGIN ISLANDS

· **Virgin Islands National Park:** Covering almost three-quarters of St. John, no natural area is more diverse or important than Virgin Islands National Park. The **Reef Bay Trail** cuts through moist and dry tropical forests before arriving at the Reef Bay ruins, now a habitat for native bats. Bird-watchers will enjoy an outing to **Francis Bay,** where a salt pond attracts local and migratory birds. Hike **L'Esperance Trail** to find the only known **baobab tree** on St. John. The scent of bay rum colors the air at **Cinnamon Bay,** a moist forest where you will see numerous specimens of the Virgin Islands' only native palm tree.

· **Buck Island, St. Croix:** Buck Island is known mostly as a snorkeling destination, but hike to the top of the island and you will pass through a dry tropical forest

where naturalists have catalogued more than 180 native plant species.

· **St. George Village Botanical Garden:** Stroll the lovingly maintained trails at this expansive garden built around the ruins of an old plantation. View showy tropical flowers, local fruit trees, a cactus garden, and medicinal herbs.

· **Magen's Bay Trail, St. Thomas:** Hike through a dry forest down the valley to beautiful Magen's Bay. Look for the telltale red bark of the turpentine tree and listen for the rustle of lizards in the undergrowth.

BRITISH VIRGIN ISLANDS

· **Sage Mountain National Park:** The highest peak in the Virgin Islands, Sage Mountain is home to old-growth forest untouched since the times of Columbus. Hike past giant elephant ears, magnificent mahoganies, tree ferns, and air-dwelling bromeliads.

· **Shark Bay National Park:** Look for bats in the bat cave and hike through a boulder-strewn landscape. Keep your eyes open for colorful butterflies and bananaquits, attracted to the fruit of the pipe organ cactus.

· **Gorda Peak National Park:** The park at the top of Virgin Gorda is home to the smallest lizard in the world; you may not spot one, but you're sure to see dozens of hermit crabs shuffling around the undergrowth of this lush forest.

· **Sandy Cay, Jost Van Dyke:** This tiny island has it all: dry tropical forest, rocky bluffs, a small salt pond, and a sandy beach. A nature trail circles the island and takes you on a whirlwind tour of Virgin Islands ecosystems.

· **Anegada Outback:** The wilds of Anegada are unlike any other place in the Virgin Islands. A mysterious landscape of frangipani trees, century plants, and wild orchids, the dry scrubby bush that blankets the island is at first glance uninviting—but venture in and you will be delighted.

monohulls and catamarans with 2–5 cabins. Yachts in its exclusive line are less than two years old; the club line features older boats.

Sunsail (Wickham's Cay II, 284/495-4740 or 888/350-3568, fax 284/495-1767, www.sunsail.com) is the second biggest fish in the BVI charter yacht market, known as a better value than the Moorings.

Smaller charter companies include family-operated Conch Charters (Fort Burt Marina, Road Town, 284/494-4868 or 800/521-1989, www.conchcharters.com); Voyage Charters (Soper's Hole Marina, 284/494-0740 or 410/956-1880, www.voyagecharters.com); and Tortola Marine Management (Road Reef, 284/494-2751 or 800/633-0155, www.sailmm.com).

USVI CHARTER COMPANIES

CYOA Yacht Charters (Frenchtown Marina, 340/777-9690 or 800/944-2962, www.cyoacharters.com) has a fleet of monohull, catamaran, and power yachts. Locally owned and operated, Island Yachts (Red Hook,

340/775-6666 or 800/524-2019, www.iyc.vi) gets high marks for its personalized service.

Setting Sail

DAY 1
Fly to Terrance B. Lettsome International Airport, Beef Island. Check in with your charter boat company, provision your yacht, and receive your safety briefing.

DAY 2
Sail to Jost Van Dyke with a pit stop for snorkeling at Sandy Spit. Head to Foxy's Taboo for lunch, and then hike to the Bubbly Pool. In the afternoon, sail around to White Bay for a Painkiller. Eat dinner on your boat.

DAY 3
Sail along Tortola's north shore to Trellis Bay, Beef Island. Pick up a mooring and dinghy ashore to browse the local art and pick up locally grown produce at Aragorn's Studio. Snorkel the reef at Marina Cay and have dinner at The Last Resort.

Loblolly Bay on Anegada's North Shore is the island's best bet, with excellent snorkeling just offshore.

DAY 4

Sail to North Sound, Virgin Gorda. Pick up a mooring and dinghy in to the beach at Prickly Pear Island. Hike the nature trail. Dine at Biras Creek Resort.

DAY 5

Rent a car and tour Virgin Gorda. Drive out to Coppermine Point and past Gorda Peak. Admire the village of Spanish Town on your way to The Baths National Park. Stop at Savannah Bay for a swim and take the Nail Bay Road back to North Sound. Have dinner at Saba Rock Resort.

DAY 6

Set sail to Anegada. Take a taxi to Loblolly Bay for snorkeling and a cocktail. In the evening, dine on Anegada lobster at one of the seaside restaurants along the island's southern coast.

DAY 7

Go for a morning swim at Cow Wreck Beach before setting sail to Cooper Island. Dine at Cooper Island Beach Club in the evening.

DAY 8

Rendezvous with a dive operator, and snorkel or dive the RMS *Rhone*. Stop at Salt Island to visit the *Rhone* graves and hike to Lee Bay. Before sunset, sail to Norman Island and pick up a mooring. Have dinner at Pirate's Bight.

DAY 9

Snorkel with colorful fish at Kelly's Cove and look for darkness-dwelling creatures at The Caves. After lunch at the *Willy T*, sail back to Road Town, Tortola. Check into a hotel and watch the sunset over dinner at Bananakeet Café in Carrot Bay. Stop in at Cane Garden Bay on your way back for live music and dancing under the stars.

DAY 10

Check out of your hotel and head to Beef Island for your flight home.

ST. THOMAS

St. Thomas is an inkblot, about 12 miles long and 3 miles wide. It is the second largest of the U.S. Virgin Islands but the most populous. A steep spine stretches from east to west, with the highest point at Crown Mountain, on the western third of the island.

The island's long history has left historic attractions dating back to the earliest days of colonization—venerable churches and forts that bring an old-world ambiance to Charlotte Amalie. The capital is one of the West Indies' most picturesque cities, with layers of elegant townhouses, narrow cobblestone walks, and handsome churches and businesses.

As the islands' center of business, commerce, services, and transport, St. Thomas long ago lost the quiet island feel of the other Virgin Islands. This is the "big city" of the Virgins—the place where people come to shop, celebrate, and meet up. The crystal blue water is abuzz with cruise ships, ferry boats, fishing skiffs, mega-yachts and seaplanes. Modern comforts including a large movie theater, fast-food restaurants, and shopping malls, will appeal to travelers who want to maintain a link to a familiar American culture. At the same time, for those who call this island home, Charlotte Amalie is still a small town where everyone knows one another.

Despite development, St. Thomas is not without natural beauty. Magen's Bay, broad, calm, and over a mile long, is quite possibly

© SUSANNA HENIGHAN POTTER

ST. THOMAS

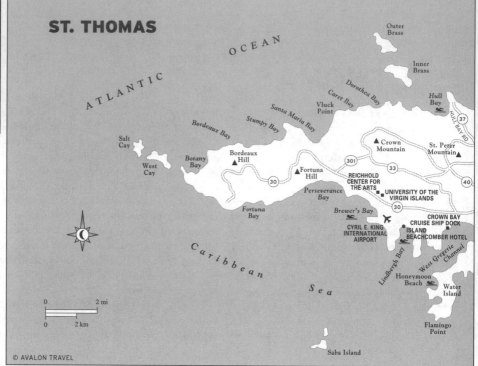

the most beautiful beach in the Virgin Islands. Coki Point attracts snorkelers and divers, and Smith Bay is an all-natural escape rivaling the unspoiled beaches of St. John and Tortola. You can also head off the beaten path to St. Thomas's western end and drive through the winding, narrow mountain roads that pass vistas rivaling any in the Virgin Islands.

PLANNING YOUR TIME

You can see St. Thomas's major sights in a few days, but plan to stay longer if you want to sample all the restaurants, attractions, and duty-free shopping, as well as have time for a day trip to one of the other Virgin Islands. St. Thomas enjoys the best air connections of all the Virgin Islands, with direct flights from a

half-dozen major U.S. cities, making a long weekend here doable.

St. Thomas is one of the most popular cruise ship stops in the Caribbean— recent years have seen upwards of 1.9 million cruise ship passengers passing through annually, or 35 times the population of the island itself. From Thanksgiving to Easter, the island is marked by traffic jams, and many sights are swamped by caravans of slow-moving taxis, weighted down with visitors off their ships. Plan your days to avoid popular sights like Magen's Bay, Drake's Seat, and the shops of Charlotte Amalie between 10 A.M. and 2 P.M., the height of the cruise ship day. Equally, be aware that many attractions close entirely on days when no cruise ship is in port.

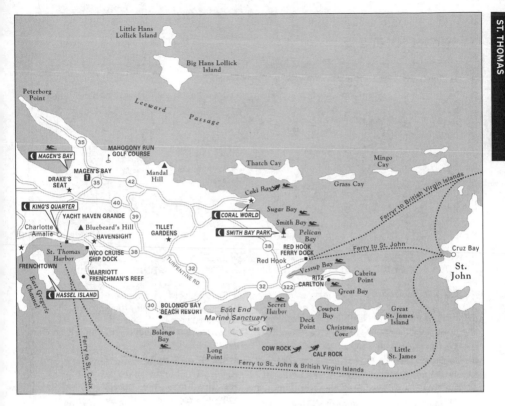

Where to Stay

Most visitors to St. Thomas stay at the large chain resorts along the beaches of the eastern and southern coast, and if resort lifestyle and a beach setting are your priorities, this is a fine choice. But also consider historic Charlotte Amalie, where travelers will find a number of small, independent hotels, many with excellent views of Charlotte Amalie Harbor and all of them steeped in the city's unique old-world ambience. You will want a rental car to explore the island, travel to the beach, and get around town at night, when street crime can be a problem.

Day Trips

St. Thomas is an easy day trip from St. Croix, St. John, and Tortola; it's not quite so easy, but doable, from Virgin Gorda and Jost Van Dyke. If you are flying into St. Thomas but headed to one of the other islands, consider adding a night in St. Thomas at the end of your trip: you'll get better flight connections and have a chance to see some sights.

If you are staying on St. Thomas, it's easy to plan day trips to Tortola, Virgin Gorda, Jost Van Dyke, St. John, or St. Croix, whether by ferry or by signing up with a day sail operator.

Ferries to St. John (15 minutes, 18 trips daily, $12 round-trip), Tortola (30 minutes, 5 trips daily, $45 round-trip), Jost Van Dyke (45 minutes, 1 trip daily, $70 round-trip) and Virgin Gorda (1 hour, 1 trip on Tuesdays, Thursdays, Saturdays and Sundays only, $80 round-trip) depart from the large **public ferry**

HIGHLIGHTS

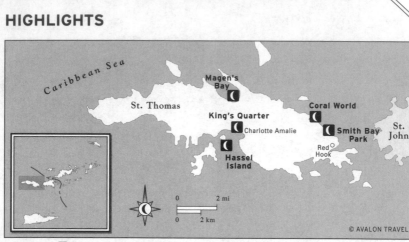

© AVALON TRAVEL

LOOK FOR **(** TO FIND RECOMMENDED SIGHTS, ACTIVITIES, DINING, AND LODGING.

(King's Quarter: The heart of historic Charlotte Amalie, King's Quarter is a neighborhood of narrow cobblestone walks, old forts, and peaceful parks (page 32).

(Hassel Island: Paddle out to Hassel Island to explore old forts and the remains of a marine railway and to enjoy unbeatable views of picturesque Charlotte Amalie (page 37).

(Magen's Bay: The jewel of St. Thomas has more than a mile of packed white sand, coconut palms, and clear water (page 41).

(Coral World: This family-friendly ocean park makes it easy to enjoy the wonders of the undersea environment. Come here to see sea turtles, rays, sharks, iguanas, colorful fish, and much more (page 42).

(Smith Bay Park: A small crescent bay fringed with coconut palms and sea grape trees, this enchanting beach, also called Lindqvist Bay, is an escape (page 44).

terminal in **Red Hook.** Passports are required for trips to any of the British Virgin Islands.

You can also catch ferries from **Charlotte Amalie** to St. John (45 minutes, 3 trips daily, $24 round-trip), Tortola (45 minutes, 10 trips daily, $45 round-trip) and St. Croix (90 minutes, 2 trips on Fridays and Saturdays, 1 trip on Sundays and Mondays, $90 round-trip).

Current schedules, fares, and telephone numbers for the half-dozen ferry operators are found in the free *St. Thomas–St. John This Week* tourist magazine, available all over the island. Advance reservations are not necessary except for the Jost Van Dyke and Virgin Gorda

trips operated by **Inter-Island Boat Services** (340/776-6597), but it is always a good idea to call ahead on the day of your trip to confirm the schedule.

A **seaplane daytrip** to St. Croix may be the highlight of your vacation: taking off and landing on the water will certainly give you something to talk about. The 15-minute flight from Charlotte Amalie to Christiansted on **Seaborne Airlines** (www.seaborneairlines.com, 340/773-6442) ranges $100–150 one-way. Advance reservations are required.

If you'd rather not fuss with ferry schedules and routes, go on a **day sail** outing. Most

CRUISING TO FORTUNE?

By design, no island in the Virgins is as touched by cruise ships as St. Thomas. Some 1.9 million cruise ship passengers come to the island annually, three times the number of overnight tourists who visit. A full three-quarters of all cruise ships departing from the United States stop at St. Thomas, and it is the most visited cruise ship destination in the Caribbean.

Cruise ships represent the bread and butter of the St. Thomas economy. Taxi drivers, excursion companies, downtown shops, and roadside vendors depend on the constant traffic of cruise ship passengers for a livelihood. The industry is credited with bringing in 40 percent of the USVI's tourism revenue. Surveys have shown that the average cruise ship party of two spends more than $550 during a day on St. Thomas, more than in any other cruise ship port.

Cruise ships are an important source of revenue for the local government, too. Ships pay a $7.50 head tax for each cruise ship passenger they bring to the island. Revenue from these taxes is used to finance expensive port development projects required by bigger and bigger cruise ships, such as the $31 million Austin "Babe" Monsanto Marine Terminal at Crown Bay, which opened in 2006. Between Crown Bay and WICO dock at Havensight, the island can now accommodate six cruise ships at dock, and additional ships may anchor in the harbor on especially busy days.

Cruise ships have a social and cultural impact on the island, too. While Charlotte Amalie feels like a bustling city during the day, it can be a ghost town at night after the ships have sailed away. The popularity of St. Thomas as a cruise ship destination has encouraged the development of a more gimmicky tourism product there, one that tends to exploit popular misperceptions and stereotypes of the Caribbean rather than break them down. Equally, the size of the cruise sector has led many islanders to develop a narrow view of what tourists are and can be. The end result: fewer opportunities for meaningful exchange of culture between visitor and resident.

outfitters depart from Red Hook and head to St. John, Jost Van Dyke, or Norman Island, with a few making the longer journey to Virgin Gorda. A typical day sail involves one or two snorkel stops plus a stop at a beach bar for drinks. Lunch is sometimes served on board; other times you will go ashore for the mid-day meal. Most day sail operators are based in St. John; Check the listings in that chapter for the greatest number of options or look for the many handbills around Red Hook, the sailing hub of St. Thomas. Day sails are typically booked at least a few days in advance and cost between $90–150 per person.

Sights

Explore Charlotte Amalie on foot or by taxi. The rest of the island is best explored by car. The countryside is largely developed, with the exception of the west end. Highways are generally well maintained, but routes are confusing and traffic can be very heavy. Drivers make liberal use of their horns and hand gestures to communicate with other drivers.

To reach the island's east end, take Route 30 (Frenchman's Bay or Bovoni Road), which follows the southeastern coast, runs into Route 32 (Red Hook Road), and continues along the shoreline (past the best beaches and large resorts) before becoming Route 30 (Smith Bay Road). To get to the north shore, take Route 35 (Mafolie Road) and follow it to Magen's Bay. Route 40 (Valdemar Hill Drive, also called Skyline Drive) follows the island's backbone from Charlotte

Amalie to the east end. Take Route 30 as far west as you dare to explore the west end.

CHARLOTTE AMALIE

The capital of the U.S. Virgin Islands, this harbor town is one of the loveliest in the region. The wide bay plays host to huge cruise ships, pleasure boats, luxury mega-yachts, and the small skiffs of traditional fishers. Long narrow warehouses, built to store hogsheads of sugar, line the waterfront and have been converted into one of the largest shopping districts in the Caribbean. Behind the shops, quiet side streets evoke the town's long history.

Visitors with a taste for history can amble along narrow alleys to the top of Government or Denmark Hills for a view of the historic district. Old churches, many of which date to the early days of Danish colonization, are among the most distinctive landmarks. Fortifications around the historic town have been converted into tourist attractions and provide some of the best views of the harbor.

Those with a preference for commerce can browse the glitzy shops on Main Street, which boast large selections of duty-free jewelry, perfume, liquor, crystal, and other fine wares. Even nonshoppers will appreciate the ambience of the old warehouse buildings and the narrow cobblestoned walks between them.

Charlotte Amalie is also a hub for dining, entertainment, and nightlife. Dozens of restaurants cater to all tastes, and during the annual St. Thomas Carnival a colorful parade makes its way up Main Street.

Orientation

There are three main roads in Charlotte Amalie. Waterfront Drive, also called Veteran's Drive, fronts the harbor and extends from Havensight Mall to Frenchtown. This four-lane road is best navigated by car or taxi. Main Street, also called Dronningen's Gade and Norre Gade, runs parallel to the waterfront.

Back Street, also called Wimmelskafts Gade, is one block farther inland, also parallel to the shoreline. The town's street names are remnants of the island's Danish past.

Parking is available at the large public lot near Fort Christian. From 7 A.M. to 6 P.M. Monday–Friday, you pay $1 for the first hour and $0.75 for each additional hour, or $5 for the whole day. Parking after hours and on weekends is free.

Explore Charlotte Amalie in the morning or late afternoon for the best experience. The noonday sun combined with slow-moving taxis that congest Main Street detract from the overall experience at other times of day. The town must be explored on foot—traffic is just too tight and parking too scarce to attempt driving, except at night, when street crime can be a problem.

History

Charlotte Amalie was founded in 1781, when four artisans built homes next to the new Fort Christian and were granted licenses to operate inns. The settlement was named after the Danish queen, but for the first century of its existence, Charlotte Amalie was better known as Taphuus (meaning "pub"). That probably says a lot. Early visitors described it variously as a freewheeling and exciting place, or as a den of pirates and scoundrels.

Charlotte Amalie grew steadily after its establishment. Warehouses were built on long narrow lots, which allowed for the most efficient use of the valuable waterfront. Homes were built on the hillward side of Main Street, and the residential portion of town steadily expanded up Denmark and Government Hills and in the valley between them. Authorities did not manage this growth, and many homes were built very close together along narrow, precarious lanes. In the mid-1700s it became clear that additional residential space would be required in the town, and Danish authorities subdivided the valleys west of Denmark Hill and east of Government Hill.

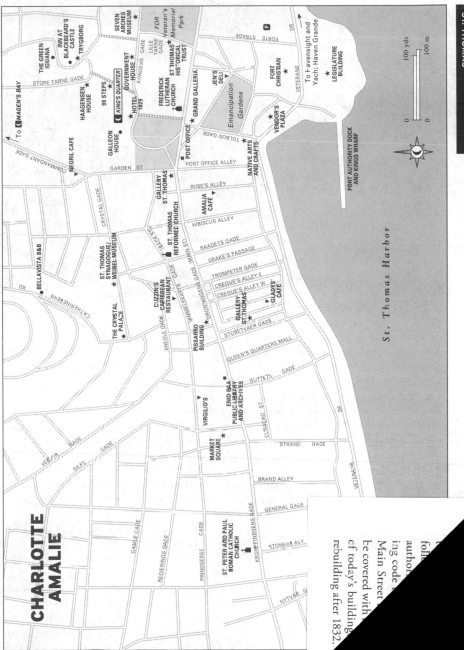

CHARLOTTE
AMALIE

St. Thomas Harbor

To ★ MAGEN'S BAY

THE GREEN
IGUANA
INN AT
BLACKBEARD'S
CASTLE ★ TRYGBORG
SEVEN
ARCHES
MUSEUM
FDR
Veteran's
Memorial
Park
P

STORE TARNE GADE
HAAGENSEN
HOUSE
99 STEPS
KING'S QUARTER
HOTEL
1829
GOVERNMENT
HOUSE
LILLE
TARNE
GADE
KONGENS GADE
ST. THOMAS
HISTORICAL
TRUST
FORTE STRADE

To ★ avensight and
Yach: Haven Grande
FORTE STRADE
DR

NEGRIL CAFE
GALLEON
HOUSE
FREDERICK
LUTHERAN
CHURCH
1829
GRAND GALLERIA
JEN'S
DELI
FORT
CHRISTIAN
LEGISLATURE
BUILDING

COMMANDANT GADE
GARDEN ST
POST OFFICE
TOLBOD GADE
Emancipation
Gardens
VETERANS
VENDOR'S
PLAZA

CRYSTAL GADE
POST OFFICE ALLEY
NATIVE ARTS
AND CRAFTS
PORT AUTHORITY DOCK
AND KINGS WHARF

GALLERY
ST. THOMAS
RIISE'S ALLEY
AMALIA
CAFÉ
HIBISCUS ALLEY

BELLAVISTA B&B
ST. THOMAS
SYNAGOGUE/
WEIBEL MUSEUM
ST. THOMAS
REFORMED CHURCH
RAADETS GADE
DRAKE'S PASSAGE
TROMPETER GADE
CREQUE'S ALLEY E
CREQUE'S ALLEY W.
GLADY'S
CAFÉ

CATHERINEBERG
RD
CUZZIN'S
CARIBBEAN
RESTAURANT
GALLERY
ST. THOMAS
THE CRYSTAL
PALACE
SNEGLE GADE
PISSARRO
BUILDING
STORETVAER GADE
QUEEN'S QUARTERS MALL

GUTTETS GADE
ENID BAA
PUBLIC LIBRARY
AND ARCHIVES
VIRGILIO'S
CURACAO ST

VEB/ER
GADE
GADE
MARKET
SQUARE
STRAND GADE
BRAND ALLEY

SILVE
GADE
GAHLE GADE
GENERAL GADE
STONEHS ALY

REGIERINGS GADE
PRINDSESSE GADE
KRONPRINDSENS GADE
ST. PETER AND PAUL
ROMAN CATHOLIC
CHURCH

100 m
0
100 yds
0

N

follo
author
ing code
Main Street
be covered with
of today's building
rebuilding after 1832.

© SUSANNA HENIGHAN POTTER

Frederik Lutheran Church is the oldest church still standing on St. Thomas.

Many of the early residents of Charlotte Amalie were free Black people. These former slaves often bought their freedom, although some were manumitted by their owners. Many were skilled artisans, and others started shops that catered to the demands of a growing town. Savanne, the area west of Denmark Hill, near the market square, was the heart of the free Black population. Today the area is called Savan (sa-VON).

The absence of building standards and the generally unplanned nature of Charlotte Amalie made it susceptible to fire. No fewer than six fires destroyed more than half the town between 1804 and 1832. Eventually, following the last of these devastating fires, [authori]ties put in place a restrictive build[ing code t]hat prohibited wood buildings on [...] [and] required that all new roofs [be of f]ire-resistant materials. Many [...] date from the period of

King's Quarter

The Danes divided Charlotte Amalie into three *kvarters* (quarters). **Kongens Quarter,** or King's Quarter, is the oldest part of the city. Stretching from Bluebeard's Hill in the east to Post Office Square in the west, this district housed the earliest government buildings, stately homes, churches and the island's first hospital.

Today, exploring the base and steep step-streets of **Government Hill** in the western environs of King's Quarter is the best way to experience Charlotte Amalie's historic charm.

FRANKLIN DELANO ROOSEVELT AND VETERANS MEMORIAL PARK

Located on Norre Gade, east of the Fort Christian parking lot, this attractive park, once called Coconut Square, pays tribute to U.S. president Franklin D. Roosevelt and to Virgin Islanders who have served in the American armed forces. Trees, benches, and historic buildings that surround the park make it a pleasant place to pause during a tour of the city. There is also a small children's playground. Look for the two baobab trees in the southeast corner of the park, distinguished by their trunks, which are widest at ground level.

FORT CHRISTIAN

This imposing Danish fortification on the eastern end of the St. Thomas waterfront is the oldest building in use on St. Thomas and a National Historic Landmark. Built between 1672 and 1680 by African laborers under the direction of Danish colonists and named for King Christian V of Denmark, the fort was the center of political and community life during the early years of Danish colonization of the Virgin Islands. The fort housed the governor's residence, town hall, the court, and the jail, as well as the island's first church.

Fort Christian has been under repair since 2005 and is now stuck in a quagmire of litigation between the government and contractor; it is unclear when it will reopen to the public. It's still worth stopping to admire the building's lovely facade. When the project is complete, visitors will be able to go inside and tour the restored courtyard, governor's quarters, and church.

VIRGIN ISLANDS LEGISLATURE BUILDING

The handsome cream-colored building across Veteran's Drive from Fort Christian is the Virgin Islands Legislature Building. This building dates back to 1874, when the Danes built it atop the site of a two-story wooden army barracks. It served as the Charlotte Amalie High School before it became the seat of the Virgin Islands Senate.

EMANCIPATION GARDENS

Catty-corner from Fort Christian is the inviting, shady square of Emancipation Gardens, built in commemoration of the island's 1848 emancipation. A model of the Liberty Bell pays tribute to the Jamestown settlers who spent three days on St. Thomas in 1607 before resuming their journey to Virginia. Lignum vitae trees provide shade. Today, the gardens are a pleasant place to rest and people-watch. Public concerts and other events are frequently held in the gazebo.

GRAND HOTEL

Across the street from the park is the restored Grand Hotel, now the Grand Galleria, a complex of shops and restaurants. The hotel opened in 1840 as the Commercial Hotel and Coffee House.

FREDERIK LUTHERAN CHURCH

Across Norre Gade (Main Street) from the Grand Galleria is Frederik Lutheran Church, the earliest church still standing on St. Thomas. Work began on Frederik Lutheran Church in the 1780s, and it was dedicated in 1793. The original church was in the simple Georgian style. It was gutted by fire in 1825 and rebuilt, with the addition of some Gothic-style trim. An 1870 hurricane blew off the roof, which was rebuilt. Inside you will see a large mahogany altar and mahogany pews—each with its own door.

Lutheranism was the official religion of the Danish colony, and while other faiths were tolerated, Lutheranism was encouraged. During the period of slavery, ministers led two services on Sunday: one for the Danish and one for people of color.

GOVERNMENT HOUSE

Take one of the narrow steep walks up to white-brick Government House, the fourth official residence of the Virgin Islands' chief executive, now used only for offices. (The governor lives at Catherineberg, atop Denmark Hill.) Built in 1867 by St. Croix carpenter Richard Bright, the house was designed by a local merchant, Otto Marstrand, and is notable for its covered balconies with slender fluted columns and ironwork rails. Inside is a handmade mahogany staircase.

Ask at the security desk if you can come in for a look around.

HOTEL 1829

Formerly the Lavalette House, this historic home (now a hotel and bar) was built around 1831 by Alexander Lavalette, a wealthy French merchant. The building's delightful historic ambience and outstanding views of the harbor below make this a pleasant place to relax with a cold drink; the bar is open to the public most afternoons. The site is also a functioning hotel.

99 STEPS

Step streets are one of Charlotte Amalie's most distinctive features, and the most famous of these is 99 Steps, a narrow, steep walkway originating between Hotel 1829 and the Lutheran Parsonage. The walk connects Government Hill with Trygborg, a Danish lookout tower that dates back to 1680 and is better known today as Blackbeard's Castle. As you'll discover if you care to count, the steps are wrongly named: there are more than 100.

Less well known but no less beautiful, the bright white step street that is a continuation of Lille Taarne Gade rises between Government House and the Lutheran Parsonage.

BLACKBEARD'S CASTLE

A Danish lookout tower dating from 1680, **Trygborg,** better known today as Blackbeard's Castle, is the centerpiece of a collection of historic buildings and museums clustered around Government Hill. Guided ($20) and self-guided ($14) walking tours of the district are available through Blackbeard's Castle (340/776-1234, www.blackbeardscastle.com), although you will find the attraction shuttered on days when no cruise ship is in port. Hours vary according to the seasons; call ahead to confirm.

Tour stops include **Villa Notman,** built in 1860 by Scottish engineer James Notman;

Britannia House, the onetime home of the British consul to the Danish West Indies; **Haagensen House,** an 1827 home built for the Danish banker Hans Haagensen; and **Hotel 1829** on Government Hill. Each of the historic homes has been restored with period furniture and decor. If you take the self-guided tour, curators are on hand at Haagensen House and Britannia House to answer your questions.

Main Street

Explore Main Street (Dronningen's Gade) and its side streets to find more historic buildings.

ST. THOMAS DUTCH REFORMED CHURCH

At the corner of Nye and Crystal Gades, one block inland from Main Street, is the St. Thomas Reformed Church, formerly the Dutch Reformed Church. This 1844 church is unique among Charlotte Amalie structures in that it has survived largely intact since its construction. An imitation Roman temple, the church was built at the height of the classical revival period, with plaster colored and grooved to resemble red sandstone. The interior reflects the colonial woodworking styles of the period. A unique feature is the building's lumber core covered by masonry, which has prevented the building from sustaining the cracks pure masonry structures suffer during the region's frequent earthquakes.

ST. THOMAS SYNAGOGUE

One of Charlotte Amalie's most notable historic buildings is the St. Thomas Synagogue (Crystal Gade, 340/774-4312, hebrewcong@ islands.vi, www.onepaper.com/synagogue, 9 A.M.–4 P.M. Mon.–Fri.), more properly called the Synagogue Beracha V'shalom V'gimilath Chasidim (Blessing, Peace, and Acts of Piety). Built in 1833 to replace an older structure, this house of worship continues to serve St. Thomas's small Jewish population. It is the

PISSARO: IMPRESSIONIST MASTER

Camille Pissarro was born on July 10, 1830, on St. Thomas. The son of a Sephardic Jewish father and Dominican mother, Pissarro went to Paris at age 12 to attend school. There, his advisor told him to "take advantage of his life in the tropics by drawing coconut trees." When Pissarro returned to St. Thomas at age 17, he took this advice to heart. He spent the next five years of his life drawing images of island life: donkey carts, women washing clothes, harbor life, and the Danish forts.

Pissarro's parents did not embrace his avocation, and they required him to continue with daily chores to assist with the family business. The young artist became frustrated, and at 23 he ran away to Venezuela with the Danish painter Fritz Melbye. Pissarro later said he "bolted to Caracas in order to get clear of the bondage of bourgeois life."

Soon, Pissarro's parents resigned themselves to his choice of profession, and he returned to St. Thomas. He later returned to Paris to study art, where he was influenced by early impressionists. His own style was developing, too—one in which light was as essential as the subject being painted.

Pissarro developed friendships with other artists on the vanguard of the impressionist movement. In 1874, he joined Monet in organizing independent exhibitions to avoid the scrutiny of the status quo, which was highly critical of this new kind of art.

After Pissarro moved to Paris, his parents followed, having left their St. Thomas business in the hands of a caretaker. His parents employed a young maidservant from Burgundy, Julie Vellay, who became Pissarro's lifelong companion.

Despite scathing reviews and poverty, Pissarro remained dedicated to the impressionist method. He became something of a teacher, providing inspiration for artists such as Renoir, Monet, Degas, and Cézanne. By the end of his life, Pissarro had finally begun to receive critical praise for his work. He died of blood poisoning in November 1903.

oldest Hebrew congregation in the United States and the second oldest in the Western Hemisphere. The building, which underwent restoration in 2000, has been designated a National Historic Landmark. The sand floor is believed to reflect a tradition of early Sephardic Orthodox congregants, who worshiped on this site beginning in 1796. Visitors are welcome as long as no service or other event is in progress. Next door, the **Weibel Museum** (15 Crystal Gade, 340/774-4312, 9 A.M.–4 P.M. Mon.–Fri., free) recounts the history of the Jewish community of St. Thomas. Donations are welcome.

PISSARRO BUILDING

The father of French impressionism, Camille Pissarro, was born on St. Thomas in 1839. His family's home is at 14 Dronningen's Gade is still known as the Pissarro Building.

ENID M. BAA PUBLIC LIBRARY AND ARCHIVES

Near the corner of Dronningen's Gade and Guttet Gade is the Enid M. Baa Public Library and Archives (Main Street, 340/774-3407, 9 A.M.–5 P.M. Mon. and Fri., 9 A.M.–8 P.M. Tues.–Thurs., 10 A.M.–4 P.M. Sat.), built in 1818 by Baron von Bretton. The handsome yellow building opened its doors as the island's library in 1940 and has functioned as such for more than 60 years. During the 19th century, the ground floor of the building contained shops and a courtyard, while the second floor was used as residential quarters. A new library is under construction next to Tutu Park Mall, but the 2012 completion date is likely to slip due to budget cuts.

MARKET SQUARE

Just west of the public library is the Market

Square, the traditional center of trade and commerce in town. The square consists of a large, open-air pavilion, surrounded by sidewalks where vendors set up tents. During the days of slavery, this was where slave auctions were held. In more recent history, it was where market women (known as hucksters) came to sell produce and other necessities.

The market is still a good place to find local farmers and artisans selling produce, arts, and crafts, especially early on Saturday morning (6–8 A.M.). A two-year restoration project to improve drainage and install cobblestones, benches, and historically accurate lighting, among other things, began in 2011.

Market Square lies at the boundary between the tourist-friendly Main Street shopping district and Savan, a colorful yet hard-edged community. It's not a good neighborhood to explore at night.

ST. PETER AND ST. PAUL ROMAN CATHOLIC CHURCH

About two blocks west of Market Square along Main Street is St. Peter and St. Paul Roman Catholic Church. Consecrated in 1848, this building replaced earlier churches destroyed by fire and hurricanes. The interior murals depicting scenes from the Old and New Testaments were painted in 1899 by Belgian artists Father Leo Servais and Brother Ildephonsus.

Museums

ST. THOMAS HISTORICAL TRUST MINI MUSEUM

Examine a collection of antique furniture, historic artifacts, and photographs of old St. Thomas at this small museum operated by the St. Thomas Historical Trust (15B Norre Gade, 340/774-5541, www.stthomashistoricaltrust.org, 10 A.M.–3 P.M. Tues.–Fri., free). The Trust sells a self-guided walking tour of Charlotte Amalie. The museum is located in the Anduze House, facing FDR Park at the base of Government Hill.

SEVEN ARCHES MUSEUM

Tucked along a narrow alley next to the Lieutenant Governor's office on Government Hill is the Seven Arches Museum (Knud Hansen Alley, 340/774-9295, www.sevenarchesmuseum.com, $7), a historic home open for public tours by appointment only. This spot was first surveyed in 1805; early structures were destroyed by hurricanes in the first half of the 19th century. Italian Andre Bonelli constructed the present building in 1857 as a gift to his daughter. The museum is furnished with antique West Indian mahogany furniture.

FRENCH HERITAGE MUSEUM

Located in a handsome yellow stone building next to the Joseph Aubain Ballpark, the French Heritage Museum (Rue de St. Barthelemy, 340/774-2320, www.frenchheritagemuseum.com, 9 A.M.–6 P.M. Mon.–Fri., free) is dedicated to preserving the traditions and history of St. Thomas's French inhabitants.

The museum is located in Frenchtown, a quaint, tight-knit community on the west side of Charlotte Amalie Harbor. It's named for the French Huguenots who left St. Bartholomew and settled here in the 1870s. The French settlers were fishermen and artisans, especially known for their straw hats, samples of which you will see at the museum. Fishing remains an important industry for residents of Frenchtown, and many mornings you will find fish for sale at the dock here.

WATER ISLAND

At 500 acres, Water Island is the larger of the two islands in Charlotte Amalie Harbor. A quiet, mostly residential place, Water Island has several miles of paved road good for walking or biking, some nice beaches, and an interesting history. In 2008, a cottage campground opened. There is regular ferry service from Frenchtown.

History

Often referred to as the fourth Virgin Island,

Water Island was the site of a series of Black-owned plantations, dating as far back as 1769, when a free mulatto named Jean Renaud had a plantation and 18 slaves there. In 1793 the plantation was sold to Peter Tararyn, another free Black man and the commander of the Free Negro Corps, established by the Danes to capture runaway slaves.

In 1944, the U.S. Department of Defense bought Water Island for $10,000 and began to build Fort Segarra, a military fort with barracks, gun emplacements, watchtowers, and underground bunkers. World War II ended while construction was under way; Fort Segarra was abandoned midstream, but not before basic infrastructure, including roads, water pipes, a sewage system, and power lines, was put in place. After the war, the army's Chemical Warfare Division used Water Island to test poisonous gases.

In 1950, the Department of Defense leased Water Island to a private developer, who built a hotel and private homes on the island. The hotel was badly damaged by Hurricane Hugo in 1989 and was not rebuilt. It is widely believed that Herman Wouk's novel *Don't Stop the Carnival* was set on a fictionalized Water Island.

Honeymoon Beach

Water Island's main attraction is Honeymoon Beach, also known as Druif Bay, a protected, clean, and quiet beach along its southwest shore. Honeymoon Beach is within walking distance of the ferry that runs regularly between St. Thomas and Water Island, and it makes a good day trip destination, especially if you are staying near Charlotte Amalie. Most days a restaurant on the beach sells casual lunch, and occasionally "da pizza boat" makes an appearance. There is nice snorkeling along the southern end of the beach.

Getting There

Get to Water Island on the **Water Island**

Ferry (340/690-4159, $10 round-trip, 10 minutes), which offers 11 scheduled trips between 6:30 A.M. and 6 P.M. Monday through Saturday. On Sundays and holidays, there are six scheduled trips between 8 A.M. and 7 P.M. Late-night ferries (9 P.M.) often run on Wednesday, Friday, and Saturday nights, but call ahead to confirm. The ferry departs from Crown Bay Marina, in the area of Charlotte Amalie known as Subbase.

◖ HASSEL ISLAND ☆

The smaller of the two islands in St. Thomas's harbor, Hassel Island was once connected to St. Thomas via a narrow isthmus. There are several historic ruins on the 135-acre island, including British fortifications and the remains of a 20th-century marine railway. Most of the island is owned by Virgin Islands National Park, which has embarked on a project to restore the island's sites, develop trails, and open the island up to visitors.

History

The Danish government first separated Hassel Island from St. Thomas in 1860 in hopes of creating better water circulation in the harbor. The U.S. Army Corps of Engineers deepened the channel by dredging in 1919. Originally called Hurricane Hole, the island came to be known Hassel Island for its owners, the Hazzell family.

In addition to the military and industrial purposes the island has served over the years, it housed a leprosarium from the 1830s until the 1860s. The government paid the equivalent of $2 per patient housed in the facility operated by the Hazzell family.

Sights

Creque Marine Railway on the northern tip of the island was the earliest steam-powered marine railway in the Western Hemisphere and is evidence of St. Thomas's importance as a 19th-century shipping depot. Opened in 1844, the marine railway lifted large vessels out of the water for cleaning and repair. The marine railway operated almost continuously for 120 years. From 1911 until 1954 it was operated by the Creque family of St. Thomas. During World War II it was leased to the U.S. Navy. The last recorded ship was hauled out there in 1965.

The ruins of the railway have recently been cleared of overgrowth, and visitors can examine an interesting collection of old-fashioned machinery and equipment, including early diving bells.

Other ruins on the island include early-19th-century British fortifications, dating back to the brief British occupation during the first Napoleonic war. The British built **Fort Shipley,** or Shipley's Battery, on the highest point of the island; hike up for excellent views of Charlotte Amalie. **Fort Willoughby,** also known as Prince Frederik's Battery, is a picturesque lookout on the island's far eastern point.

Getting There

Virgin Islands Eco-Tours (340/779-2155 or 877/845-2925 www.viecotours.com) offers guided kayak, hike, and snorkel tours of Hassel Island four days a week. The three-hour tours cost $100 and include visits to Fort Willoughby, the Creque Marine Railway, Fort Shipley, and Garden Beach. Signing up for one of these trips is the only way to visit the island, aside from sailing there in a private boat.

HAVENSIGHT

Havensight is the shopping district around the cruise ship dock, on the eastern end of Charlotte Amalie Harbor. A large outdoor mall and additional stores in the vicinity attract shoppers nearly every day of the year.

Paradise Point

The view of St. Thomas harbor is genuinely outstanding from Paradise Point, a bar perched far above Havensight. Get there aboard one of the gondolas that glide above the trees on the Paradise Point Tramway (Havensight,

340/774-9809, 9 A.M.–5 P.M. Thurs.–Tues., 9 A.M.–9 P.M. Wed., adults $21, children 6–12 $12, under 6 free). The trip up takes seven minutes. You can also drive up to Paradise Point on the road on the western side of Al Cohen's Plaza. The bar stays open late on Wednesday nights, when the gondola ride price is cut to $10.

The Butterfly Garden

Learn about the life cycle of butterflies and observe these delicate creatures at the Butterfly Garden (Havensight, 340/715-3366, 8:30 A.M.–5 P.M. daily, adults $12, children $6). Inside a netted garden near the cruise ship dock, colorful butterflies flutter amid a tropical flower garden. Photographers will delight in snapping close-ups of these normally elusive creatures. Inside a hatching house, proprietors hang pupae behind glass, making it possible for visitors to see the process of metamorphosis up close. Outside the netted garden, a native garden attracts local butterflies, hummingbirds, and bananaquits, small yellow-chested birds. A 20-minute bird show is included in the price of admission and entertains young and old four times daily, at 9:30 A.M., 11 A.M., 1 P.M., and 3 P.M. (call to confirm, especially if no cruise ship is in port). The butterflies are most active in the morning. If you are staying on the island an admission entitles you to a pass to return multiple times to check on the butterflies or look for new "hatchlings."

MORNINGSTAR BEACH

Morningstar Beach is next to the Marriott Frenchman's Reef Resort on the easternmost end of Charlotte Amalie Harbor. Long and narrow, with caramel-colored sand, Morningstar is fronted by two restaurants and is sometimes crowded with resort guests. The water is often wavy and the beach windy. The view is of open ocean, interrupted by passing ferryboats and cruise ships as they motor into the harbor. There is a volleyball court, water-sports

A Blue Morpho butterfly lands on a flower at the Butterfly Garden.

equipment for rent, beach chairs ($15 for non-guests), and a reef for snorkeling.

Getting There

Frenchman's Reef Resort operates a ferry from the Charlotte Amalie waterfront to the resort, making it possible to visit Morningstar Beach without driving there (daily Dec.–May, Mon.–Sat. June–Nov., adults $6, children 3–12 $4, under 3 free). The ferry departs from the dock opposite Vendor's Plaza every hour on the hour between 9 A.M. and 5 P.M., with a return voyage hourly 8:30 A.M.–4:30 P.M.

WEST ISLAND

Highway 30 west of town is crowded with commercial ventures: banks, warehouses, shopping centers, car rental shops, and gas stations. About four miles outside of the city center is the Cyril E. King International Airport, and past that the road narrows to two lanes and becomes decidedly less trafficked.

Estate Nisky Moravian Church

Moravians first established a mission at this site (then called Estate Niesky) 1.5 miles west of Charlotte Amalie in 1755. Church buildings were destroyed by hurricane or fire in 1771, 1819, 1867, 1871, and, finally, 1971. But each time the church was rebuilt on the same foundation. Today, the Estate Nisky Moravian Church (6 Estate Nisky, 340/774-2809) consists of a manse, a church, a cemetery, and several outbuildings, including former slave cabins. It is still a working church and school.

Lindberg Bay

Located just east of the airport, Lindberg Bay (Airport Rd.) is a long, narrow beach popular with families, locals, and guests lodging at two airport hotels. The beach has received Blue Flag certification for sustainability and environmental protection efforts. A public playground right next door is an added attraction. The bay got its name in 1929 when Charles Lindbergh landed

...g a goodwill tour of ...1927 solo crossing of

...h

...y Beach (Hwy. 30) is a ...pular among students from the neighboring University of the Virgin Islands, who can walk here from their dormitories.

The beach itself is short but wide, with medium-grain honey-colored sand. The waters are protected, making Brewer's a popular choice for families or beginning swimmers. There are bathrooms and picnic tables and a food bus or two usually park here on the weekends, selling cold drinks and snacks. If you're here at the right time (afternoon is best), you get the thrill of watching planes swoop down to land at the nearby airport.

Estate Bordeaux

This quiet, residential area of St. Thomas is where the Virgin Islands government has set aside 50 farm plots to encourage local agriculture. Bordeaux farmers, many of whom are Rastafarian, travel to Charlotte Amalie on Saturday mornings to sell at the downtown Market Square. On the last Sunday of each month they invite buyers to come to them at **We Grow Food Inc.,** an open-air food market in the heart of the Bordeaux community. Once a year, in January, the farmers host a weekend festival with music, arts, vegetarian dishes, and lots of locally raised food.

To find Bordeaux and the We Grow Food market, drive west on Highway 30 past the airport. The journey takes you up and over several large hills and through the least populated parts of St. Thomas. Once in Bordeaux, the road levels off and passes a row of homes; look for a colorful sign marking the turnoff on your right.

NORTHSIDE

The northern shore of St. Thomas is quiet, crisscrossed by narrow roads and punctuated by remarkable vistas. A series of bays wind in and out, but none is better than Magen's Bay, the broad, long public beach about midway along the island's north coast.

Overlooks

On St. Thomas, a good view is an entrepreneurial opportunity. The best vistas are popular with itinerant vendors, drink retailers, and other businesspeople out to make a buck. When the cruise ship dock is full, expect the following overlooks to be teeming.

The most famous overlook on St. Thomas is **Drake's Seat,** a few feet from the intersection of Routes 40 and 33. The legend that Sir Francis Drake stopped here is probably not true, but never mind. The view of Magen's Bay is fantastic, and you can sit on a bench to thoroughly enjoy it. On clear days you can see parts of the British Virgin Islands in the distance.

Valdemar Hill Drive Scenic Overlook is located on Skyline Drive (Rte. 40) just before it intersects with Magen's Bay Road (Rte. 35). It faces south and offers an outstanding view of Charlotte Amalie Harbor. Itinerant vendors offer t-shirts and cold drinks for sale.

World Famous Mountaintop (St. Peter Mountain Rd., 340/774-2400) is a small shopping mall atop one of St. Thomas's highest points. When there's a cruise ship in town, taxis disgorge hundreds of passengers here. When there's no ship, the place is a ghost town. The view from the front balcony is excellent: on a clear day you can see Tortola and the other British Virgins. Restrooms are available. A bar specializes in banana daiquiris.

St. Peter Great House

Come to St. Peter Great House and Botanical Gardens (St. Peter Mountain Rd., 340/774-4999, www.greathousevi.com, 9 A.M.–5 P.M. daily, adults $10, children $5) for excellent views and the chance to see showy tropical plants. Gardeners will delight in the boardwalk

water lilies at the St. Peter Great House and Botanical Gardens

nature trail, which takes you past red ginger, flamingo flowers, bougainvillea, parrot flower, coleus, crinium, amaranthus, and many more. Lovebirds, cockatoos, and macaws provide the soundtrack. After your walk, relax with a complimentary rum punch and enjoy the view of Hull Bay, Magen's Bay, and the British Virgin Islands.

Magen's Bay

A mile-long white sand bay lined with coconut palms and sea grape trees and washed by calm turquoise waters, Magen's Bay is St. Thomas's best beach. The park attracts a diverse crowd of tourists and locals, and it can be a place for quiet relaxation or high-spirited fun.

The sand is packed and white and the water almost always calm. There is plenty of shade beneath trees, and since the beach is so large, you are almost guaranteed to find a quiet patch of sand. Lifeguards keep an eye on safety and swimming buoys keep boats out. Picnic tables, large bathhouses, pavilions, a snack bar, and plenty of parking make this a comfortable place to spend the day. A small enterprise at the eastern end of the park rents water-sports gear and kayaks, but most people are content lolling around in the calm crystal water. The beachside shop has a large collection of swimwear and just about anything you might need to round out your day at the beach, from novels to sunscreen.

Magen's Bay is owned by the territorial government and administered as a public park; visitors must pay $2 per adult, $1 per child, and $2 per car to get in. The fee collection booth is open daily from about 7:30 A.M.–6 P.M.

You can explore Magen's Bay away from the beach along the 1.5-mile **Magen's Bay Nature Trail,** a facility operated by the Nature Conservancy. The trail passes through the moist lowlands before heading uphill through a dry tropical forest. The lower trailhead is tucked among the coconut palms about midway along the bay. To find it, turn left after

© SUSANNA HENIGHAN POTTER

Magen's Bay: the best beach on St. Thomas

passing the guard gate and then look for small white signs directing you to the trail. The upper trailhead is along Route 35, the road to Magen's Bay, but poor signage makes it difficult to find.

Hull Bay

This caramel-colored coarse-sand beach is the only place to catch surf on St. Thomas. During the winter months, small swells are just big enough to provide a diversion for surfers, although many head to better breaks on Tortola when they can. Hull Bay is the epicenter of the north shore French community, and the bay is often scattered with small fishing boats.

The bay here is almost always quiet, and there is plenty of shade. The beach bar is as friendly as they come, offering games such as horseshoes to while away an afternoon.

Offshore cays **Inner Brass** and **Outer Brass** provide something to look at, and adventurous beachgoers can kayak out to them.

RED HOOK AND THE EAST END

St. Thomas sheds its historical ambience on the east end, where resorts line adjacent bays. The landscape is decidedly more dry than in other parts of the island, and there are fewer steep hills. This is where you will find the best water sports and one of the island's most popular attractions, Coral World. Red Hook, the sprawling town on St. Thomas's easternmost tip, is where most people come to catch ferries to St. John and Tortola. Farther inland, Estate Tutu and the surrounding areas are the most populated portions of St. Thomas, with large shopping malls and traffic jams.

◖ Coral World

Coral World Marine Park and Undersea Observatory (Coki Point, 340/775-1555, fax 340/775-9068, www.coralworldvi.com, adults $19, children 3–12 $10, family rate $52) puts the wonder of underwater sea life within reach

© SUSANNA HENIGHAN POTTER

Children watch a shark at Coral World Marine Park.

of everyone. An undersea observatory allows you to get eye-level with the coral reef, and jewel boxes display every imaginable marine habitat of the Virgin Islands; other exhibits showcase specific marine creatures, including green turtles and stingrays. You can swim with South American sea lions ($124) and snorkel with nurse, lemon, and blacktip sharks ($51). There is even an exhibit showing the nighttime reef—including phosphorescent coral. Feedings and public demonstrations are scheduled every 45 minutes during the day, so there is always something to watch, whether it's fish feeding around the undersea observatory or a demonstration with the sea lions. A touch pool allow visitors young and old to feel sea stars, sea cucumbers, and a West Indian sea egg. Through the Sea Trek offering (adults $77, children $68) guests can enjoy the experience of scuba diving without the fuss of a tank. In addition to the marine exhibits, Coral World has an aviary where you can meet tropical birds including lorikeets and a short nature trail featuring tropical plants, endangered tortoises, and lots of iguanas.

Coral World is an excellent destination for families, but just about everyone will delight in exploring its attractions. At first blush, Coral World may seem like a tourist trap—there are plenty of opportunities to spend money here—but the park is serious about its educational mission. Each year more than 5,000 local schoolchildren tour the park free of charge to learn about the marine environment that surrounds them.

Coral World tends to be busy, especially when many cruise ships are in port. If you have your heart set on one of the add-on activities, book ahead. To avoid the crowds, come early or late.

Coral World is open daily 9 A.M.–5 P.M. (ticket booth closes at 4 P.M.) but cuts back its hours in the summer. Call ahead to confirm.

Coki Point Beach

The most popular public beach in the east

end is Coki Point Beach, next to Coral World. Neither too big or too small, Coki has fluffy white sand and a moderate amount of shade. There is good snorkeling just offshore, and a dive shop rents gear and offers scuba lessons and rentals. An array of beach vendors sell snacks, trinkets, cold drinks, and, more discreetly, marijuana. The beach gets crowded with residents on weekends and with tourists when a cruise ship is in town.

To find Coki Beach, look for signs for Coral World on Route 38 (Smith Bay Road) and take the short, potholed road to the beach. Parking is haphazard and unsecured; leave your valuables at your hotel. If you have reservations at Coki Beach Dive Club, you are permitted to park in the Coral World lot.

Sugar Bay

Sugar Bay, at the Wyndham Sugar Bay Resort, is a compact but broad ribbon of coarse white sand opposite Coki Point. A rocky bottom makes entry difficult in places but provides good snorkeling. There are lots of beach chairs and water-sports equipment for rent.

◖ Smith Bay Park

A public park, Smith Bay (also called Lindqvest Bay) is a magnificent place to spend the afternoon. The beach is curved and narrow, with the fine white sand descending at a gentle slope toward the water. Mild wave action produces a relaxing symphony of wave sounds, but does not interfere with swimming or snorkeling. Picnic tables are tucked amid shade trees. The view is largely unblemished and you look out at a series of uninhabited offshore cays. Aside from Magen's Bay, which is a different animal altogether, Smith Bay is the best beach on St. Thomas.

A $2 per car admission fee is charged. Facilities include pit toilets and security guards. A restaurant is planned for the future.

Sapphire Beach

One of the best resort beaches on St. Thomas is at Sapphire Bay, a long beach near Red Hook. Packed white sand provides the backdrop for a perfect day at the shore. A reef runs parallel to the rocky part of the bay; staff at the dive shop on the beach can provide equipment and directions to the best snorkeling. If you prefer to stay on the beach, you will enjoy views of the British Virgin Islands and Pillsbury Sound.

Locals flock to Sapphire on Sunday afternoons when bands play hot soca and calypso tunes. There is usually a game of beach volleyball going on, too.

Great Bay Beach

Great Bay, on the eastern end of St. Thomas, is not as perfect as you might expect the beach at a Ritz-Carlton resort to be. The sand is a little coarse and the bottom is rocky. But plenty of coconut palms, sea grape trees, and seaside grasses provide ambience, along with the Ritz-Carlton's distinctive blue umbrellas and beach chairs (not free to nonresort guests). The water is pure and refreshing. Great Bay is also one of two Blue Flag beaches on St. Thomas, a designation given to beaches that reach high standards of environmental stewardship.

To find Great Bay, drive all the way past the resort entrance and look for the service road that directs you to the public beach access.

East End Marine Sanctuary

The eastern shoreline of St. Thomas and several offshore cays have been declared wildlife sanctuaries by the local government. The waters around Great St. James and Little St. James Islands, Cas Cay, Cow and Calf Rocks, and Patricia Cay include important mangrove, salt pond, and seagrass habitats that help sustain the local fishery. Rules limit fishing and internal combustion engines are banned in certain areas.

Since it is protected, this area offers excellent opportunities for wildlife viewing—the best on St. Thomas. Around Cas Cay you will find healthy seagrass beds; large schools of fish, stingrays, lobster, and conch; and a mangrove ecosystem that serves as the nursery of the ocean, protecting large numbers of juvenile fish from predators. A short hiking trail on tiny Cas Cay leads you to tidal pools that are home to sea urchins and make a dramatic setting for photographs when the tide is up.

Unless you have your own boat and are familiar with local waters, the only way to access the sanctuary is with a tour. **Virgin Islands Ecotours** (No. 2 Estate Nadir, 340/779-2155, www.viecotours.com) leads daily kayak, snorkel, and hiking tours in the sanctuary. All tours begin with a kayak around the mangrove lagoon and also include an outstanding snorkel tour of the seagrass bed, sandy flats, and mangrove ecosystem. You may choose to add on a half-mile hike around Cas Cay or include a stop at Patricia Cay and lunch for the full-day tour.

Bolongo Bay

Located along the southern shore of St. Thomas, on Route 30, is Bolongo Bay, another good resort beach. Bolongo is a small crescent bay with a coarse-sand beach scattered with small stones and coral fragments. Coconut palms provide shade and the resort offers sea toys like dinghies, kayaks, and paddleboats for rent. The beach attracts a fun-loving crowd as likely to spend the afternoon at the beach bar as on the water. Beach chairs rent for $5 a day to those not guests of the resort.

Entertainment and Events

NIGHTLIFE

Nightlife on St. Thomas is generally quiet, and most of the best bars and clubs are also restaurants. Many restaurants catering to tourists have steel pan, calypso, or other live music during dinner. The venues listed here are the most popular destinations for socializing and meeting new people.

Charlotte Amalie and Frenchtown

In Charlotte Amalie, **The Green House** (Waterfront, 340/774-7998, cover varies) is the first choice for many island residents looking for a night out. Its two-for-one happy hour is the first attraction, followed by live music on weekends. The dance floor is hot and crowded, moving to the rhythm of reggae, calypso, and soca. If midweek has you down, stop by the Green House on Tuesday night for one of the liveliest school-night parties around. Ladies, beware the sharks.

If you prefer to be near the water, head to the Yacht Haven Grand and take your pick between open-air options **Wikked** (340/775-8953, no cover) and **Fat Turtle** (340/714-3566, cover varies), which draw a large late-night crowds on Fridays with live music. It's easy to ping-pong between the two. Wikked also offers live jazz on the Saturday closest to the full moon.

If you would rather forget you're in the Caribbean, grab a table at **Shipwreck** (Al Cohen's Plaza, Havensight, 340/777-1293, cover varies), a dark, cavernous, air-conditioned bar popular with statesiders. Shipwreck hosts a ladies night on Wednesdays but its big night is Saturday, when Old School and Top 40 tunes fill up the dance floor.

For a quiet evening drink without the distraction of live music, head to Frenchtown's **Oceana** (340/774-4262, no cover) for lively after-work conversation at the stylish bar with nice views of the sea.

Red Hook and the East End

What's a trip to the islands without limbo? **Iggies Beach Bar** (Bolongo Bay Beach Resort, 340/775-1800, no cover) is the best destination on the island for Caribbean-themed entertainment. Its holds "Carnival Night" every Wednesday, featuring live calypso music, a West Indian buffet and a limbo contest on the beach.

In the parking lot of Red Hook Plaza on the east end, **Duffy's Love Shack** (Red Hook, 340/779-2495, no cover) is a landmark. This is your place for genuine froufrou drinks and limbo party, and people looking for fun come here like moths to the flame. The open-air bar is a popular hunting ground for those searching for companionship, whether for the night or a little longer.

Across the street is **Caribbean Saloon** (American Yacht Harbor, 340/775-7060, no cover), a bar and nightclub open seven nights a week that caters to the marine-oriented boat crowd of the east end. There is a DJ on Wednesday, Friday, and Saturday nights.

Funky **Latitude 18** (Vessup Bay, 340/777-4552, cover varies) is a waterfront institution, attracting a laid-back crowd of salty dogs. Eclectic nightly live music ranges from blues to rock to country. There is an open mic on Tuesday nights.

THE ARTS

The premier performance venue in the Virgin Islands is the **Reichhold Center for the Arts** (2 Brewer's Bay, 340/693-1559, www.reichholdcenter.com), an open-air amphitheater affiliated with the University of the Virgin Islands. The 2,000-seat center was built in the late 1970s and has hosted performers as varied as the Moscow Ballet and Ray Charles. The center's annual arts series runs from October to May and features performances by top jazz, Latin, and reggae performers. Other shows include dance, classical, and local quelbe music. Tickets can be bought online in advance.

Many of the most exciting arts events on St. Thomas are organized by **The Forum** (340/690-4350, www.theforum.vi), a nonprofit organization that produces concerts, dance recitals, academic lectures, and film festivals. Check out the season schedule for a rundown on some of the best events on the island. Many of the Forum's presentations take place at the Reichhold Center for the Arts at UVI or Prior-Jollek Hall at Antilles School, located in Frenchman's Bay.

Pistarckle Theater (Tillett Gardens, Estate Tutu, 340/775-7877, www.pistarckletheater.com) is an amateur theater company that puts on six productions annually. It also offers a summer film series and acting classes for children and adults.

EVENTS

The largest annual event on St. Thomas is **Carnival,** which takes place in April and lasts several weeks, with events including concerts, parades, food fairs and beauty pageants.

St. Thomas's Carnival attracts islanders from St. Croix, St. John, Tortola, Virgin Gorda, and even farther afield. The Carnival Village is set up in the large public parking lot next to Fort Christian in downtown Charlotte Amalie. Admission is free, and there is top-notch live entertainment nightly, plus lots of local food and drink on sale.

The Lionel Roberts Stadium in the Hospital Ground area of Charlotte Amalie is the venue for many of the shows and contests, including a series of calypso contests culminating in the finals, where the island's Calypso Monarch is crowned. The King and Queen of the Band is a contest for the most elaborate, colorful feathered costume, and the annual steel-pan concert features the island's best steel-pan bands. A Quelbe Tramp is held down Main Street, where people dance behind a traditional quelbe band, but the crowds come out for the massive early-morning Jouvert, when soca and calypso bands pump out loud, pulsating grooves.

The climax of the Carnival is the Adult's Parade (the Children's Parade, held one day before, features lots of majorettes and children's steel-band orchestras), which wends from Western Cemetery to the Lionel Roberts Stadium. Ground zero is Post Office Square, the broad stretch of road in front of the main downtown post office, where judges and dignitaries watch the parade on risers. Onlookers line Main Street starting early in the day, staking claim to shady spots with foldout chairs and coolers.

Check with the U.S. Virgin Islands Department of Tourism (340/774-8784, www.usvitourism.vi) for a schedule for the upcoming Carnival. During the fete, check local papers for details about start times, performers, and parking restrictions.

Another major event in the spring is the **International Rolex Regatta** (www.rolexcupregatta.com), which takes place in March and is the largest single sailing event on St. Thomas.

In August is the **USVI Open Atlantic Blue Marlin Tournament** (www.ambt.vi), the largest sportfishing event in the Virgin Islands.

Every November hundreds of U.S. college basketball players come to St. Thomas for

Paradise Jam (www.paradisejam.com), usually held the week of Thanksgiving.

CINEMA
St. Thomas's lone cinema is **Caribbean Cinemas** (Weymouth Rhymer Hwy., 340/776-3666), in the same shopping center as Cost-U-Less between Charlotte Amalie and Estate Tutu. First-run movies show nightly, with matinees on the weekend.

The annual **Forum Film Festival** (www.theforum.vi) takes place in May and features offbeat, interesting films that would otherwise never find their way to the Virgin Islands.

GAMING
While there are no casinos on St. Thomas, you will find slot machines in bars, restaurants, and hotels around the island. **Southland Gaming of the Virgin Islands** (340/777-7568) operates gaming machines in some 55 locations throughout St. Thomas. Dozens of bars and restaurants have a machine or two, with larger "gaming complexes" at hotels (including the Wyndham Sugar Bay and the Holiday Inn Windward Passage) and shopping malls (including Crown Bay and Havensight).

Shopping

Main Street in downtown Charlotte Amalie is the original shopping district on the island and it has the most character. Newer additions are the mall at Crown Bay and the shops at the Yacht Haven Grande. On the east end, Red Hook offers offbeat shops in a low-pressure environment.

By far the most talked-about item for sale on St. Thomas is jewelry—from fine name brands to upscale knockoffs. In addition to jewelry you'll find perfume, name-brand skin care products, sunglasses, handbags, liquor, and crystal. Tucked amid big-name retailers like A.H. Riise,

Little Switzerland, and Cartier are unique boutiques that peddle wares ranging from Caribbean coffee to colorful Turkish imports. There is also a growing number of art galleries.

CHARLOTTE AMALIE
Main Street
The original St. Thomas shopping experience is found in downtown Charlotte Amalie, where old sugar warehouses and 18th- and 19th-century townhouses have been converted into a bustling shopping district. Cobblestone walks, old stone walls, and classic West Indian

architecture add to the enjoyment of being downtown. Don't miss Royal Dane Mall, Palm Passage, or Hibiscus Alley, narrow alleys that offer ambience in spades.

Main Street is the main artery of Charlotte Amalie's shopping district. Stores open big double doors to the street, expelling tantalizing breezes of high-powered air-conditioning (not very energy-efficient, but it's good for sales). Once a fixture of the shopping district, loud-mouthed barkers have gone mute, thanks to a law banning them, but the most enterprising entrepreneurs still find ways to badger passersby.

More than the shopkeepers, however, it is your fellow shoppers who steal the show. Cruise ships disgorge visitors of all types and stripes on St. Thomas, and most find themselves here—strolling along a Main Street glutted with taxis and crammed with tourists. Some shoppers appear merely out for a stroll, others have a distinct sense of purpose. For a bargain-hunting shopper or expert haggler, Charlotte Amalie is a trove of opportunity. The best way to haggle is to simply suggest a lower price than what's posted and begin negotiating. Haggling is most successful at the smaller, family-owned shops. At large name-brand stores, you may receive a small discount.

Most Main Street shops open by 9 A.M. and close between 4 and 5 P.M. These shops cater to tourists, and on days when no cruise ship is in town you're likely to find most shuttered, especially on Sunday.

JEWELRY

It is simply impossible to overlook the major retailers on Main Street. **Diamonds International** (340/774-1516), **Little Switzerland** (340/776-4110), **Cartier** (30 Main St., 284/774-1590), and **Cardow Jewelers** (340/776-1140) are the biggest names in jewelry. Dozens of other shops specialize in jewelry: **Okidanokh Goldcraft** (Palm

© SUSANNA HENIGHAN POTTER

The Main Street shopping district on St. Thomas is an inviting neighborhood of narrow alleys, stone buildings, and cobblestoned walks.

Passage and Royal Dane Mall, 340/775-3060) features unique work by designer Abel Fabri, and **H. Stern** (32 and 8 Main St., 340/776-1146) features the light, airy designs of Brazil.

CAMERAS
Boolchands (340/776-0302) and **Royal Caribbean** (340/776-4110) have a wide selection of cameras, other electronics, and watches.

LIQUOR AND PERFUME
Thanks to the island's duty-free status, liquor prices on St. Thomas are about half those of the U.S. mainland. Airline rules limiting liquids in carry-on luggage have complicated life for travelers, but shops will pack your purchases in boxes suitable to be checked. (Alternatively, buy your liquor at **Caribbean Host** (340/776-4000) inside the departure gate at Cyril E. King Airport and carry it on.)

A.H. Riise (37 Main St., 340/776-2303), which was founded in 1838 as the island's apothecary, is today the biggest name in downtown liquor, but it also sells perfume and a smattering of fine art prints. **Dynasty Dazzlers** (No. 1 Main St., 340/776-8935) also specializes in liquor and perfume.

ART
For island crafts, visit **Native Arts and Crafts** (488 Tolbod Gade, 340/777-1153, Mon.–Fri. 9 A.M.–4 P.M., Sat. 9 A.M.–2 P.M.), a cooperative for local artisans next to Vendor's Plaza. Here you'll find locally made lace, dolls, woodwork, decorative arts, and music.

Gallery St. Thomas (Palm Passage, 340/777-6363) features works by dozens of local and regional artists, ranging from contemporary pieces to traditional island scenery. The gallery sells paintings, wood sculpture, ceramics and glass, metal sculpture, and photography, as well as prints and reproductions.

The **Jonna White Gallery** (A.H. Riise Mall, 340/774-1201) sells colorful graphic prints.

The vibrant paintings and intricate etchings of artist David Hill are available from the **David Hill Gallery** (Royal Dane Mall, 340/714-4400). Lucinda O'Connell's abstract watercolors, as well as her charming landscapes inspired by the islands, are featured at **Cloud Nine Studio** (No. 1 Norre Gade, 340/514-2432), near the St. Thomas synagogue. The artist-in-residence at the Ritz-Carlton, O'Connell also teaches watercolor classes for visitors.

GIFTS
Down Island Traders (Waterfront and 14A Norre Gade, 340/775-7019) stocks an appealing selection of Caribbean arts, crafts, spices, and more.

The rich smell of chocolate draws shoppers into **The Belgian Chocolate Factory** (A.H. Riise Mall, 340/777-5247), which sells boxes of high-end imported chocolate, as well as hot chocolate, coffee, cookbooks, and other food-related items.

LINENS
Mr. Tablecloth, Inc. (6 Main St., 340/774-4343) is an institution that stocks a dazzling array of tablecloths, placemats, lace, and embroidered accessories, plus nightgowns, baby clothes, and lovely lace parasols, ideal for the St. Thomas sun.

CLOTHING
There are more and more shops selling clothes. **Carilooha** (Grand Galleria, 340/774-5506) has a collection of clothing manufactured from bamboo. Look like you just came back from vacation with clothes from **Fresh Produce** (A.H. Riise Mall, 340/774-0807), a store stocking tropical-toned sundresses, tops, bathing attire, and accessories. Get shorts, tops, sunglasses, and hats to pull off a surfer look at **Billabong** (5120 Dronnigens Gade, 340/774-4010, 10 A.M.–5 P.M. Mon.–Sat.).

Zora of St. Thomas (5040 Norre Gade, 340/774-2559, www.zoraofstthomas.com)

© SUSANNA HENIGHAN POTTER

Charlotte Amalie

has been making custom leather sandals for men and women since 1962. Devoted followers swear by the unbeatable comfort of sandals designed especially for your feet. Zora, located across from F.D.R. Park, also sells handmade canvas bags, locally blown glass, and jewelry.

Vendor's Plaza

Located at the eastern end of downtown, next to Emancipation Gardens, is an open-air tourist market called Vendor's Plaza. This is where to come for cheap goods: colorful sarongs, St. Thomas T-shirts, jewelry, and handbags. You can also usually find people offering to plait your hair into dreadlock-like braids. The plaza is "open" on days when a cruise ship is in port but deserted on other days.

CROWN BAY

Located alongside the Crown Bay cruise ship dock, **Crown Bay Center** (161 Sub Base, 340/774-2132) is an enclosed mall, with many

of the same retailers you will find downtown and at Havensight. There are also small kiosks selling T-shirts and other souvenirs. If Crown Bay is your port of entry, or if it's raining or otherwise unpleasant outside, this is a good place to shop.

YACHT HAVEN

Lying between downtown and Havensight, **Yacht Haven Grande** (9100 Port of Sale, www.yachthavengrande.com, 340/774-5030) is a marina and outdoor mall, with restaurants, boutiques, and condos. Catering to well-heeled visitors off of visiting mega-yachts, Yacht Haven has the island's most upscale shopping. Shops here are generally open 10 A.M.–5 P.M. daily.

Retailers include **Coach, Louis Vuitton, Gucci, bebe,** and **Bulgaria.** At **How About Your Pet** you can purchase all manner of toys, clothing, and cutesy accessories for your dog, and **Kool Kidz** sells children's clothing, including a wide selection of tutus. **Bella Vera**

(340/774-0374) is a small boutique specializing in name-brand women's clothing from cocktail dresses to jeans.

HAVENSIGHT

Havensight is the outdoor shopping mall next to the West Indian Company cruise ship dock, the main cruise ship dock on St. Thomas. Havensight has a well-worn but comfortable ambience and many of the same retailers as Main Street. Shops here are generally open 10 A.M.–5 P.M. Monday–Sunday, but some close without notice if there's no cruise ship at the dock, especially on Sundays. **Dockside Books** (Building 6, 340/774-4837) is the island's best bookstore, with a fine collection of new releases, reference, and local authors.

RED HOOK AND THE EAST END

Red Hook's American Yacht Harbor offers an alternative to jewelry and perfume stores. Stylish island-style apparel and a wide selection of Crocs, Teva, and other brands of warm-weather footwear are in stock at **Keep Left** (340/775-9964). For silver jewelry and lightweight linen clothing, stop at **Elizabeth Jane's** (340/779-1595). **Pirates of Red Hook** (340/775-5595) has a fun selection of pirate and nautical-themed gifts as well as exclusive jewelry manufactured from authentic artifacts off historic shipwrecks. For incense, wall hangings, and the island's most extensive selection of bongs, make your way to **Rhiannons** (340/779-1877). Surfers and skateboarders can buy equipment (plus clothing to look the part) at **Evolution Surf and Skate** (340/715-0012), home of the "Red Hook Low Life" T-shirts that are all the rage.

TILLET GARDENS

Located in Estate Tutu and surrounded by colorful murals, **Tillett Gardens** (Anna's Retreat, 340/779-1929, www.tillettgardens.com) is an arts community named for its founder, silk-screen artist Jim Tillett. Tillett founded the arts center on an old Danish farm in the 1960s. Today, the surrounding area has evolved into a busy shopping district, but Tillett Gardens is still a quiet oasis. It is home to a half dozen artists' studios and galleries, including **Ridvan Studio** (340/776-0901), a working clay studio specializing in raku wall sculptures, and **FStop** (340/626-0666), a photography studio featuring the work of former Virgin Islands Daily News photographer Steve Rockstein, whose contemporary compositions feature scenes from New York and the Virgin Islands. Look for Tillet Gardens opposite Four Winds shopping plaza, near Tutu Mall.

Sports and Recreation

WATER SPORTS
Snorkeling

The best place on St. Thomas for snorkeling is Coki Beach on the east end. A healthy fringing reef runs parallel to the beach, with a narrow sandbar in the middle. Gear plus orientation, if you want it, is available from **Coki Beach Dive Club** (340/775-4220, www.cokidive.com), adjacent to Coral World Marine Park. Daily gear rental runs $10, or sign up for an hour-long orientation and tour for $30, perfect for beginners. For something different, try a night snorkel ($45), when you can see octopus, sea stars, stingrays, tarpon, and other creatures that like the dark.

You can also snorkel around Cas Cay and the other islands in the East End Marine Sanctuary. **Virgin Islands Ecotours** (Estate Nadir, 340/779-2155, www.viecotours) offers kayak and snorkel tours of the area beginning at $80.

If traditional snorkeling doesn't appeal to you, there are other ways to view the underwater world. In **Sea Trek** (Coral World, 340/775-1555, adults $77, children $68), offered by Coral World at its undersea observatory off Coki Point, you wear a helmet that supplies oxygen as you explore 30 feet below the surface of the water. The cost of Sea Trek includes admission to the Coral World park.

BOSS Submersible Scooter (Crown Bay Marina, 340/777-3549, www.bossusvi.com, $100 per person) puts you on an underwater scooter to explore in water about 7–10 feet deep. In both Sea Trek and BOSS your hair stays dry and you can wear glasses or contacts without a problem.

Diving

Only **Coki Beach** has good diving from the beach, but several notable wreck and reef dive sites are accessible by boat from St. Thomas.

Miss Opportunity, an old Navy hospital barge, lies in about 55 feet of water south of the airport. One of the most popular wreck dives is the *Witshoal II,* an old tank-landing ship that spent 32 post–World War II years hauling wood pulp on the Great Lakes but sank during Tropical Storm Klaus in 1984. Today, it lies in water between 30 and 90 feet deep, west of Saba Island off St. Thomas, and is home to a thriving artificial reef. Three other wrecks, the *Witconcrete II, Grainton,* and *Witservice IV,* lie around Saba Island.

There is another cluster of snorkel and dive sites around Buck and Capella Islands, off the southeast coast of St. Thomas. Not to be confused with St. Croix's Buck Island, St. Thomas's Buck is small, rocky, and home to a lighthouse. The west end of the island offers year-round protected reef diving and snorkeling. The *Cartanza Senora* (sometimes called the *Cartenser Senior*) was sunk here as an artificial reef in 1979. Submarine sightseeing tours

bring visitors to this area, especially the north shore of Buck Island.

The **Cow and Calf,** another popular dive site, is named for its resemblance to an adult and baby whale. Below water, this dive site is a maze of arches, ledges, and tunnels.

In addition to sites mentioned here, many St. Thomas operators sail to sites around St. John and even to the British Virgin Islands.

Expect to pay about $90 for a one-tank dive; $125 for a two-tank dive.

DIVE OPERATORS

Red Hook Dive Center (American Yacht Harbor, 340/774-3483, www.redhookdivecenter.com) is one of the largest St. Thomas dive operators, offering a whole range of dive packages, instruction, and night snorkels and dives. The company also has an office at Sugar Bay Resort.

Another favorite St. Thomas dive shop is **Coki Beach Dive Club** (340/775-4220, www.cokidive.com). These folks offer some of the best and friendliest dive instruction, and you can dive right off the beach—no need to get in a boat. Also try **Aqua Action** (Secret Harbour Beach Resort, 340/775-6285, www.aadiveres.com) and **St. Thomas Diving Club** (Bolongo Bay Beach Resort, 340/776-2381, www.stthomasdivingclub.com).

Kayaking

Bovoni Cay, Patricia Cay, and Cas Cay lie within the protected mangrove lagoon offshore from the community of Nadir and are ideal for exploring in a kayak. **Virgin Islands Ecotours** (Estate Nadir, 340/779-2155, www.viecotours) offers guided kayak tours of the area, plus hiking and snorkeling tours around Cas Cay.

Tours, which range from 2.5 to 5 hours, run from $80–150 for adults and $45–80 for children under 12.

Parasailing

Parasailers ride above the water at

exhilarating speeds. To give it a try, call **Caribbean Watersports and Tours** (340/775-9360), which will pick you up from your hotel and take you to one of its 10 parasailing locations around St. Thomas. A 10-minute ride costs $80.

Windsurfing and Kiteboarding

Windsurfers glide along the surface of the water astride a board, powered by a single sail. Kiteboarders ride the surface of the sea, powered by a kite sail. Both sports are exhilarating and physically challenging ways to get out on the water. For lessons ($50–75 per hour) and gear rental call **West Indies Windsurfing** (340/774-6530).

Stand Up Paddleboarding

Easy to learn and a fun way to explore the ocean, stand up paddleboarding, or SUP, has grown in popularity in recent years. The calm waters of Magen's Bay are a good place for beginners to try out this relatively new sport; rentals are available from the water-sports center on the eastern end of the beach.

Blue Water SUP Safaris (Hull Bay, 340/774-9436, www.supvi.com) offers lessons ($65–90), rentals ($90 per day), and full-day group excursions ($1,200).

Fishing

St. Thomas is the base of the largest sportfishing fleet in the Virgin Islands. Sportfishers depart daily from marinas along the east end of the island, many headed to the North Drop, a famed fishing ground in the British Virgin Islands. Half-day inshore fishing trips are also available. Expect to pay $600 and up for a half-day trip, $1,200 and up for a full day, and more for 10-hour marlin outings. Prices are quoted per outing (not per person). Typically equipment, bait, tackle, fuel, and beverages are included.

Marlin season is in the summer, when the waters are at their warmest. Marlin are tagged and released. Other sport fish, such as barracuda, wahoo, tuna, mahimahi, and jacks can be kept; most boats will fillet up to 20 pounds for you at the end of the day.

The **Marlin Prince** (340/693-5929, www.marlinprince.com), a 45-foot comfortable Viking captained by Eddie Morrison, can accommodate up to six and features a large air-conditioned cabin. **Double Header Sportfishing** (Sapphire Marina, 340/777-7317, www.doubleheadersportfishing.net) has three boats: a 40-foot sportfisher and two 35-foot center console open sportfishers. **Mixed Bag** (340/513-0389, www.sportfishingstjohn.com), captained by Robert Richards, offers offshore and inshore fishing aboard 40-foot and 32-foot sportfishers. **About Time Charters** (340/779-9028, www.stthomassportfishing.com) offers some of the least expensive outings, aboard a 29-foot sport cat and a 31-foot Bertram express sportfisher.

The **Virgin Islands Game Fishing Club** (6501 Red Hook Plaza, 340/775-9144, www.vigfc.com) organizes fishing tournaments, including the Offshore Marine Dolphin Derby in April, the July Marlin Open, and Wahoo Wind-Up every November.

SAILING
Day Sails

Spend a day on the water, visiting snorkel sites and quiet anchorages around St. John and the British Virgin Islands. Day sails cost $100–120 per person for a full day, $60–90 per person for a half day. Sunset cruises are also offered.

Bad Kitty (340/777-7245) offers full- and half-day snorkel trips to the British Virgin Islands aboard a 49-foot motorized catamaran. **The St. John Champagne Cat** (340/775-5055, www.cruiseshipexcusions.com) offers half-day sails to Honeymoon Beach, St. John.

Boat Rentals

If you have experience at the helm, renting a boat is a fun way to explore other islands and get out on the water. Powerboat rentals are available from **Nauti Nymph** (American Yacht Harbor, 340/775-5066). The company has 25-, 29-, and 31-foot powerboats, which come equipped with a bimini top, ice cooler, and freshwater shower. Rates range $225–480 for a half day, $240–570 for a full day. Skippers are available.

Regattas

The St. Thomas Yacht Club (340/775-6320) hosts the **International Rolex Regatta** every March. The Rolex is part of the Caribbean Ocean Racing Triangle, which also includes the St. Maarten Heineken Regatta and the BVI Spring Regatta. It is the premier sailing event on St. Thomas's calendar.

Other annual regattas include the Martin Luther King Regatta in January, the Scotiabank Regatta in June, and the Columbus Day Regatta in October; all are organized by the St. Thomas Yacht Club.

Marinas

St. Thomas's marinas are clustered around Charlotte Amalie and the east end. The **Yacht Haven Grande** (340/774-9500, www.yachthavengrande.com) is located between Havensight and Charlotte Amalie and can accommodate boats up to 450 feet in length. Yacht Haven offers in-slip high-speed communications, provisioning, 24-hour security, catering, a florist, dedicated crew facilities, and tennis, just to name a few amenities.

Also near Charlotte Amalie, **Crown Bay Marina** (Gregorie Channel, 340/774-2255, fax 340/776-2760, www.crownbay.com) is a 99-slip full-service marina and host to the annual Charter Yacht Society boat show. There is a chandlery and repair shop plus shops, restaurants, high-speed communication, fuel, water, electricity, and pump-out service. Crown Bay can accommodate vessels up to 200 feet long and 15-foot drafts.

American Yacht Harbor (Red Hook, 340/775-6454, fax 340/776-5970, www.igy-americanyachtharbor.com) is a 126-slip, full-service marina in the heart of Red Hook. Amenities include refueling, pump-out, communications, ice, water, and electricity. AYH can accommodate boats up to 110 feet long, with a 10-foot draft.

Anchorages

St. Thomas has 11 official anchorages, including Bolongo Bay, Charlotte Amalie Harbor, Cowpet Bay, Hull Bay, Jersey Bay, Long Bay, Muller Bay, Nazareth Bay (Secret Harbor), Red Hook, Benner Bay, and Vessup Bay. On Water Island, you can anchor at Sprat Bay, Flamingo Bay, and Honeymoon Bay. On Hassel Island, anchor at Careening Cove.

The Reef Ecology Foundation of St. Thomas and St. John has set up a limited number of moorings for public use to protect the coral reef from anchor damage. These blue-striped buoys are free but restricted to boats less than 60 feet long. They are located at Thatch Cay, Grass Cay, Congo Cay, Carvel Rock, Great St. James, Little St. James, Cow and Calf, Capella Island, Flat Cay, and Saba Island.

These moorings are intended for day use only (three-hour limit) and not in storm conditions.

Yacht Clubs

The **St. Thomas Yacht Club** (Cowpet Bay, 340/775-6320, www.styc.net) organizes regattas and social events year-round. The International Rolex Regatta in March is the biggest sailing event of the year, but the yacht club hosts a number of other smaller-scale regattas from October to May.

LAND PURSUITS
Golf

Mahogany Run Golf Course (340/777-6006 or 800/253-7103, www.mahoganyrungolf.com) is

St. Thomas's only golf course. The 18-hole, par 70 course was first built in 1980 but has undergone recent renovations and improvements. Nestled in a small valley near Magen's Bay on northeast St. Thomas, Mahogany Run is compact and highly engineered. It was designed by George and Tom Fazio. The course is best known for the Devil's Triangle, the challenging 13th, 14th, and 15th holes, where golfers battle the windswept Atlantic coast.

Tee-time reservations are accepted up to two months in advance with full prepayment. Golf course amenities include a newly renovated clubhouse, restaurant, and pro shop. Greens fees (including cart rental) range from $165 per pair in winter to $125 per pair in the summer.

Tennis

There are six public tennis courts on St. Thomas two at Crown Bay (Subbase), two at Bordeaux, and two at Long Bay. They are open on a first-come, first-served basis.

Several hotels also have tennis courts. Near Charlotte Amalie, the **Marriott Frenchman's Reef** (340/776-8500, ext. 6818, $10 per hour) has four lighted courts. **Bluebeard's Castle Hotel** (340/774-8990, $6 per hour) has two lighted courts.

Bolongo Bay Beach Club (340/775-1800, ext. 468, $10 per hour) has four lighted courts. **Mahogany Run Tennis Club** (340/775-5000, $8–10 per hour), next to the same-named golf course, has two lighted courts.

Near the east end, there are courts at **Sapphire Beach Resort and Marina** (340/775-6100, $10 per hour) and the **Ritz-Carlton** (340/775-3333, $60 per hour).

Spectator Sports

St. Thomas has local basketball, softball, and soccer leagues, plus regular horse races, tennis

© SUSANNA HENIGHAN POTTER

Mahogony Run is St. Thomas's only golf course.

competitions, and golf tournaments. Check the Emile Griffith ball field across from the ferry dock in Charlotte Amalie for local softball and Little League action. Basketball takes place on community courts around the island; tournaments are held at the University of the Virgin Islands gym at Brewer's Bay. Check the local papers for upcoming sporting events.

Horse racing is one of the most popular local sports. Races are held monthly at **Clinton Phipps Racetrack** (Estate Nadir, 340/775-4355).

Accommodations

There are two kinds of accommodations on St. Thomas: large chain resorts and small independent hotels and guesthouses. Most people who come here stay in the large resorts; they have the longest advertising reach, and many offer attractive package deals. Chains including Best Western, Holiday Inn, Marriott, Wyndham, and Antilles Resorts have hotels on St. Thomas.

Travelers looking for accommodation that is intimate, unique, and locally owned would be wise to steer clear of chain resorts. Rooms in Charlotte Amalie's historic district are affordable, and some are quite luxurious. There are also a few independent beachfront hotels for a range of budgets.

VILLAS

St. Thomas has hundreds of villas for rent. The best-known villa agent is **McLaughlin Anderson** (Bluebeard's Castle, 800/537-6246 or 340/776-0635, www.mclaughlinanderson. com). Also try **Calypso Realty** (340/774-1620, www.calypsorealty.com).

HISTORIC CHARLOTTE AMALIE

Accommodations in Charlotte Amalie offer proximity to downtown shopping and attractions, a pleasant old-world atmosphere, and moderate prices. Street crime is a problem in the city, however, and after dark, taxis are recommended. Some downtown inns are set on steep lots; if stairs are a concern, inquire about this before booking.

Under $125

One of the best values on St. Thomas, **◖ The**

Crystal Palace (12 Crystal Gade, 340/777-2277 or 866/502-2277, www.crystalpalaceusvi. com, $119–149 winter, $99–119 summer) is a five-room bed-and-breakfast located in a historic Charlotte Amalie townhouse. The colonial manor is furnished with 18th- and 19th-century West Indian pieces and is set in a neighborhood of equally impressive colonial-era townhouses, churches, and shops. All rooms are air-conditioned; two come with private baths. Guests share a kitchenette, and a continental breakfast is served overlooking Charlotte Amalie Harbor every morning. Host Ronnie Lockhart is a treasure trove of local history and tips for visiting St. Thomas.

Perched on the edge of Government Hill, **Galleon House Bed and Breakfast** (31 Kongens Gade, 340/774-6952 or 800/524-2052, www.galleonhouse.com, $85–159 winter, $75–125 summer) offers 15 moderately priced rooms within walking distance of downtown shopping and historic attractions. Rooms lack personality but are equipped with air-conditioning, cable TV, and telephones. The cheapest rooms have shared bathroom facilities; the most expensive have private balconies and views of Charlotte Amalie. There is a small pool, and guests praise the complimentary made-to-order breakfast.

With 21 rooms, **Bunker Hill Hotel** (3207 Commandant Gade, 340/774-8056, www. bunkerhillhotel.com, $99–125 winter, $79–105 summer) is one of the largest downtown hotels. Superior rooms offer balconies and views; all rooms have basic furnishings, air-conditioning, cable TV, a telephone, and private bath. Two pools and full complimentary breakfast round out the amenities at this handy hotel.

Next door to Government House and in the middle of Charlotte Amalie's historic district, **(Hotel 1829** (Government Hill, 340/776-1829 or 800/524-2002, www.hotel1829.com, $105–190 winter, $80–145 summer) is 15-room inn with historic ambience. Built by a wealthy French sea merchant for his bride in 1829, the three-story building was a private home until 1906. The original kitchen has been turned into a bar and dining room where visitors can play backgammon or sip cocktails while looking out over Charlotte Amalie Harbor. The view is especially lovely at night. Decor includes original hand-painted tiles, life-size Italian chess pieces, and a Tiffany stained-glass mural. Rooms are furnished with mahogany furniture, cedar ceilings, and bamboo platform beds. Suites offer private balconies while "modest rooms" cater to budget-minded travelers. All rooms have air-conditioning, cable TV, private baths, and wireless Internet, and guests can cool off in the property's small pool.

The Inn at Blackbeard's Castle (37 Blackbeard's Hill, 340/776-1234 or 800/524-2002, $105–145 winter, $80–115 summer) is located atop Government Hill on the upper edge of Charlotte Amalie's historic district. The pirate theme prevails around the hotel grounds, but the rooms offer respite. Hardwood floors, four-poster beds, and private balconies overlooking the harbor make this a pleasant, even romantic, choice. Rooms are equipped with coffeemakers, refrigerators, and televisions. There is a pool on the property.

Sleep in a 150-year-old Danish manor house at **Miller Manor** (2527 Prindsesse Gade, 340/774-1535 or 888/229-0762, www.millermanor.com, $85–145), a guesthouse overlooking Charlotte Amalie Harbor. Each room features a mini-refrigerator, microwave, and air-conditioning; select rooms offer harbor views and private balconies. The view from the veranda and bar is nice, and hosts Marj and Harry win praise for attentiveness. Miller Manor is located adjacent to a sketchy part of town.

$125-175

The Green Iguana Hotel (37B Blackbeard's Hill, 340/776-7654 or 800/484-8634, www.thegreeniguana.com, $140–179 winter, $125–155 summer) wraps around the side of Blackbeard's Hill with views of Crown Bay and parts of downtown Charlotte Amalie. The rooms are clean and cozy and come equipped with modern amenities, including satellite TV, microwaves, coffeemakers, air-conditioning, telephones, and wireless Internet. Large rooms have full kitchens. The Green Iguana is within walking distance of downtown Charlotte Amalie, although climbing Blackbeard's Hill on your way back is no stroll in the park.

$175-225

A lovely location and personalized service keep guests coming back to **(Bellavista Bed and Breakfast** (2713 Murphy Gade, 340/714-5704 or 888/333-3063, www.bellavista-bnb.com, $195–265 winter, $175–235 summer). A four-room bed-and-breakfast around the corner from the governor's private residence, Bellavista lives up to its name: views are of the bright red roofs of historic Charlotte Amalie and the turquoise water of the harbor. Guests have access to the pool, an above-average collection of vacation reading, full made-from-scratch breakfasts, and the invaluable advice of hostess Wendy Snodgrass. Rooms are cozy and comfortable, but you will probably find yourself relaxing in the spacious sitting rooms and on the balcony. Amenities include air-conditioning, cable TV, and nightly turndown service. No detail goes unnoticed.

OUTSIDE CHARLOTTE AMALIE

There are a number of hotels and inns on the outskirts of Charlotte Amalie. Some are nestled in quiet residential communities, and others are right on the beach.

$125-175

Mafolie Hotel (7091 Estate Mafolie, 340/774-2790, www.mafolie.com, $170–210 winter, $105–135 summer) is a moderately priced 22-room inn overlooking Charlotte Amalie. Rooms are not luxurious, but do offer air-conditioning, cable TV, phone, refrigerator, microwave, coffeemaker, wireless Internet, and tasteful decor. Guests are offered continental breakfast and a daily hotel shuttle (one-way) to Magen's Bay or downtown. The popular on-site restaurant serves dinner nightly and there is a pool. Some rooms have balconies overlooking the picturesque harbor, but no matter where you stay, you are never far from the impressive panorama below you. The hotel is set on a busy road perched well above town; walking to town is out of the question and it can be a bit noisy, especially at rush hour.

$175-225

The **Island Beachcomber Hotel** (8071 Lindberg Beach Rd., 340/774-5250 or 800/982-9898, www.islandbeachcomber.net, $199–229 winter, $129–149 summer) has two things going for it: it is on the beach and next to the airport. Rooms are not noted for their character but come well-equipped with air-conditioning, satellite TV, wireless Internet, refrigerator, phone, coffeemaker, and hair dryer. There is a restaurant and bar on the premises.

Over $300

St. Thomas's flagship hotel is the **Marriott Frenchman's Reef** (5 Estate Bakkeroe, 340/776-8500, $350–500 winter, $250–400 summer), a 450-room hotel located on a promontory at the entrance to Charlotte Amalie Harbor. Conference facilities consisting of 31 meeting rooms make this a top choice for events on the island, but vacationers will also find a host of amenities: wireless Internet, fitness center, on-site spa, room service, four pools, and nine restaurants, just to name a few. A $48 million renovation in 2011 included construction of new pools, a new spa, and a new fitness center, plus renovation of all guest rooms. The result: some of the most modern and stylish facilities in the Virgin Islands. All water-facing rooms have private balconies overlooking the harbor, where you can watch cruise ships, seaplanes, ferries, and pleasure yachts come and go. Morningstar Beach is a short walk from the resort.

RED HOOK AND THE EAST END

The east end is where you will find large beachfront resorts, including chain resorts operated by Ritz-Carlton, Wyndham, Antilles Resorts, and Equivest, a time-share company. Listed here are hotels with a more independent feel.

$225-300

Bolongo Bay Beach Club (340/775-1800 or 800/524-4746, www.bolongobay.com, $230–395 winter, $180–310 summer) is a family-run 65-room beachfront resort that offers a warm welcome to its fun-loving clientele. While not luxurious, amenities are above average and Bolongo's genuinely friendly staff, active water sports program, and popular restaurants bring back many repeat visitors. The hotel is set on Bolongo Bay beach, a broad, curved ring of sand shaded by coconut palms. There are two restaurants, a dive shop, a plethora of nonmotorized water sports, and nightly live entertainment. An all-inclusive option, which includes food, alcohol, and some activities, is available ($530–680 winter, $400–560 summer).

Set in a sheltered, crescent-shaped bay near Red Hook, **Secret Harbour Beach Resort**

(6280 Estate Nazareth, 340/775-5550, www. secretharbourvi.com, $275–475 winter, $185–215 summer) is a 60-room, full-service resort. Rooms overlook Secret Harbour and are appointed with tasteful rattan furniture, tile floors, and exposed beams in the ceiling. Amenities include a water sports center, tennis courts, a pool, an on-site restaurant, and gift shops. Rooms are air-conditioned, with cable TV, phone, and wireless Internet. Many have balconies overlooking the ocean.

Over $300

Point Pleasant Resort (6600 Estate Smith Bay, 340/775-7200 or 800/524-2300, fax 340/776-5694, www.pointpleasantresort.com, $300–375 winter, $180–255 summer) is part of the Antilles Resort family, but it retains a unique feel. Originally a family-owned resort, Point Pleasant is a series of individual villas perched over Water Bay and overlooking Coki Point. All suites come with a full kitchen, satellite TV, air-conditioning, private balconies, and ocean views. Suites range in size from junior suites perfect for two adults to deluxe suites for as many as five people. There are pools, a beach, and walking trails leading to nearby beaches and overlooks. In addition, there are two popular restaurants on-site.

All-inclusive **Sugar Bay Resort** (6500 Estate Smith Bay, 340/779-8800 or 877/894-4461, www.sugarbayresortandspa.com, $450–650 winter, $350–550 summer) offers guests a no-fuss vacation at a beachfront location. Spend your days playing on the caramel sand at Sugar Bay Beach, relaxing by the pool, or dining in one of six on-site restaurants. A kid's club from 10 A.M.–4 P.M. daily keeps youngsters occupied with arts and crafts, games, and outdoor activities.

The classiest accommodations on St.

Thomas are at the **Ritz-Carlton** (6900 Great Bay, 340/775-3333, $550–5,000 winter, $400–5,000 summer). The dark wood and large windows of the 180 guest rooms and suites are reminiscent of the mahogany furnishings and West Indian construction of historic great houses. But the amenities are entirely modern: private terrace, soaking tub and rain showers, flat-screen TVs, wireless Internet, and a business center. On-site spa services, a fitness center, and guest facilities at two beaches provide plenty of reasons not to venture off the property.

WATER ISLAND
$125-175

The **Virgin Islands Campground** (Water Island, 340/776-5488 or 877/502-7225, www.virginislandscampground.com, $120–160 winter, $100–130 summer) is one-of-a-kind on St. Thomas, a destination not known for outdoorsy pursuits. The campground's six cottages closely resemble those at Maho Bay Camps in St. John. They consist of a wood frame enclosed with mesh screens and heavy-duty canvas. There are beds to sleep three adults (or two adults and two children), electricity, a cooler, bins for your food, a dining table, and a porch. A communal pavilion houses cooking facilities plus a communications room with Internet, telephone, and television. There is also a modern bathhouse and a hot tub for everyone at the camp to share.

The camp is atop a rise near the center of 500-acre Water Island. You can walk to Honeymoon Beach or the St. Thomas ferry, but many guests prefer to rent a bicycle from the campground to get around. The Water Island ferry runs most days (6:30 A.M.–6 P.M.) and offers late service several nights per week, making it easy to get to St. Thomas to sightsee there.

Food

Restaurants catering to tourists are generally high quality and range from moderate to expensive. More outgoing diners will enjoy trying local eateries as well.

CHARLOTTE AMALIE
Casual

Set in a restored waterfront warehouse, **Gladys' Cafe** (Royal Dane Mall, 340/774-6604, 7 A.M.–5 P.M. Mon.–Sat., 8 A.M.–3 P.M. Sun., $7–15) draws a crowd of loyal regulars for her traditional breakfast, served with lots of hot coffee or local "bush" tea. At lunch, retreat into the air-conditioning for sandwiches, soups, and salads, or better yet, order from the West Indian menu of saltfish, mutton stew, conch, and fish. Buy a bottle of Gladys's own hot sauce as a souvenir, or taste her excellent Bloody Mary. With a winning atmosphere and efficient service, you'll want to come back.

Across the street from Emancipation Gardens, **Jen's Island Café and Deli** (Grand Galleria, 43–46 Norre Gade, 340/777-4611, 7 A.M.–4 P.M. Mon.–Fri., $5–10) is more than just a deli. Choose from sandwiches, wraps, soup, salads, and made-to-order entrées such as the finger-licking mango barbecue wings. Breakfast options include burritos, bagels, and omelets. Jen's opens on Saturdays when a cruise ship is in port.

In the midst of bustling A.H. Riise Mall, look for an oasis: **Amalia Cafe** (24 Palm Passage, 340/714-7373, $15–26, 11 A.M.–9:30 P.M. Mon.–Sat.) is a popular choice for Spanish cuisine. Diners praise the tapas menu, sangria, paella, and the outstanding service provided by owners Randolph and Helga Maynard and their staff. Amalia is open on Sundays when a cruise ship is in port.

West Indian

Cuzzin's Caribbean Restaurant & Bar (7 Back St., 340/777-4711, 11 A.M.–4:30 P.M. Mon.–Sat., $13–20) is the place to come for authentic Virgin Islands and West Indian cuisine. Local dishes include mutton stew, conch salad, and fried or steamed fish, and don't miss the opportunity to sample an authentic local drink like mauby (made from a local tree bark), ginger beer, or sea moss (made from seaweed). Cuzzin's is tucked away in a restored 19th-century livery stable and cookshop away from the bustle of downtown.

Italian

For classic northern Italian cuisine served in a romantic setting, come to **Virgilio's** (18 Dronningen's Gade, 340/776-4920, 11:30 A.M.–10 P.M. Mon.–Sat., $22–40). Tucked away in a tastefully decorated restored townhouse with vaulted ceilings, this is an intimate and sophisticated place to dine. Soft music and expert service create a refined ambience. Meals are expertly created: lobster ravioli, rack of lamb, and some of the most luxurious desserts on the island.

FRENCHTOWN

Some of the island's best restaurants are found in Frenchtown, a community on the west side of Charlotte Amalie Harbor notable for its quaint West Indian cottages. Walk around this peaceful neighborhood and take your pick for fine dining.

Casual

A yachtman's favorite long ago discovered by the rest, **Hook, Line and Sinker** (2 Honduras St., 340/776-9708, 11:30 A.M.–4 P.M. and 6–10 P.M. Mon.–Sat., 10 A.M.–2:30 P.M. Sun., lunch $9–15, dinner $10–28) is a waterfront restaurant serving lunch and dinner, plus brunch on Sundays. Seafood right off the dock is the specialty, but plenty of people come here for the generous burgers, crisp Greek salad, and liver and onions.

Fusion

A Frenchtown landmark for more than 25 years, **❘ Bella Blu** (24-A Honduras St., 340/774-4349, $9–28, 11:30 A.M.–10 P.M. Mon.–Sat.) has a dizzying array of choices: Austrian specialties, pasta, Mediterranean dishes, salads, sandwiches, and fresh seafood. One diner can try souvlakia (skewered lamb) while another has veal jaeger schnitzel. The dining area is cozy yet chic, with a changing array of local artwork on the walls and bright colors all around. An outdoor wine bar is the perfect place to relax and watch the sun go down over Frenchtown. This is also a great stop for lunch and is popular with the local business crowd.

❘ Craig and Sally's (3525 Honduras St., 340/777-9949, 11:30 A.M.–3 P.M. Wed.–Fri., 5:30–10 P.M. Wed.–Sun., $14–32) is an intimate, romantic restaurant known for imaginative cuisine. The menu changes daily according to the whims of chef Sally and the availability of the best ingredients. Imagine creamy Manchego risotto, linguini putanesca, and seared local wahoo. You can also choose from one of the best wine lists on the island—and don't miss Sally's incredible pumpkin chiffon pie.

You can nibble from the extensive tapas menu, or dine more formally on fresh seafood, lamb, or beef at **Oceana** (8 Honduras St., 340/774-4262, 5–10 P.M. Mon.–Sat., $21–35) located in Villa Olga on the tip of Frenchtown. The downstairs bar attracts a lively after-work crowd. Upstairs, diners choose from a seafood-heavy menu with specialties like pan-fried trout and mussels in white wine sauce. The downstairs tapas menu includes crostini, cheese platters, and the like.

For the best pizza on St. Thomas, make your way to **Pie Whole** (24A Honduras St.,

340/642-5074, 11 A.M.–11 5–11 P.M. Sat., $14–20. B pizza comes in traditional ar binations, including a meat-lo ham, and sausage pizza and "ve with vegetable toppings. If pie isn't your thing, choose from a handful of well-executed pasta dishes, including fettuccini with arugula and goat cheese. Nothing goes with pizza like beer, and the folks at Pie Whole have gone to the ends of the earth—or so it seems—to find the best beer selection on St. Thomas, by far. If you've never had Belgian beer, come find out what you're missing.

CROWN BAY
Casual

Rub elbows with the sailing set at **Tickles Dockside Pub** (Crown Bay Marina, 340/776-1595, $10–22, 7 A.M.–midnight). This open-air waterfront eatery is casual and welcoming, with a menu reminiscent of a diner back home: hearty breakfast platters, burgers, fish and chips, spaghetti and meatballs, chicken-fried steak. Watch happenings at the adjacent marina while you dine.

WATER ISLAND

If you find yourself hungry on Water island, head to **Pirate's Ridge** (63 Water Island, 340/473-6722, 11 A.M.–7 P.M., $10–18), a pizzeria and deli located on the hill overlooking Honeymoon Beach.

HAVENSIGHT
Coffee Shops and Cafés

Bad Ass Coffee (Yacht Haven Grande, 340/775-8223, 7 A.M.–6 P.M. Mon.–Sat., 7 A.M.–4 P.M. Sun., $2–5) will get you going or keep you wired seven days a week. In addition to coffee, the shop serves bagels, pastries, and a few simple sandwiches.

Just down the road in Havensight, near Paradise Point, is **Barefoot Buddha**

777-3668, 7 A.M.–3 P.M. Mon.–Sat.,
A.M.–3 P.M. Sun., $5–12), a laid-back coffee-
house-style eatery serving organic coffee and tea,
baked goods, sandwiches, frittatas, and salads.

Casual

Shipwreck Bar and Restaurant (Al Cohen's
Plaza, 340/777-1293, 11 A.M.–4 A.M. Mon.–
Sat., 11:30 A.M.–2 A.M. Sun., $7–12) is a dark,
cavernous bar with monster-sized burgers. This
is a favorite hangout for young statesiders who
live on St. Thomas. Come here for bar food
at its best: quarter-pound hot dogs, fries, na-
chos—you get the picture.

Sushi

Ben Iguana's Sushi Bar (Havensight Mall
Building IX, 340/777-8744, 11:30 A.M.–3 P.M.
and 5–9 P.M. Mon.–Sat., $5–12 per sushi roll)
offers dozens of artfully crafted sushi rolls from
its location adjacent to the cruise ship pier.
Don't miss the steamed mussels served with
tangy-sweet dressing that will knock your socks
off. The sushi salad offers a filling alternative if
you've tired of seafood. Blindingly white decor,
a wall-sized fish tank, and dozens of leafy green
plants lend a certain 1970s vibe to your meal.

FRENCHMAN'S BAY
Fusion

Havana Blue (Morningstar Beach, 340/715-2583,
5–10 P.M., $28–48) serves Latin American –Asian
fusion at a lovely beachfront location. Leave your
flip-flops at home for this trendy and elegant
dining experience. Try ceviche to start, and for
your entrée the Havana Chicken, marinated and
stuffed with cheese, cilantro, and garlic, or the ac-
claimed Ancho Filet, a grilled filet mignon seasoned with ancho chile and espresso. There is also
an alluring tapas menu, and don't skip the cocktails: the margaritas, mojitos, and sangria are the
perfect start to your evening. A $50 prix-fixe menu
is available, or go all out with the seven-course
extravaganza starting at $125 per person.

MID ISLAND
International

One of the best-kept secrets on St. Thomas,
Randy's Bar and Bistro (Al Cohen's Plaza,
340/775-5001, 11 A.M.–10 P.M. Mon.–Sat.,
$12–37) is a gourmand's delight tucked into
a commercial storefront at the top of Raphune
Hill. Happy hour is popular here—especially
among martini fans—and many drinkers migrate to the tables set amid wine crates for dinner of roasted lamb, fresh salmon, mussels, and
more. Lunch is more casual but no less satisfy-
ing, with first-class deli sandwiches, salads, and
pasta. Then-candidate Barack Obama dined
here with his family in 2008.

NORTHSIDE
Casual

Few places on St. Thomas capture island style
better than **Hull Bay Hideaway** (Hull Bay,
340/777-1898, 10 A.M.–10 P.M. daily, $8),
serving sandwiches, burgers, and fries. Come
in bare feet and don't dare hurry. This open-air,
laid-back bar and restaurant caters to beachgoers, families, and people just looking for a little
company. Games like horseshoes and domi-
nos are popular ways to spend the afternoon.
If you're hungry, the famed Arthur Burger,
named after the proprietor, is the way to go.

Fine Dining

The best gourmet dining on St. Thomas is
found at ◖**Old Stone Farmhouse** (Mahogany
Run, 340/777-6277, 5:30–9:30 P.M. Mon.–
Sat., 11 A.M.–2 P.M. and 6–9:30 P.M. Sun.,
$25–40), a delightful and attentive restaurant
located in a 200-year-old restored plantation
house. The menu changes daily but count on
exciting taste combinations and impeccable
presentation. The signature Butcher's Block allows guests back to the kitchen to meet the chef
and choose their own cut of local or imported
meat or fish. Save room for the best desserts
on the island.

RED HOOK
Casual

What's not to love about **Duffy's Love Shack** (340/779-2080, 11 A.M.–midnight, $10–20), a colorful roadside shack serving the most outrageous drinks on the island? Choose from concoctions such as Zoom Zoom Shooter, the Funky Monkey, Taboo Lagoon, and the signature Volcano, 50 ounces of frozen tropical goodness. For eats, choose from the reliable bar menu of tacos, burgers, and wings, or go upscale with pu-pu platters and dinner entrées like grilled mahimahi and Cuban-style steak. Bring plenty of cash: Duffy's doesn't accept credit cards.

Craving Irish home-style stew or bangers and mash? Me neither, but don't let that stop you from enjoying a pleasant meal at **Molly Malone's** (American Yacht Harbor, 340/775-1270, 7 A.M.–11 P.M. daily, $10–30). Located dockside at American Yacht Harbor, Molly's is a friendly choice for breakfast, lunch, dinner, or drinks. Despite its billing as an Irish pub, Molly Malone's offers all the American standards, as well as fresh seafood. Guests praise the breakfast menu, which includes lobster omelets, pancakes, and island-style French toast. Molly's attracts a menagerie of iguanas, a fun diversion for children.

Italian

Pesce (American Yacht Harbor, 340/715-1442, 11 A.M.–10 P.M. daily, lunch $10–15, dinner $20–30) has been a popular island institution for familiar Italian cuisine for years. (It was previously called the East End Cafe.) The menu features Italian classics such as baked pasta dishes and eggplant Parmesan, as well as seafood. On weekends (11 A.M.–4 P.M.) you can also order from the brunch menu, which features omelets, eggs, toast, and other morning favorites.

Tapas

Next door to Pesce is **The Cellar** (American Yacht Harbor, 340/715-1442, 5 P.M.–2 A.M. daily, $9–18), a tapas restaurant with an extensive wine list and martinis. Small plates feature the very best in fresh greens, seafood, beef, and chicken, all with a creative and sophisticated flair. Pesce and the Cellar are proponents of the Slow Food movement, and they source local and organic ingredients whenever they can.

EAST END
Casual

Located at fun-loving Bolongo Bay Beach Resort, **Iggies** (Bolongo Bay, 340/693-2600, 11:30 A.M.–11 P.M., $10–25) is a beachfront eatery that knows how to have a good time. Iggies has live music several nights a week and special events like karaoke night, all-you-can-eat barbecue (Sundays), and the Carnival show every Wednesday. The menu does not stray far from old standbys: burgers, barbecue, and seafood take center stage. This is a good choice for a fun casual meal on the beach.

Fine Dining

The beachfront **Blue Moon Cafe** (Secret Harbour Resort, 340/779-2262, 8 A.M.–10 P.M. daily, $14–36) transforms from a casual beachfront café during the day to a refined and romantic spot at night. The breakfast menu features traditional and island favorites such as eggs Benedict and stuffed French toast. At lunch, choose from a lineup of fresh salads, sandwiches, and wraps. For dinner, the menu includes seafood dishes, pasta, risottos, and grill favorites, including double-cut pork chops and fresh grilled mahimahi. There is also a bar menu. Sunsets are glorious, but the sand flies can be a pest.

Bolongo Bay's upscale eatery is **The Lobster Grill** (Bolongo Bay, 340/775-1800, breakfast daily 7:30–10:30 A.M., lunch Mon.–Fri. 11:30 A.M.–3 P.M., dinner Fri.–Sun. 6–9 P.M., $20–45), a gourmet restaurant that offers a view of the water and an intimate setting for a special dinner out. Friday night is lobster night, Saturday is surf and turf, and Sunday is prime rib. In addition, you can order seared tuna, herbed mahimahi, glazed duck, or other traditional favorites, including shrimp, pasta, and steak. Lunch is a casual affair ($10–14), with salads, burgers, and sandwiches.

Seafood

Known for its fresh seafood and lovely down-island views **Agave Terrace** (Point Pleasant Resort, 340/775-4142, 6–10 P.M. daily, $20–50) fuses Italian, Asian, and Caribbean styles for seemingly effortless and impeccable meals. Seafood risotto, Thai-style curry shrimp, and charbroiled New York strip steak are among the options, but it is the fresh, local fish and lobster that draw the most raves. Muted piano, guitar, and steel-pan music four nights a week add to the sensuous atmosphere.

SMITH BAY
Italian

For upscale Italian cuisine, look no further than **Romano's Restaurant** (6697 Estate Smith Bay, 340/775-0045, $23–42). Proprietor Tony Romano is equally passionate about food and art, and the result is a restaurant that caters to all the senses. Art adorns the walls and each of the 12 tables is set with the exactitude you expect from a fine restaurant. The menu features the simple, yet delectable, cuisine of northern Italy: Ossobucco, Salmone in Gratella, and Lasagne Quattro Formaggio.

MARKETS

St. Thomas's largest grocery store is **Plaza Extra** at Tutu Park Mall at mid-island. **Gourmet Gallery** (Havensight Mall, 340/774-4948) is an upscale grocery store with a good takeout deli.

Farmers markets may be found on Saturday mornings at the market square in downtown Charlotte Amalie, every other Sunday morning at Yacht Haven Grande, and on the last Sunday of the month at We Grow Food in Bordeaux.

Information and Services

TOURIST OFFICES

The Department of Tourism operates an information office at Havensight, near the cruise ship dock, but don't go out of your way to find it: it's pretty useless unless all you want are numerous advertising handbills.

MAPS AND CHARTS

The free pocket map of St. Thomas and St. John widely available at tourist information booths, hotels, and car rental agencies is clear and well drawn. Pick one up when you arrive—it will be adequate for most people's purposes. There is also a map inside *St. Thomas This Week*, the free tourist magazine. Additional maps are available at Dockside Bookshop in Havensight Mall.

LIBRARIES

The **Enid M. Baa Public Library** (Main St., 340/774-3407, 9 A.M.–5 P.M. Mon. and Fri., 9 A.M.–8 P.M. Tues.–Thurs., 10 A.M.–4 P.M. Sat.) is located on Main Street next to Market Square, in the historic Bretton House. You can still see the original "charge desk," dedicated in 1943 by poet Edna St. Vincent Millay, who was a frequent visitor to the Virgin Islands at the time. There is public Internet access here for $2 an hour. A new, much larger public library is under construction at Estate Tutu.

MEDIA

The *Virgin Islands Daily News* publishes Monday–Saturday and is the best source for up-to-date news and events information. A weekend section on Thursday includes a dining guide and entertainment calendar. The *Daily News* is for sale at numerous establishments, plus along the roadside for people on their morning commute.

You can also buy the *St. Croix Avis* at many places on St. Thomas. And try the bright yellow *St. Thomas–St. John This Week* for useful visitor information.

EMERGENCIES

There is a full-service hospital on St. Thomas. The **Roy L. Schneider Hospital** (Estate Thomas, 340/776-8311, www.rlshospital.org) recently expanded to include a cutting-edge cancer treatment facility. Schneider Hospital has a decompression chamber for diving accidents; call 340/693-6215 to reach it directly. Despite the advances, many island residents still feel better traveling to Puerto Rico or the mainland United States for specialist and even routine services.

Walk-in medical centers can help with minor health problems and are convenient for visitors. The **Walk-In Medical Center** (6th St., Estate Thomas, 8 A.M.–6 P.M. Mon.–Fri., 340/775-4266) is a good choice.

Police headquarters is located in the Alexander Farrelly Justice Center on the waterfront, next to the Fort Christian parking lot. You can reach the police by calling 340/774-2211. Dial 911 in an emergency.

Mariners can call for help on Channel 16, or call Virgin Islands Radio on Channels 24 or 85.

BANKS

U.S., Canadian, and Puerto Rican banks do business in the U.S. Virgin Islands. You will find **Banco Popular** (340/693-2777) branches at Hibiscus Alley in downtown Charlotte Amalie, at Red Hook Plaza, and Lockhart Gardens, near Havensight. The **Bank of Nova Scotia** (340/774-0037) has branches at Havensight, Tutu Park Mall, and Nisky Center (west of town). **FirstBank** (340/775-7777) can be found at Red Hook and Port of Sale Mall, Havensight.

POST OFFICES

There are five post offices on St. Thomas. The main post office, **DeLugo Post Office** (5046 Norre Gade, 7:30 A.M.–5 P.M. Mon.–Fri., 7:30 A.M.–noon Sat.), is in central Charlotte Amalie. **The Havensight Post Office** (9 A.M.–4:30 P.M. Mon.–Fri., 9 A.M.–1 P.M. Sat.) is in the Havensight Mall.

COMMUNICATIONS

There is a cluster of cybercafés and shops selling overseas telephone calls across the street from Havensight Mall. They cater to cruise ship crew members who want to contact friend and family during their time off the ship.

CUSTOMS AND IMMIGRATION

People arriving in St. Thomas from the British Virgin Islands or other international destinations must clear immigration and customs on their arrival. People returning to the U.S. mainland from St. Thomas undergo immigration and customs screening on their departure, although a passport is not required (a government-issued ID is, however). There are Customs and Immigration officers stationed at the Weymouth Blyden Ferry Terminal on the Charlotte Amalie waterfront 8 A.M.–4:30 P.M. daily. They meet all ferries arriving from international destinations (principally the British Virgin Islands) and any private yachts that need to check in. Call 340/774-2378 to reach the immigration office at the ferry dock.

In addition, there are customs, immigration, and other border security officials at the Cyril E. King International Airport. For more information, call **Customs** (340/693-2250 or 800/981-3030) or **Immigration and Naturalization** (340/774-1390). The INS has an administrative office at Nisky Center on the western outskirts of Charlotte Amalie.

LAUNDERETTES

There are many different launderettes on St. Thomas, most with long hours. Almost all provide drop-off service in addition to letting you do your own wash. Plan on paying about $2 per wash wherever you go. One of the largest is **La Providence Laundromat** (Tutu Park Shopping Center, 340/777-3747, 6 A.M.–11 P.M. daily) behind Tutu Park Mall. Near town, try **Lover's Lane Laundromat** (Barbel Plaza, 340/714-1658, 6:30 A.M.–6 P.M. Sun.–Fri., 6:30 A.M.–7 P.M. Sat.). At Red Hook, there is **Harbor Laundromat** (American Yacht Harbor, 340/714-7672, 8 A.M.–7 P.M. daily), located behind Pesce restaurant.

Getting There

BY AIR

More direct flights from the mainland arrive in St. Thomas than on any other Virgin Island. During the winter travel season, Delta, U.S. Airways, American, Jet Blue, and United fly nonstop from major North American cities including New York, Baltimore, Miami, Charlotte, Boston, Toronto, and Chicago.

In addition, several commuter airlines, including Cape Air, provide daily service from San Juan, Puerto Rico. Seaborne Airlines flies daily from the Old San Juan harbor to St. Thomas and Charlotte Amalie Harbor.

The **Cyril E. King International Airport (STT)** is near Lindberg Bay, about four miles west of Charlotte Amalie. You will pay $8 for a taxi from the airport to town, and between $12 and $15 if you're heading to the east end resorts. Car rental companies Avis and Hertz have desks at the airport.

BY CRUISE SHIP

Most people who visit St. Thomas come aboard a cruise ship. Nearly every major cruise line calls on the island, including Carnival, Holland America, Norwegian, Royal Caribbean, Princess, and Celebrity. Cruise ships dock at the West Indian Company Dock in Havensight or the Crown Bay Marina on the west side of Charlotte Amalie. Check the back cover of *St. Thomas This Week* for an up-to-date cruise ship schedule.

BY FERRY
From St. John

Transportation Services (tel. 340/776-6282) and **Varlack Ventures** (tel. 340/776-6412) operate 20 daily round-trip journeys between St. John and St. Thomas, connecting Cruz Bay, St. John with Red Hook and Charlotte Amalie. Ferries to Red Hook leave every hour on the hour 6 A.M.–11 P.M.; round-trip fare is $12. The journey between St. John and Red Hook takes about 15 minutes and from St. John to Charlotte Amalie takes about 30 minutes.

If you have a car, consider taking the car barge from St. John which departs every hour on the half hour 7:30 A.M.–5:30 P.M. The round trip rate for an average car is $50. Call **Boyson Inc.** (340/776-6294) for details.

From St. Croix

V.I. Seatrans (340/776-5494) operates ferry service from Christiansted to Charlotte Amalie four days a week. The 90-minute journey costs $90 round-trip. Call ahead to confirm availability; the schedule is often more limited during the summer.

The seaplane is an alternative to the ferry for transportation between St. Croix and St. Thomas. The 15-minute flight on **Seaborne Airlines** (340/773-6442, www.seaborneairlines.com) costs between $200–300 round trip.

© SUSANNA HEN GHAN POTTER

the Charlotte Amalie waterfront, as seen from the deck of an approaching ferry

From the British Virgin Islands

There are more than a dozen daily ferry trips between Tortola and St. Thomas, with trips originating from both Road Town and West End. **Native Son** (340/774-8685 or 284/495-4617, www.nativesonferry.com) operates green and white boats from West End to both Charlotte Amalie and Red Hook. **Smith's Ferry Service** (340/775-7292, www.smithsferry.com), also known as the Tortola Fast Ferry, departs from both Road Town and West End with service to Red Hook and Charlotte Amalie. The **Road Town Fast Ferry** (340/777-2800, www.roadtownfastferry.com) runs exclusively from Road Town to both Charlotte Amalie and Red Hook.

Round-trip fare on all operators is $45, with a $5 departure tax due in the BVI before leaving. Passports are required.

There is ferry service four days a week between Virgin Gorda and St. Thomas. **Inter-Island Boat Service** (340/776-6597 or 284/495-4166) operates on Thursdays and Sundays, while Virgin Gorda-based **Speedy's** (284/495-5240) runs on Tuesdays, Thursdays and Saturdays. The fare is $70–80 round trip.

Inter-Island (340/776-6597 or 284/495-4166) also provides service between Red Hook, St. Thomas, and Jost Van Dyke every day except Thursday. The fare is $70 round trip. Call to confirm the schedule and make reservations.

ST. THOMAS

Getting Around

BUSES

The public bus system, **Vitran** (340/774-5678), has routes covering St. Thomas from the far west to the far east. Country buses ($1) travel between Red Hook and Charlotte Amalie every hour beginning at 5:30 A.M. and ending at 8:30 P.M. Additional buses travel from town to Bordeaux in the west. City buses ($0.75) travel between the hospital on the east side of town to the western end of town between 6:15 A.M. and 10:15 P.M. Some travel to the airport and the University of the Virgin Islands. In general, Vitran is unreliable, however. If you happen to catch a bus, be sure to have exact change.

But don't be disheartened—there is another way. For budget travelers, one of the delights of St. Thomas is its **dollar buses.** These unofficial, highly efficient buses follow a set route with stops including Red Hook, Tutu Park Mall, Charlotte Amalie, and the University of the Virgin Islands. They do not go to the north side, beaches, or west end. Passengers pay $1 for a ride, no matter how long or short it is. Dollar buses are actually the same open-air "safari" taxis—converted from pickup trucks—that bus cruise ship and other tourists around the island. The only differences are the passengers and the route they follow.

Dollar buses stop at established Vitran bus stops, marked with a brown and white sign. Some of the easiest places to catch a dollar bus are in Red Hook, next to the ferry dock; in front of Tutu Park Mall; in front of the Fort Christian parking lot; and in front of the Roy L. Schneider Hospital.

You need to be sprightly, confident, and have some knowledge of island geography to ride dollar buses comfortably. Some bus drivers may pass you by if you don't look like their average passenger. Stick your arm out as a signal to stop; if you're on a road frequented by tourist taxis (especially Waterfront Drive in Charlotte Amalie), they may be more likely to stop for you instead. When in doubt, just ask, "Is this the dollar bus?" and someone will set you straight.

TAXIS

Taxis are readily available at the airport, around Charlotte Amalie, and at resorts and major attractions. Many are 6- to 12-passenger vans; others are open-air "safari" buses, ideal for sightseeing. Taxi rates are set by the government. Official licensed taxis have a special license plate beginning with the letters TP. Drivers will display their taxi commission ID cards. Per-person taxi rates are lower if you have more than one person going to the same destination. The single-person rate from Charlotte Amalie to Red Hook is $13, to the airport is $7, and to Magen's Bay is $10. For a complete list of current taxi rates, check *St. Thomas This Week.*

CAR RENTALS

Renting a car is the best way to get around St. Thomas if you want to explore widely. The best rental rates are available from the major car rental chains, especially if you book in advance. Per-day rental rates for an economy car run $30 and up from most rental agencies; some quote rates as high as $60 a day. There is a $2.50 per day government tax on car rentals, and additional fees for those rented at the airport. Four-wheel drive will not usually be necessary; St. Thomas roads are well maintained. Chain rental companies include **Avis** (340/774-1468), **Hertz** (340/774-1879), **Budget** (340/776-5774), and **Thrifty** (340/776-1500). You could also try **Dependable Car Rental** (340/776-2253).

ST. JOHN

For many travelers, St. John is as near to perfection as a Caribbean island can be. More than 60 percent of the 20-square-mile island is national park, so its beaches, vistas, underwater coral gardens, and peaceful hiking paths are quiet and unspoiled. For outdoors enthusiasts, there is no better place to explore a tropical wilderness. St. John may be small, but its bays, hills, and reefs hold a seemingly infinite array of sights and sounds; as you peel off the layers, you will be surprised, enchanted, and inspired.

St. John is a playground. It is the type of place where you're tempted to live in your swimsuit, and where less is definitely more. The simple pleasures are divine: driving around with the windows down, reading a book from cover to cover on the beach, basking in turquoise water, and sitting down with a glass of wine. There is certainly an upscale bent to St. John—just check out some of the prices—but it is an upscale that prefers flip-flops to heels.

The loveliness of St. John can be almost shocking. Blinding white sand is lapped by crystal-clear water; the hillsides are a palette of greens; and the sky above is a sheer blue canvas. Tucked within St. John's scenic coves, bays, and mountainsides is a remarkable history. In 1733 the island was the site of a successful slave revolt. Ruins of sugarworks and great houses from the plantation era remain, and provide visitors the opportunity to consider this dramatic past.

HIGHLIGHTS

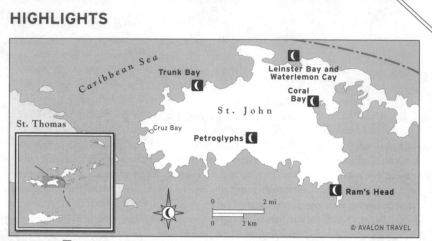

LOOK FOR ◖ TO FIND RECOMMENDED SIGHTS, ACTIVITIES, DINING, AND LODGING.

◖ **Trunk Bay:** With fine white sand, lots of shade, and good snorkeling, this is the most beautiful beach on St. John (page 78).

◖ **Leinster Bay and Waterlemon Cay:** The colorful reef around this offshore cay teems with life, making this a snorkeler's paradise (page 80).

◖ **Coral Bay:** Unwind with a cold beer and dance under the stars to live music in this funky, laid-back village on the east end (page 83).

◖ **Ram's Head:** Hold on to your hat at this remote headland, where the sound of waves crashing and the wind blowing will fill your ears. The view is spectacular here at the island's southernmost point (page 85).

◖ **Petroglyphs:** These mysterious stone carvings may have been made by some of the island's first residents, but no one knows for sure. Stop by and ponder their origins while hiking at Reef Bay (page 87).

St. John complements its natural beauty and historic sites with two laid-back hamlets, Cruz Bay and Coral Bay. These small towns have pretty much everything a visitor needs to feel at home: gourmet coffee, trendy restaurants, cold beer, and Internet access, for starters. While Cruz Bay often vibrates with the day-to-day comings and goings of car barges, passenger ferries, trucks, cars, and gangs of tourists, Coral Bay is a sleepy row of bars, restaurants, and shops.

St. John's perfection has consequences. So many people have come here and loved it that real estate agents, development companies, and construction firms are trying to build on every piece of the island's undeveloped privately held land. In some parts of the island, the sound of waves crashing is drowned out by the scream of air brakes, the ringing of hammers, and the hum of construction generators. Equally problematic, the influx of wealthy snowbirds and young Continentals has created a social divide between native St. Johnians and their American guests.

PLANNING YOUR TIME

It is safe to assume that no matter how much time you spend on St. John, it won't be enough. A tired joke is that most of the Continentals

ST. JOHN

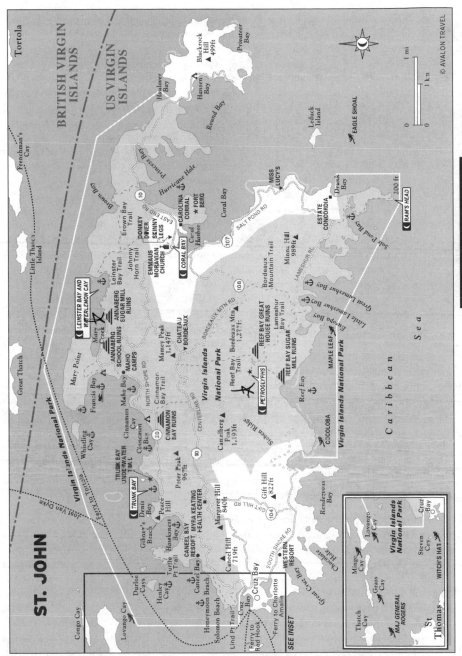

ST. JOHN

BRITISH VIRGIN ISLANDS

US VIRGIN ISLANDS

Tortola

Frenchman's Cay

Little Thatch Island

Great Thatch

Congo Cay

Lovango Cay

Jost Van Dyke to Tortola

Virgin Islands National Park

Mary Point

Whistling Cay

Hanover Bay

Blackrock Hill 499ft

Hansen Bay

Privateer Bay

Round Bay

Leduck Island

EAGLE SHOAL

Princess Bay

Hurricane Hole

Brown Bay

Brown Bay Trail

10

EAST END RD

Carolina Corral

FORT BERG

DONKEY DINER

SKINNY LEGS

Coral Bay

MISS LUCY'S

Drunk Bay

RAM'S HEAD

200 ft

Coral Harbor

SALT POND RD

107

ESTATE CONCORDIA

Salt Pond Bay

LEINSTER BAY AND WATERLEMON CAY

Leinster Bay Trail

EMMAUS MORAVIAN CHURCH

CORAL BAY

ANNABERG SUGAR MILL RUINS

Johnny Horn Trail

108

Bordeaux Mountain Trail

LAMESHUR RD

Minna Hill 989ft

Mary Creek

ANNABERG SCHOOL RUINS

MAHO CAMPS

Maho Bay

CHATEAU BORDEAUX

Mamey Peak 1,147ft

BORDEAUX MTN RD

Bordeaux Mtn 1,277ft

REEF BAY GREAT HOUSE RUINS

Reef Bay Trail

Lameshur Bay Trail

REEF BAY SUGAR MILL RUINS

MAPLE LEAF

Great Lameshur Bay

Little Lameshur Bay

Europa Bay

Francis Bay

Cinnamon Cay

Cinnamon Maho Bay

NORTH SHORE RD

Cinnamon Bay Trail

Virgin Islands National Park

PETROGLYPHS

Reef Bay

Reef Key

Caribbean Sea

Trunk Cay

TRUNK BAY UNDERWATER TRAIL

20

CINNAMON BAY RUINS

Cinnamon Bay

CENTERLINE RD

10

Camelberg Peak 1,193ft

Sieben Ridge

COCOLOBA

Virgin Islands National Park

TRUNK BAY

Denis Bay

Peter Peak 967ft

Peace Hill

MYRA KEATING HEALTH CENTER

Margaret Hill 840ft

Gift Hill 827ft

GIFT HILL RD

Rendezvous Bay

Gibney's Beach

CANEEL BAY RESORT

Caneel Hill 719ft

SOUTH SHORE RD

WESTERN RESORT

104

Durloe Cays

Henley Cay

Hawksnest Bay

Turtle Pt Trail

Caneel Bay

Honeymoon Beach

Solomon Beach

Cruz Bay

Great Cruz Bay

Chocolate Hole

Lind Pt Trail

Cruz Bay

Ferry to Red Hook

Ferry to Charlotte Amalie

SEE INSET

St Thomas

Thatch Cay

Mingo Cay

Grass Cay

MAJ GENERAL ROGERS

Congo Cay

Lovango Cay

Steven Cay

Cruz Bay

Virgin Islands National Park

WITCH'S HAT

1 mi

1 km

0

0

living there came down for vacation and never left. It's hackneyed, but there is definitely a kernel of truth to the belief: St. John is just that enchanting.

But if you can't pick up and move, a week is a good length of time to be on St. John. You'll have time for a couple beaches, a couple hikes, and a day sail: just about what you need to properly unwind.

Where to Stay

The best beaches are along the island's north shore. Nature lovers should find accommodations at one of the campgrounds in this part of the island. If you prefer to be near restaurants and nightlife, look for digs in Cruz Bay. If you want to get away from the crowds, head to Coral Bay, where you'll find the greatest concentration of vacation villas. If you prefer all-inclusive accommodations, St. John has two standard-setting choices near Cruz Bay.

Day Trips

St. John is a good day trip if you're based on St. Thomas or Tortola. If all you have is a day, take an open-air taxi along the lovely north shore to Annaberg and then spend a few hours at Cinnamon Bay, hiking the nature trail and then sunning on the beach.

If you're staying on St. John, the most popular day trips are to the British Virgin Islands. Book an outing with a day sail operator headed to Norman Island, Virgin Gorda, or Jost Van Dyke. Alternatively, take a ferry to West End (Tortola), Great Harbour (Jost Van Dyke) or Spanish Town (Virgin Gorda) and explore at your own pace.

Ferries and day sails depart exclusively from **Cruz Bay.** Ferries to Tortola and Jost Van Dyke run about three times a day and cost $50–70 round trip. The ferry to Virgin Gorda runs on Thursdays and Sundays only and costs $80 round trip. Ferry trips last 20–45 minutes.

While it's not necessary to make reservations for ferries to Tortola, call ahead to confirm the availability of service to Jost Van Dyke and Virgin Gorda. Day sail outings should be scheduled several days in advance (or several weeks in peak season).

Sights

St. John is mountainous, with very little flat land. Cruz Bay, on the far western end of the island, is where ferries and boats from neighboring islands arrive. Many of the best and most popular beaches are along the north coast of the island, accessible by scenic North Shore Road (Route 20). Coral Bay is a sprawling settlement along a wide, horseshoe-shaped bay on the far eastern end of the island. Centerline Road (Route 10) connects Cruz Bay and Coral Bay.

From Coral Bay you can drive to the remote eastern tip of the island on the East End Road (Route 10) or head south through remote seaside communities and luxury villas on Salt Pond Road (Route 107). Both drives take you to remote beaches with good snorkeling and few crowds.

CRUZ BAY

Named by the Spanish, Cruz Bay is St. John's first and only real town. The heart of Cruz Bay lies within about six square blocks immediately adjacent to the **Franklin A. Powell Sr. Park,** which faces the passenger ferry terminal. This is a good place to people-watch.

Cruz Bay's streets are lined with shops, open-air bars, and courtyard restaurants that cater to visitors. The town is steadily expanding, with

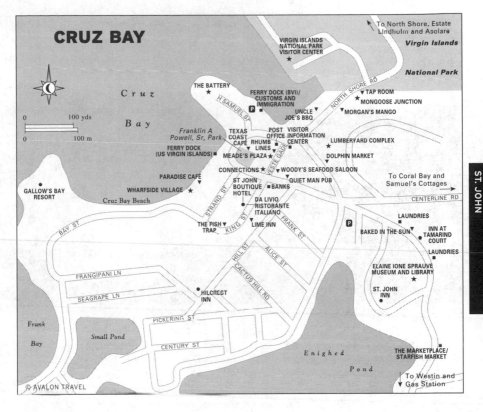

CRUZ BAY

To North Shore, Estate Lindholm and Apolare

Virgin Islands

National Park

VIRGIN ISLANDS
NATIONAL PARK
VISITOR CENTER

C r u z

B a y

THE BATTERY

FERRY DOCK (BVI)/
CUSTOMS AND
IMMIGRATION

TAP ROOM
MONGOOSE JUNCTION
MORGAN'S MANGO

NORTH SHORE RD

UNCLE
JOE'S BBQ

0   100 yds

0   100 m

Franklin A. Powell, Sr. Park

TEXAS
COAST
CAFE
RHUMB
LINES

POST
OFFICE

VISITOR
INFORMATION
CENTER

LUMBERYARD COMPLEX

FERRY DOCK
(US VIRGIN ISLANDS)

MEADE'S PLAZA

DOLPHIN MARKET

PARADISE CAFÉ

CONNECTIONS

WOODY'S SEAFOOD SALOON

QUIET MAN PUB

To Coral Bay and
Samuel's Cottages

GALLOW'S BAY
RESORT

WHARFSIDE VILLAGE

Cruz Bay Beach

ST JOHN
BOUTIQUE
HOTEL

BANKS

DA LIVIO
RISTORANTE
ITALIANO

CENTERLINE RD

STRAND ST

BAY ST

KING ST

THE FISH
TRAP

LIME INN

FRANK ST

LAUNDRIES

BAKED IN THE SUN

INN AT
TAMARIND
COURT

LAUNDRIES

HILL ST

ALICE ST

CACTUS HILL RD

ELAINE IONE SPRAUVE
MUSEUM AND LIBRARY

FRANGIPANI LN

SEAGRAPE LN

HILCREST
INN

ST. JOHN
INN

Frank

Bay

Small Pond

PICKERING ST

CENTURY ST

E n i g h e d

Pond

THE MARKETPLACE/
STARFISH MARKET

To Westin and
Gas Station

© AVALON TRAVEL

ST. JOHN

the construction of upscale shopping centers, condominiums, and homes around the outskirts of the original village.

For decades, the pace was slow and the attitude was casual in Cruz Bay. While some of this low-key ambience remains, old Cruz Bay is quickly being replaced by another sort of town, one where SUVs rule the road, parking is a nightmare, and people are in a hurry.

For visitors, Cruz Bay is a necessary part of any journey to St. John. This is where the passenger and car ferries arrive and depart and where the greatest number of restaurants and shops are found. It is home to the largest grocery stores and St. John's most happening nightlife. It is also where you will find the visitors center for Virgin Islands National Park, the

best starting point for any tour of the island. Two excellent beaches are a short hike away from the town center.

Logistically speaking, a car is a liability in central Cruz Bay. Parking is atrocious, and the maze of one-way streets is confusing for a first-time visitor. Walking is the best way to get around, but beware the narrow sidewalks, hills, and hot sun.

Finding your way around can be challenging since there are few road signs in town. Directions are often given in relation to community hubs such as Mongoose Junction, the post office, and the churches. Pick up a glossy hand-drawn *St. John Guidebook* map, which is the best tool for finding your way around Cruz Bay.

© SUSANNA HENIGHAN POTTER

Cruz Bay is St. John's largest town.

Virgin Islands National Park Visitor Center

The Virgin Islands National Park Visitor Center (Waterfront, 340/776-6201, www.nps. gov/viis, 8 A.M.–4 P.M.) is a good first stop for visitors to the island. A permanent exhibit describes the human and natural history of St. John, and a three-dimensional map helps you get your bearings. Park rangers are on duty to answer questions and hand out maps and brochures. Outside, the visitors center has shaded picnic tables and public restrooms. A public playground is right next door.

The Battery

Built on the finger of land jutting out in the center of Cruz Bay, the Battery is the headquarters of island administration. The present building sits atop the foundation of Christian's Fort, built in 1734 in response to an island-wide slave revolt a year earlier. Note that the cannons face landward—colonial authorities

feared another slave revolt more than an attack from the sea.

In 1825 Christian's Fort was expanded to include a prison, courthouse, dungeon, and so-called "justice post," where slaves were beaten, sometimes to death, for breaking the restrictive slave code. The additions were supposed to improve life for island slaves, as they allowed punishment to be prescribed and delivered by state authorities rather than by individual overseers, some of whom were known for their extreme brutality.

Today, the Battery contains government offices and is not open for tours. However, no one will stop you from poking around during regular business hours.

Solomon and Honeymoon Beaches

The beach at Cruz Bay is too crowded and built up for swimming, although it is nice to look at. Grab a seat at one of the bars that line the water for the best view. The nearest nice beaches are a one-mile hike from town. **Solomon Beach** is

© SUSANNA HENIGHAN POTTER

The Virgin Islands National Park Visitor Center in Cruz Bay is the best source of information about the island.

a secluded white sand beach with good snorkeling; it is unofficially known as the nudist beach on St. John (nude bathing is illegal in the U.S. Virgin Islands). **Honeymoon Beach** is a slightly larger, equally charming white sand beach, just beyond Solomon, where people tend to keep their clothes on. The rocky headland between the two is good for snorkeling. Since you can't drive to these beaches, you will almost always have them to yourself, unless you have the bad luck of choosing to visit at the same time day sail operators drop in with a boatload of tourists.

To get to Solomon and Honeymoon Beaches, take the Lind Bay Trail, which begins behind the national park visitors center in Cruz Bay. It is 0.9 mile to Solomon Beach and 0.1 mile farther to Honeymoon. After your swim, you can make the short walk on to Caneel Bay Resort and catch a taxi back to town, or you can hike back the way you came.

Although the distances are short, don't underestimate the walk to these beaches, especially on a hot day. Bring lots of water.

NORTH SHORE

As you head north out of Cruz Bay on Route 20, also called North Shore Road, you leave behind the bustle of town, and in less than half a mile, enter Virgin Islands National Park. Immediately, the air feels cooler, the sounds of traffic are gone, and you can smell the forest through your open windows. This is quintessential St. John: powder-white beaches, pristine coral reefs, hiking trails, and awesome overlooks. No trip to St. John is complete without traversing this part of the island.

You can drive along most of the north shore; the journey takes about 20 minutes one way, or longer if you make a point of stopping at each of the half-dozen overlooks. If you have time for only one driving tour of St. John, make it the North Shore Road.

′33 SLAVE REBELLION

ｅre were 1,295 adults living on St. John; 1,087 of them were slaves, many who had only recently arrived from Africa. The island was in the throes of a very hard year. There had been drought, a hurricane, and a plague of insects, and starvation was a very real problem, especially for slaves.

With such dire living conditions on the plantations, an increasing number of slaves began running away. Maroon camps popped up in remote parts of the island—Ram's Head was the site of a large one. To address planters' fears of more runaways, the Danish governor issued a new slave code in September that prescribed brutal punishment for runaways and cash incentives for slaves who informed on a maroon.

It was all more than some of the slaves—especially those recently arrived from Africa—could take. At night, the sound of drumbeats could be heard around the island, as slaves at different plantations planned and prepared for what would come next.

The St. John slave rebellion began in the early morning of November 23, 1733, when a dozen slaves entered Fort Berg in Coral Bay, carrying cane knives and cutlasses hidden in bundles of wood. The rebels killed all but one of the Danish soldiers—the one who survived hid beneath a bed—and fired the fort's gun three times to signal to slaves that the planned rebellion was now under way. In the days that followed, two bands of rebels circled the island, looting and burning many plantations. Some whites were killed, others were spared, and many were able to escape by sea to outlying cays, either by their own initiative or because of warning and assistance from "loyal" slaves. Able-bodied white men, as well as a significant number of loyal slaves, set up camp at the Duurloo Plantation at Klein Caneel Bay, which remained their encampment for the duration of the rebellion.

The standoff continued for six months. Attempts by the local militia, the free black corps, and British army companies from Tortola and St. Kitts failed to round up the remaining African rebels. Meanwhile, the Africans, who had set up camps at Leinster Bay, Maho Bay, and Catherineberg, were running out of weapons and gunpowder. Their leaders, including King Bolombo and Prince Aquashi, quarreled over which of them would rule the island after their rebellion succeeded. This power struggle distracted them from organizing any significant offensive against the remaining whites. In retrospect, many historians say that if the Africans had continued their attack on St. John's whites, they might have found themselves in control of the whole island.

In the end, the rebellion failed. In May 1734, a company of more than 200 French soldiers came to the Danes' rescue. They spent a whole month scouring every part of the island, capturing several Africans and finding many more who had committed suicide. Five months after the French left, 14 remaining rebels were captured after being tricked into returning to their old plantation. Their leader was beheaded. Four more died in prison, four were sentenced to be worked to death building St. Croix's new forts, and the rest were tortured to death.

When it had all ended, less than one-quarter of the island's 208 whites had been killed. Danish authorities determined that 146 slaves, or 14 percent of the slave population, had taken part in the rebellion. All these were killed—in battle, by their own hand, or by torture and execution. Of the island's 92 plantations, 48 had been damaged.

St. John's planters rebuilt following the rebellion, and four years after the revolt was put down, the island's population exceeded its 1733 level. But relations between slave and master on St. John were never the same.

Caneel Bay

Now the setting for St. John's most famous resort, Caneel Bay is a picturesque straight bay on the western side of Hawksnest Point. During the colonial period, this area was known as Klein Caneel Bay, or Little Cinnamon Bay. Ruins of the Duurloo great house have been preserved and are open to the public. The house served as the headquarters for white plantation owners during the 1733 slave rebellion and was never taken by the Africans.

Nonguests can explore the ruins, shop or dine at the resort, or go to Caneel Bay beach. There is an offshore platform for diving and decent snorkeling to the right of the pier. You can also walk around the Caneel property, which includes a two-mile fitness trail and acres of open lawns and landscaped grounds. Hiking trails take you to Little Hawksnest Beach, Turtle Point, and Turtle Bay Beach.

To visit, drive into the resort (you may be asked to give your name at the guard gate) and park in the guest lot. A $20 parking fee per vehicle applies. Go to the concierge desk for maps and other information.

Hawksnest Bay

Hawksnest Bay is a deep bay home to several excellent beaches. The most prominent is glorious **Hawksnest Beach,** a wide, long strip of pale sand fringed by a canopy of mature trees and sandwiched between rock promontories. Small reefs lie in the shallow water, perpendicular to the beach. On calm days, it's fun to snorkel around the rocks on the eastern end of the beach.

Hawksnest is the closest beach you can drive to from town, making it popular with day-trippers and residents. You will find some of the newest facilities in the park here, including picnic tables, grills, group pavilions (reservations are required), bathhouses, and showers.

East of Hawksnest is **Gibney's Beach,** also called Oppenheimer Beach or Little Hawksnest Beach. This lovely shoreline is often less crowded than the main bay, mainly because it's a bit harder to access. To find it, drive past the Hawksnest parking lot and look for an unmarked white gate on the seaward side of the road. Parking is extremely limited; be sure not to block the road or the fence.

The history of Gibney's Beach is rather involved, but interesting. Beatniks Robert and Nancy Gibney bought 40 acres of land here in 1950. In 1957, the Gibneys sold a small piece of beachfront land to J. Robert Oppenheimer, inventor of the atom bomb. When Oppenheimer's daughter died, she left the land and house to "the children of St. John." The upshot of this is that the yellow building you can see on the shoreline (the old Oppenheimer house) is maintained by the Virgin Islands government and can be rented for community functions.

Peace Hill

At the top of the headland between Hawksnest and Trunk Bays is Peace Hill, a grassy knoll and windmill ruin with beautiful views of the British Virgin Islands and the north shore of St. John. The land was donated to the national park in the 1950s by Colonel Julius Wadsworth, who wished that "Peace Hill be perpetually dedicated as a place where people might meditate and find inner peace, in the hope that in some way this might contribute to world peace." In 1953 Wadsworth commissioned a statue of Jesus, which he named "Christ of the Caribbean." The statue gradually deteriorated and was eventually knocked down by Hurricane Marilyn in 1995. The Park Service put up a plaque in its place.

Today, the main attractions at Peace Hill are the ruins of the windmill and the spectacular views. This is a nice place to take pictures.

There is a small parking area with a sign marking the trailhead to Peace Hill. It is a 0.25-mile uphill hike to the hill. An unmaintained steep foot trail to **Denis Bay** veers off to the right about 50 yards up the Peace Hill trail when you are hiking in. Denis Bay is a pretty, rarely visited beach. Be aware that the home at the eastern end of Denis Bay is private property.

Jumbie Beach

A small crescent of sand, ringed by low-growing sea grape trees and coconut palms, Jumbie Beach is a retreat. Only four parking spaces are provided, naturally limiting the number of people who visit this humble destination. Legends of ghosts (jumbies) haunting the beach do not help to draw crowds. The sand is coarse but fluffy, and there is shade. Snorkeling is good along the shallow reef, but be careful not to get too close, especially when the sea is rough. Sit on the beach for views of Trunk Bay and Jost Van Dyke, plus distant ferry traffic.

Jumbie Beach is usually quiet, and if you have it to yourself you'll be especially glad you came. Access is via stairs and a short path from North Shore Road. The parking spaces are about 40 yards west of the trailhead, on the opposite side of the road. Be careful of traffic.

◖ Trunk Bay

Trunk Bay is St. John's most magnificent beach and its most popular. The bay is a vision of fluffy white sand, sea grape trees, and coconut palms. Trunk Cay, just off shore, is a tiny island of rocky cliffs, tufted by hardy palm trees. It takes about half an hour to traverse the National Park Service's underwater snorkel trail, which lies alongside the cay and is good for beginners.

Trunk Bay is named for the leatherback turtles, locally called trunks, that nest here. It is a long beach and even at its most crowded you will find a semblance of solitude at either extreme end. Facilities (7:30 A.M.–4:30 P.M.) include lifeguards, barn-like bathhouses and showers, and a group pavilion. A snack bar ($4–9) serves burgers, hot dogs, fries, sandwiches, and ice cream, and you can pick up

sunscreen, a new bathing suit, and beach toys at a small gift shop tucked under the trees. Rent chairs ($7), snorkel gear ($5), and an umbrella ($5) from the counter adjacent to the gift shop for a perfectly provisioned day at the beach. All equipment requires a deposit, so don't forget your credit card.

If you'd like to learn a thing or two, sign up in advance for the ranger-led snorkel tour that departs from the Trunk Bay lifeguard station at 9:30 A.M. every Monday. Call the Cruz Bay Visitor Center (340/776-6201) to confirm.

Trunk Bay is the only beach on St. John that you must pay to enter. The NPS collects $4 per person (under 17 free) 9 A.M.–4 P.M.

Trunk Bay is often mobbed, since it is the most popular stop for organized day trips from St. Thomas and the cruise ships. Parking is also limited. To avoid the crowds come early or late, but do come—this is what Caribbean beach dreams are made of.

Cinnamon Bay

At the other side of the steep switchbacks that corkscrew up and over Peter Ridge is Cinnamon Bay, another standout spot in the national park. In addition to an excellent beach, there are extensive ruins, a short hike, and some of St. John's best conditions for water sports.

The shore at Cinnamon is long and winding and gives way to an expansive beach. Fine white sand drops off somewhat steeply at first and then levels out, creating a wide, shallow bank ideal for water play. Most visitors are content to bathe, but you can also snorkel on the reef around Cinnamon Cay, about 100 yards from shore.

Because of its generally windy conditions, Cinnamon is the best St. John beach for windsurfing. You can rent equipment and get lessons from the water-sports center in the whitewashed concrete shed near the shore. You can also rent a kayak and paddle up and down the beach or out to Cinnamon Cay. The watersports center also sells snack and drinks; for more substantial refreshment, there is a restaurant near the parking lot.

When there is a strong swell, surfers head to Cinnamon. On days like this, waves pound the shore, making it a difficult beach for swimming or snorkeling and limiting the amount of sandy real estate for beachgoers.

HISTORIC SITES

Early archaeologists identified Cinnamon Bay as the site of a Taino village, and recent excavations have uncovered evidence that the area was a site of social and spiritual significance for these early people. Digs discovered religious zemis (statues of ancestral spirits), remnants of a chief's house, and evidence of religious observations.

Colonial settlement at Cinnamon Bay dates back to 1680, when a small-scale cotton plantation was established. During the 1733 slave rebellion, the plantation buildings were looted and burned. Following the rebellion, the plantation was rebuilt and expanded to include a sugar factory. In the early 20th century a mechanized bay rum distillery was built on site, and Cinnamon Bay became the leader in producing this refreshing tonic.

You can explore the remains of the bay's colonial history at the **Cinnamon Bay Ruins.** A self-guided half mile walk begins about 200 feet east of the entrance to the campground and beach and takes you through the ruins of the sugar factory, estate house, and bay rum still. It then loops through the nearby forest, with markers that identify common trees, animals, and insects, as well as historical remnants such as a small Danish cemetery. A raised boardwalk and paved pathways make the first part of the trail—which explores the ruins—accessible to wheelchairs.

For information about Cinnamon's prehistory, stop at the **Cinnamon Bay Archeological Museum,** housed inside a whitewashed concrete shed on the beach. The museum, open most weekdays from 8 A.M.–4 P.M., houses a collection of pottery and other artifacts found by archeologists at Cinnamon Bay. Among the finds are a large number of zemis depicting bats, thought to be of spiritual importance to the Taino people who lived here beginning in about A.D. 1000. Above the older items, scientists are finding pottery and other remains of colonial times.

Cinnamon Bay is an active archeological site: the focus at present is on the sites nearest to the water's edge, which are threatened by beach erosion. Groups of student interns assist the park's archeologist.

Park rangers lead a free weekly nature and culture walk through the museum and ruins at Cinnamon Bay every Tuesday 9:30–10:30 A.M. The hike begins at the benches next to the museum on the beach. Call the Cruz Bay Visitor Center (340/776-6201) to confirm that the event is on.

Maho Bay

Maho Bay is a long, narrow beach well protected from surf and just a few steps from North Shore Road. The sand is punctuated by overhanging sea grape trees, which create a sense of privacy and containment. Since it is almost always calm, Maho is a popular anchorage and it's also a good destination for stand up paddleboarding, children, and insure swimmers.

Swim out to the rocky outcropping between Maho and Little Maho to the east for good snorkeling.

Though it's been a popular destination for years, Maho was not part of the national park until 2007, when the efforts of the National Park Service, the Friends of Virgin Islands National Park, and the Trust for Public Land to contact the landowners and raise the $19 million necessary to purchase the bay and 419 acres of adjoining hillside bore fruit. Since then

ST. JOHN

the Park Service has begun to improve the site with more parking and the addition of restrooms and a small group pavilion.

Annaberg School Ruins

The 1840s saw the construction of the first government schools in what were then called the Danish West Indies. Governor-General Peter von Scholten saw universal compulsory education as a way to prepare the colony for the eventual elimination of slavery. Government schools were first built on St. Croix, and in 1844 funds were made available for the construction of two schools on St. John. One was situated at Bethany, near Cruz Bay, and the other was near Annaberg, on the north shore of the island.

The ruins of the Annaberg School are a short distance from the road to the Annaberg Plantation. Steps have been built so you can better view the ruins, and a small display describes the history of the school and efforts to preserve it.

Little Maho Bay

Little Maho Bay is a small, sandy, not-quite-so-calm beach on the other side of Maho Bay point from Maho Bay. Land access is through Maho Bay Camps. There is a water-sports shop near the beach, and nonguests are welcome to use the beach. Just park up by the dining pavilion and take the stairs down. (It's a long way down!) You can also scramble along a goat trail from the eastern end of big Maho Bay beach.

Francis Pond and Bay

This crescent bay on the western side of Mary Point is a great place for a peaceful swim and home to the best bird-watching on St. John. The water at **Francis Bay Beach** is invariably calm—most days it is like a pond. For this reason it is a favored anchorage for sailboats and a good place for children. Its western outlook makes it a popular venue for sunset weddings.

Because it's a ways off the beaten track, Francis Bay is also almost always quiet. There are picnic tables and pit toilets.

A small area of coral reef at the western end of the beach (nearest Maho) is good for beginning snorkelers. Strong swimmers can snorkel out from the eastern end of the beach, where a narrow reef begins about halfway to the point. You can also launch here for a kayak trip to Whistling Cay, but be sure to keep clear of ferry traffic.

Francis Bay Pond is a salt pond and mangrove area behind the beach, and it's a great place for bird-watching. The Francis Bay Trail passes through a crumbling great house "ruin" (which was clearly used in modern times as well) before reaching an overlook with benches and a view of the pond. Sit here with binoculars (and insect repellent) to watch the birds. The path continues around the pond on sandy earth to the north end of Francis Bay Beach.

Park Service rangers host a weekly bird-watching walk at Francis Bay on Friday mornings (7:30–9 A.M.). Walkers meet at the Francis Bay trailhead; call the Cruz Bay Visitor Center (340/776-6201) to confirm and to arrange taxi service if necessary.

◖ Leinster Bay and Waterlemon Cay

The combined attractions of Leinster Bay and Waterlemon Cay are a snorkeler's dream. Calm and protected, Leinster has extensive sea grass, with turtles, fish, and sea stars. Waterlemon Cay is home to a healthy and expansive coral reef. Together, they make a good half-day, or even full-day, destination for energetic snorkelers.

Leinster Bay is covered with packed coarse yellow sand, but shade and calm waters make it a decent place to swim. Put on a mask and snorkel to peer down at swaying sea grass, conch, and other creatures. From the beach, hike 0.25 mile up the Johnny Horn Trail to reach great house ruins once associated with the Annaberg estate and nice views of the bay below.

Waterlemon Cay, named for a type of shark, has hard-packed sand on the southern tip (facing the shore) and rocky edges on the seaward-facing side. Begin at the sand and make a counterclockwise ring around the island for the best snorkeling. In rough weather, don't attempt a complete circumnavigation. Look for squid, fish, and other reef-dwelling creatures. For many people, this is the snorkeling highlight of a trip to St. John.

Hiking is the only way to reach Leinster Bay and Waterlemon Cay. The Leinster Bay Trail (0.8 mile) departs from opposite the driveway for the Annaberg Plantation. The hike is flat and follows the shoreline. From Leinster Bay, you can swim out to Waterlemon Cay or continue walking another 0.5 mile along an unofficial trail that hugs the shoreline and takes you closer to the cay.

There are no facilities at Leinster Bay; pack plenty of food and water.

Annaberg Plantation

The ruins of the Annaberg sugar mill are the best place to learn about the colonial-era life of both planters and slaves on St. John. The site includes the ruins of a windmill, a sugar factory, a mill round, a rum still, and slave quarters. A 0.25-mile paved trail meanders through the grounds past interpretive signs describing elements of the ruins.

A nondescript hillside overgrown with dense shrubs near the beginning of the trail was once the site of a sprawling village of 65 slave cabins, mostly wattle and daub huts long lost to time. The slaves of Annaberg labored under a succession of owners from 1721 until 1796, the year that Irish-born James Murphy purchased the estate. At his death in 1808, Murphy was the single largest producer of sugar on the island, with 1,300 acres and 662 enslaved people to his name; Annaberg alone frequently produced more than 100,000 pounds of raw sugar annually.

ST. JOHN

© SUSANNA HENIGHAN POTTER

the remains of a windmill which once powered the Annaberg sugar factory

The windmill at Annaberg, built by slaves with fieldstone, coral, and hand-mixed mortar, was one of five windmills on St. John during the plantation era. The ruins of the windmill, mill round, and boiling house are what remains today of Murphy's massive sugar operation. Look around and imagine gangs of workers cutting cane on a steeply terraced hillside above. The cut cane would have been loaded on wooden skids and slid down the hill to the factory. Water also flowed downhill; Murphy used slave labor to build a reservoir and elevated aqueduct to complement the 20,000-gallon rainwater cistern that lies alongside the boiling house.

Other structures still standing include a traditional stone oven used to bake large batches of bread and a dungeon outfitted with a post, handcuffs, and chains, evidence of the means used by overseers to control the enslaved population, especially after the 1733 rebellion in which Annaberg slaves took part.

The last European owner of Annaberg was Thomas Letsom Lloyd of Tortola, who sold the plantation to George Francis in 1871. Francis had been born into slavery at Annaberg in the early 1820s. His acquisition of the plantation came at a time when the industry was in steep decline. After Francis died in 1875, his descendents turned to subsistence farming, cattle grazing, and the manufacture of charcoal. The property was purchased for the establishment of the National Park in 1954.

The National Park Service organizes cultural demonstrations here three days a week, when rangers tend the garden and bake bread in the oven (10 A.M.–2 P.M. Tues.–Thurs.). Annaberg is also a pleasant place just to be; from the crest of the hill you will find lovely views of Mary's Point and Tortola. During the summer, broad flamboyant trees bloom flaming red, and year-round this is a breezy and quiet place to pass time or enjoy a picnic.

© SUSANNA HENIGHAN POTTER

Coral Bay is a sprawling community that lies next to a large, protected natural harbor.

◖ CORAL BAY

Technically, "Coral Bay" refers to the expansive broad bay that stretches from Sabbat Point in the west to Long Point in the east. It encompasses Round Bay, Hurricane Hole, and Coral Harbor, plus dozens more creeks, bays, and points.

For most people, however, "Coral Bay" means the sprawling, laid-back hamlet that lines the shore here. This village is the last frontier of St. John, and one of its unique places. It takes some 30 minutes to drive here from Cruz Bay, and by the time you make the dramatic descent into town, you feel as if you have left the rest of the world far behind.

For many decades, this part of St. John was practically undeveloped. The tight-knit local community that lived here for generations had closer ties with nearby Tortola (only a short sail away) than it did with Cruz Bay. But as St. John was discovered by outsiders in the middle part of the 20th century, so was Coral Bay. The area's breathtaking views of the British Virgin Islands and enchanting sense of isolation attracted successive waves of American and European transplants. The first were free spirits who built small homes or lived aboard their sailboats, but recent arrivals have not been so modest. These days, luxurious homes peer down from the hillsides around Coral Bay, and upscale markets, restaurants, and boutiques have opened to cater to the changing clientele.

Despite the changes, however, Coral Bay is still the most laid-back part of St. John and the best place to feel the magical calm that is St. John's greatest attraction.

The area got its name from the Dutch word *kraal* (corral), an indication of the importance of cattle and livestock in the bay's early history. Coral Bay did not always play second fiddle to Cruz Bay; when the Danish settled St. John in the early 1700s, they took note of Coral Bay's large natural harbor and established their capital and only fortification there because of the protected harbor. The Danish W[...] Guinea Company secured the choi[...] on the island for its plantation: Car[...] flat plain facing Coral Harbor. A [...]ades later, the slave revolt of 1733 began when a dozen slaves attacked the Danish fort atop Fort Berg, overlooking the bay.

Orientation

Route 107 follows a north–south path along the western coast of Coral Bay, ending just past Salt Pond Bay. Route 10, also called the East End Road, follows the eastern coast of the bay through some of St. John's most remote territory and over a series of thrilling roller-coaster hills. The two roads meet up at the head of Coral Harbor, which can be thought of as the center of Coral Bay. Most bars, restaurants, and shops are within a mile of this crossroads, on either Route 107 or Route 10.

It is fun to explore Coral Bay and the surrounding communities by car. Trying to get around here on foot would be frustrating and slow-going. Plan a few hours if you want to see the whole bay, more if you want to refresh yourself at one of the nearby beaches or restaurants.

Emmaus Moravian Church

The handsome church that overlooks Coral Bay was built by German Moravian missionaries who arrived in the Danish West Indies in 1732 to minister to the slaves. The Emmaus manse was built around 1750, and the original church was constructed in 1782. Both were rebuilt after a destructive hurricane in 1916. The masonry foundation, which survived the storm, was built of rubble, ballast brick, and coral. The one-story church has a belfry attached to the west end. The property on which the church sits was once owned by the Danish governor, Thomas de Malleville, who deeded it to the Moravians in 1782 after he converted to the faith.

This is still an active congregation

© SUSANNA HENIGHAN POTTER

The Emmaus Moravian Church stands watch over Coral Bay.

(340/776-6713), but visitors are welcome to look around as long as a service is not taking place.

Fort Berg

The ruins of the Danish fort that were the opening scene of the 1733 slave revolt sit atop Fort Berg (Fort Hill), the sugarloaf that juts out between Coral Harbor and Hurricane Hole.

The fort was constructed in 1717, the same year Danish settlement of St. John began in earnest. In 1760, four bastions and a gun deck were added to the fort. During the Napoleonic Wars, the fort and adjacent battery were occupied by the British in 1801 and again from 1807 to 1815.

The ruins, and the hill on which they stand, are on private property and there is no public access. Once a year, around November 23, the date of the start of the 1733 rebellion, locals commemorate the slave revolt by hiking to the hilltop and holding a ceremony of remembrance. An announcement of this event is published in local newspapers.

THE EAST END

The east end of St. John is remote and beautiful. Where other parts of the island are lush and tropical, the east end is arid and windswept. There are no glorious white sand beaches here, but the landscape of low hills, protected bays, and crystal clear water is still spectacular.

Hurricane Hole

This deep bay consisting of Borck Creek, Princess Bay, and Water Creek is so well protected that it is the traditional safe port for boats during a hurricane. Ringed by mangroves and contained on three sides by land, Hurricane Hole offers natural protection from wind and storm surge.

East End Road skirts Hurricane Hole, but access from land can be tricky because of the dense mangrove forest that lines the shore. The best way to explore Hurricane Hole is by kayak; it takes about an hour to paddle here from the water-sports shop in Coral Bay. Bring a snorkel to explore the unlikely but enchanting world that exists amid the knobbed knees and underwater roots of the mangrove trees.

Brown Bay

A quiet, shallow bay on the north shore of the island, Brown Bay is accessible only by foot. A 0.8-mile trail from the East End Road deposits you on an unremarkable coarse-sand beach. Large masses of sea grass grow in the bay, and nestled among them is the largest population of conch and West Indian sea egg you are likely to see on your snorkels. If you're lucky, a ray or sea turtle will swim by.

The water in Brown Bay is so shallow and clear that wading is a reasonable alternative to snorkeling if you don't feel like getting completely wet. Just be careful not to step on a sea egg.

Haulover Bay

A rocky beach facing Tortola, Haulover Bay is so named because mariners hauled their boats over land here rather than sail the long circle around the far eastern tip of St. John.

Today, Haulover is best known as an off-the-beaten-track destination for snorkeling. Look for star coral boulders and fish along the rocky shoreline, but be careful, especially in rough weather. The Coral Bay side is invariably calm and offers scattered corals, rocks, and moderate numbers of fish.

Hansen Bay

The beach at Hansen Bay is a mixture of sand and rocks, and the snorkeling offshore can be good. This bay is home to Vie's Campground and Snack Bar; it makes a good pit stop for your tour of the east end.

SOUTH SHORE

The south coast of St. John is remote and largely unspoiled. It is home to excellent snorkeling and some of the island's best hikes.

Salt Pond Bay

For many St. John residents, Salt Pond Bay is a favorite beach, if for no other reason than that it tends to be uncrowded, even on weekends. This is partly due to the bay's remote location near the end of Route 107, and partly due to the 10-minute hike to the beach.

Salt Pond's wide, white beach is speckled by small pebbles. It offers some shade, several picnic tables, and pit toilets. The water here is invariably calm; when north shore beaches are being pounded by waves, Salt Pond Bay is dead calm.

Be sure to bring your snorkel to explore the underwater landscape around the jagged rocks in the middle of the bay. Also worth checking out is the shoreline on the eastern side of the bay. Rocks and small patches of reef attract a pleasing variety of fish; it gets better the farther out you go.

Salt Pond Bay is a jumping-off point for hikes. A short dogleg from the beach takes you to **Drunk Bay,** a rocky shore good for beachcombing. Remember, however, that this is park land, so you can look but not take.

The trail to Ram's Head leaves from the end of the beach and is a much longer and more challenging hike.

◀ Ram's Head

The extreme southeastern tip of St. John is a narrow finger of land called Ram's Head. Here, waves crash on rocks 200 feet below and howling wind carries your voice far away. The view is of the Caribbean Sea to the south and the irregular foothills of southern St. John to the west. Ram's Head is a dramatic place that inspires silence and awe. During the 1733 slave uprising, Ram's Head was one of the Africans' camps, chosen because it was easily defended and difficult to reach.

The only way to get to Ram's Head is on foot. It is a 1.2-mile hike (one-way) from the parking lot for Salt Pond Bay through dry forest, along rocky shorelines, and then through the open, grassy landscape that defines Ram's

Head. Turk's head cactus dot the hillside, and as you walk, look back for outstanding views of Salt Pond Bay and Concordia.

Though the round-trip to and from the parking lot is just 2.4 miles, do not underestimate the difficulty of this hike and the amount of water you will need. Sun protection is a necessity.

Lameshur Bay

Some of St. John's best snorkeling is found around Great Lameshur Bay and Little Lameshur Bay—side-by-side bays along the island's south coast. Great Lameshur is scattered with rock and coral; the best snorkeling is on its eastern side. The remains of *Tektite,* an underwater living habitat for aquanauts (built in the late 1960s), lie submerged under 50 feet of water here. Little Lameshur has a sand and rubble beach. There is good snorkeling around the rocks that jut out in the middle of the bay. If you are lucky enough to visit on a calm day, follow the western shoreline as far as Europa Bay for some exquisite snorkeling.

On land, hike the short trail (less than half a mile) to Yawzi Point, the tip of the headline that divides Great and Little Lameshur Bays. The trail travels through an arid landscape of cactus, bromeliads, thorny bushes, and trees. There are pleasant views of both bays and a cooling breeze at the end.

The road to Lameshur Bay is improved. The two-lane blacktop Route 107 ends a few miles past Salt Pond Bay, but don't worry. After a few hundred yards of easy dirt road, the pavement returns. It is a steep ascent and then a steeper descent into Lameshur. Drive slowly and watch for oncoming traffic. After you reach Great Lameshur Bay, the road is again unpaved. Parking is available off the road at both Great Lameshur and Little Lameshur.

Reef Bay

This broad, wooded bay was the site of one of the

The Reef Bay petroglyphs have intrigued people for centuries.

© SUSANNA HENIGHAN POTTER

most productive sugar plantations on St. John. Par Force, as the estate was called, was owned by the Rif family. "Reef Bay" is a corruption of this name; it has nothing to do with coral.

The sugar mill ruins are at the edge of the bay. They are marked by National Park Service signs explaining the sugar production process. The old sugar factory is home to a rare species of bat—look up when you step inside.

Most people get to Reef Bay by hiking (the only other alternative is by boat). On the trail down, you pass several other sugar mill ruins and the foundation of an old worker's cottage. The Reef Bay Great House is a short detour off the Lameshur Bay Trail. The old great house is one of the largest on St. John, but it's in disrepair, and the NPS does not encourage visits here.

◖ Petroglyphs

Stone carvings along the Reef Bay Trail are a reminder of St. John's rich history, although their origin is something of a mystery.

The most widely accepted explanation of the carvings' origin is that they were made by Taino people who lived on St. John beginning around A.D. 200. Petroglyphs like these have been found at former Taino settlements on Puerto Rico, Hispaniola, and other islands in the Caribbean. It is believed that many of the petroglyphs are representations of bats, animals of significance to the Tainos.

But there are other theories. One is that Africans carved the petroglyphs during a pre-Columbian journey to the Caribbean and Central America. This idea stems from similarities between the St. John petroglyphs and an Ashanti symbol that means "accept God." It has also been argued that the symbols resemble a script used by peoples of southeast Libya.

The petroglyphs make a nice pit stop along the Reef Bay Trail. When there has been recent rain, there is also a waterfall (at other times, the pool remains, but there won't be any running water). The petroglyphs are cut into the rock above the main pool; splash a little water on them and you'll see them better.

ST. JOHN

Entertainment and Events

People don't come to St. John for the party, but they'll find one once they're here. Nightlife is relaxed but fun, and the island's annual event calendar includes live music festivals, sporting events, and Carnival. Bands and live music are usually on tap a couple times a week; pick up the *Sun Times* or *Tradewinds* for a rundown of upcoming gigs.

NIGHTLIFE

After a day in the wilds of the national park, many people head to bars in Cruz Bay and Coral Bay for companionship, music, and a chance to share stories. Cruz Bay's nightlife feels increasingly spring break-ish, but Coral Bay is mellow and laid-back. Nights out tend to start early, often over happy hour.

Cruz Bay

In Cruz Bay the party begins and ends on the sidewalks along Route 10, near its intersection with King Street, amid a cluster of bars, restaurants, and the town's only bank.

The bell rings at 3 P.M. to announce the start of $1 beers at **Woody's Seafood Saloon** (Cruz Bay, 340/779-4625, 11 A.M.–1 A.M. Sun.–Thurs., 11 A.M.–2 A.M. Fri.–Sat.), a hole-in-the wall where the waitresses wear short-shorts and the deep fryer is always on. Twenty-somethings and their brethren flock here for happy hour and stay late into the night, spilling out on the sidewalk in a scene that may remind you of a college house party.

If voyeurism is more your thing, grab a stool

at **Quiet Mon Pub** (Cruz Bay, 340/779-4799), a generally peaceful bar with a second-story view. Nurse draft Irish beer or hard cider while peering down at the mayhem unfolding below.

If the view you prefer is of sand and ocean, there are no fewer than four bars lining Cruz Bay beach. These establishments come and go with some frequency, so the best way to get the current lay of the land is to stroll the sand and see which watering hole appeals. At the time of research, the **Beach Bar** (Wharfside Village, 340/777-4220, www.beachbarstjohn.com) at the far end of the sand was attracting a crowd with cocktails like painkillers and bushwackers, a smattering of tables scattered in the sand, and live music on Sundays. A couple of doors down, the **Waterfront Bistro** (Wharfside Village, 340/777-7755) is the most upscale of the town's beachfront bars; it's a pleasant place for a drink and turns out above-average food as well.

Get off the tourist track and mingle with locals at two of Cruz Bay's oldest watering holes. **Mooies** (Strand St., 340/776-6464, open at 6 P.M.), just steps from the ferry dock, serves beer and mixed drinks in a dimly lit room, staying open until the last people go home—usually between midnight and 2 A.M., but sometimes even later on weekends. It's perfect for a discreet assignation. **Cap's Place** (340/777-2379), on the other hand, is an open-air sidewalk bar where you can see and be seen while drinking some of the coldest brews in town.

Finally, beer fans should not miss the **Tap Room** (Mongoose Junction, 340/715-7555, 11 A.M.–9 P.M., www.stjohnbrewers.com), where you choose from a dozen different microbrews on tap, including six designed by St. John's only microbrewery. Tropical Mango, Island Summer Ale, Island Hopping IPA, and Amber Jack are a few of the options—and nothing tastes better after a day at the beach. St. John Brewers also cooks up kegs of root beer and ginger beer, both of which are also on tap.

Sun Dog Cafe (Mongoose Junction, 340/693-8340, 6–9 P.M. daily) hosts a mid-week live music jam in the courtyard at Mongoose Junction every Wednesday beginning at 7 P.M. Just down the road, **Morgan's Mango** (next to Mongoose Junction, 340/693-8141, 6–10 P.M. daily) has live music after dinner four nights a week.

Coral Bay

By and large, nightlife in Coral Bay is mellower than in Cruz Bay. Live blues, rock, and acoustic music can be found five nights a week at **Island Blues** (340/776-6800, www.island-blues.com, 6–10 P.M. daily), a seaside bar and restaurant. Local regulars and stateside bands, Island Blues gets them all.

Skinny Legs (340/779-4982, 11 A.M.–9 P.M. daily) is the original Coral Bay watering hole, catering to sailors and other salty dogs. The open-air dining room faces a bar that is full by noon many days and remains so into the night.

The bar at **Aqua Bistro** (Cocoloba Center, 340/776-5336, 11 A.M.–11 P.M. daily) is often filled for happy hour, and live music on Friday nights draws a crowd.

Miss Lucy's (Salt Pond Rd., 340/693-5244, 11 A.M.–9 P.M. Tues.–Sat.) hosts a full moon party monthly.

EVENTS

The biggest event on St. John is the annual July 4 Carnival, but the island throws some other parties, too.

Carnival on St. John starts in mid-June and lasts through July 4, when a small but energetic parade winds through Cruz Bay. The Carnival Village is erected in the parking lot next to the Customs and Immigration building on the waterfront. There's lots of live music, a food fair, and much more.

Athletes swim 0.5 mile, bike 14 miles, and run 4 miles in the **Love City Triathlon** (340/779-4214, www.stjohnlandsharks.com). Love City is St. John's nickname, redolent of the hippie attitude many early residents embrace. The triathlon, which takes place in

September, usually attracts athletes from the U.S. and British Virgin Islands, as well as Puerto Rico.

Runners and walkers brave St. John's hills in the annual **8 Tuff Miles** (www.8tuffmiles.com) road race in February. The route from Cruz Bay to Coral Bay, along Centerline Road, climbs 1,400 feet in less than six miles and in recent years has attracted nearly 900 participants.

A few weeks later, the island holds a **St. Patrick's Day parade** through Cruz Bay: "8 tuff minutes for the rest of us."

The National Park Service and the Friends of the Virgin Islands National Park host an annual **St. John Folklife Festival** in late February at the Annaberg sugar mill ruins. Traditional music, food, crafts, stories, and dance are featured. For information, contact the Friends of the Virgin Islands National Park at 340/779-4940.

Shopping

St. John has an increasing number of small, unique boutiques catering to the upscale and funky tastes of its visitors. Shoppers won't find acres of gold jewelry, as on St. Thomas, but they will find some of the most upscale and trendy shopping in the Virgin Islands.

CRUZ BAY

St. John has less shopping than nearby St. Thomas, but its shops have more character. This is a good place to find unique clothing, jewelry, and art to commemorate your Virgin Islands vacation. Navigate Cruz Bay's shops by heading to various shopping plazas around town.

Mongoose Junction

The best place for shopping in Cruz Bay is Mongoose Junction, a maze-like outdoor mall located at the extreme northern end of town. Here, amid cobblestone walls and tropical plants, you'll find a pleasant array of clothes, jewelry, beach gear, art, and souvenirs. Shops at Mongoose Junction are generally open from 9:30 A.M. to at least 8 P.M. Monday–Saturday. On Sundays most shops close by 6 P.M.

It is difficult to leave **Caravan Gallery** (340/779-4566) empty-handed: something from its wide selection of silver jewelry and semiprecious stones will find its way into your jewelry box. **The Fabric Mill** (340/776-6194) offers distinctive imported textiles from South America, plus breezy ladies' attire. **Bamboula** (340/693-8699) is a long-standing favorite for its bohemian clothing, batik bedspreads, stylish handbags, jewelry, and art.

Nest & Co. (340/715-2552) has a fresh vibe and a little bit of just about everything: spunky greeting cards, high-end body products, and stylish picnic gear, plus ladies' and children's clothing.

Absolutely don't miss the **Friends of Virgin Islands National Park Gift Shop** (340/779-8700). Here you can buy books, T-shirts, posters, prints, art, and conversation starters like paper made from donkey poop. Purchases here support the national park.

The island's best all-around art gallery is **Bajo El Sol** (340/693-7070), which sells a wide variety of high-quality paintings, prints, sculptures, and decorative pieces by St. John artists.

Browse jewelry inspired by the St. John petroglyphs and zemis at **R&I Patton** (340/776-6548). Partial proceeds from some of the pieces go toward archaeological projects in the national park.

Wharfside Village

Located facing Cruz Bay's tiny beach, Wharfside Village is the shopping and dining plaza closest to the ferry dock. The smell of spices and fresh-roasted coffee greets you at the door at **St. John Spice** (340/693-7046), a treasure trove of culinary goodies including the widest selection of pepper and hot sauces this side of hell.

You can watch the manufacture of silver and gold jewelry at **Bamboo Studio** (340/776-0669) and then pop into the neighboring shop to buy St. John–inspired charms, pendants, and bracelets.

Around Town

Deck your home in art, ornaments, figurines, and various other island-inspired frills available from **Pink Papaya** (King St., 340/693-8535), a venerable St. John gift shop located in a pink and peach cottage.

For the best selection of water gear, including snorkels, swimsuits, cover-ups, and water booties head to **Low Key Watersports** (Bay St., 340/693-8999), a dive shop located at the southern frontier of Cruz Bay, at the foot of Grande Bay Resort.

For books, maps, and children's toys with an educational bent, browse the small selection at the **Virgin Islands National Park Visitor Center** (Waterfront, 340/776-6201). St. John's only real bookstore is **Papaya Cafe** (Marketplace, Enighed, 340/693-8535), where you'll find bestsellers, paperbacks, and some Virgin Islands–inspired works.

CORAL BAY

Coral Bay's shopping is offbeat and unique. It is also growing. The opening of the Cocoloba Shopping Center on Route 107 doubled shopping outlets in this far-flung community, for better or for worse. In addition to some practical things like a mailbox service and grocery store, Cocoloba contains art, clothing, and souvenir shops.

The original Coral Bay shopping complex is at Skinny Legs, just east of the main Coral Bay crossroads of Routes 107 and 10. Here, **Mumbo Jumbo** (340/779-4277) sells island clothes, handbags, sunglasses, and footwear.

Over at Cocoloba, **Full Moon of St. John** (Cocolobo Shops, Coral Bay, 340/774-9033) sells original artwork, jewelry, and designs by some 40 different St. John artists. Ladies, meanwhile, can order custom-made bikinis at **Ranifly** (Cocoloba Shops, 631/204-7452). Choose your style and fabric and get measured for a custom fit; designs start at $120. If you'd rather just look, Ranifly also produces and sells an annual St. John swimsuit calendar.

A great stop for everyone, especially families, is the **Tall Ship Trading Company** (340/776-6816), next to Shipwreck Landing along Route 107. Here you can watch an old-fashioned silkscreen T-shirt press in operation and choose from the latest designs. Neighboring shops sell postcards, T-shirts, hats, and other island-inspired accessories and gifts.

THE NORTH SHORE

For brand-name resort wear, magazines, art, and high-priced gifts, check out the boutique at **Caneel Bay** (340/776-6111).

The most interesting shop on St. John is at **Maho Bay Camps** (340/776-6226, www.maho.org), right next door to the campground restaurant: At **Trash to Treasures Art Center,** artists convert discarded glass and fabric into works of art. Many days you can watch a master glassblower at work. Also at Maho Bay Camps is **Maho Bay Clay Works** (Maho Bay, 340/776-6226, ext. 226), perhaps St. John's most fascinating gallery. There are frequent classes and detailed demonstrations at both places. Check out the website for a schedule.

Sports and Recreation

Recreation on St. John generally has one aim: to bring you closer to the exquisite natural beauty of the island. Hiking and snorkeling are the most popular pursuits because they are rewarding, easy, and require little gear. For people seeking something a little more involved, there are also opportunities for biking, kayaking, scuba diving, windsurfing, and sailing.

For some of the most rewarding activities, check with the **Friends of Virgin Islands National Park** (340/779-4940, www.friendsvinp.org), which organizes guided hikes, workshops, arts and crafts lessons, and other fun educational activities. Past workshops have showcased traditional island cooking, how to take better nature photographs, and stargazing. The organization accepts donations in support of its conservation work.

WATER SPORTS
Snorkeling

Snorkeling is probably the most popular activity on St. John, and for good reason. It requires minimal equipment and allows you to explore the underwater cornucopia of fish, coral, shellfish, turtles, and other marine creatures that live in the waters around St. John. Because of strict rules governing fishing, anchoring, and pollution in national park waters, the snorkeling around St. John is excellent.

You can snorkel anywhere. Most people gravitate toward coral reefs, but snorkeling over sea grass or in the mangroves can be just as interesting. The National Park Service publishes a brochure, *Where's the Best Snorkeling?*, which provides detailed descriptions of snorkeling at the major beaches on St. John.

CORAL REEF SITES

On the north shore, the **Trunk Bay Underwater Trail** is a good reef for beginners. Signs along the sea floor identify types of coral and fish, and lifeguards are on duty for safety. **Jumbie Beach** has a shallow, maze-like reef along the eastern (right-hand) side, where you may see lobsters and nurse sharks. **Waterlemon Cay,** accessible via Leinster Bay, has excellent coral reef snorkeling.

When the north shore is too rough for snorkeling, try south shore bays, which are normally calm. On the south shore, **Salt Pond Bay** has good reef snorkeling around the two jagged rocks that break the surface of the bay. There is also good snorkeling on the eastern shoreline (nearest Ram's Head), which gets better the farther out you go. At **Great Lameshur Bay,** the snorkeling is best along the eastern shore. You may see the sunken foundation remains of *Tektite*, an underwater habitat for aquanauts (used from 1969 to 1970). **Little Lameshur Bay** has snorkeling for beginners just off the western end of the beach. If it is calm, strong swimmers can explore the western shoreline, which features deep cliffs, canyons, and schools of fish.

SEA GRASS SITES

Maho Bay has offshore sea grass beds that provide food for green turtles, especially in the early morning and late afternoon. **Leinster Bay** near Annaberg, on the extreme northwestern end of the island, has nice sea grass beds, where you may see sea stars, conch, and turtles. **Brown Bay,** accessible only on foot, has a sea grass bed just offshore. Not part of the national park, **Chocolate Hole** has a thick sea grass bed where you can see juvenile fish, rays, conch, and sometimes turtles. Chocolate Hole was named for the color of the rocks along the shore. It is located on Route 104, on the southern coast.

ST. JOHN

SNORKELING 101

Every visitor to the Virgin Islands should try their hand at snorkeling. It is a simple, low-tech, and easy way to explore the wonderland of reefs, sea grass beds, mangrove forests, and sandy bottoms that exist around the islands. These tips will help you enjoy a successful and safe snorkel experience.

- 1. Test your mask to see if it fits properly. Do this by placing it on your face without the band, taking a deep breath in, and holding it. If the mask fits properly, it will stay on your face. If your mask does not stay put, try another size or check for things that could be breaking the seal: beards or mustaches, hair, eyeglasses, or sunscreen.

- 2. Fogging is also a problem. You can prevent fogging by rubbing the inside of your mask with spit or mild dish soap. Commercial defogging solutions are also available.

- 3. Make sure that your mask strap is not too tight and that it is positioned just below the widest part of your head. Your mask should be secure, but comfortable.

- 4. Fins help because they reduce the amount of energy you have to use to get around. Your kick should be smooth and nearly effortless. Be careful not to accidentally kick or brush up against coral.

- 5. If you tend to get chilled easily, it is a good idea to wear a wetsuit or surf shirt.

- 6. A floatation belt or jacket helps snorkelers who do not naturally float or who want extra security.

- 7. Underwater visibility is best on sunny days, when the sea is calm.

- 8. If you're entering the water from shore, you can walk backwards with your fins on until the water is deep enough to swim. Or carry your fins in hand and put them on in the water. Don't enter the water where there are a lot of sea urchins, sharp coral, or wave action.

- 9. Protect yourself from the sun; while snorkeling, your back and legs are subject to terrible sunburns. Wear a T-shirt and shorts or wetsuit. A bathing cap is a good idea for bald heads. If you are only using sunscreen, apply a reef-safe brand at least 15 minutes before you go in the water and reapply frequently. (Ladies— and Speedo-loving gentlemen—pay special attention to the skin of the backs of your upper thighs, right below your bathing suit.)

- 10. Be sure to tell someone where you are going and when you will be back. Always snorkel with a buddy, and agree ahead of time how far you will separate from each other in the water. If you feel tired, get out and rest.

- 11. Ask about currents before you go in the water. If you do get caught in a current, do not fight it. Swim across it until you can get out or are washed toward the shore.

MANGROVE SITES

Mangroves are not as flashy as reefs or sea grass, but they provide a fascinating glimpse into an important marine habitat. Mangroves are where juvenile fish, lobsters, and crabs live until they get big enough to fend for themselves in the great big ocean. Mangroves are often referred to as the nursery of the ocean. The best place for mangrove snorkeling is **Princess Bay** along Route 10 (East End Road). Get as close to the knobby trees as you can, and look carefully for the marine life. The water is shallow,

and fins will disturb the sea bottom; it is best not to wear them.

SNORKEL EQUIPMENT

If snorkeling appeals to you at all, it's a good idea to rent snorkel gear for the duration of your stay. It is cheaper than renting it by the day or hour, and that way you will always have gear on hand. Check first to see if your lodging has or rents snorkel equipment; most hotels do. You can also rent gear from any water-sports or dive operation on the island. In Coral Bay,

Crabby's Watersports (Cocoloba Shopping Center, 340/714-2415) rents a full set of snorkel gear for $10 a day or $50 a week. Near Salt Pond Bay, **Concordia Eco-Resort** (Concordia, 340/693-5855, 8 A.M.–7:30 P.M. daily) rents gear for $8 per day.

In Cruz Bay, **Low Key Watersports** (Bay St., 340/693-8999) rents gear for $7 a day and $35 a week. Water-sports shops at Trunk Bay, Cinnamon Bay, and Little Maho Bay also rent gear.

SNORKEL TOURS

Low Key Watersports (Bay St., 340/693-8999) will take snorkelers out on a boat to shallow reefs and wrecks around St. John. A two-site snorkel costs $50 and a full-day three-site safari plus lunch runs $115 per person.

The National Park Service (340/776-6201) offers ranger-guided snorkeling trips (9:30–10:30 A.M. Mon., adults 17 and up $4, children under 17 free) along the **Trunk Bay Underwater Snorkel Trail.** A fee is required to enter Trunk Bay; the guided snorkel is free. Meet at the Trunk Bay lifeguard station.

Diving

St. John has a half dozen good dive sites off its southeastern shore, as well as two good sites just off Cruz Bay. The string of cays between St. John and St. Thomas—from Carval Rick to Thatch Cay—is also popular with divers. The **Maj. Gen. Rogers,** a 1940 army freighter, was sunk in 1972 to become an artificial reef. The excellent reefs around **Grass Cay** and **Mingo Cay** are good for beginning divers. And there is a dizzying array of sea life at **Witch's Hat** on the southern tip of Steven's Cay, just off Cruz Bay.

South shore dives include **Cocoloba,** an easy, sandy reef dive, and **Maple Leaf,** a large offshore reef east of Reef Bay. The most famous east end dive site is **Eagle Shoal,** between Ram's Head and Leduck Island. The shoal, known for its massive underwater cave, has been the site of underwater weddings. Access

to Eagle Shoal is limited because of its exposure to southeasterly swells.

Low Key Watersports (Cruz Bay, 340/693-8999) offers daily dive trips as well as certification courses. Captain Bob Carney leads dive trips with **Paradise Watersports** (Caneel Bay Resort, 340/779-4999, www.paradisevi.com), which specializes in small groups. **Cruz Bay Watersports** (Cruz Bay and the Westin Resort, 340/693-8720) departs from the national park dock in Cruz Bay. Its office is located below Chilly Billy's in the Lumberyard Complex. **Maho Bay Watersports** (340/776-6226) at Maho Bay Camps offers certification, resort courses, and a regular schedule of one- and two-tank outings.

Dive rates vary, but expect to pay about $75 for a single-tank dive and $100 for a double-tank dive. Discover Scuba courses, also called resort courses, which give inexperienced divers a brief introduction to the sport, run about $125 and include one shallow reef dive. Many dive shops offer economical packages of multiple dives for scuba enthusiasts.

Kayaking

Kayaking is a good way to get from bay to bay or out to the small cays around St. John, where you can picnic or just enjoy a day on a desert island. How easy or hard it is to kayak around St. John depends a lot on the weather and sea conditions; calm weather means easy kayaking, so check the marine forecast or a water-sports center before planning a trip. The most popular area for kayaking is off St. John's north shore, where you can paddle up to beaches or out to offshore islets, like Whistling Cay, Waterlemon Cay, or the Durloe Cays. A kayak is the ideal means to explore the creeks and bays that make up Coral Bay or reach the remote east end of the island.

GEAR AND TOURS

On the north shore, kayak rentals are available

Kayak

at **Cinnamon Bay Watersports** (Cinnamon Bay, 340/776-6330 or 340/693-5902) and at **Maho Bay Watersports** (Little Maho Bay, 340/776-6226, 9 A.M.–4 P.M.). For exploring around Coral Bay, **Crabby's Watersports** (Cocoloba Shopping Center, 340/714-2415) rents single and two-seater kayaks. Expect to pay $50–75 for a full-day kayak rental.

For a little bit more than you would spend for a kayak rental, you can go on a kayak trip with a guide. **Arawak Expeditions** (340/693-8312, www.arawakexp.com) offers guided kayak tours to Henley and Lovango Cays, leaving from Cruz Bay. Half-day tours cost $65; full-day tours are $110 including lunch. Arawak also offers multiday guided paddle trips, such as a four-day circumnavigation of St. John.

Hidden Reef Eco Tours (East End Rd., 877/529-2575, www.kayaksj.com) offers two-hour, three-hour, full-day, and sunset guided paddle trips around St. John's east end. All tours depart from Haulover Bay and explore remote and relatively inaccessible snorkel sites. Rates range $55–110, and there are tours for every ability level, including one designed especially for children. All tours are naturalist-led and include snorkeling; the full-day tours incorporate hiking as well.

St. Thomas–based **Virgin Islands Ecotours** (340/779-2155, www.viecotours.com) has teamed up with Caneel Bay to offer guided kayak tours of Caneel Bay, Paradise and Scott Beaches, and Turtle Point. The three-hour excursion ($80) usually takes place on Mondays and Thursdays and includes snorkeling and hiking, too. Reservations are essential and can be made through Virgin Islands Ecotours or the Caneel Bay activity desk (340/776-6111, ext. 7218).

Fishing

Opportunities for sportfishing and fly-fishing immediately around St. John are limited by national park restrictions. Local guides, however, know where to go to put a line in the water. **Arawak Expeditions** (Mongoose Junction, 340/693-8312, www.stjohnflyfishing.com) offers full- and half-day fly-fishing outings with Captain Arthur Jones. You'll fish for bonefish and tarpon aboard his 18-foot Edgewater.

If you want to hook a marlin, tuna, mahimahi, wahoo, or kingfish, sign up for a sportfishing excursion with a St. Thomas–based sportfisher.

SAILING
Day Sails

A number of day sail operators offer sailing trips around St. John and to the nearby British Virgin Islands. Choices typically include half-day snorkel trips around St. John; full-day expeditions to Jost Van Dyke, Norman Island, or Virgin Gorda in the British Virgins; and sunset sails around St. John. Many trips include extras like free drinks and lunch. Rates range $65–85 for half-day sails and $100–120 for a full-day sail.

Instead of contacting sailing operators yourself to check availability and prices, save time by using one of the clearinghouse activity desks around St. John. Desks include **St. John Adventures Unlimited** (Gallow's Point and Cruz Bay, 340/693-7730, www.stjohnadventures.com), **Connections** (Coral Bay and Cruz Bay, 340/776-6922), **Crabby's Watersports** (Coral Bay, 340/714-2415, www.crabbyswatersports.com), and **Low Key Watersports** (Cruz Bay, 340/693-8999).

SAILING YACHTS

The *Pepper* (340/776-6226, ext. 212, www.sailpepper.com) offers the most distinctive sailing excursions on St. John. Modeled after a traditional island sloop, the 23-foot *Pepper* can accommodate up to six passengers. With Captain Fred at the helm, you will travel to off-the-beaten-path snorkel sites during the daytime snorkel sail ($95 per person). Alternatively, sign up for a sunset cruise ($50 per person). The *Pepper* departs from Maho Bay on the north shore.

Also departing from Maho Bay from December to April, **Heron** (340/776-6226, www.woodenboatco.com) is a beautiful three masted schooner offering five-hour snorkel sails ($95 per person) and three-hour sunset cruises ($55). The *Heron* summers in Maine.

Captain Philip Chalker runs a popular day sail operation on his 30-foot Islander sloop, the **Wayward Sailor** (340/776-6922, www.waywardsailor.net), notable for its red sails. Full- and half-day expeditions visit snorkel sites around St. John and the British Virgin Islands. There is a six-person maximum, guaranteeing personalized service.

Kekoa (340/244-7245, www.blacksailsvi.com) is a 50-foot wooden catamaran departing daily from Cruz Bay for sites around St. John and Jost Van Dyke. You'll recognize it by its black sails and silver hull.

For smaller groups and personal service, sign up with **Fly Girl** (340/626-8181, www.flygirlvi.com), a six-passenger Stiletto Catamaran that heads out to secluded coves and uncrowded reefs around St. John and the British Virgin Islands.

Other day sail boats include **Cloud 9** (340/998-1940, www.cloud9sailingadventures.com), the motor yacht **Cinnamon Bay** (631/946-9292, www.motoryachtcinnamonbay.com), and **Cimarron Yacht Charters** (207/415-6405, www.cimarronyachtcharter.com).

MOTOR YACHTS

Bad Kitty (340/777-7245, www.calypsovi.com) is a power catamaran that, because of its speed, is able to cover a lot of territory in a full-day tour: stops include the Baths, Cooper Island, Norman Island, and Jost Van Dyke.

For a luxurious day aboard a plush power yacht, call **Blue Tang Yacht Charters** (340/776-9070, www.bluetangyachtcharters.com). A professional crew will greet you and help you board the 51-foot *SeaRay* yacht, and

then it's off to the British Virgin Islands for a day of snorkeling and sightseeing. This is truly an upscale day out. All charters are exclusive, and groups of up to six can be accommodated.

The **Sadie Sea** (340/514-0779, www.sadie-sea.com) specializes in half-day snorkel trips to outlying cays aboard a 40-foot trawler, not unlike a mini ferry.

Boat Rentals

If bareboating is more your style, and you're competent at the wheel, consider renting a small powerboat you can captain yourself. **Nauti Nymph** (340/775-5066) is a St. Thomas–based rental company with an office at the Westin Resort on St. John. It offers 28-foot to 32-foot Fountain powerboats and 26-foot to 28-foot catamarans. High-season rates range $375–670 for a full-day rental.

Copeland Boat Charters (Cruz Bay, 340/777-1368, www.copelandboatcharters.com) offers full- and half-day powerboat rentals. Captain are available for hire.

Anchorages

If you are sailing into St. John from the British Virgin Islands or another foreign port, you will have to clear U.S. Customs and Immigration in Cruz Bay.

There are National Park Service moorings at Caneel Bay, Hawksnest Bay, Cinnamon Bay, Maho Bay, Francis Bay, Leinster Bay, Salt Pond Bay, Great Lameshur Bay, and Little Lameshur Bay. Each bay has its own specific anchoring regulations; check with the National Park Service guide before dropping anchor.

At Coral Bay, don't pick up any of the private moorings; instead, drop your anchor. There is a dinghy dock in front of Skinny Legs.

LAND PURSUITS
Hiking

There are more than 28 miles of hiking trails on St. John, ranging from easy 15-minute

ST. JOHN

rambles to challenging all-day outings. Trails wind through moist tropical forest and scrubby woods, passing Danish plantation ruins and quiet bays. Despite the development occurring on St. John, hiking remains the only way to reach some of the island's most remote, and most beautiful, places. If you're feeling a little crowded walking around Cruz Bay or on the beach at Trunk Bay, go for a hike and you will quickly reacquire the sense of quiet that makes St. John so appealing.

Official national park trails are detailed in a free NPS trail guide, which includes brief descriptions of each trail and a somewhat hard-to-read map. The guide is available at the Cruz Bay Visitor Center; don't hike without it. If you plan to do a lot of hiking, it's worth buying a copy of National Geographic's *Trails Illustrated* St. John map, available from the Virgin Islands National Park Visitor Center, Arawak Expeditions, and other island retailers. You may also see the *Trail Bandit Guide,* a pocket-size map of hiking trails, including unofficial paths. The guide includes a clearly labeled full-color map, trail descriptions, and GPS waypoint locations.

Don't be fooled by the fact that most hikes on St. John are short; hiking in the island's tropical climate is grueling. Bring twice the water you think you will need, and cover up to protect yourself from the sun and insects. The best time to hike is in the early morning or late afternoon, but be aware that darkness comes quickly this close to the equator. In the winter it is dark at 6 P.M., in the summer at 7 P.M.

The National Park Service offers weekly educational hikes, evening lectures, and cultural demonstrations. Call the visitor center at 340/776-6201 to confirm the schedule ahead of your visit.

There are more than 30 official and unofficial trails on St. John, plus secondary spurs. The hikes described here are some of the best.

SPECIAL NPS PROGRAMS

In addition to guided hikes, the National Park Service offers evening lectures and cultural demonstrations. Call the Visitor Center at 340/776-6201 to confirm the schedule ahead of your visit. Here are some highlights:

· **Annaberg Cultural Demonstrations** (10 A.M.-2 P.M. Tues.-Thurs., free): Go back in time to St. John's "subsistence years," when residents fished, farmed, and engaged in small-scale industry to survive. Dressed in period costumes, docents bake bread and tend a traditional garden.

· **Sky Watch** (7:30-8:30 P.M. Mon., free): Get an orientation to the stars at a tropical latitude from the beach at Cinnamon Bay. Meet at the Cinnamon Bay Campground Amphitheater.

· **Ranger's Choice** (7:30-8:30 P.M. Thurs., free): An evening ranger-led lecture on a facet of the park: history, plants, or animals. Meet at the Cinnamon Bay Campground Amphitheater.

· **Friends of the Park Seminar Series** (340/779-4940, Jan.-Apr., $25-125): Enjoy a sequence of educational and fun hikes, workshops, lectures, and hands-on activities. Ranging from guided botanical hikes to photography workshops, the seminar series is an excellent way to support the park while adding to your knowledge and experiences. Advance reservations are required.

LIND POINT TRAIL

A relatively easy and very rewarding hike, the Lind Point Trail (1.1 miles) connects the Cruz Bay Visitor Center with Honeymoon Beach at Caneel Bay. It has an upper and a lower track; the upper trail climbs more than 150 feet to Lind Point, with nice views of Cruz Bay and

Pillsbury Sound, before heading back down toward the beaches. The lower trail goes straight to the bay. In both cases, a side trail branches off to Solomon Beach, while the main track continues on to Honeymoon Beach, one of Caneel Bay Resort's seven beaches. Nonguests are welcome at the beach. You can either hike back the way you came or continue on to Caneel Bay Resort and catch a taxi back to town.

TURTLE POINT TRAIL ✦

This 0.5-mile hike is fully contained within the grounds of Caneel Bay Resort. Nonguests must check in at the resort front desk, where you will be given a map and instructions on where to meet the shuttle that will take you to the trailhead. The trail circles Hawksnest Point, where there are convenient benches and beautiful views, and ends at Turtle Bay Beach.

CINNAMON BAY LOOP

This is an easy 0.5-mile walk, but plan on about an hour if you want to absorb all the information along the way. The trail starts among the ruins of the old sugar factory across the road from the entrance to Cinnamon Bay Campground. It continues through the woods behind the ruins; markers identify prominent trees, animals, and insects. The hike ends by the ruins of the estate house.

The National Park Service also offers a guided Cinnamon Bay History & Culture Walk (9:30–10:30 A.M. Tues., free). Walk with a ranger along the half-mile Cinnamon Bay loop trail, past sugarworks and estate house ruins, through a moist tropical forest, and past sites of prehistoric significance. Meet at the benches next to the Cinnamon Bay Archaeology Exhibit.

CINNAMON BAY TRAIL

Don't confuse this trail with the self-guided loop. The Cinnamon Bay Trail is a 1.1-mile uphill trail that begins about 100 yards east of the campground entrance and follows an Danish road all the way to Centerline Road. Of course, if you start at Centerline Road, it is all downhill. The trail passes through land that would have been cultivated with sugarcane during the plantation era; it is now all secondary forest.

FRANCIS BAY TRAIL

This is a good hike for bird-watchers. The beginning of this 0.5-mile trail is well marked on the west end of the Mary Creek paved road. It passes through dry forest, goes past estate house ruins, and skirts a mangrove forest and salt pond. The trail ends at Francis Bay Beach.

The National Park Service also offers a guided bird walk on this trail (7:30–9 A.M. Fri., free), traversing the seashore, past a salt pond and through dry tropical forest. Meet at the Francis Bay trailhead or call to inquire about shared taxi service from Cruz Bay.

LEINSTER BAY AND JOHNNY HORN TRAILS

This 2.6-mile trail, often considered two separate trails, connects the Emmaus Moravian Church in Coral Bay with Annaberg Plantation on the north coast.

From Annaberg, the trail follows the shoreline of Leinster Bay for 0.8 mile before striking out over Leinster and Base Hills, past the ruins of a great house. The hike includes several flat sections, as well as steep uphill and downhill segments as you prepare to enter Coral Bay. Seven-tenths of a mile past Leinster Bay, the Brown Bay Trail veers off and heads to remote Brown Bay. The Johnny Horn Trail finishes at the driveway of the Moravian Church. At the end, only the sturdiest of hikers would want to turn around and hike back the way they came.

The National Park Service also offers the Water's Edge Walk (9:30–10:30 A.M. Wed., free), which explores the area between sea and shore. Learn about the creatures who thrive in on this family-friendly outing. nster Bay trailhead.

...RAIL

This 0.8 mile (one-way) hike heads from the East End Road to Brown Bay on the island's north shore. The path climbs up and over a low ridge and then skirts the bay before depositing you on a rough sand beach. Brown Bay is home to large sea grass beds and is good for snorkeling. Return the way you came, or continue on for another 0.8 mile to Johnny Horn Trail, for a longer outing that could end at Coral Bay or Annaberg.

RAM'S HEAD TRAIL

This 1.2-mile hike takes you to the windswept end of Ram's Head, the southernmost point of St. John. Take Route 107 nearly to the end, to Salt Pond Bay, and then follow the wide sunny 0.25-mile path down to Salt Pond Beach. The Ram's Head Trail starts at the eastern end of the beach, climbing through dry, scrubby woods before reaching a rocky bay. The final ascent is 200 feet up to Ram's Head—the views and general atmosphere are spectacular. This hike is the perfect prescription to calm the mind and energize the spirit.

Near the beginning of the Ram's Head Trail is a 0.25-mile spur trail to Drunk Bay, an excellent spot for beachcombing.

YAWZI POINT TRAIL

This 0.5-mile easy hike follows the headland that separates Little Lameshur and Great Lameshur Bays. People suffering from yaws, a tropical skin disease, were sent to a quarantine camp here in the 18th and 19th centuries. The trail cuts through a dry forest before reaching the point.

REEF BAY TRAIL

The most popular hike on St. John is the

hikers near the summit at Ram's Head on St. John's South Shore

2.1-mile Reef Bay Trail, which descends from Centerline Road to the shore at Reef Bay. The trail passes through both moist and dry tropical forests and the remains of four different sugar factories, including the extensive Reef Bay ruins. The hike descends 600 feet from start to finish. Plan on two hours to hike down, three to hike up.

Several markers along the way identify significant plants, trees, and landmarks. You may see white-tailed deer along the trail. Despite being introduced years ago as game for planters, the deer are not fearful of people.

The 0.25-mile spur trail to the **Reef Bay Petroglyphs** branches off 1.6 miles down. Just past the petroglyph trail is the beginning of the Lameshur Bay Trail. It's a 1.5-mile hike to that bay. The Reef Bay Great House Ruins are a short distance up this trail. If you keep going straight, you come to the Reef Bay Sugar Ruins

and a short spur trail to Little Reef Bay, where you can swim.

The National Park Service leads guided hikes down the Reef Bay Trail several days a week (9:30 A.M.–3 P.M. Mon.–Wed. and Fri., $30 per person). Advance reservations are a necessity for this hike, the most popular ranger-led activity in the park. Contact the Friends of the National Park (340/779-8700) to reserve a spot. Sign up early, preferably before you arrive on St. John, because the hike is almost always fully subscribed.

Participants taxi to the Reef Bay trailhead, and then hike the 2.6 miles down to the Reef Bay sugarworks ruins, with a detour to the petroglyphs. Rangers lead groups of about 30 people down the trail, stopping regularly to describe the natural and historic landmarks along the way. It's a great opportunity to learn about the island, but the biggest perk of the outing is that you don't have to hike back up. The park service arranges a boat to pick you up at the end of the trail and sail back to Cruz Bay.

L'ESPERANCE TRAIL

The long way to Reef Bay, this 2.6-mile trail passes ruins of the L'Esperance Great House and the island's only baobab tree before heading up, and then down, into Reef Bay. Return the way you came or choose to hike back up along the Reef Bay trail, stopping at the petroglyphs on the way, for a strenuous, long, and rewarding day of hiking

Biking

St. John's hills make biking a strenuous pursuit. If you want to take on the challenge, contact **Arawak Expeditions** (340/693-8312, www.arawakexp.com), which provides guides and routes tailored for beginning, intermediate, and advanced bikers. Rates are $50 for a half day or $90 for a full day.

© SUSANNA HENIGHAN POTTER

Hikers stand next to St. John's only baobab tree, found along the L'Esperance trail.

Horseback Riding

Guided trail rides around Coral Bay are offered by **Carolina Corral** (East End Rd., 340/693-5778, www.carolinacorral.vi). Trips depart daily at 10 A.M. and 3 P.M. and run $65 for one hour.

Tennis

There are two public tennis courts in Cruz Bay, next to the Department of Motor Vehicles. Tennis classes and pro shop services are available at the **Westin** (340/693-8000) and **Caneel Bay Resort** (340/776-6111).

Accommodations

St. John's accommodations run the gamut from luxurious resorts to bare-bones campsites. The island's hotels and villas are among the priciest in the Virgin Islands, but top-notch campgrounds, eco-resorts, and a growing number of moderate hotels in Cruz Bay make St. John an affordable destination for budget-minded travelers, too.

VILLAS

The fastest-growing sector of St. John's accommodation market is villas, private homes rented out for a week or more at a time. Many are owned by snowbirds, who rent the house out when they are not using it. Others were constructed specifically for vacation rentals. Villas come in a wide variety of styles and sizes, but most have two or more bedrooms, with capacity to sleep large groups of people. One-bedroom villas are hard to find.

Villa rental rates vary widely but generally start around $2,500 per week in the winter and top out at over $10,000. Average rates are $3,000–5,000 per week.

The best way to book a villa is to contact a villa rental agency. These agencies represent villas, make reservations, and, in many cases, manage the properties for the owners. **Carefree Getaways** (340/779-4070 or 888/643-6002, www.carefreegetaways.com) specializes in villas south of Cruz Bay, in Chocolate Hole, Rendezvous Bay, and Gift Hill. **Windspree Vacation Homes** (Coral Bay, 340/693-5423 or 888/742-0357, www.windspree.com) represents several dozen villas around Coral Bay and the east end.

Catered To (Marketplace, Cruz Bay, 340/776-6642 or 800/424-6641, fax 340/693-8191, www.cateredto.com) represents some 50 villas in the Cruz Bay and north shore areas. **Virgin Islands Vacations and Villas** (Boulon Center, Cruz Bay, 340/779-4250 or 888/856-4601, www.vivacations.com) and **Caribbean Villas and Resorts** (800/338-0987, www.caribbeanvilla.com) have a wide selection of villas all over the island.

Caribe Havens (340/776-6518, www.caribehavens.com) is a small rental agency specializing in inexpensive rentals. Despite the lower price tags, these comfortable and clean homes offer good locations and views. Many of the properties predate the recent large-scale building boom. Weekly rates range $1,100–2,500 in winter and $875–1,500 in summer.

AROUND CRUZ BAY
Under $125

The three one-bedroom cottages at **Samuel's Cottages** (Rte. 10, tel./fax 340/776-6643, www.samuelcottages.com, $100) are cute, clean, and a good home base for exploring Cruz Bay and the rest of St. John. Each peach-colored cottage has a full kitchen, cable TV, and phone and can sleep up to five people. The views are of Cruz Bay and Enighed Pond. It is a five-minute walk along a busy street to the heart of Cruz Bay, and the road traffic and general noisiness of Cruz Bay mean that this is not necessarily a quiet retreat. The cottages generally rent by the week ($700 for seven nights); if you are staying for three nights or less, the rate is $150 per night.

$125-175

The Inn at Tamarind Court (340/776 6378 or 800/221-1637, www.tamarindcourt.com, $150–240 winter, $110–170 summer) is a 20-room hotel about three blocks from the heart of Cruz Bay. Rooms include standard motel-style accommodations and self-catering apartments furnished in chunky bamboo. The on-site courtyard restaurant serves breakfast daily and dinner five nights a week; guests receive a free continental breakfast. Single economy rooms with shared bath are available for $60–75 depending on the season. These airless dorm-style rooms have little, save the price tag, to recommend them.

Treetops (Fish Bay, 340/779-4490, www.treetops.vi, $115–160 winter, $85–135 summer) is a three-room bed-and-breakfast tucked into a forested hillside three miles east of Cruz Bay. Lots of decks, exposed wood, and the chirping of neighborly birds give the property a treehouse vibe. Rooms, which range from a single studio to a two-room air-conditioned suite, have their own private entrance and bath; guests share an outdoor grill and hot tub. You'll need a rental car at Treetops, which may seem out of the way or perfectly secluded depending on your point of view. Guests under 25 years old are not permitted.

$175-225

Set on the mildly industrial side of Cruz Bay **St. John Inn** (Enighed, 340/693-8688, www.stjohninn.com, $175–275 winter, $105–165 summer) is an 11-room inn for travelers with modest budgets. Colorful tropical bedspreads provide a splash of color in the mostly plain rooms, which are outfitted, sometimes to a jumbled effect, with air conditioning, cable TV, wireless Internet, a refrigerator, a coffeemaker, and a microwave. Guests can also use the inn's outdoor grill or relax around its teeny

pool. Meet your fellow guests over breakfast and sunset happy hour on the inn's pool deck.

The ◖ **St. John Boutique Hotel** (Cruz Bay, 340/642-1702, www.cruzbayhotel.com, $190–265 winter, $105–200 summer) is an airy and unpretentious six-room inn in the heart of Cruz Bay. A palette of white and muted greens sets a relaxing tone in the guest rooms, which have balconies overlooking one of Cruz Bay's busiest streets. The rooms are small, but comforts include air conditioning, satellite TV, wireless Internet, mini refrigerators, queen-size beds, and continental breakfast daily. Guests praise the cleanliness of the rooms and the warm welcome provided by owners Denise and Dave.

A family-run inn since 1966, **Hillcrest Guest House** (Cruz Bay, 340/776-6774, www.hillcreststjohn.com, $200–245 winter, $165–195 summer) sits atop a low hill on the outskirts of Cruz Bay. Six guest rooms are outfitted similarly with modest white frills, cable TV, kitchenettes, and queen-size beds. In most rooms, futons provide sleeping space for up to four guests, making Hillcrest an economical option for groups willing to share close quarters. Mediocre views from top-floor rooms are of Cruz Bay. Hostess Phyllis Hall stocks your fridge with fruit, bacon, eggs, bagels, and an assortment of beverages, so breakfast is yours to make. Hillcrest is a short, but steep, walk to the heart of town.

$225-300

Ensconce yourself in island-style charm at ◖ **Garden by the Sea** (Turner Bay, 340/779-4731, www.gardenbythesea.com, $250–275 winter, $160–180 summer), a three-bedroom bed-and-breakfast in the residential outskirts of Cruz Bay. Walls are washed in pastel purple, pink, green, and blue; private baths are furnished with skylights and tropical plants; and the common room feels just like home. There are no phones or televisions, but guests fork into frittatas, piña colada French toast, and made-from-scratch muffins each morning on the deck. At the time of research, Garden by the Sea was for sale; check current reviews to ensure that the high quality of service is maintained by the new owners.

Over $300

Estate Lindholm (Lindholm, 340/776-6121 or 800/322-6335, www.estatelindholm.com, $340–380 winter, $170–210 summer) is a family-run bed-and-breakfast overlooking Cruz Bay. Cobblestone walkways and weathered stone walls lend an old-world feel to this modern retreat. Rooms have a clean, calm atmosphere with white walls and polished wood finishes and furnishings. Some of the 10 rooms have views of the ocean, and all come with air conditioning, cable TV, refrigerators, microwaves, and coffeemakers. A free continental breakfast is served daily, and a fine on-site restaurant serves dinner nightly. Additional perks include a fitness room and pool.

A condo village on the outskirts of Cruz Bay, **Gallow's Point Resort** (Gallow's Bay, 340/776-6434 or 800/323-7229, fax 340/776-6520, www.gallowspointresort.com, $465–595 winter, $265–395 summer) is an adults-only alternative to the island's major resorts. Each unit has a private outdoor patio, ocean or harbor views, a full kitchen, living and dining areas, air-conditioning, cable TV, and a pull-out sleeper couch. A major renovation in 2011 saw most units redone from floor to ceiling; those not updated now rent for $50 less per night. A pool and restaurant are on site, and Cruz Bay is a short, downhill walk away.

One of the two large resorts on St. John, **The Westin** (Great Cruz Bay, 340/693-8000 or 888/627-7206, www.westinresortstjohn. com, $500–1,400 winter, $250–1,000 summer) sprawls along the beach at Great Cruz Bay. Guests have no real reason to leave the resort; it has a beach, water sports, shopping, a pool, three restaurants, a spa, a gym, and tennis courts on the grounds. The 175 rooms come with all the amenities you would expect, plus free Starbucks coffee, Nintendo game systems, and, of all things, two voicemail boxes. Across the street are the Westin Villas, which offer added privacy and luxury with the bonus of resort amenities.

EAST END
$125-175

The environmentally friendly design of the popular Maho Bay Camps was improved upon at Maho's sister resort, ◖ **Concordia Eco-Resort** (Concordia, 340/693-5855 or 800/392-9004, www.concordiaeco-resort. com), overlooking Salt Pond Bay in southeastern St. John. Concordia has two kinds of accommodation, eco-tents and studios ($160–255 winter, $110–165 summer). The eco-tents, which can sleep up to six people, are constructed with recycled material and employ modern eco-friendly technology to keep their environmental footprint minimal. Four are accessible to disabled travelers. Though they are called tents, these accommodations are more like treehouses. The studios, which were half-built condominiums when developer Stanley Selengut bought the estate, are more traditional villa-style accommodations, but they have been retrofitted, where possible, with environmentally friendly appliances and furniture. Selengut is steadily expanding the resort; there were some 40 units at the end of 2011 and more planned for the future.

Guests at Concordia enjoy a few luxuries absent at Maho Bay Camps. Each unit has a private bath with a solar-heated shower and the property has a pool. There are fully equipped kitchens and composting toilets (newer units are connected to a sewage treatment system). Many of the units also have spectacular views of Salt Pond Bay and Ram's Head. A 15-minute hike takes guests directly to the beach at Salt Pond Bay, which boasts excellent snorkeling.

The Concordia Eco-Resort restaurant serves dinner nightly during the high season, using organic and local ingredients. Yoga classes, dancing, and special events take place on the covered pavilion next to the restaurant.

Over $300
About halfway down the East End Road, past Coral Bay, are the beach houses at **Estate Zootenvaal** (Hurricane Hole, 340/776-6321, www.estatezootenvaal.com, $275–550 winter, $180–360 summer). The setting is serene—the sound of the gentle surf is about the only noise around—and the cottages are unpretentious yet comfortable. Sea green, peach, and white walls complement the bright greens and blues of the gardens and sea outside. Accommodations include two one-bedroom cottages and one two-bedroom apartment, each with a full kitchen and large screened-in porch. There are no televisions. The property faces the south shore of St. John and offers walking trails and a lovely bay for beachcombing. Good swimming beaches are a 10-minute drive away.

NORTH SHORE
$225-300
Part of the Maho Bay Camps property, **Harmony Studios** (340/776-6240 or 800/392-9004, www.maho.org, $225–250 winter, $130–155 summer) combines the comforts of traditional vacation villas with eco-friendly building and design. The studios, located on the hillside overlooking Little Maho Bay, use recycled building materials and solar power and employ water-saving technology. They also have private bedrooms, equipped kitchenettes, private baths, and decks. Studio guests can also join in the Maho Bay Camps universe of dining, activities, and happy nature-loving camaraderie.

Over $300
For decades, **C Caneel Bay Resort** (Caneel Bay, 340/776-6111, U.S. 212/758-1735, www.caneelbay.com, $550–1,700 winter, $395–1,025 summer) has set the standard for barefoot elegance in the Caribbean. Laurance Rockefeller created Caneel Bay in the 1950s in the bosom of the new national park he helped create. Today, Caneel Bay still attracts guests looking for a luxurious vacation that emphasizes natural beauty and time-honored tradition. The resort's 166 rooms are nestled discreetly into the resort's lush and painstakingly tended landscaping. A half-dozen accommodation types range from modest-sized rooms with garden views to expansive suites with walls of windows overlooking the ocean. All guest rooms are faultlessly clean and have a tasteful, understated style underlined with neutral tones and native stonework. Inside you will find a coffeemaker, minibar, beach towels, and bathrobes but no telephone or television to disturb the solace.

Outside your room, delight in the wide range of resort activities: a pool, seven beaches, tennis courts, free continental breakfast and afternoon tea, art classes, spa, shopping, evening turndown service, and use of Sunfish sailboats and kayaks, among others.

Caneel Bay does not have the pizzazz of a bright new resort like Scrub or the energy of the more family-oriented Westin. But it does offer a refreshingly old-fashioned Caribbean experience that focuses on the simple pleasure of being well cared for in a truly spectacular setting.

CAMPGROUNDS
Camping is the best way to immerse yourself in the natural beauty of St. John, and the best choice for visitors who don't want to shell out big bucks for a hotel room. Campsites on the island range from bare tent sites to completely equipped eco-cottages. Take note that NPS rules forbid camping anywhere but on established commercial campsites.

© SUSANNA HENIGHAN POTTER

a tent cottage at Maho Bay Camps

Maho Bay

Maho Bay Camps (Maho Bay, 340/715-0501 or 800/392-9004, www.maho.org, $130–135 winter, $80 summer) sets the standard for Caribbean camping and eco-friendly development. Accommodations are "tent-cottages," built out of wood, canvas, and mesh screening on elevated platforms. The accommodations meld creature comforts usually unknown in camping with an unbeatable natural setting and eco-friendly *esprit de corps*.

The 114 cottages are set among the trees and connected by broad wooden walkways with names like Mongoose Highway and Sandy Landing. Little Maho Bay, a quiet, protected beach, is at the foot of the camp's hill. Great Maho Bay is a 10-minute hike down a steep goat trail. Each cottage is furnished with two twin beds, a sleeper couch, a two-burner propane stove, a cooler, dishes, fresh linens, towels, a porch, a clothesline, lights, a

fan, and electrical outlets. There are toilets and cold-water showers in the camp's communal bathhouses.

For many people, Maho Bay is a truly magical place. Yes, you have to carry your own water to your tent and bathe in a shared bathhouse, but you also get to delight in the fresh air, night sounds, and wildlife of Maho Bay. Iguanas perch on trees just outside your tent windows, and you will fall asleep to the sound of waves and tree frogs. Maho is especially great for families. The camp has the feeling of a world apart, which appeals to many youngsters, and daily activities for children make it easy to keep them entertained.

If you want, Maho can be much more than just a place to stay. The camp restaurant serves moderately priced breakfasts and dinners, and its sunset happy hour with free popcorn is especially popular. There's a full-blown on-site activities desk that coordinates Maho's own activities and hooks guests up with outside

333334333333333333

activity providers. There are art classes, daily yoga sessions, a water-sports center, and regular shuttles to town.

Get here while you can. Maho's lease expires in 2013, and Maho founder Stanley Selengut has declared that unless the landowners agree to a long-term lease, the campground will close. Selengut says he is developing the sister resort, Concordia Eco-Resort, in preparation for Maho's probable closure.

Cinnamon Bay

The other big campground on St. John is **Cinnamon Bay Campground** (Cinnamon Bay, 340/776-6330, www.cinnamonbay.com), a sprawling facility with less character but just as much beauty as Maho. Accommodations are in fully screened cottages ($81–160 winter, $81–105 summer), some of which are beachfront, each with concrete walls, electric lights, a terrace, four twin beds, linens, ceiling fans, charcoal grill, propane stove, ice chest, and cooking and eating utensils; prepared tents

($93 winter, $67 summer), which are large canvas tents furnished with four twin beds and elevated on a wooden platform; and bare sites ($30). Prepared tents have an outdoor kitchen with a picnic table, ice chest, lantern, propane stove, and cooking and eating utensils. Bare sites fit one large tent or two small ones; a picnic table and charcoal grill are provided.

Cinnamon Bay beach is where campers spend their days: a long, meandering beach good for water sports, sunbathing, or just bobbing in the water. Having the sand a few hundred yards (or less) from your door is a real luxury and it is what keeps many Cinnamon Bay campers coming back year after year.

Cold-water showers and lavatories for all guests are in shared bathhouses. There are group campsites. An on-site restaurant serves three meals a day, and a small store sells basic food and supplies (at exorbitant prices).

Cinnamon Bay closes during the month of September.

Food

St. John is a wonderland of restaurants, large and small, casual and elegant. Plan to sample a variety during your visit.

CRUZ BAY
Breakfast

It's mostly breakfast that draws folks to **Jakes** (Lumberyard Complex, 340/777-7115, 7:30 A.M.–7 P.M., $8–16), an open-air dining room where more is more. Monster-sized breakfast platters, tall stacks of pancakes, overstuffed breakfast burritos, and the island's best corned beef hash will keep you fueled well past noon. Jake's breakfast is served all day, but so is his bar menu of burgers, BLTs, hot dogs, and the like. Grab a seat at the open window to watch the comings and goings around busy Cruz Bay.

Hearty breakfast fare with a side of the American Southwest is what's on tap at **J.J.'s Texas Toast Café** (Cruz Bay, 340/776-6908, 7 A.M.–9 P.M. daily), an easy-to-find storefront facing Franklin Powell Park. Choose from the likes of breakfast burritos, huevos rancheros, and biscuits and gravy, and wash it down with coffee or a bloody Mary. J.J.'s also serves lunch and dinner.

Delis and Bakeries

All the sandwiches at **Baked in the Sun** (Hill St., 340/693-8786, 6 A.M.–5 P.M. Mon.–Fri., 6 A.M.–2 P.M. Sat., $4–10) clock in at under $10, but it is the quality that makes this a popular place to eat. It begins with bread baked daily on the premises and continues with sandwich

ST. JOHN

fillings such as tangy-sweet curry chicken salad and a homemade veggie burger voted best on the island. A wide selection of fresh baked goods, cookies, coffee, and tea round out the menu, and at breakfast, grab a hefty breakfast sandwich or roll. Carry out or eat in the cheerful dining room, where it seems most of St. John passes through on their way about town.

A deli for grown-ups, **Sam & Jacks** (The Marketplace, 340/714-3354, 9 A.M.–5 P.M. Mon.–Sat., $9–12) occupies a stripped-out storefront on the third floor of the Marketplace shopping center. The vibe is more Manhattan than Maho, with bare concrete floors, loud rock music, and a suitably hip staff. But the food, oh, the food: Sam & Jack's top-notch deli meats and cheeses are used to dazzling effect in a dozen or so house sandwiches, such as Uncle Peep, two slices of whole wheat sandwich bread filled to capacity with roasted turkey and Havarti cheese and topped with arugula and raspberry aioli. Salads are available as well. Sam & Jack's is mostly takeout, but there is a small area for dining.

International

Greek for "an agreeable and leisurely passing of time," **Asolare** (Caneel Hill, 340/779-4747, 5:30–10 P.M., $29–38) is the place for a romantic dinner. The setting is marvelous; come early to watch the sun set over Cruz Bay and then tuck into a very special meal. The Asian-inspired menu changes daily and offers a half-dozen appetizers and entrées—the focus here is on good food, not on extensive selection. Popular main courses include rack of lamb, locally caught mahimahi, and seared tuna. If you have room, finish with the chocolate pyramid for dessert. A four-course tasting menu with wine pairings runs $85 per person.

At **La Tapa** (Centerline Rd., Cruz Bay, 340/693-7755, $35–45), chef Alexandra Ewald serves Mediterranean cuisine, with an emphasis on fresh seafood and creativity. Diners can choose entrée-sized large plates or sample several small plates. Specialties include Prince Edward Island mussels and paella-for-two. La Tapa's high-end cuisine is at odds with its crowded sidewalk setting adjacent to two noisy bars, but most folks don't mind.

Barbecue

You will smell **Uncle Joe's Bar-B-Q** (Waterfront, 340/693-8806, 11 A.M.–9 P.M. daily, $7–14) before you see this tiny barbecue stand on the waterfront, often teeming with people. Order his grilled chicken or ribs to go, or eat at one of a few tables on the sidewalk. Meals come with hearty sides like rice and peas, coleslaw, and macaroni salad. You'll be hard-pressed to find a more filling and better-tasting meal for under $10.

West Indian

Tour the Caribbean and South American over dinner at **Morgan's Mango** (340/693-8141, 5:30–10 P.M., $19–36), an inviting open-air restaurant tucked away among the trees on Cruz Bay's waterfront. Dishes on the menu are labeled according to their island of origin and include Cuban, Jamaican, Haitian, and Virgin Island specialties. Seafood is handled well here, and there are vegetarian options. The salads are huge and filling. Live music is on tap a couple of nights each week.

At lunchtime, St. Johnians head in numbers to the back of **Dolphin Market** (Centerline Rd., 11 A.M.–1 P.M. Mon.–Fri., $5–10), where the takeout deli serves generous plates of local dishes like grilled fish, barbecued chicken, and stewed oxtail. Side dishes include boiled plantain, sweet potatoes, macaroni pie, and rice and peas. Takeout only.

Think soul food with a Caribbean twist at **Windy Level Bar and Restaurant** (Centerline Rd., 340/715-2000, 6:30 A.M.–10:30 P.M. Mon.–Sat., $10–20), a dining room about two miles out of Cruz Bay. Chef and owner Carryn Powell offers a changing menu of local specialties, such as fish, conch, pork chops, and baked chicken served with generous helpings of rice, macaroni, coleslaw, and other side dishes. In true island style, the service is slow but friendly.

Ital is Rastafarian-friendly food, and you can sample generous plates of homemade *ital* cuisine at ◖ **Roaryal Abeba** (Palm Plaza, 340/677-0497, noon–6 P.M. Mon.–Sat., $10–13), a family-run vegetarian restaurant tucked into a storefront near the entrance to the Westin. The menu changes daily but includes generous portions of all-vegetarian options such as tofu burgers, peanut stew, lentil patties, coconut rice and beans, and steamed pumpkin. Or stop in to sample a wide selection of natural local drinks: sea moss, tamarind, ginger, sorrel, peanut punch, and more. You won't regret departing from the same-old to explore new cuisine with Roaryal Abeba as your guide. Come early for the best selection.

Italian

The cuisine of northern Italy is presented with exacting attention to detail and a naturalness that can only come from experience at ◖ **da Livio** (King St., 340/779-8900, 5:30–10 P.M. daily, $19–33). Tucked beneath a small hotel on a not-so-busy street of Cruz Bay, this intimate eatery is worth seeking out when you've grown tired of Caribbean cuisine and just want something really good to eat. Thin-crusted pizza is baked in an outdoor oven on the stoop and the kitchen at the back turns out masterful pasta dishes, ranging from simple to complex, including handmade lobster-filled ravioli and pappardelle with bolognese sauce. Salads and bread come doused with a swirl of olive oil and balsamic vinegar that will awaken even the most over-tired taste buds. Finish with a morsel of delectable tiramisu or panna cotta the texture of clouds. You'll want to linger over espresso in the stylish dining room decorated with corks

and black-and-white movie stills featuring Italian food.

Café Roma (340/776-6524, 5–10 P.M. daily, $12–30) has been pleasing diners with homestyle Italian dinner fare for more than two decades. Now under new ownership, Café Roma continues to serve consistently good lasagna, spaghetti bolognese, baked penne, ravioli, and pizza. The atmosphere is cozy and the service is genuinely friendly.

Seafood

A long-standing island favorite, **The Fish Trap** (Raintree Court, 340/693-9994, 4:30–9:30 P.M. Tues.–Sun., $12–44) serves pasta, steaks, and burgers, but seafood is the reason to come. Frequent visitors swear by the conch fritters and fresh fish; also try the shrimp, scallops, and hand-cut steaks. If you prefer to do the cooking yourself, you can buy fresh seafood here, too.

Though not strictly seafood only, fresh local fish and lobster feature heavily on the menu at **Lime Inn** (Lemon Tree Mall, 340/779-4199, 11:30 A.M.–3 P.M. Mon.–Fri., 5:30–10 P.M. Mon.–Sat., dinner $24–35), a long-time Cruz Bay pick for unpretentious good food. The courtyard setting is nothing special and the service, though friendly, runs slow, but the food is carefully prepared and tasty. Come early, before the daily catch of Caribbean lobster, whole red snapper, and fillets of mahimahi, tuna, and grouper run out. Nightly steak, chicken, and pasta specials cater to the non-seafood-lovers, and save room for homemade apple crisp. Wednesday night is a popular all-you-can-eat shrimp fest.

Asian

Located in a colorful courtyard in the heart of Cruz Bay, **Rhumb Lines** (Mead's Plaza, 340/776-0303, 11 A.M.–2 P.M. and 5:30–10 P.M. Wed.–Mon., $17–28) serves Pacific Rim cuisine with a Caribbean touch. Entrées

ST. JOHN

include dishes like pad Thai, fresh grilled seafood, and mojo pork; or try a few of the "pupu portions" of tempura shrimp, spring rolls, dumplings, and samosas. Service is cheerful, and the decor is an east-meets-west tropical, with lots of bamboo, plants, and vibrant colors.

NORTH SHORE

There are not many eateries inside the national park boundaries. There are plenty of picnic tables, though. If you don't pack your own food, here are your choices.

Casual

While geared mostly to guests and staff at nearby Maho Bay Camps, **Pavilion Restaurant** (Maho Bay Camps, 340/776-6226, 7:30–9:30 A.M. and 5:30–7 P.M. daily, $14–20) is open to the public for breakfast and dinner. There are no waiters; order and pay for your food at the counter and wait for your name to be called at the window. At breakfast you can get muffins, cereal, and fruit, or more substantial omelets, pancakes, and French toast. For dinner, each evening has its own theme, ranging from Italian to West Indian. Call ahead to find out the flavor of the day. Sunsets are spectacular here, and happy hour drinks come with free popcorn. The camp's shop sells sandwiches, ice cream, drinks, and other picnic supplies.

T'ree Lizards (Cinnamon Bay Campground, 340/776-6330, $14–24) at Cinnamon Bay serves breakfast, lunch, and dinner daily. The food is nothing special, really—sandwiches, burgers, seafood and pasta—but if you're at the beach, you can't beat the convenience. Dining is in the open air, beneath a huge, spreading rain tree.

International

No restaurant can claim a better view than ◖ **Chateau Bordeaux** (Bordeaux Mountain, 340/776-6611, 11 A.M.–3 P.M. daily, 5:30–10 P.M. Tues.–Thurs., $12–38). Tucked amid banana and papaya trees, the dining room looks down into the broad valley that is Coral Bay, with the East End and the British Virgin Islands in the background. At lunch grab a seat on the deck and enjoy chicken wraps, burgers, and sweet potato fries along with the view. As the sun sets, the action moves inside the wood-paneled dining room, where fantastical light fixtures, a multitude of textiles, and mix-and-match furniture make it feel like your Great Aunt Marsha's old summer house. The evening menu here is classy and sophisticated; try the Caribbean lobster crepe or Chilean sea bass, and don't skimp in your choices from the excellent wine list. If you're here for a full moon, come early to watch the moon rise over Coral Bay. Reservations are required for dinner.

CORAL BAY
Breakfast

M&M Donkey Diner (East End Rd., 340/693-5240, 8 A.M.–1 P.M. Mon.–Tues., Thurs., Sat.; 8 A.M.–8 P.M. Wed., Fri., Sun.) presents an unlikely combination: kickass breakfasts daily plus made-from-scratch pizza three nights a week. Islanders swear by the café's bloody Marys, ricotta pancakes, home fries, and French toast, served daily until 1 P.M. in the sunny dining room whose cheer is subdued enough not to interfere with a bad hangover. On Wednesday, Friday, and Sunday evenings, slide into a booth for pizza night. Toppings range from traditional marinara and cheese to offbeat: roasted chicken, potato, and rosemary. Calling itself "a pretty OK place," **Skinny Legs** (Coral Bay, 340/779-4982, 11 A.M.–9 P.M. daily, $8–15) embodies Coral Bay when it was just a remote and unpretentious community of free spirits, salty dogs, and welcoming locals. Come here to fill your belly and bask in the fun-loving and laid-back atmosphere of the island's eastern end. The open-air dining room looks out over Coral Bay and the many boats and dinghies that congregate there. As for the food, Skinny Legs is the place for burgers, sandwiches, and cold beer. And don't be impatient; the motto "same day service" says it all.

West Indian

Sweet Plantains (Salt Pond Rd., 340/777-4653, 6–9 P.M. Tues.–Sat., $18–25) delivers an imaginative menu with fresh flavors and style. The menu was crafted by owners Rose and Prince Adams, who are very much present in the kitchen and behind the bar. Entrées include braised short ribs, fresh fish, roti, and fantastic West Indian and East Asian curries. Many meals come with the namesake sweet plantains.

Set on a quiet bay a few miles south of Coral Bay, **Miss Lucy's** (Friis Bay, 340/693-5244, 11 A.M.–9 P.M. Tues.–Sat., 10 A.M.–2 P.M. Sun., $14–38) is a seafood restaurant with a strong and long following. Miss Lucy, a taxi driver, gifted cook, and all-around supreme human being, died in 2007, and her presence is missed. But the restaurant she created is still a favorite place for fresh snapper, grouper, tuna, and a plate of traditional St. John fried fish. On Sundays, Miss Lucy's is crowded with folks tucking into Black Strap French Toast, Eggs Benedict, and Fish and Johnny Cakes as live jazz plays in the background.

Make a point to find **Sylvia's Clean Plates** (Sputnik Complex, 340/775-7373, 8 A.M.–8 P.M. daily, $10–17), a Jamaican restaurant inside the Sputnik II Nightclub. Fork into dishes like curried goat and peanut rice in Sylvia's homey dining room, and for your beverage pass up the usual suspects in favor of homemade ginger beer, limeade, or even a beet smoothie.

International

With an emphasis on fresh and a lovely view of Ram's Head, **C Cafe Concordia** (Concordia Eco-Resort, 340/693-5855, 5:30–9:30 P.M. Thurs.–Sat. and Mon., 9 A.M.–1:30 P.M. Sun., $18–28) is a mighty fine place to eat. The menu changes daily based on what's available and in season, but expect well-portioned entrées such as yellowtail snapper, hangar steak, and spiced pork tenderloin. Concordia always has a veggie option, and don't rush to your entrée: salads of local organic greens, appetizers such as the Fisherman's Platter, and flatbread topped with gorgonzola and pear are the right start to your meal.

If you eat only once at Concordia, however, make it Sunday brunch, when chefs turn out meals that hit all the right notes: the breakfast platter comes with prosciutto and basil oil; the French toast is stuffed with passion fruit and cream cheese; and lunchtime appetites may prefer the seafood roll, stuffed with fried clams, scallops, and shrimp. Despite the smart menu and excellent execution, Concordia is not stuffy or overpriced.

THE EAST END
Casual

Vie's Snack Shack (Hansen Bay, 340/693-5033, 11 A.M.–6 P.M., $4–8) is the only place to get food and drink after you leave Coral Bay proper and head out onto St. John's eastern tip. Stop by for a hot dog, a johnnycake, or some of Vie's famous conch fritters. She is open most afternoons until sunset but sometimes closes early.

GROCERIES

Groceries are expensive on St. John, but they still cost less than eating out every night. To stock your larder, your best bet is **Starfish Market** (The Marketplace, 340/779-4949, 7:30 A.M.–9 P.M. daily), the island's largest and most complete grocery store. In Cruz Bay proper, **Dolphin Market** (Centerline Rd., 340/776-5322, 7:30 A.M.–11 P.M. daily) has most everything you will need.

In Coral Bay, choose between **Love City Mini-Mart** (7 A.M.–9:30 P.M. daily), a small but well-stocked grocery just past the crossroads in Coral Bay, and **Lily's Gourmet Market** (340/777-3335), an upscale market in the Cocoloba Shopping Center, just past Island Blues.

ST. JOHN

Information and Services

TOURIST OFFICES

The **Department of Tourism Visitor Center** (Cruz Bay, 340/776-6450, 8 A.M.–5 P.M. Mon.–Fri.) is located next door to the post office. **Virgin Islands National Park Visitor Center** (Waterfront, 340/776-6201, www.nps.gov/viis, 8 A.M.–4:30 P.M. daily) orients visitors to the park and its resources. This is where you can find out about upcoming park service hikes, lectures, and demonstrations, as well as pick up a calendar of events sponsored by the Friends of Virgin Islands National Park organization. You'll also find an exhibit about the park, public restrooms, and a picnic table.

MAPS AND CHARTS

The best map of St. John is published by the National Park Service. The full-color foldout map shows roads, hiking trails, beaches, and park facilities and offers a short introduction to the history and natural features of the island. It is available free from the Cruz Bay Visitor Center.

Widely available, the free *St. John Guidebook* map is useful for finding restaurants and stores and for making sense of the mishmash of streets that are Cruz Bay.

The St. John map inside the pocket road map available at car rental agencies is about the size of a postage stamp, but it can be helpful in a pinch.

If you require nautical charts, you will have to buy them on St. Thomas before you come over to St. John. The National Park Service publishes a guide for mariners that details rules on anchoring, mooring, vessel size, and safety. The guide also has a map that shows the locations of NPS moorings, but it should not be used for navigation.

LIBRARIES

The **Elaine Ione Sprauve Library** (340/776-6359, 9 A.M.–5 P.M. Mon.–Fri.) is in a beautiful but aging colonial-style building overlooking Cruz Bay. It has a good collection of fiction and nonfiction, magazines, and newspapers. When the system is working, you can log onto the Internet for $2 per hour.

MEDIA

St. John events and happenings are covered in the St. Thomas–based *Virgin Islands Daily News,* which you will find for sale at stores around the island. For more detail, and the best listings of local events, pick up the two St. John papers.

St. John Tradewinds (www.stjohntradewindsnews.com, $1) is a weekly paper published every Monday. *St. Thomas–St. John Sun Times* (www.stjohnsuntimes.com, free) is published monthly. Both are a good source of information on events, live music, and the issue du jour.

Kapok Chronicles is the free quarterly newspaper of the Virgin Islands National Park, available from the NPS visitor center in Cruz Bay.

EMERGENCIES

There is no hospital on St. John; emergency medical care must be obtained off-island on St. Thomas or Puerto Rico. Doctors and nurses at the **Myra Keating Health Center** (340/693-8900) at Susannaberg provide routine medical care.

Cruz Bay Family Practice (Cruz Bay, 340/776-6789) is another choice if you need to see a doctor.

For a pharmacy, try **Chelsea Drug Store** (The Marketplace, Cruz Bay, 340/776-4888, 9 A.M.–7 P.M. Mon.–Fri., 9 A.M.–6:30 P.M. Sat., and 9 A.M.–4:30 P.M. Sun.) or **St. John Drug Center** (Boulon Center, Cruz Bay, 9 A.M.–6 P.M. Mon.–Sat.).

Police can be reached by calling 340/693-8880, 340/776-6262, or 911.

BANKS

There are two banks on St. John. FirstBank is located in downtown Cruz Bay, near Connections; you'll find Scotiabank at the Marketplace. Both have ATMs that accept major U.S. debit and credit cards.

Nonbank ATMs can be found at the Love City Mini-Mart and Cocoloba Center in Coral Bay.

Most businesses on St. John accept credit cards and travelers checks. Personal checks are not accepted, and cash is preferred by some smaller outfits.

POST OFFICES AND COMMUNICATIONS

St. John's lone post office is in Cruz Bay, near the waterfront. Postal rates are the same as in the continental United States.

Connections (Cruz Bay, 340/776-6922, 8:30 A.M.–5:30 P.M. Mon.–Fri., 8:30 A.M.–1:30 P.M. Sat.) is a all-purpose hub of helpfulness: these guys can help you mail letters and packages, make phone calls, send faxes, check your email, make copies, notarize documents, and wire money. They can also answer questions, book excursions, and provide tourist information. There is a bulletin board with help wanted, for rent, and for sale postings, as well as the best-stocked gallery of handbills on the island. You'll pay $3 for 15 minutes on the Internet.

In Coral Bay, **Keep Me Posted** (Cocoloba Shopping Center, 340/775-1727, 8 A.M.–6 P.M. Mon.–Fri., 8 A.M.–2 P.M. Sat.) has Internet access: $3 gets you 15 minutes. It also provides mail forwarding, faxing, and local and long-distance phone calls. **Connections East** (Skinny Legs Complex, 340/779-4994, 9:30 A.M.–5:30 P.M. Mon.–Fri., 9:30 A.M.–1:30 P.M. Sat.) offers many of the same services as Connections in Cruz Bay: Internet access, stamps, mail service, faxes, and tourist information.

LAUNDERETTES

There is a high density of laundries on the South Shore Road near Tamarind Court Inn. Try **Superwash** (no phone), **Santos Laundromat** (340/693-7733), or **Kilroy's Dry Cleaning and Laundry** (340/693-8741). At the Lumberyard Complex, you'll find washers at **Superclean Laundromat** (340/693-7333).

A wash will cost about $3.

ST. JOHN

Getting There and Around

GETTING THERE

There is no airport on St. John; the only way to get here is by boat.

From St. Thomas

Transportation Services (340/776-6282) and **Varlack Ventures** (340/776-6412) operate ferries between Red Hook, St. Thomas, and Cruz Bay. Ferries depart Red Hook daily at 6:30 A.M., 7:30 A.M., and then hourly 8 A.M.–midnight. Return ferries leave Cruz Bay every hour 6 A.M.–11 P.M. The fare for the 20-minute ride is $6 one-way for adults and $1 for children 2–11 years.

From Charlotte Amalie, daily ferries leave at 10 A.M., 1 P.M., and 5:30 P.M. Fare for the 45-minute trip is $12 one-way for adults and $3.50 for children 2–11 years. The Charlotte Amalie route is canceled from time to time; call ahead.

The rates given here include a fuel surcharge, which varies with the price of fuel. You can expect rates to change from time to time. There is also a charge of $2.50 per piece of luggage on both routes.

Caneel Bay and the Westin provide private ferries that bring guests directly to the resorts.

ST. JOHN

From the British Virgin Islands

Inter-Island Boat Services (Tortola, 284/495-4166, and Cruz Bay, 340/776-6597) provides daily ferry service from West End, Tortola, and Great Harbour, Jost Van Dyke, to Cruz Bay. Fare is $45 round-trip. The trip takes about 20 minutes; boats make the journey between the islands four times daily Monday through Saturday and three times on Sundays.

GETTING AROUND

Taxis

Taxis are widely available on St. John, especially in Cruz Bay and at the popular north shore beaches. When you disembark from the St. Thomas ferry in Cruz Bay, you will be bombarded by taxi drivers offering to take you where you need to go. Taxi rates are set by the government. From Cruz Bay to Trunk Bay you will pay $8; from Cruz Bay to Maho Bay, it's $13 per person; and from Cruz Bay to Salt Pond Bay, the rate is $20 per person. Per-person rates are lower for groups of two or more.

If you need to call for a taxi, try **C&C Taxi Service** (340/693-8164) or **St. John Taxi Services** (340/693-7530). To complain about a taxi, contact the Taxi Commission at 340/774-3130. This agency can also help trace lost or missing luggage.

Rental Cars

Rental vehicles are a popular way to get around St. John. This is the kind of place where you want the wind in your hair and the freedom to go wherever you want.

Rental companies based on St. John only rent four-wheel-drive sport utility vehicles suitable for the island's roads. Rates start at $80 per day. Book ahead, since rentals are often fully booked up, especially in the winter season.

Many agencies have a three-day minimum rental for advance reservations, however.

None of the big rental chains serve St. John. Rental companies are exclusively located in or around Cruz Bay and include **Best Rent A Car** (340/693-8177), **Courtesy Car Rental** (340/776-6650), **Delbert Hill Jeep Rental** (340/776-6637), **O'Conner Car Rental** (340/776-6343), **Varlack Auto Rental** (340/776-6412), **Sun and Sand Car Rental** (340/776-6374), **L&L Jeep Rental** (340/776-1120), **Hospitality Car and Jeep Rentals** (340/693-9160), **Cool Breeze Jeep and Car Rental** (340/776-6588), **C&C Car & Jeep Rental** (340/693-8164), **Paris Rentals** (340/776-6171), **Spencer's Rentals** (340/693-8784), and **St. John Car Rental** (340/776-6103).

Most rental agencies not located in central Cruz Bay will pick you up from the ferry if you ask.

Buses

One of the best things about St. John is its bus, which runs hourly from Cruz Bay to Coral Bay and Salt Pond Bay, along Centerline Road. It costs just $1 no matter how far you go along this route. The bus picks up passengers in Cruz Bay at the passenger ferry dock and stops along the way at the orange and brown Vitran bus signs. It turns around in Coral Bay at the base of Fort Berg hill and turns around again at the parking lot for Salt Pond Bay. The bus usually departs from Cruz Bay at 20 past the hour; call 340/774-0165 for a schedule.

Gas Stations

There is only one gas station on St. John. The E&C Service Station is on South Shore Road, on the way to the Westin, near Cruz Bay. Prices are higher here than on any of the other Virgin Islands. Plan ahead to avoid running out of gas.

ST. CROIX

The largest of the U.S. Virgin Islands is the richest in history, culture, and landscapes. St. Croix (pronounced CROY) lies 40 miles south of St. Thomas and St. John, on the other side of the cavernous Virgin Islands trough. The 84-square-mile island is 22 miles long and 6 miles wide. Beaches line the straight west coast, giving way to a dense tropical forest in the northwest. To the south, rolling hills slope toward the sea. The island tapers to a point at its extreme east end, where the spare landscape is characterized by cactus and wild frangipani trees. The Taino, among the island's earliest inhabitants, called the island Ay Ay (the River). The Kalinago, who lived on St. Croix several centuries later, named it Cibuquiera (the Stony Land).

Frederiksted, on the west coast, is a quiet, Victorian-style town where Crucians (CRU-shuns) come to enjoy the sunset and some of the island's hippest bars. Christiansted, on the north coast, is a bastion of historic sites, shopping, and creative eateries. In between, the countryside is dotted by great house and windmill ruins, built by African slaves when the island was a major sugar-producing colony. Place names like Work and Rest, Humbug, All for the Better, and Patience Grove evoke the island's colorful past.

St. Croix sees the fewest tourists of any of the U.S. Virgin Islands and its economy is the most diverse. Two large rum factories brew gallons of grog for export and Senepol cattle

© SUSANNA HENIGHAN POTTER

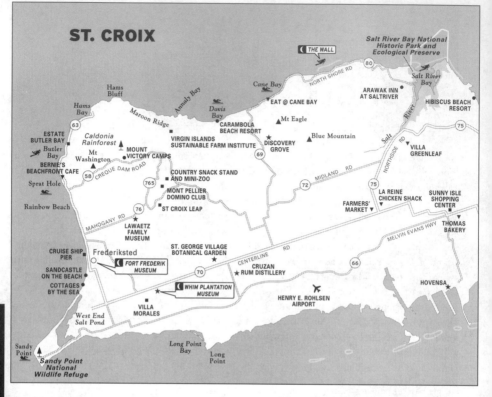

ST. CROIX

Salt River Bay National Historic Park and Ecological Preserve

THE WALL

Salt River Bay

Hams Bluff

Cane Bay

ARAWAK INN AT SALTRIVER

HIBISCUS BEACH RESORT

Hams Bay

Maroon Ridge

Annaly Bay

Davis Bay

EAT @ CANE BAY

NORTH SHORE RD

80

CARAMBOLA BEACH RESORT

Mt Eagle

75

ESTATE BUTLER BAY

63

Caldonia Rainforest

VIRGIN ISLANDS SUSTAINABLE FARM INSTITUTE

Blue Mountain

Salt River

Butler Bay

MOUNT VICTORY CAMPS

Mt Washington

69

DISCOVERY GROVE

NORTHSIDE RD

VILLA GREENLEAF

BERNIE'S BEACHFRONT CAFE

58

CREQUE DAM ROAD

COUNTRY SNACK STAND AND MINI-ZOO

MIDLAND RD

Sprat Hole

765

MONT PELLIER DOMINO CLUB

72

75

LA REINE CHICKEN SHACK

SUNNY ISLE SHOPPING CENTER

Rainbow Beach

76

ST CROIX LEAP

FARMERS' MARKET

MAHOGANY RD

LAWAETZ FAMILY MUSEUM

MELVIN EVANS HWY

THOMAS BAKERY

CRUISE SHIP PIER

Frederiksted

ST. GEORGE VILLAGE BOTANICAL GARDEN

CENTERLINE RD

FORT FREDERIK MUSEUM

66

SANDCASTLE ON THE BEACH

70

CRUZAN RUM DISTILLERY

HOVENSA

COTTAGES BY THE SEA

WHIM PLANTATION MUSEUM

HENRY E. ROHLSEN AIRPORT

West End Salt Pond

VILLA MORALES

Sandy Point

Long Point Bay

Long Point

Sandy Point National Wildlife Refuge

graze in pastures. Tourism, while critical to the St. Croix economy, has never held the revered status that it has on other islands. St. Croix is foremost a place where people live, not a place where people visit.

Just over 50,000 people make their home on St. Croix, a few more than St. Thomas, but the island's ample proportions mean a lot more elbow room. Descendants of St. Croix's African slaves make up the majority of the population, but successive waves of Caribbean immigrants, many from Puerto Rico, have enriched the native society. Settlers from the Middle East, the U.S. mainland, Canada, and Europe, including Danes who can trace their roots back to the days of slavery and sugar, complete the island's diverse population.

Nowhere is St. Croix's diversity more evident than in its music, food, and arts. You can spend an evening dancing to the infectious sounds of traditional scratch music or grooving to modern guitar jazz. Meals range from sophisticated fusion cuisine served in an historic townhouse to spicy fire-roasted chicken served from an open-air booth.

St. Croix is the most overlooked of the U.S. Virgin Islands, in part because it has been unwilling to smooth out all of its kinks for the benefit of tourists. Visitors who recognize the value of this realism will be rewarded by a dynamic, fascinating, and ultimately awesome island. While the Big Island is unable to match the pizzazz of St. Thomas or the untouched natural beauty of St. John, it has something neither of the other islands does: a whole package.

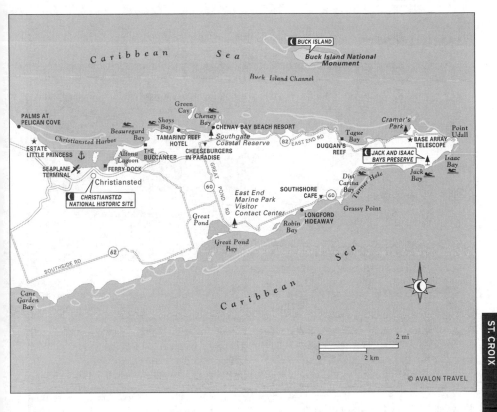

ST. CROIX

PLANNING YOUR TIME

They don't call St. Croix "The Big Island" for nothing. It can take all day just to circle the island, and more than a week to tap into all the attractions and activities it has to offer. It is an island that deserves to be explored at a leisurely pace.

Where to Stay

If you are looking for oceanfront accommodations, consider those located south of Frederiksted or west of Christiansted. If you prefer to be within walking distance of lots of different restaurants and sites, look for a hotel room in Christiansted. If you want to truly get away, consider staying a bit farther from the beaten track: in the rainforest, along the

southern shore, or in a villa on the quiet east end.

When to Come

St. Croix puts on some great annual events, and it is worth considering whether you can plan your visit to coincide with one. The annual Crucian Christmas Festival, which begins in mid-December and continues until Three Kings Day in January, is the biggest annual showcase of Crucian culture, arts, and music. The Agriculture Fair in late February, Half Ironman in April, and Mango Melee in July are also worthwhile.

Day Trips

St. Croix is an easy but expensive day trip

HIGHLIGHTS

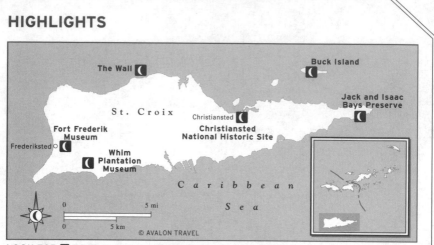

LOOK FOR ◖ TO FIND RECOMMENDED SIGHTS, ACTIVITIES, DINING, AND LODGING.

◖ **Christiansted National Historic Site:** Once St. Croix's economic and administrative core, Christiansted is still the center of its historic attractions. Fort Christiansvaern, the Steeple Building, and other attractions make this the best place to begin exploring the island's rich past (page 117).

◖ **Buck Island:** Protected by the National Park Service, Buck Island is surrounded by a huge barrier reef. Hiking trails cut through dry, tropical brush (page 123).

◖ **The Wall:** This massive underwater ledge on the north coast plunges 3,200 feet. Teeming with marine life, it is a perfect playground for divers (page 127).

◖ **Fort Frederik Museum:** The brick-red colonial-era fort in Frederiksted houses a museum that interprets St. Croix's rich history, especially the painful story of slavery (page 130).

◖ **Whim Plantation Museum:** St. Croix is dotted with the ruins of great houses, sugar factories, and windmills, but Whim is the only place where you can see a fully restored versions, even down to the working cookhouse (page 135).

◖ **Jack and Isaac Bay Preserve:** These beautiful, unspoiled bays on the east end of the island are the place to come for seclusion, white beaches, turquoise water, and peace (page 141).

from St. Thomas: seaplanes make the 15-minute flight between Charlotte Amalie and Christiansted a dozen times a day. Unless you charter your own transport, St. Croix is not an easy day trip from any of the other Virgin Islands. If you're on the island only a day, explore Christiansted for a couple of hours in the morning and then get a taxi to Cane Bay Beach, Whim Plantation, or the St. George's Botanical Gardens in the afternoon.

Sights

CHRISTIANSTED

Picturesque and brimming with history, the first city of St. Croix is an oasis of sophistication with a small-town feel. By day the sidewalks fill with people exploring the town's historic sites and browsing its unique shops. By night, people from all over St. Croix come to dine at fine restaurants and enjoy lively nightlife.

Exploring Christiansted on foot is a pleasure. It is compact and easy to navigate, and most sidewalks are shaded. Leave your car at one of the public parking lots in town and plan on a day to explore the town's attractions.

History

Christiansted was founded following the Danes' purchase of St. Croix in 1733. Located in a good natural harbor and near the earlier French settlement of Bassin, Christiansted was carefully planned by St. Croix's first Danish governor, Frederik Moth. Moth's vision was a grand and beautiful city, with boulevards, promenades, and beautiful lines of buildings. Many of the buildings in the center of the town were built in the decades the followed, and Moth's vision came to life. During the plantation era, Christiansted was the leading city for trade into and out of the growing Danish colony; life revolved around the wharf.

Orientation

Most attractions and restaurants in Christiansted are found within the four-square-block area contained by King Cross Street on the west, Queen Street at the south, and the waterfront on the north and east sides. A boardwalk extends from the seaplane terminal to the old wharf.

Use common sense if you explore areas outside of this central area—Christiansted is well acquainted with urban problems like street crime, vandalism, and drug abuse, especially in the areas untouched by tourism. Avoid the areas beyond Market Street and Hill Street at night.

◖ Christiansted National Historic Site

Comprising five historic structures dating to the earliest days of Danish colonization, Christiansted National Historic Site (340/773-1460, www.nps.gov/chri, 8 A.M.–5 P.M. Mon.–Fri. and 9 A.M.–5 P.M. Sat.–Sun., adults $3, children under 16 free) is the natural starting point for any exploration of historic Christiansted. Located on the waterfront and surrounded by expansive lawns, the historic site is immediately identifiable by the yellow color of the fort and other buildings. The stunning contrast between the yellow buildings, blue water, and green grass is reason enough to come. Indeed, the benches scattered around the lawns are an excellent place to pass a few minutes with a book, in conversation, or simply enjoying the view. Explore inside the buildings to delve into their history, beginning with the fort.

FORT CHRISTIANSVAERN

Built on the site of an earlier French fortification, Fort Christiansvaern (Christian's defenses) was designed to protect the port from attacks, enforce collection of customs duties, house Danish troops, and prevent slave insurrections on the island. Its bright yellow color was typical of Danish construction of the day.

The fort was completed in 1749, with significant additions made between 1835 and 1841. After 1878, when laborers rioted throughout the island, the fort was converted into a police station and courthouse. The National Park Service has restored the fort to its 1830s appearance.

The tour of the fort is self-guided, although park rangers are around if you have any

ST. CROIX

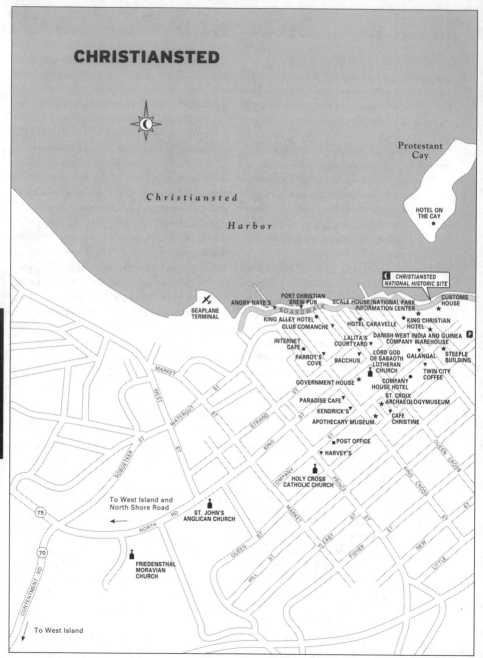

CHRISTIANSTED

Christiansted

Harbor

Protestant
Cay

HOTEL ON
THE CAY

CHRISTIANSTED
NATIONAL HISTORIC SITE

FORT CHRISTIAN
BREW PUB
ANGRY NATE'S   SCALE HOUSE/NATIONAL PARK   CUSTOMS
                                INFORMATION CENTER   HOUSE
                    BOARDWALK
SEAPLANE   KING CHRISTIAN
TERMINAL   KING ALLEY HOTEL   HOTEL CARAVELLE   HOTEL
                CLUB COMANCHE
                                    LALITA'S   DANISH WEST INDIA AND GUINEA
            INTERNET   COURTYARD   COMPANY WAREHOUSE
            CAFE
                                                 LORD GOD   STEEPLE
                PARROT'S   OF SABOTH   GALANGAL   BUILDING
                COVE   BACCHUS   LUTHERAN
                                                 CHURCH
                                                              TWIN CITY
            GOVERNMENT HOUSE   COFFEE
                                                 COMPANY
                                                 HOUSE HOTEL
                PARADISE CAFE   ST. CROIX
                                                 ARCHAEOLOGYMUSEUM
                    KENDRICK'S
                APOTHECARY MUSEUM   CAFE
                                              CHRISTINE

                        POST OFFICE

                    HARVEY'S

                    HOLY CROSS
                    CATHOLIC CHURCH

To West Island and
North Shore Road   ST. JOHN'S
                        ANGLICAN CHURCH

75

70   FRIEDENSTHAL
                MORAVIAN
                CHURCH

MARKET
WEST
WATERGUT ST
SOBOETKER ST
STRAND
KING
COMPANY
MARKET
PRINCE
ST EAST
FISHER
QUEEN
HILL
NORTH RD
QUEEN CROSS ST
KING CROSS ST
NEW
LITTLE
CONTENTMENT RD

To West Island

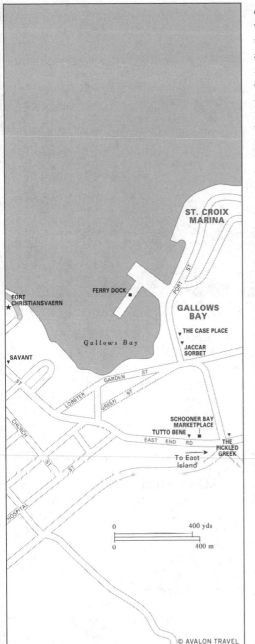

ST. CROIX MARINA

FORT CHRISTIANSVAERN ★

FERRY DOCK

FORT ST

GALLOWS BAY

THE CASE PLACE

JACCAR SORBET

Gallows Bay

SAVANT

GARDEN ST

GREEN ST

LOBSTER

CHURCH ST

SCHOONER BAY MARKETPLACE

TUTTO BENE

EAST END RD

THE PICKLED GREEK

To East Island

HOSPITAL

| 0 | 400 yds |
| 0 | 400 m |

© AVALON TRAVEL

questions. Some rooms have been furnished with period furniture to depict the lifestyle of the Danish soldiers and officers. There is also an arsenal stocked with small arms and equipment for the fort's cannons, and a few boards detail the fort's construction and the life of St. Croix native Alexander Hamilton. The tour also takes you to the underground cells, where slaves and convicts were punished, and to the fort's latrines, which emptied right into the sea. The views of Protestant Cay and the Christiansted waterfront from the upper deck are reason enough to come.

THE STEEPLE BUILDING

The attractive white Steeple Building (corner of Company and Hospital Streets) was the first Danish Lutheran Church on St. Croix. Construction began in 1750, and the building was consecrated in May 1753 as the Church of the Lord of Sabaoth. The distinctive tower, with its four tiered octagonal cupola, was added 40 years later. Pay attention to the large spans of tray ceilings, restored in 2004 but largely intact from the building's 1750s construction.

Lutheranism was the official religion of the Danish, so church attendance by military officers, government officials, and members of Danish colonial society was considered mandatory. During the time the Steeple Building functioned as a church, there were two Sunday services. The first, at 9 A.M., was conducted in Danish for the white congregation. The second, at noon, was conducted in Creole for nonwhites.

In 1831 the congregation moved to a new church building at the corner of King and Queen Cross Streets, where it remains today. Many of the original church furnishings are still in use at the present-day church. The Steeple Building was then used variously as a warehouse, hospital, bakery, and school before becoming part of the National Historic Site.

Visitors to the building can view a life-size mural depicting the way the building

© SUSANNA HENIGHAN POTTER

Christiansted still bears the stamp of its Danish colonial founders.

would have been laid out during a church service. There are also a few small exhibits, and National Park Service staff and volunteers may be present to answer your questions.

DANISH WEST INDIA AND GUINEA COMPANY WAREHOUSE

From 1733, when the Danes bought St. Croix, until 1754, the island was administered by the Danish West India and Guinea Company, a royally chartered slave-trading company that also sold land, traded in sugar and rum, and generally ran every business on the island. The Danish West India and Guinea Company Warehouse (1749), located across Company Street from the Steeple Building, was the administrative and commercial headquarters of the company. During the second half of the 18th century, the warehouse complex was about three times its present size, containing customs offices, warehouses, and quarters for company staff and slaves. The open yard in the center of

the warehouse was used for slave auctions, and historians estimate that 40,000 Africans were sold here during the island's slavery era. It is the only historic slave market under U.S. government protection, having been purchased by the park service in 2001. Today the warehouse contains offices and public restrooms.

There are plans to convert part of the building into a slavery museum and research archives.

THE SCALE HOUSE

The two-story Scale House, steps from the waterfront, is where hogsheads of sugar and puncheons of rum were weighed for the purposes of taxation before being loaded on ships to Europe and North America. Imports were also carefully measured, logged, and taxed here. The building you see today was built in 1856 and replaced a wooden weighing house first built in 1740.

A scale dating from 1861 is on display on the ground floor, which also houses a National Park Service gift shop and information desk.

THE CUSTOMS HOUSE

The taxes levied at the Scale House were paid at the Customs House next door, a colonial-style building with a wide, sweeping staircase facing the sea. It is perhaps the loveliest of all the buildings in Christiansted. Part of the first floor dates to 1751, when it was part of a row of buildings in the Danish West India and Guinea Company's warehouse. The existing structure was completed in 1841. The Customs House was the site of the town's post office until 1927 and then housed the public library until 1972, when it became a part of the historic site. It is not open to the public.

GOVERNMENT HOUSE

This imposing U-shaped building, at Nos. 7–8 King Street, still functions as the governor's living quarters and office when he is on St. Croix and houses numerous government offices. Government House is no longer part of Christiansted National Historic Site, but it is still a nice place to visit. Governor-General Peter von Scholten combined two large townhouses—the Schopen and Sobotker houses—and added the eastern facade in 1830 to create the building as it appears today. A small red sentry box at the foot of the entrance staircase is an authentic Danish guardhouse.

As long as no official function is going on, visitors are welcome to tour the building, walking around the interior garden and visiting the elegant ballroom on the second floor, where you can see reproductions of original Danish furnishings and fixtures as well as paintings of King Frederik VII of Denmark and Peter von Scholten. Admission is free.

St. Croix Archaeology Museum

The local Archaeological Society maintains the tiny St. Croix Archaeology Museum (6 Company St., 340/692-2365, 10 A.M.–2 P.M. Sat., free), which is dedicated to promoting interest in the island's pre-Columbian past. Artifacts from the island's Taino and Saladoid periods are on display. In addition, a display recounts the events that took place when Christopher Columbus's fleet sailed into Salt River Bay.

Apothecary Museum

Calling this a museum is a little bit of a stretch, but it is worth a stop nonetheless. Located in Apothecary Hall at No. 4 Queen Cross Street, the glass-enclosed exhibit (visible from the sidewalk) shows an apothecary's office from the 19th century, complete with vials, bottles, and handwritten ledgers. The site was a functioning apothecary's shop from 1827 until 1970, when it was deeded to the St. Croix Landmarks Society.

Historic Churches

LORD GOD OF SABAOTH LUTHERAN CHURCH

St. Croix's oldest extant church, the Lord God of Sabaoth Lutheran Church (4 King St., 340/773-1320) was built around 1740 as the Dutch Reformed Church. When the Lutheran congregation left the Steeple Building in 1831, they moved in here. The most distinctive feature is the neoclassical tower, built in 1834.

HOLY CROSS CATHOLIC CHURCH

The Holy Cross Catholic Church (20 Company St., 340/773-7564) was built in 1755 and extensively altered in the 1850s. Holy Cross combines the molded facades of San Juan's 17th-century churches with the neo-Gothic elements favored in the 19th century.

ST. JOHN'S ANGLICAN CHURCH

St. John's Anglican Church (27 King St., 340/778-8221) sits prominently at the entrance to downtown Christiansted. St. John's was built in the mid-19th century, replacing a 1772 building. A fire in 1866 destroyed much of the church's original interior, but the exterior is

ST. CROIX

ALEXANDER HAMILTON: FAMOUS SON

Alexander Hamilton, the first Treasury Secretary of the United States and one of the authors of the Federalist Papers, grew up in obscurity in Christiansted, the illegitimate son of a shopkeeper. Hamilton's years on St. Croix, from age 10 to 18, provide a glimpse into social realities of the time; his story provides insight into the early influences of one of America's most important early statesmen.

Hamilton's mother, Rachel Faucett, moved to St. Croix when she was 16 and was married to John Lavien, who owned a cotton plantation in the new colony. Rachel and John's marriage was not a happy one. In 1749 John publicly accused Rachel of infidelity and had her jailed at Fort Christiansvaern for several months. When she was released, Rachel left St. Croix for St. Kitts, where she met and fell in love with James Hamilton, a Scotsman. Alexander Hamilton was born in 1755, the second of two sons born to Rachel and James, who never married. In 1765, the family moved to St. Croix, where James had some business. Soon after the move, James moved out, and he later returned to the island of Nevis. He never saw his sons again.

Rachel rented a house and shop in Christiansted at 34 Company Street. Alexander helped his mother with the business while his brother was apprenticed to a carpenter. In February 1768, Rachel caught yellow fever and died, at the age of 38. Alexander was 11 years old. What little property Rachel had was inherited by Peter Lavien, her legitimate son by her ex-husband. Alexander and his brother were left penniless.

Alexander moved in with a local merchant, Thomas Stevens, and began working as a clerk for an import-export house, Beckman and Cruger, located at 7-8 King Street. Alexander's natural intelligence and business sense attracted the attention of his employers, and soon he was making important decisions for the company. Hamilton later told his children that his years

at Beckman and Cruger were "the most useful part of [my] education."

During this time Hamilton also developed a friendship with Presbyterian Reverend Hugh Knox, who shared with him his library of books on philosophy, reason, and law. Hamilton's account of a 1772 hurricane published in the *Royal Danish America Gazette* so impressed those who read it that Hamilton's friends and supporters raised money for him to travel to the United States for an education. In June 1773, Hamilton sailed from St. Croix for New York, where he would spend one year at the Barber Academy before enrolling in King's College, the institution later to become Columbia University.

© LIBRARY OF CONGRESS/JOHN TURNBULL

Alexander Hamilton spent his teenage years on St. Croix.

© SUSANNA HENIGHAN POTTER

the reception hall at Government House

faithful to the Gothic Revival style prescribed at the time for Anglican churches around the world.

FRIEDENSTHAL MORAVIAN CHURCH

Moravian missionaries arrived in St. Croix in the 1730s to minister to enslaved Africans. Christiansted's Friedensthal Moravian Church (New St., 340/772-2811) was founded in the 1750s. The parish house, or manse, was built in the 1830s, and the present church was built between 1852 and 1854. The manse was used as both a home and a school.

PROTESTANT CAY

Located in the middle of Christiansted Harbor, Protestant Cay is a tiny islet home to a small, inviting beach, a water-sports center, a restaurant, and a hotel.

To get there, hop on the ferry (adults $3 round-trip) that runs 7 A.M.–midnight daily. The ferry departs from the Christiansted wharf in front of the old Customs House. Look for a small step marked Hotel on the Cay near a bench, where you can sit while you wait. The ferry does not run according to schedule; as soon as the captain sees anyone waiting on either side, he comes out to carry you across.

◖ BUCK ISLAND

Buck Island, a 180-acre island surrounded by almost 20,000 acres of protected coral reef and seabed, is located less than two miles from St. Croix's northern coast. Noted for excellent snorkeling, hiking, and one of the nicest beaches on St. Croix, Buck Island packs a lot of punch for nature-loving visitors. The island and surrounding reef make up **Buck Island National Monument** (340/773-1460, www. nps.gov/buis, 6 A.M.–6 P.M.), which was declared by President Kennedy in 1961. President Clinton added 18,135 acres of seabed and reef to the monument as part of the U.S. Coral Reef Initiative in 1998.

Buck Island is a nesting ground for

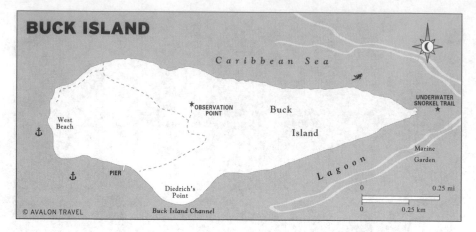

endangered brown pelicans, hawksbill, leatherback and green sea turtles, raptors, and the threatened least tern. An endangered native ground lizard has recently been reintroduced to the island. The barrier reef that surrounds Buck has extraordinary coral formations, deep grottos, abundant reef fishes, sea fans, and gorgonians. An underwater snorkel trail on the east end showcases a small part of the reef, while hiking trails cut through the dry forest and provide views of the surrounding sea.

The National Park Service manages Buck Island, and human activity is carefully managed. A half-dozen concessionaires are licensed to provide day trips to the island. Private boats must adhere to strict regulations; fishing and scuba diving are prohibited. The Park Service provides basic infrastructure to give the public access to Buck Island's attractions. There are moorings near the underwater snorkel trail to accommodate concessionaires and a concrete dock at Diedrich's Point on the western shore. Picnic tables and pit toilets are at West Beach and Diedrich's Point, and interpretive signs describe some of the island's most noteworthy natural characteristics.

A challenging 1.5-mile hiking trail connects West Beach and Diedrich's Point and passes through a dry coastal forest where flowering frangipani, Turk's head cacti, and orchids grow. The trail climbs steeply to an observation point at mid-island, from which you can see St. Thomas, St. John, and the British Virgins on a clear day. There is also an easy quarter-mile loop trail along the beach and through the forest at West Beach.

Getting There

Licensed concessionaires offer half- and full-day trips to Buck Island. Half-day trips typically include snorkeling on the underwater trail and a short visit to the western beach. Full-day trips give visitors more time underwater and enough time to hike the island's trail.

It is easy to feel like a member of the herd at Buck Island, especially since the Park Service requires tour operators to guide you through the underwater trail. For the best experience, try to get on a trip with fewer than six people. If you want to hike the complete trail, be sure to tell the tour operator your wishes so you will get on a trip that will give you at least 1.5 hours on the island.

Most concessionaires leave from Christiansted, and the trip to Buck Island takes between 30 and 80 minutes, depending on the type of boat (sailboats are slower). Other trips leave from Green Cay Marina, which is closer to Buck. Full-day trips include lunch, normally a beach barbecue or picnic. Expect to pay between $65 and $75 for a half-day trip and between $85 and $110 for a full day.

For the smallest and most private Buck Island excursion, book with **Teroro II and Dragonfly** (340/773-3161). Both sailing yachts depart from "H" dock at Green Cay Marina, east of Christiansted.

Caribbean Sea Adventures (59 King's Wharf, 340/773-2628, www.caribbeanseaadventures.com) offers full- and half-day trips to Buck Island on sailboats or powerboats. The company's glass-bottomed powerboat is a draw.

Jolly Roger (Christiansted Boardwalk, 340/513-2508, www.jollyrogervi.com) sails small groups (up to 6) and private groups (up to 20) over to Buck Island to hike, snorkel, and relax.

Probably the biggest Buck Island tour company, **Big Beard's Adventure Tours** (Queen Cross St., Christiansted, 340/773-4482, www.bigbeards.com) takes guests out on the sailboat *Adventure* and the power catamaran *Renegade*.

Private boats must obtain a permit from the National Park Service before anchoring or mooring at Buck Island. Permits must be applied for in person or via fax through the National Park Service headquarters in Christiansted (340/773-1460) at least four days in advance. On application you will be informed about current rules regarding anchoring and the use of park service moorings.

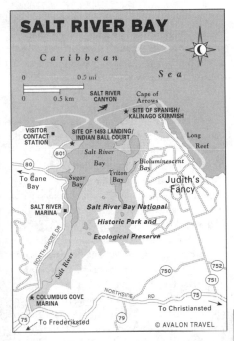

NORTH SHORE

Northshore Road winds along Salt River Bay before striking out along the dramatic northern coast. Offshore and underwater, the celebrated Wall teems with marine life, beckoning divers.

Estate Little Princess

Located less than two miles west of Christiansted, the ruins of Estate Little Princess are under the stewardship of the Nature Conservancy (3052 Estate Little Princess, 340/718-5575, 9 A.M.–5 P.M. Mon.–Fri.,

www.nature.org). Visitors can amble through the 250-year-old plantation ruins and appreciate the small garden. This is also the site of the Nature Conservancy's Eastern Caribbean headquarters.

St. Croix's first governor, Frederick Moth, bought the estate in 1738 and gradually established a full-fledged sugar plantation and factory. It operated as a sugar plantation for nearly 200 years. In the 1950s an American couple bought the 25-acre estate, and in 1990 the property was bequeathed to the Nature Conservancy.

Salt River Bay National Historic Park and Ecological Preserve

A wide estuary on the northern coast of St. Croix, Salt River Bay National Historic Park and Ecological Preserve (340/773-1460, www.nps.gov/sari) is a site of both natural and historical significance.

HISTORY

Archaeological studies have shown that the pottery-making Igneri people settled at Salt River Bay as early as A.D. 50, attracted by its protected waters, fertile fishing grounds, and nearby sources of freshwater. By A.D. 700 the Taino people arrived at Salt River. They absorbed the remaining Igneri and lived there for centuries. In 1914 Danish archaeologists found evidence of a large ceremonial ball court on Salt River Bay's western shore, proof of the settlement's size and importance to the Taino people. Petroglyphs, stone belts, and zemis associated with the ball court are in the possession of the National Museum in Copenhagen.

There is evidence of habitation by Kalinago people from around 1400, and when Christopher Columbus sent a longboat ashore at Salt River Bay in search of water on November 14, 1493—on his second voyage—the party encountered several Kalinago in a canoe. The two parties fought, with both sides suffering casualties in the first recorded instance of Native American resistance to European encroachment. Columbus named the site Cape of Arrows.

Salt River Bay was the site of successive fledgling European settlements during the early years of colonization on St. Croix. In the 1580s John Smith stopped here on his way to Roanoke Island, and between 1641 and 1655, the English, Dutch, French, and Knights of Malta (through a lease from the French) sited settlements on the bay's western shore. Remains of an unusual triangular earthwork fort called Fort Flammand or Fort Salé, started by the English in 1641 and finished by the Dutch in 1642, sit on the western point of the bay.

ECOLOGY

In addition to its historical importance, Salt River Bay is a dynamic coastal habitat that plays a critical role in the area's marine environment. Extensive mangrove forests that line the estuary act as a buffer between the sea and the land, providing a sheltered home for juvenile fish and filtering runoff from the land. The area is also a major bird habitat. Just past the mouth of the bay the sea floor falls away, creating the deep Virgin Islands Basin and its coral-covered walls. At night, certain parts of the bay glow with bioluminescence.

Many visitors to Salt River Bay gravitate to the **Columbus Landing Beach,** a sandy shore at the western mouth of the bay. This is where an Native American ball court once lay, where Columbus's longboat came ashore in 1493, and the site of Fort Salé. Today, it is a somewhat unremarkable beach for swimming which is, nonetheless, popular with residents on weekends.

VISITING THE PARK

If it is open, start at the Salt River Visitor Contact Station (9:30 A.M.–4:30 P.M. Tues.–Thurs. Nov.–June), located on the western side of the bay in what was once a private home. The center sits atop a knoll and has dramatic views of the mouth of the bay. If the station is closed when you visit, pick up a map and guide from the Christiansted National Historic Site and explore on your own.

To reach the Cape of Arrows, on the eastern side of the bay, take Route 75 west from Christiansted and then turn north onto Route 751. You will have to pass through a security gate to enter the residential community of Judith's Fancy. A number of unofficial and unmarked trails on the eastern shore take you through the mangrove forest and to the top of the point overlooking the site of the 1493 skirmish.

One of the best ways to explore Salt River Bay is in a kayak. Rentals and guided tours are available from **Caribbean Adventure Tours** (Salt River Marina, 340/778-1522 or 800/532-3483, www.stcroixkayak.com), **Virgin Kayak Co.** (Cane Bay, 340/778-0071 or 340/514-0062, www.virginkayak.com), and **Sea Thru Kayaks VI** (340/244-8696, www.seathrukayaksvi.com).

ST. CROIX'S BIOLUMINESCENT BAY

Paddle out into certain parts of Salt River Bay after sunset and you will be treated to one of nature's most remarkable shows. Bioluminescence is a natural scientific phenomenon, created by a species of plankton called a dinoflagellate that lives in the water of the bay.

Dinoflagellates are a microorganism, invisible to the naked eye, that lives in ocean water. In certain conditions—often to do with the temperature, salinity, and amount of movement— dinoflagellate blooms occur, where millions of these tiny organisms gather in one place. When this happens, you can get bioluminescence that's visible to the human eye.

It is not unusual for marine creatures to emit some form of bioluminescence, especially species that live in the deep parts of the ocean where little if any sunlight penetrates. Undersea divers have long marveled at the glowing eels, fish, sharks, and coral that they see at night—which is why night diving is such a magical experience. Terrestrial creatures—most famously fireflies and glowworms—also emit bioluminescence.

Bioluminescence occurs in just a few parts of the Salt River Bay, and the quality of the display varies from day to day. When the glow is "on," a cool, bluish light is visible when the water is disturbed—whether by a hand, paddle, or fish swimming below the surface. The result is a magical experience—where the seemingly electrified water becomes a source of almost endless fascination. It is especially fun to paddle quickly through the dark water, startling fish, who swim ahead of your craft and look like meteors flashing through the water.

Both **Caribbean Adventure Tours** (Salt River Marina, 340/778-1522 or 800/532-3483, www.stcroixkayak.com) and **Virgin Kayak Co.** (Cane Bay, 340/778-0071) can take you on a guided moonlight bioluminescence tour of the Salt River Bay.

Ras Lumumba Corriette of **Ay-Ay Eco Hikes and Tours** (340/772-4079, ayatours@gmail.com) offers an excellent hike along the eastern shore of Salt River Bay, which focuses on the ecological importance of the area.

◘ The Wall

St. Croix's greatest underwater sight is the Wall, a massive ledge that runs parallel to the island's north shore for seven miles between Christiansted and Ham's Bluff on the northwest coast. From the shore, the sea floor slopes gradually to about 30 feet before plunging to depths of 3,200 feet.

The Wall teems with marine life: extensive hard and soft coral, turtles, eagle rays, barracuda, damselfish, butterfly fish, cleaner wrasses, gobies, squirrelfish, and more. Since the wall faces deep, open water, large pelagic species such as snappers, jacks, and sharks can be seen here too.

There are more than 20 different established wall dive sites, but a good place to start is **Cane Bay,** a sandy beach about halfway between Christiansted and the northwest point of the island. No dive boat is necessary here (although some operators use small dinghies) because you can easily swim the 300 feet offshore to where the Wall begins. Snorkelers can explore the shallow parts of the Wall, but divers get the best views of its intricate holes, passages, and the awesome precipice below.

If one Wall dive is not enough for you, try the **Salt River Canyon** dives at the mouth of Salt River Bay. Here, healthy coral gardens border the east and west sides of the large undersea canyon. For experienced divers, **Vertigo,** at Annaly Bay, is the holy grail of St. Croix diving. Here the Wall slopes back under itself, creating an overhang that puts divers in the middle of wide, dark ocean. This is a challenging, dangerous dive (it has been known to be deadly) and not all dive shops will take you there.

© SUSANNA HENIGHAN POTTER

Crowds of locals and visitors enjoy Cane Bay.

Cane Bay

Wide, sandy Cane Bay is a destination for water-sports enthusiasts with a penchant for good times. After a morning or afternoon out exploring the celebrated Cane Bay Wall, divers and snorkelers share stories over a cold one at one of the friendly beach bars. If you feel more like taking it easy, the palm-lined beach has plenty of shade, sand, and space to relax. Cane Bay is a favorite destination for Crucians, especially on weekends, when there is usually a party atmosphere.

Gain perspective on the beach and you will see the windmill ruin that stands guard at the rear of the bay—it is located behind the Cane Bay Dive Shop complex.

Davis Bay

Davis Bay, the setting of Carambola Beach Resort, is a lovely beach. The bay is sandwiched between two dramatic stone bluffs, and the packed white sand is littered with small rocks.

Drive past the guard gate and walk to the far western end for the easiest entry into the water. When the sea is calm, there is nice snorkeling.

Annaly Bay

A remote, rocky bay on the northwest coast of St. Croix, Annaly Bay has a sandy beach, good snorkeling, and unique tide pools. There are no facilities here, but the setting and seclusion make roughing it worthwhile.

To hike into Annaly Bay, drive into Carambola Beach Resort and ask at the guard gate to be pointed toward the trail to Annaly. It is approximately 2 miles of moderate to difficult hiking from there to Annaly. You can also reach the bay via the Scenic Route, an unpaved and often very rough road. The best way to get here, though, is to come with a guide. **Ay-Ay Eco Hikes and Tours** (340/772-4079, ayaytours@gmail.com) offers a guided hike to Annaly, and **Tan Tan Tours** (340/773-7041 or 340/473-6446, www.stxtantantours.com) does open-air, off-road jeep tours.

FREDERIKSTED

With dramatic views of the wide open Caribbean Sea and streets lined with historic Victorian-era buildings, Frederiksted on St. Croix's western coast is a lovely town. Smaller and quieter than Christiansted, Frederiksted is home to what may be the island's best historic site: Fort Frederik, a dramatic red Danish fort that houses an excellent museum. The town also boasts some of the island's most interesting restaurants and the best sunsets on St. Croix. Dive shops in and around the town specialize in the island's west coast dives, including the Ann Abramson Pier. Lovers of historic architecture will enjoy touring the town's back streets.

Frederiksted is St. Croix's cruise ship port, and during the winter months as many as three ships may visit each week (but rarely more than one ship per day). During summer this number drops off dramatically. On ship days the town hums with activity: shops and attractions open, tour operators are fully booked, and the beaches and parks around the city fill.

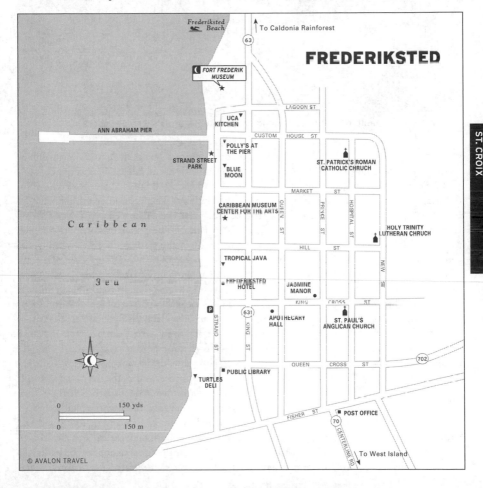

© SUSANNA HENIGHAN POTTER

Fort Frederik was built in 1752 to stop smuggling along St. Croix's western shore.

History

Frederiksted was founded in 1751 to put a stop to the growing illegal trade taking place along the island's western coast, where merchants could easily skirt import taxes. It was here that Governor General Peter von Scholten, faced with 8,000 slaves demanding freedom, emancipated slaves in the Danish West Indies in 1848. Thirty years later, black laborers again marched into Frederiksted to protest unfair working conditions. They set fire to the town and 30 neighboring estates in what is now called the Fireburn. The town was rebuilt in the Victorian style of the day, with elaborate gingerbread trims, wide porches, and covered sidewalks. This architecture is still evident today.

◖ Fort Frederik Museum

The Fort Frederik Museum (Fort Frederik, 340/772-2021, 8:30 A.M.–4:30 P.M. Mon.–Fri., $3) is well worth a visit. Set on the town's waterfront, this deep red fort served as the focal point of two of St. Croix's most important historic events: the 1848 abolition of slavery and the 1878 labor riots, better known as the Fireburn. The fort houses exhibits that describe these events, as well as a UNESCO exhibit titled "The Slaver Fredensborg," which remembers the slave trade by recreating the 1768 journey of the slave ship *Fredensborg* from Copenhagen to Christiansted via the Gold Coast of Ghana. The museum also regularly houses local art and photography exhibits.

In addition to housing exhibits, the fort is an attraction in itself. Built between 1752 and 1760 to discourage smuggling along the island's western shore, the fort was named for the reigning Danish monarch of the day, Frederik V. It was built on the site of an earlier earthen fortification, Fort St. James, which had been constructed by the English in the 1640s and was later used by both the Spanish and the French. It is said that the cannons at Fort Frederik fired the first-ever salute to the new United States flag on October 25, 1776. Deep red in color with stunning views of the electric blue sea, Fort Frederik is a photographer's dream.

Unlike Fort Christiansvaern, which is owned by the federal government, Fort Frederik is maintained by the local government. Until 1973, the fort housed government offices. Between 1974 and 1976 the fort underwent restoration before being opened as a museum.

Caribbean Museum Center for the Arts

The Caribbean Museum Center for the Arts (10 Strand St., www.cmcarts.org, 340/772-2622, 10 A.M.–4 P.M. Wed.–Sat., free) is a gallery and community arts organization whose mission is to nurture St. Croix's artists. It has two primary gallery spaces that house the work of local artists. The center is also a venue for purchasing local art, and it produces an annual wall calendar featuring the work of local artists.

Strand Street Park

Frederiksted is a seaside town and it has a lovely waterfront park. The long, narrow park, which runs parallel to Strand Street, consists of palm trees and other landscaping, paved walks, and benches. The centerpiece is the Ann Abraham Pier—if there isn't a cruise ship in port, walk out for lovely views of the town and the western shore.

Inland, directly opposite the entrance to the pier, is a landmark statue depicting a slave blowing the conch shell—this was how, in 1848, the island's enslaved population spread the word from plantation to plantation that the day to demand their freedom had arrived. The statue stands in front of the **Customs House,** a two-story masonry building and an example of 18th-century Danish colonial architecture. Originally where goods such as cotton, sugar, and rum were weighed and taxed, the building is now occupied by government offices.

Strand Street is home to several notable historic buildings. **Victoria House** (Nos. 7 and 8

Strand St.) is a residential townhouse that was badly damaged in the 1798 Fireburn. During reconstruction the elaborate Victorian "icing" was added. Today the building is considered to be the best example of Victorian Caribbean architecture in the city.

Meanwhile the large masonry structure at 10 Strand Street survived the Fireburn; it represents typical Danish construction of the 1750s.

Apothecary Hall

This two-story townhouse at the corner of Queen and King Cross Streets, which has long served as a pharmacy and shop, was built in 1839. It is said that the shop was an important gathering place for discontented laborers in 1878 and that it was here the first stirrings of the great Fireburn played out.

Historic Churches

Frederiksted's numerous historic churches are evidence of the city's long history, and of the long-standing importance of religion in island life. **Holy Trinity Lutheran Church,** at Hill and New Streets, is the oldest church in Frederiksted. Built in 1791 to replace an original wood structure built 25 years earlier, Holy Trinity has changed some over the years but still reflects the original design. The Frederiksted town cemetery is across the road from Holy Trinity.

At Market and Hospital Streets, **St. Patrick's Roman Catholic Church** was built in 1848 to replace an earlier wooden structure destroyed in an 1825 hurricane. Built from local cut stone, the church shows elements of Gothic revival, neoclassical, and Spanish mission styles. The church cemetery contains a monument to 14 sailors from the *U.S.S. Monongahela,* who perished in an 1867 tidal wave that deposited their vessel several hundred yards inland.

St. Paul's Anglican Church at King Cross and Hospital Streets dates from the British occupation of St. Croix in the early 19th century.

Apothecary Hall in Frederiksted is an example of the town's Victorian architecture.

© SUSANNA HENIGHAN POTTER

The church as seen today combines an 1812 West Indian hipped-roof structure with a neo-Gothic three-tiered tower built in 1848. The tower was constructed with local limestone and Danish brick. The church was completely restored after an electrical fire in 1996.

WEST COAST

Western St. Croix is a long, mostly straight shoreline dotted by white, sandy beaches. Come here to swim, scuba dive, or ponder the horizon. Sunsets are glorious.

South of Frederiksted

A great deal of the shoreline south of Frederiksted is sandy and good for swimming. Many locals head to the patches of sand immediately south of town, near the fisherman's dock. Here large stones litter the shore and trees provide pleasant shade.

Farther south is the beach commonly called **Sandcastle Beach,** or Dorsch Beach, where the sand widens and you can take advantage of a restaurant and other facilities at Sandcastle hotel.

The coastal road ends at **Vincent F. Mason Coral Resort,** an attractive and popular public park with lots of parking, picnic tables, grills, bathrooms, a swimming pool (9 A.M.–4 P.M. daily), and a beautiful sandy beach.

Sandy Point National Wildlife Refuge

A finger of land that protrudes from St. Croix's southwestern corner, Sandy Point National Wildlife Refuge is a 380-acre wildlife preserve managed by the U.S. Fish and Wildlife Service. The beach here is wide and covered with soft white sand. It is also the single most important nesting site for leatherback turtles in the Virgin Islands: an estimated 150 animals nest here in an average year. At least 100 species of birds have been spotted in the refuge, including endangered brown pelicans, peregrine falcons, black-bellied plovers, and roseate terns.

FREEDOM CITY

Moses Gottlieb, better known as General Buddhoe, is the hero of the 1848 St. Croix slave uprising that led to emancipation in the Danish West Indies. He is credited with not only leading the uprising, but also with keeping the peace during the days after emancipation was achieved.

Like many legends, there are differing accounts of Buddhoe's personal history. Some say that he was a skilled sugar boiler who often traveled from plantation to plantation. Others say that Buddhoe was a freeman and a blacksmith who operated a blacksmith shop at Estate Butler Bay, north of Frederiksted. There is also a story that Buddhoe came from Tortola, in the British Virgin Islands, where slavery was abolished in 1834. In any event, it is clear that Buddhoe was known and respected by slaves around the island and that he was a persuasive leader.

Late on July 2, 1848, the sound of a conch shell told slaves around the island that the rebellion had begun. By the morning of July 3, more than 2,000 slaves were on the roads, making their way to Frederiksted. Legend has it that as they marched, the black men, women, and children sang, "Mek way, we comin fo ahwe freedom." Before midday, General Buddhoe arrived from Estate La Grange atop a white horse, dressed in full military uniform.

Buddhoe was the spokesman for the slaves, telling the authorities that their demand was simple: freedom. A deadline of noon came and went with no sign of freedom, so the slaves tore up the hated whipping post and threw it in the sea. Reports indicate that at the peak of the insurrection, the city of Frederiksted contained some 8,000 enslaved people, or half of all slaves on the island.

Buddhoe gave the authorities a final ultimatum: If the slaves did not receive their freedom by 4 P.M., the town would burn. Minutes before 4 P.M., Governor-General Peter von Scholten rode into Frederiksted, quickly consulted with the planters inside the fort, and came outside to make his announcement. His words are famous: "From this day onward, all unfree in the Danish West Indies are today free."

With the objective met, Buddhoe set about keeping the peace. He interceded to save the life of fire marshal Jacob Gyllich and even helped round up former slaves who continued to loot. But Buddhoe was not thanked for his efforts. After the discord ended, Buddhoe was imprisoned at Fort Christiansvaern. He was not tried but was deported to Trinidad on January 8, 1849. There are reports he eventually made his way to the United States, but to this day, no one is certain what became of the former hero of St. Croix's emancipation.

A bust of Moses Gottlieb sits prominently in the public park, named in his honor, immediately south of Fort Frederiksted.

Because of its importance to wildlife, Sandy Point is closed most days. From September to April the refuge is open to the public on weekends only (10 A.M.–4 P.M. Sat.–Sun.), when the Fish and Wildlife Service posts officers there to ensure the safety of visitors and of the endangered animals. The refuge is closed during the summer turtle nesting season. The St. Croix Environmental Association offers guided tours and turtle-watch programs in the refuge throughout the year.

North of Frederiksted

Just north of Frederiksted, within walking distance, is **Frederiksted Beach,** a pleasant, wide, sandy beach with nice views of the waterfront and cruise ship pier. A grassy public park with picnic tables and benches buffers the beach from the road and adds to the appeal. This is the location of monthly free Sunset Jazz concerts (Friday evenings).

Farther north, the coast is really one long beach. Drive along and choose a spot that appeals to you. Many people opt for a patch of sand next to one of the beach bars that line the shore: **Rainbow Beach,** next to Coconut's, is close to town. Farther north **Sprat Beach** is especially popular on Sunday afternoons.

Nestled among the northern foothills of the rainforest is **Estate Mount Washington,** sugar estate ruins about 1.5 miles off Route 63 in the island's northwest corner. Look for a small yellow sign at the turnoff. Estate Mount Washington began as a cotton plantation in 1750 but turned to sugar production in 1779. The current owners have preserved the ruins while planting an orchard and building a labyrinth on the grounds. The ruins are open to the public during daylight hours.

Estate Butler Bay, located just north of the turnoff to Creque Dam Road, will attract your attention as you drive along the west coast; you'll see large stone buildings in various states of ruin, a wide drive, and some of the largest trees on St. Croix. The ruins of the Butler Bay sugar plantation consist of a large sugar factory, a well, and various other outbuildings, including the old blacksmith's shop, which has been converted to a modern house. During the plantation era, Butler Bay was one of the largest plantations on St. Croix, and it is believed that William Gotlieb, better known as Buddhoe, the leader of the 1848 slave uprising, lived here. The ruins are on private property, but visitors are allowed during daylight hours and some tour groups stop here. Be respectful and careful as you explore.

While at Butler Bay, take time to look at the trees. In addition to tamarind, papaya, and genip trees, Butler Bay has one of the island's largest baobab trees. This distinctive-looking tree is native to Africa, where it has spiritual and cultural significance. The baobab trees on St. Croix were planted by slaves, and as such, they serve as a meaningful connection to the past. During dry months it is not uncommon for the limbs of the baobabs to be completely bare, but when rains come the trees leaf out and produce extravagant hanging flowers. Baobabs have silvery wide trunks that become narrow and spindly towards the top of the tree.

Baobab trees grow at Estate Butler Bay, north of Frederiksted.

© SUSANNA HENIGHAN POTTER

© SUSANNA HENIGHAN POTTER

Estate Whim great house

WEST ISLAND

From the broad plain in the south to the rainforest in the north, no part of St. Croix offers as much diversity and richness as the west island. Museums here pay tribute to the island's past, while other attractions showcase its rich natural resources.

Whim Plantation Museum

The best place to begin an exploration of St. Croix's history is at the Whim Plantation Museum (52 Estate Whim, 340/772-0598, fax 340/772-9446, www.stcroixlandmarks. com; 10 A.M.–4 P.M. Mon.–Sat. Nov.–Apr.; 10 A.M.–3 P.M. Mon., Wed., Fri., and Sat. May–Oct.; adults $10, seniors $5, children $4). The elegant 18th-century Whim great house is the centerpiece of the museum. Oval-shaped and constructed of white stone, the great house is furnished with period furniture handmade from local hardwoods on St Croix. Polished wood floors, broad windows, and airy breezes add to the atmosphere, while displays including a census of slaves and the ornaments of everyday life provide an glimpse into the running of the plantation. Guided tours of the house are included with admission, while a self-guided tour of the grounds takes you to the only fully restored windmill on the island, a sugar factory, a watch house, a cookhouse, and a garden. There is also a small exhibit hall and museum.

Whim was first developed as a plantation in the 1730s, but it was not until 1754 that sugar cultivation began on the estate, fueled by the labor of enslaved Africans. Whim was a medium-size plantation: in 1810, a peak year for sugar production on the island, there were 105 slaves at Whim and 130 acres under cultivation. Sugar continued to be produced until 1920, when the estate turned to livestock. This was short-lived; in 1932, the federal government bought the plantation as part of a Depression-era homestead program. In 1954, 11 acres at Whim, including the great

© SUSANNA HENIGHAN POTTER

St. George Village Botanical Garden

house, were deeded to the St. Croix Landmarks Society for preservation and education. A library and archives on site has an excellent collection of material about St. Croix and the Virgin Islands, including extensive genealogical resources.

St. George Village Botanical Garden

Tropical flora combines with history at the St. George Village Botanical Garden (127 Estate St. George, 340/692-2874, www.sgvbg.org; 9 A.M.–5 P.M. daily Nov.–Apr.; 9 A.M.–4 P.M. Tues.–Sat. May–Oct.; adults $8, children $1). Set on the site of Taino and Danish settlements, the 16-acre garden contains a botanical collection of more than 1,500 native and exotic species. It takes an hour or more to stroll leisurely through the garden, which includes fruit trees, orchids, local herbs and vegetables, cactus, and numerous examples of flowering trees and shrubs. There is also a rainforest trail that traverses a damp forest of tall trees and lush

greenery. The gardens coexist happily with ruins of the old sugar mill and sugarworks.

Every July the gardens come alive for the annual Mango Melee, a celebration of the juicy fruit that features food, music, educational presentations, garden tours, and mangoes galore. Other regular events cater to gardening enthusiasts. The gift shop is one of the best on the island.

Cruzan Rum Distillery

You can witness rum production from fermentation to bottling at the Cruzan Rum Distillery (No. 3 Estate Diamond, 340/692-2280, 9 A.M.–11:30 A.M. and 1–4:15 P.M. Mon.–Fri., adults $4, under 18 $1). The half-hour tour takes you past massive vats of fermenting liquid and through the warehouse where Cruzan rum is aged in wooden barrels. A complimentary rum punch is included in your tour.

Rum has been produced at Cruzan's Estate Diamond factory since 1760. Today, the molasses used in the rum production is imported from Central or South America, and most of the rum leaves the island in huge containers. It arrives in Florida, where it is bottled and then sold around the world. About 15 percent of the rum produced on St. Croix is bottled on the island and stays in the Caribbean.

Captain Morgan Visitor Center

Stop at the new $5 million Captain Morgan Visitor Center (Estate Annaberg and Shannon Grove, 340/713-5699, 8 A.M.–5 P.M., $10) for immersion in the history and manufacture of rum. The visitor's facility built as part of Diageo's Captain Morgan Rum Distillery opened in 2012 and consists of history and artifacts of the rum industry, a movie theater, a bar, and a gift shop.

CALDONIA RAINFOREST

No, this is not a real rainforest (there's not enough rain), but that's what everyone on St. Croix calls the damp northwestern corner of the island, so don't quibble. This is the most mountainous and thickly forested part of St. Croix, a land of running streams, damp air, and huge trees. It is a world apart from the arid east end or the gentle rolling hills of the south, and it's well suited for a driving tour.

To explore the rainforest by car, take Route 76, Mahogany Road, which winds through dense forest. You can also take Route 765, Annaly Road, to Route 58, Creque Dam Road, and follow that west to the coast. You will need four-wheel drive to explore unpaved Route 78, Scenic Drive, which heads east toward Route 69.

Beware: The asphalt truck makes infrequent trips to the rainforest, and the roads—though paved—are relatively rough. Take your time and drive gently over the potholes and broken asphalt. Venture off the pavement at your own risk.

ST. CROIX

© SUSANNA HENIGHAN POTTER

the Lawaetz Family Museum

Lawaetz Family Museum

Set in the foothills of the rainforest, the Carl and Marie Lawaetz Family Museum (Rte. 76/Mahogany Rd., 340/772-1539, www.stcroixlandmarks.com, 10:30 A.M.–3:30 P.M. Tues., Thurs., and Sat., adults $10, seniors $5, children 6–12 $4, under 6 free) depicts the history of a St. Croix family farm that reached its zenith in the first half of the twentieth century.

Carl Lawaetz left Denmark to seek his fortune in St. Croix in the early 1890s, and he found work on one of the island plantations. In 1896 he bought the run-down sugar factory, land, and estate house at Little LaGrange, north of Frederiksted. Five years later, he married, and the estate soon became home to Carl and Marie's growing family. The Lawaetz name is closely associated with the St. Croix cattle industry and its specially bred Senepol cattle.

Carl and Marie's home was turned over to the St. Croix Landmarks Society in 1996 to become a museum. Inside are period furniture and family heirlooms. Outside are nicely tended gardens and walking trails. Visitors to the museum receive a guided tour of the house and are invited to stroll the grounds on their own.

St. Croix LEAP

Another interesting rainforest stop is St. Croix LEAP, or Life Environmental Arts Project (Rte. 76/Mahogany Rd., 340/772-0421, 8 A.M.–5 P.M. Mon.–Sat., free), a woodworking shop located deep within the rainforest. LEAP has been producing housewares and art from mahogany and other tropical hardwoods for some 40 years. Drop by the barn-like workshop to meet the artisans and browse locally made wall art, clocks, kitchenware, and furniture.

Mount Victory Camps

This eco-retreat located in the heart of the rainforest is a campground and venue for concerts and other special events. Casual visitors to Mount Victory Camps (Rte. 58/Creque Dam Rd., 340/772-1651, www.mountvictorycamp.com) can see red-legged tortoises, sample organic bush tea, and meet interesting people. There is an organic farm at the rear of the campground. Call ahead and ask if someone will be able to give you a guided tour.

Virgin Islands Sustainable Farm Institute

The 200-acre property tucked away in the rainforest is part organic farm, part training institute, and part eco-retreat. You can buy the produce at weekly farmers markets in Christiansted and Frederiksted, but enthusiasts should schedule a two-hour tour of VISFA (Creque Dam Rd., 340/220-0466, www.visfi.org), where you will see the farm's fruit and vegetable cultivation, meet farm staff, and learn about the medicinal and practical uses of dozens of tropical trees and plants. You'll also see the farm's bamboo grove, community house, and farm animals including chickens, rabbits, goats, and sheep, as well as an authentic replica of a Taino bohio (hut). Tours cost $25 per person.

VISFA also offers occasional Slow Down Dinners, which are an extremely popular way for visitors to sample farm produce and learn more about sustainable farming and lifestyles. Call ahead to find out if one is in the cards during your visit.

VISFA is located about a mile past Mount Victory Camps on Creque Dam Road. The driveway is unpaved; four-wheel drive is recommended.

Mount Pellier Domino Club

Another recommended pit stop in the forest is the Mount Pellier Domino Club (Rt. 76/Mahogany Rd., 340/772-9914, 10 A.M.–5 P.M. daily). The casual bar is famous for three things: beer-drinking pigs, potent mamajuana (spiced rum), and excellent down-home hospitality from host Norma George. The pigs switched to nonalcoholic brew a few years ago, but it is still fun to watch them crack open a can and chug its contents. Norma also serves an enticing menu of home-cooked food and as the name suggests, there is sometimes a spirited domino game in progress.

Country Snack Shack and Mini-Zoo

Near the eastern end of Mahogany Road is the Country Snack Shack and Mini-Zoo (28 Mahogany Rd., 340/772-0604, 10 A.M.–6 P.M. daily, free), a fruit and vegetable stand, smoothie bar, and petting zoo. Family-owned and operated, the snack shack sells seasonal local produce—mangoes, grapefruit, starfruit (carambola), tomatoes, papaya, bananas, and much more. The signature smoothie, the "Country Blend," is a mixture of six different local fruits with ice and no added sugar. It's highly refreshing on a hot day. The Snack Stand also serves sandwiches, snacks, and juices. Behind the stand is a homegrown complex of caged rabbits, iguanas, peacock, ducks, parrots, mongeese, turtles, hamsters, and more,

plus a little brown pig named Cocoa. Admission to the zoo is free, but donations are requested.

EAST ISLAND

Arid and relatively undeveloped, eastern St. Croix looks and feels different from the rest of the island. Unlike western St. Croix, which is dominated by rainforests in the north and the flat plain in the south, the eastern end of the island is dry and scrubby. During the plantation era, farms in this part of the island were smaller and produced cotton and indigo rather than the more lucrative sugar. Socially, the east end is a land of ostentatious homes, quiet drives, and American snowbirds. There is less of the cultural richness so evident in the island's two towns or western suburbs.

Nonetheless, there are several very good reasons to head east. East St. Croix has some of the island's best beaches, pristine natural areas, and a beautiful rolling landscape. Windswept Point

ST. CROIX

A road cuts through the sparse, windswept landscape of eastern St. Croix.

© SUSANNA HENIGHAN POTTER

Udall is the easternmost point in the United States and offers stunning views of the Atlantic. The East End Marine Park provides opportunities for bird-watching, recreational fishing, kiteboarding, and snorkeling.

The east end is easy to navigate. Route 82 heading east out of Christiansted follows the coast, taking you past a string of beaches, resorts, and restaurants, and eventually to Point Udall. Along the way, you pass Cramer Park, a popular beach and picnic site, and the starting point of hikes to Jack and Isaac Bays.

Route 60 follows the southern coast, past the island's most elite estates, the Carina Bay Casino, and the wide open plain surrounding Great Pond Bay, an important wetland. Pressing on, you enter St. Croix's cattle country, home to the hearty Senepol breed.

Buccaneer Bay

A beautiful white sand beach often crowded with guests from the Buccaneer hotel and resort, Buccaneer Bay is convenient to Christiansted and endowed with beach chairs, a seaside restaurant, water-sports rentals, and lovely views of the sea. Nonguests of the resort must pay $6 to use the beach.

Shoy's Beach

Shoy's is a quiet, protected, honey-colored beach without facilities about a mile east of Christiansted. To get there, follow signs to the Buccaneer, but turn right immediately before passing through the Buccaneer guard gate. You will pass another guard, who will probably ask your name and can give you directions to the beach. The parking area is about half a mile down paved roads and past exclusive homes. The beach here tends to be a bit rocky, but the water is calm and clear, and it is a good place to snorkel.

Southgate Coastal Reserve

Created in 1999 to protect the Southgate salt pond and surrounding area, the Southgate

Coastal Reserve (East End Rd., www.stcroix-environmental.org) is a 100-acre nature preserve owned and managed by the St. Croix Environmental Association. An important bird habitat, the preserve encompasses a coastal salt pond, mangrove forest, beach forest, and upland grassland. The pond and surrounding area provide habitat for many species of resident and migratory birds, and the beach is used for turtle nesting. The environmental association offers guided tours of the reserve from time to time, many focused on showcasing the birds of the area. There are plans for a visitor center when funding becomes available.

The preserve faces **Cheney Bay,** a long protected crescent of honey-colored sand with views of Green Cay offshore. Swimming here is good because there are not a lot of offshore rocks and you can snorkel along the eastern end of the bay. Cheney is also accessible from Cheney Beach Resort, where there is a restaurant and resort.

Look for the Southgate Preserve just east of Cheeseburgers in Paradise on Highway 82, also called East End Road. The dirt track to the preserve is unmarked and unpaved. If you reach Cheney Beach Resort, you've gone too far.

East End Marine Park

The East End Marine Park is a protected area entirely consisting of marine resources: the reefs, sea grass beds, fishing grounds, turtle nesting beaches, and mangroves that encircle nearly 17 miles along the eastern end of St. Croix. Though the park was established by the Virgin Islands government in 2003, it is only in recent years that it has been staffed and an office and visitor contact center established (5005 Estate Great Pond, 340/718-3367, www.stxeastendmarinepark.org, 9 A.M.–4 P.M. Mon.–Fri.). The park's primary role is management—establishing rules for fishing, recreation, and development along St. Croix's eastern coastlines. But the park also welcomes people who want to explore the shore and coordinates regular recreational activities within the park.

The East End Marine Park begins at the Southgate Coastal Reserve east of Christiansted and continues around the entire eastern tip of the island to the western side of Great Pond Bay. Within the park, Cheney Bay, Cramer's Beach, Jack Bay, Isaac Bay, Grapetree Bay and Turner Hole all offer sandy beaches. There is snorkeling at Jack and Isaac Bays and Boiler Bay on the road to Point Udall. Coakley Bay on the north shore and Great Pond Bay are used for kiteboarding when conditions are right. Cramer Park and Rod Bay are both areas with a local camping tradition, especially at Easter (but there are no formal camping facilities).

Cramer Park

Cramer Park, near the island's eastern tip, is a popular public park with picnic tables, bathrooms, shelters, and plenty of parking. Crucians flock here on holidays and weekends, many of them setting up camp, especially at Easter. This is the sort of place where you will see families celebrating a child's birthday, courting couples, and beachgoers just like yourself. It is not necessarily a quiet retreat, although you may well have it to yourself, especially on weekdays.

The beach has medium-grain honey-colored sand and just a few offshore rocks to look out for. Inland there are plenty of shade trees.

Base Array Telescope

At 82 feet wide and 10 stories high, the radio telescope that sits just across the road from Cramer Park stands out from its surroundings. The telescope is part of the national **Very Long Baseline Array** (340/773-0196, www.vlba.nrao.edu), a system of 10 identical radio telescopes located across the continental United States and Hawaii. Funded by the National Science Foundation, the 10 telescopes intercept radio waves to look deep into the universe. They are controlled at the National Radio Astronomy Observatory in New Mexico. Group tours are available by prior appointment only.

Point Udall

Up until 1999, Point Udall, named for Stewart Udall, secretary of the interior (1961–1969), was simply a remote lookout point on the far eastern end of St. Croix. But when millennium fever struck, the local government paved the road to Point Udall and built a monument in recognition of the fact that, as the easternmost point on U.S. soil, Point Udall would be first in to welcome the new millennium.

After the excitement of the millennium, Point Udall returned to being a remote, windswept place, although with the added bonus of a nicely paved road and interesting monument. It is a nice drive out here, through wild, scrubby landscape, and the view of wide open ocean is captivating. Early birds are advised to make a sojourn here to watch the sun rise.

◖ Jack and Isaac Bay Preserve

St. Croix's best secluded beaches are located side by side in the 300-acre Jack and Isaac Bay Preserve (340/718-5575, www.nature.org) on the southeastern end of the island. These pristine, quiet beaches are part of a coastal wildlife reserve managed by the Nature Conservancy. The reefs, beaches, and near-shore waters of the bays are part of the East End Marine Park, and they are protected by local law. Hiking trails at the reserve cut through a dry, open landscape dominated by guinea grass, wild frangipani, and manjack trees. The beaches are important nesting sites for green, hawksbill, and leatherback turtles.

Jack Bay, a broad crescent of white sand shaded by sea grape trees, is the farther west of the two bays. Isaac Bay is longer, straighter, and equally inviting. Some people bathe in the nude here, although the practice is illegal in the U.S. Virgin Islands. There are no facilities, so

Point Udall is the easternmost point on St. Croix.

© SUSANNA HENIGHAN POTTER

bring plenty of water and don't forget to carry your trash out with you.

Hiking is the only way to access Jack and Isaac Bays. The primary trailhead is located a couple dozen yards west of Point Udall. There is space for a few cars, and the hike takes you down across East End Bay into Isaac and then Jack Bays. Along the way a side-leg trail takes hikers to the top of Goat Hill (600 ft.) for awesome views of St. Croix, Buck Island, and Point Udall. There are trail markers along the way.

The other way to get to the preserve is to hike an unmarked trail just east of the Base Array Telescope.

Whichever way you hike in, plan at least a half day for the excursion and bring twice as much water as you think you will need. An early morning start allows you to avoid hiking at the hottest part of the day.

Turner Hole

On the south coast, Turner Hole at the Divi Carina Bay is a long, straight stretch of sand with good swimming. Snorkels, kayaks, and small sailboats are available for rent.

Great Pond

A large salt pond and surrounding landscape about three miles west of Divi Carina Bay, Great Pond is stunning landscape. Green-tufted hills covered in golden guinea grass surround a wide, flat basin and pond. It is a landscape virtually unseen in other Virgin Islands, more reminiscent of the American midwest than the subtropical Caribbean. The pond is a good place for bird-watching; experienced bird-watchers can talk to the staff at the East End Marine Park for directions and go out on their own. Local environmental groups offer occasional guided bird-watching walks for beginners.

Great Pond Bay is also a protected anchorage; boats that maneuver the tricky offshore reef can enjoy a peaceful and almost certainly private bay. It is a popular place for kiteboarding.

Developers have been trying to build a resort at Great Pond Bay since 1999. The plans call for a major conference center, golf course, hotel, and casino, but the project has been tied up in a long-running legal dispute with environmentalists.

HOVENSA

Hess Oil established an oil refinery on the south shore of St. Croix in 1966. In 1998, a corporate restructuring led to a new name for the facility, HOVENSA. In 2012, after more than 40 years in operation, the plant closed because of three consecutive years of financial losses. Some 2,000 island residents lost their jobs, creating a vacuum in the economy unlikely to be filled in the near future. The facility now functions as a transhipment depot.

Sports and Recreation

St. Croix's scenery is lovely to look at, but even nicer when you experience it firsthand. Outdoor pursuits like hiking, horseback riding, snorkeling, and diving bring you up close to St. Croix's unique environment.

WATER SPORTS
Diving

St. Croix offers the best and most diverse diving in the Virgin Islands. Its main attraction is the Wall, a deep undersea ledge that runs parallel to the island's northwestern shore, providing divers with a remarkable number of interesting, exciting, and rewarding dives. But what sets St. Croix apart most of all is the diversity of its diving: in addition to Wall dives, there are reef dives, wreck dives, and a world-class pier dive. As dive operators like to say, St. Croix is the only island in the Virgins where you can dive a wreck, a reef, a wall, and a pier in one day.

St. Croix's dive sites are located along the northwestern and western shore—draw a line from Frederiksted to Christiansted along the shore, and you have defined the diving territory. Wall dives are located along the north coast, while the best wreck, reef, and pier dives are on the western shore. As a rule, west coast dives are calmer (they are in the lee of the island), and so they are the best choice when the sea is rough.

Standout dives on St. Croix include the **Cane** Bay Wall, a beach dive, which is the perfect starting point for exploring the north shore Wall. **Salt River Canyon East and West** are two more outstanding Wall dives. For wreck diving, try **Butler Bay,** where five different wrecks were intentionally sunk between 1984 and 1999 for the benefit of divers. Two of the most unusual dive sites on St. Croix are the old and new **Frederiksted Piers.** These shallow, protected dive sites bring you up close to some of the sea's wackiest creatures: seahorses, bat fish, octopi, eels, sponges, and anemones. The pier is especially neat at night.

Dive shops on St. Croix tend to specialize in the dives closest to them. Christiansted and Salt River Bay shops take divers to the Salt River Canyon or reef dives along the Christiansted Harbor. Cane Bay shops head to the north shore Wall, while west coast shops specialize in the pier, wreck, and reef dives on that side of the island. When choosing a dive operator, consider proximity; the longer you have to travel to get to a site, the less time you will have to explore it.

Expect to pay $65–85 for a one-tank dive and $90–110 for a two-tank dive on St. Croix, or a bit more if it is a night dive. All dive shops also offer dive packages that may include daily dives and accommodations at select hotels for a week or more. New divers or those who have not dived in a while can sign up for a wide range of refresher and certification courses,

ST. CROIX

including some you can start online before you arrive. A full certification course, which includes classroom sessions and confined and open-water dives, costs between $300 and $500; many shops charge more for an accelerated, one-on-one course.

St. Croix Ultimate Bluewater Adventures (14 Caravelle Arcade and Sandcastle by the Beach, 340/773-5994 or 877/567-1367, www.stcroixscuba.com) goes by the convenient acronym SCUBA. Ed and Molly Buckley came to the island to work for an airline decades ago, but now they run one of the most popular dive businesses on the island. They have two shops: their Christiansted operation takes divers to north shore dive sites including the Wall, while the west end location specializes in pier, wreck, and night dives.

Another choice is **Dive Experience** (1111 Strand St., Christiansted, 340/773-3307 or 800/235-9047, www.divexp.com), operated by divemaster and Women Divers' Hall of Fame inductee Michelle Pugh.

Cane Bay Dive Shop (340/773-9913 or 800/338-3843, www.canebayscuba.com) has locations in Christiansted and Frederiksted, and at Divi Carina Bay and Caramola resorts, but its main base is at Cane Bay, where divers can swim or dinghy out to the famous Cane Bay Wall.

For personalized service, try **N2 The Blue Diving Adventures** (Customs House St., Fredriksted, 340/772-3483, www.n2blue.com), which takes no more than six passengers per trip. It specializes in west coast dives and is located a quarter mile north of the cruise ship pier in Frederiksted.

Headquartered inside Salt River Bay National Park, **Anchor Dive Center** (Columbus Cove, 340/778-1522 or 800/532-3483, www.anchordivestcroix.com) is a five-minute ride to the Salt River Canyon dives.

Scuba West (330 Strand St., 340/772-3701 or 800/352-0107, www.divescubawest.com) is located in Frederiksted, right across the road from the waterfront.

Snorkeling

St. Croix is best known for superior diving, but there are excellent snorkel spots as well. **Buck Island** has an underwater snorkel trail at its eastern tip, with signs identifying key features of the reef. The trail is heavily used, however, and while it's good for beginners, it's not the most pristine snorkel spot around St. Croix. **Cane Bay** offers easy access to a large, shallow reef and is a popular snorkeling location. Easily accessible from the shore, the Cane Bay "garden" features elkhorn, brain, and star coral as well as a variety of colorful sponges and fish. Snorkelers wishing to get a glimpse of the famed St. Croix Wall can go under at **Northstar Beach,** just west of Cane Bay, where the drop-off begins in just 30 feet of water. This is a popular haunt for sea turtles.

On the east side of the island, **Shoys Beach** and **Grapetree Beach** both have shallow reefs and usually calm waters.

Snorkel equipment is available from any of the island's dive shops. Water-sports centers at Carambola Beach Resort, Divi Carina Bay, Protestant Cay, and the Buccaneer also rent gear for exploring shallow reefs around the resorts.

St. Croix SCUBA (340/773-5994, www.stcroixscuba.com) offers two-hour snorkel tours ($50 per person, $25 for children under 10) from its west coast location at Sandcastle by the Sea. The tours include a reef or shipwreck location followed by the Frederiksted Pier. Call ahead to make a reservation.

Kayaking

The best place to kayak on St. Croix is Salt River Bay, a quiet estuary protected from waves and currents. Just put in your kayak and start exploring. Go at early morning or late afternoon for exceptional bird-watching or at night to experience bioluminescence. You can explore the expansive bay on your own or with a guide, who will provide added safety and be able to explain the history and ecology of the area. Expect to pay $45–50 per person for a 2.5-hour guided tour and $25 per hour for a two-person kayak rental.

There are two kayak tour and rental companies that specialize in Salt River Bay. **Caribbean Adventure Tours** (Columbus Cove, 340/778-1522 or 800/523-3483, www.stcroixkayak. com) offers three different 2.5-hour trips per day, including a historical tour, an ecological tour, and a moonlight tour. **Virgin Kayak Co.** (Cane Bay, 340/778-0071) offers a tour that focuses on the Taino settlement of Salt River Bay.

For something different, try **Sea Thru Kayaks VI** (340/244-8696, www.seathrukayaksvi.com), which uses clear kayaks on its guided tours of Salt River Bay, Altona Lagoon, the East End Marine Park, and other locations. The visibility through the floor of your kayak makes the experience a cross between snorkeling and kayaking.

Fishing

There is a fertile deep-sea fishing ground a short sail away from St. Croix, where anglers can troll for mahimahi, marlin, tuna, and wahoo. Expect to pay about $700 for a half-day offshore charter and $900 for a full day. Inshore fishing charters target species such as snapper, tarpon, and bonefish and start around $400 for a half day and $600 for a full day. Fishing rates are always quoted per charter, not per person, and typically include the boat, fuel, crew, and all gear.

Captain Carl Holley (340/277-4042, www. fishwithcarl.com) operates the 36-foot *Mocko Jumbie* and the 29-foot *Keep It Reel* and gladly crafts sportfishing charters for experienced or novice anglers and welcomes children, too. **St. Croix Deep Blue Fishing Charters** (340/626-0060, www.stxdeepbluecharters.com) operates fishing excursions off a roomy 46-foot sportfishing yacht. Another option is fishing with Captain Bunny Jones aboard the 38-foot **Catch-22** (340/778-6987).

St. Croix Inshore Fishing Charters (340/514-6078, www.fishstcroix.com) specializes in rod and-reel and fly-fishing from a 17-foot Key West along St. Croix's inshore reefs and flats. Captain Ryan DiPasquale operates **Jade Hook Fishing Charters** (340/244-9062, www.jadehookcharters.com) and offers both inshore and offshore fishing charters.

SAILING
Yachting Facilities

It is a day's sail to St. Croix from the other Virgin Islands, but well worth the journey. The seaward approach to Christiansted Harbor is one of the most picturesque in the Caribbean. If you are sailing from the British Virgin Islands, be sure to visit **Customs and Immigration** (Gallows Bay, 340/778-0216, 8 A.M.–4 P.M.) first. The best chandlery is **St. Croix Marine** (Gallows Bay, 340/773-0289, 7:30 A.M.–5 P.M.). This full-service boatyard and marina is just east of the customs dock. It can accommodate boats up to 200 feet with up to 10-foot drafts. Gallows Bay is convenient to restaurants, services, and grocery stores.

Also near Christiansted are **Jones Maritime Company** (1215 King Cross St., Christiansted, 340/773-4709 or 866/609-2930, www. jonesmaritime.com), which has 15 slips and all services except fuel. **Silver Bay Dock** (Christiansted, 340/778-9650) can accommodate boats up to 40 feet long.

East of Christiansted, there's **Green Cay Marina** (340/773-1453), located opposite Green Cay, a small offshore nature preserve. It is well protected and has 140 slips, a hotel, a restaurant, fuel, laundry, electricity, showers, a pump-out station, and ice. It monitors Channel 16 and can accommodate boats with depths up to 10 feet.

West of Christiansted, **Salt River Marina** (Salt River Bay, Channel 16) is a small marina within the protected Salt River Bay Historic Park and Ecological Preserve. Boats with more

ST. CROIX

than six-foot drafts should not attempt to sail in here. Marina facilities include fuel, water, electricity, ice, and laundry. There is a restaurant and bar ashore.

Anchorages

The area in the lee of Protestant Cay in **Christiansted Harbor** is the best anchorage there, but it is often crowded. The harbor is also busy with seaplane traffic. Instead, visiting yachts should anchor east of Protestant Cay or in Gallows Bay.

Frederiksted is an open, exposed harbor protected from wind, but it is not safe during a storm. Visiting yachts are asked to anchor north of the cruise ship pier. You can also sail farther north and anchor near any of the west coast beaches north of town.

Yacht Clubs

The **St. Croix Yacht Club** (Teague Bay, Channel 16) is on the east end of St. Croix. There are moorings for visiting yachts. This is a good place to meet other sailors and learn about upcoming regattas. There is a bar and restaurant, showers, and garbage disposal.

Day Sails

Built in 1925 in Massachusetts, *Roseway* (Port Authority Dock, Gallows Bay, 340/626-7877, www.worldoceanschool.org) is a beautiful 137-foot schooner and a registered National Historic Landmark. From November to May, guests can book private day sails or sign up to join the daily sunset sail which departs Gallows Bay at 4 P.M. and returns at 6:30 P.M. Rates for the evening sail are $45 for adults and $30 for children. *Roseway* spends its summers in Massachusetts.

BOARD SPORTS
Stand Up Paddleboarding

Stand up paddleboarding, often known by the SUP, has grown in popularity in recent years.

Teres Veho (Frederiksted Beach, 340/227-0682, www.standuppaddleconnection.com) is the place to try it on St Croix. Proprietor Nikki Cicero views SUP as a way to get fit and enjoy nature. It's easier to learn than surfing and other board sports and lets you gain a unique perspective on the water. Depending on the weather and your skill, popular places to SUP are at the Frederiksted Beach, Altona Lagoon, or the East End Marine Park. Teres Veho offers equipment rentals, lessons, and SUP training programs. Surfboards are also available for rent.

You can also rent SUP equipment from **Kite St. Croix** (340/643-5824, www.kitestcroix.com).

Kiteboarding

Surf the surface of the water under the power of the wind. **Kite St. Croix** (Cotton Valley, East End Rd., 340/643-5824, www.kitestcroix.com) will introduce newbies to the exciting sport of kiteboarding, or rent gear to experienced adrenaline hounds.

Motorcraft

Island Flight Jet Ski Rentals (Christiansted Boardwalk, 340/778-7541, www.stcroixvijetskirentalsandtours.com) offers Jet Ski rentals, tube riding, and Jet Ski snorkeling tours.

LAND PURSUITS

St. Croix's relatively flat topography combined with its large size make the island a natural setting for a wide range of land pursuits. St. Croix is the first choice for golfers in the Virgin Islands, and its winding back roads are ideal for biking.

Golf

With its flat valleys and dramatic views, St. Croix is a natural setting for world-class golf. The leading golf course is the 18-hole **Carambola Golf and Country Club** (River Rd., 340/778-5638, fax 340/779-3700, www.

St. Croix has the finest golf courses in the Virgin Islands, including Carambola.

golfcarambola.com), designed in 1966 by Robert Trent Jones Sr. and built by Laurance Rockefeller. Carambola features rolling terrain with excellent views. Expect to pay $135 for 18 holes or $110 after 2 P.M.

The other principal golf course on St. Croix is at **The Buccaneer** (340/712-2144, www.thebuccaneer.com) east of Christiansted. The par 70, 18-hole course was designed by Bob Joyce in 1973. It boasts nice sea views, a putting green, a chipping area, and practice nets. Greens fees are $60–100, depending on season.

The Reef Golf Course (Teague Bay, 340/773-8844) is a nine-hole course and driving range. The greens fee is $13 for nine holes.

Tennis

There are public tennis courts at D.C. Canegata Ballpark outside of Christiansted and near Fort Frederik in Frederiksted. **The Buccaneer** (Gallows Bay, 340/773-3036,

www.thebuccaneer.com) has eight courts and has been cited as one of the best tennis facilities in the Caribbean by *Tennis Magazine*. The rate is $18 per court per hour ($22 for one of two lighted courts). Lessons are available. There are also tennis courts at **Cheney Beach Resort** (Cheney Bay, 340/773-2918) where the cost is $5 per person per hour.

The Reef Golf Course (Teague Bay, 340/773-8844) also offers tennis courts for $5 per person per hour.

Hiking

There are dozens of exceptional hikes on St. Croix, but most of them are on unmarked, unofficial trails difficult for visitors to find. The best and most accessible hike on the island is the hike from Point Udall to Jack and Isaac Bay, managed by the Nature Conservancy. The trailhead is located a few hundred yards west of Point Udall, and the hike travels about two miles down to twin pristine and stunning white sand bays. Bring a swimsuit, snorkel equipment, food, and plenty of water, and make a day of it.

To explore other trails, including walks that take you to remote tidal pools and dramatic viewpoints, call Ras Lumumba Corriette of **Ay-Ay Eco Hikes and Tours** (340/772-4079, ayaytours@gmail.com). Lumumba leads hikes through St. Croix's most beautiful natural areas, including Jack and Isaac Bays, Annaly Bay, Salt River Bay, Maroon Ridge, and Mount Eagle. Fees range $50–60, depending on the length of the hike.

The **St. Croix Hiking Association** (www.stcroixhiking.org) also organizes regular hikes.

Biking

St. Croix's rolling hills, quiet back roads, and impressive scenery make it the best Virgin Island for bicycling. Many bikers prefer the northwest part of the island. Coastal Route 63 is relatively quiet, and the roads that branch off it are great for exploring. The far eastern end of St. Croix is equally nice; the road to Point Udall is never busy, and the views are spectacular.

Bike rentals and tours are available from the friendly and knowledgeable folks at **Freedom City Cycles** (2E Strand Sq., Frederiksted, 340/277-2433, www.freedomcitycycles.com). Mountain bike rentals are $5 per hour, $35 per day, and $75 per week, and hotel pick-up and delivery is available. For something more structured, choose a half-day guided coastal bike ride through Frederiksted and along the northwestern coast, or go off-road on a guided mountain bike ride through the forest. Guided trips cost $40–50 for adults. You may find the bike shop closed on days when no cruise ship is in port; it's a good idea to call ahead.

Horseback Riding

Paul Wojciechowski and Jill Hurd lead rainforest, beach, ruins, and nature trips on friendly

Horseback riding tours traverse the western beaches of St. Croix.

© SUSANNA HENIGHAN POTTER

ST. CROIX

and willing horses at **Paul and Jill's Equestrian Stables** (Creque Dam Rd., 340/772-2880 or 340/772-2627, www.paulandjills.com). The couple, who have been leading horse tours for more than 30 years, cater to all experience levels and ages. The two-hour tours take riders through forest and field and along the white sand beach. As Jill leads the tour she identifies common plants and notable trees, including large tamarind, mango, baobab, and sandbox trees. The tours cost $80 per person and leave in the morning or afternoon; advance reservations are recommended, especially during high season.

For a more adventurous ride, ideal for those with some riding experience, call Stephen O'Dea of **Equus Riding Tours** (340/513-4873, equus@gotostcroix.com), who leads tours at Cane Bay. An Irishman with an interesting life story and a laid-back approach, Stephen guides his riders along a short forest trail and uphill to a knoll with lovely views of the North Coast. You will be able to walk, trot, and canter according to your skill level. Then it's down to Cane Bay Beach, where you ride along the sand, look for sea turtles, and then ride straight into the sea to swim with your horse. It's a magical moment as the sun sets behind you.

Motoring

Slow down and enjoy Frederiksted and the West Coast aboard an open-air, four-seater electric car. **Sunbug LLC** (69C King St., Frederiksted, 340/719-7555, www.sunbugelectriccars.com) rents small electric cars that travel up to 22 miles per hour and run off electricity and solar power. The recommended route begins with a spin through town, stopping at some of the historic sites, and then sets off to explore the western end of the island. Pit stops can be made at the beach, to explore historic ruins, or to visit the beer-drinking pigs in the rainforest. Rentals are $39 per hour.

Guided all-terrain vehicle (ATV) tours of western St. Croix are available from **Gecko Island Adventures** (Strand Street Square, Frederiksted, 340/713-8820, www.geckosislandadventures.com).

Fitness

The **V.I. Family Sports and Fitness Center** (23 Beeson Hill, 340/778-5144, www.vihealth.com) has a pool, fitness classes, aerobics, a weight room, cardio equipment, and a sauna and steam room. Day and weekly passes are available.

Entertainment and Events

St. Croix's greatest strength is its diversity, and this diversity is manifested in the range of cultural events, entertainment, and nightlife on the island. On any given weekend, you may be able to choose from an arts festival, community theater, or a blistering nightclub. Some entertainment events are geared to tourists, but most are meant for the enjoyment of locals, too. Getting out is a great way to get a feel for the pulse of this happening island.

Check *St. Croix This Week* for a rundown of live music, festivals, fairs, theater, and more.

Also check the *St. Croix Avis* entertainment column on Friday.

NIGHTLIFE
Christiansted

The **Fort Christian Brew Pub** (Waterfront, 340/713-9820) is the only microbrewery on the island, and it's the best place for draft beer. The downstairs bar draws a young crowd during happy hour. It is especially popular among young Continentals.

Hotel on the Cay (Protestant Cay, 340/773-2035) hosts a family-friendly West Indian

ST. CROIX

beach buffet with live entertainment including mocko jumbies (stilt walkers) and steel-pan musicians on Tuesdays.

Frederiksted

The most popular gathering place in Frederiksted is **Blue Moon Café** (17 Strand St., 340/772-2222), a jazz club especially popular on Friday nights.

East Island

Divi Carina Bay Casino (Southshore Rd., 340/773-7529, www.carinabay.com) is St. Croix's first and only casino. Located across the street from its partner resort, Divi has video poker, slot machines, live poker, table games, bingo, and live entertainment. The casino draws a diverse crowd; lots of Crucians come here, especially on weekends when the live music heats up.

EVENTS
Jump-Ups

Four times a year, Christiansted retailers throw a block party. These Jump-Ups ("jump-up" is slang for a party, especially one that involves dancing) happen in July, October, January, and April. If you are on island for one, don't miss it. The heart of downtown is closed to traffic, local bands set up on street corners, and retailers often offer significant discounts. Mocko jumbies perform in the streets, face painters delight children, vendors sell street food and beer, and everyone seems to have an excellent time. Jump-Ups generally run 6–9 P.M., but many revelers don't go home. Christiansted bars and nightclubs are especially hopping well into the night of a Jump-Up.

Agriculture Fair

St. Croix celebrates its agricultural heritage at the annual Agriculture Fair, usually held in late February. The three-day event is like a traditional American county fair, but with a distinctly Caribbean twist. Come here to buy, or just admire, local fruits and vegetables including papayas, carambolas, cassava, pumpkin, and bananas. This is also a great place to try local food, take in local music, or watch cultural demonstrations, such as dancing and traditional games.

The Ag Fair, as it is called, is held on the Department of Agriculture's Fair Grounds at Estate Lower Love, in central St. Croix. The fair normally runs for three days, opening on a Friday and closing on a Sunday. Admission is $5 for adults, $2 for children. For information, or to confirm the dates, contact the Department of Agriculture (340/778-0997).

St. Croix International Regatta

St. Croix's premier sailing event is the St. Croix International Regatta, which takes place in February. Boats from St. Thomas, the British Virgin Islands, and around the Caribbean converge on St. Croix for a long weekend of racing. The regatta is organized by the St. Croix Yacht Club (www.stcroixyc.com).

Taste of St. Croix

Diners get to sample a buffet of mammoth proportions at the annual Taste of St. Croix (www.tasteofstcroix.com), a food- and wine-tasting event held every April. Nearly every major restaurant on St. Croix takes part, preparing appetizers, main dishes, desserts, salads, and cocktails. Tickets to this event tend to sell out very quickly; buy them online to avoid disappointment. Proceeds benefit the St. Croix Foundation, which supports a number of charitable and economic development projects on the island.

St. Croix Half Ironman

Hundreds of athletes converge on St. Croix every May for the St. Croix Half Ironman (340/773-4470, fax 340/773-7400, www.stcroixtriathlon.com), where they battle heat, humidity, hills, and headwinds over a punishing course. The race includes a 2-kilometer (1.24-mile) swim in Christiansted Harbor, a 90-kilometer (56-mile) bike race across the St. Croix countryside, and a 21-kilometer (13.1-mile) run around Christiansted. The race is nicknamed "Beauty and the Beast" by those who know: beauty for the unbeatable views along the way, beast for the tough 600-foot climb 21 miles into the bike segment.

The best athletes finish the 70.3-mile course in just over four hours, and top finishers qualify for the 70.3 Ironman World Championships. There is also a sprint triathlon that features a 750-meter swim, eight-mile bike, and four-mile run.

Race Week is a fun time to visit St. Croix. There are more than the usual number of parties and events; there is always a Christiansted Jump-Up a few days before the race. Spectators are encouraged to line the racecourse and cheer on athletes; people line up early at "Hot Corner," at Strand Street and Strand Lane in Christiansted, and at the top of the Beast, where they cheer on flagging bikers.

Emancipation Day

St. Croix was the setting of the momentous events that led to Emancipation in the Danish West Indies in 1848, and every July islanders celebrate and remember this historic milestone. Events include panel discussions, performances, and donkey and horse races, and culminate with a remembrance ceremony and reenactment on Emancipation Day, July 3, in Frederiksted. Check local papers and *St. Croix This Week* for schedule details.

Mango Melee

Mangoes begin to ripen in late May and early June, and by July these silky sweet fruits are for sale by the bucket at roadside stands and supermarkets. St. Croix celebrates the mango at the annual Mango Melee, held in early July

at the St. George Village Botanical Gardens (340/692-2874). There are mango displays, mango desserts, mango preserves, mango demonstrations, mango seed crafts, and plenty of opportunities to taste the unadulterated fruits. In addition to mangoes, vendors sell local food, drinks, arts, and crafts.

Crab Races

Entertaining hermit crab races are hosted weekly at popular watering holes around the island. Pay $2 to pick out a crab from the bucket (or bring your own), and then watch to see which crab claws past the finish line first. Sponsors of the winning crab get a prize. The crab races are held at the Fort Christian Brew Pub on Mondays, Divi on Wednesdays, and the Deep End at Tamarind Reef Hotel on Fridays. Races begin around 5 P.M. and you should arrive early for the best selection of crabs. This is a good event for kids, but adults like it just as much.

ARTS

St. Croix's rich history and diverse community engenders a robust number of arts events. *St. Croix This Week* lists upcoming events. Also check *The St. Croix Avis* for listings, or read its entertainment column on Friday.

Caribbean Community Theatre

Caribbean Community Theatre (No. 18 Orange Grove, 340/773-7171, www.cct.vi) puts on five plays between October and May, and two each summer. The theater is located behind Pueblo at the Orange Grove Shopping Center.

Island Center

St. Croix's premier venue for live music and performances is Island Center (Rte. 79, 340/778-5271), near the hospital. You may be able to catch performances by leading reggae, calypso, and jazz musicians, as well as shows by the Heritage Dancers.

Sunset Jazz

On the third Friday of every month, the Frederiksted Economic Development Association hosts Sunset Jazz, a free, open-air jazz concert held on the Frederiksted waterfront. Music starts around 6 P.M. and runs until 9 P.M. Bring a blanket or chairs. This is a family-friendly event.

Art Thursday

Christiansted's art galleries have collaborated to organize Art Thursday, a monthly event for which galleries stay open late for gallery walks. Restaurants and other retail shops get into the mix by opening late and offering specials. Art Thursday takes place on the first Thursday of the month from 5–9 P.M.

Shopping

CHRISTIANSTED

There are a multitude of inviting shops in Christiansted. In fact, while Christiansted's shopping may not compete with that on St. Thomas in terms of sheer volume, it is the hands-down winner when it comes to the offbeat, unique, and original. The town's shops are located on Company Street, King Street, and the alleys that run between these thoroughfares. Hours are typically 10 A.M.–5 P.M. Monday–Saturday.

Jewelry

St. Croix is famous for the Crucian bracelet, a silver or gold bracelet featuring a range of unique clasps. All downtown jewelers have their own style of bracelet, and if you look, you will soon notice that most Crucians sport at least one or two on each wrist. Dozens of shops sell Crucian bracelets, and more than a few claim to be the originator of the concept. Some of the most popular of these are **Sonya's** (1 Company St., 340/773-8924), which specializes in silver jewelry, **Crucian Gold** (Strand St., 340/773-5241), with nature-inspired designs by Nathan Bishop, and **ib designs** (Company and Queen St., 340/773-4322), which offers a unique array of so-called "feel good" jewelry by metalsmith Whealan Massicott.

Another unique keepsake is jewelry made from chaney, colonial-era pottery shards found on St. Croix. Colorful earrings, bracelets, and pendants are widely available.

Galleries

Christiansted has a variety of art galleries that sell paintings, photographs, and other work by local artists. Most galleries open from 10 A.M.–5 P.M. Monday–Saturday, and one Thursday a month many galleries to stay open late for **Art Thursday,** which encourages people to visit galleries in the evening.

D&D Studio Fine Art Photography (55 Company St., 340/719-1201) is a clean, modern gallery showing the fine art photography of Ted Davis. Large-format prints depict Caribbean scenes but often with a graphic, almost abstract, eye. Prints, cards, and posters are also available.

Design Works (6 Company St., 340/713-8102) sells fine art as well as an array of island-inspired housewares, including fabrics and home furnishings. The style here favors colonial over colorful.

Marie Henle Studio (55 Company St., 340/773-0372) shows the works of sisters Marie and Tina Henle, as well as selected St. Croix artists. The gallery is open only on Saturdays from 11 A.M.–3 P.M., and by appointment.

A cozy little gallery, **Yellow House Gallery** (3A Queen Cross St., 340/719-6656) shows the works of Judith King, whose pieces offer a colorful and whimsical portrait of Caribbean urban life. She also sells handmade jewelry and masks. Upstairs, **Watch Your Step Art Studio** (3A Queen Cross St., 340/626-1554)

GUIDED TOURS

Some of St. Croix's most remarkable historic and natural sights are located far from the main roads. Often unmarked, and sometimes on private property, these sights are accessible only if you have a guide. These organizations and companies offer noteworthy tours of St. Croix.

ST. CROIX ENVIRONMENTAL ASSOCIATION

If you're interested in combining recreation with education, contact the St. Croix Environmental Association (Gallows Bay, 340/773-1989, www.stxenvironmental.org) before you come. SEA is the island's leading voice for environmental protection, but it also organizes a smorgasbord of educational outings for residents and visitors, ranging from stargazing to kayak trips. Every summer, SEA organizes popular turtle-hatching excursions to Sandy Point Beach. Most activities are free for association members; visitors are asked to pay $10-20, depending on the activity. It is worthwhile to check the calendar of events before you arrive and reserve a spot on any trips that catch your eye, as many activities fill up quickly.

ST. CROIX HIKING ASSOCIATION

The friendly folks at the St. Croix Hiking Association (www.stcroixhiking.org) are passionate about exploring their home Island on foot. In addition to advocating for the environment and promoting outdoor literacy, the association organizes monthly hikes in some of St. Croix's best- and least-known areas. Nonmembers are welcome; nominal fees are charged.

CHANT

Crucian Heritage and Nature Tourism Inc., or CHANT (3B Strand St., Suite 5, Frederiksted, 340/719-5455, www.chantvi.org) is a community-based coalition that promotes heritage- and nature-based tourism in St. Croix. The

group can hook you up with historical walking tours of Frederiksted and Christiansted, farm tours, medicinal plant guides, and tours of historic sites such as Estate Hermitage, Parasol Mill, and Butler Bay.

ST. CROIX LANDMARKS SOCIETY

Concerned with the preservation of St. Croix's historic sites, especially its colonial-era ruins, the St. Croix Landmarks Society (52 Estate Whim, Frederiksted, 340/772-0598, www.stcroixlandmark.org) is best known as the owner and operator of the Whim Plantation and Lawaetz Family Museums. But the society also organizes a number of house tours and "ruins rambles" during the winter months, which showcase historic sites and noteworthy private properties that would otherwise be off-limits to the public.

AY-AY ECO HIKES AND TOURS

Ay-Ay Eco Hikes and Tours (340/772-4079, ayaytours@gmail.com) offers educational walking tours to some of St. Croix's most beautiful and remote natural areas with naturalist Ras Lumumba. You will learn about native plant and animal species, medicinal herbs, and the cultural and historical uses of certain parts of the island. He offers tours of Salt River Bay, the rainforest, Annaly Bay, Ham's Bluff, Maroon Ridge, and much more.

FREEDOM CITY CYCLES

A bike rental and tour outfit in Frederiksted, Freedom City Cycles (2F Strand Sq., Frederiksted, 340/277-2433, www.freedomcitycycles.com) offers guided bike tours of the west coast of St. Croix, as well as off-road treks into the rainforest. The West Coast tour takes you around Frediksted's historic sites and to Butler Bay Plantation, among other stops.

showcases the colorful, graphical paintings of Diane Given Hayes.

Arts and Crafts

Tesoro (36C Strand St., 340/773-1212) is an expansive shop that specializes in arts and crafts imported from around the Caribbean, especially Haiti. The shop sells handmade hardwood bowls and plates, metal wall art, baby quilts, dolls, paintings, banana-leaf art, and hand-carved stone figurines. Interspersed throughout are photos and descriptions of the people in Haiti who make the crafts.

For island-inspired decorative glass platters and ornaments, visit the **Mitchell Larsen Studio** (58 Company St., 340/719-1000), where you can also purchase scenic photography of the island. Jan Mitchell's glass Christmas ornaments are collector's items, and a set go on the White House Christmas tree every year.

Clothing

In the islands you should wear loose-fitting, lightweight cotton; if you didn't pack enough, stock up at **Pacific Cotton** (1110 Strand St., 340/773-2125), which sells ladies' pants, skirts, tops, and dresses, all ideal for the Caribbean climate.

For batik-print dresses and skirts or colorful beaded jewelry, visit **Island Tribe** (2106 Company St., #2, 340/719-0936).

Hotheads (1000 King St., 340/773-7888) is a small shop that packs a big punch with swimsuits, a wide selection of hats, and cocktail and island-style dresses for a special night out.

Satisfy your craving for a new outfit at **From the Gecko Boutique** (1233 Queen Cross St., 340/778-9433), a small shop that stocks a surprisingly rich selection of fashionable ladies' and men's apparel.

Books

The best all-around bookshop on St. Croix is **Undercover Books and Gifts** (5030 Anchor Way, Gallows Bay, 340/517-1567), which stocks a nice selection of new fiction and children's and young adult titles, as well as local- and Caribbean-related books.

Treasure Attic Bookshop (16 Company St., 340/778-5520), located on the second floor above a fabric shop near downtown Christiansted, sells new and used books and has a large selection of local-interest titles.

The **National Park Service** shop in the Scale House (340/774-1460) sells books, maps, and children's educational toys and games.

You can also find good selections of local books at gift shops at the St. George Botanical Garden, Whim Museum, and the Fort Frederik Museum.

FREDERIKSTED

There are a handful of shops along Strand Street in Frederiksted, selling T-shirts and other souvenirs. For local art, shop at the **Caribbean Museum Center for the Arts** (10 Strand St., 340/772-2622), a gallery and exhibit space dedicated to promoting local artists.

Another source for local arts and crafts is the **Fort Frederick Museum Shop** (Fort Frederick, 340/772-2021, 9 A.M.–4 P.M. Mon.–Fri.), which sells local art, jewelry, music, paintings, books, and some food items, including hot sauces and honey.

On days when a cruise ship is in port, vendors set up stalls at Strand Park selling cheap T-shirts, sarongs, jewelery, and more.

Accommodations

St. Croix has accommodations for every taste: luxury resorts to rainforest camps and just about everything in between.

To be near restaurants, nightlife, and shopping stay in Christiansted. For solitude and quiet, stay at one of the hotels or guesthouses in the countryside. If you are looking for a beachfront vacation, look at hotels along the west and south coasts.

St. Croix has one openly gay-friendly hotel (Sand Castle on the Beach) and more that provide an equally warm, but more discreet, welcome to gay and lesbian travelers.

VILLAS

Villas are private houses for rent, usually by the week. They range in size from one-bedroom condos to six-bedroom homes and are ideal for large family groups. Most St. Croix villas are located on the east end and north shore areas of the island.

The best way to arrange a villa rental is through a rental agency, which will help identify a villa that suits your needs, keeps a database of availability, and handles payment. Rental agencies include **Donna Ford Villa Rentals** (57 Estate Solitude, 340/778-8782, www.enjoystcroix.com) and **Vacation St. Croix** (340/718-0361 or 877/788-0361, www.vacationstcroix.com).

CHRISTIANSTED
Under $125

Affordable rooms and a good location are the primary calling cards at **Company House Hotel** (2 Company St., 340/773-1377, www.companyhousehotel.com, $115–125). Formerly the Danish Manor Inn, this historic property is located two blocks from the waterfront and next-door to the historic Steeple Building. The facade and foyer have an upscale, historic feel, but the guest rooms offer little in the way of ambience or views. Nonetheless, guests can enjoy basic comforts including air-conditioning, cable TV, a pool, an outdoor patio, and complimentary breakfast.

Named for the first boat to provide scheduled day trips to Buck Island, **Club Comanche** (1 Strand St., 340/773-0210, www.clubcomanche.com, $90–170) has been housing guests on St. Croix continuously since 1948. This 23-room landmark hotel underwent much-needed renovations in 2009, but it still maintains its historic feel. Rooms and suites have safes, flat-screen TVs, Internet access, fans, and air conditioning, and the location is steps away from dining, nightlife, and the Christiansted boardwalk. All-in-all, Comanche offers a good combination of location, value, and character.

$125-175

One of the best small inns on St. Croix, **Carrington's Inn** (4001 Estate Herman Hill, 340/713-0508 or 877/658-0508, www.carringtonsinn.com, $125–165) is a five-room bed-and-breakfast located in the hills overlooking Christiansted. You'll need a car, but it's worth the drive to reach the comfortable beds, attractive city views, and warm hospitality of the inn. A hot breakfast is included daily, and there is a pool and wireless Internet. No children.

The 39-room **King Christian Hotel** (340/773-6336 or 800/524-2012, www.kingchristian.com, $120–140) faces the Christiansted wharf and is centrally located in the middle of the town's historic district. Guests choose between standard and superior rooms; superior rooms have balconies and waterfront views and can sleep up to four people. All rooms have air-conditioning, phones, TV, refrigerators, and coffeemakers. There is a pool on the property.

ST. CROIX

Hotel Caravelle (44 Queen Cross St., 340/773-0687, fax 340/778-7004, www.hotelcaravelle.com, $170–190) is a small, stalwart hotel facing the waterfront. Many of its 33 rooms have harbor views, and there is a pool, a sundeck, and free Internet access for guests. All rooms have air-conditioning, refrigerators, and cable TV.

Recently refurbished with all new fittings and furnishings, the **King's Alley Hotel** (Kings Alley Walk, 340/773-0103 or 800/843-3574, $170–229) offers another waterfront alternative in Christiansted. Its 22 rooms feature either one or two king-size beds, refrigerators, full-size ironing boards, satellite TV, and views of the King's Alley courtyard. The single suite has an oceanfront view. There is no pool.

PROTESTANT CAY
$125-175

With a beach right outside your room and bustling Christiansted a 90-second ferry ride away, it would be hard to imagine a better arrangement than the one enjoyed by guests at **Hotel on the Cay** (Protestant Cay, 340/773-2035 or 800/524-2035, www.hotelonthecay.com, $150), a 53-room hotel located on a small spit of land in the middle of Christiansted Harbor. Rooms at the hotel are dated, but have excellent views, as well as basic comforts such as coffeemakers, toaster ovens, and cable TV. The property itself is a rather charmless concrete block, but hotel management has done its best to camouflage it with plenty of trees and landscaping. A restaurant on the cay serves three meals a day and the beach is small but nice. Some days it may be crowded with day-trippers.

NORTH SHORE
$125-175

Located on the dramatic north shore, about a mile from Salt River Bay, **⟨ Arawak Bay: The Inn at Salt River** (62 Northshore Rd.,

340/772-1684, www.arawakhotelstcroix.com, $140) is an attractive, welcoming bed-and-breakfast that offers an uncommon package of quality and value. Each of the 14 rooms has a private balcony, two king or double beds, air-conditioning, cable TV, and wireless Internet access. There is private on-site parking. A continental breakfast is served daily in the inn's dining room, and guests rave about the hospitality and care shown by proprietors Jennifer and Lionel. The bed-and-breakfast is located in a quiet residential area, where the sound of the surf drowns out the occasional passing car. The inn is convenient to Cane Bay and Salt River, and about a 10-minute drive from Christiansted.

About a 10-minute drive inland from Cane Bay, **Discovery Grove** (Estate Canaan, 340/642-8322, www.discoverygrovestx.com, $115–140) is a collection of cottages nestled together on a quiet hillside. Accommodations include cute bamboo bungalows with a shared bathhouse and kitchen and fully equipped cottages with one, two, or three bedrooms. In addition to serving individuals and families, Discovery Grove is equipped for groups.

$175-225

Hibiscus Beach Resort (4131 La Grande Princess, 340/718-4042 or 800/442-0121, fax 340/773-7668, www.hibiscusbeachresort.com, $200) is a friendly beachfront hotel just east of Christiansted. Hibiscus's 36 rooms are dated but clean and have air-conditioning, coffeemakers, refrigerators, microwaves, and cable TV. There is a pool, but it doesn't get much use, since the rooms are steps away from a lovely white beach. The on-site restaurant serves three meals a day.

Villa Margarita (Salt River Bay, 340/713-1930, www.villamargarita.com, 145–280) offers three apartments of various sizes with kitchenettes and dramatic views of the sea. There is also a pool on site.

$225-300

Located next to the Hibiscus Beach Resort, the **Palms at Pelican Cove** (4126 La Grande Princess, 340/718-8920 or 800/548-4460, fax 340/778-9218, www.palmspelicancove.com, $230–280) is a venerable but much-loved hotel whose 40 beachfront rooms are set picturesquely amid coconut palms. Rooms are tastefully decorated and come equipped with air-conditioning and coffeemakers; hotel amenities include free snorkel gear (there is great snorkeling in front of the hotel), tennis courts, a business center, and a pool. The on-site beachfront restaurant serves three meals a day and hosts live entertainment many evenings. This hotel was formerly the Cormorant Beach Club.

Expect to be pampered at the intimate **◖ Villa Greenleaf** (Estate Rattan, 340/719-1958 or 888/282-1001, fax 340/772-5425, www.villagreenleaf.com, $275–300), a bed-and-breakfast overlooking Salt River Bay. Guests are treated to gourmet breakfasts, evening cocktails, and the hospitality and helpful assistance of the innkeepers. Rooms are luxurious and modern. There is a pool, an entertainment center, and the largest kapok tree on St. Croix on the grounds.

Over $300

Carambola Beach Resort (Davis Bay, 340/778-3800 or 888/503-8760, fax 340/778-1682, www.carambolabeach.com, $450–550) is a perfect getaway. Tucked away at lovely Davis Bay, 151-room Carambola was built by Laurance Rockefeller in 1986. The red-roofed resort has elegant rooms finished with rich mahogany, featuring air-conditioning, screened-in porches, rocking chairs, satellite TV, coffeemakers, refrigerators, hair dryers, irons, and king-size beds. The resort has two restaurants, an on-site dive shop, Internet access, a fitness center, and a freshwater pool, and it sits steps away from the powder-white sand of Davis Bay.

FREDERIKSTED
Under $125

The 40-room **Frederiksted Hotel** (442 Strand St., 340/772-0500 or 800/595-9519, fax 340/772-0500, www.frederikstedhotel.com, $80–110) has seen better days, but it is a clean, comfortable choice for budget travelers, and it is the only hotel in Frederiksted proper. Rooms have air-conditioning, cable TV, microwaves, and refrigerators, and some offer nice views of the Frederiksted waterfront.

Jasmine Manor (18 Prince St., Frederiksted, 340/227-1908, www.jasminemanorvi.com, $75–95) is a recently renovated 200-plus-year-old Frederiksted townhouse. Owner Vicky Pedersen lives in the compound and rents four apartments to visitors, who delight in the historic ambience of the unique property. Stonework, deep wood finishes, and airy breezes characterize the manor's accommodations, and a large garden provides additional space for guests to relax. There are no televisions, clocks, or air-conditioning, but each apartment is equipped with a full kitchen.

WEST COAST
$125-175

Sand Castle on the Beach (127 Smithfield, 340/772-1205, U.S. toll free 800/524-2018, fax 340/772-1757, www.sandcastleonthebeach.com, $149–349) is a small hotel set on lovely Dorsch Beach, a couple miles south of Frederiksted. Its 23 rooms vary from standard hotel-style studios with garden views to expansive beachfront villas. All rooms have air-conditioning, a fan, cable TV, a VCR, a kitchenette, and a cooler; complimentary breakfast is provided at the adjoining beach bar and restaurant. Sand Castle is the best-known hotel for gay and lesbian travelers on St. Croix, but it's welcoming to guests of all orientations.

Location plus low-key comfort add up to a great package at **◖ Cottages by the Sea** (127A Smithfield, 340/772-0495 or 800/323-7252, www.caribbeancottages.com, $160–220), a complex of 16 brightly painted wooden cottages on Dorsch Beach. Some cottages have beach views, but all are steps away from the sand. Each cottage has cable TV, a full kitchen, air-conditioning, fans, and a patio; they sleep between two and six people. Though not luxurious, Cottages offers a simplicity that many travelers will find exceptional.

CALDONIA RAINFOREST
Under $125
Tucked away in the rainforest, **(Mount Victory Camp** (Creque Dam Rd., 340/772-1651 or 866/772-1651, www.mtvictorycamp.com, $85–95) is a unique outdoor retreat. Bruce and Mathilde Wilson have constructed five hardwood bungalows on the hillside below their garden and home. Each is equipped with beds, a cold-water sink, a two-burner gas stove, dishes, and a dining table. Screens keep unwanted critters out at night. All campers share the tidy bathhouse and solar-heated showers. Campers fall asleep to the sounds of tree frogs and wake to birdsong.

EAST ISLAND
$125-175
Longford Hideaway (Longford Estate, 340/773-2386, www.longfordhideaway.com, $125) is a fully equipped one-bedroom cottage set on a working cattle and organic vegetable farm. Guests at the hideaway will be welcomed by the whole farm family—Velaria and Chicco Gasperi, their children, grandchildren, resident dogs, cats, chickens, and, of course, the Senepol cattle. The neat cottage has a full kitchen, air-conditioning, a pool, a porch, and TV. Guests can walk on trails around the farm and along the southern coast.

Accommodations at **Chenay Bay Beach Resort** (East End Rd., 340/718-2918 or 866/226-8677, www.chenaybay.com, $150–200) are in one- and two-bedroom Caribbean-style cottages, many of them with beach views.

Each air-conditioned cottage is equipped with a kitchenette, cable TV, and a private porch. The property could do with some updates, but it offers a good value and location. The beach is a long crescent with clear, calm water.

Over $300
Nearly all 46 rooms at **Tamarind Reef Hotel** (5001 Tamarind Reef, 340/773-4455 or 800/619-0014, www.tamarindreefresort.com, $275–325) have ocean views. The two-story hotel is right next door to Green Cay Marina and the Tamarind Reef Beach. Rooms have air-conditioning, cable TV, a coffeemaker, a refrigerator, a hair dryer, and a iron. Suites have a kitchenette and a dining area for four.

If luxury and exclusivity are what you want, **(The Buccaneer** (Gallows Bay, 340/712-2100 or 800/255-3881, www.thebuccaneer.com, $350–1,000) will provide them. The 138-room resort, which includes an 18-hole golf course, eight tennis courts, a spa, a beach, and three restaurants, set the standard for luxury on St. Croix when it opened in 1947 and continues to do so today. Rooms are well appointed, with window seats, generous balconies, and all the amenities you would expect from a classy resort. Rates include breakfast. Unique among large resorts these days, the Buccaneer has been owned and operated by the same family since it was established, and the resulting dedication to service is evident. The Buccaneer is located about two miles east of Christiansted.

Divi Carina Bay Resort (Turner Hole, 340/773-9700 or 877/773-9700, fax 340/773-6802, www.divicarina.com, $400–500) is the only large-scale accommodation on St. Croix's beautiful southeast shore. The 53-room beachfront resort is across the street from the casino that shares its name, but guests here don't necessarily have to be interested in gambling. Rooms at the all-inclusive resort sport a bright, modern decor, and all have balconies or patios overlooking the beach. Amenities include in-room refrigerators, coffeemakers, microwaves, cable TV, and data ports, as well as a pool, a water-sports center, a fitness center, and tennis courts. Room rates include all meals taken at the hotel's two restaurants

The Gasperi family operates **Castle Nugent Farm Caribbean Guesthouse** (340/773-1508, www.caribbeanguesthouse.com, $300), a three-bedroom historic guesthouse that is part of a working cattle farm.

Food

MARKETS
The original **St. Croix Farmer's Market** is a colorful, vibrant open-air market where farmers and fishermen come to sell locally grown produce, seafood, and baked goods. Located in La Reine, at the northwestern corner of the intersection between Highways 75 and 70, the market is open Saturday mornings from 7 A.M.–noon. Come before 9 A.M. for the best selection. Small-scale producers set up under an open-air pavilion with seasonal harvests: during the peak growing months (December to March) you will find tomatoes, eggplant, cucumbers, peppers, and a large selection of greens. If you don't need fresh vegetables, look for pastries, jams, and jellies available from some vendors. The fishermen set up on the outskirts and sell locally caught lobster, conch, snapper, tuna, and more. This is a great place to soak up St. Croix's diverse local culture and to find the fixings for dinner, too.

Other local farmstands include the **VI Farmer's Cooperative** (340/773-3276 or 340/277-6046), which sets up opposite the VI Health & Fitness Center at Beeston Hill, just outside of Christiansted, on Saturday mornings and other days in season; **ARTfarm** (340/514-4873, www.ARTfarmllc.com), along the South Shore Road on Wednesdays and Saturdays; and **VI Sustainable Farm Institute** (340/220-0466 or www.visfi.org), which has a market stand in Frederiksted weekly. Call ahead for details and to confirm opening days, especially during the summer, when things typically quiet down. In addition to advertised markets,

dozens of small-scale farmers and fishers set up daily along St. Croix's roadways and near busy stores. Pull over and see what you find.

For groceries of a more mundane nature, head to one of the island's many grocery stores. **Schooner Bay Marketplace** (Gallows Bay, 340/773-3232) is St. Croix's gourmet market with fresh produce, a large deli, and ready-made meals. There is a large **Pueblo** (340/773-0118) grocery store on Route 75, near the Orange Grove stoplight. A little farther west, on Route 75, is **Food Town** (LaGrande Princess, 340/692-9990), a good all-purpose supermarket. Many locals prefer the large **Plaza Extra** (14 Mount Pleasant, 340/719-1870) for size and selection. Plaza Extra is located on the Queen Mary Highway about midway between Sunny Isle and Frederiksted.

CHRISTIANSTED
Christiansted restaurants have some of the most creative and eclectic menus in the Virgin Islands. While there are a number of casual choices for lunch and breakfast, many Christiansted eateries are decidedly upscale at dinnertime.

Cafés and Coffee Shops
Take a break at the cool oasis **Lalita's Courtyard** (54 King St., 340/719-4417, 9:30 A.M.–9 P.M. Mon.–Sat., $6–22), a natural food restaurant specializing in raw, vegan, and otherwise wholesome food. The quiet gurgle of a fountain sets the mood for meals that nourish the body and awaken the senses.

© SUSANNA HENIGHAN POTTER

bananas, avocados, and other produce for sale at a roadside stand

Soups, salads, sandwiches, and light entrées are the mainstays of the menu; dishes like the spicy carrot soup, vegetable lasagna, and vegan cheesecake will win over meat eaters and delight vegetarians. Lalita also serves a wide selection of natural fruit smoothies and hot and cold herbal teas.

Twin City Gallery and Coffee Shop (2 Company St., 340/773-9400, 7 A.M.–3 P.M. Mon.–Sat., $6–15) is a small sidewalk café and the place to come for a good cup of coffee. The shop also serves breakfast and lunch.

International

Located a block east of Fort Christensvaern, **◖ Savant** (Hospital St., 340/713-8666, 6–10 P.M. Mon.–Sat., $19–39) serves a sophisticated menu that fuses Asian, Mexican, and Caribbean cuisine. Fresh seafood, inventive flavors, and an intimate, convivial atmosphere are the best reasons to come here. Whitewashed walls and the quiet murmur of jazz make for a

romantic setting, despite the nondescript exterior appearance. The flavors favor Mexico and Thailand but borrow Caribbean ingredients. The frozen key lime pie is a good ending to just about any meal. Reservations are highly recommended; otherwise, come early.

Bacchus (Queen Cross St., 340/692-992, 6–10 P.M. Tues.–Sat., $28–35) is a world-class restaurant serving American and French cuisine inside an old townhouse in historic Christiansted. Specialties include hand-cut steaks, local lobster, duck confit, lamb shank, and blackened salmon. Bacchus is noted for its extensive wine list, one of the best on the island, and the restaurant bakes its own sourdough bread daily. Finish off your meal with French-press coffee and red curry coconut cheesecake, and then enjoy an after-dinner drink and a game of billiards in the poolroom.

A long-time favorite for fans of truly fine food, **Kendricks** (Company St., 340/773-9199, 5–9:30 P.M. Tues.–Sat., $19–35) features the sophisticated cuisine of chef and owner Dave Kendrick, who has more than 25 years of experience in the kitchen. Dinner, served in the leafy courtyard of an historic Christiansted townhouse, features classics like pork loin, duck, lamb, tuna, and salmon. The homemade dinner rolls are spectacular. Kendricks also offers a bar menu ($10–14) with casual fare including potstickers, stuffed manicotti, and tuna tacos.

Take a culinary journey far away from the Virgin Islands at **Galangal** (17 Church St., 340/773-0076, 5:30–10 P.M., Tues.–Sat., $18–36), an impeccably run upscale restaurant serving southeast Asian cuisine. Stylish decor, attentive service, and authentic flavors make this a popular destination for locals who have tired of the same-old. Using local seafood and vegetables when possible, Galangal offers a selection of Thai curries, as well as steamed fish, Asian-style short ribs, and grilled pork tenderloin. Portions are modest. Proprietor Arthur Mayer has taken great care with the wine list, importing directly from Europe, and offers excellent pairing recommendations. Galangal is not a large restaurant, so reservations are highly recommended.

A charming courtyard restaurant with a loyal local following, **Cafe Christine** (6 Company St., 340/713-1500, 11:30–2:30 P.M., $8–15) serves salads, sandwiches, pastas, and entrées inspired by the native France of the café's owner. The small menu changes daily, but the food is consistent and above-average: no greasy fries or poorly conceived salads here. Fresh-baked bread, superior pâtés, crisp salads, and heavenly desserts are just a few of the reasons to make your way here. Call ahead to secure one of the charming courtyard tables (or any table at all). Christine's closes down for a couple months every summer.

Casual

Parrot's Cove (1102 Strand St., 340/773-6782,

11 A.M.–2 P.M. daily, $8–15) may have muddled the metaphor in its name, but the place does know a thing or two about mini burgers. This expansive upper deck bar and restaurant serves up the usual suspects (burgers, sandwiches, and salads), but also no fewer than 10 versions of its "sliders": mini burgers served by the six-pack. These hot, handmade burgers come in what must surely be fresh-baked rolls. Go for the original or try varieties including chicken-fried, blue cheese, jalepeño, or even fish.

Despite its name **Angry Nate's** (Christiansted Boardwalk, 340/713-9820, 11 A.M.–10 P.M. Mon.–Sat., 11 A.M.–8 P.M. Sun., $15–30) is a laid-back place for breakfast, lunch, or dinner, boasting an eclectic menu, bright yellow walls, and a lovely waterfront view. Seafood features prominently, and on Friday nights Nate's is the place to come for local lobster and fish fresh from the grill (and the sea). Nate's also serves a popular pub menu, hearty breakfast platters, and bottomless champagne at its Sunday brunch.

The **Fort Christian Brew Pub** (Christiansted Boardwalk, 340/713-9820, 11 A.M.–10 P.M. Mon.–Sat., 11 A.M.–8 P.M. Sun., $9–22) is a good go-to choice for a meal in Christiansted, if only for the setting. Located in the heart of the Christiansted boardwalk, the Brew Pub gives you a pleasant vantage point on the harbor and the foot traffic in town. The menu includes barbecue, burgers, salads, pastas, and steak, but some of the best dishes come with a spicy Cajun accent. The pub is also a microbrewery.

West Indian

For local Crucian fare, the best destination in Christiansted is **Harvey's** (11B Company St., 340/773-3343, 11 A.M.–4 P.M. Mon.–Sat., $10–24), an island institution easily located by the mural of St. Croix native and NBA star Tim Duncan on the exterior. Chefs prepare a half-dozen daily specials, ranging from stewed mutton to fried fish to conch. Meals are served with traditional side dishes such as fungi, peas and rice, fried plantain, and potato salad, and you can finish your meal with a slice of homemade guava, coconut, or pineapple tart.

Mediterranean

Italian for "everything good," **Tuttu Bene** (Boardwalk Building, Hospital St., 340/773-5229, 6–10 P.M. nightly, $14–35) is the gold standard of Italian eating on St. Croix. Specialties include pizza, veal saltimbocca, spaghetti bolognese, and oven-roasted duck. Tuttu Bene is located in a small shopping plaza just east of Christiansted, before the turnoff for Gallows Bay. In season Tuttu Bene serves a limited lunch menu from 11 A.M. (Tues.–Fri.).

Drive about half a mile east of Christiansted to find **The Pickled Greek** (5A Estate St. Peter, 340/713-1868, 11 A.M.–10 P.M. Mon.–Fri., 3–10 P.M. Sat., $15–25), a friendly little Greek restaurant serving homestyle food and hospitality. The menu offers all the standard Greek favorites: moussaka, kebabs, roasted chicken, falafel, baklava, and more. Or be adventurous and try Yia-Yia Stew, a vegetarian house specialty. The Pickled Greek offers $12 lunch specials during the week, and also a kid's menu.

Ice Cream

Sorbet made from organic island fruits is on the menu at **Jaccar Organic and Natural Sorbet** (Arawak Building, Gallows Bay, 340/719-6999, 10 A.M.–5:30 P.M. Tues.–Sat., $3–5). Try mango mint, pineapple ginger, carambola, soursop, strawberry sorrel, or any one of the dozens of other inventive flavors. Jaccar also serves Italian-style gelato in a range of flavors, as well as cookies and fruit drinks.

FREDERIKSTED
International

A Frederiksted institution, **Blue Moon** (7 Strand St., 340/772-2222, 11 A.M.–2 P.M. Tues.–Fri., 6 P.M.–late Tues.–Sat., 11 A.M.–2 P.M. Sun.) is known for good food and mellow jazz. Set on the Frederiksted waterfront, this cheery restaurant serves an eclectic menu with a Cajun flair. At lunch ($10–18), order fresh salads or sandwiches. For dinner ($25–28), choose from dishes like roasted duck in Asian-style glaze or the Blue Moon's signature New Orleans pasta with sausage, shrimp, and creamy alfredo sauce. The Sunday brunch with pancakes, French toast, and omelets is also popular. There is live jazz on Wednesday and Friday nights.

A mile or so south of Frederiksted at Sandcastle by the Sea, the **Beachside Café** (127 Smithfield, 340/772-1205, 6–9 P.M. Fri.–Mon., 11 A.M.–3 P.M. Mon.–Sat., 10 A.M.–3 P.M. Sun., $12–35) serves salads, sandwiches, and burgers at lunch and more upscale fare at dinner. The mussels, fresh-baked bread, lamb chops, and scallops are popular, and wine lovers will appreciate the extensive wine list and pairing option. Flavors span the globe, with Asian, French, and Caribbean influences especially apparent. The café is a popular choice for Sunday brunch; after mimosas and French toast it's just a few steps to some of the best beach real estate for your Sunday afternoon. Like at all the eateries along the west coast, the sunsets here are spectacular.

Casual

For the best sandwiches on St Croix, head to the southern end of Fredricksted and **Turtles Deli** (37 Strand St., Prince Passage, 340/772-3676, 8:30 A.M.–5:30 P.M. Mon.–Fri.), an island institution where the staff bake the bread and take their time with each and every sandwich. Step inside to the dimly lit counter to place your order, and then grab a seat in the seaside courtyard to wait for your meal. Signature choices include the Mushroom Melt, BLT, Tuna Melt, and Smoked Turkey Special. If you're really hungry, go for the Turtles Sub, a massive sandwich with three kinds of meat and two types of cheese. You can order halves of most sandwiches and combine that with a side salad if you choose.

Fredricksted stands out as home to two excellent, but very different, vegetarian restaurants. **Polly's at the Pier** (3 Strand St., 340/719-9434, 7 A.M.–6 P.M. Mon.–Fri., 8 A.M.–5 P.M. Sat.–Sun., $9–12) has a few carnivorous options daily, but the stars of the show are her creative salads and wraps made with locally grown produce, the homemade veggie burgers, stellar grilled cheese sandwiches, and Polly's smoothies, which come in a wide variety of local fruit blends. Polly's also serves a wide selection of coffees and teas, as well as baked goods. Light, airy, and a hub for locals and tourists, Polly's is a pleasant place for a lunch hour or pit stop. When it's crowded, service can be a bit slow.

Rastafarian vegetarian cooking, better known as *ital*, is what's on the menu at the barn-like ◖ **UCA Kitchen** (71B King St., 340/772-5063, 12:30 P.M. until the food is finished Mon.–Sat., $6–12), located across the street from Buddhoe Park, near Fort Frederick. Daily specials vary, but expect choices like stewed tofu, ital soup, and spicy black-eyed peas. Portions are hearty. UCA Kitchen is also a great place to sample local drinks made from fruits (soursop, tamarind), flowers (hibiscus), plants (chlorophyll, made from a mixture of grasses, including local guinea grass and lemongrass), and even nuts (peanut punch, a traditional island drink made from peanuts, milk, and a selection of spices). For a snack, buy a bag of spiced popcorn or one of the vegan muffins. Venture away from the familiar and enjoy a meal here. It will be one of the more memorable of your vacation.

WEST COAST
International
Near the turnoff to Creque Dam Road, **Bernie's Beachfront Cafe** (Rte. 63,

340/772-5855, 11:30 A.M.–9 P.M. daily, $9–27) serves both an all-day bar menu and daily sandwich, salad, and dinner specials. Dining is either on the open-air patio or on the beach with the sand between your toes. Both afford excellent views.

NORTH SHORE
Casual
Occupying a prime piece of real estate in the center of popular Cane Bay, ◖ **eat @ cane bay** (Cane Bay, 340/718-0360, 11 A.M.–9 P.M. Mon. and Wed.–Sat., 11 A.M.–4 P.M. Sun., $10–14) is not your average beach bar. Waitstaff deliver classy build-your-own burgers and meal-sized salads to diners in the open-air dining room that blurs the line between youthful hangout and sophisticated eatery. An extensive wine and cocktail menu, kids' specials, and a handful of distinctive sandwiches and entrées, including the Cane Bay Rueben and "drunks-up" mussels round out the options. Don't forget tempting add-ons like sweet potato fries, hand-cut onion rings, grilled garlic bread, and a knock-your-socks-off rum cake. eat also serves a popular Sunday brunch menu.

WEST ISLAND
West Indian
For good local food in a homey, welcoming setting, try **Villa Morales** (Estate Whim, 340/772-0556, 10 A.M.–10 P.M. Thurs.–Sat., $16–35). This family-run restaurant serves traditional Crucian dishes, many with a Spanish accent. Chef Angela Morales prepares dishes like conch in butter sauce, roast pork, grilled fish, and lobster. This is a casual outdoor restaurant with plenty of seating and a warm welcome.

Ice Cream
Armstrong's Homemade Ice Cream (Queen Mary Hwy., 340/772-1919, 7 A.M.–7 P.M. Mon.–Sat., 11 A.M.–7 P.M. Sun., $4–8) is a favorite stop for locals. Ice cream

cones start at $2. The shop also serves hearty American-style breakfasts and lunch sandwiches. The grill closes at 2:30 P.M. daily.

MID ISLAND

The center of St. Croix is a mangle of traffic lights, shopping centers, and open space and not the most obvious destination for excellent food. The adventurous diner will find some reasons to venture off the beaten track, however.

West Indian

Bring an appetite to **La Reine Chicken Shack** (Estate LaReine, 340/778-5717, 10:30 A.M.–5 P.M. daily, $8–13), a local favorite for specialties such as stewed mutton (goat), conch in butter sauce, and fried fish. The most popular item at the Chicken Shack, however, is the $9 plate of roasted chicken, which includes seasoned rice, stewed red beans, salad, and half a slow-roasted chicken, expertly seasoned and hot off the fire. Ask for a side of tangy BBQ sauce if you like. You can choose to substitute or add other side items, including Crucian-style macaroni pie, coleslaw, and potato stuffing, a baked casserole of mashed potatoes like nothing you've had before. Portions at the Chicken Shack are generous to say the least—a plate of food will easily feed two or even three people.

To find the Chicken Shack, turn north on Route 75 at La Reine and look for the smoke escaping from the grill. It is located adjacent to the site of the weekly La Reine farmers market.

Bakery

The smell of fresh-baked bread, cakes, and pastries greets you at the door of **Thomas Bakery** (1Da Estate Diamond, 340/778-2625, 5 A.M.–7 P.M. Mon.–Sat., 5 A.M.–1 P.M. Sun., $1–4), an island institution. Come for a loaf of traditional bread (white or wheat), cakes such as St. Croix's signature seven-layer Vienna cake,

and an assortment of sweet buns, popovers, and irresistible single-serving fruit tarts, made the old-fashioned St. Croix way. To find Thomas, look for a faded white sign on Route 70, just past the Carib Do-It-Best building supply store and across from the side entrance to Sunny Isle Shopping Center. Then follow your nose (and all the other cars) to the nondescript two-story white building that houses the bakery.

EAST ISLAND
Casual

One of the best casual restaurants on the east end, **Cheeseburgers in Paradise** (Estate Southgate, 340/773-1119, 11 A.M.–10 P.M. daily, $8–15) serves burgers of every stripe, as well as burritos and daily specials. This roadside joint is a popular stop for east enders on their way home or for families looking for an affordable, kid-friendly place to eat.

International

Chef Diane Marie Scheuber serves handmade pasta, homemade bread, generous salads, and fresh meat and fish at the **Southshore Café** (Petronella Dairy, 340/773-9311, 6–8:30 P.M. Wed.–Sun., $17–27). Set in an old dairy farm, the Southshore Café has nice views of Great Pond and the south shore. The atmosphere is relaxing and classy, with a little twist of funk.

Long associated with some of the best fresh seafood on the island, **Duggan's Reef** (East End Rd., Teague Bay, 340/773-9800, 6–9 P.M. daily, 11 A.M.–2 P.M. Sun., $18–35) offers some of the most reliably good food on the island. Steaks and seafood—especially lobster—are the specialties, but you'll also find excellent chicken and pasta. The informal setting overlooking Buck Island belies the quality of the food you'll be eating. Call ahead to find out if it's open for lunch.

Practicalities

INFORMATION AND SERVICES
Tourist Offices
The **U.S. Virgin Islands Department of Tourism** (Government House, 340/773-1404, 8 A.M.–5 P.M. Mon.–Fri.) has a visitor information center in Christiansted. The office is accessible via Government House or from a storefront on King Cross Street.

For information on the island's three national parks—Christiansted, Salt River Bay, and Buck Island—contact the **National Park Service** (Old Scale House, Christiansted, 340/773-1460, 8 A.M.–5 P.M. Mon.–Fri., 9 A.M.–5 P.M. Sat.–Sun.). The park rangers and other staff on duty there are helpful and stock a wide variety of useful brochures behind the counter—just ask.

Maps and Charts
The free, pocket-size map of St. Croix that is widely available from car rental agencies and hotels will meet the needs of most visitors. Roads and major attractions are clearly marked. **St. Croix This Week,** the free monthly tourist magazine, publishes an island map that also shows the locations of most hotels and restaurants, which can be helpful.

Detailed topographical maps are available from the **National Park Service** shop in Christiansted. Nautical charts can be found at **St. Croix Marine** (Gallows Bay, 340/773-0289).

Libraries
In Christiansted, the **Florence Williams Public Library** (King St., 340/773-5715, 9 A.M.–4:45 P.M. Mon.–Fri.) has a good collection of books and magazines and Internet access for a small fee.

Frederiksted's **Althalie Peterson Library** (Strand St., 340/772-0315, 10 A.M.–4:45 P.M. Mon.–Fri.), located in the historic Bell house, also has Internet access and a nice collection of books.

Media
The **St. Croix Avis** is headquartered and published on St. Croix. The St. Thomas–based **Virgin Islands Daily News** (www.virginislandsdailynews.com) also covers St. Croix happenings. The *Avis* comes out every day but Monday; the Daily News takes Sundays off. Both are widely available at newsstands.

St. Croix–based **WSVI,** an ABC affiliate, broadcasts local news, complete with a weather forecast, weekdays at 7 P.M. on channel 8. St. Thomas–based **TV 2** does the same on channel 2. Tune in to **95.1 FM (Isle 95)** for music and news.

Emergencies
The **Juan Louis Hospital** (Rte. 79, 340/778-1634) in Kingshill is a modern, full-service facility, with complete emergency services. The **Virgin Islands Police Department** (340/778-2211) has stations around the island. Call 911 in an emergency. **V.I. Search and Rescue** (340/773-7150) responds to reports of missing persons and vessels at sea.

Banks
Several U.S. and Canadian banks operate on St. Croix. Both **Banco Popular de Puerto Rico** and **First Bank VI** have branches and ATMs at Orange Grove and Sunny Isle.

Most establishments welcome credit cards, but always check. Personal checks are generally not accepted from visitors.

Post Offices
The U.S. Postal Service operates on St. Croix, and rates are the same as in the continental United States. Post offices are located in downtown Christiansted (100 Church St.,

340/773-3586), outside Christiansted (103-104 Richmond, 340/773-1505), in Gallows Bay (No. 118 Estate Welcome, 340/773-4538), in Frederiksted (No. 1 Mars Hill, 340/772-0040), in Kingshill (No. 2 Estate LaReine, 340/778-0199), and at Sunny Isle Shopping Center (340/778-6805).

Communications

In Christiansted, the best place to check your email is **Strand Street Station Internet Café** (1102 Strand St., 340/719-6245, 8 A.M.–6 P.M.). You will pay $4 for 15 minutes. Staff can also help you with copies, faxes, calls, and photo processing.

Customs and Immigration

You must clear customs when you leave St. Croix. Departing passengers will be asked to fill out a customs declaration form (members of a family residing together may make a joint declaration), and your bags are subject to search. U.S. Customs officers are on duty at the airport and at their offices at Five Corners on Route 75 (340/773-5650).

U.S. Immigration and Naturalization officers are stationed at Henry E. Rohlsen Airport (340/778-1419). The INS department's administration offices are located at Sunny Isle Shopping Center (340/778-6559).

Launderettes

La Reine Laundry (Barren Spot, 340/778-2801, 5:30 A.M.–11 P.M. Mon.–Thurs., 4 A.M.–11 P.M. Fri.–Sun.) is a large launderette on Centerline Road, where you will find supersize washers and plenty of dryers.

Another large full-service laundry is **S&S Laundry** (Grove Pl., 340/692-1010, 6 A.M.–9 P.M. Mon.–Thurs., 5:30 A.M.–10 P.M. Fri.–Sun.). A single wash will cost about $1.50.

GETTING THERE
By Air

St. Croix's **Henry E. Rohlsen Airport (STX)** is located on the island's southwest coast, nine miles south of Christiansted and six miles southeast of Frederiksted. The terminal is open from 5:30 A.M. to 11 P.M. daily; the 10,000-foot runway remains open 24 hours a day. Taxis meet all scheduled flights; car rental counters are open during business hours, and sometimes later. Arrangements can be made for late arrivals.

From the United States: Delta Airlines (www.delta.com), American Airlines (www.aa.com), and U.S. Airways (www.usairways) offer seasonal nonstop service to St. Croix from Atlanta, Miami, and Charlotte. If you cannot get a direct flight, route through San Juan, Puerto Rico, where you can catch a commuter flight with American Eagle (www.aa.com) or Cape Air (www.flycapeair.com) to St. Croix. You can also fly through St. Thomas and take Seaborne Airline's airport shuttle to St. Croix.

From Puerto Rico: Commuter airlines American Eagle and Cape Air provide regular scheduled service between San Juan International Airport and St. Croix's Rohlsen Airport. In addition, Seaborne Airlines (34 Strand St., Christiansted, 340/773-6442 or 888/359-8687, www.seaborneairlines.com) provides seaplane service from Old San Juan Harbour to Christiansted Harbor, via St. Thomas.

From St. Thomas: Seaborne Airlines (34 Strand St., Christiansted, 340/773-6442 or 888/359-8687, www.seaborneairlines.com) has up to 15 flights daily between St. Thomas and St. Croix, leaving from the seaplane terminals on the Christiansted and Charlotte Amalie waterfronts. Nothing beats the convenience of the seaplane—there are no airport hassles—but beware the baggage restrictions; you will be charged 50 cents for every pound over 30. Seaborne also flies between the St. Thomas and St. Croix airports several times per day.

From the Eastern Caribbean: Leeward Islands Air Transport, or LIAT (340/778-9930, www.liatairline.com) flies to St. Croix from Caribbean destinations including Antigua and Barbados.

By Sea

Sea Trans (340/776-5494) provides ferry service between St. Thomas and St. Croix four days per week. The 75-minute trip costs $90 roundtrip. Call ahead to confirm availability.

GETTING AROUND
Taxis

Taxis are widely available on St. Croix. Taxi stands are located on King Street in Christiansted, near Government House, and on Market Street. In Frederiksted, there is a taxi stand near Fort Frederik. If you need a pick-up, try **Richardson's Taxi** (340/778-8392 or 340/690-8871), **Frederiksted Taxi Service** (Frederiksted, 340/772-4775), **Rudy's Taxi** (340/773-6803 or 340/514-4600), or the **St. Croix Taxi Association** (Henry E. Rohlsen Airport, 340/778-1088).

Taxi rates are set by the government's Taxi Commission (340/773-8294), which also fields complaints on taxi service and can help trace lost luggage. The rate for one or two people from the airport to Christiansted is $16 per person, from the airport to Frederiksted is $12 per person, and from Christiansted to Frederiksted is $24 per person. Check *St. Croix This Week* for current rates. Luggage is charged at $2 for each bag. For oversized luggage, agree on a price ahead of time. A premium of $2 is charged on trips between midnight and 6 A.M. The minimum fare in town is $5. Taxis that have been called will charge the base rate plus a premium of one-third the base rate.

Buses

VITRAN buses operate between 5:30 A.M. and 9:30 P.M. Monday–Saturday. The bus route begins at Tide Village east of Christiansted and ends at Fort Frederik, following Centerline Road. The fare is $1 for adults, and 25 cents for transfers. Adults over 55 pay 55 cents. Exact change is required. For schedule information, call 340/778-0898 or 340/773-1290, but remember that the only thing certain about VITRAN is that it will not run on schedule. Look for the VITRAN signs marking pick-up locations.

Informal, open-air taxis, called the "dollar bus," run frequently between Frederiksted and Christiansted along Centerline Road, stopping at Sunny Isle Shopping Center. Although there is no official schedule or route, these are a pretty reliable way to get around during daylight hours if you already know your way around the island. The fare is $2 per person. At night, stick to official taxis.

Car Rentals

Reserve your rental car early for the best rates. Expect to pay between $45 and $55 per day, although you can sometimes find a better rate if you book early or for an extended period. National rental chains including **Hertz** (340/778-1402, www.rentacarstcroix.com), **Budget** (888/264-8894, www.budget.com), and **Avis** (340/778-9355, www.avis.com) have counters at the Henry E. Rohlsen Airport and at resorts and other locations throughout the island. Avis and Budget have locations at or very near the seaplane terminal in Christiansted.

Independent rental agencies include **Centerline Car Rental** (LaReine, 340/778-0450 or 888/288-8755, www.centerlinecarrentals.com); **Judi of St. Croix** (4017 Herman Hill, 340/773-2123 or 877/903-2123, www.judiofcroix.com); **Olympic-Ace Rent-a-Car** (1103 Richmond, 340/773-8000 or 888/878-4227, www.stcroixcarrentals.com); and **Skyline Rentals** (LaReine, 340/719-5990 or 877/719-5990).

TORTOLA

Tortola is the hub of the British Virgin Islands: home to its quaint capital, its modern airport, its magnificent beaches, and the most wide-ranging array of activities, accommodations, and restaurants in the territory. The island's spine runs east to west, punctuated by ridges that descend to the Atlantic Ocean to the north and the Caribbean Sea to the south. Between these ridges are bays, some edged by sandy beaches and seaside communities. High hills and steep, winding roads make exploring exciting (or terrifying, depending on your perspective), and the views that greet you from the top will take your breath away. At its longest, Tortola extends 12 miles; at its widest, it is 3 miles across. Its southern shore, washed by the Caribbean Sea, is generally calm and is home to marinas and the largest settlements. The north shore has the best beaches and, in season, the best waves.

Tortola is an island of contrasts—a place where stray chickens share the roadways with the latest-model cars and trucks. Of all the British Virgin Islands it is the most developed—three-quarters of the territory's 23,000 people live here—and as such it is the island most acquainted with the scourges of development: crime, traffic jams, and environmental damage. But despite the inroads of change, Tortola is still by and large a sleepy, green jewel willing to content itself with the daily rhythms of life.

Though it is touched in places by large-scale

HIGHLIGHTS

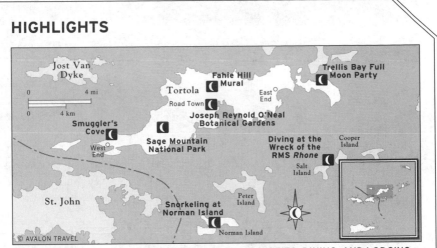

LOOK FOR ◖ TO FIND RECOMMENDED SIGHTS, ACTIVITIES, DINING, AND LODGING.

◖ **Joseph Reynold O'Neal Botanical Gardens:** A four-acre oasis in the heart of Road Town, these botanical gardens are a living museum of colorful and unusual tropical plants and animals (page 177).

◖ **Fahie Hill Mural:** An ode to Tortola's past, this colorful mural painted on a roadside retaining wall depicts islanders' way of life after emancipation but before widespread development (page 179).

◖ **Sage Mountain National Park:** Cool, moist, and remote, Tortola's Sage Mountain is the highest point in the Virgin Islands and a hiker's dream (page 180).

◖ **Smuggler's Cove:** Is this a perfect beach, or is it just me? Coconut palms, fine white sand, a small reef, protected waters, and an utterly peaceful atmosphere—this is the reason you came to the Caribbean (page 189).

◖ **Trellis Bay Full Moon Party:** This funky full moon celebration on Beef Island features traditional music, arts, and Aragorn Dick-Read's flaming fireballs (page 191).

◖ **Snorkeling at Norman Island:** Explore underwater caves and the remarkable reef surrounding the Indians at Norman Island, one of the best destinations in the BVI for snorkeling and diving (page 215).

◖ **Diving at the Wreck of the RMS** *Rhone:* Swim past portholes, cabins, and the propeller of the RMS *Rhone*, sharing the experience with a dizzying variety of fish. This is believed by some to be the best wreck dive in the Caribbean (page 220).

development, Tortola remains a rustic island. For visitors, it offers a comfortable balance between creature comforts (grocery stores, nice restaurants, a hospital) and the obscure (dirt roads, braying donkeys, quiet mountain peaks, and dusty mom-and-pop shops). Tortola has a more "regular people" feel than Virgin Gorda and St. John—there are accommodations and

attractions for nearly every budget—and it is far less commercial than St. Thomas.

Tortola is an island that caters to a wide range of tastes and interests. It is an ideal jumping-off point for water-based pursuits: Sailing, diving, snorkeling, and windsurfing are the most popular. Its marinas are home to the Virgin Islands' largest fleet of charter yachts.

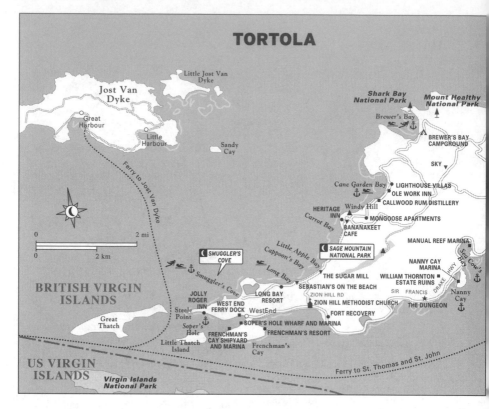

Landlubbers will find two excellent national parks, several historical attractions, and dozens of quiet, undisturbed beaches. Meals can be had from the capital's jerk chicken stands or under the stars at a fine restaurant.

Planning Your Time

You could visit all of Tortola's major attractions in a day, but why would you want to? People don't exhaust themselves with that kind of frenzied activity here, and you would be silly to buck the trend. The whole point of vacationing in a place like Tortola is to slow down. Ten days is enough time to explore Tortola, figuring in a few do-nothing days spent on the beach and one or two day trips to surrounding islands.

Where to Stay

Look for accommodations outside of Road Town—the capital city offers little in the way of ambience. If your first priority is the beach and your second is the beach bar, you will be happiest at Cane Garden Bay, the island's premier beach, with the widest array of accommodations, restaurants, and entertainment choices. The only downside—and it can be significant depending on your disposition—is the throngs of cruise ship visitors that descend on the bay many days from October to March.

If you prefer to make a quieter beach your home base, look for places to stay near Apple Bay, Brewer's Bay, or Josiah's Bay—all nice beaches that lean toward the quiet side. Remember that accommodations away

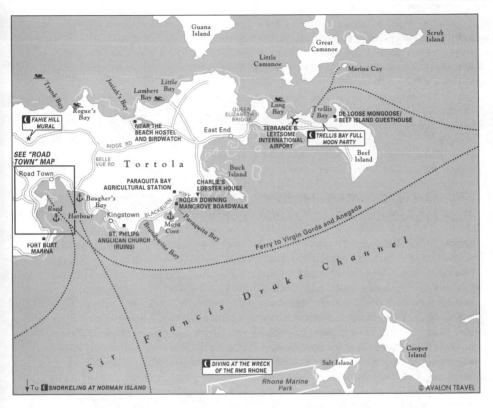

from the beach can be a good value, and hillside rooms generally have better views and more breeze than those directly on the water. Nowhere on Tortola is more than 10 minutes from a beach.

Day Trips

Tortola makes a convenient day trip from St. Thomas, St. John, or Virgin Gorda. If you have only a day, take an open-air island tour and spend a few hours at one of the beaches: Cane Garden Bay if no cruise ship is in port; Smuggler's Cove, Josiah's Bay, or Brewer's Bay otherwise. Add on a hike at Sage Mountain National Park or a stroll through the Joseph Reynold O'Neal Botanical Gardens if you have time.

If you're staying on Tortola, you have a lot of options for day trips: St. John and St. Thomas, Virgin Gorda, Jost Van Dyke, Anegada, Peter Island, Marina Cay, and Norman Island are all popular and convenient choices.

Ferries depart from docks and marinas all over the island; they range from large interisland catamarans to supply boats with room for a few passengers. From West End, you can catch ferries to St. Thomas (30 minutes, $45 round-trip), St. John (20 minutes, $45 round-trip) and Jost Van Dyke (30 minutes, $25 round-trip). From Road Town, boats sail to St. Thomas (1 hour, $45 round-trip), Virgin Gorda (30 minutes, $30 round-trip), and Anegada (75 minutes, $50 round-trip). You can also take a ferry from Trellis Bay to Virgin Gorda (30 minutes, $45).

Many resorts and restaurants offer **free ferry service;** you only have to dine at the resort or restaurant giving you a ride to the island. These private ferries operate from Baugher's Bay, near Road Town, to Peter Island (20 minutes, free); from Palastina to The Bight, Norman Island (20 minutes, free); and from Trellis Bay to Marina Cay (5 minutes, free) and Scrub Island (10 minutes, free). While advance reservations are not required for public ferries, it's a good idea to call ahead to confirm the private ones. It is also possible to hitch a ride to Cooper Island with dive guides **Sail Caribbean** (Hodges Creek, www.sailcaribbean.com, 284/495-3244), for $15 round trip.

Day sail operators are scattered around the island, but you will find most operators in Sopers Hole (West End), Road Town, or Hodges Creek Marina (East End). Advance reservations for day sails are essentia, especially during high season.

Sights

ROAD TOWN

The capital of the British Virgin Islands, Road Town sprawls along the shore of Road Harbour, its namesake, a deepwater port on the south-central Caribbean coast of Tortola. ("Road" was once a common word for a harbor. Early writings refer to this area of Tortola simply as "The Road.") Steep hillsides rush down to the shore on all sides, creating what looks like a giant amphitheater, with Road Town as the stage.

Road Town is like an adolescent who has reached the awkward stage. Planning here has been haphazard, the effects being poor traffic design, lack of parking, and spotty sidewalks. A recent effort to build more sidewalks, plant trees, install traffic signals, and create crosswalks has improved things slightly but has not resolved the traffic gridlock that strikes at rush hour.

Road Town possesses little of the old-world charm found in other port towns of the Virgin Islands. After all, it operated in the shadow of ports like Charlotte Amalie and Christiansted during the plantation era. A townwide fire in 1853 did not help things.

Despite its flaws, Road Town has a certain appeal, embodied by its ramshackle appearance, roaming chickens, and constant ebb and flow of people.

Road Town's main thoroughfare is Waterfront Drive, which follows the waterfront as far as the Crafts Alive shopping area before turning inland. Waterfront Drive ends at Road Town's main roundabout, where the town's central arteries meet, and runs roughly parallel to Main Street.

The best bets for parking in Road Town are the public lots on either side of the Road Town ferry terminal, on the waterfront.

Road Town is generally safe, although occasional muggings and break-ins at night signal a need for caution. Scatliffe Alley, a narrow road that runs from the Sunday Morning Well to the Fire and Rescue Station, is best avoided.

Main Street

There is no better place to soak up Road Town's charm, such as it is, than on narrow and winding Main Street, home to historic buildings, museums, boutiques, and cafés. It is a wonderful place for an early morning or late afternoon stroll and has the best shopping on Tortola.

Explore Main Street on foot; it simply is not practical or pleasant to navigate it in a car. The sights presented here can easily be turned into a walking tour that begins at Old Government House, on the western end of Main Street, and concludes at the House of Assembly in the center of town. From there you can easily find the

Joseph Reynold O'Neal Botanical Gardens, about two blocks away. Plan on at least one hour for this one-mile walk, more if you spend a lot of time in the shops and museums.

OLD GOVERNMENT HOUSE MUSEUM

Old Government House Museum (284/494-4091, www.oghm.org, 9 A.M.–3 P.M. Mon.–Fri., adults $3, children under 10 free), on the hill behind the Governor's Office at the western end of Main Street, is a study of the island's colonial past and present. The white, Spanish-inspired home was built in the late 1920s after the original Government House was destroyed in a powerful 1924 hurricane. The building served as the home of the island's British governor until the mid-1990s, when it was decided it was no longer up to the task. While in use, it was often referred to as "Olympus" by islanders because of its position overlooking Road Town and, presumably, because of the superior attitude of those who inhabited it.

After years of debate over the future of the building—and a very real proposal to tear it down—Government House underwent modest restoration and reopened as a museum in 2003. A new residence for the governor was built next to the old one.

The museum's exhibits include historic paraphernalia, such as a guest book signed by Queen Elizabeth II and the plumed pith helmet worn by governors at parades and ceremonial occasions up until 2000. The dining and sitting rooms of the museum are set up as they would have been during earlier days. Upstairs is a library that contains an ad hoc but rich selection of books and articles about the British Virgin Islands. Other rooms are dedicated to the British Virgin Islands' Quaker history and its stamps.

The best thing about the museum is being able to see inside this stately and singular building, an experience that will take you back in time if you let it. There are also nice views of Road Harbour from the museum's second-floor veranda and a small garden at the rear, where you can stroll or sit. The museum's shop sells books, crafts, and gifts.

Old Government House Museum occasionally opens on Saturdays for tours; call ahead.

SIR OLVA GEORGES PLAZA

Across from the downtown ferry jetty is the Sir Olva Georges Plaza, named for the first British Virgin Islander to be knighted by the queen. Sir Olva lived on Main Street in a home that has now been converted into a trendy restaurant. Before reclamation changed the shoreline, Sir Olva Georges Plaza served as the main jetty and market square for Tortola. During slavery, it was the site of slave auctions. After emancipation, the square retained its prominence as a center for trade and commerce. A 1920s visitor described the weekly market held there:

> The sellers mostly squatted on the ground with their produce in front of them in calabashes, in trays, or displayed on old sacking. Everyone appeared radiant as the sun and the sea, exchanging greetings of the marketplace, chattering and gesticulating whether anyone attended or no?.... A row of brown sloops from the islands lay moored alongside the white glare of the wharf, their sails furled, lazily rocking in the blue-lit waters.

Today, the plaza is a quiet place to sit, rest, and watch the comings and goings of Road Town. It comes to life for occasional events and performances, especially at Christmas.

Across Main Street from Sir Olva Georges Plaza is the **Old Administration Building,** which today houses government offices. It was from this building that the British Virgin Islands were administered for many years, until the mammoth Central Administration Building was completed in 1993 and most offices moved there.

TORTOLA

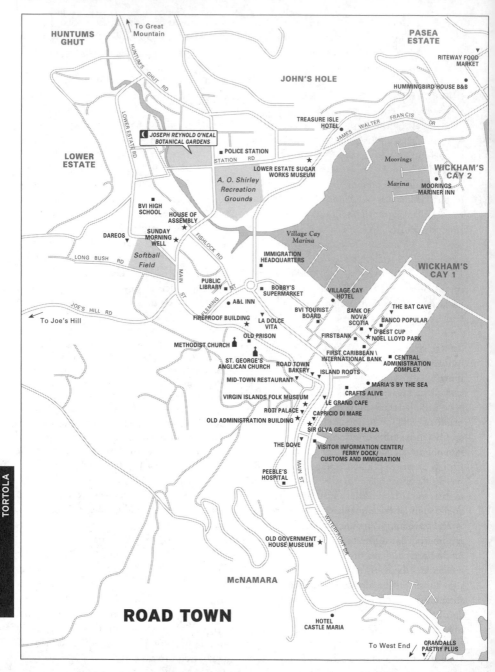

HUNTUMS
GHUT

To Great
Mountain

PASEA
ESTATE

RITEWAY FOOD
MARKET

JOHN'S HOLE

HUMMINGBIRD HOUSE B&B

TREASURE ISLE
HOTEL

JOSEPH REYNOLD O'NEAL
BOTANICAL GARDENS

POLICE STATION

Moorings

WICKHAM'S
CAY 2

LOWER
ESTATE

LOWER ESTATE SUGAR
WORKS MUSEUM

Marina

MOORINGS
MARINER INN

A. O. Shirley
Recreation
Grounds

BVI HIGH
SCHOOL

HOUSE OF
ASSEMBLY

DAREOS

SUNDAY
MORNING
WELL

Village Cay
Marina

LONG BUSH RD

Softball
Field

IMMIGRATION
HEADQUARTERS

WICKHAM'S
CAY 1

JOE'S HILL RD

To Joe's Hill

PUBLIC
LIBRARY

BOBBY'S
SUPERMARKET

VILLAGE CAY
HOTEL

THE BAT CAVE

A&L INN

BVI TOURIST
BOARD

BANK OF
NOVA
SCOTIA

BANCO POPULAR

FIREPROOF BUILDING

LA DOLCE
VITA

FIRSTBANK

D'BEST CUP
NOEL LLOYD PARK

OLD PRISON

METHODIST CHURCH

FIRST CARIBBEAN \
INTERNATIONAL BANK

CENTRAL
ADMINISTRATION
COMPLEX

ST. GEORGE'S
ANGLICAN CHURCH

ROAD TOWN
BAKERY

ISLAND ROOTS

MID-TOWN RESTAURANT

MARIA'S BY THE SEA

CRAFTS ALIVE

VIRGIN ISLANDS FOLK MUSEUM

LE GRAND CAFE

ROTI PALACE

CAPRICIO DI MARE

OLD ADMINISTRATION BUILDING

SIR OLVA GEORGES PLAZA

THE DOVE

VISITOR INFORMATION CENTER/
FERRY DOCK/
CUSTOMS AND IMMIGRATION

PEEBLE'S
HOSPITAL

OLD GOVERNMENT
HOUSE MUSEUM

McNAMARA

ROAD TOWN

HOTEL
CASTLE MARIA

To West End

CRANDALLS
PASTRY PLUS

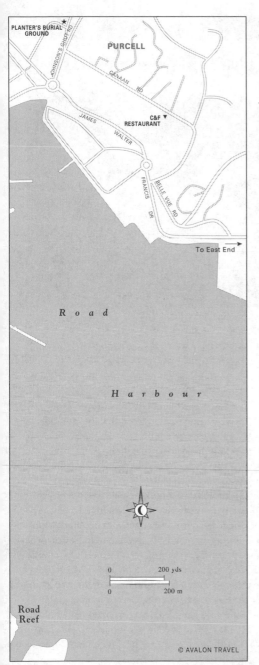

THE VIRGIN ISLANDS FOLK MUSEUM

The Virgin Islands Folk Museum (98 Main St., 284/494-3701, ext. 5005, 8:30 A.M.–4:30 P.M. Mon.–Fri., free) is up a short flight of stairs in a traditional home built by shipwright Joseph Wilfred Penn in 1911. The three-room museum houses a small collection of pre-Columbian and plantation-era artifacts, an exhibit of traditional architecture, and crockery salvaged from the wreck of the RMS *Rhone,* which sank off Salt Island in 1867. There is no razzle-dazzle to the exhibits, but if you are truly interested in the BVI's history, the museum is a valuable resource. A small shop in the rear sells contemporary arts and crafts, books, and T-shirts. The museum is occasionally closed during its regular hours; call ahead to confirm.

UPPER MAIN STREET

The long, low **Old Customs House,** home to a coffee shop, marks the division between Lower Main Street and Upper Main Street, where the street makes a sharp left turn and heads farther inland. The corner is known locally as Fonseca Corner, named after a prominent Road Town family that lived there.

The picturesque **St. George's Anglican Church** (170 Main St., 284/493-3894) is one of the oldest houses of worship on Tortola. All the early church records were lost in 1819 when a hurricane destroyed the building. Following emancipation, the church served as a school and community center for the residents of Road Town.

A few steps farther up Main Street is the **Road Town Methodist Church** (186 Main St., 284/494-2198), centerpiece of the other long-standing denomination of the British Virgin Islands. The first Methodist missionary came to Tortola in 1789 and quickly converted thousands of slaves to the faith. In 1796, the church had 3,168 members in the British Virgins, more than any other Methodist mission in the West Indies. It remains the single largest denomination in the BVI. Today's Road Town Methodist

Road Town

© BRITISH VIRGIN ISLANDS TOURIST BOARD

TORTOLA

Church was built in 1926 after the original structure was destroyed by hurricane in 1924.

Sandwiched between the two churches is the **Old Prison,** with high white walls and a broad red door. The prison was in use continuously from the late 17th century until the mid-1990s, when a new prison, financed by the British government, opened on Tortola's remote northeastern corner. For a brief period in the early 2000s, the old prison was put to use again to ease overcrowding at the main facility. It is now empty once more.

The prison yard hosted the territory's hangings, the most famous of which occurred in 1811 when Arthur Hodge, a wealthy planter, was hanged for the murder of his slave. The last execution to take place here is a distant memory, and in 1999 the U.K. government forced the territory to take capital punishment off its books—which it did, but over loud local protests.

Across Main Street from the Methodist church is a large, pink concrete structure known as **The Fireproof Building.** The building got its name in 1853 when it was one of the only buildings to remain standing after rioters set fire to Road Town in protest against an increase in the cattle tax. The unrest eventually spread throughout the countryside, as residents set fire to many of the remaining plantations and estate homes.

SUNDAY MORNING WELL

Located two blocks past the intersection of Joe's Hill Road and Main Street is the Sunday Morning Well, the place where some historians believe emancipation was announced on August 1, 1834. Others say it was read in churches around the territory. The Sunday Morning Well is the site of an annual emancipation remembrance ceremony that takes place during the August Festival. Today there is a sheltered seating area and a fountain. It's a popular place for people to gather and talk.

TORTOLA AND THE TURTLEDOVE MYTH

It is said that Tortola was named by Christopher Columbus, who christened the island "Land of the Turtledove" after the birds he saw here. This story, while quaint, is untrue.

In truth, Columbus named the island Santa Ana, a moniker that did not stick. It was Dutch settlers who gave the island the name it kept. These early settlers were reminded of Tholen, a small island off the western coast of the Netherlands. They called it Tor Tholen (New Tholen) after this island. When English settlers came, the Dutch name was anglicized to today's Tortola.

Turtledoves, properly called Zenaida doves, do live on Tortola, as well as on many other islands in the Caribbean. Reddish brown with light-brown heads, turtledoves are best identified by the iridescent purple on their necks and their white-tipped tail feathers.

HOUSE OF ASSEMBLY

The white, colonial-style, two-story building next to the Sunday Morning Well is the House of Assembly and courthouse. The 13 members of the House meet downstairs to pass laws and approve the annual budget. High Court convenes upstairs most days. Busts of the first four elected representatives sit in front of the building.

🅲 Joseph Reynold O'Neal Botanical Gardens

A short foot trail loops around the four-acre Joseph Reynold O'Neal Botanical Gardens (Botanic Station, 284/494-4557, 8 A.M.–4 P.M. daily, adults $3, children under 10 $2), an oasis of quiet in bustling Road Town. The gardens were opened in 1986 on part of what was once the island's 60-acre agricultural station, the rest of which has been consumed by schools, roads, and commercial development.

Named for the founder and first chairman of the BVI National Parks Trust, the gardens are the place to come to get acquainted with the rich variety of tropical plants and animals that live in the BVI. The gardens include an orchid house, a fern collection, and a garden of local medicinal herbs. You will also find a wide range of fruit trees, such as mango, passion fruit, and breadfruit. Look out as well for the collection of palm trees, including the native tyre palm, traditionally used to make brooms.

Ask at the ticket booth for a printed guided walk, which provides detailed information about many of the species you see. Look around Fishlock Hall, the one-room wooden building at the center of the gardens, for staff who can answer any other questions you may have.

The gardens are a popular venue for weddings. Call the **BVI National Parks Trust** (284/494-2069, www.bvinationalparkstrust. org) for more information.

Lower Estate Sugar Works Museum

Situated in a 300-plus-year-old sugar factory next to the Sir Rupert Briercliffe Hall, the Lower Estate Sugar Works Museum (Station Rd., no phone, 9 A.M.–4 P.M. Mon.–Fri., free) is a pleasant hodge-podge of historical artifacts, local art, and natural history. The museum is housed in a complex of buildings that have served successively, since the 1780s, as sugarworks, cotton gin, agricultural station, courthouse, government offices, and headquarters of the police maintenance unit. Before the reclamation of Wickham's Cay in the 1960s, the building sat on the shore of Road Harbour; now it sits along the busy James Walter Francis Drive.

Several rooms contain relics of everyday life, such as coal-powered irons and old-time sewing machines, which depict the self-sufficiency and work ethic of earlier generations of Virgin Islanders. Another room is dedicated to exhibitions of local artists' work. Toward the rear, a room houses photographs and detailed

TORTOLA

Old Government House, built in the 1920s, is now a museum.

© SUSANNA HENIGHAN POTTER

TORTOLA

descriptions of some of the BVI's animals and plants. Downstairs are exhibits about the territory's maritime history, including artifacts from the wreck of the RMS *Rhone*.

Unfortunately there is no telephone at the museum and opening hours are subject to change.

Noel Lloyd/Positive Action Movement Park

Named for the Virgin Islander who led the movement against outside development of Road Town's waterfront in the 1960s, this pleasant little park sits in the middle of Road Town, behind First Bank and next to the Palm Grove House. There are benches, gazebos, pathways, and lots of picturesque coconut palm trees.

The park, also called the Palm Grove Park, is the scene of occasional free concerts, fairs, and other community events. On many afternoons it is the preferred place for families to unwind and catch up.

Queen Elizabeth II Park

A small park on the western outskirts of Road Town, the QEII Park, as most locals call it, is nothing to write home about. But it does offer swings, a jungle gym, a slide, a shelter, and a picnic table—perfect for families looking for a place to burn off some energy.

Find the QEII Park by heading west from the Road Town ferry dock. A small parking area is across the street from Macnamara Road, just before the road makes a sharp left turn.

Planter's Burial Ground

During the plantation era, a formal burial was a privilege granted only to the white planter class. One of the sites of these burials was the Planter's Burial Ground at Johnson's Ghut, a valley lying to the east of Road Town. A low wall and fence keep wandering livestock from damaging the gravestones. You can open the gate and walk among the gravestones, which remember former governors, governors' wives,

THE HANGING OF ARTHUR HODGE

For a brief moment in the spring of 1811, events on Tortola held all the West Indies and much of Great Britain transfixed. The happening in question was the trial and execution of an influential and wealthy planter, Arthur Hodge, on charges that he murdered a slave.

The evidence was strong. Two witnesses at the trial, which ran for 22 consecutive hours in Road Town's tiny courthouse on March 29, 1811, described the events that led to the slave's death in 1808. They said Hodge ordered Prosper to be flogged for over an hour on two consecutive days after he was unable to pay Hodge the six shillings the planter demanded for a mango Prosper had picked up from the ground. His skin in shreds, Prosper languished in the estate's sick house for five days before crawling to his own cabin. He died days later, alone, and was buried in a pit behind his cabin.

The jury of 13 white men took three hours to return its guilty verdict. While a majority of the jurors recommended mercy, the governor of the Leeward Islands, Hugh Elliot, who had traveled to Tortola to observe the trial, refused the plea. Hodge was hung on May 8 in the yard behind the prison. It was the first time a white person in the British colonies had been convicted and executed for killing a slave.

Days before the trial began, Governor Elliot wrote to his wife in England, noting "The eyes of all the West Indies are turned towards this cause and it will create a no less general sensation in Great Britain."

Elliot's prediction was not overstated. In July, reports of the trial appeared in *The Times*, *The Globe*, and two leading magazines. The transcript of the trial, taken by Road Town merchant Abraham Belisario, was published in London in September and in the United States the next year. The *Annual Register* included the Hodge trial in its list of significant events of 1811, and the trial was often referenced, years later, in the debate that led to the eventual abolition of slavery in the British colonies in 1833.

and planters. The burial ground has been the subject of study by Caribbean Volunteer Expeditions (www.cvexp.org), which has cataloged the gravestone information and done simple maintenance work.

To find the burial ground, take the first left immediately after the Riteway Supermarket in Pasca. Follow this road until it forks; take the left fork to the burial ground, which is right next to the island's animal shelter.

RIDGE ROAD

As you climb up any of the steep roads that rise spectacularly to the top of Tortola's spine, the air gets cooler, the breeze intensifies, and the views become more and more fantastical. Once at the top, the narrow Ridge Road winds past hillside communities and cool roadside bars. This is what Tortola residents refer to as "up country," and in many ways it is truly the most rural part of the island.

The Ridge Road extends seven miles along Tortola's backbone. A half dozen roads climb from sea level on both the north and south shores of the island to meet the road.

The Ridge Road is also nice to explore on foot, but few people do it. Traffic is not too heavy, the breezes are cool, and you will have time to savor the views along the way. For the least uphill climbing, walk from west to east.

C Fahie Hill Mural

In 2001 a local artist, Reuben Vanterpool, decided to turn a retaining wall in his Great Mountain community into a gallery of its history; he sketched a series of scenes on the wall and, with the help of other artists, painted them in vivid colors. The result was the Fahie Hill Mural, an excellent depiction of life on Tortola after emancipation but before widespread development.

Panels show how islanders raised and

gathered their food: They depict young men fishing, older men watering cattle, and the whole family working together to terrace land for crops. One panel illustrates women baking bread in traditional Dutch brick ovens.

Other panels show the schoolhouse where children once studied, a sugar factory at harvest time, and men working at the nearby rum distillery. The mural also shows how islanders had fun: One panel depicts a fungi band at work, and another shows traditional dancing.

The mural is along the Ridge Road between Great Mountain Road and Johnson's Ghut Road.

C Sage Mountain National Park

Hikers at Sage Mountain National Park (Sage Mountain Rd., 284/494-2069, www.bvinationalparkstrust.org, adults $3, children $1) can climb to the highest point in the U.S. and British Virgin Islands, 1,716 feet above sea level. The 92-acre park in west-central Tortola

is also home to scenic overlooks, a forest untouched for over 500 years, and a host of delightful tropical trees, flowers, and animals.

The National Parks Trust has erected dozens of signs that identify trees and plants along the trails, including the West Indian mahogany, elephant-ear vine, and bulletwood tree. Bromeliads, air-dwelling tropical plants, bejewel parts of the forest, and ferns carpet moist parts of the park. Visitors will hear the sounds of resident birds and bo-peeps, one of the most common kinds of tree frogs. You may also catch glimpses of the fast-moving bananaquit, a tiny yellow-breasted bird, and will certainly see lizards.

The entrance to Sage Mountain National Park is about 0.3 mile from the parking lot, at the end of an unpaved road that cuts through private property. Once inside the park, you can choose to follow the North Trail, which descends slightly before passing through some of

the roots of a huge fig tree in Sage Mountain National Park

the oldest and most lush parts of the forest; the South Trail, which cuts through drier forest; or the Central Trail, which follows the spine of the ridge. All three trails meet at a giant old fig tree at the western end of the park. Other trails track eastward from the park entrance and climb past an impressive lookout to the highest point in the park.

Shelters have been built at several spots along the trails, and there is a picnic table on the North Trail just past the park entrance. There is a pit toilet about midway along the Central Trail. Brochures, which include a map of the park, are sometimes available at the park entrance, and there is a map on display at the parking lot.

Sage Mountain is almost always cool and damp; the air here can be a real relief on hot days. Wear sturdy shoes and plan to spend about two hours to see most of the park.

CANE GARDEN BAY

If you've ever seen a brochure promoting the British Virgin Islands, chances are you've seen a photo of Cane Garden Bay, a picture-perfect crescent beach along the northern coast of Tortola. Located just a 10-minute drive from Road Town, Cane Garden Bay is what many people dream of when they think of the beach. The setting is lovely, with expansive white sand, a smattering of long-necked coconut palms, and the quaint feel of a seaside village. The atmosphere is fun: There are a half dozen beachfront restaurants, lots of beach chairs, and—on most days—plenty of people. Island-style music spills out from restaurants, bikini-clad patrons sip cocktails in the sun, and youngsters make sand castles and splash around in the sea.

Cane Garden Bay is well protected from the swells that crash other north shore beaches, so it is a popular anchorage for yachts. Because of this, there is a defined swimming area, cordoned off by buoys. On days when the waves are very strong—about a dozen days a

year—surfers flock to "The Point" at the far eastern end of the bay for the ride of their lives.

Cane Garden Bay is the preferred destination for cruise ship visitors, who are taxied over the mountain and disgorge onto the beach between the hours of 10 A.M. and 4 P.M. If you don't like crowds, you may want to avoid Cane Garden Bay when a ship is in port.

Callwood Rum Distillery

The Callwood family runs the only rum distillery still operating in the British Virgin Islands, about 100 yards from the beach at Cane Garden Bay. Located on what was once better known as Estate Arundel, the Callwood Rum Distillery (284/495-9383, 8 A.M.–5 P.M. Mon.–Sat., free) still produces rum in much the same way it was done 300 years ago—the biggest concession to modernity is that instead of animal power they use a small diesel engine to crush the sugarcane. Inside, things appear to have changed very little over the years. Wooden barrels and demijohns of aging rum line the stone walls. The air carries a pleasant smell of rum, and the light is dim. It doesn't take much imagination to picture this place in the days of planters and pirates.

Admission to the distillery is free, but you should definitely splurge on the $2 tour, which involves an explanation of the process of rum production. If you want to take pictures, you'll have to pay for a tour or buy at least one bottle of rum. The season for rum production is March to October.

BREWER'S BAY

Quiet and largely undeveloped, Brewer's Bay Beach is the reward for people brave enough to drive down one of the two steep roads that plummet from Tortola's Ridge Road into Brewer's Bay. A long, straight, hard-packed beach with fine caramel-colored sand, Brewer's Bay attracts both residents and tourists. Located between two long fingers of land, the

© SUSANNA HENIGHAN POTTER

Callwood Rum Distillery is the oldest still-operating distillery in the Virgin Islands.

bay is protected and the water is usually very calm. A shallow, sandy shelf extends a long way from the beach, making this an ideal beach for swimming and water play. Snorkelers should head to the western end of the bay and explore along the rocky shore. Watch out for sea urchins among the rocks.

On the land, development has been limited to a campground, and a grove of coconut and sea grape trees provides plenty of shade. A casual beach bar on the western end of the bay sells drinks, hot dogs, hamburgers, and snacks.

Shark Bay National Park

Located on the promontory between Brewer's Bay and Shark Bay to the east, Shark Bay National Park (284/494-3904, free) is a nice place to hike. One trail at this small 18-acre park leads to "bat caves," rooms created by huge boulders that provide hikers with a destination and a quiet, cool place to rest. Another trail tracks to the headland through a dry landscape of wild

frangipani, Turk's head cactus, and lovely views. There is a lookout platform near the top.

None of the distances are long: It takes no more than two hours to thoroughly explore the park. But trails are somewhat rough, so good shoes are advised. To find Shark Bay, look for a one-lane estate road at the first switchback as you depart Brewer's Bay heading east. Park your car along the main road and walk about 10 minute along the estate road to find the park entrance, which is marked.

Mount Healthy National Park

A well-preserved 18th-century windmill is the main attraction at Mount Healthy National Park (284/494-3904, www.bvinationalparkstrust.org, free), a one-acre park perched atop a foothill overlooking Brewer's Bay on the north shore. Built around the turn of the 19th century, the Mount Healthy windmill provided power to crush sugarcane grown on the surrounding plantation, owned by Tortola's

© SUSANNA HENIGHAN POTTER

inside the "bat cave" at Shark Bay National Park

wealthiest planter, Bezaliel Hodge. All other plantations on Tortola used an animal round—a simple mill operated by mules, horses, or oxen—to power their cane-crushing machine, as windmills were expensive to build and required 360-degree exposure to winds to be worthwhile.

In addition to the main windmill ruins, you can see other remnants of the Mount Healthy sugar mill at the park. A short trail circles the edge of the park, and there's a picnic table.

EAST ISLAND

The Blackburne Highway follows the southern coast of Tortola east of Road Town, up and down through a series of small bays, to East End, the second most populated area of Tortola. Josiah's Bay beach, just over the hill from East End, is popular among surfers. Beyond East End, a bridge connects Tortola to Beef Island, home to the territory's airport and one of its best undeveloped beaches.

St. Philips Anglican Church

The ruins of St. Philips Anglican Church are the most visible remains of the Kingstown settlement of free Africans. The village was established as a settlement for Africans liberated from slaving vessels after Britain outlawed the slave trade in 1808. In 1831, the king gave land grants to the settlers, and within a year some 100 cottages were erected to house 300 people.

The church was built between 1831 and 1834 by settlers and served as a house of worship and school. The ruins are the property of the Anglican church, and some basic steps have been taken to prevent the building from collapsing. Visitors can pull off the road to look more closely at the ruins, but please don't climb on them.

Paraquita Bay Agricultural Station

The Department of Agriculture leases garden plots to local farmers in Paraquita Bay, one of the largest areas of undeveloped flat land on Tortola. Farmers raise livestock or produce

TORTOLA

© SUSANNA HENIGHAN POTTER

The windmill at Mount Healthy National Park is the only one of its kind in the British Virgin Islands.

TORTOLA

crops including sugarcane, bananas, mangoes, tomatoes, and okra. Narrow paths between the plots make the area ideal for walking, and the station is an excellent place to see unusual fruits and vegetables. If you go in the early morning or late afternoon, you are likely to meet some of the farmers, who can answer your questions or sell you whatever's in season.

Centre for Applied Marine Studies

Across the Blackburne Highway from the agricultural station is the Centre for Applied Marine Studies, part of the H. Lavity Stoutt Community College (284/494-4994, www.hslcc.edu.vg, 8:30 A.M.–5:30 P.M., free), a two-year college named for the first chief minister of the British Virgin Islands. Students at the center study navigation, outboard engine mechanics, marine biology, and Virgin Islands history. A sculpture outside the building depicts a traditional Tortola sloop, and an exhibit on the second floor details attempts to preserve these vessels. Also on display are artifacts from the 1867 wreck of the RMS *Rhone* off Salt Island.

A partially completed boardwalk winds through the mangroves in front of the center. The **Roger Downing Mangrove Boardwalk** is being funded by the British government and the local Rotary club. A visitors center was hurriedly built in 2005 for the visit of Princess Anne, who dedicated the building, but it remains empty. At some point in the future, you will find information about the importance of mangroves here. In the meantime, it is a pleasant place to walk if you are interested in seeing a mangrove forest up close.

Josiah's Bay

One of two surfing beaches on Tortola, Josiah's Bay is a long, straight stretch of sand on the northeastern coast. Two casual beach bars sell food and drinks on the eastern end, and there

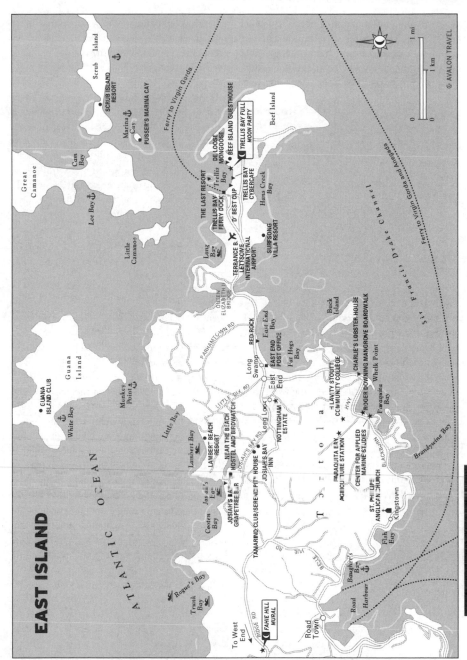

EAST ISLAND

ATLANTIC OCEAN

Scrub Island

SCRUB ISLAND RESORT

PUSSER'S MARINA CAY

Marina Cay

Cam Bay

Great Camanoe

Lee Bay

Little Camanoe

Ferry to Virgin Gorda

DE LOOSE MONGOOSE

BEEF ISLAND GUESTHOUSE

TRELLIS BAY FULL MOON PARTY

Trellis Bay

Beef Island

THE LAST RESORT

TRELLIS BAY FERRY DOCK

D' BEST CUP

TRELLIS BAY CYBERCAFE

Hans Creek

Long Bay

TERRANCE B.
LETTSOME INTERNATIONAL AIRPORT

SURFSONG VILLA RESORT

QUEEN ELIZABETH II BRIDGE

Sir Francis Drake Channel

Ferry to Virgin Gorda and Anegada

Guana Island

GUANA ISLAND CLUB

White Bay

Monkey Point

PARHAM TOWN RD

East End Bay

RED ROCK

Buck Island

CHARLIE'S LOBSTER HOUSE

ROGER DOWNING MANGROVE BOARDWALK

Whelk Point

EAST END POST OFFICE

Fat Hogs Bay

Long Swamp

East End

LITTLE DIX RD

T o r t o l a

Paraquita Bay

LAVITY STOUTT COMMUNITY COLLEGE

Little Bay

Lambert Bay

LAMBERT BEACH RESORT

NEAR THE BEACH HOSTEL AND BIRDWATCH

Long Look

JOSIAH'S BAY RD

NOTTINGHAM ESTATE

JOSIAH'S BAY INN

PARAQUITA BAY AGRICULTURE STATION

CENTER FOR APPLIED MARINE STUDIES

Paraquita Bay

Brandywine Bay

Josiah's Bay

JOSIAH'S BAR & GRAPETREE BAR

PIT HOUSE

Centers Bay

TAMARIND CLUB/SERENDIPIT HOUSE

BLACKBURN HWY

ST. PHILIPE ANGLICAN CHURCH

Kingstown

Fish Bay

Rogue's Bay

Trunk Bay

FAHIE HILL MURAL

RIDGE RD

BELLE VUE RD

Baugher's Bay

To West End

Road Town

Road Harbour

© AVALON TRAVEL

1 mi

1 km

0

TORTOLA

is often an informal game of beach volleyball under way. A half dozen shelters provide shade along the vast expanse of white sand. Stay close to the eastern end to feel like part of the action, or strike out to the far western side for a more solitary experience.

During the winter, waves here attract local surfers, but the beach is especially good for boogie boarding, the sport of riding smaller waves close to shore. You can rent gear from the beach bars. This is also a great beach for walking.

Josiah's Bay beach is at the head of a large, flat bay that is also home to a salt pond and farms. The shady, flat road that leads to the beach is a nice place for walking or bike riding.

Josiah's Bay Salt Pond

Salt ponds are important to the delicate balance of tropical ecosystems and are good places for bird-watching. Many ponds have been filled in over the years to create flat land for development, but the pond at Josiah's Bay remains and is one of the largest on Tortola.

Vernon and Marie Blyden, who operate a hostel about a hundred yards from Josiah's Bay beach, advertise bird-watching from their property, which adjoins the pond. At the **Near the Beach Birdwatch** (Josiah's Bay, 284/443-7833) enthusiasts can set up a chair and look for sandpipers, spotted rail, bananaquits, grey heron, osprey, red-tailed hawk, and more. Bring your own binoculars and call ahead to ask if Vernon can arrange a kayak to paddle out to the middle of the pond.

Lambert Bay

A beautiful stretch of coarse caramel sand lines Lambert Bay, also known as Elizabeth Beach. From the shore, there are views of Guana Island, and there's plenty of shade beneath large sea grape trees along the sand. The sea here can be rough; on many days there are strong waves and a powerful undertow, which makes it a poor choice for weak swimmers. There is

a beach volleyball net, and water-sports equipment is available to rent from the resort that fronts the bay. Food and drinks are for sale at the hotel restaurant.

Little Lambert Bay

East of Lambert is Little Lambert Bay, also called simply Little Bay. Once a retreat known to few, Little Bay is experiencing a massive growth spurt. Dozens of high-end homes have recently been built, and more are under construction. Getting to the beach can feel a bit like driving through a construction site, but once you reach the shore you will find your reward.

Little Bay is a quiet, sunny bay with fluffy white sand and moderate surf. Sit on the shore and look out at the open ocean, or bathe among the waves. There is not a lot of shade, so you may want to bring an umbrella.

Find Little Bay by heading east past the turnoff to Lambert Beach Resort and looking for a narrow paved road on your left. Construction traffic may be apparent. Follow the road down to the beach, and look for parking near a weathered old Tourist Board sign that indicates the location of the public access.

East End Methodist Church

This picturesque chapel set on the top of a low rise in East End celebrated its bicentennial in 2010. In commemoration, local artists painted a series of murals entitled "The Church in the Community" on the wall just outside the church's gates. It's worth a stop to admire the vibrant colors and thoughtful depictions of the way in which church life and community life have been intertwined for two centuries.

BEEF ISLAND

Many a traveler flying to the British Virgin Islands has been perplexed to see that Beef Island, not Tortola, is his or her final destination. The reason is simple: Beef Island, which is connected to the southeastern coast of Tortola by a two-lane bridge, is home to the Terrance B. Lettsome International Airport, the port of entry for many visitors to the British Virgin Islands.

Beef Island got its name from the cattle that were raised there during the plantation period. A popular legend tells of a widow who lived on Beef Island, raising cattle, during the age of piracy: It is said that she became fed up with losing livestock at the hands of pirates, who used the waters around Beef Island for a rendezvous point. One day she invited the whole pirate gang to dinner and poisoned them with rum tainted with juice from the toxic manchineel fruit. The island's pirate legacy lives on in name—Bellamy Cay, just off the coast, is named for Black Sam Bellamy, a pirate said to have used the cay as his base while prowling the northern Caribbean in the early 1700s.

Long Bay

Though technically on Beef Island, Long Bay is easily accessible from Tortola and is one of the most popular beaches among visitors and residents. The fine white-sand bay forms a perfect half moon, providing plenty of elbow room even on the busiest days of the year. The water is almost always calm, but the sea bottom slopes steeply, making it important to keep a close eye on children and inexperienced swimmers.

Long Bay is ideal for long walks, and there can be rewarding beachcombing at the far eastern end. Coconut and sea grape trees provide plenty of shade, but there are no permanent restaurants or bathroom facilities. Its location next to the airport means that you can hear the sounds of departing and arriving aircraft, and sometimes see them too. In 2005, the government bought nearly 100 acres of land around the beach to protect it from development.

WEST ISLAND

Heading west from Road Town, Drake's Highway runs parallel to the Sir Francis Drake Channel, its namesake, all the way to the western tip of Tortola. The road passes through Sea Cow's Bay, a community that borders a wide bay once home to manatees. After that, the road passes through a series of more sparsely populated bays until reaching the end of the island.

Two cays lie just offshore from Tortola; both are connected to the main island by bridges. Nanny Cay lies about halfway between Road Town and West End and is home to a large marina, a hotel, and two restaurants. Frenchman's Cay lies near the western tip and houses a marina, several shops, a hotel, and a small community. Soper's Hole, the body of water between Tortola and Frenchman's Cay, also refers to a waterfront complex of bright Caribbean-style buildings on the western end of the cay.

On the north shore, western Tortola is a series of lovely bays, from Smuggler's Cove, a remote and protected crescent of sand, to Carrot Bay, a traditional village where many islanders still make their living from the sea and the land.

William Thornton Estate Ruins

Located in aptly named Pleasant Valley, just west of Sea Cow's Bay, are the ruins of an estate house where William Thornton drew the design of the U.S. Capitol building. Thornton, a Quaker, was living at his Pleasant Valley plantation in March 1792 when Secretary of State Thomas Jefferson advertised a contest to design the capitol building and president's home, which would be built in the new city of Washington.

By the time Thornton learned of the contest and sailed to Philadelphia with his design, the contest was closed. But the commissioners, who had not been impressed by any of the other designs, waived the deadline and accepted his entry. Thornton won $500 in gold and a plot in the new city.

Little remains of the Thornton estate, which is privately owned and used as a storage facility for a local water company. A few crumbling walls are visible through the trees.

TORTOLA

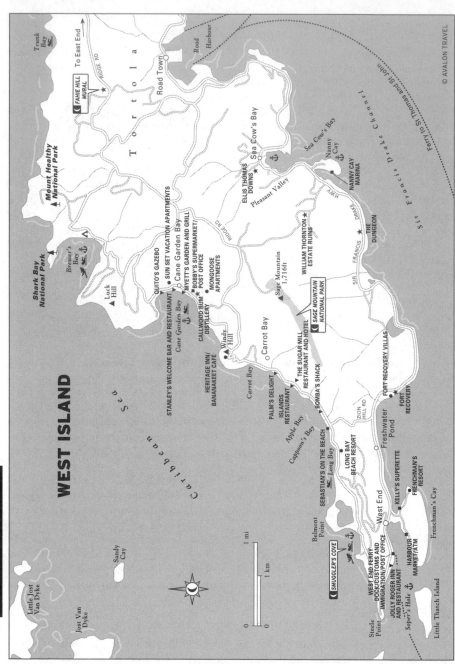

WEST ISLAND

Caribbean Sea

Little Jost Van Dyke

Jost Van Dyke

Sandy Cay

Little Thatch Island

Steele Point

Soper's Hole

Belmont Point

WEST END-FERRY DOCK/CUSTOMS AND IMMIGRATION/POST OFFICE

JOLLY ROGER INN AND RESTAURANT

SMUGGLER'S COVE

HARBOUR MARKET/ATM

West End

KELLY'S SUPERETTE

FRENCHMAN'S RESORT

Frenchman's Cay

Freshwater Pond

SEBASTIAN'S ON THE BEACH

LONG BAY BEACH RESORT

Long Bay

ZION HILL RD

FORT RECOVERY

FORT RECOVERY VILLAS

Cappoon's Bay

Apple Bay

ISLANDS RESTAURANT

PALM'S DELIGHT

BOMBA'S SHACK

THE SUGAR MILL RESTAURANT AND HOTEL

Carrot Bay

SAGE MOUNTAIN NATIONAL PARK

Sage Mountain, 1,716ft

Windy Hill

HERITAGE INN/ BANANAKEET CAFE

Cane Garden Bay

STANLEY'S WELCOME BAR AND RESTAURANT

QUITO'S GAZEBO

SUN SET VACATION APARTMENTS

CALLWOOD RUM DISTILLERY

MYETT'S GARDEN AND GRILL

BOBBY'S SUPERMARKET/ POST OFFICE

MONGOOSE APARTMENTS

RIDGE RD

Carrot Bay

WILLIAM THORNTON ESTATE RUINS

THE DUNGEON

SIR FRANCIS DRAKE HWY

Luck Hill

Brewer's Bay

Shark Bay National Park

Mount Healthy National Park

Tortola

RIDGE RD

Pleasant Valley

ELLIS THOMAS DOWNS

Sea Cow's Bay

Sea Cow's Bay

Nanny Cay

NANNY CAY MARINA

Sir Francis Drake Channel

Ferry to St. Thomas and St. John

Road Town

FAHIE HILL MURAL

To East End

Trunk Bay

Road Harbour

1 mi

1 km

0   0

© AVALON TRAVEL

To find the Thornton Estate, turn off Drake's Highway at the E&D Convenience Store in Pleasant Valley, also called Palistina, and pass the Cable and Wireless complex. The road crosses a small stream and turns to the right before passing the estate ruins on the right.

The Dungeon

The ruins of Fort Purcell, just east of Pockwood Pond along Drake's Highway, are more commonly known as the Dungeon because of a below-ground magazine that looks more sinister than it probably ever was.

First built in the 17th century by Dutch settlers, Fort Purcell was expanded and strengthened by the British in the mid-18th century. Located on about five acres of land, the fort complex included dozens of buildings, including water catchments and storage facilities. It was named for an influential governor, James Purcell, who oversaw construction of a number of the fortifications that once ringed Tortola and the other British Virgin Islands.

The Governor's Office announced plans to turn the ruins into a national park in 2011, but at the time of writing they remain badly overgrown and there is no sign marking their location from the road. Look for a dirt access road on the hillward side of the highway between Havers and Pockwood Pond. You can park along the highway and walk in, but be careful crossing the road.

Fort Recovery

The remains of **Tower Fort** on the southwestern coast are better known by the name of the adjacent resort, Fort Recovery. The Tower Fort is believed to be the oldest building still standing in the British Virgin Islands, built in the 17th century by early settlers.

Zion Hill Methodist Church

The West End Methodist Chapel was first built in the early 1800s and was located on top of Zion Hill, with views looking north to Jost Van Dyke and south to St. John. In 1834, emancipation was proclaimed from the altar. The chapel was destroyed or damaged in successive hurricanes, and in 1926 it was rebuilt at the foot of Zion Hill, where it would be less exposed to high winds. The church served not only as a place of worship but as a school as well.

In 2002, a new, larger church was built next door, but the old chapel, where the territory's first chief minister, H. Lavity Stoutt, was educated, remains.

Apple Bay

A humble place, Apple Bay, also called Cappoon's Bay, may not rate among the top beaches in the British Virgin Islands, but it is not without charm. Surfers flock here during the winter months when the surf is up. The best waves come in right in front of Bomba's Surfside Shack. Grab a seat along the shore in the afternoon to watch the humans surf and the pelicans dive.

For swimming, head to the sand in front of Sebastian's on the Beach or to the pleasant but small sandy beach in front of the Sugar Mill Hotel.

Long Bay

A long, straight stretch of sand set next to a picturesque sugarloaf mountain, Long Bay is a good beach for walking, sunning, and beachcombing. A buffer of rocks just offshore makes swimming difficult in most places. The best swimming area is near the western end of the beach, opposite a low rock bluff. The far western end of the beach is excellent for beachcombing. Food, drink, and restroom facilities are available at Long Bay Beach Resort's beachfront restaurant.

◖ Smuggler's Cove

One of Tortola's best all-around beaches, Smuggler's Cove is a small crescent of sand fringed by sea grape trees and coconut palms, bookended by two sugarloaf mountains. Almost always calm, Smuggler's Cove is as popular with residents as it is with tourists. A small reef at the western end provides some entertainment for those who need more than crystalline water and soft sandy shore. Three impermanent beach bars sell cold drinks and snacks and rent beach chairs.

Smuggler's Cove is at the end of a bumpy gravel road. To get there, drive past Long Bay and continue past a steep uphill segment at the end of the beach. Here the road turns to gravel and you can choose from the low or high road: Either route takes you to the beach.

Carrot Bay

Located between Apple Bay and Cane Garden Bay on the north shore, Carrot Bay is as traditional a village as you will find on Tortola. Many men here continue to fish for a living, and most afternoons you can buy fresh catch from the wharf. The hillsides around Carrot Bay are verdant and moist, a good setting for farming. Fruit and vegetable stands offer fresh produce to residents and passersby.

The pace and style of life in Carrot Bay is peaceful and community-focused. It is a nice place to go for a walk or to sit on the waterfront and pass the time of day with whomever you meet.

Entertainment and Events

Tortola is not exactly New York or London, but enterprising people will find something interesting to do most weekends, whether it is catching a concert, seeing a play, or being seen at the hottest club.

For the most up-to-date and comprehensive guide to nightlife, events, and sporting events, check out the entertainment listings in the *Limin' Times,* a free guide published every Thursday and available from supermarkets, hotels, and restaurants.

NIGHTLIFE

Nightlife on Tortola is hit or miss. On certain nights, and at certain times of the year, Road Town, Cane Garden Bay, and other parts of the island are downright buzzing. At other times, it is deadly quiet. The clubs and bars listed here are some of the most reliable.

Road Town

On the waterfront you'll find several popular watering holes, ideal for meeting up with the after-work crowd. The second-story bar on the southwest corner of the Sir Olva Georges Plaza has gone through a number of iterations recently, but the rooftop deck is always a good place to wind down and enjoy the view of Road Town, such as it is. At the time of research, the spot was occupied by **Origins** (Sir Olva Georges Plaza, 11 A.M.–midnight Tues.–Thurs., 11 A.M.–2 A.M. Fri.–Sat.), which also serves sushi and bar food. **Pusser's** (Waterfront Dr., 284/494-3897) is a popular happy hour haunt, especially on Friday nights, when it is downright jammed with young residents and islanders looking to kick off the weekend. **Le Grand Cafe** (Waterfront Dr., 284/494-8660, 11 A.M.–2 A.M. daily), set among the trees next to Pusser's, is a late-night hangout especially popular with expats.

For a more refined nook, grab a seat at **The Dove** (67 Main St., 284/494-0313, 6 P.M. till late Tues.–Sat.), a wine bar popular with professionals.

For the best Caribbean dance hall and an intense immersion into Caribbean culture, head to **Stone's** (Long Bush, 284/494-6776), a venerable club with hot music and an even hotter clientele on Friday and Saturday nights. The party gets going late—after midnight—and goes till dawn. Don't dare come underdressed (and for the ladies, less is definitely more).

CARIBBEAN FRIENDS

In 1727 an important new group of settlers began to arrive in the British Virgin Islands: Quakers. The Quakers fled England some years before to escape religious persecution and settled throughout the West Indies. Tortola's Quakers first settled in Anguilla but left that island after a major drought made survival difficult.

The Quakers eventually settled throughout the present-day British Virgin Islands. The largest group lived at Fat Hog's Bay, Tortola, but smaller Quaker settlements were found in Road Harbour, Virgin Gorda, and Jost Van Dyke. One of the first lieutenant governors of the Virgin Islands was John Pickering, a Quaker, who was later stripped of the post when he refused to bear arms.

Several other Quakers are still remembered today. William Thornton, who owned an estate in present-day Sea Cow's Bay, won the contest to design the U.S. Capitol Building in Washington, D.C. Another Quaker, Dr. William Coakley Lettsome, who was born on Little Jost Van Dyke, went on to found the London Medical Society.

Samuel and Mary Nottingham, both Quakers, made history when they not only freed all their slaves in 1776, but also gave them land to live on at Nottingham Estate, now Long Look in Tortola's East End. The action, and the subsequent success of the now-free people at Nottingham, was cited by abolitionists as evidence that the end of slavery need not lead to social instability.

The Quaker era did not last long in the Virgin Islands. The faith was unpopular with many planters, as the upright and moral Quaker attitudes ran counter to the West Indian planter lifestyle and philosophy. As the Tortola meeting reported to London in 1750: "The love that had kept them in fear of the Lord appears to be much abated and the too eager pursuit after the things of the World that choke and hinder the growth of Truth, too much sought after."

The last meeting took place in 1762, although individual Quakers remained. The ruins of the Quaker burial ground and meeting house at Fat Hog's Bay still exist and were purchased by the local government in 2005, although they are overgrown and deteriorating.

You can learn more about the BVI Quakers in the Quaker Room at Old Government House Museum in Road Town.

Cane Garden Bay

If dancing under the stars is more your cup of tea, head to Cane Garden Bay, where several beach bars offer the quintessential Caribbean night out. All these establishments are open all day—from lunch (in some cases breakfast) until late night. You can expect evening entertainment to begin at around 8 P.M. and last until midnight or later.

The most famous of Tortola's musicians, Quito Rymer, performs several nights a week at his **Gazebo** (Cane Garden Bay, 284/495-4837). Quito plays acoustic on Tuesdays and Thursdays, while on weekends he plugs in with his band, The Edge. The sound is an upbeat combination of reggae and calypso. The crowd here tends to be an equal mix of tourists and island residents, and this is a good place for dancing. Friday night is especially popular among locals, and the dance floor remains crowded well into the wee hours.

Myett's (Cane Garden Bay, 284/495-9649) has live music Friday–Monday, and the garden atmosphere is relaxing. There is often DJ music at other beach bars, including **Big Banana** (284/495-4606).

Beef Island
◀ TRELLIS BAY FULL MOON PARTY
Beef Island's Trellis Bay is an artsy and hip place to be every day of the year, but under full moons its funky atmosphere boils over at the Trellis Bay Full Moon Party, a joint production of Aragorn's Studio (284/495-1849) and the Trellis Bay Cybercafé (284/495-2447). The parties may share a name with Bomba's

full moon parties on the west end of the island, but the similarities end there. Trellis Bay's fetes feature local musicians, a top-notch barbecue buffet, stilt walkers, and local artist Aragorn Dick-Read's flaming fireballs.

Musical entertainment often includes steel-pan tunes or Tortola's traditional music, scratch-band music called fungi. Mocko jumbies, colorful stilt-walking characters, perform impressive moves at heights of up to 10 feet, and there are artist demonstrations.

Aragorn's fireballs are a story unto themselves. Spherical metal sculptures about five feet in diameter, the fireballs are stuffed with flammable material, fastened on stands over the water, and lit afire. The effect is mesmerizing; flames dance over the crystal water, allowing glimpses at the balls' intricate carved designs.

Trellis Bay also throws a great New Year's Eve bash.

West Island

The Bomba Shack (Apple Bay, 284/495-4148) is western Tortola's most distinctive bar. Built of flotsam and painted an array of colors (and with colorful words), "The Shack"—as it is known—is one watering hole you won't soon forget. Bomba's is legendary in the Virgin Islands for its raucous full moon parties and risqué shack decor. Ladies' underwear hangs from the rafters, often shed after imbibing Bomba's potent rum punch or his even more potent mushroom tea, brewed from locally grown hallucinogenic mushrooms. Photographs adorning the walls depict other X-rated shenanigans that have gone on at the Shack and cross the line from raunchy to—quite frankly—offensive.

Bomba's tea is served at midnight during the full moon parties, which also feature live bands and dancing. If you want a Shack experience that is a bit more tame, try it out on a Sunday or Wednesday night, when there is live music and more mellow company. Or stop by any afternoon to benefit from the pieces of wisdom previous partygoers have scrawled on the shack's walls over the years, and to watch the pelicans and the surfers out in the water.

One of the most reliable places for a night out is the **Jolly Roger** (Soper's Hole, 284/495-4559), a seaside restaurant that also boasts a friendly bar and live music several nights a week. Acts sometimes include rockers from the United States.

THE ARTS

Several amateur acting companies put on plays throughout the year, many in the H. Lavity Stoutt Community College Auditorium. Check the *Limin' Times* for information.

There are regular "jams" on Tortola—concerts by visiting entertainers, many of them stars in the reggae, soca, or calypso genres. Jams are advertised locally by posters and ads in newspapers. Admission is usually $20–25, and shows invariably start late—often after midnight.

EVENTS

Check the *Limin' Times* and local newspapers for details of these annual events.

Spring
BVI SPRING REGATTA

The BVI Spring Regatta (www.bvispring-regatta.org) is one of the premier regattas in the Caribbean, often attracting entries from Europe, North America, and all over the Caribbean. A Sailing Festival before the regatta provides a week of rally-style sailing and parties for less competitive sailors. The regatta itself has five classes (racing, cruising, classic, multihull, and bareboat) and takes place over three days.

The regatta is at Nanny Cay Resort and Marina in early April. The regatta village, a grassy area with bars, restaurants, seating, and music, draws a diverse crowd of racers, residents, and landlubbers who come out to soak in the yachty atmosphere.

© SUSANNA HENEGHAN POTTER

A costumed troupe participates in Tortola's annual August Festival parade.

BVI MUSIC FEST

Held over Memorial Day weekend, the BVI Music Fest (www.bvimusicfestival.com) brings popular reggae, R&B, and calypso acts to the BVI. The three-day event usually boasts at least one big-name act. Past headliners have been Jimmy Cliff, Boyz II Men, and Maxi Priest. Admission is usually $25 per night. Traditionally, the fete takes place in Cane Garden Bay, but there has been talk about moving it to a larger venue.

Summer

AUGUST FESTIVAL

Tortola's biggest party of the year commemorates the end of slavery on August 1, 1833. The August Festival starts in late July with the opening of the Festival Village and lasts through the first week of August. There is entertainment nightly in the village, where you can sample authentic local food like goat water (goat soup), stewed conch, roti, and patés (fried meat-stuffed bread). Entertainers from all over the Caribbean perform, including some well-known reggae and soca artists. A favorite night is the calypso competition, when local singers perform calypsos touching on island politics, culture, and current events.

The centerpiece of the August Festival is the parade, held the first Monday of August. Beginning around noon (never mind any schedule that says it will start sooner), colorful troops, dancers, and floats parade down Waterfront Drive to the Festival Village. If you plan to attend, it is wise to bring chairs and scope out a shady spot early.

Other popular festival events are the horse races, the Miss BVI pageant, watersports events, the food fair, and Carrot Bay Fiesta, a mini-festival that takes place on the Thursday, Friday, and Saturday after the festival parade.

Contact the **BVI Tourist Board** (284/494-3134, www.bvitourism.com) for the festival schedule.

HIGHLAND SPRING HIHO
Some of the world's best windsurfers descend on the BVI every July for the Highland Spring HIHO (www.go-hiho.com), a weeklong windsurfing race that takes competitors throughout the British Virgin Islands. The name HIHO derives from the windsurfing lingo "hook in and hang on." During the annual event, windsurfers skit across the waters, followed by a fleet of sailboats. Wherever the HIHO leads, there's a party to be found.

Fall

HLSCC PERFORMING ARTS SERIES
H. Lavity Stoutt Community College presents a Performing Arts Series (284/494-4994, www.hlscc.edu.vg) every year from September to May. Performers include local and international artists. Concerts take place from September to May at the auditorium at the college's Paraquita Bay campus.

Winter

FUNGI FEST
Fungi is the traditional music of the Virgin Islands, and at no time of the year is it more appreciated than during the Christmas season. Fungi Fest takes place in November and features traditional performers from the Virgin Islands and farther afield. For information contact the government's Department of Culture (284/494-3701).

CHRISTMAS ON MAIN STREET
Taking place in early December, this weekend festival includes musical performances, vendors, and the lighting of a Christmas tree in the Sir Olva Georges Plaza. It marks the unofficial beginning of the holiday season in the BVI.

FARMER'S WEEK
Usually taking place in February, Farmer's Week is organized by the Department of Agriculture (284/494-3701) and local farmers. It includes farm and garden competitions, demonstrations for school groups, and workshops. But the main event is the agricultural exhibition that takes place over the weekend at Paraquita Bay. Here you will see livestock and have a chance to buy a wide variety of local fruits and vegetables from farmers. There are also games, entertainment, and speeches.

CINEMA
UP's Cineplex (284/494-2189, ext. 21) is a multiscreen high-rise movie theater next to the House of Assembly and the Elmore Stoutt High School, unmissable for its grotesquely pastel exterior color scheme. In addition to seven movie screens, there is a bowling alley in the basement and a food court and indoor play area at street level.

Shopping

Shopping is not a reason to come to Tortola, but once you're here, it can be rewarding. There are virtually no major-name stores here, but locally owned boutiques offer unique gifts and souvenirs to remember your trip by.

ROAD TOWN
Main Street
The best place to shop in Road Town is along Main Street, which has the greatest concentration of shops and a pleasant atmosphere. Most shops are open by 10 A.M. and close around 5 P.M. Many are closed on Sundays. **Latitude 18** (Fonseca Corner, 284/494-3811) sells beachwear, sunglasses, Crocs, and island-style dresses; **The Gallery** (102 Main St., 284/494-2096) features framed and matted paintings; and **Allamanda Gallery** (124 Main St., 284/494-6680) is a photo gallery featuring the work of Amanda Baker.

Another good place to browse is **Little Denmark** (147 Main St., 284/494-2455), which has an intriguing mix of goods including Cuban cigars, jewelry, luggage, and kitchenware. For jewelry, go to **The Jewelry Box** (101 Main St., 284/494-7278) for gold or silver pieces or **Samarkand** (94 Main St., 284/494-6415), which specializes in the Virgin Islands gem larimar. You will be hard-pressed to leave **Sunny Caribbe Spice Shop and Art Gallery** (121 Main St., 284/494-2178) empty-handed. Here you will find a wide array of spices, sauces, relishes, and body products, as well as Caribbean postcards, prints, and crafts.

Bamboushay (109 Main St., 294/494-0393) sells colorful locally made pottery, and the best place for books is **Serendipity Books** (151 Main St., 284/494-5865).

Around Road Town
Across from Main Street, facing the waterfront, is **Crafts Alive**, an open-air market of brightly painted Caribbean-style houses. Space is rented to local artisans, but, sadly, the local art is overshadowed by cheap tourist goods—T-shirts, bags, and hats. But if you make an effort you will also find locally made hot sauce, soaps, drinks, preserves, and crafts: look for the booth selling goods produced by the Road Town Senior Citizens group and Ermine Mathavious's local drinks. You may find some Crafts Alive vendors absent if there is no cruise ship in port.

If you are in the market for brand-name jewelry, browse at **Little Switzerland** (Administration Dr., 284/494-3730) and **Columbian Emeralds** (Romansco Place, 284/494-7477).

For surfer-inspired clothing and gear, head to **Cane Garden Bay Surfboard Company** (Christopher Building, Mill Mall, 284/494-5423), in the shopping plaza opposite Banco Popular in Road Town.

CANE GARDEN BAY
The best shopping in Cane Garden Bay is at **Olivia's Corner Store** (Myett's, 284/495-9649), which has crafts, island beachwear, local music, books, and more.

EAST ISLAND
Trellis Bay is the best place for shopping in the east. **Aragorn's Studio** (Trellis Bay, 284/495-1849) has unique local arts, Carib crafts, pottery, and silk-screened T-shirts of Aragorn Dick-Read's woodcut prints. **HIHO** (Trellis Bay, 284/494-7694), a BVI-based brand of Caribbean-inspired clothing and beachwear, sells sundresses, hats, swimsuits, and surfer shorts.

WEST ISLAND
There are some nice shops along the boardwalk at Nanny Cay, a full-service marina and hotel

complex located about midway between Road Town and West End. **Arawak Gifts** (284/494-5240) sells clothing, jewelry, and beachwear. About 20 yards from the waterfront, on the main road to the marina, you will find **Bamboushay** (284/494-0393), which has locally made pottery and other arts.

Soper's Hole, a marina and retail complex at West End, has several nice shops, including **Latitude 18** (284/495-4347), which sells island-style clothing and footwear. **Samarkand Jewellers** (284/495-4137) and **Zenaida's** (284/495-4867) are good places for unique jewelry.

Sports and Recreation

Tortola is a land of plenty for sailors and watersports enthusiasts. This is ground zero for the territory's charter yacht industry, one of the largest in the Caribbean. The island also hosts the largest annual windsurfing race in the region, has the best surfing in the entire Virgin Islands, and is an excellent home base for anyone wanting to scuba dive on the reefs and wrecks that lie all around the BVI.

Praises of Tortola's land-based pursuits are not as commonly sung, but they should be. There is good hiking in the island's largest national park, exciting bicycling, and opportunities for tennis and horseback riding.

WATER SPORTS
Snorkeling
While the British Virgin Islands' most impressive snorkeling is generally found around outer islands, you should not write Tortola off completely. There are several nice snorkel sites easily accessible from the beach.

Good snorkeling is found at Marina Cay, a small island just off the coast of Beef Island. Smuggler's Cove on the west end has a shallow offshore reef best explored in calm weather. Other good snorkel sites are Gun Point, at the western point of Smuggler's Cove, and at both the western and eastern points of Brewer's Bay.

Snorkel equipment can be rented from any of the dive operators listed under *Diving*.

Diving
There are more than 60 popular dive sites in

the British Virgin Islands, and dive operators on Tortola lead trips to many of them every day. Most famous is the RMS *Rhone,* the remains of which lie submerged between Salt and Peter Islands. Other popular sites include the Indians off Norman Island, the Dogs between Virgin Gorda and Tortola, and Blonde Rock between Salt Island and Dead Chest. Weather conditions will dictate the best sites on any given day.

There are more than a dozen Tortola-based dive operators, and the competitive nature of the industry means that only the best survive. Expect to pay $70–90 for a one-tank dive; $100–120 for two tanks. Resort (learn to SCUBA) courses run about $120.

In the Road Town area, try **Aquaventure Scuba Services** (Wickham's Cay I, 284/494-4320, www.aquaventurebvi.com), which specializes in small groups, or **BVI Scuba Co.** (Inner Harbour Marina, www.bviscubaco.com).

With locations at Nanny Cay and Soper's Hole, **Blue Water Divers** (Nanny Cay Marina, 284/494-2847; Soper's Hole Marina, 284/495-1200; www.bluewaterdiversbvi.com) is one of the BVI's largest dive operators, with a complete selection of certification courses and a variety of dive trips.

On the east end, **Sail Caribbean Divers** (Hodge's Creek Marina, 284/495-1675, www.sailcaribbeandivers.com) gets high marks for friendly service. **UBS Dive Center** (Harbour View Marina, 284/494-0024, www.scubabvi.com) is another good choice.

Dolphin Swimming

Opened amid a furor of controversy back in the early 2000s, **Dolphin Discovery** (Prospect Reef Resort, 284/494-7675, www.dolphindiscovery. com) soldiers on, selling "dolphin encounters" to willing tourists. Critics objected to the captive dolphins and said that the attraction did not fit with the BVI's generally responsible nature-based tourism product. These days, the debate has died down, but there are still those with strong views on dolphin swimming.

It costs $80 for a brief dolphin encounter and up to $140 for a longer swim. Many of the facility's customers are from cruise ships that visit Tortola.

Surfing

Tortola has the best and most reliable surfing of any of the Virgin Islands. On weekends surfers from St. John and St. Thomas sojourn to Tortola in search of waves. The surf is generally up during the winter, from December through March, when cold fronts come off the east coast of North America and create swells along Tortola's Atlantic shore. September and October can be good months as well, but they are less reliable.

The best surfing beaches are Apple Bay on the west end, Josiah's Bay in the east, and Cane Garden Bay. Apple Bay sees reliable two- to four-foot waves during the season and is probably the most heavily surfed location on Tortola. Josiah's Bay is popular among longboarders and is considered "on" when it has one- to three-foot waves. Josiah's is known for its dangerous riptide, so be careful in rougher conditions.

"The Point," at the far eastern end of Cane Garden Bay, is mythic among surfers. When it's on, Cane Garden Bay delivers six- to seven-foot waves that last up to 200 yards. Cane Garden Bay is on only about a dozen days a year; when it is, word spreads quickly among all who surf.

© SUSANNA HENIGHAN POTTER

catching a wave at Apple Bay

TORTOLA

Surfers also sometimes paddle to Cooten Bay, west of Josiah's Bay, for a change of scenery and nice meaty waves.

Island Surf and Sail (Soper's Hole Marina, 284/494-0123, www.bviwatertoys.com) offers surf equipment rentals and lessons and organizes the annual Tortola Surf Classic in February, a youth surf competition. On the east end, rent surfboards and equipment from **HIHO** (Trellis Bay, 284/494-7694), starting at $20 per day.

Debi and Bob Carson build custom boards at their studio in Cane Garden Bay, **Cane Garden Bay Surfboards** (www.canegardenbay.net).

Windsurfing

Windsurfing, a cross between sailing and surfing, is exhilarating and physically challenging. When conditions are right, windsurfers skim across the water at speeds rivaling those of a speedboat. Beginners can get a taste of this sport with lessons, while experienced windsurfers will find plenty of gear to rent and a community of kindred spirits.

Island Surf and Sail (Soper's Hole Marina, 284/494-0123, www.bviwatertoys.com) rents windsurfing equipment starting at $50 per day. You can also rent a range of gear or take lessons at **Boardsailing BVI** (Trellis Bay, 284/495-2447, fax 284/495-1626, www.windsurfing.vi, 7 A.M.–6 P.M. daily). A two-hour beginner's lesson costs $75.

Stand Up Paddleboarding

Stand Up Paddleboarding, or SUP, is just what it sounds like: stand on a paddleboard and use an oar to push yourself around the water. Easier to learn than windsurfing, SUP offers a great physical workout and the ability to explore shallow marine environments otherwise inaccessible. From your elevated vantage point, you will catch sight of fish and other marine life through crystal waters.

SUP lessons, rentals, and advice are available from **Island Surf and Sail** (Soper's Hole Marina, 284/494-0123, www.bviwatertoys.com). Lessons cost $75–100 per person.

Kayaking

When there's no wind, water-sports enthusiasts often turn to kayaks for a little excitement. Seaworthy one- and two-person kayaks are a good way to explore coastal areas, especially on the southern shore of Tortola and other protected areas.

Kayaking can be hard work, especially if there is strong wind, current, waves, or all of the above. But it is a great way to maneuver around mangroves, rocky shores, and other hard-to-reach areas.

You can rent kayaks from **Island Surf and Sail** (Nanny Cay Marina, 284/494-0123, www.bviwatertoys.com) or **Boardsailing BVI** (Trellis Bay, 284/495-2447, www.windsurfing.vi). For a guided kayak tour, contact **Tortola Kayak Snorkel & Eco Tours** (UBS Dive Centre, Harbour View Marina, East End, 284/494-0024 or 284/496-8475, www.tortolakayak-tours.com). The guided tour, only available to groups with advance reservations, explores the mangroves, sea grass beds, and secluded sand beaches of East End, as well as some off-the-beaten-track historic sites of the area.

Fishing

Pursue tarpon, permit, and bonefish with Nanny Cay–based **Caribbean Fly Fishing** (Nanny Cay Marina, 284/494-4797, www.caribflyfishing.com), which leads fly-fishing trips around Tortola. Rates for two people are $650 for three-quarters of a day and $850 for a full day. The company also offers wading trips ($325 for a half day, $480 for a full day).

SAILING

The British Virgin Islands are the sailing capital of the Caribbean and Tortola is home to nearly all the BVI's 800-plus charter yachts, dozens of day-sail operators, sailing schools, two yacht clubs, and a community of enthusiastic sailors. While Tortola may lag behind the rest of the world in many things, don't be surprised to find the latest sailing technology, services, and equipment here.

Day Sails

For visitors who have chosen land-based accommodation over a charter yacht, a day sail is often the easiest and best way to see what this sailing fuss is all about.

Day sail operators usually take guests to a handful of popular sites: Norman Island, the Baths, and Jost Van Dyke are the most common. Each operator fosters a different kind of atmosphere aboard, ranging from party-hardy to family-oriented. If you have a large group, many operators will offer a private charter where you get to choose your destinations. Most operators offer both half- and full-day trips. Full-day sails range $100–125 per person, while half-day sails run $80–100. Most serve lunch on board. This is one aspect of your vacation that you should plan in advance; many day-sail companies book up, especially in high season.

Patouche Charters (Harbour View Marina, East End, 284/494-6300, www.patouche.com) wins the prize for friendliest crew and is an especially good choice if there are inexperienced snorkelers in your group. The company offers a wide variety of trips, including sails to the Baths, Norman Island, Peter Island, and sunset cruises.

White Squall II (Village Cay Marina, 284/494-2564, www.whitesquall2.com) is an 80-foot traditional schooner that takes day sailors to the Baths, Norman Island, and Cooper Island. It tends to book large groups.

Departing from West End, three different catamarans offer day sails to Jost Van Dyke, Norman Island, and other destinations: **Aristocat Charters** (284/499-1249, www.aristocatcharters.com), **Kuralu** (284/495-4381,

www.kuralu.com), and **Mystique** (284/494-0740, www.voyagecharters.com) all depart from Soper's Hole Marina.

Motorboat Rentals

Renting a boat is a good way for experienced boaters to chart their own course for a day or more. It's not cheap, though; powerboats go for $200 and up for a day's rental, excluding fuel. Expect to pay twice that, at least, if you need a skipper.

Island Time (Nanny Cay Marina, 284/495-9993, www.islandtimeltd.com) offers 22-foot Contenders and rigid-hull inflatables for long- and short-term rentals. Rates are $220 and up. **King Charters** (Nanny Cay Marina, 284/494-5820, www.kingcharters.com) rents 30-foot Bradleys, perfect for day trips to the outer islands, from $375 per day. **C&D Powerboat Rentals** (Major Bay, 284/542-9104 or 284/495-2646, www.cdpowerboats.com) rents a wide range of motor boats, from 12-foot dinghies to 40-foot luxury yachts.

Marinas
ROAD TOWN
Road Harbour is home to a half dozen different marinas, which offer a place to dock your boat, plus amenities like electricity, water, showers, restaurants, and hotels.

Village Cay (Wickham's Cay, 284/494-2771) is a 100-slip marina that can accommodate boats up to 150 feet in length. It is home to a popular restaurant, bar, and hotel. Services include a spa, laundry, showers, phone service, and cable TV.

Fort Burt Marina (284/494-4200) in Road Reef on the western end of Road Harbour has permanent and overnight slips, water, fuel, ice, and power.

SEA COW'S BAY
Manual Reef Marina (Sea Cow's Bay, 284/495-2066) is a 40-slip marina offering electricity, water, showers, wireless Internet, and yacht

management. **Nanny Cay Marina** (Nanny Cay, 284/494-2512) is a full-service boatyard and marina with a 40-room hotel, two restaurants, a chandlery, a spa, Internet access, and much more.

WEST END

On the west end, **Soper's Hole Wharf and Marina** (Frenchman's Cay, 284/495-4589) has 50 slips, a small hotel, and services. It also has moorings. Also at Soper's Hole, **Frenchman's Cay Shipyard and Marina** (284/495-4353) has dockage for ships up to 150 feet, a chandlery, and repairs. It specializes in wooden yachts, multihulls, and teak decking.

EAST END

Hodge's Creek Marina (Maya Cove, 284/494-5000) is one of the largest marinas on the east end of Tortola. In East End Bay, **Penn's Landing Marina** (East End, 284/495-1134) and **Harbour View Marina** (East End, 284/495-0165) provide services and overnight accommodation.

Anchorages

Probably the favorite anchorage on Tortola, **Cane Garden Bay** is usually comfortable for overnight use. Be sure to stay out of the swimming area. There is a dinghy dock on the eastern end of the bay, near Quito's Gazebo.

On the west end, **Soper's Hole** has moorings for visiting yachts, plus restaurants, groceries, and other supplies.

A nice anchorage on the east end is **Buck Island,** off Maya Cove. Anchor on the southwestern shore in 7–10 feet of water. Also on the east, **Trellis Bay,** Beef Island, is a great stop for yachters. Check on the latest regulations in the area, however, as the presence of the international airport has rendered some parts of the harbor off limits.

Yacht Clubs

Both the **Royal BVI Yacht Club** (Road Reef, 284/494-3286, www.rbviyc.net) and the **"Loyal" West End Yacht Club** (Soper's Hole, www.weyc.net) put on a series of regattas every year. Hang out among the yacht crowd long enough and you are bound to be invited along if there's a regatta coming up.

Some of the West End Yacht Club's most popular local races are the Firecracker Regatta held every July 4, the Anegada Dark and Stormy in March, and the Sweethearts of the Caribbean in February.

The Royal BVI Yacht Club puts on the Road Tortola Race every November, the Virgins Cup (where the skipper must be a woman) in October, and the Anegada Pursuit Race in July.

LAND PURSUITS
Hiking

Hiking trails on Tortola are found at **Sage Mountain National Park** off the Ridge Road and **Shark Bay National Park** at Brewer's Bay. Other nice places for walking are the quiet roads around Belmont, West End, and the road that traverses the easternmost tip of Tortola, beginning near the Beef Island Bridge.

Biking

Biking is an increasingly popular sport on Tortola, and it is not unusual to see bikers out in the early morning or late afternoon, especially along Drake's Highway, the flat road that connects West End and Road Town. If you want a challenge, there is no shortage of hills to choose from. Two of the best are the fearsome "East End Wall," a steep road between Greenland and Lambert in East End, and Trellfall, which climbs to Sage Mountain from the westernmost end of Sea Cow's Bay. Once you get there, the ride along the Ridge Road is pleasant and relatively flat.

The **BVI Bicycling Federation** (www.bvi-cycling.com) puts on a series of bike races, including the Jason Bally Memorial in October, which often attracts racers from around the Caribbean. Serious bikers are welcome to join in for a race, and many races feature a novice/ fun class for less-seasoned riders. Nature's Little Secrets Cycle Club also puts on time trials and road races throughout the year.

Road and mountain bikes can be rented from **Last Stop Sports** (Purcell, 284/494-1120, 9:30 A.M.–6 P.M. Mon.–Fri., 9:30 A.M.–3:30 P.M. Sat.) for $30–40 a day.

Tennis

There are no public tennis courts on Tortola, but you can pay to use courts at many of the larger resorts. Expect to pay $5–15 per hour. In the west, there are courts at **Long Bay Beach Resort** (284/495-4252) and **Nanny Cay** (284/494-2512). Out cast, try **Lambert Beach Resort** (284/495-2877). In Road Town, the **Tortola Sports Club** (Pasea Estate, 284/494-3457, www.tortolasportsclub.com) has tennis and squash courts. Visitors can purchase temporary membership to the club, which puts on the BVI Tennis Open every June.

Golf

There are no golf courses on Tortola, but if you want to practice your swing in a laid-back environment, try **Captain Mulligan's** (Nanny Cay, 284/495-4414, noon–dusk), where you can drive golf balls into the ocean and watch them float back in to shore.

Spectator Sports

Sports including cricket, basketball, and softball are played in the BVI. The best way to find out about upcoming sporting events is to consult the *Limin' Times,* a free weekly entertainment guide that includes a sports calendar.

Men's and women's fast-pitch **softball** is played at the Old Recreation Grounds next to the BVI High School in Road Town. The season usually begins in March and wraps up in July. Games are played on Friday, Saturday, and Sunday nights.

Basketball is played in the Multi-Purpose Complex on Botanic Station Road in Road Town. The season usually opens in May and concludes in July.

Cricket is played on the Greenland field in East End, and pickup games take place sometimes on the open space next to the cruise ship pier at the waterfront or at the Festival Grounds near the Road Town roundabout.

Horse racing is very popular among islanders, and there is always a crowd for the races at the Ellis Thomas Downs in Sea Cow's Bay. Races are held about seven times a year on Sunday afternoons, except for the annual August Festival races held on the second Tuesday in August and the Boxing Day Races on December 26.

Athletics are also popular, and meets take place at the A.O. Shirley Recreation Grounds in the center of Road Town. Consult the local media to find out if any events are planned during your visit.

Accommodations

Tortola has small inns, locally-owned villas, and resorts.

VILLAS

Tortola, like other Virgin Islands, is well endowed with a variety of private villas. While most of these are luxurious (and expensive), some can fit more modest budgets, especially during summer. Winter rates generally range $1,200–4,000 a week for one- to two-bedroom homes. In summer, rates drop, ranging $700–2,000.

Private villas are completely equipped homes: They have full kitchens, several bedrooms, entertainment centers, and water-sports gear. Many have a private pool. Villas are a great choice for families or large groups, or for visitors who want independence and privacy.

The easiest way to find a private villa is to use a villa rental agency. These agencies represent dozens of villas, making it easy to find one that fits your needs. The best villa rental agencies on Tortola are **Areana Villas** (P.O. Box 263, Road Town, Tortola, 284/494-5864, www.areanavillas.com) and **Purple Pineapple Rental Management** (284/495-3100, fax 305/723-0855, www.purplepineapple.com).

ROAD TOWN

Stay in Road Town only if you are traveling for business or need a convenient hotel before or after your Road Town–based yacht charter. The town atmosphere is simply not the best Tortola has to offer.

Under $125

Hotel Castle Maria (Macnamara Rd., 284/494-2553, $110–120 winter, $90–115 summer) is a 30-room hotel in a shady residential neighborhood outside Road Town, but it's within walking distance of shops and marinas. The hotel facilities here are adequate but nothing more. The rooms are small and the decor is dated, but the neighborhood is pleasant and quiet (with the exception of the roosters) and there is a mature garden on the property. The Hotel Castle Maria is a good alternative if you need to stay near town but don't want to shell out big bucks for a fancy hotel.

Located on one of Road Town's busiest and most colorful commercial side streets, the **A&L Inn** (Fleming St., 284/494-6343, www.aandlinn.com, $110–120 winter, $90–115 summer) is a good choice if you need affordable but comfortable accommodation in the capital. The inn's 14 air-conditioned rooms are clean; some have kitchenettes.

$125-175

Hummingbird House Bed and Breakfast (Pasea Estate, 284/494-0039, www.hummingbirdbvi.com, $140–155) offers homey accommodations in a residential neighborhood about 10 minutes walk from downtown Road Town. Guests choose from four rooms, including three that can sleep up to four people (though you pay $30 for each additional person after two). Rooms have air-conditioning (you'll pay a $20–35 surcharge for using it), televisions, refrigerators, and coffeemakers. The house is surrounded by mature trees, and the pool and deck offer an inviting place to relax. Hostess Yvonne is a cat lover; those with allergies should book elsewhere. A hot made-to-order breakfast is included in the rates.

$175-225

Located at Road Town's largest marina, **Village Cay Hotel** (284/494-2771, www.villagecayhotelandmarina.com, $150–225 winter, $125–195 summer) is convenient for yachters and businesspeople. The 19 air-conditioned rooms come with TV and phone, and the best have nice views of the marina. Two-bedroom suites ($305) are also available. A popular restaurant and bar are downstairs, and the hotel is within walking distance of dozens of other places to eat.

Maria's by the Sea (Waterfront Dr., 284/494-2595, www.mariasbythesea.com, $160–205 winter, $130–200 summer) has attractive views of Road Harbour but no beach. Facilities at the hotel, which began a major expansion in 2011, include a pool, restaurant, and conference room. The air-conditioned rooms come with telephones and TV. There is one wheelchair-accessible room here and a two-bedroom suite. Maria's is next door to the government administration building and is within easy walking distance of restaurants and the business center.

A bit more upscale than other Road Town hotels, **Treasure Isle** (James Walter Francis Dr., 284/494-2501, www.pennhotels.com, $190–275 winter, $170–225 summer) caters to business travelers. One of Road Town's oldest hotel properties, Treasure Isle underwent a major overhaul in the mid-2000s and now boasts some of the most modern rooms in the capital city. All have pleasant views of Road Harbour and the surrounding landscape, although those on the upper stories are better. Amenities include wireless Internet access, large work desks, in-room coffeemakers, and flat-screen televisions. The property has a pool and restaurant. The heart of Road Town is a five-minute walk away.

$225-300

Located at charter boat hub the Moorings, **Moorings Mariner Inn** (Wickham's Cay II, 284/494-2333, www.bvimarinerinnhotel.com, $220–395 winter, $160–320 summer) has a block of motel-style unrenovated rooms (which frankly are overpriced and best avoided) and a small number of new, upscale waterfront rooms. Convenient before or after a charter, the

new rooms, with vaulted ceilings, stylish bathrooms, and dark wood finishes, are also a good choice for business travelers. Three restaurants on site serve breakfast, lunch, and dinner daily.

CANE GARDEN BAY

The most happening of Tortola's beachfront communities, Cane Garden Bay is also home to a wide selection of affordable accommodations.

Under $125

Sun Set Vacation Apartments (284/495-4751, fax 284/495-9114, www.sunsetvacationapartments.com, $100–130) has a loyal following of guests who come back year after year for modest but comfortable rooms just steps from Cane Garden Bay beach. The two-story, family-operated apartment complex has eight one-bedroom and two two-bedroom units, each with air-conditioning, ceiling fan, kitchen, and cable TV. The proprietors, who operate a colorful local shop next door, will rent local mobile phones to guests.

Another good choice for no-frills accommodation is **Carrie's Comfort Inn** (284/495-9220, www.stanleycomfort.com, $100 winter, $65 summer), located 220 yards uphill from the beach. Carrie's provides all the basics: bed, bath, and living rooms; a kitchenette; air-conditioning; and a balcony. Under the same management, **Stanley's Welcome Villas** (284/495-9544, www.stanleycomfort.com, $850–1,500 per week) offers one- and two-bedroom villas in a cheerful pink concrete apartment building overlooking Cane Garden Bay. Villas have full kitchens, air-conditioning, living rooms, dining rooms, and balconies. Both properties are located on a hillside facing Cane Garden Bay and offer lovely views of the bay.

Just steps from the beach and across the street from Quito Rymer's Gazebo Bar and Restaurant, the **Ole Works Inn** (284/495-4837, www.quitorymer.com, $100–200 winter, $90–185 summer) provides no-frills accommodation for beach lovers. Rooms range from modest pool-side options to a honeymoon suite with a balcony and lovely views of the ocean. There is a pool, and rooms have air-conditioning, cable TV, telephones, coffeemakers, and refrigerators. The inn can be noisy, especially on weekends, when there is live music across the road at the Gazebo.

$125-175

◖ **Mongoose Apartments** (284/495-4421, www.mongooseapartments.com, $200–240 winter, $145–175 summer) is a brightly painted and well-managed inn a short walk from Cane Garden Bay beach. The eight one-bedroom apartments include full kitchens, outdoor grills, air-conditioning in the bedrooms, TVs, and sleeping accommodations for up to four people. A phone is available in the office, and guests can use the inn's beach chairs, snorkels, floats, and kayaks for free. Hosts Elroy and Sandra Henley will happily help you arrange activities during your stay, and don't miss the wall of newspaper clippings recounting Elroy's success as a minor league baseball star in Chattanooga, Tennessee, in the late 1970s. There are no dramatic ocean views here, but the inn's location nestled among coconut and banana trees is so charming you probably won't mind.

$175-225

Steps away from the beach, the **Cane Garden Bay Cottages** (284/495-9649, www.virginislandsholiday.com, $190 winter, $135 summer) are two cute cottages surrounded by coconut trees. Each cottage is divided into two one-bedroom units, each with a small kitchen, sitting area, screened-in dining room, and porch. Larger groups may rent both sides of a cottage. There is air-conditioning in the bedrooms.

Over $300

The Lighthouse Villas (284/494-5482, fax 284/495-9101, www.lighthousevillas.com) is

a few (steep) steps above the beach at Cane Garden Bay. The three-story concrete structure rises above the surrounding buildings, giving guests lovely views of the bay. The best views are from the two penthouse suites on the third floor. The one- and two-bedroom villas are neat, clean, and homey, with full kitchens, private balconies, phones, cable TV, and air-conditioning. Guests share a hot tub. Stays of at least a week are preferred. In winter for double occupancy, weekly rates range $1,225–2,000. Two-bedroom suites are available for $2,000–3,000 per week. For short-term rates, add 10 percent.

BREWER'S BAY
Under $125

Brewer's Bay Campground (284/494-3463, $50) has a dozen campsites nestled under the palms at beautiful Brewer's Bay beach. Prepared sites come with a platform tent, beds, bedding, a two-burner propane stove, a cooler, a table, chairs, and cooking equipment. You must provide your own ice and drinking water. Bare sites, which come with a table, chairs, and a place to pitch your tent, are available for $25 per night. Shared bathrooms are at a concrete bathhouse, with utility sink, toilets, and (cold water) showers.

The greatest attraction here is being able to sleep just a few steps away from Brewer's Bay beach, one of the best and least disturbed beaches on Tortola. Area bars and restaurants close at night, making evenings peaceful. The campground facilities are increasingly run-down, and the unsophisticated approach to guest services may be charming or frustrating, depending on your perspective.

Consider logistics if you stay here; Brewer's Bay has no grocery store and few restaurants, and taxis charge upwards of $20 for a one-way trip to town. Walking to the nearest market in Cane Garden Bay will easily take several hours. It is a good idea to either stock up on groceries before you come or plan to rent a car.

EAST ISLAND
Under $125
Located a 10-minute walk from Josiah's Bay Beach, **Serendipity House** (284/495-1488, www.serhouse.com, $90–105) is a sprawling villa complex with one-, two-, and five-bedroom suites, including full kitchens, TV, telephone, and a shared pool. **Near the Beach Hostel** (284/443-7833, www.josiahsbaybvi.com, $70–90) offers four rooms, two with private baths, to visitors seeking a no-fuss place to lay their heads. Rooms are equipped with double beds and kitchenettes and the beach is about 100 yards away.

$125-175
Located on Trellis Bay, **The Beef Island Guesthouse** (284/495-2303, www.beefislandguesthouse.com, $130 winter, $100 summer) is a homey bed-and-breakfast convenient to the airport and the ferry to North Sound. The guesthouse's four rooms boast comfortable beds, ceiling fans, and private baths (no air-conditioning). There is a shared living room, a full kitchen, and a screened-in porch. Amenities include satellite TV, high-speed Internet, and continental breakfast.

The guesthouse is set right on Trellis Bay, where you can swim or relax in a hammock. There is a restaurant and a beach bar next door. The guesthouse is the only place to stay within walking distance of the airport and is a popular choice for people who need a room the day before or after a sailing charter.

The Tamarind Club (284/495-3477, www.tamarindclub.com, $139–199 winter, $115–155 summer) is a small inn set amid flamboyant trees on the road to Josiah's Bay beach. The nine rooms face either the pool or the garden and come equipped with air-conditioning, phone, and television (no cable, but plenty of videos). There is a continental breakfast for guests.

Over $300
Lovely, quiet, and elegant, ◖ **Surfsong Villa**

Resort (Beef Island, 284/495-1864, www.surfsong.net, $500–1,000 winter, $400–885 summer) is a small estate in secluded Well Bay on Beef Island. The six well-equipped one- and two-bedroom villas are tucked amid tropical gardens with views of crystal blue waters. The villas feature exposed wood ceilings and offer courtyards, porches, and balconies that make it easy to feel a part of the beautiful surroundings. Comforts include satellite TV, wireless Internet, ceiling fans, resort robes, fully equipped kitchens, ceiling fans, and air-conditioning in all bedrooms. Expert concierge service is provided by owner-operators Cate and Mark Stephenson, who pay attention to every detail for the benefit of their well-cared-for guests.

WEST ISLAND
Under $125
Budget travelers look to **The Jolly Roger Inn** (284/495-4559, fax 284/495-4184, www.jollyrogerbvi.com, $85–106 winter, $67–89 summer) for cheap accommodation near the West End ferry dock, Soper's Hole, restaurants, and car rental. Rooms are as basic as they come; there are no telephones, TVs, or kitchenettes; not all rooms have air conditioning and some share a bathroom.

$225-300
Perched above one of the most picturesque beaches on Tortola, ◖ **Long Bay Beach Resort** (284/495-4252 or 866/237-3491, www.longbay.com, $300–440 winter, $260–385 summer) is the island's largest hotel. Open since 1963, it is one of Tortola's oldest resorts, too, although you wouldn't guess it from the modern facilities. The 153 rooms range from small one-bedroom beachside cabanas to spacious two-bedroom villas on the hillside above. The resort also manages a half dozen privately owned estate homes, which boast the best views of the mile-long beach below. All rooms have air-conditioning, TV, phone, and refrigerator, and many have full

kitchens. Resort amenities include a pool, three restaurants, a nine-hole pitch-and-putt golf course, tennis courts, a spa, a gym, a dive shop, car rental agencies, and water-sports equipment rental. The large pool with a swim-up bar and lots of space for sunning is popular. Breakfast and dinner in the resort restaurants can be included for $50 more per person per night.

The **Heritage Inn** (284/494-5842, www.heritageinnbvi.com, $225–275 winter, $135–185 summer) is atop Windy Hill, overlooking Carrot Bay and points farther west. Its spectacular view of western Tortola and the U.S. Virgin Islands is its most outstanding attraction. Its nine modern rooms are equipped with phones, TVs, full kitchens, private balconies, and air-conditioning in the bedrooms. Amenities include an on-site pool and restaurant. Beaches are about 10 minutes away in either direction by car. Both one- and two-bedroom accommodations are available

Sebastian's on the Beach (Apple Bay, 284/495-4212 or 800/336-4870, www.sebastiansbvi.com, $250–350 winter, $150–250 summer) is a 26-room boutique hotel facing picturesque Apple Bay, a favorite for surfers. In addition to beachfront and garden rooms, Sebastian's has several new luxury villas at the west end of the beach. For an additional $50 per day, guests can add breakfast and dinner daily at the on-site restaurant.

Over $300

⟨ The Sugar Mill (284/495-4355, fax 284/495-4696, www.sugarmillhotel.com, $340–365 winter, $260–300 summer) is as good as a luxury Caribbean hideaway can get. The hotel is set amid almond, breadfruit, and mango trees, and many of its 23 air-conditioned rooms have superb ocean views. Accommodations range from well-appointed hotel-style rooms to one- and two-bedroom luxury villas. There is a pool on the property, but most guests prefer to bathe at the idyllic beach right across the road. Ruins of a centuries-old sugar mill have been incorporated into the hotel's award-winning restaurant, which is one of the best places to eat on Tortola. Given that, the hotel's $70-per-day meal plan is worth considering. Children under 11 are not allowed during the winter months, and the hotel closes every August and September.

Fort Recovery Villas (284/495-4467 or 800/367-8455, fax 284/495-4036, www.fortrecovery.com, $310–360 winter, $210–250 summer), a complex of 24 one- to four-bedroom beachfront villas, lies in the shadow of a 17th-century Dutch fort, the oldest extant building on Tortola. The rooms, which are small but comfortable, face the hotel's private beach and offer pleasant views of St. John and the Sir Francis Drake Channel. Amenities include a pool, continental breakfast, yoga classes, Internet access, and a library; for $47 per person per night guests can add breakfast and dinner in the hotel's private restaurant. Family-owned and operated since 1969, Fort Recovery offers a number of attractively priced package deals.

Frenchman's Resort (284/494-8811, www.frenchmansbvi.com, $425 winter, $365 summer) is an intimate villa resort on Frenchman's Cay, a tiny island that lies alongside western Tortola. Frenchman's consists of nine one- and two-bedroom villas, all newly refurbished in a swank Balinese-Caribbean style. The resort is located on a dramatic headland and offers guests views of the Sir Francis Drake Channel and St. John. Snorkeling is good off the small private beach, and guests may also pass the time on the regulation tennis courts, at the pool, or kayaking the waters around the resort. Frenchman's also has a resident masseuse and offers on-site fine dining at the Watermark restaurant. Villas come with a fully equipped modern kitchen, comfortable sitting areas, balconies, and, of course, private baths and spacious bedrooms. Frenchman's offers attractive packages that include spa treatments, day sails, and car rental, among other enticements.

Food

You won't find the sophisticated dining of the U.S. Virgin Islands on Tortola, but you will still find good food. In addition to a handful of truly gourmet restaurants, Tortola has a number of homey beachfront eateries and a whole range of local food choices.

ROAD TOWN

Road Town has the greatest variety of food choices, especially at lunchtime.

Coffee Shops

Head to either one of the town's coffee shops for a good cup. The island's first coffee shop, **D'Best Cup** (Mill Mall, 284/494-3280, 7 A.M.–8 P.M. Mon.–Wed., 7 A.M.–9 P.M. Thurs.–Fri., 7 A.M.–1:30 P.M. Sat., $3–8) still serves the best brew. It shares its premises with a wine bar specializing in South African *vino* and has a few small tables both inside and out on the lawn. **Island Roots** (Old Customs House, Main St., 284/541-9182, 7:30 A.M.–4 P.M. Mon.–Fri., 8:30 A.M.–4 P.M. Sat., $3–9) serves coffee, pastries, and panini in a charming old storefront on Main Street. Snag a window seat for good people-watching.

Ice Cream

For homemade Italian ice cream, head to **La Dolce Vita** (Waterfront Dr., 284/494-8770, 10 A.M.–9 P.M. Mon.–Thurs., 10 A.M.–10 P.M. Fri.–Sat., 10:30 A.M.–9:30 P.M. Sun., $3–5). No kidding—this is the real thing. Try some of the unique flavors like soursop, cantaloupe, and ginger. The shop also serves soy ice cream, frozen yogurt, milkshakes, and banana splits.

Bakeries

Sample the work of H. Lavity Stoutt Community College's culinary students at the **Road Town Bakery** (123 Main St., 284/494-0222, 7 A.M.–7 P.M. Mon.–Fri., 7:30 A.M.–3 P.M. Sat., $5–10), one of three hands-on culinary training centers on Tortola. Don't worry about the quality of the students' work; the bakery produces top-notch pastries, cakes, and breads, as well as a popular lunch menu.

For an authentic Tortolian breakfast, don't be afraid to fight the crowds at popular **Crandalls Pastry Plus** (284/494-5156, 5 A.M.–4 P.M. Mon.–Sat., $3–8). Don't miss the patés (fried bread stuffed with seasoned beef, chicken, or seafood) and local bush tea (a sweetened tea made from herbs including lemongrass and mint). Or try locally made coconut bread sliced and served with scrambled eggs and cheese. Most folks take their food to go, but there are a handful of tables if you want to dine in. At lunch, Crandalls serves local specials including curries, rotis, and barbecue.

West Indian

For authentic West Indian roti, there is nowhere better than the **Roti Palace** (94 Main St., 284/494-4196, 11 A.M.–8 P.M. Mon.–Sat., $10–24). Up a narrow flight of stairs next to Samarkand Jewellers, the Roti Palace serves nothing but rotis, the Indian style wraps filled with curried meat and vegetables. Fillings on offer include chicken, conch, whelk, lobster, goat, and vegetable. The generous wraps come with rice, salad, homemade chutney, and *kuchela*, a spicy condiment made on the premises from hot peppers, green mango, and vinegar. Stepping into this family-run restaurant, in a converted second-story apartment, feels a bit like entering someone's house. Choose to dine in a small courtyard or in the dining room overlooking Main Street. The Roti Palace sometimes closes without notice, especially for the evening meal. Call ahead.

For Tortola's take on the greasy spoon, visit **Mid-Town Restaurant** (132 Main St., 284/494-2764, 7 A.M.–10 P.M., $4–10). Located at the midpoint of Main Street, this aptly named restaurant has a genuine lunch counter as well as about a dozen tables. In addition to local daily specials, such as boiled fish, oxtail soup, and stewed mutton (goat meat), you can get sandwiches and fries. Full American-style breakfasts are available.

Tucked away at the end of a narrow alley in Purcell, a residential community just east of Road Town, is **❐C&F Restaurant** (284/494-4941, 6:30–10 P.M. Thurs.–Tues., $12–25), one of the best West Indian restaurants on the island. Chef Clarence serves fresh fish, steak, lobster, barbecue, and curries. That may sound familiar, but it all just tastes better here. Red-checkered tablecloths and a jumbled decor give the restaurant a homey feel. Takeout is popular, since one dinner plate can easily serve two people.

Munch on Jamaican-style jerk chicken and pork at **Dareo's** (Lower Estate Rd., 6–10 P.M. Fri.–Sat., $4–12), a street vendor that sets up next to the softball field behind the Elmore Stout High School after dark on the weekends. Dinner plates come with your choice of sides, such as macaroni and cheese, peas and rice, salad, coleslaw, and baked potato pie. Dareo's is mobbed many nights, especially Fridays, when a little bit of assertiveness and a lot of patience are necessary to get through the line.

Casual

Village Cay (Wickham's Cay, 284/494-2771, 7:30 A.M.–10 P.M. daily, $7–25) is a casual waterfront restaurant at Road Town's largest marina. Enjoy the view of boats big and small as you tuck into a burger, sandwich, steak, grilled fish, or salad. The bar is popular at happy hour and later and is good place to meet the sailing set.

Italian

Steps away from the Road Town ferry dock, **Capricio di Mare** (Waterfront Dr., 284/494-5369, 8 A.M.–9 P.M. Mon.–Sat., $7–18) is a casual Italian-themed sidewalk café. For breakfast try croissant French toast, fruit, and a cappuccino. The lunch and dinner menu features salads, pastas, pizzas, and focaccia sandwiches.

Fine Dining

Located in a refurbished traditional Caribbean home, **❐The Dove Restaurant** (67 Main St., 284/494-0313, 6:30–10 P.M. Tues.–Sun., $18–55) is an oasis of sophistication in the heart of Road Town. Its upscale clientele come for specialties like the honey and sesame Peking duck and peppercorn-crusted tuna, but the menu changes daily depending on the availability of ingredients and the whim of the chef. The Dove has one of the best wine lists on the island. It is a popular choice for happy hour, and rightfully so: Sink into one of the comfortable alcoves with a glass of wine and you'll soon be unwound.

RIDGE ROAD
Indian and Sushi

Good food meets a one-of-a-kind view at **Sky** (Meyers, 284/494-3567, 6 P.M. till late daily, $12–36). Located high up in the hills, Sky offers dramatic views and an escapist ambience, plus the best ethnic food on Tortola. Choose your pleasure between sushi and Indian: Both are surprisingly good. Come before the sun sets to enjoy the view, and be sure to bring a light jacket to keep warm against the cool breezes that blow up here.

CANE GARDEN BAY
International

Myett's Garden and Grill (284/495-9649, 7 A.M.–9:30 P.M. daily in winter, 11 A.M.–9:30 P.M. daily in summer, $12–35) is a pleasant oasis at the western end of Cane Garden Bay. Its dining area, built amid lush gardens, is a cool retreat from the heat of the beach, just steps away. Lunch here is a casual affair of wraps, salads, rotis, and burgers. For dinner, things get more sophisticated with seafood pasta, roasted duck, and fresh lobster, plus a loaded grill menu.

Get a bird's-eye view of Cane Garden Bay beach at **Sailor's Rest** (Cane Garden Bay, 284/494-5482, 7 A.M.–8 P.M. daily, $6–18), a charming hole-in-the-wall perched near the eastern end of the bay. For breakfast try Coconut Rum French Toast, and during the day choose from a low-key bar menu or local specialties like Fried Fish in Creole Sauce. The decor pays tribute to Tortola sloops and their captains.

EAST ISLAND
Coffee Shops

Gourmet coffee, coffee drinks, smoothies, ice cream, sandwiches, and bar drinks are served at **D'Best Cup** (Trellis Bay, 284/495-0259, 7:30 A.M.–6:30 P.M. Tues.–Sat., $3–7). The coffee here is excellent, and you can enjoy it seated on the inviting and shady patio.

Casual

Charlie's Lobster House (Fat Hog's Bay, 284/495-1010, 11 A.M.–10:30 P.M. daily, $8–20) wins marks for its setting on the water's edge and reasonable prices. The menu features sandwiches, pizza, Pusser's fried chicken, and the namesake lobster.

Casual is the name of the game at **Josiah's Bay Grapetree Bar and Restaurant** (284/495-2818, 11 A.M.–4 P.M., $5–10), where you can grab a burger, sandwich, or barbecue chicken plate, not to mention a whole array of cold drinks. It's perfect for a day at the beach.

The **Trellis Bay Kitchen and Cybercafé** (Trellis Bay, 284/495-2447, 9 A.M.–6 P.M., $5–12) attracts windsurfers, artists, and those hungry for the fruit juice smoothies and Caribbean-inspired lunch and breakfast dishes

on offer. Breakfast is served all day, and lunch includes sandwiches, rotis, and seafood dishes. Try the "awesome sandwich" of mahimahi, vegetables, and tasty sauce on whole wheat. The atmosphere is low-key; seating ranges from picnic tables to comfy couches, and a never-ending loop of groovy chill-out music immediately takes the edge off. The food here is consistently good, and there's an Internet café on the premises.

De Loose Mongoose (Trellis Bay, 284/495-2303, 8:30 A.M.–10 P.M. Tues.–Sun., $5–25) serves casual fare on the water's edge. Try the rotis, burgers, or fish and chips for a substantial lunch. For dinner, favorites include burritos, steak, and grilled fish. Dining is inside a screened-in porch (a plus when mosquitoes are out) or out front at a picnic table. De Loose Mongoose does a Sunday night barbecue in season.

International

Uncommonly sophisticated, **Red Rock Restaurant and Bar** (Penn's Marina, 284/495-1646, www.redrockbvi.net, 3–10 P.M. Tues.–Sun., $18–36) serves upscale dishes in a casual seaside environment. Popular entrees include rosemary-crusted halibut, veal escalope, and pasta primavera. Red Rock also serves homemade pizza and calzone.

WEST ISLAND
West Indian

Don't be turned off by the somewhat ramshackle appearance of **🄲 Palm's Delight** (Carrot Bay, 284/495-4863, 6:30–9 P.M. daily, $8–16), a real gem among restaurants on Tortola. This is simply the best place on the island for local food. Specialties include fried and steamed fish, shrimp, rotis, and a special chicken dish made with Stone's Ginger Wine. Try the generous portions of peas and rice, fried plantain, coleslaw, and vegetables, or ask for fungi, dumplings, and ground provisions. On weekends or in season, come early so you don't have to wait for a table. Service is careful, but slow; don't come here if you're in a rush.

If you're catching an early ferry from West End, try **Zelma's Courtesy** (West End, 284/495-4211, 6 A.M.–4 P.M. daily, $2–8) for breakfast. Zelma's, right across the road from the dock, serves fresh johnnycakes, patés (fried stuffed bread), fried fish, and bush tea. Or try hot "dumb bread" (so called because it is unleavened and does not rise) with cheese.

International

Probably the best restaurant on Tortola, **《The Sugar Mill Restaurant** (Great Apple Bay, 284/495-4355, 7–9 P.M., $18–32) fuses traditional gourmet fare with Caribbean ingredients and style. The service here is second to none. Run by food writers Jeff and Jinx Morgan, the Sugar Mill changes its menu nightly based on what's fresh and in season. Salads, pastas, seafood, and remarkable dessert concoctions are among the favorites. Come early for a sunset cocktail on the patio. Dinner is served in a restored 18th-century sugar factory; Caribbean artwork adorns the walls.

Bananakeet Café (Windy Hill, 284/494-5842, 5:30–9:30 P.M. Mon.–Sun., 10 A.M.–2 P.M. Sun., $18–35) has one of the best views on Tortola: looking west towards Long Bay and then onwards to Jost Van Dyke and St. Thomas. Sunsets are outstanding, so come early for happy hour. Specialties include seafood pasta, Coconut Rum Fish, and Banana Chutney Jerk Pork. The Sunday Pimm's Cocktail Brunch draws a crowd.

Appropriately, the skull and crossbones fly over the **Jolly Roger** (284/495-4559, 8 A.M.–midnight daily, www.jollyrogerbvi.com, $8–32), a bar and restaurant as popular with locals as it is with tourists. Choose to dine upstairs by the bar or downstairs by the waterfront. Regular menu items include barbecue, rotis, pizzas, and salads, while the daily specials always feature fresh seafood, pasta, and meat,

often with an Asian flair. This is a good place for hearty breakfasts, too, and is within walking distance of the West End ferry dock.

For cuisine that reflects the traditions of France and the ingredients and sensibility of the Caribbean, go to **The Club House** (Frenchman's Cay Resort, 284/495-4862, 6:30–10:30 P.M. Tues.–Sat., 11 A.M.–2 P.M. Sun., $18–35). Treat yourself to house-made patés and sausages and the inventive dishes of Chef Paul Mason. The prix-fixe Sunday brunch ($24) is always popular, and Mojito Happy Hour beginning at 4:30 P.M. is a perfect place to unwind.

Casual

The Sugar Mill Restaurant goes casual for lunch at its seaside **Islands Restaurant** (Great Apple Bay, 284/495-4355, noon–2 P.M. daily, $7–15), where you can watch the pelicans dive for food while you enjoy yours. In addition to its regular menu of sandwiches and salads, Islands has daily soup, seafood, and pasta specials. After you eat, relax on the beach next door. This is a great place to while away a few hours.

MARKETS
Grocery Stores

The largest grocery store on Tortola is **Rite Way Food Market** (Pasea Estate, 284/494-2263), located near Wickham's Cay II outside of Road Town. **Bobby's Supermarket** (Wickham's Cay I, 284/495-2140) is smaller but closer to the city center and within walking distance of downtown hotels and marinas.

Smaller markets in East End, Cane Garden Bay, and Soper's Hole provide convenience at slightly higher prices.

Local Seafood

The **BVI Fishing Complex** (Baugher's Bay, 284/494-3491, 8:30 A.M.–5 P.M. Mon.–Fri., 8:30 A.M.–noon Sat.) buys fresh local seafood from local fishermen and passes it on to consumers. Selection depends on the day's catch, but you can usually find a wide variety of reef fish as well as pelagic species such as swordfish, tuna, and snapper.

Farmers Markets

The official weekly farmers market (Agriculture Department, 284/494-3701) is in flux, but you will find vendors selling locally grown fruits and vegetables near the roundabout in Road Town most days. Local goods are also available at Aragorn's Studio (Trellis Bay, 284/495-1849). The Agricultural Station at Paraquita Bay is also a good place to find local farmers.

Information and Services

Tourist Offices

The **BVI Tourist Board Waterfront Office** (Road Town ferry dock, 284/494-7260, 8:30 A.M.–4:30 P.M. daily) has helpful staff and a large selection of brochures and information. Other Tourist Board information booths are located at the airport and the cruise ship dock.

Maps and Charts

Free pocket maps published by American Express are available from car rental agencies, tourist information booths, and many businesses. This map will be adequate for most people. There is also a good map printed in the middle of the free *Welcome Magazine.* For a more detailed map, visit the **Survey Department** (Waterfront Dr., 284/494-3459, 8:30 A.M.–3 P.M. Mon.–Fri.) for the official "tourist" map ($12).

Imray-Iolaire charts are available from **Golden Hind Yacht Services** (Wickham's Cay II, 284/494-2756).

Libraries and Bookstores

The run-down **Road Town Public Library** (Fleming St., 284/494-3428, 8:30 A.M.–7 P.M. Mon.–Fri., 9 A.M.–1 P.M. Sat.) has adult, children's, and reference sections, as well as a West Indian collection. It offers free public Internet access.

The most charming bookstore on Tortola is **Serendipity Books** (Main St., 284/494-5865), which has books by West Indian and BVI authors, as well as an extensive children's collection. **National Educational Services** (Road Reef Plaza, 284/494-3921) has a good collection of works by local authors.

Media

There are three newspapers published on Tortola. *The BVI Beacon* comes out on Thursday; *The Virgin Islands StandPoint* is published on Wednesday; and *The Island Sun* comes out Friday. All three can be obtained from supermarkets and a number of smaller stores around the island.

Major U.S. newspapers are available (for a small fortune) at supermarkets in Road Town, while British papers can be found at **Best of British** (Mill Mall, 284/494-3462).

ZBVI Radio (780 AM) broadcasts local and international news, including the BBC world roundup, daily at 7 A.M., noon, and 5:45 P.M. For music, try **ZROD (103.7 FM)** or **ZVCR (106.9 FM)**.

Emergencies

The British Virgin Islands' only hospital is located in Road Town. **Peebles Hospital** (Main St., 284/494-3497) is named for the British governor who saw to its construction more than 80 years ago. The hospital provides 24-hour emergency, diagnostic, surgical, and obstetric services, as well as regular dialysis and laboratory service. A new hospital is under construction with plans for completion in 2014. Dial **999** in an emergency. There is no

TORTOLA

decompression chamber, and many advanced services are not available. Air ambulance service is provided by **Island Helicopters** (284/499-2663) and VI Airlink (284/495-1652).

There are also private medical clinics. **B&F** (Mill Mall, 284/494-2196, 7 A.M.–5 P.M.) is open seven days a week and has its own pharmacy. **Eureka Medical Clinic** (284/494-2346, 8:30 A.M.–6 P.M. Mon.–Fri., 8:30 A.M.–1 P.M. Sat.) provides numerous doctors and specialists as well as operating a walk-in urgent care center from 6 A.M.–midnight daily. **Vanterpool's** (284/494-2702) and **Medicure** (284/494-6189) are well-stocked pharmacies, both near the Road Town roundabout.

Banks

There are four commercial banks in the British Virgin Islands, clustered in central Road Town, in the area between Village Cay and the Central Administration Complex. They are Puerto Rico–based **Banco Popular** (284/494-2117) and **FirstBank** (284/494-2662); Canadian **Scotiabank** (284/494-2526); and Barbados-based **First Caribbean International Bank** (284/494-2171), the only bank providing currency exchange services.

There are ATMs at Soper's Hole Marina, Paraquita Bay, Pasea Estate (next to Riteway Food Market), in East End, and in Cane Garden Bay.

Banks generally open at 9 A.M. and close as early as 3 P.M. Monday–Friday, although some stay open later on Friday.

Post Offices

The island's main post office is located in the Qwomar II Building at the Port Purcell roundabout, on the east side of Road Town. The post office (284/494-3701, ext. 5160) is open 8:30 A.M.–3:30 P.M. Monday–Friday and 9 A.M.–noon Saturday. You can arrange money orders, mail letters and packages, and buy collectible stamp sets.

Other post offices are located at the West End ferry dock, East End, Carrot Bay, Cane Garden Bay, and at the Terrance B. Lettsome International Airport. You can also buy stamps from J.R. O'Neal Drug Store, next door to the old Post Office building on Main Street in Road Town. The letter drops are still active at the old post office.

International air courier companies FedEx and DHL operate on Tortola.

Communications

You can get online in Road Town, at **Bits and Pieces** (Mill Mall, 284/494-5954, 9 A.M.–5 P.M. Mon.–Fri., $5 for 30 minutes) and the **Road Town Library** (Fleming St., 284/494-3428, 8:30 A.M.–7 P.M. Mon.–Fri., 9 A.M.–1 P.M. Sat., $1.50 for 30 minutes).

On the East End, go to **Trellis Bay Cybercafé** (Beef Island, 284/495-2447, 8 A.M.–11 P.M. daily, $5 for 2 hours). In Cane Garden Bay, try **Myett's** (284/495-9649, 9 A.M.–5 P.M. daily, $5 for 15 minutes).

Customs and Immigration

Immigration and Customs officers are stationed at Tortola's official ports of entry: the West End ferry dock, Road Town ferry dock, and the Terrance B. Lettsome International Airport. As long as you are on a scheduled ferry or plane, there will be an officer on duty to check your passport and clear your goods. If you plan to arrive on a private boat or plane outside of normal working hours, call ahead for instructions.

If you plan to stay more than 30 days, you will have to visit the **Immigration Department** (RJT Edifice Building, Wickham's Cay, 284/494-3471, 8:30 A.M.–4:30 P.M. Mon.–Fri.) for an entry permit renewal. The **Road Town Customs Office** (284/494-3475) is at the Road Town ferry dock on Waterfront Drive.

Launderettes

There are laundries in nearly every community

on Tortola, so ask around to find the one closest to where you are staying. Nearly all provide drop-off service or let you do your own wash. In Road Town, try **Freeman's Launder Centre** (Palm Grove Shopping Center, 284/494-2285,

8 a.m.–5 p.m.), which also provides dry cleaning. If you have a car, it is worth the drive to air-conditioned **Speed Clean** (284/494-9428, 6 a.m.–midnight) in Baugher's Bay, which has plenty of machines and hot water and is open late.

Getting There

By Air

There are no nonstop flights from the U.S. mainland to Tortola. U.S. and Canadian travelers destined for Tortola arrive via San Juan, Puerto Rico, or St. Thomas, U.S. Virgin Islands. American Airlines (www.aa.com), Cape Air (www.capeair.com), and Air Sunshine (www.airsunshine.com) are the main airlines providing scheduled service between the Terrance B. Lettsome International Airport and San Juan. Visitors from Europe can also fly to Antigua or St. Maarten and connect to the BVI on BVI Airways (www.gobvi.com) or LIAT (www.liat.com).

Other travelers fly into St. Thomas and catch a ferry to Tortola. If you choose this route, remember that the last ferry to Tortola usually leaves St. Thomas at 5 p.m.

By Sea

At least four ferry companies offer daily ferry service between Tortola and St. Thomas. Ferries run between Charlotte Amalie and Red Hook, St. Thomas, and Road Town and West End, Tortola. The trip from West End to Red Hook is about 30 minutes; from West End to Charlotte Amalie is about 45 minutes; and from Road Town to Charlotte Amalie is about an hour. Expect to pay about $50 round-trip, regardless of the route you choose. There is an additional $5 departure tax payable to the BVI

Ports Authority at the departure gate. If you are going to the St. Thomas airport, it's best to get a ferry that will take you all the way to Charlotte Amalie (you'll save on the taxi).

Up-to-date ferry schedules are printed in *The Welcome* (www.bviwelcome.com) and on its website. There is no need for advance ferry reservations, but it is essential to confirm the schedule on the day of your journey, as ferry schedules are subject to change.

Ferry companies operating between the U.S. and British Virgin Islands are **Native Son** (284/494-4617 or 340/774 8685, www.nativesonferry.com, Charlotte Amalie and Red Hook to West End and Road Town); **Smith's Ferry Service** (also called Tortola Fast Ferry) (284/494-4495 or 340/775-7292, Charlotte Amalie and Red Hook to West End and Road Town); and **Road Town Fast Ferry** (284/494-2323 or 340/777-2800, www.roadtownfastferry.com, Charlotte Amalie to Road Town).

From St. John, **Inter-Island Boat Services** (284/495-4166, www.interislandboatservices.com, Cruz Bay to West End, $45 round-trip) makes four trips daily.

If you eschew crowds, charter the **Virgin Islands Water Taxi** (Red Hook, St. Thomas, 340/775-6501, www.watertaxi-vi.com) for $325 and up from Red Hook to West End and other points in the British Virgin Islands (five-person minimum).

Getting Around

Tortola is a relatively small place—12 miles long and about 3 miles wide—but it is not necessarily easy to get around. There is no public transportation, except for an ad-hoc system of private shuttle buses; the steep hills make walking and biking challenging for most of us; and taxis and rental cars are pricey.

If you expect to do a lot of exploring, it is wise to rent a car. Taxi fares add up. Many visitors on a budget choose to rent a car for one or two days to explore the island and then stay put for the rest of their vacation.

Nearly any taxi will take you on a two-hour island tour ($110 for two people), stopping at the best-known sights. But for that price, most people are better off renting a car and driving themselves.

Taxis

Taxis and the rates they charge are regulated by the government, but it is still a good idea to agree up front on a rate. The fare between the airport and Road Town for one person is $27; two people will pay $14 each; three people, $12 each. From Road Town to Cane Garden Bay is $24 for one; $12 each for two; $8 each for three.

Taxi stands are located at most heavily trafficked places. In Road Town, try the **Waterfront Taxi Stand** (284/494-6456) next to the Road Town ferry dock or the **Road Town Taxi Stand** (284/494-6362) on Wickham's Cay. The **Beef Island Taxi Association** (Terrance B. Lettsome International Airport, 284/495-1982) operates at the airport. The **West End Taxi Association** (284/495-4934) is opposite the West End ferry dock. **Nanny Cay Taxi Stand** (284/494-0539) is next to Nanny Cay Hotel.

If you need an early morning taxi, call the night before. Choose the taxi association closest to you, and expect to pay extra if they come to pick you up.

Rental Cars

There is a plethora of car rental agencies on Tortola. Almost all of them rent two- and four-door SUVs, ranging from small Suzuki Sidekicks to large Mitsubishi Pajeros. Expect to pay about $60 per day for a rental that seats four people, more for larger ones. It is usually worthwhile to compare prices, because there can be substantial variation among rental companies. You will have to pay $10 more for a temporary driver's license (obtainable at the rental agency) and can choose from a range of insurance packages.

U.S.-based rental chains including **Hertz** (West End and Terrance B. Lettsome International Airport, 284/495-4405, www.hertzbvi.com), **Avis** (Road Town, Terrance B. Lettsome International Airport, and West End, 284/494-3322), and **Dollar** (East End and Long Bay, 284/494-6093, www.carrentalsbvi.com) have offices here.

In Road Town, **Itgo Car Rental** (Mill Mall, 284/494-2639) has some of the cheapest rates on the island. **International Car Rentals** (Fishlock Rd., 284/494-251, www.carrentals.vg) has a good selection of Suzuki vehicles. Other reliable agencies include **Denzil Clyne Jeep and Car Rental** (West End, 284/495-4900), **Jerry's Car Rental** (West End, 284/495-4111), and **Del's Jeep and Car Rental** (Cane Garden Bay, 284/495-9356).

Out Islands: Sir Francis Drake Channel

If Road Town is just too crowded for your taste, get out your map and discover some of the British Virgin Islands' small outer islands. Some are home to relaxed beach bars and restaurants; others house full-service resorts; and still more are home to nothing more than seabirds and a few goats. Under the sea surrounding these islands are some of the Virgin Islands' best snorkeling and diving sites, including its most famous shipwreck dive, the wreck of the *Rhone.*

An out island can be home base for your vacation or a day trip destination. Almost without exception, a private boat—charter or otherwise—is the best (and in some cases only) way to reach these islands. They are, by definition, off the beaten track.

Several of the BVI's most popular "outer islands" lie across the Sir Francis Drake Channel from Tortola. Schoolchildren in the BVI learn the phrase "Norman gave Peter salt so Cooper could buy ginger" to remember the order of these islands. These islands can be visited in sequence over the course of a day if you have your own boat. Sailboats often cruise up the row, stopping here and there to eat, snorkel, or overnight. Necker and Mosquito Islands are generally only hospitable to registered guests.

NORMAN ISLAND

Long associated with pirate treasure, Norman Island is a one-square-mile island and the westernmost of the row of islands that line the Sir Francis Drake Channel. It is claimed that the island was the inspiration for Robert Louis Stevenson's 1883 novel *Treasure Island.* True or no (Stevenson never traveled here, but he may have seen a map of the island), it is easy enough to be convinced that Stevenson's imagined island was much like Norman Island. In modern times, a legend flourished that a local fisherman found pirate booty in one of the underwater caves on Norman Island.

The Bight is Norman Island's largest bay and most popular anchorage. There are two bars and restaurants here, and it is a short dinghy trip to some excellent snorkeling. Those seeking solitude may prefer anchoring at Benure's or Money Bay instead.

◖ Snorkeling at Norman Island

Norman Island has some great snorkeling and is one of the most popular destinations for day sail snorkeling trips in the British Virgins. **The Caves,** to the west of the Bight, are one of the few places where you can see darkness-dwelling coral and fish in the middle of the day. Bring an underwater flashlight if you want to plumb the full 70-foot length of the largest of the caves. **Kelly's Cove,** east of the Bight, is a shallow, diverse reef great for beginning snorkelers. **The Indians,** near neighboring Pelican Rock, is considered one of the best reef dives in the BVI, but it is rewarding for snorkelers, too. Other good sites are **Angelfish Reef, Spyglass Wall,** and **Sandy Ledge,** all a short boat trip from the Bight. And for those without access to a boat, the reef just offshore the beach at the Bight is surprisingly rewarding. **Sail Caribbean Divers** (The Bight, 284/495-1675) operates a dive shop on Norman. In addition to offering diving excursions, classes, and gear, Sail Caribbean also rents kayaks and snorkel gear.

Food

At Norman Island you can choose between dining on land or the sea. ◖ **Pirate's Bight** (The Bight, 284/496-7827, channels 16 and 69, www.normanislandpirates.com, 11 A.M.–9 P.M., $12–40) sits square in the middle of the Bight, in front of the dinghy dock and just a few yards away from a peaceful sandy beach. There are hammocks and beach chairs where you can sip a piña colada and while away an afternoon. At

TORTOLA

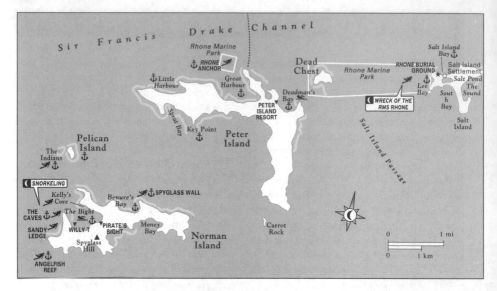

4 P.M. the bartender sets off a mini cannon, signaling the beginning of happy hour. A good deal of happiness ensues. Lunch is a casual affair of burgers, rotis, and sandwiches. At dinner expect delectable fresh lobster, seafood, and expertly grilled steak.

If you would rather dine on the water, your choice is the **Willy T** (284/496-8603, channel 16 or 74, www.williamthornton.com, 11 A.M.–9 P.M., $9–24), one of the BVI's most celebrated watering holes. A 100-foot steel schooner, the *William Thornton* (its proper name) has been serving cold beer, belly shots, and the shotski since 1989. It specializes in booze of all kinds (no blended drinks, however) and serves lunch and dinner, too. The menu features burgers, sandwiches, seafood, steak, and pasta, but, frankly, folks don't come here for the food.

Getting There

There are many ways to get to Norman Island, but they all include a boat and point to The Bight, the island's best harbor. The most popular way to reach Norman is aboard one of the

day sail and dive operators from Tortola, St. Thomas, or St. John which head to Norman daily. Call the operator of your choice several days in advance to reserve your place. Operators departing from Road Town and Nanny Cay will have the shortest sail, about 20 minutes; from East End or West End plan on 30 minutes or more. Trips from St. John and St. Thomas take between 45 minutes and 1 hour (you will also need to clear customs and immigration).

Boaters can also get to Norman Island on a day-long powerboat rental. Rent a boat from the Nanny Cay area on Tortola for a short 20-minute drive across the channel to Norman.

If all else fails, you can always take the informal ferry operated by Pirate's Bight Restaurant. Departure is usually around 11 A.M., with returns at 4 P.M. and 9 P.M. You'll ride over with the restaurant staff; you're expected to dine in the restaurant in exchange for the trip. The ferry lands at The Bight, where there is a small but pleasant beach, good snorkeling and ready access to drinks and food. The ferry's schedule and availability is subject to change and there is a limit to the number of passengers who can be

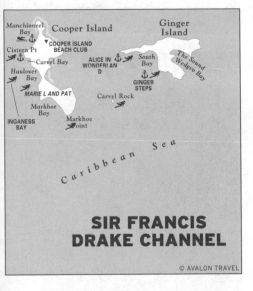

Manchioneel Bay
Cooper Island
Ginger Island
Cistern Pt
COOPER ISLAND BEACH CLUB
Careel Bay
ALICE IN WONDERLAND
South Bay
The Sound Wedgeo Bay
Haulover Bay
GINGER STEPS
MARIE LAND PAT
Carvel Rock
Markhoe Bay
INGANESS BAY
Markhoe Point
Caribbean Sea

SIR FRANCIS DRAKE CHANNEL

© AVALON TRAVEL

accommodated. Call 284/496-7827 for more information.

PETER ISLAND

Home to one of the Virgin Islands' most famous luxury resorts, Peter Island is a tiny universe unto itself. Resort guests can spend their days on Deadman's Beach, one of the prettiest in the Virgin Islands, or take advantage of the world-class spa and water-sports facilities. Day-trippers looking for luxury come over to eat lunch and enjoy treatments at the spa. The more adventurous come to walk the paths and roads that traverse miles of untouched forest on the 1,800-acre island.

Peter Island has a unique history. In the late 1600s a group of slave traders from Brandenburg, Germany, settled the island, intending to establish a large settlement. They got as far as building several forts before the Danes chased them out. Peter Island was cultivated during the plantation era, and remains of an island church, homes, and a burial ground have been found there. In 1855 a coaling station was opened on Peter Island, where steamships

could load up. The Peter Island coaling station was an alternative to one on St. Thomas, which was closed regularly because of yellow fever outbreaks on that island.

In the 1930s, British diplomat John Brudnell-Bruce moved his family to Peter Island, where they lived for several decades. In 1950, Brudnell-Bruce was one of the four men elected to the first Legislative Council of the British Virgin Islands.

Peter Island was also the home to generations of Virgin Islanders who fished, grew crops, and traded with residents of other islands to get by. *The Way We Were* by Andria D. Flax is a charming memoir of life on Peter Island in the 1950s and 1960s.

In the late 1960s, a Norwegian millionaire, Peter Smedwig, became smitten with Peter Island, bought it, and had a fleet of luxury A-frame chalets shipped there from Norway. He built a small clubhouse and opened the first guesthouse on the island. In the late 1970s, U.S. entrepreneurs linked to the Amway Corporation bought Peter Island and have continued to expand and upgrade the resort.

Accommodations

Peter Island Resort (284/495-2000, 770/476-9988, or 800/346-4451, www.peterisland.com, $600–1,200) often finds itself near the top of lists of best Caribbean resorts, winning points not just for its luxury accommodations and world-class dining, but also its spectacular setting. For no additional charge, guests can visit some six beaches on the island with a gourmet picnic lunch, go hiking through the forest, snorkel under the sea, or just relax on the sand with a book. Amenities include free tennis, a fitness center, water-sports equipment, movie nights, a swimming pool, horticultural tours, and beach volleyball. Spa services, snorkel and dive trips, tennis lessons, and outings to other Virgin Island destinations are available for an extra charge.

TORTOLA

TREASURE ISLAND

The inspiration for Treasure Island came to Robert Louis Stevenson while he was on a wet Scottish holiday with his father and stepson. Encountering an old, hand-painted map of an imaginary island, Stevenson made notes about his new idea. "It was to be a story for boys; no need of psychology or fine writing; and I had a boy at hand to be a touchstone," he wrote. The story's most famous character, Long John Silver, was modeled after his friend and collaborator W. E. Henley.

Stevenson's story was first published in 17 weekly installments under the title The Sea-Cook in Young Folks magazine. He wrote using the pseudonym "Captain George North" and was paid £30.

Two years later Stevenson revised the periodical text and created Treasure Island, published In 1883 by Cassell and Company in London. It sold briskly and has become a classic. The original map that served as its inspiration was lost, and Stevenson considered the replacement, included in some early editions, to be a poor copy. Today, the legend lives on that the island setting of Treasure Island is the British Virgin Islands' Norman Island.

© LIBRARY OF CONGRESS

Robert Louis Stevenson

The resort's 52 guest accommodations include beachfront, ocean-view, and garden-view rooms, plus a few luxury villas. The 32 ocean- and garden-view rooms feature standard hotel-style accommodations with a small balcony and are housed in the resort's original A-frame cottages. They are tastefully furnished in an island style that isn't over the top, a five-minute walk from Deadman's Beach, the resort's most beautiful and popular beach. Beachfront junior suites overlook the bay and offer added extras like a bar, a Jacuzzi, and a bit more elbow room. Up to three people can stay in a junior suite. Guests can choose between room-only rates ($600–1,000) or all-inclusive rates ($800–1,200), which include three meals a day. Children under 12 can stay in their parents' room for $75 per night.

Peter Island's spa is an attraction in itself, with hydrotherapy tubs, private steam rooms, private whirlpools, a spa lounge, a meditation area, indoor treatment suites, and movement classes. It is located in a dramatic bay a mile or two away from the resort itself. Call about day trip spa packages that include transportation, spa treatments, and lunch.

Food

◖ **Tradewinds Restaurant** (284/495-2000, $25–50) is Peter Island's flagship eatery. Elegant yet welcoming, this upscale restaurant sits next to the pool, but diners also feast on ocean views. Low lighting, exposed stone walls, dark-hued wood, and white tablecloths set a tone of refinement, even for the Saturday night West Indian buffet. The food is of a high standard and the menu is creative, with meat, seafood, and vegetarian options. After 6 P.M. the dress code at Tradewinds and the adjoining **Drake's Lounge** is "smart" for ladies and trousers and collared shirts for gentlemen. The lounge is also the scene of lunch, when the menu offers upscale salads, hot and cold sandwiches, and soups. Breakfast is more casual and features a beautiful morning buffet of fresh breads, fruits, and cereal, as well as hot-from-the-kitchen choices including pancakes, waffles, and eggs.

Deadman's Beach ($17–30) is a more casual affair. This seaside café serves lunch and dinner daily. At dinner you can expect grilled seafood, steak, jerk chicken, pasta, or pizza direct from the stone oven.

Getting There

Peter Island Resort guests ride the **Peter Island Ferry** (Baugher's Bay, 284/495-2000) free, as do people with dinner reservations at Tradewinds Restaurant or an all-day spa booking. Everyone else pays $20 round-trip. The ferry, which also carries resort staff, usually departs Tortola at 8:30 A.M., 10 A.M., noon, 2:30 P.M., 5:30 P.M., 6:30 P.M., 8 P.M., and 10:30 P.M. Call to confirm departure times.

Private yachts are welcome at Peter Island. There are anchorages at the extreme southeast corner of Deadman's Bay, Little Harbour, Great Harbour, and Key Point, or you can dock at the marina.

DEAD CHEST

The sheer rock face of Dead Chest island is said to be the final resting place of the 16 mutineers immortalized in the old sea song: "16 men on a dead man's chest. Yo ho ho and a bottle of rum." Others say that the 16 men left here by the pirate Blackbeard tried to swim to nearby Peter Island but drowned, washing ashore on what is now Deadman's Bay. For now, the impenetrable rocky face of Dead Chest isn't betraying the truth.

SALT ISLAND

Before refrigeration, islanders relied on salt to preserve meat. Many islands in the Virgins have salt ponds where crystal salt was collected, but no island had a larger or more productive pond than Salt Island, a small T-shaped island about five miles from Tortola. For centuries the small settlement on Salt Island thrived on the salt industry.

Salt is harvested in the early spring, before the rainy season begins. Traditionally, the Salt Island harvest was a time of great festivity. Residents from nearby islands would travel there to watch as a government agent supervised the "breaking of the pond." After it was harvested from the pond, the salt was dried in a special salt house. Up to 1,000 pounds of salt were harvested annually from Salt Island. Today, islanders still harvest salt, but on a much smaller scale. Most of it is finely ground and mixed with local seasonings to make "seasoning salt" for fish and meat.

No one still lives on Salt Island year-round, although some Salt Islanders who live on Tortola come back regularly and tend the smattering of houses in the bay. The settlement along the north coast is a cluster of simple homes, set amid coconut palms. There are no restaurants, snack bars, or stores, and no electricity or potable water. But the settlement provides a unique glimpse into the past.

When you visit, look around the settlement for signs of life. If someone happens to be home, be sure to extend them the courtesy of a greeting and an explanation of what you intend to do. Someone may even agree to show you around. Hiking trails circle the pond, or you can trek over to South Bay in the west or the Sound in the east. There is a cemetery of *Rhone* shipwreck victims a few dozen yards from the settlement in Lee Bay. And remember: Don't disturb the salt pond or take any salt unless you have permission.

© SUSANNA HENIGHAN POTTER

The settlement at Salt Island lies alongside the salt pond which gives the island its name.

TORTOLA

◖ Diving at the Wreck of the RMS *Rhone*

The wreck of the RMS *Rhone* is the preeminent dive site in the British Virgin Islands and one of its most visited attractions. The 310-foot twin-masted steamer, which sank during a ferocious hurricane in 1867, lies in three sections west of Salt Island and has beckoned underwater explorers for decades. In 1977 it was the primary filming location for the movie *The Deep,* starring Nick Nolte and Jacqueline Bisset.

Lying in 65–80 feet of water, the bow is the deepest, largest, and most intact section of the *Rhone.* Here divers can enter the interior of the vessel and will find the mast and crow's nest still attached to the ship. The midsection, lying in about 60 feet of water, is dominated by a series of support beams—all that remains of the ship's deck. The stern, the shallowest part of the wreck, can be explored by snorkelers as well as divers. It features the ship's large rudder and 15-foot propeller.

Divers should not try to explore the whole wreck in one dive. It is too deep, and there is too much to see. The best way to explore the ship is to start with a dive on the deepest section, the bow, and follow that with another dive on the stern and midsection. If you really want to get to know this wreck, however, you will need to plan more than two dives and include one at night, when it comes alive with unusual and colorful sea life.

Visibility around the wreck is usually good—between 60 and 100 feet. The bow and midsection are sometimes susceptible to currents. For ease and safety, always go diving with a local dive company, since staff will be familiar with local conditions and dangers.

Local dive boats visit the *Rhone* every day of the year. In fact, many days it seems like a whole fleet makes the journey. For the best experience, choose a dive boat that specializes in small groups and avoid the busiest times; 9 A.M.–noon and 2–4 P.M.

THE WRECK OF THE *RHONE*

On October 29, 1867, the RMS *Rhone* was at anchor in Great Harbour, Peter Island. The 310-foot *Rhone* had left St. Thomas, her usual port of call, days earlier because of a yellow fever outbreak there and was taking on passengers and cargo for a journey to Europe. A member of the Royal Mail Steam Packet Company, the *Rhone* transported mail, passengers, and goods between England and its colonies in the West Indies and South America.

During the morning, Captain Robert Wooley noticed that the barometer was falling but thought it was too late in the season for a hurricane. He decided that the *Rhone*, which had weathered terrible gales in the open sea, would remain at anchor off Peter Island for the incoming weather. It was a deadly decision. At about 11 A.M., the barometer fell dangerously low, and the hurricane began in earnest. The *Rhone* was knocked about but remained whole and upright. Captain Wooley became worried, however. When there was a lull in the storm about an hour later, he decided to flee for the open ocean. Unable to free the ship's 3,000-pound anchor, the crew cut the chain, and the *Rhone* steamed out of Peter Island, through the Salt Island Passage, toward the open sea.

As it turned out, the lull was the passage of the eye, and as the *Rhone* rounded Dead Chest and headed out to sea, it was battered by full-force hurricane winds. The ship was blown backward onto Salt Island's Black Rock and split in half. Cool ocean water ran into the ship's overheated boiler, causing a massive explosion. The ship sank in minutes.

'Only six people survived—five crew members and one passenger who clung to debris for six hours before washing ashore. Witnesses reported seeing Captain Wooley washed onto a skylight before being thrown overboard into the roiling sea. He was never seen again. Residents of Salt Island did what they could to collect the bodies of those who perished—a dozen or so are buried on the west end of the Salt Island settlement. The burial ground is the only memorial in the BVI to the more than 150 souls lost—except of course the wreck itself. Sadly, many people think that if the *Rhone* had remained at anchor off Peter Island, it would have fared far better, since the hills of the island would have shielded it from the worst of the winds.

In the years following the wreck, treasure-seekers gathered nearly everything of value from the wreck. An 1870 article in the Port-of-Spain, Trinidad, *Gazette* recounts a party held by visiting divers who took cases of champagne, beer, brandy, lemonade, and soda water from the wreckage: "The liquors were as good as they were the first day and it is nearly three years since they have been down; the champagne was first rate, as cool as possible."

Getting There

There is no ferry service to Salt Island, so if you want to come you will have to sail yourself. Strangely, even though Salt Island is unique among the BVI's outlying cays, it is off the radar of most visitors and likewise is not featured on any regular day sail itineraries. This is all the more reason to go. Dive operators regularly head to the wreck of the Rhone.

Sailors can anchor at Salt Island Bay or moor at Lee Bay. Both are exposed, however, and are considered day-use only.

Descendants of Salt Island residents usually organize a day trip, including ferry and lunch, on a bank holiday in the springtime. Ask around or check the local papers and radio stations for advertisements of this outing.

COOPER ISLAND

Located about four miles from Tortola and just east of Salt Island, Cooper Island got its name from the skilled coopers who practiced their trade during the plantation era. About 1.5 miles long and 0.5 mile wide, Cooper Island is undeveloped except for a small hotel and clutch of vacation homes at Manchioneel Bay on the north end of the island.

TORTOLA

No fewer than nine dive sites form a ring around Cooper Island. **Cistern Point,** at the southern tip of Manchioneel Bay, is one of the most popular since it is shallow, easy, and equally good for snorkeling. There are three nice wrecks around Cooper Island, all sunk intentionally by the BVI Dive Association. The *Inganess Bay* lies in about 50 feet of water halfway between Salt and Cooper Islands. The *Marie L* and *Pat* lie side by side off Hallovers Bay on Cooper Island's western shore. Other good dives around Cooper Island include **Carvel Rock,** between Ginger and Cooper, and **Markhoe Point,** an isolated and geologically interesting dive on the extreme southern tip of Cooper Island.

Accommodations

Rarely has a private island experience been so cheap and yet so fulfilling as that at ℂ **Cooper Island Beach Club** (284/495-9084, 413/863-3162, or 800/542-4624, www.cooperisland-beachclub.com, $250 winter, $200 summer). Don't expect frills—there are no room phones, TVs, or air-conditioning—but do expect a warm welcome, idyllic setting, and one of the greenest resorts in the BVI. The recently refurbished cottages are powered by the sun, watered by rain, and furnished with pieces repurposed from salvaged materials. The trade winds, helped along with ceiling fans, will keep you cool. Weeklong packages including three meals daily and government taxes cost $1,500 per person in high season. Days at Cooper Island are spent sunbathing, swimming, reading, or exploring the island trails and reefs. The hotel boasts a cadre of annual visitors who bask in the relatively unknown delights of this simple seaside resort.

Cooper Island Hideaways (513/232-4126, www.cooperisland.com, $270 winter, $150 summer) operates two villas at Manchioneel Bay. The Beach House can sleep two people, while the Hideaway sleeps up to six. Both are equipped with full kitchens, balconies, and solar-powered lights, fans, and appliances. They rent by the week.

Food

The ℂ **Cooper Island Beach Club** (Manchioneel Bay, 284/495-9084, $18–35) serves classy but relaxed meals to visiting yachtsmen and hotel guests. Set sail here for lunch ($12–18) for traditional West Indian roti, seafood and chicken wraps or a burger. At dinner chefs put a new twist on familiar dishes, such as the pork tenderloin served with roasted pineapple or the mahimahi seasoned with coconut and wasabi. The bar at Cooper Island is a pleasant place to relax, and house cocktails, including the excellent Painkiller, make it easy to linger.

Getting There

There is no public ferry service to Cooper Island, although visitors on private boats are welcome and guests get here on the resort's daily shuttle from Road Town. Some day sail operations include Cooper Island in their itinerary; dive shops also take visitors to its most popular dive spots. **Sail Caribbean Divers** (Hodges Creek Marina, Tortola, 284/495-1675) will bring small groups out for the day for $15 per person round-trip. Cooper Island maintains overnight moorings at Manchioneel Bay for visiting yachts.

GINGER ISLAND

Uninhabited and undeveloped, Ginger Island lies between Salt Island and Round Rock. The island is shaped like a two-pronged pitchfork. There are sheer cliffs on the north and south sides, plus protected Wedgeo Bay in the center, between the pitchfork prongs.

There are some excellent diving and snorkeling sites around Ginger Island. In South Bay you will find **Alice in Wonderland,** one of the best deep-water reef dives in the territory. Staghorn coral here grow to heights of 15 feet and more. You are likely to encounter pelagic species like rays, sharks, and barracuda at **Ginger Steps,** another deep coral site in South Bay. The north shore of Ginger Island, near Grapetree Landing, is a long, healthy, and shallow reef, good for either diving or snorkeling.

Out Islands: Off Tortola's East End

GUANA ISLAND

Named for a rock outcropping that looks like an iguana head, 850-acre Guana Island lies off Tortola's northeastern tip, a short sail from Trellis Bay. In the 18th century, Quakers settled the island, building sugar mills and houses and cultivating sugar, cotton, and other crops. Following the end of slavery, Guana was mostly undeveloped until 1935, when Beth and Louis Bigelow bought the island and built a small clubhouse on the saddle of the main ridge. The Bigelows invited intellectuals and artists to Guana, which was known as a rustic retreat with spectacular natural beauty and good conversation. In 1975, Henry and Gloria Jarecki bought Guana and expanded the guest facilities to accommodate up to 32 people. They also hired a naturalist and began a project to reintroduce native animal species to the island. Every summer, Guana Island hosts research scientists who stay on the island, perform research on environmental topics, and then present their findings at a community science symposium.

Unfortunately for those without deep pockets, Guana does not welcome non–resort guests to come ashore, although you can anchor out, snorkel, and swim onto the beaches, which are, by law, public up to the high-water mark. The resort's slogan says it all: "Imagine the Caribbean before it went public."

Accommodations and Food

The **C Guana Island Club** (Guana Island, 284/495-9786, 914/964-6050, or 800/544-8262, www.guana.com, $1,550 winter, $695 summer) is one of the best private island retreats in the BVI. Guest accommodations are in private stone and masonry cottages along the ridge, with commanding views of the beaches and bays below. Options also include one private beach cottage on North Beach and two hillside villas elsewhere. Three meals daily, plus afternoon tea and evening cocktails, are served in the clubhouse, which also has a comfortable library and sitting room. Many of the tropical fruits, vegetables, and herbs served in the dining room are grown in Guana's own garden near White Bay. Guana Island's restaurant is not open to nonguests, and the whole resort can hold only about 30 people, so you won't feel crowded.

Guests can spend their days hiking some of the 22 marked and maintained trails, swimming at any of the island's seven beaches, or just relaxing on their balconies with a book. In addition, guests have access to kayaks, snorkel equipment, sailboards, and small sailboats for exploring the ocean. There is also tennis, croquet, volleyball, table tennis, waterskiing, and badminton. Visitors seeking total privacy can book the whole island for between $22,000 and $31,000 per night; up to 32 people can be accommodated.

BELLAMY CAY

A speck of land just off the beach at Trellis Bay, Bellamy Cay is home to **The Last Resort** (Bellamy Cay, 284/495-2520, 6:30–9:30 P.M. daily, $16–30), a destination for dinner and entertainment. Founder Tony Snell is now enjoying his retirement in the United Kingdom, but his daughter has carried on the tradition of a fun-loving atmosphere and high-quality food. Gourmet fish, meat, and

TORTOLA

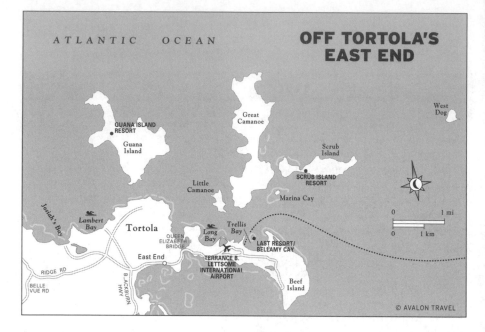

ATLANTIC OCEAN

OFF TORTOLA'S EAST END

Guana Island
GUANA ISLAND RESORT
Great Camanoe
West Dog
Scrub Island
SCRUB ISLAND RESORT
Little Camanoe
Marina Cay
Josiah's Bay
Lambert Bay
Tortola
Long Bay
Trellis Bay
QUEEN ELIZABETH II BRIDGE
LAST RESORT/ BELEAMY CAY
East End
TERRANCE B. LETTSOME INTERNATIONAL AIRPORT
RIDGE RD
BELLE VUE RD
BLACKBURN HWY
Beef Island

0   1 mi
0   1 km

© AVALON TRAVEL

vegetarian dishes are on offer at this welcoming place where even the chef sings. Use the hotline phone at the Trellis Bay dock to summon a free ferry to the island, or dinghy in from your boat.

MARINA CAY

This seven-acre island is about 10 minutes by ferry from Beef Island, near Tortola's east end. Home to a small hotel, restaurant, gift shop, and dive shop, Marina Cay was immortalized in Robb White's 1953 memoir *Our Virgin Island*. The book describes the two-year sojourn of White and his wife, Rhodie, on the island in the late 1930s. In 1958, the book was made into the movie *Our Virgin Island*, which starred Sidney Poitier and John Cassavetes and was filmed on Marina Cay and Long Bay, Beef Island.

The one-room house that Robb and Rhodie built largely by hand atop the island still stands; its present owners have converted it into a happy hour bar. You can see photographs of the Whites and other images from 1930s and 1940s Tortola at the restaurant.

The reef around Marina Cay is good for snorkeling. Virgin Gorda–based **Dive BVI** (284/495-9363, www.divebvi.com) operates an outpost on Marina Cay, providing dive instruction, dive trips, and gear rentals.

Accommodations & Food

Pusser's Marina Cay (284/494-2174, www.pussers.com, $175 winter, $150 summer) consists of a beachfront restaurant and a handful of hilltop villas and smaller double rooms. The restaurant serves breakfast, lunch, and dinner. The resort's four guest rooms have private balconies and refrigerators and enjoy views of Trellis Bay, while villas gaze out toward the open ocean.

Getting There

A free ferry (284/494-2174) to Marina Cay leaves Trellis Bay, Beef Island, every hour on

© BRITISH VIRGIN ISLANDS TOURIST BOARD

Marina Cay, off Tortola's East End, is a good stop for a meal and snorkeling.

the half hour 10:30 A.M.–12:30 P.M. and every hour on the hour 3–7 P.M.

SCRUB ISLAND

Lying a short sail from Beef Island, Scrub Island is home to the first major new resort to be built in the British Virgin Islands in the last 15 years. **Scrub Island Resort** (284/440-3440 or 877/890-/444, www.scrubisland.com, from $525 in winter, from $400 in summer) is a 50-room resort with 55 slips for visiting yachts. The Marriott-branded resort has a modern Mediterranean atmosphere, three restaurants, boutiques, and all the amenities one would expect from a high-end resort. Day-trippers can enjoy lunch by the pool, while hotel guests lavish themselves at the day spa or chill out at North Beach. The view of the marina is spectacular at night.

TORTOLA

VIRGIN GORDA

Virgin Gorda is a spectacularly beautiful island. The third largest of the British Virgins and the second most populated, Virgin Gorda is home to exquisite beaches, remarkable vistas, and quiet upscale resorts. The Baths National Park, a world-famous natural attraction where huge boulders and turquoise grottos invite exploration, lies at the far southern tip. The entire southwestern peninsula of the island is a flat, dry landscape colored by vivid bougainvillea and lined by perfect white beaches: Devil's Bay, Spring Bay, and Valley Trunk Bay are a few.

At mid-island the topography begins to change, flat and dry giving way to mountainous and lush. Roads wind steeply through wild forest, past Gorda Peak National Park and breathtaking viewpoints, and down to the quaint village of North Sound, which clings to the hillside overlooking the eponymous harbor. Sir Francis Drake used North Sound as a staging area for a 1595 attack on Puerto Rico, but today it is a playground for sailboats, motor yachts, kite surfers, and anyone who feels at home on the water.

Virgin Gorda's calling card is its natural beauty. The Baths National Park is a stunning white-sand beach littered with large, dramatic boulders; Savannah Bay is a near-perfect crescent beach with an excellent offshore reef for snorkeling; Gorda Peak is a peaceful wild forest home to rare birds, lizards, and plants; and all around Virgin Gorda the island is bestowed with

VIRGIN GORDA

HIGHLIGHTS

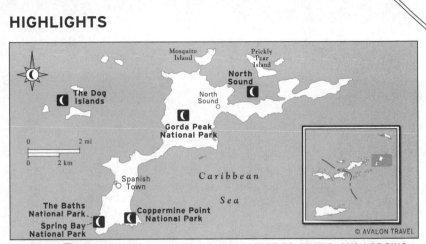

© AVALON TRAVEL

LOOK FOR ☾ TO FIND RECOMMENDED SIGHTS, ACTIVITIES, DINING, AND LODGING.

☾ **Coppermine Point National Park:** A crumbling stone chimney breaks through the bright blue sky at Coppermine Point, a wind-swept headland. Watch the waves crash below and the birds fly overhead (page 230).

☾ **The Baths National Park:** Huge granite boulders create an endless array of pools and grottos perfect for exploration at the British Virgin Islands' most famous sight (page 230).

☾ **Spring Bay National Park:** The "other" Baths, this beach maintains its serenity most days, making it a venue popular with locals and ideal for relaxation (page 232).

☾ **Gorda Peak National Park:** On an island where so much revolves around the sea, this mountaintop park offers the diversion of its verdant canopies, wild birdsongs, and expansive views (page 234).

☾ **North Sound:** Called by some a saltwater lake, this broad bay is protected from rough seas and ideal for sailing. Secluded beaches and friendly beach bars await exploration (page 235).

☾ **The Dog Islands:** Protected by the National Parks Trust, this cluster of islands near Virgin Gorda has some of the BVI's most pristine reefs for snorkeling or diving (page 249).

brilliant blue waters, the sights and sounds of wildlife, and exceptional views in every direction.

Just about 3,000 people call Virgin Gorda home, and they are a particularly welcoming bunch. At Spanish Town, the main settlement in the south, life revolves around the marina and the ferry dock. The side streets are lined with neat West Indian–style homes, many fronted by colorful gardens. Others are built imaginatively around the giant granite boulders of the area. Goats and sheep wander through the village, causing occasional traffic jams.

Virgin Gorda is classically Caribbean: the Caribbean the way it once was. A simple yet captivating package of spectacular beauty, blissfully laid-back lifestyle, friendly people, and the comfort of fine accommodations keep many visitors returning year after year.

PLANNING YOUR TIME

Your Virgin Gorda vacation should simply be as long as you need to unwind. Virgin Gorda is a beautiful and relaxing place, and a week or two is the perfect duration to recharge and

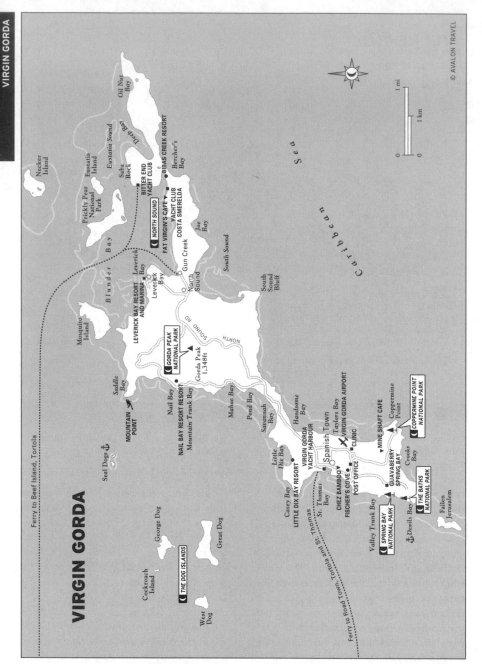

VIRGIN GORDA

© AVALON TRAVEL

refresh. The aim, after all, is not to be busy but to be relaxed.

Getting to Virgin Gorda is a bit of a haul: most visitors have to take multiple planes plus a ferry to get here. All the more reasons to make your trip as long as possible.

Where to Stay

Accommodations in or around the Valley are close to the Baths, Spring Bay, and town— home to most of the island's restaurants, shops, and ferries to Road Town and St. Thomas. If you stay in North Sound, you'll be close to sailing and water sports and far away from the rest of the world. A clutch of good restaurants, shops, and services are here, too, and there are ferries to Beef Island, near Tortola's airport.

Getting Around

Depending on how many amenities and activities are available to you at your hotel, you may want to rent a car for at least part of your stay, so you can easily reach sights like Coppermine Point and Gorda Peak. But remember that around North Sound, it is boats, not cars, that allow you to get around.

Day Trips

At less than nine square miles, Virgin Gorda is easy to explore in a single day. **Ferries** make at least 10 daily trips connecting Road Town and Spanish Town, making Virgin Gorda a convenient day trip from Tortola. The journey is about 30 minutes, costs $30 round trip. You'll arrive at the island's largest public dock: the St. Thomas Bay jetty. Open-air "safari" taxis meet every arriving ferry; it costs about $7 to make the 15-minute trip to the Baths. If you are staying on St. Thomas or St. John, look for one of the many **day sail operators** offering trips to the Baths, or take a public ferry operated by **Inter-Island Boat Service** (340/776-6597, $80 round-trip) on Thursdays and Sundays, or **Speedy's** (284/495-5240, $70 round-trip) on Tuesdays, Thursdays and Saturdays.

Ferry service is also available between Trellis Bay, Beef Island; Spanish Town, Virgin Gorda; and North Sound, Virgin Gorda. Though used primarily by people arriving at the airport, travelling from Beef Island is also a convenient choice if you are staying on the eastern end of Tortola. Companies operating ferries on this route are **Speedy's** (284/495-5240) and **North Sound Express** (284/495-2138).

If you're staying on Virgin Gorda, snorkeling day trips to the Dog Islands are available with one of the local sail or dive operators. Or travel to Tortola aboard one of the 10 ferries which sail from Spanish Town to Road Town (30 minutes, $30 round-trip). You can also take the ferry to Anegada (60 minutes, $50 round-trip) which operates six days a week. It's necessary to call ahead to confirm the Anegada ferry because the boat doesn't stop at Virgin Gorda unless they know someone wants to get on. You can also get to Anegada aboard the *Sea Lion*'s weekly Anegada day trip through **Dive BVI** (284/495-5513), departing Virgin Gorda every Friday.

Sights

ORIENTATION

Virgin Gorda is a long, meandering island. The southern portion of the island is known as the Valley; it is flat and the most populated part of Virgin Gorda. Spanish Town is the residential and commercial center located around the ferry dock and marina. It is a 10-minute drive from Spanish Town through quiet residential areas to the Baths, at the southern tip of the island.

The northern half of Virgin Gorda is essentially a single large mountain that rises to 1,370 feet at Gorda Peak National Park. At mid-island are a clutch of villa resorts and fine beaches. On the other side of Gorda Peak is North Sound, a large natural harbor home to luxury resorts and seaside restaurants. Much of North Sound is accessible only by boat.

THE VALLEY

The Valley is the wide, flat southern end of Virgin Gorda, home to Spanish Town, four national parks, a marina, and the giant boulders that define this island. Many travelers arrive on Virgin Gorda aboard one of the ferries that dock at the St. Thomas Bay jetty, a short walk from the marina and town center.

Spanish Town

Some say that Virgin Gorda's main settlement, Spanish Town, got its name from the Spaniards who settled there in the early 1500s. Others say that Spanish Town is a corruption of the town's early name, Penniston.

In 1680, Spanish Town became the first seat of government in the British Virgin Islands. In 1717, the first census of the island found 317 Whites living on Virgin Gorda and 303 Blacks, more people than were living on Tortola at the time. In 1742, the capital of the territory moved to Tortola, where it has remained since.

Today, Spanish Town is one of the most picturesque villages in the British Virgin Islands. Unrestrained by hills, it sprawls along a gentle slope, an attractive mix of homes, shops, churches, and schools. It is a nice place to walk.

◖ Coppermine Point National Park

Coppermine Point (Coppermine Rd., no phone, free) is a remote, windswept spot overlooking the rocky, rough north coast and the island's airport. Legend has it that Spanish settlers first mined silver here in the mid-1500s, and indigenous people may well have built mines here even earlier than that. The ruins you see date back to 1838, when Cornish miners established a copper mining operation here. It had a short, unprofitable life and closed four years later. The mines were reopened in 1859 and were worked until 1867.

Today, the spot's greatest appeal is the dramatic beauty of the stone ruins silhouetted against the blue sky. Windy even on calm days, Coppermine Point looks eastward over the Atlantic Ocean, where the view is of nothing except the disappearing horizon. Linger awhile and perhaps an airplane will land at the airstrip below, adding to the drama. Or come before dawn to witness the sun appearing, as if by magic, from the ocean. At night, the stars glitter overhead. Also keep a eye out for the birds that frequent this corner of the island—one called the Black Witch is a large, hulking beast that flies around the rocks.

Facilities consist of a parking lot, sign, and trail.

◖ The Baths National Park

Virgin Gorda's Baths National Park (Tower Rd., 284/496-6314, adults $3, under 11 free) is one of the most famous sights in the British Virgin Islands. Formed tens of millions of years ago when volcanic lava cooled into huge chunks of granite, the Baths are a landscape of

SPANISH TOWN

Little Dix Bay

To ◀NORTH SOUND

HANDSOME BAY RD

LITTLE DIX BAY RESORT

VIRGIN GORDA VILLAGE

St. Thomas

Bay

CRABBE HILL

LITTLE RD

FERRY DOCK

DIXIE'S BAR AND RESTAURANT

CHEZ BAMBOO

POLICE STATION

LEE RD

Virgin Gorda Yacht Harbour

TOURIST INFORMATION CENTRE/BUCK'S FOOD MARKET/BATH AND TURTLE

METHODIST CHURCH

MILLIONAIRE RD

CRABBE HILL RD

VIRGIN GORDA AIRPORT

BANKS

VANTERPOOL ADMINISTRATION BUILDING/ POST OFFICE

0   200 yds

0   200 m

ROMAN CATHOLIC CHURCH

FISCHER'S COVE HOTEL AND RESTAURANT

PRINCESS QUARTERS

Taylors

TOWER RD

NORTH RD

Bay

THE ROCK CAFÉ

Little Fort National Park

LSL BAKE SHOP

TOWER RD

CHURCH HILL RD

ST. MARY'S EPISCOPAL CHURCH

TO ◀THE BATHS NATIONAL PARK

To ◀COPPERMINE POINT NATIONAL PARK

© AVALON TRAVEL

building-size boulders, clear saltwater grottoes, and powder-white beaches. There are endless pools for exploring and swimming and offshore reefs provide opportunities for snorkeling.

The Baths proper is a small cove beach, shaded by sea grape and coconut palm trees and littered with boulders. The largest are as tall as a three-story building; the smallest are the size of a person. Time has worked its magic on the rocks: Pockmarked by water flows, colored by mineral deposits, and strewn about by

the shaking of earthquakes, the boulders are beautiful in their disorder. They create a landscape like a playground, where even grown-ups are tempted to climb over and around, looking for a quiet pool or hidden room.

To truly experience the Baths, take the quarter-mile trail south from the beach to **Devil's Bay,** a slightly larger white-sand beach with more space for beaching and swimming. The trail is an obstacle course that travels over, around, and through large rocks. It's great fun.

© SUSANNA HENIGHAN POTTER

The Cathedral is one of the Baths' most beautiful features.

Steps and handrails are carefully maintained by the National Parks Trust, but the walk is still recommended only for the sure-footed.

On the trail to Devil's Bay is **The Cathedral,** a pool formed by the intersection of two large rocks that allow in a small shaft of sunlight. The water here is about waist height, and if it looks familiar, it is because the spot has been the scene of numerous magazine and television shoots. It is a romantic place when it's not crowded.

If you don't arrive at the Baths by land, you will also enjoy a pleasant quarter-mile hike through not-so-rocky forest to the beach. Another trail through dry scrubby forest connects Devil's Bay with the parking area at the Top of the Baths, allowing visitors to make a complete loop.

Facilities at the Baths include a modest beach bar, lockers, and restrooms. Occasionally there are also a few vendors offering to braid hair or sell you a sarong.

The Baths can be crowded: tour operators bring day sails here from visiting cruise ships and from Tortola and the U.S. Virgin Islands. If you can, avoid visiting during peak hours—10 A.M.–4 P.M. It's also important to know that the sea around the Baths can be rough during a swell, making it dangerous to swim or snorkel. The BVI employs a flag system on its beaches: If the flag on display is red, you shouldn't swim. If it's yellow, take caution.

◖ Spring Bay National Park

Spring Bay National Park (Tower Rd., no phone, free), about half a mile north of the Baths, has the same captivating landscape as the Baths, but often with far fewer people. A moderately sized crescent bay is fringed by shade trees and equipped with picnic tables. A swimming area is framed by large boulders, while smaller pools are ideal for explorers. Hunt for the "crawl," a magical calm pool of water entirely surrounded by boulders.

Exploration around Spring Bay reveals further pleasures. Walk south along the shore and you'll find another beach: This one is longer and straighter and bordered by the vacation cottages of Guavaberry Spring Bay. To the north, there is an unmarked trail through the boulders that takes you to **Valley Trunk Bay,** yet another boulder-strewn beach lined by sea grape trees.

Look for signs to Spring Bay just before Guavaberry Spring Bay Apartments on the road to the Baths. Park in the lot and follow the trail about 50 yards to the beach.

MID-ISLAND

At 1,370 feet, Gorda Peak is the highest point on Virgin Gorda and one of the highest in the Virgin Islands. The peak and all land above the 1,000-foot contour is national park and much more remains unspoiled because of the difficult topography. On the western shore, the green hillsides cascade down to a string of white-sand beaches.

Two paved roads wind through this terrain:

THE STORY OF THE BOULDERS

© SUSANNA HENIGHAN POTTER

boulders at Virgin Gorda's Baths National Park

During the Tertiary Period of geologic history, about 70 million years ago, molten rock seeped through the floor of the young Caribbean Sea. The lava was hot, reaching temperatures as high as 2,000 degrees Celsius (over 3,600 degrees Fahrenheit). When it came into contact with the cool seawater, it solidified into granite.

As it cooled, the rock also shrank, causing cracks to form. Because of the characteristics of granite, it cracked at right angles, creating a series of rectangular rocks, stacked neatly on top of one another, like a block of cheese cut into cubes. Through faulting and uplifting over the next 60 million years, many of these granite cubes reached the earth's surface.

Over the last one million years, the boulders have been aged and weathered by the elements. The rhythm of waves, jolt of earthquakes, and flow of water have been written on the faces of the boulders. Time has also caused many of the right-angled boulders

to transform into smooth-sided or spherical shapes.

Before running water made its way to Virgin Gorda in the 1960s and 1970s, the island's boulders played an important role in water collection. Pools of rainwater formed on top of many of the large rocks, which islanders used to water livestock, wash clothes, and bathe. In places, the boulders also provided shelter from the wind, sun, and rain if you happened to need it.

War journalist Martha Gellhorn visited Virgin Gorda in 1942 as part of a Caribbean tour to assess World War II's impact on the region. The war, she observed, seemed too far away to be true on Virgin Gorda. She spent an afternoon at the Baths and described it like this: "This cove was a place where nothing had changed since time began, a half circle of white sand, flanked by huge squarish smooth rocks, the rocks overlapping to form cool caves and the water turquoise blue above the furrows of the sandy bed."

Spring Bay National Park is Virgin Gorda's "other" Baths: beautiful but often less crowded.

the main road, which traverses steeply past Gorda Peak National Park and vistas to the southeast, and an alternative route, which circles the peak passing through Nail Bay, providing views of Tortola and the Dog Islands before intersecting with the main road just above the village of North Sound.

Gorda Peak National Park

Gorda Peak National Park (North Sound Rd., no phone, free), designated in 1974, after the land was donated by Laurance Rockefeller, is one of the best examples of dry forest remaining in the region. Although the park is relatively small (just 265 acres), the percentage of rare and endangered species is remarkably high. For example, keep a lookout for the billbush, a shrub you won't find elsewhere in the Virgin Islands. While it appears to have leaves, the stiff dark appendages are really modified stems. It puts out tiny scarlet flowers that smell, surprisingly, like boiling potatoes.

Other rare species include the Christmas orchid, St. Thomas prickly ash, and the Virgin Gorda gecko, the smallest lizard in the world. Gorda Peak's richness led it to be chosen as a U.K. Darwin Initiative site for the preservation of biodiversity.

Two trails cut through the forest to a lookout tower near the peak. The main trail (the second you will encounter when driving from the Valley) provides the most direct route (about 0.75 mile) to the summit. The other trail is less steep and meanders pleasantly through the forest before climbing to the summit. Near the summit a lookout tower climbs above the treetops and provides a stunning view of North Sound below. On a clear day, you can see Anegada.

Besides the trail and the tower, facilities here include picnic tables, in a flat clearing a few hundred yards below the lookout tower, and a pit toilet.

The National Parks Trust publishes an informative brochure on Gorda Peak. Look for

Lush plants grow along Gorda Peak's rock footpaths.

a copy at the BVI Tourist Board office at the marina (none are available at the park).

Savannah Bay

If you feel constrained by boulder-strewn beaches or just want a change of scenery, head to Savannah Bay, a white-sand beach about a mile north of Spanish Town and the best beach for snorkeling on Virgin Gorda. The sand is narrow but long, with plenty of sea grape bushes for shade and the same exquisite white sand as other Virgin Gorda beaches. Savannah Bay is shallow a good distance out and is protected from swells, making it a good beach for small children or unsure swimmers and a good anchorage for yachts. A healthy offshore reef teems with life in the shallow, usually calm waters. The bay is also a good place for running or walking in the early morning or late afternoon.

You'll need a car or a taxi to get to Savannah, but the journey is well worth it. There are no facilities, except a few trash cans.

Along the Western Shore

Several villa resorts line the western shore of Virgin Gorda north of Savannah Bay. Take the road immediately north of Savannah to explore this territory, which is seeing a steady stream of development as new homes are built. **Pond Bay,** just north of Savannah Bay and accessible by a steep foot trail, shares many of Savannah Bay's characteristics: white sand, calm waters, good reef. **Mahoe Bay** is a pretty, tree-lined beach serving two resorts, and farther on, **Mountain Trunk Bay** is located at the Nail Bay development. Mahoe and Mountain Trunk have hard-packed, caramel-colored sand that may prove a disappointment to visitors spoiled by the quality of other Virgin Gorda beaches.

◖ NORTH SOUND

North Sound is a protected circular body of water formed by the narrow northernmost finger of Virgin Gorda and a smattering of small islands and cays. The sound is almost always calm, and it's usually a beehive of marine activity. Mega-yachts and small cruise ships drop anchor, the North Sound Express ferry chugs across the water, bareboat charters pass a night at anchor, and dinghies and Boston whalers criss-cross the waters while kiteboarders play.

The tiny, colorful village of North Sound overlooks the water. Homes here cling to the hillside, and rum shacks that look deserted during the day turn lively at night. On Sundays, church bells ring out over the valley, and during the week children walk to school. The road drops steeply down through the village, passing what was once the world's smallest post office.

Leverick Bay, on the western end of North Sound, is a hub for entertainment and services and the only marina development in North Sound accessible by car. There are shops, restaurants, a water-sports center and dive shop, a spa, laundry, a tiny beach, and a small grocery. The road to North Sound dead-ends at **Gun Creek,** a small inlet and jetty where

© SUSANNA HENIGHAN POTTER

Savannah and Pond Bays are long, pristine . . . and almost always empty.

you will find ferries to other North Sound establishments.

North Sound is accessible only by boat. Take a ferry to the Bitter End, Biras Creek, or Saba Rock for a meal and explore. There are walking trails that connect Biras Creek and Bitter End. Or if you prefer to chart your own course, rent a dinghy or small powerboat from the water-sports center at Leverick Bay (from $90 per day). You will have a great time roaming around the quiet bays, empty beaches, and beach bars of the Sound.

Saba Rock

Too small to call an island, Saba Rock is a fleck in the middle of North Sound and home to a popular restaurant, hotel, marina, carefully tended garden, and nautical museum. The **Saba Rock Nautical Museum and Gift Shop** (284/495-9966, www.sabarock.com/museum, 9 A.M.–9 P.M. daily, free) showcases some of the treasure discovered on shipwrecks around

the BVI by underwater explorer Bert Kilbride. Kilbride, who died in 2008 at the age of 94, is said to have discovered and dived more than 91 wrecks around Anegada. A few years before his death, Kilbride claimed to know the location of some 138 wrecks around the BVI and was planning to explore another, the *San Ignacio*, a Spanish ship that sank on the Anegada reef in 1742, carrying gold and jewels. A resident of the BVI for more than 50 years, Kilbride aroused admiration from many for his underwater daring but anger from some for taking as his own what many considered to be the property of the BVI as a whole.

You can see some of Kilbride's remarkable underwater finds at the Saba Rock museum. Coins, jewelry, cannons, and many more artifacts are on display daily from early until late. In addition, an anchor and cannon from the RMS *Rhone*, famously wrecked near Salt Island in 1867, are displayed in the lighted shallows around Saba Rock, providing a good reason to come here at night. Day or night you can also enjoy the perfectly manicured and tended garden.

Prickly Pear National Park

This 243-acre island in the center of North Sound was declared a national park in 1988. Head here in a dinghy or small boat (no ferry service) for a near-perfect day. Vixen Point, the beach visible from Virgin Gorda, is a beautiful white-sand beach home to a casual beach bar, the Sand Box. You can hike from Vixen Point to the north shore, passing several of the island's four salt ponds and seemingly thousands of prickly pear cactus. On the north shore are two more lovely beaches with good reefs for snorkeling.

Entertainment and Events

NIGHTLIFE

Virgin Gorda nightlife is quieter than on other islands but lively enough to satisfy most. Residents spend their evenings at basketball games, church events, neighborhood cookouts, sing-alongs, and local bars. Every so often, one of the nightspots will host a jam featuring local or visiting artists. These events are usually advertised with fliers posted all around the island. You can also pick up a copy of the free weekly *Limin' Times* for a complete rundown on nightlife and events.

The Valley

There is occasional live music at **The Rock Café** (Tower Rd., 284/495-5482), where you can always count on a crowd around the bar. Piano jazz at dinner gives way to up-tempo calypso, reggae, and soca later in the night. **The Bath and Turtle** (Yacht Harbour, 284/495-5239) and its neighboring **Rendezvous Bar** are good places for happy hour. Perhaps the most celebrated nighttime entertainment takes place on Fridays, when **Chez Bamboo** (Lee Rd., 284/495-5752) offers live jazz. **The Mine Shaft** (Coppermine Rd., 284/495-5260) has live music on Tuesday and Friday nights, and proprietor Elton Sprauve throws a popular full moon party once a month.

North Sound

The **Bitter End Yacht Club** (284/494-2745) and **Leverick Bay Resort** (284/495-7421) have entertainment most evenings, of the resort variety. The bar at **Saba Rock** (284/495-7711) is often crowded with visiting yachters; there is sometimes live music or a DJ.

One of the best weekly events on Virgin Gorda is the Friday night beach party at **Leverick Bay,** offering live music, a barbecue, and entertainment by stilt-walking mocko jumbies.

EVENTS
Spring

Every Easter, Virgin Gorda puts on a swinging, high-spirited festival. Smaller than the carnivals on Tortola and St. Thomas, Virgin Gorda's annual celebration makes up for its size with an abundance of spirit. The **Virgin Gorda Easter Festival** includes nightly entertainment in the Festival Village, set up in the schoolyard. There are also beauty pageants, calypso competitions, a food fair, and J'ouvert, an early-morning street party with thumping bass lines and energetic dancing. Fischer's Cove Beach Hotel (284/495-5252) hosts a fishing tournament on Easter weekend during the festival. The weigh-in always winds up as a rollicking party with music and plenty of fish tales. The festivities climax with a parade through the streets of Spanish Town on the Monday following Easter. The parade ends at the Festival Village, which hosts many musical performances, amusement park rides, and general good fun throughout the night.

The Easter festival normally gets going

during the week before Easter. Call the BVI Tourist Board office at the Yacht Harbour (284/495-5181) for a schedule and more information.

Winter

The entire holiday season is a festive time in Virgin Gorda. In addition to church and school concerts, there's the annual **Christmas in Spanish Town street fair** (mid-December). There is also a tree-lighting at the Vanterpool Administration Building in early December, and look for extravagant fireworks displays by Little Dix Bay and other resorts on New Year's Eve.

Shopping

Virgin Gorda is not known for its shopping, and it won't ever be. Many islanders make regular journeys to Tortola or St. Thomas to stock their households, although the necessity of this has diminished in recent years, with the opening of new wholesale food outlets and even a health food store. Gifts and souvenirs are not hard to find, however.

The Valley

The marina at the Virgin Gorda Yacht Harbour, is the shopping hub of the Valley. Shops here cater to visitors and residents; there are souvenir shops right next to food markets and banks. **Dive BVI** (284/495-5513) has a good selection of snorkel and dive equipment, plus T-shirts and gifts with a nautical theme. Check out **Thee Artistic Gallery** (284/495-5104) for crafts and books and **Next Wave Designs** (284/495-5623) for stylish gifts and household items. There are also stores selling perfume, electronics and local music.

There is also a clutch of gift shops at the Top of the Baths, where you can buy T-shirts, Caribbean spices, sarongs, sunscreen, disposable cameras, and gifts.

North Sound

Bitter End Yacht Club (284/495-9448) has several shops. The Reeftique has clothing, books, and gifts, while the Trading Post has postcards, magazines, film, sunscreen, and the like.

On Saba Rock, **The Saba Rock Nautical Museum** (284/495-9966) is part museum, part gift shop. Here you can see artifacts collected by diving legend Bert Kilbride and buy wreck-inspired jewelry and gifts. At Leverick Bay, a **Pusser's Company Store** (284/495-7369) sells resort wear and nautical-themed gifts and accessories.

Sports and Recreation

Most recreation around Virgin Gorda takes place on or near the water.

WATER SPORTS
Snorkeling

The favorite place to snorkel on Virgin Gorda is at **The Baths.** Within the pools, you can examine the underwater boulders; to see fish, swim beyond the boulders on the ocean side or head to **Devil's Bay** and snorkel around the rocky edge of the bay. There are also reefs off **Spring Bay, Valley Trunk Bay,** and **Savannah Bay.**

You can rent snorkel gear for a few hours or a few weeks from any of the dive operators listed under *Diving*.

Diving

Dive operators around Virgin Gorda often take

divers to **Mountain Point** at the end of the island's westernmost tip, where overhangs and caves make for exciting diving. Conditions here can be rough in the winter. Another nice dive site is **The Invisibles,** named because it lies almost invisibly under the sea east of Necker Island, north of Virgin Gorda. A twin-rock pinnacle here attracts reef fish as well as the occasional pelagic species.

Dive operators and day sails from Virgin Gorda often take passengers to the Dogs, a cluster of islands that lie between Virgin Gorda and Beef Island. **The Chimneys,** at the western end of Great Dog, is a site popular with both divers and snorkelers, who can admire underwater archways and tunnels. Other popular sites are **Bronco Billy's,** reputedly named by Jacques Cousteau himself, between Cockroach Island and Seal Dog, and **Wall-to-Wall,** which is usually packed with schooling fish.

Another popular site for Virgin Gorda dive operators is the **Chikuzen,** a wreck lying northwest of the island. The *Chikuzen,* a 246-foot refrigeration ship, sank in 1981, and its carcass attracts pelagic fish, eagle rays, sharks, and many more species.

There are dive shops in the Valley and North Sound. **Dive BVI Ltd.** (Yacht Harbour and Leverick Bay, 284/495-5513 or 800/848-7078, www.divebvi.com) has been around for more than 35 years and gets consistently high marks from customers. On Fridays, Dive BVI offers a day trip to Anegada, and its BVI Safari day trip can be customized for divers or snorkelers. Dive BVI also offers nitrox diving and is among the handful of dive shops using new equipment that allows divers to hear and talk to instructors underwater.

Or try **Kilbride's Sunchaser Scuba** (Bitter End, 284/495-9638 or 800/932-4286, www.sunchaserscuba.com), which offers dive packages and picks up guests from resorts in North Sound or from the government jetty in Spanish Town. Expect to pay about $110 for a two-tank dive.

Kiteboarding

Bitter End is the place for kiteboarding, a high-energy cross between surfing and windsurfing that involves being airborne for up to eight seconds. **Carib Kiteboarding** (Bitter End Resort, 284/495-7740, www.caribkiteboarding.com) offers classes and gear for all levels, from beginner to experienced. A 90-minute introductory course costs $150.

Equipment

North Sound is the perfect place to try water sports of any kind, and the best place to start is **Leverick Bay Watersports** (Leverick Bay Resort, 284/495-7376, fax 284/495-7014, www.watersportsbvi.com). Here you can rent gear ranging from a snorkel and fins to a Hobie Wave sailboat. Kayaks, dinghies, and wakeboards are also available. Talk to the friendly folks here to plan your day on the water. **Bitter End Resort** (284/494-2746) is the epicenter of water sports on North Sound, and you can also rent dinghies and take lessons there.

SAILING

Day sail operators will take you out for a day of sailing and snorkeling around Virgin Gorda. **Double D Charters** (Yacht Harbour, 284/495-6150 or 284/499-2479, www.doubledbvi.com) offers a wide range of sailing excursions on a 40-foot motor yacht and 50-foot catamaran. The 48-foot **Bravura** (Leverick Bay, 284/443-2586, www.sailbravura.com) is available for private day sails to Anegada or full- and half-day sails to the Baths, Cooper, Ginger, Great Camanoe, and other islands. Full-day sail excursions for up to five people cost $700; half-day sails are $400 and up.

If you would rather set your own course, **Euphoric Cruises** (Yacht Harbour, 284/495-5542 or 284/494-5511, www.boatsbvi.com) rents a range of powerboats.

In North Sound, **Leverick Bay Watersports** (Leverick Bay Resort, 284/495-7376, fax

284/495-7014, www.watersportsbvi.com) rents four-person dinghies, monohull sailboats, and two-person sea kayaks for $50–90 per day. It also rents more upscale powerboats for $300–450 per day. **Bitter End Yacht Club** (North Sound, 284/494-2746) offers a whole range of sailing excursions, classes, and rentals. If you're interested in a sailing course, call the Bitter End.

Marinas

There are four major marinas on Virgin Gorda. **Virgin Gorda Yacht Harbour** (The Valley, 284/495-5500, www.virgingordayachtharbour.com) is a 120-slip, full-service marina and boatyard just south of St. Thomas Bay, the ferry terminal in the Valley. Overnight rates vary from $1.25–$3 per foot per day, and they go down if you stay for a week, a month, or longer. If you're in transit, you can dock here free for 30 minutes and at $10–15 for each hour

after that, depending on size. There are moorings outside the marina; pay for them at the Yacht Harbour.

At North Sound, **Leverick Bay Resort** (284/495-7421, www.leverickbay.com) has 36 moorings and 15 slips with a controlling draft of 22 feet. Amenities include fuel, water, laundry, Internet access, a hotel, a restaurant, and a chandlery. Yachts can stop in here for a few minutes at no cost.

Bitter End Yacht Club (284/494-2745, www.beyc.com) has 20 slips and a draft of 30 feet, as well as 75 moorings. Bitter End is a full-service marina, including a repair shop, with all the expected amenities except laundry service.

Saba Rock Resort (North Sound, 284/495-7711, www.sabarock.com) has overnight slips and moorings, electricity, water, and boater rates for its hotel rooms.

The newest marina on Virgin Gorda is **Yacht Club Costa Smerelda** (Oil Nut Bay,

The Yacht Club Costa Smerelda on Virgin Gorda's remote northeast corner is the BVI's newest marina for luxury yachts.

284/346-2000, www.yccsmarina.com), which has 38 slips for yachts up to 328 feet (100 meters). The marina caters to super-yachts and is part of the ambitious Oil Nut Bay development, which also includes an ultra high-end residential development. Oil Nut Bay is located on the northeastern tip of Virgin Gorda, behind Bitter End and Biras Creek.

Accommodations

Accommodations on Virgin Gorda range from modest apartment-style suites to all-inclusive luxury hotels. The total number of rooms is quite small, however, so book early, especially in high season.

VILLAS

There are dozens of luxury villas on Virgin Gorda, many of which provide privacy in extraordinary settings. There are villas near the Baths, the Coppermine, Mahoe Bay, Nail Bay, and Leverick Bay.

Villa rental agencies will help match you with a villa that fits your needs and budget and assist with trip planning if you like. Villas typically rent by the week, although shorter or longer stays can usually be arranged. Rates typically range $1,500–5,000 (or more) per week.

Virgin Gorda Villa Rental (Leverick Bay, 284/495-7421, 800/848-7081, or 800/463-9396, fax 284/495-7367, www.virgingordabvi.com) manages 40 different villas at Leverick Bay and Mahoe Bay. **Purple Pineapple Rental Management** (284/495-5100, fax 305/723-0855, www.purplepineapple.com) also rents villas on Virgin Gorda.

THE VALLEY
$125-175

You will receive a hearty welcome at the **Bayview Apartments** (Spanish Town, 284/495-5329, www.bayviewbvi.com, $140 winter, $95 summer), a complex of three two-bedroom apartments set amid lush gardens in a residential section of Spanish Town. Rooms are furnished in rattan with tropical colors and

have full kitchens and balconies. There is air-conditioning in the bedrooms only. The apartments are within walking distance of the yacht harbor and other sites in Spanish Town; the Baths are a short taxi ride away.

A good option for moderate budgets is **《Fischer's Cove Hotel** (The Valley, 284/495-5252, fax 284/495-5820, www.fischerscove.com, $160–200), where you can choose between a private studio cottage and a more traditional hotel room. Cottages come with kitchenettes, ceiling fans, and a comfortable sitting room, but most importantly they line the hotel's own white-sand beach. Hotel rooms, housed in a colorful apartment-style concrete unit, have balconies that face either the garden or the ocean. Some rooms are air-conditioned. If having the most up-to-date furnishings is important to you, go elsewhere, but if you're keen on an unfussy and friendly place to lay your head, close to Virgin Gorda's beaches, this is one of the best choices on the island. Owned and operated by the Flax family, Fischer's Cove also has an on-site restaurant that serves three meals daily.

$225-300

For accommodations near the Baths, your first and best choice is **《Guavaberry Spring Bay** (The Valley, 284/495-5227, www.guavaberryspringbay.com, $240 winter, $150 summer). Circular, with high ceilings and exposed beams, these guesthouses are comfortable, private, and within walking distance of the island's best beaches. There are one-, two-, and three-bedroom units. Each comes with a full kitchen and an AM/FM radio. There is no cable TV or Internet. Air-conditioning is available for an additional fee in some of the smaller units; otherwise count on breezes and ceiling fans to do the cooling. There is a small commissary (but no restaurant) on the property, so you can even avoid a trip to the grocery store if you like. The best thing about Guavaberry Spring Bay is the charming setting—units are nestled between giant boulders, coconut palms, and brightly colored bougainvillea. Guests can walk down to Spring Bay right next door or take a slightly longer hike to the Baths. Also noteworthy is the knowledgeable and friendly staff (messages are delivered in person). A family atmosphere permeates the property.

Some of the newest rooms on Virgin Gorda are at **Virgin Gorda Village** (formerly Olde Yard Village; The Valley, 284/495-5544, www.virgingordavillage.com, $250–295 winter, $180–210 summer), an attractive condominium development on the outskirts of Spanish Town. The village includes one-, two-, and three-bedroom condos, all of which come with a full kitchen, air-conditioning, telephone, and cable TV. Units are individually owned but centrally managed. A pool and restaurant are on the property.

Over $300

◖ Little Dix Bay Resort (Little Dix Bay, 284/495-5555 or 888/767-3966, fax 284/495-5661, www.littledixbay.com, $300–1,300 summer, $700–2,300 winter) was the first resort in the British Virgin Islands and continues to set the standard for barefoot elegance in the region. Opened by Laurance Rockefeller in 1964, Little Dix offers comfortable accommodations in a spectacular setting. Rooms are tastefully decorated with exposed stone, wood finishes, and tile floors. The grounds are truly exquisite.

Guests are treated to a free bottle of rum and mixers upon arrival; complimentary morning and afternoon coffee; and use of the resort's snorkel gear, Sunfish boats, waterskiing equipment, fitness center, and tennis courts. There is a lovely beach, three fine restaurants, and a world-class spa where you can partake in the most up-to-date curative and restorative treatments. The resort prides itself on top-notch service, and with a guest-to-staff ratio of 3-to-1, you can count on individualized attention. All in all, Little Dix epitomizes class.

MID-ISLAND

The hotels at mid-island are a real getaway. If you want to see the island or sample its restaurants and shopping, you will need a rental car.

$225-300

Nail Bay Resort (Nail Bay, 284/494-8000, 800/871-3551, or 800/487-1839, fax 284/495-5875, www.nailbay.com, from $240 in winter, from $185 in summer) is a secluded estate of one- to three-bedroom luxury villas sprawling across a quiet hillside. Each villa is unique, but they feature common amenities including satellite TV, maid service, and air-conditioning. Guests may also use central tennis courts, two beaches, and an on-site restaurant. Prices at the resort range from $240 in season for a well-appointed apartment in the resort "village" to $600 and up for a high-end villa. Guests praise attentive staff and the peacefulness of the retreat.

Over $300

Located along a quiet beach halfway between the Valley and North Sound, **Mango Bay Resort** (Mango Bay, 284/495-5672, fax 284/495-5674, www.mangobayresort.com, $345–595 winter, $205–360 summer) has six beachfront villas with front doors just steps away from the ocean, plus additional private villas on the hillside overlooking the bay. All units come with air-conditioning, telephone, wireless Internet, and daily maid service. All but the most modest rooms have a full kitchen, and you will be steps away from a lovely beach.

NORTH SOUND
$125-175

Nestled amid an upscale community of snowbirds and vacationers on North Sound, **Leverick Bay Resort Hotel** (Leverick Bay, 284/495-7421, 800/848-7081, or 800/463-9396, fax 284/495-7367, www.leverickbay.com, $149 winter, $119 summer) has 18 hillside rooms and suites overlooking the resort marina. Rooms are basic but reasonably equipped with air-conditioning, cable TV, phone, coffeemaker, refrigerator, and double beds; there are also a handful of two-bedroom apartments for larger groups. Leverick Bay is not as plush as many resorts on Virgin Gorda, but you won't find a better value on the island. On-site amenities include a restaurant, a swimming pool, laundry, a water-sports center, a spa, shops, and a small grocery.

$175-225

Saba Rock is a speck of an island in middle of North Sound, home to a cheerful nine-room boutique hotel, the **Saba Rock Resort** (North Sound, 284/495-7711, fax 284/495-7373, www.sabarock.com, $125-235 winter, $100-225 summer). Rooms, which range from small studios to suites, are equipped with air-conditioning, satellite TV, coffeemakers, wireless Internet, and small fridges. In addition, the two-bedroom villas ($395-450) have full kitchens. In addition to tranquility, guests rave about spectacular views in every direction. The resort has pleasant gardens and seaside hammocks, as well as an on-site restaurant. There is no pool, although guests can swim off the dock.

Over $300

◖ **Biras Creek Resort** (North Sound, 284/494-3555, 877/883-0756, or 800/883-0756, www.biras.com, $690-870 winter, $505-590 summer) is a 31-suite North Sound resort delivering elegance, seclusion, and blissful relaxation. Accommodations are in individual cottages, many of which face the beach, and all of which are tucked tastefully and spaciously amid coconut palms and sea grape trees. Bercher's Bay is a picturesque string of windswept white sand, ideal for beachcombing and walks. There are miles of hiking trails on the property, and guests also have free use of the resort's water-sports equipment, bicycles, and dinghies.

Suite amenities include air-conditioning, outdoor showers, ceiling fans, telephones, CD players and iPods, refrigerators, tea- and coffeemakers, wireless Internet, flat-screen televisions, and private verandas. With an award-winning restaurant on site, many guests opt for the all-inclusive option ($970-2,250 winter, $715-1,990 summer), which includes three meals a day, plus afternoon tea. Children under four years old are not permitted at Biras.

Accessible only from the water, **The Bitter End Resort** (North Sound, 284/494-2746 or 800/872-2392, fax 284/494-4756, www.beyc.com, $720-1,895 winter, $620-1,480 summer) is an all-inclusive resort for sailors and water lovers. Guests may choose daily from a wide array of water sports (most of them free), hikes, fishing and snorkeling expeditions, and sailing classes. Three sand beaches and a pool adorn the property. With movie nights and kid's club activities as well, Bitter End specializes in family vacations.

Eighty-five guest suites are scattered around the hillside overlooking Bitter End's bustling marina and beaches. Rooms offer views, breezes, and the comforts of home: air-conditioning, ceiling fans, refrigerators, coffeemakers, wraparound porches, hammocks, and TV (upon request). Guests staying at least seven nights are enrolled in the resort's Admiral's Club and enjoy three meals a day at the resort's restaurants plus additional perks.

Food

Eating out on Virgin Gorda is generally expensive, but in many cases, it is worth the cost. Entrées at most "nice" restaurants in the evening run between $20 and $30. Adventurous visitors should seek out some of the local restaurants, where you can taste West Indian food and meet and mingle with island residents.

THE VALLEY
Casual
For fun, unpretentious dining and excellent sunsets, try **⟨ Mine Shaft Café and Pub** (Coppermine Rd., 284/495-5260, 10 A.M.–10 P.M. daily, $7–25). In the same neighborhood as Coppermine Point National Park, the Mine Shaft overlooks a landscape of cacti and flowering frangipani trees. The diverse menu features roti, curry shrimp, jerk chicken, and steak, plus fresh fish and lobster. Barbecue ribs are a house specialty, and don't miss the deadly Cave-In house drink.

The **Bath and Turtle** (Virgin Gorda Yacht Harbour, 284/495-5239, 7:30 A.M.–10 P.M. daily, $8–25) is a handy patio pub located at the marina in Spanish Town. Good for pizza, burgers, and breakfast, this is a casual and convenient spot to satisfy hunger; moderate your expectations and you will be satisfied. A few steps away is **Rendezvous Bar,** an outdoor bar overlooking the marina, which often attracts a happy hour crowd.

Village Cafe (Spanish Town, 284/495-5544, 7 A.M.–8 P.M. Mon.–Sat., 7 A.M.–7 P.M. Sun., $22–42) is a casual poolside restaurant with reliable food and a warm welcome. At dinner choose from seafood, pasta, or steak; at lunch ($10–16), the menu is a nice selection of sandwiches, pizza, wraps, and salads. The café is also open for breakfast. Guests may chose to dine inside in the a/c, at the bar, or at one of the covered tables set around the pool. The

atmosphere here is decidedly welcoming, and the service is pleasant and not stuffy.

There is something extra special about the piña coladas at **⟨ Mad Dog** (The Baths, 284/495-5830, 9 A.M.–7 P.M. daily, $6–10), but don't bother trying to find out the secret—they won't tell you. This inviting, open-air café serves hot and cold sandwiches all day, but it's the cold and blended drinks that bring in the crowds. Beat the rush to get one of the comfortable loungers on the porch, and you won't know where the afternoon has gone. Mad Dog is next to the Top of the Baths parking lot.

The food plays second fiddle to the view at **Top of the Baths** (The Baths, 284/495-5497, 8 A.M.–10 P.M. daily, $12–32), where the dining room overlooks spectacular boulders. The menu features pasta, salads, sandwiches, and fresh seafood; quality is hit or miss. Diners can take advantage of the freshwater pool.

West Indian
Dixie's (Spanish Town, 284/495-5640, 7 A.M.–9 P.M. Mon.–Sat., $5–12), near the ferry dock, is a popular diner serving hearty West Indian and American food at breakfast and lunch. It is also a great place to soak up local culture, especially in the morning, when it seems that just about everybody in Virgin Gorda stops by for a cup of bush tea and something to eat. Try a "bake" (round baked bread) with egg and cheese for breakfast. At lunch you can dine on local specialties like stewed mutton and curried chicken, but many people opt for Dixie's ever-popular fried chicken.

On Friday nights, look around the Fire Station on Lee Road to find a full-blown barbecue with fish, chicken, pork, and all kinds of West Indian side dishes, including peas and rice, plantains, and coleslaw.

Creole

C Chez Bamboo (The Valley, 284/495-5752, 5–10 P.M. daily, $20–40) is a stylish New Orleans–style supper club located between the ferry dock and marina. A wraparound mural depicts a jazz band, and the menu borrows heavily from Creole traditions, throwing in occasional Caribbean touches. Try the conch gumbo, Nassau grouper *en papillote*, or strip steak with a creamy Worcestershire sauce. Desserts include delicacies like chocolate bourbon mint cake. There is often live jazz or blues on the veranda Friday nights. The food here is imaginative—some of the best on the island.

International

At **The Rock Café** (The Valley, 284/495-5482, 4 P.M.–midnight, $19–40), you can enjoy Caribbean and international cuisine at tables set amid boulders or inside the air-conditioned dining room. With a friendly barkeep and big-screen television, this is a popular stop for happy hour, and there is live music at the piano bar most nights, especially during the winter tourist season. The menu is diverse but leans toward Italian, with house specialties including Sicilian-style swordfish and spaghetti with fresh Anegada lobster.

Treat yourself to a meal at **C Little Dix Bay Resort** (The Valley, 284/495-5555), which delivers the best fine dining this side of Gorda Peak. Little Dix has three main restaurants: The Pavilion ($36–50), an open-air dining room with a highly pitched roof, serves elaborate breakfast, lunch, and dinner buffets featuring some of the freshest ingredients available in the BVI. You can also order from an à la carte menu. The Sugar Mill ($45–80) is the place to go for intimate, upscale dinners in a romantic setting. Menu options include the likes of miso-glazed grouper, Mediterranean sea bass, and five-spice pork belly. Collared shirts and slacks are expected for men at the Sugar Mill; ladies should wear "suitable evening attire."

The Beach Grill (11:30 A.M.–6 P.M., $12–20) is a casual waterfront restaurant near the resort dock that serves cold drinks, burgers, sandwiches, and the like.

Ice Cream

For a cold treat, drop by **Yum Yums** (Spanish Town, 284/495-6990, 11 A.M.–7:30 P.M. Mon.–Thurs., 10 A.M.–8 P.M. Fri., call for weekend hours) for ice cream or a wide selection of chocolates and candy.

Markets

Buck's Food Market (Yacht Harbour, 284/495-5423, 7 A.M.–8 P.M. Mon.–Sat., 7 A.M.–7 P.M. Sun.) has canned and packaged food, carries lots of frozen meat and vegetables, and serves inexpensive hot lunches daily except Sunday.

NORTH SOUND
Casual

Fat Virgin's Cafe (Biras Creek, 284/495-7052, 10 A.M.–9 P.M., $8–20), on the dock at Biras Creek Resort, serves casual but hearty fare for lunch and dinner. Ask about the soup of the day, or try the chicken roti, baby back ribs, or flying-fish sandwich. This is a pleasant respite from the fine dining that otherwise dominates North Sound.

Fine Dining

C Creek (284/494-3555, www.biras.com) welcomes nonguests to dine at its excellent standard-setting restaurants. Breakfast ($30 per person, 8–10 A.M.) and dinner ($85 per person, seatings at 6:30 P.M. and 8:45 P.M.) are served in the Hilltop Restaurant, a breezy, open dining room with views of North Sound. Lunch ($35 per person, 1–2 P.M.) is served beachside. Dinner is an upscale, four-course affair with a dress code. Advance reservations are required.

Bitter End Yacht Club (North Sound, 284/494-2745, www.beyc.com, $40–50 dinner) has four restaurants and a bakery. The

Clubhouse Grille is its flagship dining room, serving generous buffets at breakfast and lunch, as well as a dinner menu that spans the spectrum from casual grill food to elegant seafood. The resort's Sunday brunch is a destination for visitors and residents. The **Crawl Pub** (lunch and dinner, $10–18) offers casual pub fare, including pizza from brick ovens on the premises. Nonguests can catch the free Gun Creek ferry to the resort. Dinner reservations are requested.

Another fine choice for excellent food and good company is **The Restaurant at Leverick Bay** (Leverick Bay, 284/495-7154, lunch and dinner daily), overlooking the beach and water-sports center at this buzzing corner of North Sound. Lunch ($12–28) is focused on the grill, with burgers and steaks, as well as gourmet pies from the pizza oven. Dinner ($28–45) is elegant with fine salads, soups, and entrées like prime rib, fresh Atlantic grouper, and Anegada lobster. The rotisserie chicken is deservedly popular. On Friday nights the Restaurant at Leverick Bay throws a Caribbean-style beach party with a barbecue, live music, and mocko jumbies.

Markets

The biggest market in North Sound is **Buck's Food Market** (Gun Creek, 284/495-7368), about 100 yards from the Gun Creek dock. Yachters can provision at the Bitter End Yacht Club's **Emporium,** and **The Chef's Pantry** (Leverick Bay, 284/495-7154) has groceries, a deli, and bakery.

Information and Services

TOURIST OFFICES

The **BVI Tourist Board** (284/495-5181, 8:30 A.M.–4:30 P.M. Mon.–Fri.) operates a visitor information office at the Virgin Gorda Yacht Harbour. Friendly and knowledgeable staff here can give you maps, brochures, and advice about visiting Virgin Gorda.

There is a visitor welcome center at **Gun Creek** with bathrooms, seating, and staff to assist with inquiries and transportation needs. Sometimes this center is not open, however.

MAPS AND CHARTS

The best map of Virgin Gorda is found in the pocket-size, free, and widely available road map of the BVI. For a detailed topographical survey map, you will have to visit the Survey Department (Road Town, 284/494-3459, 8:30 A.M.–3 P.M. Mon.–Fri.) on Tortola.

Nautical charts, plus a lot of other marine equipment, can be purchased at the **Virgin Gorda Yacht Harbour Chandlery** (The Valley, 284/495-5628, www.vgmarina.biz), which also has a shipyard and repair service.

LIBRARIES AND MEDIA

The **Virgin Gorda Public Library** (Crabbe Hill Rd., 284/495-5516, 9 A.M.–5 P.M. Mon.–Fri., 9 A.M.–1 P.M. Sat.) has a small collection of books and magazines.

There are no Virgin Gorda newspapers; the national BVI papers are available at supermarkets around the island. The free Tortola-based *Limin' Times,* published on Thursdays, includes Virgin Gorda nightlife and upcoming events.

Listen to Radio ZBVI (780 AM) at 7 A.M., noon, and 5:45 P.M. for local, regional, and international news.

COMMUNICATIONS

If your lodging does not offer Internet access, you can go online at Trintek (Yacht Harbour, 284/495-6562, 9 A.M.–6 P.M. Mon.–Fri., 9 A.M.–1 P.M. Sat.) for $2 per 10 minutes.

EMERGENCIES

There is no hospital on Virgin Gorda. The **Iris O'Neal Clinic** (Crabbe Hill Rd., 284/495-5337) sees patients 8:30 A.M.–4:30 P.M. on weekdays. Nurses are available after hours: call 554. **Apex Medical Center** (Millionaire Rd., 284/495-6557) and **Medicure Ltd.** (Ocean View Hotel, 284/495-6833) are the island's two private medical clinics. Medicure also operates a pharmacy (284/495-5479, 9 A.M.–5 P.M. Mon.–Fri., 9 A.M.–1 P.M. Sat.).

Virgin Gorda's main police station is in the Valley (Crabbe Hill Rd., 284/495-2222), with an outpost in North Sound. In an emergency, dial 999 or 911. For maritime search and rescue, contact **Virgin Islands Search and Rescue** (284/494-4357, emergency 767).

BANKS

FirstBank (Lee Rd., 284/495-6229), **FirstCaribbean International Bank** (Virgin Gorda Yacht Harbour, 284/495-5217), and **Scotiabank** (Yacht Harbour Village, 284/CHECK) have ATMs and can assist with banking transactions.

POST OFFICES

There are post offices in the Valley (Vanterpool Administration Building, Millionaire Rd., 284/495-5224) and North Sound (284/494-1898), where you can buy stamps and money orders and send mail all over the world. For courier services, try **Rush-It** (284/495-5821).

CUSTOMS AND IMMIGRATION

Immigration and customs officers meet all international flights and ferries arriving on Virgin Gorda. Tourists must have a return ticket and prearranged accommodations and can receive a tourist visa of up to 30 days in the first instance. If you need to apply for an extension, visit the **Immigration Department** (Vanterpool Administration Building, Millionaire Rd., 284/495-5621). Customs officers can be reached at their headquarters at the ferry dock (284/495-5173).

LAUNDERETTES

Steven's Laundry and Cleaners (Virgin Gorda Yacht Harbour, 284/495-5525, 8 A.M.–noon and 4–8 P.M. daily) is the best choice for doing laundry in the Valley. You'll pay $3 for a wash.

Getting There

BY AIR

Virgin Gorda's tiny airport (VIJ) is along the eastern shore of the Valley, about a mile from the ferry dock. The 3,160-foot runway is wedged between two hills, so takeoffs and landings can be heart-stopping. Because of the conditions, flights can arrive and depart only in daylight. Nonetheless, flying is the most convenient way to arrive. You can avoid the hassle of arriving on Tortola and then arranging taxis and ferries to Virgin Gorda. You also get the pleasure of short lines and quick service at the small airport.

Air Sunshine (284/495-8900 or 800/327-8900, www.airsunshine.com) has four flights daily from San Juan to Virgin Gorda. Expect to pay $145 one-way.

BY SEA

Ferries sail daily to Virgin Gorda from St. Thomas (1 hour, 4 days per week), Tortola (30 minutes, daily), and Beef Island (30 minutes, daily). Ferries from St. Thomas and Tortola arrive at the St. Thomas Bay jetty in Spanish Town. Those from Beef Island arrive at North Sound. You don't need advance reservations on most of the ferries (with the exception of certain routes on North Sound Express), but always call to confirm the schedule ahead of time.

From St. Thomas to Virgin Gorda: Speedy's (284/495-5240) has round-trip ferries from St. Thomas to Virgin Gorda on Tuesday, Thursday, and Saturday. Boats depart St. Thomas at 8:45 A.M. and 5 P.M. on Tuesday and Thursday and 4 P.M. on Saturday. The fare is $70.

From Tortola to Virgin Gorda: Two ferry companies run boats from the Road Town ferry dock to the Spanish Town ferry dock. Round-trip adult fare is $30; one-way fare is $20. **Speedy's** (284/495-5240, www.speedysbvi.com) comfortable, air-conditioned catamaran departs Road Town Monday–Saturday at 9 A.M., 10:30 A.M., noon, 1:30 P.M., and 4:30 P.M. There are additional trips on Saturday at 5 P.M.; on Monday and Friday at 6 P.M.; on Tuesday and Thursday at 10 A.M. and 2:45 P.M.; and on Wednesday and Saturday (December–July) at 6:45 P.M. and 11 P.M. On Sundays and public holidays, Speedy's departs Road Town at 9 A.M., 1:30 P.M., and 5:15 P.M.

Smith's Ferry Service (284/495-4495, www.smithsferry.com) departs Road Town Monday–Friday at 7 A.M., 8:50 A.M., 12:30 P.M., and 3:15 P.M. On Saturday, Smith's departs Road Town at 7 A.M., 8:50 A.M., 12:30 P.M., and 4:15 P.M. On Sunday, Smith's departs Road Town at 8:50 A.M., 12:30 P.M., and 4:15 P.M.

From Beef Island to North Sound and the Valley: Two ferry companies depart from Trellis Bay, Beef Island for Virgin Gorda. The **North Sound Express** (284/495-2138) runs a circular route between Beef Island, Spanish Town, Virgin Gorda, and North Sound, Virgin Gorda. Ferries leave the Trellis Bay, Beef Island, ferry terminal at 8 A.M., 11 A.M., 1:45 P.M., 4:15 P.M., 6 P.M., and 8 P.M. The fare is $30 round trip to Spanish Town and $65 round trip to North Sound. Alternatively, **Speedy's** (284/495-5240) runs three trips from Beef Island to Spanish Town daily, departing Trellis Bay at 6:30 A.M. 12 noon, and 10:30 P.M. The fare is $30 round trip.

The ferry terminal is within walking distance (about 0.3 mile) of the Terrance B. Lettsome International Airport, but if you are carrying lots of luggage, opt for a taxi. (Better yet, get a taxi to deliver your luggage and walk off your airplane legs.) The fare is $45.

Getting Around

TAXIS

Taxis are plentiful in the Valley, especially from the ferry dock to the Baths. Expect to pay $4–7 per person one-way from anywhere in the Valley to the Baths, Spring Bay, Valley Trunk Bay, Savannah Bay, Pond Bay, and the Coppermine. It is a whopping $30 to travel from the Valley to Leverick Bay or Gun Creek.

A two-hour island tour including the Valley, the Coppermine, the Baths, Gorda Peak, and Leverick Bay costs $110 for 1–2 people.

If you need a taxi pickup, call **Mahogany Rentals and Taxi Service** (284/495-5469), **Gafford Potter Taxi Service** (284/495-5329), **Andy's Taxi and Jeep Rental** (284/495-5511), or the taxi stand at the Virgin Gorda Yacht Harbour (284/495-5252).

CAR RENTALS

Getting a rental car gives you the freedom to explore Virgin Gorda at your own pace, although at a hefty price. The most bare-bones rentals here run more than $50 per day and quickly climb to over $90. You will need to buy a temporary BVI driver's license for $10 if you rent a car.

Speedy's (Crabbe Hill Rd., 284/495-5240) has a large fleet of Jeeps and sometimes offers special ferry and car rental packages. Other rental companies, all in the Valley, are **L&S Jeep Rental** (284/495-5297), **Mahogany Car Rentals** (284/495-5469), and **Island Style**

Jeep and Car Rental (284/495-6300). Book early to avoid being stuck with the biggest and most expensive vehicle.

BY BOAT
If you want to explore North Sound, you have to do it in a boat. **Leverick Bay**

Watersports (Leverick Bay Resort, 284/495-7376, fax 284/495-7014, www.watersports-bvi.com) rents four-person dinghies for $80 per day, monohull sailboats for $60 per day, and two-person sea kayaks for $50 per day. It also rents more upscale powerboats for $350–400 per day.

Out Islands: Around Virgin Gorda

These islands are popular for snorkeling and diving trips. Almost without exception, a private boat—charter or otherwise—is the best, and in some cases only, way to reach these islands. The exclusive resort at Necker Island is accessible by invitation only.

FALLEN JERUSALEM
As its name suggests, this island evokes the ruined ancient city of Jerusalem, with a landscape that resembles tumbled-down buildings. It lies between Round Rock and the southern tip of Virgin Gorda and looks like a tail extended off Virgin Gorda's Baths. The 30-acre island is a national park, and National Parks Trust moorings on the north side of the island

enable visitors with private boats to explore it. On calm days, the snorkeling here is exceptional—imagine the beauty of the Baths without the crowds. But there are very few calm days. If you get ashore, the entertainment is clambering around the rocky shore. Likely, the only other creatures you will see are the seabirds that nest here.

◀ THE DOG ISLANDS
West Dog, Seal Dog, West Seal Dog, East Seal Dog, and Great Dog Islands join with Cockroach Island to form the Dogs, the site of some of the best snorkeling and diving in the British Virgins. Totally undeveloped and uninhabited, the Dogs lie scattered between Virgin Gorda and Tortola. Their closeness to Virgin Gorda makes them a popular destination for dive operators based there. Dive boats leaving from Tortola's eastern end may also visit here. These islands are protected by the National Parks Trust, and visitors should use the NPT moorings provided.

The Chimneys, at the western end of Great Dog, is a site popular with both divers and snorkelers, who can admire underwater archways and tunnels. Other popular sites are **Bronco Billy's,** reputedly named by Jacques Cousteau himself, between Cockroach Island and Seal Dog, and **Wall-to-Wall,** which is usually packed with schooling fish. Your underwater sojourn here will almost certainly be the most memorable of your entire trip.

AROUND VIRGIN GORDA

Necker Island

NECKER ISLAND RESORT

0   0.5 mi

0   0.5 km

Prickly Pear Island

Eustatia Island

Prickly Pear National Park

Eustatia Sound

Blunder Bay

Saba Rock

Deep Bay

Oil Nut Bay

BITTER END YACHT CLUB

North Sound

YACHT CLUB COSTA SMERELDA

Gun Creek

BIRAS CREEK RESORT

Bercher's Bay

© AVALON TRAVEL

THE DOG ISLANDS

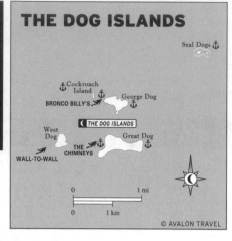

Seal Dogs

Cockroach Island

BRONCO BILLY'S   George Dog

THE DOG ISLANDS

West Dog   Great Dog

THE CHIMNEYS

WALL-TO-WALL

0   1 mi

0   1 km

© AVALON TRAVEL

NECKER ISLAND

It really does not get any more exclusive than at Necker Island (284/494-2757, www.necker.com, $4,100 and up), the 74-acre private island owned by Sir Richard Branson of Virgin Atlantic and hot-air balloon fame. A house fire caused by lightning in 2011 provided fodder for English tabloids: actress Kate Winslet was said to have carried Branson's elderly mother out of Balinese-style Great House, which was totally destroyed in the blaze.

The fire did disrupt operations at Necker, but not for long. You and 27 of your friends can rent the entire island for $50,000 per night. Needless to say, guests are treated to gourmet dining and luxurious pampering and can choose from a wide array of activities, from boat excursions to board games. A staff of 50 is at your beck and call. Several times a year Necker Island invites not-quite-so-moneyed guests to "Celebration Weeks" and "Revitalization Weeks," where you can rent a room "house-party style." The rate for these events starts at $29,000 per week, per couple.

Getting There

Information about getting to Necker Island is provided to guests on a need-to-know basis. Suffice it to say that there are no public ferries, and day sail operators will not take you here. If you try to anchor your boat here and swim ashore to one of the beaches, you will certainly have a story to tell back home (although the law is on your side: all beaches are public up to the high-water mark).

MOSQUITO ISLAND

This 125-acre island sits off the northeastern coast of Virgin Gorda, forming part of the barrier that keeps the North Sound calm and protected. Sir Richard Branson bought Mosquito Island several years ago and plans to construct an eco-friendly resort there.

JOST VAN DYKE

A short sail from Tortola and St. Thomas, Jost Van Dyke is a getaway among getaways. The five-square-mile island shares a common topography with the other Virgin Islands: rich green hillsides that cascade toward perfect white beaches. But Jost Van Dyke (YOST van dike) possesses a character of its own, thanks to the thousands of sailors who visit every year and the influence of one world-famous islander. Named after an early Dutch settler (some say pirate), Jost Van Dyke was a sleepy island community well into the 1960s. Islanders fished, farmed, and traveled to nearby islands for work. But then, in 1968, a young Philicianno "Foxy" Callwood changed things when he started selling drinks and food from a beach shack at Great Harbour. It turned out that Foxy had a serious knack for hospitality. As his reputation as an easygoing entertainer and gracious host grew, so did the number of sailors putting Jost Van Dyke in their sights.

Today, Foxy's is still the best-known thing on Jost Van Dyke, but it is by no means the only reason to come here. Watering holes in Great Harbour, Little Harbour, White Bay, and the east end cater to the yachting crowd. If you are happiest with a drink in your hand and the sand beneath your feet, you can't do much better than Jost Van Dyke.

If you have the will to wander away from the beach bar, you will find an idyllic island

© SUSANNA HENIGHAN POTTER

JOST VAN DYKE

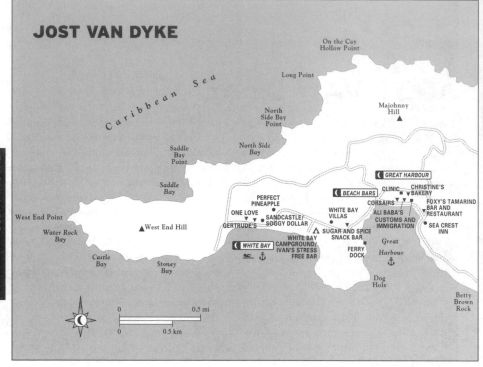

JOST VAN DYKE

On the Cay
Hollow Point

Long Point

Caribbean Sea

Majohnny
Hill ▲

North
Side Bay
Point

North Side
Bay

Saddle
Bay
Point

Saddle
Bay

◀ GREAT HARBOUR

CLINIC   CHRISTINE'S
◀ BEACH BARS   ▼ ▼ BAKERY
PERFECT   CORSAIRS   FOXY'S TAMARIND
PINEAPPLE   ▼ ▼   BAR AND
ONE LOVE   ●   WHITE BAY   ALI BABA'S   RESTAURANT
▼ ▼   SANDCASTLE/   VILLAS   CUSTOMS AND   ● SEA CREST
GERTRUDE'S   SOGGY DOLLAR   ●   IMMIGRATION   INN
▲ SUGAR AND SPICE
WHITE BAY   SNACK BAR   Great
◀ WHITE BAY   CAMPGROUND/   Harbour
⚓   IVAN'S STRESS   FERRY
FREE BAR   DOCK   ⚓

West End Point

Water Rock
Bay   ▲ West End Hill

Castle
Bay   Stoney
Bay

Dog
Hole

Betty
Brown
Rock

0   0.5 mi
0   0.5 km

still content with the simple life. White Bay, on the south shore, is one of the best beaches in the whole Virgin archipelago. A network of mostly unpaved roads through the island's hills can double as hiking trails and afford explorers unmatched views. Adventurers can hike to the mysterious Bubbly Pool and snorkel at Diamond Cay National Park. Jost is a great jumping-off point for exploring the out islands of Sandy Cay, Sandy Spit, and Little Jost Van Dyke, where visitors will find still emptier beaches and the remains of an 18th-century sugar plantation.

Most people get to Jost Van Dyke on charter yachts, which explains why there are still relatively few hotel rooms on the island. Still, you can find high-quality, low-fuss places to stay on Jost, including an excellent beachfront

campground. Daily ferry service makes Jost accessible to those without their own yachts.

PLANNING YOUR TIME

Jost is a quiet place—most visitors will be ready to move on after a few days. But if you want to get on the fast track to complete relaxation, by all means, plan a longer stay. Just don't forget to pack some books.

Jost makes a good **day trip** from St. John, Tortola, or St. Thomas, all of which are within a 45-minute ferry ride. Ferries arrive at Great Harbour, within walking distance of White Bay and Foxy's. **New Horizon Ferry Service** (284/495-9278, 25 minutes, $25 round-trip) makes five daily round trips between Great Harbour and West End, Tortola. **Inter-Island Boat Service** (340/776-6597, 45 minutes, $70

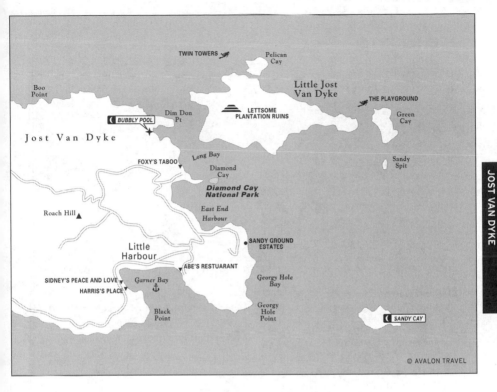

JOST VAN DYKE

round-trip) makes two round-trip journeys daily between Cruz Bay, St. John and Great Harbour, plus at least one round trip between Red Hook, St. Thomas and Great Harbour, Jost Van Dyke.

If you arrive by ferry, catch a taxi out to the Bubbly Pool and then head over to White Bay for an afternoon on the beach. Or stroll through Great Harbour before hiking out to White Bay for the rest of the day.

Reservations are not necessary for the Tortola to Jost Van Dyke ferry, but call ahead

to confirm the schedule and availability of the ferries connecting St. Thomas and St. John with Jost Van Dyke.

Another way to get to Jost is aboard a **day sail** or **dive excursion.** Your captain may skip Great Harbour altogether and head straight to White Bay, Sandy Cay, Sandy Spit, or Diamond Cay, depending on passengers' requests and sea conditions. Advance reservations are required for day sail outings. Call the operator of your choice several days in advance (choose someone close to where you are staying).

JOST VAN DYKE

HIGHLIGHTS

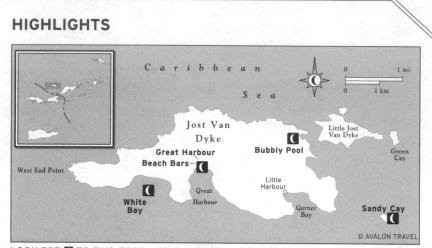

© AVALON TRAVEL

LOOK FOR ◖ TO FIND RECOMMENDED SIGHTS, ACTIVITIES, DINING, AND LODGING.

◖ **Great Harbour:** The most picturesque sea-side village in the Virgin Islands, the "capital" of Jost Van Dyke consists of a sandy track along the waterfront and a few quiet side streets. Coconut palms, a majestic harbor, and a stately old church round out the appeal (page 255).

◖ **White Bay:** One of the nicest beaches in the Virgin Islands, White Bay is divided in two by a rock promontory. The offshore reef is good for snorkeling; the sand is good for relaxing (page 255).

◖ **Bubbly Pool:** Tucked away on the remote east end of Jost, this is a favorite of hikers and explorers. A nice, private place for a dip, the pool fills with froth and bubbles when the surf is up (page 257).

◖ **Sandy Cay:** A perfect desert island. Relax on the white sand beach, snorkel on the reef, or hike the loop trail and look for bananaquits and boobies (page 257).

◖ **Beach Bars:** No island has better beach bars than Jost Van Dyke. Foxy's is the most famous, thanks to master entertainer Foxy Callwood, but others such as Soggy Dollar, Taboo, and Sidney's Peace and Love, are just as memorable and even more welcoming (page 259).

Sights

Jost Van Dyke is four miles long and three miles wide at its broadest point. Its ridge climbs to 1,054 feet at Majohnney Point and stretches from east to west like a meandering backbone. Traditionally, development was limited to four bays along the southwestern coast of the island, although a few hilltop homes have now been built. A single road connects White Bay, Great Harbour, Little Harbour, and the east end; it

takes about 15 minutes to drive the four miles from end to end. A new road has been cut along the ridge. It is mostly unpaved and treacherous without four-wheel drive.

Ferries arrive at Dog Hole, on the far western end of Great Harbour. It is easy to walk from the ferry to any place in Great Harbour, and as long as you don't mind a bit of exercise, you can walk from there to White Bay as well.

SOUTH SHORE

Three bays along the southeastern shore of Jost Van Dyke constitute the greatest extent of human settlement on the island.

◖ Great Harbour

Great Harbour looks like paradise: a fringe of white sand, coconut palms rising above the village, a beautiful old church, and unblemished green hillsides towering above it. Whether you arrive by ferry or private boat, your first real glimpse of Jost Van Dyke will probably be of Great Harbour. Get your camera ready. Great Harbour's main street is a sandy path that runs parallel to the beach. Fronting this are most of the town's restaurants and bars, as well as the Jost Van Dyke Methodist Church and the island's two-story Administration Building, where police, customs, immigration, and an island administrator have offices. Foxy's Tamarind Bar is on the far eastern end of the harbor. At Foxy's you can look in on the construction of a traditional island sloop, being built by local teenagers with help from a nonprofit, the Jost Van Dyke Preservation Society.

The heart of Great Harbour proper lies on the narrow side roads that veer off from the main street and on Back Street, which runs parallel to Main Street at the back of the village. This is where you will find the school, library, shops, laundry, gas station, and other evidence that people actually do live on Jost Van Dyke.

◖ White Bay

As you reach the top of the hill heading west out of Great Harbour, look down for the spectacular sight of White Bay before you, a ribbon of snow-colored sand and turquoise waters. White Bay is by far the nicest beach on Jost, and it's one of the best in the entire Virgin Islands. The sand is smooth and clean; it is fringed by low palms, sea grapes, and a few rustic buildings. The beach is cut in half by a small rock promontory. You can follow a path

over the rocks or swim around them. An offshore reef rewards snorkelers. The bay is popular with the yachting crowd despite the fact that there is no dock. Boats weigh anchor and passengers wade or swim ashore; hence the Soggy Dollar Bar at the beach's western end, named for the damp money fished from wet pockets and wallets.

The eastern end of White Bay is quiet; a campground huddles among the sea grape trees and a few tasteful guesthouses look down from the hillside above. The western end is home to a half dozen beach bars and restaurants and a small hotel. The only real nod to commercialism here is at the far western tip of the beach, where on some days small cruise ships unload hundreds of passengers for a beach picnic. A sports center there rents kayaks, pedal boats, and other water toys and takes visitors on ATV tours of the island. The good news is that if this type of thing doesn't appeal to you, it's pretty easy to ignore.

Little Harbour

About 2.5 miles to the east of Great Harbour is its smaller sister, Little Harbour. Small houses cling to the hillside here, overlooking the small bay and a narrow beach. A handful of shoreside restaurants, bars, and shops attract visiting yachts. The road dips down into Little Harbour, then steeply up and then down again toward the east end. East End

A few years ago, the east end of Jost Van Dyke was largely unknown to visitors. There was no reason for most people to venture that way since only a few people lived there and there were no restaurants, hotels, or well-known attractions. But in 2003 Foxy Callwood opened Foxy's Taboo, built a dock, and began to draw visitors to one of the most beautiful parts of Jost Van Dyke. The east end differs in character from other parts of Jost. The land around Taboo is flat and somewhat desolate; the flora includes cacti and other dry-weather plants.

ISLAND SLOOPS

© GEOFFREY BROOKS

a Virgin Islands sloop under sail

Before the age of modern yachts, motorboats, and cruise ships, a different breed of watercraft plied the waters around the Virgin Islands. Small, wooden, and high-bowed, sloops were once the primary means of water transportation around the island. Known by the misnomer "Tortola sloop," these vessels were built and used throughout the British Virgin Islands.

The sloops were built by Virgin Islanders, often using white cedar (*Tabebuia heterophylla*), a tree native to the Virgin Islands. Shipwrights scoured the island for cedars that were the appropriate size and shape for their next project. As a result white cedar eventually became the national tree of the British Virgin Islands.

Boatbuilders learned how to construct the sloops from one another, and they kept their construction plans in their heads, not on paper. The construction process was carried out primarily using basic carpenters' tools such as a saw, hammer, chisel, and—most importantly—adze.

Island sloops are notable for their high bow and pronounced sheer, with a long overhang at both bow and stern. The mast is stepped on the keel and located one-third of the way between the bow and stern. The boom extends well beyond the transom and is usually the same length as the overall boat. Most Tortola sloops are less than 30 feet long.

As the islands' economy grew and diversified in the second half of the 20th century, the art of boatbuilding faded from prominence in the community. For many years, the only active shipwrights were elderly men; the younger generation showed no interest in learning this art form.

But there is hope still for the island sloop. The Virgin Islands Studies Programme at the H. Lavity Stoutt Community College in Tortola has bought three Tortola sloops: *Moonbeam*, a 20-foot sloop built in the 1980s, *Youth Instructor*, a 25-foot boat built in 2000, and *Vigilant*, a 25-foot sloop built in the 1880s. Steps have also been taken to interview shipwrights and educate the community about its rich maritime heritage.

A highlight of the annual August Festival on Tortola is a sloop race in Road Harbour between boats captained by the governor and the premier.

Meanwhile, the Jost Van Dyke Preservation Society is building a traditional island sloop with the help of high school students, island residents, and some marine experts. Ask about the project around Foxy's Tamarind Restaurant in Great Harbour.

There is also an exhibit about Tortola sloops and their makers at the **Lower Estate Sugar Works Museum** (Botanic Station) in Road Town.

JOST VAN DYKE

Jost Van Dyke Methodist Church

The small beach next to Taboo is rocky—not good for swimming—but the area is beautiful in an empty kind of way. The 1.25-acre **Diamond Cay National Park** juts out from the mainland just south of Taboo and is a nesting site for boobies and pelicans.

◖ Bubbly Pool

Ask at Foxy's Taboo for a map to the Bubbly Pool, or just head northward from the restaurant and look for the path—it's not hard to find. You will bypass the salt pond and climb over a low rise before descending into the cove where you will find the pool. The Bubbly Pool is a small grotto formed by rocks and faced by a half-moon beach of coarse sand and rubble. The pool is large enough to fit about four swimmers comfortably. When the sea is calm, the pool is a private and quiet place for a dip. But when the northern swell is up and waves crash violently on the north-facing rocks, the show begins. On these days, large waves crash

into the pool, dissipating into mounds of bubbles that crack and pop. It's fun to play in the waves, and the bubbles have been likened to a high-priced spa treatment.

From the pool you can clamber up a short footpath on the eastern side of the pool that leads to an overlook and views of Jost Van Dyke's rugged north coast—a landscape of sheer cliffs, pounding waves, and windswept vegetation.

The hike from Foxy's Taboo to the Bubbly Pool takes about 20 minutes and passes loblolly trees, mangroves, and a large number of Turk's head cacti. It's best to wear sturdy shoes.

◖ Sandy Cay

Sandy Cay, a six-acre island less than a mile offshore Jost Van Dyke, is in many respects a perfect desert island. It has a sandy white beach, coconut palm trees, a nice offshore reef, and a wooded interior. Most visitors can pass a few hours here relaxing on the beach, swimming, or snorkeling. Others take the 20-minute hike that circles the interior salt pond and traverses rocky cliffs favored by nesting seabirds. Naturalists will admire the diversity of ecosystems—beach, swamp, cliff, forest—that exist on such a tiny island. Look for the flowering lilies that grow near the beach and the seeming millions of hermit crabs that maneuver around the island in borrowed shells. Keep your eyes out for a glimpse of the tiny bananaquit, a yellow-breasted bird that flits around with great speed and favors the pipe organ cactus, especially when it is flowering. If you can't see the birds, look for their nests, untidy masses of twigs and grass that hang just about at eye level in parts of the forest. For many decades, Sandy Cay was owned by multimillionaire philanthropist Laurance Rockefeller. Just before his death in 2005, Rockefeller donated the island to the British Virgin Islands government on the condition that it become a national park, which it has. Rockefeller always believed in maintaining public access to the island, and the short trail that circles the island is well maintained. There are no moorings, however, and no trash cans, picnic tables, or bathrooms. Visiting sailboats should anchor off the sandy beach. The beach is susceptible to swells, especially in winter.

Sandy Spit

Add two shipwrecked souls to Sandy Spit and you have the desert island depicted in so many cartoons. It takes about five minutes to walk around the island, which consists of a beach and couple of palm trees. An offshore reef on the southern side is good for snorkeling. Sandy Spit is a popular stop for charter boats, day sails, and day-trippers from Jost Van Dyke. You can also kayak here from the east end of Jost Van Dyke.

Little Jost Van Dyke

Little Jost Van Dyke lies so close to its namesake that you can wade there. Little Jost, a 155-acre (0. 25-square-mile) island, is most famous as the birthplace of Dr. John Coakley Lettsome, the esteemed Quaker doctor and founder of the London Medical Society. Lettsome was born on Little Jost in 1744 while the islands were beginning their transition from cotton and indigo production to sugar. Lettsome was one of a pair of twin boys—reputedly the seventh pair borne by his mother and the only to survive! Lettsome was schooled in England and returned to the Virgin Islands as a young doctor for six months in 1768, during which time he freed the family's slaves and quickly earned the princely sum of 2,000 pounds, which he used to further his education when he returned to England. Dr. Lettsome never returned to his birthplace again, and the ruins of the Lettsome estate remain virtually untouched on Little Jost Van Dyke. They sit atop the low hill on the far western point of the island and are visible from Jost Van Dyke. In 2008 archaeologists from the United States began a project to study the Lettsome ruins as well as pre-Columbian settlements on the island.

You can wade across to Little Jost from Big Jost on your own (wear water shoes or booties). Charter yachts will also find quiet anchorages, and there is good snorkeling along the shore facing big Jost Van Dyke.

Entertainment and Events

◖ BEACH BARS

No island in the Virgins has a better handle on the beach bar than Jost Van Dyke. Indeed, this island's beach bars may seem like the stuff of fantasy, but they are as real as can be. Sand between your toes, a cool ocean breeze, the low hum of calypso, deadly sweet concoctions, and an abundance of good cheer—that is the Jost Van Dyke beach bar. It is never too early to go pub crawling, and if you arrive at a bar that seems closed, don't fret. Just help yourself. Many bars on Jost employ the honor bar system, and nothing embodies the generous spirit of the island better than this. (Don't forget to leave your payment on the way out.) Invariably, the afternoon hours, from 3 P. M. until sunset, are the best time to visit a beach bar. That is when you are sure to find a few new friends at the bar and some fitting calypso music in the background.

You really must try a Painkiller while you are on Jost. This concoction of rum, pineapple juice, coconut, and nutmeg is the quintessential island cocktail and goes perfectly with Jost Van Dyke's laid-back feel. For beer drinkers, the best news is that Foxy has a small microbrewery in Great Harbour, so you can get fresh, high-quality brews.

Jost Pub Crawl

You will need a boat to embark on this entire pub crawl, and it should go without saying that your skipper needs to sip on virgin coladas to stay safe. A good starting point is **Foxy's Taboo,** the most straitlaced of the island's beach bars. Taboo is actually a bit removed from the beach; it is built on a wooden platform overlooking Diamond Cay and Little Jost Van Dyke. Sail around to Little Harbour and stop at **Sidney's Peace and Love** (help yourself in the freezer if no one is around) and **Harris' Place,**

beach bars separated only by a narrow strip of sand ideal for children. These places are generally quiet and uncrowded. Bring your own entertainment.

Great Harbour has the greatest number of beach bars, and you can explore them on foot. Sail into the harbor, pick up a mooring, and dinghy in to the shore. **Foxy's Tamarind Bar** on the eastern end of the harbor is the biggest and best-known of these. T-shirts left (or lost) by previous visitors adorn the walls, and you can study the business cards of attorneys, businesspeople, and other type-A personalities who succumbed to Foxy's Painkillers and piña coladas. There is live entertainment on weekends, and Foxy sings calypso some afternoons. When you're ready for a change of scenery, wander down the main drag at Great Harbour, and you will also find **Ali Baba's** and **Corsairs.**

Save the best for last: Jost Van Dyke's quintessential beach bars are at White Bay. Start at **Ivan's Stress Free Bar,** next to the White Bay Campground. Mix your own cocktail at the honor bar, enjoy it out on the beach, and then head down to the **Soggy Dollar Bar,** the reputed originator of the Painkiller.

ENTERTAINMENT

For all its quietude, Jost Van Dyke is not a dull place. Several bars and restaurants offer live entertainment regularly, and the whole island lights up a couple of times a year for festivals and parties. Foxy is the main entertainer at **Foxy's Tamarind Bar** in Great Harbour, probably the most popular nighttime establishment on the island. Live music can also be found on certain nights at **Corsairs.** At White Bay, **Ivan's Stress Free Bar** has live entertainment on Thursdays, the same time as his weekly barbecue. The **Soggy Dollar Bar** has live music

JUST WHAT THE DOCTOR ORDERED

Exact recipes vary, but everyone agrees that rum, orange juice, pineapple juice, and cream of coconut are key ingredients in Jost Van Dyke's famous cocktail, the **Painkiller.** Here's one take on this popular drink, now served all over the Virgin Islands. If you prefer, you can serve this drink over ice cubes instead of blending it with crushed ice.

1 cup crushed ice
2 oz. dark rum
3 oz. pineapple juice
3 oz. orange juice
2 oz. cream of coconut (Coco Lopez)

Blend ingredients together. Garnish with a slice of orange and grating of fresh nutmeg.

Sunday afternoons, and other bars in White Bay have entertainment occasionally.

EVENTS

Jost Van Dyke knows how to throw a party. From its earliest days as a tourist destination, Jost was famous for its special style of island revelry, thanks in large part to the influence of Foxy Callwood, proprietor of Foxy's Tamarind Bar in Great Harbour.

Winter

The biggest party of the year takes place on **New Year's Eve** (known locally as Old Year's Night). Hundreds of boats fill the anchorages around Jost and people throng to bars in all four bays. Foxy normally brings in some high-profile entertainers for the event. Over at White Bay, Ivan Chinnery hosts a low-key musical weekend at his campground. What small-scale charm existed during the early years of Jost's New Year's celebration is long gone. In 1999 Foxy's made several high-profile lists of places to ring in the year 2000. While the number of revelers has receded slightly since that millennial year, Jost is still jam-packed by a party-hardy crowd every New Year's. Special ferries run between Jost and St. Thomas, St. John, and Tortola for the big event.

Spring

The island's annual events also include **Foxy's Wooden Boat Regatta,** a celebration of classic wooden boats held Memorial Day weekend. Recently, the regatta has also become a showplace for the traditional island sloops being preserved and maintained by H. Lavity Stoutt Community College on Tortola. Foxy also throws a Music Fest every March, with headliners from throughout the Caribbean, and hosts smaller parties on Halloween, Christmas Eve, and Thanksgiving. Find out more at www. foxysbar. com.

Summer

Jost holds its annual island festival, complete with a rag-tag parade, over Labor Day weekend. Don't expect much—but as with all things Jost, expect it to be a good time.

Sports and Recreation

WATER SPORTS
Snorkeling and Diving

With plenty of equipment available for rent, good guides for hire, and a number of excellent snorkel and dive sites, Jost Van Dyke is a great place for the water-sports enthusiast. There is good snorkeling at White Bay, but the best reefs are found at Diamond Cay and the surrounding out islands of Sandy Cay, Sandy Spit, and Little Jost Van Dyke. The best nearby dive sites are **The Playground,** between Green Cay and Little Jost, and **Twin Towers,** a challenging site north of Little Jost. **Watson's Rock, Tobago Canyons,** and **Mercurius Rock** are dive sites near Great Tobago, a small island bird sanctuary off the western tip of Jost. Exploring underwater can be as simple as donning a snorkel and going for a look around or as involved as spending a day diving unmarked dive sites with a guide.

Kayaking and Motorcraft

The layout of Jost and the number of nearby cays make the area ideal for kayaking. Armed with food, water, sunblock, and plenty of energy, visitors can craft their own expeditions. If you are going to paddle away from shore, be sure to equip your kayak with a flag or other marker to catch the eye of passing motorboats. A collision between a kayak and motorboat off Jost Van Dyke in 2002 tragically killed an American tourist and demonstrated that accidents can, in fact, happen in paradise. If high-powered water sports are more your cup of tea, you can rent water skis or jet boats or even spend hours bouncing on a huge trampoline over the water at White Bay.

Equipment and Guides

You can rent a wide range of equipment or sign up for guided ecotours at **Jost Van Dyke Scuba** (Great Harbour, 284/495-0271, www.

bvi-ecotours. com). More than just a dive shop, this outfit is one of the best water-sports operations in the British Virgin Islands. It has developed a range of ecotours that combine water sports, land exploration, and education and it will craft a special day trip to meet your needs if you like. Guides will take you off the beaten track (if such a thing exists on Jost!) and are excellent sources of information about the island. Ecotours cost $50–80; a daylong kayak rental will run $25; and you'll pay $400 for a full-day boat rental, including captain (but excluding fuel). For divers, Jost Van Dyke Scuba boasts 30 unmarked and mostly unknown dive sites around Jost Van Dyke and the surrounding cays. The company will take experienced divers on real blue-water expeditions. Expect to pay about $115 for a two-tank dive or $120 for a four-hour course for beginners. JVD Scuba's sister company BVI Scuba operates dive shops at Long Bay, Tortola, Marina Cay, and Road Town.

SAILING
Anchorages

White Bay is a popular anchorage, although in winter the ground swells can make it uncomfortable for overnight stops. **Great Harbour** is a large, well-protected anchorage, although it can be difficult to get your anchor to hold. Dinghy ashore. You can anchor on the western end of **Little Harbour** or pick up one of the moorings on the eastern end. On the east end, **Foxy's Taboo** (284/495-0218) has moorings and slips for boats wishing to visit the restaurant and bar.

LAND PURSUITS
Hiking

There are no formal hiking trails or maps on Jost. Nonetheless, those who enjoy exploring on their own two feet will find plenty of ground to cover. The ridge road is a great place for walking, and once you climb the steep hills to get there, it is not too demanding. You can reach the ridge by following the roads up from the western end of White Bay, the western end of Great Harbour (behind Rudy's), and the eastern end of Little Harbour. If you hike, do not underestimate the punishing sun, the steep hills, or the possibility that the weather could suddenly change or that you could be walking much longer than you expect. The potential to get lost or hurt grows if you venture into the wilderness. Don't forget to bring plenty of water, sun protection, and food. Tell someone where you are going and when you expect to be back. Bring a means of communication with you if you can.

Accommodations

The largest hotel on Jost Van Dyke has six rooms, and most accommodations are in individual villas. There are a few no-frills apartment-style rooms and a campground. Most visitors to the island sleep aboard sailboats.

UNDER $125

At ☾ **White Bay Campground** (White Bay, 284/495-9358 or 284/495-9312, www. ivanscampground. com), guests sleep steps away from the best beach on the island. The campground is well maintained and perfectly low-key. It offers a choice of bare campsites (you bring the tent), large canvas tents (already equipped with beds and linens), and charming, simple wooden cabins (equipped with bed, linens, electricity, and a light). Expect to pay about $25 for a bare site, $45 for a tent, and $65–75 or more for a cabin. Discounts are available in the summer, when the bar and restaurant close down. Campground guests can use the community kitchen (simple but adequate for basic meal preparation) and a shared bathhouse. The campground kitchen, office, and honor bar are decorated with seashells, island fliers, and photos left by previous guests. The aptly named Ivan's Stress Free Bar on the premises serves lunch most days.

Campers are vulnerable to the scourge of insects, but good strong insect repellent, mosquito coils, and vigilance in keeping your cabin door or tent flaps closed will prevent these pests from ruining your vacation. Keep in mind that dry weather and wind keep mosquitoes at bay. Sand flies, tiny gnat-like nuisances, come out around sunrise and sunset.

$125-175

The brightly painted **Sea Crest Inn** (Great Harbour, 284/495-9024 or 340/775-6389, www. bviwelcome. com/seacrestinn/seacrestinn. html, $150–165 winter, $125–130 summer) overlooks Great Harbour and is just steps away from most of its bars and restaurants. The concrete block structure houses a half dozen one-bedroom apartments, each equipped with a balcony, kitchen, queen-size beds, and cable TV. Guests praise the chilling air-conditioning, friendly hostess, cleanliness of the rooms, and views of Great Harbour. ☾ **Perfect Pineapple Guest Houses** (White Bay, 284/495-9401, www. perfectpineapple. com, $160–221) operates a cluster of colorful guest cottages and apartments a short walk from lovely White Bay. Host Gregory Callwood inherited his knack for hospitality from his father, Foxy, and has put it to good use making his well-traveled guests feel at home. The cottages, which are scattered across the hillside overlooking the beach, are clean and equipped with full kitchens, air-conditioning, satellite television, and some of the funkiest island-style color schemes around. A two-bedroom unit ($320) is also available. The Purple Pineapple complex also serves breakfast, lunch, or dinner in a casual on-site restaurant.

© SUSANNA HENIGHAN POTTER

JOST VAN DYKE

camping at White Bay

$225-300

The six-room **Sandcastle** (White Bay, 284/495-9888, fax 284/495-9999, www. sandcastle-bvi. com, $285–310 winter, $210–250 summer) lies under the shade of coconut palms along beautiful White Bay. The hotel's four octagonal cottages are modest but comfortable, with king-size beds, outdoor showers, and a lounge area. The two newer concrete block apartments are air-conditioned. The hotel and its many return guests prize peace and quiet, so rooms don't come with television or phones and children under 16 are not permitted. But there is not much you can do about the day-trippers who noisily descend on the beach each day, drawn by the Soggy Dollar Bar and its world-renowned Painkillers. For $2,700–$3,000, guests can enjoy a seven-night stay including five dinners and breakfast daily. It doesn't get much better than the ◖ **White Bay Villas and Seaside Cottages** (White Bay, 410/571-6692 or 800/788-8066, www. jostvandyke. com, $220–600 winter, $170–460 summer), a handful of one-, two-, and three-bedroom villas perched on the hillside

overlooking White Bay and the most upscale accommodations on Jost. The three one-bedroom seaside cottages are nestled in the trees a short walk from beautiful White Bay. Larger hillside villas are higher up, providing better views and breezes, but you'll probably want a car to get to the beach. Besides the exquisite location, White Bay Villas offer guests amenities including cable TV, VCR, telephone, barbecue grills, and full kitchens. Some units have air-conditioning. Knowledgeable on-site staff deal with requests efficiently and can help arrange activities and even child care.

Seclusion is the name of the game at **Sandy Ground Estates** (East End, 284/494-3391, www. sandyground. com, $280 winter, $200 summer) on the east end of the island. The property consists of eight unique one- and two-bedroom villas overlooking beautiful Sandy Ground beach. No beaches in the BVI are private, but this one might as well be, because it is all but blocked from the sea by an extensive reef and impossible to reach by car. A seven-day minimum stay is required.

Food

Dining options on Jost Van Dyke have increased in recent years, and there is a fair amount of variety for such a small island. Most island eateries specialize in West Indian food, but you can find international favorites, too. Prices are generally high; expect a modest dinner for two to cost $50 or more. Lunch is a bit more affordable. If you are staying somewhere with a kitchen and plan to cook, it is wise to shop for most groceries on Tortola or St. Thomas—selection is generally poor and prices high in the small shops on Jost. Consider the opening and closing times given here approximations, since most restaurants on Jost have flexible hours, to say the least. As one White Bay restaurant proprietor said, "I have no doors, so I'm always open. " But stroll in at 8 P. M. and ask for a steak, and you are likely to be disappointed. In fact, many restaurants, especially the smaller ones, ask for dinner reservations. Most restaurants that serve breakfast claim to be open by 8:30 A. M. , but take that with a grain of salt. If you're on a tight schedule, it is a good idea to call the night before and make sure someone will be there in the morning.

GREAT HARBOUR

The largest settlement on Jost Van Dyke also has the greatest number of places to eat and drink. A stroll down the sandy main street is all you need to introduce yourself to the choices. At the eastern end of Great Harbour sits **Foxy's Tamarind Bar** (284/495-9258, 11:30 A. M. –9 P. M. , $18–40), Jost Van Dyke's first and foremost eatery and watering hole. Foxy Callwood started out with a small shack on the beach, where he sold rum and soft drinks. Today, his Tamarind Bar is a sprawling complex that includes three bars, a stage, a microbrewery, and a gift shop. Foxy performs

his signature mix of lovable calypso and comedy most afternoons, though he has cut back his hours in recent years.

As a restaurant, Foxy serves up some of the most reliable food on the island. Don't miss the Friday and Saturday night barbecue feast featuring chicken, ribs, and seafood, followed by live music. At lunch Foxy also serves salads, pasta, rotis, and burgers. An on-site brewery makes craft beer, and this is also the only place on the island you'll find espresso. Dinner reservations are requested, but not required, by 5 P. M.

Near the middle of Great Harbour's main street is **Corsairs** (Great Harbour, 284/495-9294, 8:30 A. M. –late daily, breakfast $10, lunch $12–22, dinner $25–40), where pirate kitsch meets an international menu and winning service. Corsairs were French privateers who terrorized Dutch and Spanish settlers in the earliest days of European settlement of the British Virgins. Today, this beachfront restaurant serves the most eclectic menu on Jost: outstanding made-from-scratch pizza, a wide range of northern Italian pastas, and professional sushi rolls, plus a sampling of the fresh local seafood and lobster Jost is known for. Breakfast is a substantial meal at Corsairs and the overstuffed breakfast burritos are especially popular.

For fresh seafood, lobster, and finger-licking ribs, head to **Ali Baba's** (284/495-9280, 8:30 A. M. –10 P. M. daily, $12–40), just a few steps from the beach in Great Harbour. Proprietor Ali Baba pours a mean rum punch and the Baileys Banana Colada will have you smiling. Breakfast is also served. Dinner reservations are requested by 5 P. M.

For a change of pace, **Christine's Bakery** (284/495-9281, 8 A. M. –5 P. M. daily, $4–10) is a short walk down the side street next to the police station. This casual café is easy on budgets and serves omelets, pancakes, and French toast for breakfast, plus sandwiches at lunch. It is also the place to come for fresh homemade bread, including locally made coconut bread.

Sugar and Spice Snack Bar (Great Harbour, 284/543-9016, 8 A. M. –5 P. M. daily, $6–12) is a handy choice for breakfast or a no-fuss lunch. It's located a few steps from the ferry dock; drop in for a cup of Joan Chinnery's local herbal tea, more commonly called bush tea.

WHITE BAY

It is, indeed, hard to hold onto your worries at **Ivan's Stress Free Bar** (White Bay, 284/495-9358, 11 A. M. –4 P. M. Fri. –Wed. , 11 A. M. –late Thurs. , $10–14) on the beach at White Bay. The bar is open all day—if no one is there to serve you, just serve yourself and leave the money. Lunch includes sandwiches and burgers, nearly all for under $10. Seating is under a huge tamarind tree in the yard or on a beach chair in the sand. On Thursday nights, proprietor Ivan Chinnery goes all out with his popular barbecue buffet. The number of eateries on the western end of White Bay has grown in recent years, but the most popular remains the **Soggy Dollar Bar & Sandcastle Restaurant** (White Bay, 284/495-9888, 9 A. M. –3:15 P. M. daily, $8–18), named after the damp bills handed over by sailors who wade ashore from visiting yachts. The Soggy Dollar claims to be the birthplace of the Painkiller, a delicious concoction of rum, pineapple juice, orange juice, and cream of coconut. If you want food to go with your rum, try cinnamon rum French toast at breakfast or the flying-fish sandwich for lunch. At night, the Soggy Dollar undergoes a Cinderella-type metamorphosis to become the **Sandcastle** (6 P. M. –9 P. M. daily, 284/495-9888, $24–42), serving gourmet meals by candlelight under the stars. Cuisine is upscale yet accessible and always includes fresh fish and seafood. A favorite is the Painkiller ice cream.

Farther down the beach, **Gertrude's Beach**

Bar (284/495-9104, 9 A. M. –late daily, $10–22) serves omelets, eggs, and sandwiches for breakfast. Try garlic shrimp, chicken roti, ribs, or grilled mahimahi for lunch or dinner.

Also on White Bay you will find **Jewel's Snack Shack** (284/495-9286, 11 A. M. –4 P. M. daily, $4–8), which is exactly what it sounds like—a stand selling burgers, hot dogs, fries, and cold drinks. **One Love** (284/495-9829, 10 A. M. –5 P. M.) sells cold beer and tropical drinks, but it is best known for its Bushwhacker. This is a popular choice for lunch away from the crowd at the Soggy Dollar. Dinner is available by reservation.

EAST END

Who can argue with a place called **Sidney's Peace and Love?** Especially if it serves fresh lobster and lets you mix your own drinks. Sidney's (Little Harbour, 284/495-9271, 8 A. M. –late daily, dinner $24–45) lives up to its name with its friendly staff and low-key attitude. Lobster is the specialty here, but you can also get fresh steamed fish, conch, ribs, chicken, and more. Come Monday or Thursday for all-you-can-eat lobster, a rarity in the islands. Dinner reservations are requested by 5 P. M. , and dinner is served at 7:30 P. M. Breakfast is bacon, eggs, and toast and runs about $6. Across the bay is **Abe's by the Sea** (Little Harbour, 284/495-9329, 11 A. M. –9 P. M. daily, $16–45), where you can get lunch and dinner daily. Abe serves fresh fish, conch, and barbecued chicken, but his specialty is fresh lobster. Dinner is served at 7 P. M. Reservations are essential.

Foxy's Taboo (East End, 284/495-0218, 11 A. M. –11 P. M. daily, $12–35) is a world away from other restaurants on Jost. Physically, it is set on the dramatic and remote east end of the island. Foodwise, Taboo offers much greater variety than other restaurants. Lunch includes fresh fish, pasta, homemade pizzas, and the best burgers on Jost Van Dyke. Dinner features gourmet seafood, steak, lamb, and chicken dishes for $18 and up. Taboo is a good base for exploring Diamond Cay, Little Jost Van Dyke, and the Bubbly Pool. Staff there can help point you in the right direction and may even furnish a map.

MARKETS

Jost has a number of small groceries selling canned foods, frozen meats, water, drinks, bread, and other staples. They are: **Rudy's** (Great Harbour, 284/495-9024, 8 A. M. –8 P. M. daily); **Nature's Basket** (Great Harbour, alley between Main St. and Back St. , 8:30 A. M. –noon and 2–6 P. M. daily); **Little Harbour Marina** (Little Harbour, 284/495-9835, 8 A. M. –6 P. M. Sun. –Fri.); and **Abe's** (Little Harbour, 284/495-9329, 8:30 A. M. –8:30 P. M.).

Information and Services

There are no banks or ATMs on Jost, so plan ahead.

TOURIST OFFICES

There is no official tourist information booth on Jost; check the covered bulletin board near the Administration Building for notices and announcements. **Jost Van Dyke Scuba** (Great Harbour, 284/495-0271, 8 A. M. –5 P. M. daily) runs an unofficial tourist information center out of its dive shop and is a good source of information about the island. Libraries

The diminutive **Jost Van Dyke Public Library** is in a building near the island school and is open 11 A. M. –5 P. M. Monday–Friday.

EMERGENCIES

If you have an emergency, dial 999. Police officers are stationed in the two-story administration building in the center of Great Harbour (284/495-9345). The island's health clinic (Great Harbour, 284/495-9239) is staffed by a live-in nurse; a doctor visits one day a week.

COMMUNICATIONS

Mail service is provided by the District Officer, whose office is in the back of the Administration Building (Great Harbour, 284/495-3450, 8:30 A. M. –4:30 P. M. Mon. –Fri.).

CUSTOMS AND IMMIGRATION

If Jost is your first stop in the British Virgins, be sure to check in with Customs and Immigration as soon as you arrive. Officers can be found in the two-story Administration Building in the center of Great Harbour (284/494-3450 or 284/495-9374).

SHOPPING

As would be expected, there is no large-scale shopping on Jost, but its small boutiques can be fun to explore. In Great Harbour, stroll the sandy main street along the bay. Stop at **Wendell's World** (284/495-9969) for jewelry, crafts, and natural beauty products. **Jost Van Dyke Scuba** (284/495-0271) sells snorkeling and diving equipment as well as a small selection of gifts and books. The **Foxhole** (294/495-9258) at Foxy's Tamarind Bar stocks bathing suits, cover-ups, flip flops, and other Jost Van Dyke essentials. Over on the East End, **Foxy's Taboo** (Diamond Cay) sells T-shirts, gifts, and all sorts of Foxy-inspired items. At White Bay, **Soggy Dollar** (284/495-9888) has a large gift shop where you can obtain further evidence of your visit to this lovely paradise.

The island's police station, customs office, post office, and administration building are at the center of Great Harbour, along the village's sandy "main street."

Getting There and Around

People who don't get to Jost on a private or charter yacht come by ferry. **New Horizon Ferry Service** (284/495-9278) makes the 25-minute trip between Tortola's West End and Jost five times a day. It leaves West End, Tortola, at 8 A. M. , 10 A. M. , 1 P. M. , 4 P. M. , and 6 P. M. Monday–Friday, and 9 A. M. , 10 A. M. , 1 P. M. , 4 P. M. , and 6 P. M. on weekends. Round-trip fare is $25 per person. There is no need for advance reservations, but expect to pay with cash. **Inter-Island Boat Service** (284/495-4166 or 340/776-6597) offers service between St. John, St. Thomas, and Jost by reservation only.

Jost's small size and limited road network make renting a car a luxury, not a necessity. If you are willing to do some walking, it is fairly easy to navigate White Bay and Great Harbour on foot—although you should be prepared for a tough climb in between them. Walking to Little Harbour on the east end is possible, but a much more serious undertaking. If you opt for wheels, **Abe and Eunicy Rentals** (Little Harbour, 284/495-9329) will rent you a two-door or four-door Suzuki for $60–75 a day.

Taxis will happily run you between the various bays on Jost or take you on a sightseeing tour along the Ridge Road. **Abe's Taxi** (284/496-8429) and **Jost Van Dyke Safari Service** (284/495-9329) are good bets. Taxi rates are set by the government. Expect to pay $10 for a journey from Great Harbour to the Sandcastle and $20 from Great Harbour to the Bubbly Pool. Per-person rates go down when you have more than three people. Ask upfront about rates to avoid any confusion.

JOST VAN DYKE

ANEGADA

Flat, empty, and so low-lying that early explorers feared it would slip beneath the sea, Anegada and its accompanying charms are singular among the Virgin Islands. Its attractions are simple: fresh seafood, solitude, and miles of empty white beaches. Adventurers can complement the quiet times with expeditions through the island's wild interior, a land of epiphytes, wild orchids, and rare iguanas. Wherever you go, there is little chance of meeting a crowd. More likely, you won't see anyone at all.

Anegada lies 14 miles north of Virgin Gorda and is perched on the windward edge of a massive underwater plateau. The 15-square-mile island stands guard over the Anegada Passage, a 6,000-foot underwater chasm used as a thoroughfare by ocean liners and cargo ships. The nearby North Drop, where the sea depth plunges from 180 feet to more than 1,200, teems with large game fish. The island is buffered by the Horseshoe Reef, the third largest reef in the world, which extends south and east of the island like an underwater tail. The reef is as famous for the danger it poses to mariners as it is for its size and beauty.

Anegada peaks a mere 25 feet above sea level at its highest point. The west end of the island is dominated by salt ponds, wetlands home to rare and endangered wading birds, including flamingos. The eastern third of the island is a scraggly limestone wilderness, a surprising land of loblolly trees, cacti, epiphytes, wild orchids,

© SUSANNA HENIGHAN POTTER

HIGHLIGHTS

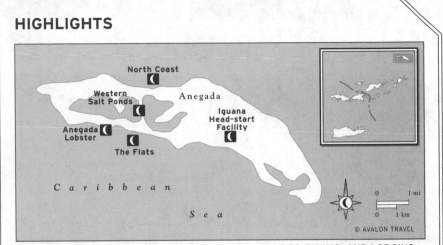

LOOK FOR **C** TO FIND RECOMMENDED SIGHTS, ACTIVITIES, DINING, AND LODGING.

C North Coast: Want a beach? You got it. Anegada's north coast is more than 10 continuous miles of powder-white sand. Walk, beachcomb, snorkel, kayak, swim, or sunbathe (page 273).

C Western Salt Ponds: The Western Salt Ponds are home to fish, wading birds, and a flock of wild flamingos. In 1999 they were declared a wetland of international importance (page 273).

C Iguana Head-Start Facility: The critically endangered Anegada rock iguana—which looks like a remnant from the dinosaur age—

is the focus of intense conservation efforts and can be seen at a head-start facility in The Settlement (page 277).

C The Flats: Silver and elusive, the bonefish that populate the flats are every fly fisher's dream. Try your hand at catching one, or hunt for easier prey such as tarpon or permit (page 277).

C Anegada Lobster: Sweet, succulent, and fresh from the sea, Anegada lobster is legendary. Enjoy it under the stars at quaint seaside restaurants on the island's southern shore (page 283).

and bright yellow century plants. The island is home to the Anegada rock iguana, an ancient-looking lizard that has been the focus of intense conservation efforts since 1997.

The island's only town, The Settlement, is a sparse collection of homes, shops, churches, and government buildings barely touched by the current of change that has swept through other Virgin Islands. Anegada's laid-back lifestyle is not an invention for tourists. It's the real thing.

Most visitors arrive by boat—either by charter boat or on one of the ferries that travel from Tortola and Virgin Gorda three days per week. The flurry of activity generated by an arriving ferry is probably the most you will see during your whole stay.

Boats can sail up to several docks along the island's southwestern shore, but only after navigating a perilous course through reefs that have ensnared more than 300 ships since people started to keep track. While beautiful to look at, the beaches along the southern coast are not standouts for swimming and snorkeling.

ANEGADA

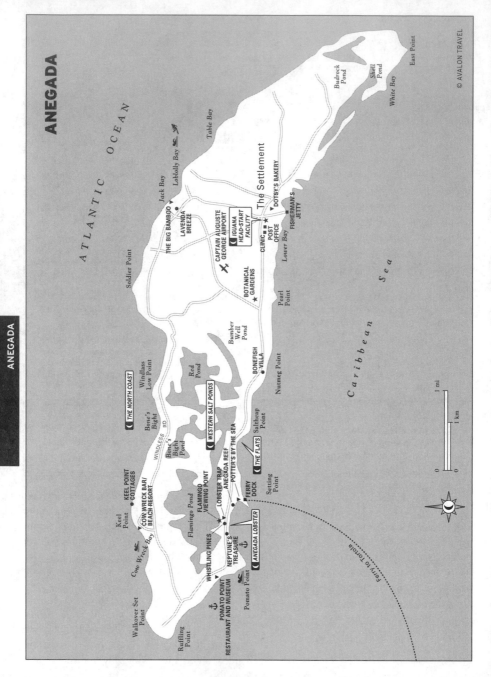

ANEGADA

ATLANTIC OCEAN

Shell Pond

East Point

Budrock Pond

White Bay

Table Bay

Loblolly Bay

Jack Bay

THE BIG BAMBOO

Soldier Point

LAVENDA BREEZE

CAPTAIN AUGUSTE GEORGE AIRPORT

The Settlement

IGUANA HEAD-START FACILITY

DOTSY'S BAKERY

BOTANICAL GARDENS

CLINIC

POST OFFICE

Lower Bay

FISHERMAN'S JETTY

Caribbean Sea

Pearl Point

Bumber Well Pond

Windlass Low Point

THE NORTH COAST

Bone's Bight

WINDLASS RD

Bone's Bight Pond

Red Pond

WESTERN SALT PONDS

BONEFISH VILLA

Nutmeg Point

Keel Point

KEEL POINT COTTAGES

COW WRECK BAR/ BEACH RESORT

Cow Wreck Bay

Flamingo Pond

FLAMINGO VIEWING POINT

Saltheap Point

WHISTLING PINES

LOBSTER TRAP

ANEGADA REEF

POTTER'S BY THE SEA

THE FLATS

FERRY DOCK

Setting Point

NEPTUNE'S TREASURE

ANEGADA LOBSTER

Walkover Set Point

Ruffling Point

POMATO POINT RESTAURANT AND MUSEUM

Pomato Point

Ferry to Tortola

1 mi

1 km

0

0

© AVALON TRAVEL

That honor belongs to the north coast beaches: windswept, wild, and nearly always empty. No land stands between Anegada's north coast and the other side of the Atlantic, and the waves that beat these beaches deposit an intriguing jumble of natural and manmade rubbish.

Anegada is spectacular, but it's not for everyone, least of all people who want to do something besides enjoy the beauty of their surroundings and the society of their companions. But for travelers wishing to truly get away, this is the place to be.

HISTORY

Pre-Columbians used Anegada as a supply station on their interisland voyages, drawing water from wells underneath the rock shelf and gathering fish and conch from the sea. Later on, pirates took shelter along Anegada's secluded shores and tempted passing ships onto its dangerous reefs. It is said that Bone's Bight on the island's north coast was named after a pirate who favored this patch of the island.

Anegada's arid climate, poor soil, and relative isolation precluded the development of the large-scale plantations that were widespread in the Virgin Islands during the 18th and 19th centuries. Instead, early settlers on Anegada quickly realized that the "wrecking industry" was the most lucrative the island offered. A Royal Geographic Society writer who visited Anegada in 1832 reported that the cry "vessel on the reef" was the only thing that roused the island's inhabitants. "Scarcely is the news announced than boats of every description, shallops and sailing vessels, are pushing off with all haste toward the scene of the action," he wrote. These settlers supplemented their wreck booty with small-scale farming of cotton, corn, and livestock.

Toward the end of the 19th century, the number of wrecks dwindled with the establishment of a lighthouse on nearby Sombrero Island and the identification of the dangerous current responsible for pushing so many ships onto Anegada's reef. Without the wrecks, Anegadians turned to farming and, increasingly, fishing to survive. Before refrigeration, the fishermen's catch was preserved using salt from the Western Salt Ponds. Islanders also gathered wood for charcoal production or collected the gummy sap of a native tree used in traditional boatbuilding. For many, however, the best way to survive these difficult years was to leave. Anegadians emigrated in large numbers to the U.S. Virgin Islands, the Dominican Republic, and the U.S. mainland, seasonally or permanently. Those who remained continued to farm and fish, buoyed by regular remittances sent by family abroad.

All this changed in 1967, when a British businessman, Kenneth Bates, made a deal with the British administrator of the islands to lease, for 199 years, four-fifths of Anegada and to build a hotel, marina, and accompanying infrastructure—all tax free. Anegadians were to be left on what some termed "a reserve" in the area around The Settlement.

This sweetheart deal soon went sour. Islanders objected to the generosity of the giveaways and complained that the agreement had been negotiated without their input. At the same time, the government had given Bates a similarly generous offer to reclaim and develop land at Road Harbour on Tortola. The public protested this, too.

Bates was eventually run out of town, but not before the British government paid him off to the tune of $5.8 million. As a result of the failed Bates development, Anegadians continue to wrestle with a landownership quagmire and remain skeptical of any government proposal for their island.

Although flawed, the Bates episode left Anegada with some basic infrastructure it desperately needed: roads and an airstrip, for example. It also stoked desire among islanders for some kind of development that would bring them greater prosperity and demonstrated that Anegadians wanted to be the ones to lead it.

EARLY VISITOR

In 1831, Robert Schomburgk, a member of the nascent Royal Geographical Society, was staying on St. Thomas when an American ship, the *Lewis*, was wrecked on the Anegada reef. Having heard that this was, by far, not the first ship to suffer such a fate, Schomburgk visited Anegada to make soundings of its passages and chart the reefs around it. Schomburgk wrote about this visit in the *Journal of the Royal Geographical Society* the next year, and his account remains one of the most keenly observed descriptions of the island.

Schomburgk found more than wrecks to report on when he visited the "strange spot" of Anegada. He found a gray siliceous substance covering the southern shore, in which he claimed to have found footprints of birds, animals, and indigenous people.

The southern part of the island was a mass of shelves, between which were large crevices and caves. The island's only trees grew out of these shelf holes, thriving in the rich, damp soil found within. Nearby, Schomburgk found a number of funnel-shaped shelf-hole wells, from which vast supplies of fresh water could be pulled. More remarkably, while camping near Cow Wreck Beach, Schomburgk was shown how to dig a hole into the sand to procure an abundant supply of fresh water.

Schomburgk was impressed by the relative health of Anegada; its people did not suffer from elephantiasis and knew nothing of fish poisoning. Schomburgk theorized that the latter was due to the absence of poisonous manchineel trees on the island. The only real scourge Schomburgk noted was the mosquitoes, which swarmed day and night, sometimes in such force as to kill wild goats.

But Schomburgk's greatest observations were of the currents that swept around Anegada. In his studies, Schomburgk found evidence of a strong northwesterly current in the area, which he believed to be responsible for pushing many ships bound for other ports in the Caribbean onto Anegada's reefs. Schomburgk's findings were later confirmed, a discovery that led to significantly fewer ships being lost on the Anegada reefs.

In 1977 Lowell Wheatley opened the island's first hotel, the Anegada Reef, which quickly became popular among sailors who delighted in Anegada's beaches, seafood, and end-of-the-earth atmosphere. Gradually, more Anegadians opened guesthouses, hotels, and restaurants to cater to tourists who turned up on visiting sailboats or small planes.

PLANNING YOUR TIME

For most people, Anegada's chief attraction is *not* planning your time. The established must-dos—seeing the rare **Anegada rock iguanas,** taking a stroll along the dramatic **north coast,** eating a **lobster dinner,** and spotting flamingos at the **Western Salt Ponds** —can easily be accomplished in a day.

But the closer you look at Anegada, the more there is to see and the more there is to do. During an extended stay you will have time to try **fishing** on the Anegada flats or the North Drop or to kayak the beautiful southern shore. You could also hike in the **Anegada Outback** and spend a day bird-watching around the ponds. Visitors wanting to experience the Anegada wilderness, above or below water, should not expect any frills. Aside from a couple of people offering fishing trips, you will be on your own.

Overnight visitors to Anegada should assess just how much of the island's jarring solitude they want. Some people stay for weeks and leave rejuvenated; others feel stir-crazy after just a few nights. Regardless of your disposition, it is wise to pack a good book (or two) and a deck of cards, since most hotels do not have television and there is next to no nightlife.

Day Trips

Anegada is a good day-trip destination from Tortola or Virgin Gorda. Take the **ferry** that runs six days a week (75 minutes from Tortola, 60 minutes from Virgin Gorda, $50 round-trip). Eight hours on the island is plenty of time to take an open-air island tour followed by snorkeling, eating, and relaxing at either Loblolly Bay or Cow Wreck Beach.

Because of the dangerous reef that virtually surrounds Anegada, all boats, whether public or private, arrive at the government jetty at Setting Point, on the south shore. From there taxis are available to carry you to your final destination.

As an alternative to the ferry, package day trips are also available from **air charter** and **day sail** operators. **Fly BVI** (284/495-1747, www.flybvi.com) offers air charter excursions from Beef Island and Virgin Gorda which include lunch and ground transportation for about $175 per person. **Dive BVI** (284/495-5513 or 800/848-7078, www.divebvi.com, $85 adults, $65 children 10 and under) offers a weekly Anegada day sail from Beef Island (Thursdays) and Virgin Gorda (Fridays) to Anegada; rates include ground transportation to Loblolly Bay.

Sights

Anegada's main road circles the Western Salt Ponds, following the south, west, and north shores of the island before cutting through the center of the island, past the one-room airport. The southern coast has the greatest concentration of restaurants and hostelries; the north coast is empty but for a few beach bars and a handful of guesthouses. The island's main town, The Settlement, east of Setting Point, is the location of the ferry dock. About half the island's roads are paved; the rest are sandy, bumpy tracks. The eastern third of the island is inaccessible by car; some narrow rough footpaths are all there is. Businesses are open mostly by schedule, but also by whim. Especially during the summer, it is wise to call ahead.

◖ NORTH COAST

The north coast is what most people come to Anegada for, and it does not disappoint. Stretching from Loblolly Bay at the east and winding all the way to West End Point, the north coast is more than a dozen miles of unblemished, uncrowded, perfectly white beaches. The waves from the often-wild Atlantic Ocean crash onto the barrier reef several hundred yards offshore; smaller waves make their way onto the beach, depositing intriguing ocean riffraff. Beach quality varies along the shore, depending on predominant currents and waves, but nowhere are the beaches rough or rocky.

A number of small roads branching off from the main loop road provide access to the coast, but many people choose to base themselves at either **Cow Wreck Bay** or **Loblolly Bay,** home to two of the most popular restaurants and beach bars. Both have good snorkeling, but the reef is closer to shore and easier to access at Loblolly.

It is possible to walk the six miles from Cow Wreck to Loblolly, but be sure to prepare for the powerful sun and make plans for a pickup. You can also kayak along the inside of the barrier reef; just remember that the current runs east to west. Beachcombing is another fun way to explore the coast.

◖ WESTERN SALT PONDS

Anegada's Western Salt Ponds, declared a wetland of international importance under the Ramsar Convention in 1999, cover more than a third of the island. They are home to migrating

ANEGADA

ANEGADA

the beach bar at Cow Wreck Bay

seabirds and shorebirds and are an important spawning area for a type of mullet fish. Before refrigeration, islanders used salt from the ponds to preserve meat and fish.

The ponds are a bird-watcher's paradise. The U.K.-based Darwin Initiative (www.seaturtle.org/mtrg) created a comprehensive list of species present. A trained eye will spot ducks, plovers, sandpipers, herons (including great blue herons), kingfishers, falcons (including peregrine falcons), and flamingos.

The ponds are surrounded by scrubby plants, including several species of mangrove and a number of succulents, including one that Anegadians add to salads for a sharp, briny flavor. You will need a guide to help you identify this plant; don't start nibbling on everything you see. Keep your eyes open for Anegada's endemic plant species: *Acacia anegadensis* (poke-me-boy), *Metastelma anegadensa* (wire wist), and *Cordial rupicola* (black sage).

The Western Salt Ponds are a minimalist landscape: flat, mostly empty, with understated colors. Most tourists don't give them a second glance. But those who do are rewarded; they are uniquely beautiful and can be a nice place to walk if you grow weary of the beach—just keep track of your route so you don't get lost. A number of narrow roads feeding off the main road that circles the island provide easy access to the ponds. Keep in mind that the ponds expand and contract depending on the amount of rainfall, so be careful not to drive too close and get stuck in soft spots. Also be mindful that these lands are protected, so fishing, hunting, and otherwise extracting materials or animals from the ponds are illegal.

SETTING POINT

The public ferry dock is at Setting Point, which is also the entrance to Anegada's most popular anchorage for visiting yachts. Walk out to the end of the dock for views of Virgin Gorda and Anegada and to watch the sun set.

© SUSANNA HENIGHAN POTTER

PINK FLAMINGOS

Flamingos are by far the most well-known birds to inhabit Anegada's Western Salt Ponds. Robert Schomburgk, writing in the *Journal of the Royal Geographical Society* in 1832, described the flocks of roseate flamingos that then lived in Anegada's salt ponds:

It is a splendid sight to see several hundred drawn up in a regular form, resembling the figure of a cross, approaching from the west, flapping their mighty wings, and the sun reflecting his rays upon their rose-coloured breasts, the air resounding with their cry, which, consisting of several cadences, has been compared by the inhabitants to singing.

Flamingos were prized for their feathers and meat, however, and by the 1950s the elegant pink birds were all gone. So it was good news in the 1990s when the joint efforts of the BVI National Parks Trust, the Bermuda Aquarium and Natural History Museum, and several private individuals resulted in the reintroduction of flamingos to the island. The 20 birds were settled in the Western Salt Ponds, where, to the delight of conservationists, they have reproduced steadily and attracted several volunteers looking for a new place to live.

It can be difficult to see the shy creatures, who spend most of their time wading in the parts of the salt ponds farthest away from roads and people. As you drive around the ponds, keep your eyes peeled for small dots of pink in the distance. Ask around in advance to find out which pond the birds have been frequenting recently. Regardless, binoculars are the best way to watch the birds, and a telephoto lens is required if you want to take good pictures of them. These wild flamingoes are not accustomed to people, so above all else don't try to get near them. Your presence will interfere with nesting, breeding, and feeding, and therefore threaten their continued survival.

A cluster of shops around the jetty serve as the island's commercial center: You will find the only gas station, a laundry, an ice cream parlor, a bulk grocery, a car rental agency, and gift shops.

POMATO POINT MUSEUM

On the picturesque southwestern point of Anegada is the Pomato Point Restaurant, home of the Pomato Point Museum (Pomato Point, 284/495-9466, 8 A.M.–8 P.M. Mon.–Sat., free), where you can inspect a private collection of Anegada shipwreck paraphernalia. The collection features old coins, cannonballs, crockery, silverware, and other items salvaged from some of the hundreds of shipwrecks off the coast of Anegada. The museum is in a small room off the dining area and is open whenever the restaurant is; it is open limited hours some Sundays.

THE SETTLEMENT

The Settlement, Anegada's only village, is as low-key as the rest of the island. Located a few hundred yards from the southern shore and a short drive from the island's airport or ferry dock, The Settlement is where you can pick up basic supplies, see a nurse, mail a letter, and find most of the island's 150 residents.

The village sprawls along a couple of miles of road, with the newer concrete buildings—including a power plant—at the outskirts of town. Homes are simple and yards barren, aside from clotheslines, parked cars, and the occasional flowering plant. Many homes here have been in use for several generations and are excellent examples of traditional Virgin Islands architecture and building practice. The village center is a simple crossroads, identifiable by the general store and small grocery that sit there.

ANEGADA

© SUSANNA HENIGHAN POTTER

The birthplace of Theodolph Faulkner in The Settlement is an example of a traditional Anegada home.

The Settlement is a pleasant place for a leisurely stroll or bike ride, especially if you want to take in something of the way of life of Anegada's residents. As on the rest of the island, there are no road signs here, so ask someone for directions if you are having trouble finding your way around.

At the end of the road heading south from the village center is the fishing jetty, a dilapidated public dock used by local fishers and protected by mangroves. The piles of discarded conch shells have been placed here by several generations of fishers. This is a good place to put in a kayak if you want to explore the southern shore.

The island's school, community center, and Methodist church lie along the road heading north from the village center. The roadsides here are lined by low walls, many now crumbling. These walls were built by previous generations of Anegadians to protect their garden plots. As impossible as it may seem, Anegadians have long been farmers, growing guinea corn, cotton, ground provisions, and fruit.

A short distance west of the village center is the **birthplace of Theodolph Faulkner,** an Anegadian who was instrumental in leading a 1949 march in Road Town to demand greater self-government for the territory. A bust of Faulkner and a small plaque have been placed outside the old home.

Most cars just whiz by Anegada's unofficial **botanical gardens,** an oasis of color and greenery on the outskirts of The Settlement. The privately maintained garden is at the intersection of the road that follows the island's southern coast and the road that slants northward to the airport and Loblolly Bay. There is no sign, and the white picket fence protecting the gardens from marauding livestock is often locked, but you can easily look over the fence to admire the tropical plants. Ask at Faulkner's Country Store in The Settlement if you want to know more about the gardens.

◖ IGUANA HEAD-START FACILITY

Low cages adjacent to the government administration building are home to dozens of critically endangered Anegada rock iguanas. The BVI National Parks Trust operates the head-start facility, where hatchlings are housed until they grow large enough to survive on their own.

Iguanas do live in the wild, but they are difficult to find. The animals are shy, and they sense your presence long before you know they are there. If you do get near one, you will likely hear it scampering away through the bush before you can lay eyes on it. If you really want to glimpse an iguana—and they are worth seeing—visit the head-start facility.

The facility is open daily during daylight hours; just be sure to close the gate behind you when you leave. For information, contact the National Parks Trust headquarters (Road Town, 284/494-2069, www.bvinationalparkstrust.org).

THE ANEGADA OUTBACK

The eastern end of the island, outside The Settlement, is a wild, unspoiled, and impenetrable land, called by some the Anegada Outback. Residents just call it the Bush. It is, at first glance, unwelcoming and harsh, but those who brave the thorns and sun of this landscape are richly rewarded by sights of unusual foliage, beautiful flowers, and a sense of silence remarkable even for Anegada.

Flora includes wild orchids, delicate pink flowers that poke up above the neighboring bushes on a single thin stem. There are also thickets of white frangipani, and huge century plants that bloom bright yellow in the late spring and early summer. Anegada is home to several species of plants that exist nowhere else in the world, including a prickly flowering bush known to islanders as "poke-me-boy" and a small flowering vine once used to manufacture fish traps. In many places, the plants grow miraculously from gnarled limestone earth.

To get started, drive the road that connects The Settlement with Loblolly Bay on the north coast. Keep your eye out for a promising gap in the bush. When you find one, pull off the road, park, and start to explore. Be sure to keep good track of your route, as there are no official trails and it is easy to get turned around. Long pants and closed-toe shoes are a good idea, too.

THE NORTH DROP

The North Drop is a deep ocean trench that runs north of the Virgin Islands, reaching depths of 1,200 feet and more in places. Anegada is the closest of the Virgin Islands to this famed sportfishing ground, where anglers battle with blue marlin, wahoo, dorado, tuna, and other prized fish.

The game fish are attracted by clouds of baitfish—squid and flying fish among them—that congregate to feed off the upwelling currents that come out from the Drop. Even those who do not troll the North Drop themselves can enjoy its fruits; most island restaurants serve fresh tuna, swordfish, and others plucked from the deep.

The Anegada Reef Hotel (284/495-8002) arranges sportfishing charters.

◖ THE FLATS

Anegada's other fishing ground is the flats, the shallow expanse of sea along the southern coast of the island, where fly fishers come to hunt bonefish, one of the most elusive and challenging game fish around. Former president Jimmy Carter dedicated an entire chapter in a memoir, *An Outdoor Journal,* to his experience fishing on Anegada and concluded that the tiny torpedoes are indeed one of the ultimate challenges of fly-fishing. Bonefish, or "gray ghosts," have strength disproportionate to their small size and spook easily; the smallest disturbance can cause

ANEGADA

ANEGADA

ANEGADA'S IGUANA

Before the 1960s, iguanas outnumbered people on Anegada. The creatures, which look like holdovers from the dinosaur age, roamed the island's limestone wilderness, nesting in the summer, while finding plants, fruit, and the occasional centipede for food.

The Anegada rock iguana, also called the stout iguana, grows up to six feet long and can live up to 80 years. It is native to the entire Puerto Rican bank—the islands that stretch from Puerto Rico to St. Croix—but development has pushed the animals out of every island except Anegada, where for many years it was unbothered by hunting, human encroachment, or predators.

But following the failed Bates development in the late 1960s, the iguanas' luck ran out. The stone walls that once partitioned islanders' agricultural land were demolished, releasing livestock, including cows and goats, which promptly moved into large areas of the iguanas' habitat. Then the population of feral cats started to grow. Cats, it turned out, have quite a taste for iguana hatchlings. The combination of cat predation and competition for habitat from livestock caused the number of iguanas to plummet.

By the early 1980s, the situation was dire; estimates put the population at fewer than 300 animals. In response, an American scientist working with the local government began an effort to save the iguanas. In 1984 and 1986, Dr. James Lazell arranged for a total of eight Anegada iguanas to be relocated to Guana Island, which had been rid of all iguana predators. The lizards thrived; the original eight have begotten a population of more than 300. Animals from the Guana Island population have since been relocated to both Necker and Norman Islands.

Back on Anegada, islanders grew unhappy that the iguanas closely associated with their island were being removed to other places while nothing was being done to protect the diminishing population on Anegada. So, in 1997 the BVI National Parks Trust opened an iguana head-start facility with a half dozen young hatchlings collected from the wild. Six years later, the first of the head-started animals were reintroduced into the wild. Animals are now released annually, and the head-start facility has been expanded.

The head-start facility is designed to prevent young iguanas from falling prey to cats, but it does not address the long-term challenges that face Anegada's iguanas. Scientists say their survival will depend on the establishment of a formal national park on Anegada, as well as a program to eradicate feral cats. Island residents, while largely supportive of both plans, point out that land titles need to be given to residents before a national park is created. Many feel the iguanas removed in the 1980s were taken without permission and so are skeptical of an alternative plan to relocate some iguanas to uninhabited Fallen Jerusalem, where they would have a better chance of survival.

In the meantime, the National Parks Trust continues to maintain the head-start facility while efforts are made to address the longstanding land conundrum that stands in the way of a permanent refuge for the iguanas.

© SUSANNA HENIGHAN POTTER

an Anegada rock iguana in the wild

a whole school to beat a frenzied retreat. They feed on the flats from Setting Point eastward to the end of the island, but if you really want to catch one, you will need a guide who knows how to find them. **Captain Kevin Faulkner** (284/547-0550 or 284/540-5100, www.flyfishinganegada.com) is an experienced guide who has been fishing on the flats since he was a boy. **Danny Vanterpool** (284/441-6334) also offers fishing excursions, or call the **Anegada Reef Hotel** (Setting Point, 284/495-8002, www.anegadareef.com). Expect to pay about $350 for a half-day trip and $600 for a whole day.

The flats are also a good area for kayaking, wading, or, if you bring your own gear, stand up paddleboarding. In the shallows, the water is perfectly clear; you will see sand flats, patches of sea grass, barracuda, tarpon, jacks, and sea cucumbers. Paddle along the mangroves to find multitudes of juvenile fish.

The easiest access point is from the fisherman's dock near The Settlement. Alternatively, look for a small bridge along the southern coastal road and an abandoned bar and restaurant called the Pink Flamingo. Here you can park and wade right in.

Sports and Recreation

WATER SPORTS
Snorkeling and Diving
With its expansive reefs and numerous shipwrecks, Anegada might at first blush seem to be a snorkeling and diving paradise. But it is not as simple as that. Most of the Horseshoe Reef lies just a few feet below the open ocean, exposed to powerful ocean swells that prevent delicate coral from growing—most of the reef here is stubby and compact. And since most of the 300-plus ships wrecked off Anegada were wooden, they rotted away on the ocean floor long ago. A no-anchor policy on the Horseshoe Reef also makes the logistics of snorkeling and diving here difficult, and dive operators have been asked not to take guests there.

But don't despair. There is excellent snorkeling at **Loblolly Bay** on the island's north coast. Enter the water just west of the Big Bamboo restaurant and swim the short distance out to the reef, where you should look for a series of deep holes and caves that cut through the reef. You can dive here, as well, if you bring your own gear, but the area is pretty shallow and snorkeling is considered the best way to view it. Watch out for the waves; if the swell is up, snorkeling or diving here can be dangerous and unrewarding—the waves stir up sand that blocks visibility. You can also snorkel the reef in front of **Flash of Beauty** on the western end of Loblolly Bay. On the other end of the island, **Cow Wreck Beach** also has a near-shore reef for snorkeling.

For the most outstanding snorkeling, book a snorkeling excursion with **Captain Kevin Faulker** (284/547-0550 or 284/540-5100, www.flyfishinganegada.com), who takes guests to parts of the reef inaccessible by land.

If you are determined to dive an Anegada shipwreck, you will have to find a knowledgeable guide willing to take you out. Ask around at dive shops on Tortola and Virgin Gorda (there are no functioning dive shops on Anegada). Two of the best wreck dives around Anegada are the *Parmatta* and *Rocus*, both of which lie several miles offshore on the southeastern tip of the Horseshoe Reef and are for experienced divers only.

Kayaking
Kayaks are ideal crafts to explore Anegada's shoreline, as they coast over reefs that snare other kinds of sea craft. Kayak parallel to the shoreline inside the reef along the north coast, or put in at the fishing dock south of The Settlement and

ANEGADA

paddle through the mangroves and flats along the southern shore to Setting Point.

Kayaks are available for rent from **Cow Wreck Beach Resort** (284/495-8047) and **Fun in the Sun** (Setting Point, 284/495-9143 or 284/540-5860). Expect to pay between $40 and $50 to rent a two-person kayak for a full day and about $10 for an hour.

Fishing
Hire a local guide to take you out fishing on the famed North Drop or on Anegada's beautiful and fecund flats. For trip information, contact **Captain Kevin Faulker** (284/547-0550 or 284/540-5100, www.flyfishinganegada.com) or the **Anegada Reef Hotel** (284/494-8002).

Board Sports
Anegada attracts surfers and kiteboarders in search of the most remote waves in the Virgin Islands. Kiteboarding is best around Bone's Bight, Windlass Bight, and Pomato Point; call the Bitter End Yacht Club on Virgin Gorda (284/494-2745) to reach the only kiteboarding school and outfitter in the BVI.

Surfers, meanwhile, come by boat to the break off the extreme northwestern tip of the island. Sometimes you can see them from the beach at Cow Wreck.

SAILING
Visiting charter yachts will need special permission to sail to Anegada; the barrier reef is dangerous. Most companies require boats have a hired skipper or significant sailing experience to make the trip.

The **Anegada Reef Hotel** (Setting Point, Channel 16) and **Neptune's Treasure** (Bender's Bay, Channel 16) have moorings for visiting yachts. At both establishments you will also find ice and a restaurant.

The shore off Pomato Point on the far western end of the island is a popular anchorage.

LAND PURSUITS
Hiking
Hiking on Anegada is an adventure, not just an outing. There are no marked trails, no hiking guides, and no maps. But there are lots of opportunities for exploration along goat paths that crisscross the eastern wilderness, the Anegada Outback.

A good place to start hiking is at the end of the main road heading east through The Settlement. Or look for any promising gap along the road to Loblolly Bay.

Take safety precautions if you decide to hike. Tell someone where you are going and when you expect to be back. Bring water and food and wear good shoes, long pants, and long sleeves to protect yourself from thorny plants and trees (of which there are a lot). Wear a hat and sunscreen. If you can, bring a cell phone (but don't count on service) or, better yet, a handheld radio. Take a map and remain alert to where you are going so you won't get lost. Start early in the morning when it is cooler, and never hike at night (when it is easy to get hurt or lost).

Biking
Being flat, Anegada presents easier terrain for bicycling than any of the other Virgin Islands. On the paved roads, biking is an easy way to get around and explore. You can also bike the miles of packed sand roads, a challenging but by no means impossible undertaking. Be sure to bring plenty of water and wear sun protection; there is not much shade out there. It takes about three hours to cycle the road that circles the Western Salt Ponds, more if you stop frequently to rest or investigate the narrow paths that crisscross the area.

You can rent bikes from **T&A's Bike Rental** at the Cash and Carry grocery store (Setting Point, 284/495-9932, 9:15 A.M.–6 P.M. Mon.–Sat., 1–5 P.M. Sun.) for about $20 a day.

Accommodations

Accommodations on Anegada are no-frills, and most folks like it that way. This is a destination where simple is a pleasure.

$125-175

Located on a shady corner of the island's south shore is the clean and cozy **◖ Neptune's Treasure Guesthouse** (Bender's Bay, P.O. Box 2711, 284/495-9439, www.neptunestreasure. com, $150 winter, $120 summer). The nine-room guesthouse is owned by the friendly and welcoming Soares family, who also operate a long-line fishing business. The family's catch winds up at restaurants on Anegada, Virgin Gorda, and Tortola. The guesthouse has nice views looking south to Virgin Gorda and Tortola. Guests enjoy air-conditioning, in-room coffeemakers, and first dibs on the day's catch at the hotel restaurant.

$175-225

The Anegada Reef Hotel (Setting Point, 284/495-8002, fax 284/495-9362, www.ane-gadareef.com, $175–310 winter, $160–275 summer) is an island institution. Located at Setting Point and equipped with a large dock, the hotel and adjoining restaurant are well positioned to attract the yachting crowd. It is a gathering place for locals, too. The 20-room hotel is intentionally no frills; if you want television, wireless Internet, and telephones, go elsewhere. The rooms are clean, neat, and comfortable, however. Choose from ocean or garden view. You can also opt for a package that includes breakfast and dinner and costs $265–400 daily in the high season.

$225-300

Located less than 20 feet from the water's edge, **◖Keel Point Cottages** (Keel Point, 284/441-0296, www.keelpointcottages.com, $250 winter, $200 summer) is a cluster of well-kept and homey cottages ideal for a beach vacation.

Three of the cheerful pastel-painted cottages have one bedroom; a fourth has two. Hosts Lucia and Rudolph Francis take pride in their property and have even coaxed attractive landscaping out of the sandy earth. Cottage amenities include ceiling fans, air-conditioning in the bedrooms, kitchens, cable television, and open-air porches. By the beach you'll find a shared outdoor kitchen and grill area for guests. Perhaps the greatest perk is that cottages come with a rental car included in the room rate.

Located just steps from the awesome white sand of Cow Wreck Beach, **Cow Wreck Beach Villas** (Cow Wreck Bay, 284/495-8047, www. cowwreckbeach.com, $275–350) is a cluster of three bright yellow cottages, each equipped with one or two bedrooms, a kitchen, air-conditioning in the bedroom, and a perfect ocean view. Excellent swimming and snorkeling is a few steps away from your front door. The Cow Wreck Bar and Restaurant next door can provide your meals, or cook for yourself.

Bonefish Villa (Nutmeg Point, 284/495-8045, $235) is a two-bedroom shoreside villa well equipped with air-conditioning, television, a phone, and full kitchen. It is on the southern coast between Setting Point and The Settlement. The villa also rents through St. Thomas–based McLaughlin Anderson (340/776-0635 or 800/537-6246, fax 340/777-4737, www.mclaughlinanderson.com).

OVER $300

If you want luxury and room to stretch out, choose **Lavenda Breeze** (Loblolly Bay, 284/495-8045, 845/255-1616, or 888/868-0199, www.lavendabreeze.com, $500) a three-bedroom villa with a wraparound porch and views of beautiful Loblolly Bay. Amenities include satellite television, a full kitchen, VCR, DVD, washer and dryer, maid service, and

ANEGADA

© SUSANNA HENIGHAN POTTER

A cottage at Keel Point looks out over the island's beautiful north coast.

ANEGADA

more. If you would rather not cook, the house is a short walk from two restaurants.

The newest accommodations on Anegada are four guesthouses at the **Big Bamboo** (Loblolly Bay, 284/495-2019, $500 winter, $300 summer). Round, green, and set behind a low screen of beachfront shrubbery, the cottages enjoy spectacular views of beautiful Loblolly Bay. They are equipped with full kitchens, a sitting area, cable television, porches, and either one or two bedrooms. Day-trippers and restaurant guests provide company during the day; at night this is a quiet and remote getaway.

Food

Eating out on Anegada means one thing: seafood. Fresh lobster, fish, and conch are the island's specialties, and restaurants serve little else. Consequently, they do them well. Seafood is caught by local anglers and is a source of income for many island families.

Nearly all restaurants ask you to make dinner reservations, including your choice of entrée, by 4:30 P.M., either by phone, in person, or on VHF radio. Some will let you choose a time for dinner; others have established seatings. Plan on paying $50 for a lobster dinner and $30 for fish or conch. Dinners include generous side dishes, often served family-style.

Also be aware that because restaurants on Anegada all require reservations, if no one is booked for dinner they may not open. And sometimes they will close without warning for a day or two.

◖ ANEGADA LOBSTER

No trip to Anegada is complete without a lobster dinner enjoyed at one of the five seaside restaurants (Potter's By the Sea, Anegada Reef Hotel, Lobster Trap, Whistling Pines, and Neptune's Treasure) between Setting Point and Bender's Bay, within walking distance of the public jetty. Served whole and hot from the grill, lobster on Anegada is as fresh and as sweet as you will ever find it. All of the restaurants in this area are masters of lobster, served at dinner under the stars and at a leisurely pace.

During daylight hours, stroll out onto any of the restaurants' docks. You will find living lobsters, lots of them, kept in traps just below the surface. Spiny, pink, and plump, these crustaceans were plucked from the reef by island fishers. They are destined for someone's dinner plate—perhaps yours?

Come out as the sun sets and you will find island chefs preparing the lobsters for dinner: cleaning, seasoning, and grilling them over open-air fires on the beach. It's a ritual that is interesting to watch and that represents Anegada to the core.

Reservations by 4:30 P.M. are essential for a lobster dinner at any of the southern coast restaurants. Make them in person, over the phone, or by calling on Channel 16.

NORTH COAST

Ask most people, and they will tell you that the best food on Anegada is served aFt the ◖ **Big Bamboo** (Loblolly Bay, 284/495-2019, 10 A.M.–5 P.M. daily), a family-run beachfront institution on beautiful Loblolly Bay. Open daily for lunch, the Big Bamboo specializes in pan-scared fish and grilled lobster, which are served with generous sides of rice, potatoes, and vegetables. You can also order lighter items such as crabcakes and chicken fingers. The adjacent bar serves blended drinks and ice-cold beers, and

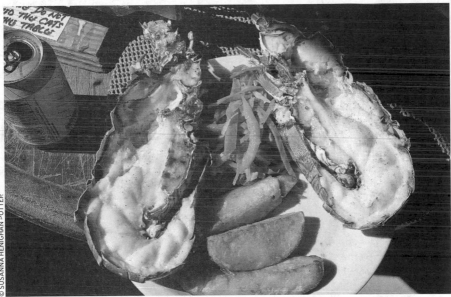

© SUSANNA HENIGHAN POTTER

an Anegada lobster dinner

ANEGADA

you can even get ice cream if you're hankering for dessert. After you eat, relax in a hammock under the sea grape trees, lie on the sand under a beach umbrella, or go for a snorkel at Loblolly Bay. It doesn't get much better than this.

You'll feel like you've reached the end of the world when you get to the **Cow Wreck Resort** (Cow Wreck Bay, 284/495-8047, 9 A.M.–5 P.M. daily). At the end of a series of low sand dunes, this bar and restaurant squats on one of the most dramatic stretches of beach on Anegada. The area got its name when the *Rocus,* a ship carrying animal skeletons to a bonemeal factory in the United States, wrecked off Anegada in 1929 and the bones washed ashore here in great numbers. You can still see some of them scattered around the restaurant as part of its decor. Lunch ($15–30) is a casual affair with burgers, salads, seafood, and some of the best hot wings on Anegada. Cow Wreck is also known locally for its superb conch dishes. After lunch, spread out on the sand, where you can watch surfing and kiteboarding when conditions are right. The offshore reef is good for snorkeling.

THE SETTLEMENT

Dotsy's Bakery (The Settlement, 284/495-9667, 9 A.M.–7 P.M. Mon.–Sat.) serves breakfast, lunch, and dinner in a small West Indian–style building in the heart of the island's only town. This is the best place for an economical meal on the island. The menu includes West Indian specialties like conch, fish, and barbecued chicken for about $15, and burgers, sandwiches, and pizza for about $10. A standard breakfast will cost $5–10. Dotsy's also sells fresh bread and local pastries.

SOUTH SHORE

Restaurants cluster around Setting Point, where visiting yachts moor. They are presented here from east to west.

Colorful **Potter's by the Sea** (Setting Point, 284/499-9637, 5–10 P.M. daily, reservations required, hours may vary, $25–50) is a cheerful restaurant with superb sunset views and a small sandy beach. The menu features all the Anegada standards: lobster, fish, and conch, as well as grilled ribs and chicken, just steps from the ferry dock.

The largest restaurant on the southern shore is the **Anegada Reef** (Setting Point, 284/495-8002, 8:30 A.M.–9 P.M. daily, reservations required, hours may vary, $24–50), which has been serving lobster dinners under the stars for more than 30 years becoming a model that by nearly all Anegada restaurants have followed. The specialty here is undoubtedly lobster, which is grilled alongside fresh fish, chicken, ribs, and steak. Meals include salad, fresh rolls, two sides, and coffee or tea. "The Reef," as it is called, is the only restaurant on the southern shore consistently open for lunch ($10–14); choose from burgers, salads, and sandwiches. Breakfast is also served daily from 8:30 A.M., and if you are looking for company after dark, the Anegada Reef's bar is the place to go.

◖ The Lobster Trap (Setting Point, 284/495-9439, 5–9 P.M. daily, reservations required, hours may vary, $25–50) is a neat, pink low-slung restaurant next to the Anegada Reef. Wilfred Creque, who also owns Pomato Point restaurant, runs this establishment with precision. Dinner is served on a deck over the water, with Christmas lights adding to the romantic ambience. Lobster, fish, and conch are the specialties, and meals come with bread, salad, rice, vegetables, and dessert.

Whistling Pines (Setting Point, Channel 16, 5–9 P.M. daily, reservations required, hours may vary, $30–50), a bright yellow restaurant set beneath a cluster of Anegada's distinctive whistling pine trees, serves lobster and seafood dinners under the stars.

Look for a cluster of coconut palms at the far western end of the bay to find **◖ Neptune's Treasure** (Bender's Bay, 284/495-9439,

8:30–10 A.M. and 5–9 P.M. daily, reservations required, hours may vary, $26–52), a family-run seafood restaurant on the southern coast. The swordfish, grouper and mahimahi on your plate come directly off the family's long-line fishing boat. Lobster is also a specialty, but if you've tired of seafood, Neptune's offers some refreshing variety in the form of pasta, orange chicken, and curry. Meals are served family-style, with fresh bread and a medley of sides. You can dine outdoors on the deck or inside the screened dining room, a plus when mosquitoes are particularly bothersome. Classic jazz played behind the bar sets a tone of refinement. Breakfast is also available daily.

Tucked behind Neptune's Treasure is **Pam's Kitchen** (Bender's Bay, 284/495-9439, 8 A.M.–5 P.M. daily, reservations required, hours may vary, $8–14), a good choice for breakfast or lunch. Pam Soares rises before dawn to bake cinnamon rolls, cookies, and bread, which draw an interesting mix of visitors and locals to her friendly kitchen. She serves breakfast and lunch sandwiches on hand-crafted sandwich rolls and offers jars of homemade mango chutney and pepper jelly. Each evening just before sundown the "Bakery Lady" peddles her fresh bread aboard a dinghy to visiting yachts.

WEST COAST

At the extreme western tip of Anegada's south shore is Pomato Point, home to the **Pomato Point Restaurant** (284/495-9439, 8 A.M.–9 P.M. daily, $28–50) and the best blended drinks on the island. The breezy dining room, decorated with lush tropical plants, is a short walk away from the beautiful and calm Pomato Point beach, perfect for swimming, walking, and sunbathing. The sunset view here is spectacular. Dinner and lunch specialties include lobster, fish, and conch and are served with homemade bread, salad, and rice and peas. Diners can examine the shipwreck artifacts at the Pomato Point Museum while they wait for their food or sip a cocktail.

GROCERIES AND SUPPLIES

Groceries and a hodgepodge of other sundries can be obtained at the **Faulkner's Country Store** (The Settlement, 7 A.M.–noon and 3–7 P.M. Mon.–Sat., 8 A.M.–noon Sun.). Come here for unbeatable small-island ambience, too. The newer **Cash and Carry** (Setting Point, 284/495-9932, 9:15 A.M.–6 P.M. Mon.–Sat., 1–5 P.M. Sun.), across the street from the Anegada Reef, sells bulk groceries and some produce.

Information and Services

There are no luxury hotels on Anegada, nor courier services, bookstores, or tourist information desks. Visiting here is an adventure; if you need something, bring it with you.

TOURIST INFORMATION AND MAPS

The best sources of information are the people you encounter. Your hotel proprietor, waiter, or taxi driver will be able to answer most of your questions. He or she may even provide the service you are looking for.

Good maps of Anegada are hard to find. The road maps provided by car rental agencies provide enough information to get around, but just barely. If you expect to do a lot of exploring, especially off-road, obtain detailed survey maps on Tortola before you arrive. The Purple Turtle at Setting Point sells nautical maps of the southern coast.

SHOPPING

Needless to say, Anegada is not a place for serious shopping. Getting what you need is the focus here.

The best recreational shopping is found at **The Purple Turtle** (Setting Point, 284/495-8062, 8:30 A.M.–6 P.M. daily), which is stocked with beachwear, gifts, children's books, toys, and practical items including toiletries and food.

LIBRARIES

The **Anegada Community Library** (The Settlement, 284/495-9464, 8:30 A.M.–4:30 P.M. Mon.–Thurs., 1–4:30 P.M. Fri., 8:30 A.M.–noon Sat.) keeps a tiny collection of books and magazines.

EMERGENCIES

The **Anegada Clinic** (The Settlement, 284/495-8049, 8:30 A.M.–4:30 P.M. Mon.–Fri.) is staffed by a nurse, with a doctor visiting from Tortola once a week.

The **Anegada Police Station** (The Settlement, 284/495-8057) can be contacted 24 hours a day. For emergencies, dial 911 or 999. For emergencies at sea, contact Virgin Islands Search and Rescue by dialing 767 from any landline or cellular phone in the BVI.

BANKING

FirstBank (The Settlement, 284/494-2662) provides banking services on Wednesdays from 9 A.M.–3 P.M. in an office near the island's administration building. There is no ATM.

COMMUNICATIONS

Communications on Anegada are still quite basic. After all, it wasn't long ago that most people communicated by radio only (in fact, calling a restaurant or business on Channel 16 is still a good way to get in touch). Most hotels do not provide phones for guests; you will have to ask to use a phone at the office or your mobile. Cellular coverage is quite good on Anegada, owing to two large towers and a flat topography.

The **Purple Turtle** (Setting Point, 284/495-8062, fax 284/495-2231, 8:30 A.M.–6 P.M. daily) has Internet, phone, and fax service. You can go online for 15 minutes for $7. Staff here can also help you plan outings and fishing trips or make dinner reservations.

Public notices and announcements are posted on telephone poles around The Settlement and Setting Point; a good place to look is on the bulletin board at the Anegada Reef. No one sells newspapers on Anegada, so the best way to stay in touch with the outside world is to tune in on a radio.

Getting There and Around

Anegada is a 10-minute flight from Tortola, and about 75 minutes by ferry, depending on sea conditions.

BY AIR

Several air carriers provide charter flights to the island on small three- to nine-seater aircraft. The views alone are worth the trip. **Fly BVI** (Beef Island, 284/495-1747, www.fly-bvi.com) offers an Anegada day trip for parties of four, five, six, or nine that runs $175 per person; the price includes airfare, taxis on Anegada, and a lobster lunch (when lobster is in season). Also from Tortola you can charter a ride over with **Island Birds** (Beef Island, 284/495-2002, www.islandbirds.com). From St. Thomas, charter a flight with **Ace Flight Center** (Cyril E. King Airport, St. Thomas, 340/776-4141). The flight from St. Thomas is about 30 minutes; from Beef Island (Tortola) plan on 20 minutes. Costs depend on the size of the plane and the number of passengers, but plan on $700 and up for the day.

BY SEA

Road Town Fast Ferry (Road Town, Tortola, 284/495-2323) makes two round-trips to Anegada every Monday, Wednesday, and Friday. The ferry departs Road Town at 6:45 A.M. and 3:30 P.M., and returns from Anegada at 8:10 A.M. and 5:10 P.M. Fare is $50 round-trip. Call ahead to confirm availability.

A number of day sail operators on Virgin Gorda and Tortola will make a day trip to Anegada if you reserve ahead.

TAXIS

Taxis will be at the dock if you arrive with a scheduled ferry on Anegada. If you are traveling with a charter, ask your charter company to arrange for a taxi or recommend one to you or call for one on Channel 16. **Tony's Taxi** (284/495-8037) is a good bet.

CAR RENTALS

A rental car will give you the freedom to explore all corners of the island at your own pace. Expect to pay about $60 a day for a four-door four-wheel drive vehicle. Rental agencies include **D.W. Jeep Rentals** (Nutmeg Point, 284/495-9688), **Anegada Reef Hotel** (Setting Point, 284/495-8002), and **Cow Wreck Beach Resort** (Cow Wreck Bay, 284/495-8047).

There are no road signs, few landmarks, and no streetlights, so expect to get a little turned around when you're driving—especially at night—even if you have a map. Driving hazards are few, but be aware of the livestock that roam the island, sometimes stopping to rest in the middle of the road.

A scooter rental is less expensive than a car and can be a fun way to get around the island. A daylong scooter rental will cost you about $40. Scooters are available from **Anjulienas** (Setting Point, 284/495-9002 or 284/544-0958).

ANEGADA

BACKGROUND

The Land

The Virgin Islands are small specks of green in the Caribbean Sea, 1,075 miles from Miami and 40 miles from Puerto Rico. Steep and forested, their hillsides plunge to the shoreline. Their coasts, lined by powder-white sand and fringed by protective coral reefs, are pleasantly scalloped. Some bays are especially wide, flat, and sheltered.

GEOGRAPHY

The Virgin Islands are at the northernmost tip of the Lesser Antilles, the string of islands that form an arc stretching from Puerto Rico in the north to Trinidad in the south.

The islands are at latitude 18°25' north and longitude 64°40' west, roughly the same latitude as Mumbai, Honolulu, and Mexico City. They lie at the confluence of the Atlantic Ocean and the Caribbean Sea. The Atlantic Ocean is north and east of the islands, while the Caribbean is to the south and west.

The Virgin Islands comprise more than 90 individual islands, many of them nothing more than uninhabited rocks surrounded by sea. They have a combined coastline of 167 miles and a combined land area of 193 square miles, about twice the size of the Vatican City.

© SUSANNA HENIGHAN POTTER

With the exception of Anegada, which is a coral island, the Virgins are volcanic. They emerged from the Caribbean Sea some 65 million years ago as a result of alternating periods of undersea mountain-building, followed by periods of uplift and periods of explosive volcanism. The highest point in the islands is Sage Mountain (1,709 feet above sea level) on Tortola.

Up until the Pleistocene era, about 100,000 years ago, the British Virgin Islands, St. Thomas, and St. John, plus their related satellite cays, were joined with Puerto Rico to form a single landmass. When the sea level rose, all but the uppermost mountains and highest valleys were submerged by water, and the islands we know today were formed.

St. Croix, divided from St. Thomas by a two-mile-deep trench, was always separate from the rest of the Virgin Islands, however. As a result, unique plant and animal species can be found there.

While the Virgin Islands form a single geographical unit, they are divided into two distinct territories with separate histories, economies, and administrations. The U.S. Virgin Islands, the more westward of the Virgins, comprise St. Thomas, St. Croix, and St. John. The British Virgin Islands comprise Tortola, Virgin Gorda, Jost Van Dyke, Anegada, and dozens of smaller islands and cays. The primary cities are Charlotte Amalie on St. Thomas, Christiansted on St. Croix, and Road Town on Tortola.

The boundary between the U.S. and British islands winds between St. John and Tortola and between Hans Lollick (U.S.) and the Tobagos (U.K.). The territories are separated by as little as one mile of water in places.

Earthquakes

The Virgin Islands lie within an active earthquake zone registering some 900 measurable quakes each year. Most are minor—so weak you don't feel them—but occasionally there are more significant events, usually marked by a loud rumbling noise and shaking.

The possibility exists for the islands to experience a major earthquake. The most significant earthquake in modern history took place in 1867, causing tsunamis that inundated the cities of Charlotte Amalie, Frederiksted, Christiansted, and Road Town. Massive seagoing ships at anchor were deposited well inland.

The islands' seismicity comes from the fact that they lie just south of the boundary of the North American and Caribbean plates, where there is gradual subduction and displacement. The Puerto Rico Seismic Network at the University of Puerto Rico (http://redsismica.uprm.edu/english) and the Seismic Research Unit at the University of the West Indies (www.uwiseismic.com) monitor the islands' seismic activity.

CLIMATE

The climate of the Virgin Islands is subtropical and humid, moderated by easterly trade winds. Seasonal changes in weather are subtle. The hottest month of the year is July, when high temperatures can reach 90°F. During the coolest winter months, December and January, high temperatures are in the low 80s. Humidity generally ranges from 70 to 80 percent, peaking in July.

Historically, the Virgin Islands receive about 40 inches of rain per year. The wettest months are September, October, and November, when it seems to rain just about every day. January, February, and March are the driest months. Rain arrives quickly, falls heavily, and moves off just as suddenly as it came. If you visit during a rainy month, you will quickly realize that the best prescription against getting wet is to seek shelter and wait out the rain.

In the last decade, serious rain events have been the most significant weather hazard in the Virgin Islands. In November 2010, 24 inches of rain (more than half the total rainfall expected in an entire year) fell on already saturated soils

BY THE NUMBERS

U.S. VIRGIN ISLANDS

· **Size:** 144 square miles
· **Population:** 109,666
· **Annual Overnight Tourists:** 664,000
· **Annual Cruise Ship Tourists:** 1.9 million
· **Life Expectancy:** 79.3 years
· **GDP:** $1.577 billion
· **Annual Budget:** $837 million

BRITISH VIRGIN ISLANDS

· **Size:** 59 square miles
· **Population:** 25,383
· **Annual Overnight Tourists:** 309,000
· **Annual Cruise Ship Tourists:** 530,000
· **Life Expectancy:** 77.6 years
· **GDP:** $853 million
· **Annual Budget:** $300 million

Days are longer in the summer, with sunrise coming close to 5 A.M. and sunset around 7 P.M. At the peak of winter, sunrise is much closer to 6 A.M. and the sun sets at 6 P.M. Tides are minimal this close to the equator, with a range of about 12 inches; you probably won't even notice tidal fluctuations.

Climate Change

Climate scientists predict that by the 2080s the Caribbean will be between 2 and 9 degrees hotter, on average; drier, receiving up to 25 percent less rainfall; and vulnerable to stronger and more frequent hurricanes. Sea levels are also expected to rise by up to two feet.

While the world debates climate change and the best response to it, residents of the Caribbean are being urged to adapt by building so as to withstand stronger storms; improving drainage and run-off around their properties; protecting mangroves and reefs; and installing low-use water fixtures. Governments have a great deal of work to do to improve the resilience of infrastructure, slow or stop development in especially vulnerable areas, and develop an agricultural sector that can withstand higher temperatures and less water.

Coral reefs are especially vulnerable to climate change. Coral is extremely sensitive to sea temperatures, and bleaching episodes in 2005 and 2010 caused by high water temperatures affected more than half the coral around the Virgin Islands. Global climate change is also expected to make oceans more acidic, which could cause corals to dissolve.

Hurricanes

The Atlantic hurricane season begins on June 1 and ends November 30, peaking in September. An old rhyme puts it fairly accurately: "June, too soon. July, stand by. August, it must. September, remember. October, all over."

The word "hurricane" comes from the Taino deity Jurakan, the god of malevolence

over a three-day period. The impact was significant: Homes and roads flooded, retaining walls collapsed, roads were undermined, and landslides damaged property. Scientists warn of a growing risk of rain events like this one as a result of climate change.

The windiest months are December and January, when the so-called Christmas Winds pass through. These delightful air currents of 25–30 knots bring cool air from northern climes, making these months ideal for sailing and generally cooler. From November to June you can count on northeast winds of 15–20 knots consistently. In May, June, and July the summer doldrums hit and winds taper off; southeast winds of 10–15 knots are common. These are the worst months for sailing, and some of the hottest. In September and October the weather tends to be unsettled.

MAGICAL MANGROVES

When most people think of snorkeling they think of coral reefs, and for good reason. Reefs are exciting, with their colorful coral formations and large numbers of fish. But a snorkel and a mask is your ticket to explore other ocean habitats as well.

Mangroves are forests that lie between the sea and the land. One of the few plants that can live—and in fact thrives—in a saltwater habitat, mangroves protect the land from erosion during storms and high seas. They provide natural hurricane protection for boats: When a storm is approaching, boats move to mangrove-protected bays, often called hurricane holes. Mangroves and the wetlands they create are a habitat for migratory birds, and among the mangroves' knobby underwater branches juvenile fish find protection from predators.

Miles and miles of mangroves have been destroyed in the Virgin Islands for coastal development. Virtually the entire southern coastlines of Tortola and St. Thomas were once blanketed by mangroves—today those coasts are home to some of the highest centers of population.

The good news is that there is growing awareness of the importance of mangroves. In St. Thomas mangroves around Cas Cay and the St. James islands are protected as wildlife sanctuaries. On Tortola, the destruction of mangroves has stopped for the most part and replanting efforts are underway. Many other islands are untouched by development, and in St. John, which is largely protected by the national park, mangrove ecosystems remain intact.

Snorkelers who explore the mangrove will be rewarded by the sight of thousands of tiny fish: miniature versions of the yellowtails, parrot fish, snappers, angel fish, and grunt you see on the reefs. Take your time and you may see baby lobster, crab, and shellfish. Inside, among the darkness of the mangrove branches, lurk larger species, such as the shy mangrove snapper. Snorkeling around the edges of the mangroves, you may see mangrove jellyfish, also called cassiopea jellies, bottom-dwelling jellyfish that resemble cauliflower (but keep your distance, these creatures have a mild sting that can be very itchy).

Don't wear fins when snorkeling around the mangroves: they are not necessary in these calm, protected areas and will only serve to kick up sand and reduce visibility. Here are some of the best areas for mangrove snorkeling:

- **Mangrove Lagoon and Cas Cay, St. Thomas:** Protected by law, this mangrove forest near Red Hook is expansive. Virgin Islands Eco Tours (340/779-2155, www.viecotours.com) offers daily snorkel tours of the mangroves.

- **Princess Bay, St. John:** Located on the East End Road, past Coral Bay, this humble bay on the south shore of the island provides access to the extensive mangrove forests of this part of St. John.

- **Hans Creek, Beef Island:** Near the Beef Island bridge, the flats around Hans Creek are buffered by a large, healthy mangrove forest. Access the water via a concrete fisherman's dock along the road.

- **Paraquita Bay, Tortola:** Walk along the Roger Downing Mangrove Boardwalk at the HLSCC Marine Studies Centre to explore the mangroves without getting wet.

- **Salt River Bay, St. Croix:** The shore of this large bay and protected marine ecosystem is made of thick mangrove forests. Talk to one of the companies offering kayak tours of the bay about snorkeling around the mangroves.

- **The Flats, Anegada:** The southern shore of Anegada is covered in thick mangrove forests, one reason why the fishing around the island is so good. You can access the Flats on an ecotour or by wading out near The Flamingo on the southern coast road.

and destruction. For ancient seafarers, the destructive capacity of hurricanes was compounded by the fact that they arrived virtually unannounced.

In more modern times, the only warning one had of a storm was a sudden drop in barometric pressure just beforehand. Older residents of Road Town, in the British Virgin Islands, can still remember the days when a government agent would monitor the barometer and ride through town on horseback warning people when the pressure took a sudden downward turn.

Today, the National Hurricane Center in Florida tracks and predicts hurricanes, and islanders have several days' notice before a storm strikes. Keeping an ear out for the tropical weather forecast is a daily feature of life in many households.

Evacuation is not generally practiced—except by tourists. Most people ride out storms by boarding up windows and hunkering down with canned food, lots of extra water, flashlights, and battery-operated radios. Some homes also have standby generators. Builders use the latest hurricane-resistant building technology: impact glass for windows and hurricane clips for roofs, for example. Mariners moor their boats at established hurricane holes, coves where wind and wave action are blocked. On top of that, local disaster management offices are well equipped and experienced in mitigation and response.

The Virgin Islands have experienced several devastating hurricanes. Storms in 1867, 1916, and 1924 wiped out whole towns. In 1989, Hurricane Hugo razed the Virgin Islands, St. Croix in particular. Hurricane Marilyn in 1995 dealt an especially devastating blow to St. Thomas. In 1999, Hurricane Lenny doused the entire region with heavy rains. In 2010 the eye of Hurricane Earl passed just north of the Virgin Islands as a Category 3 hurricane. Damage from Earl was worst for the marine industry: many docks were damaged or destroyed and boats sunk or damaged.

In addition to damage to buildings, roads, and boats, hurricanes can exact a cost on the natural environment. Waves from a hurricane can damage coral reefs, and the terrestrial destruction affects habitat for a number of creatures. Trees are stripped of leaves and branches. Some species, however, including many predators, benefit from the disturbance of a hurricane.

Travelers who book trips to the Virgin Islands during hurricane season, and especially during the peak month of September, would be wise to also buy trip insurance in case their plans are disrupted by a storm.

ENVIRONMENTAL ISSUES
Coral Reefs

Coral reefs around the world are dying, and those in the Virgin Islands are no exception. Coral disease, pollution, and careless humans take a high toll on these delicate ecosystems. Global warming and the ensuing rise of sea temperatures is also a major threat, as reefs are highly sensitive to even a minor change in temperature.

Discharge of raw sewage into the sea causes algae growth, which smothers the coral reef. Dirt and other sediment washed out to sea following rains also causes the reefs to be smothered. Marine pollution, such as oil spills or industrial wastewater discharge (such as at the rum factory on St. Croix), can have a direct, deadly impact on reefs. Careless boaters, snorkelers, and divers can kill coral just by stepping, anchoring, or otherwise touching it.

Recently, disease has been the greatest killer of reefs in the Virgin Islands. Scientists at the Virgin Islands National Park reported that between 2005 and 2006 some 60 percent of reefs in the Virgin Islands were killed, mostly because of a devastating disease they call white plague. The disease attacked reefs that had already been bleached—but not

Better management of the fishery is needed to ensure it remains healthy.

killed—by high temperatures experienced in 2005. Since the massive die-offs in the mid-2000s, reef death has slowed but not stopped, making protection of the reefs that remain all that more important.

Some steps have been taken to address these threats, although more needs to be done if the islands are going to avoid even more destruction of their greatest resource. In the U.S. Virgin Islands, fairly stringent local and federal environmental regulations are applied to control pollution and check coastal development. However, there continue to be problems with marine pollution and development that occur despite loud and reasoned environmental-based argument. In both territories, moorings have been placed in some popular anchorages to prevent anchor damage. Little can be done about coral disease, except to provide support and training to the scientists who are studying it.

Other problems still exist. The British Virgin Islands still don't have a public sewage treatment system, and raw sewage is pumped directly into the ocean. Likewise, in the sailing capital of the world, there is no rule requiring holding tanks, so yachts are free to discharge sewage directly into the sea. In both territories, no one seems able, or willing, to put a check on coastal or hillside development.

Fishing

Virgin Islanders have fished for centuries to feed their families and bring in income. Many fishers use seine or gill nets to capture schooling mackerel, yellowtail snapper, and jacks. Others use fish traps, locally known as fish pots. These traps are made of wire mesh built on a wooden or metal rectangular frame. Depending on local conditions, they are set singly or strung together. Some fishers use buoys to identify where they left their pots—others rely on memory or GPS coordinates. Fish caught in these traps are sometimes called pot-fish. You will also see children and adults standing near the water's edge with a line—they are hoping to bring home supper.

Used in moderation by fishers who appreciate the need for balance in nature, none of these fishing methods is necessarily destructive. But there is increasing evidence that the Virgin Islands fishery is declining. A 1991 study on the fishery in the U.S. Virgin Islands found that the average size of many popular species, including parrot fish, grunt, and triggerfish, is declining while large grouper, the single most important commercial species, is all but gone. Another study of the fishery around St. Croix conducted from 1997 to 2001 showed a 10 percent decrease in the average fish weight over the period and a 40 percent decline in the number of fish per fish-pot haul. There is no data on the British Virgin Islands fishery, although anecdotal evidence suggests that fish numbers and sizes are decreasing there as well.

The fishery decline is due to several factors, but it boils down to this: Too many fish are being taken from the sea. Conservationists say that fish pots are one source of the problem, because if they are lost—if they come loose from the rope or the fisher can't find them—they become floating death traps. Fish swim in but can't swim out. The fish that enter the trap eventually die, attracting more fish. Others say that more and more fishers are not following traditional fishing rules: They take fish that are too small or while they are spawning. Scarcity of fish has also pushed some fishers to use scuba gear and fish guns—a practice that also upsets the balance between humans and nature.

Quite a bit is being done about the loss of fish stock, but success depends on better enforcement and on viewing fishers as partners, not adversaries. Both the U.S. and British Virgin Islands have closed seasons for many of the most popular, and most vulnerable, species of fish, as well as other creatures like lobster and conch. There are also size limits. Both territories also have no-take areas. In the U.S.

Virgin Islands, there has been a push for fishers to use biodegradable fish pots, which break down if they are lost in the ocean.

The 2010 enactment of the Magnuson-Stevens Reauthorization Act in the United States requires more aggressive fishery management in U.S. waters, which led to some local resistance from fishers. As a result federal funds have been allocated to better measure and monitor the local fishery in order to more clearly document its health.

Consumers should not be afraid to buy fish because of overfishing concerns. Instead, familiarize yourself with closed season rules. If someone tries to sell or serve you something that should be off-limits, it has either been frozen or caught illegally. Ask.

Garbage Disposal

Garbage disposal is a major logistical challenge for islands where land is at a premium and shipping is expensive. Neither the U.S. nor the British Virgin Islands have mastered the challenge—at least not yet.

There is virtually no recycling in either territory, apparently because the cost of shipping recyclables off-island cannot be recouped through recycling revenue. An on-again, off-again can recycling program on St. Thomas is a private initiative, as are small battery and glass recycling programs in the British Virgin Islands. On St. John, Maho Bay Camps has gone farthest to embrace the concept of zero waste, using glass bottles in art and finding creative uses for other types of waste. On Tortola, Green VI opened a glass studio in Cane Garden Bay in 2010; the facility is designed to raise funds for recycling and clean energy initiatives.

Instead of recycling, the U.S. Virgin Islands have landfills on St. Thomas, St. Croix, and St. John. These cannot handle the growing amount of waste being produced. Landfill fires—sparked by spontaneous combustion from the heat generated by the garbage—pose health and environmental risks, although some strides have been made in recent years.

In the British Virgin Islands, authorities openly burn trash on the smaller islands of Jost Van Dyke, Anegada, and Virgin Gorda. On Tortola, garbage is incinerated at Pockwood Pond.

Reduction of waste has posed challenges for both territories, since so many goods arrive on container ships, wrapped in cardboard or plastic and on wooden pallets. Packaging is a big part of life. Sadly, there has been little to no political leadership on this issue, which could probably be solved, or at least addressed in a more successful way, with a clear vision and commitment. But then again, investing in garbage is a difficult political sell.

Freshwater

You will notice discreet signs in many bathrooms and kitchens asking you to preserve water. Water is a precious resource on these islands with no lakes or rivers and few springs. Most homes, and a good many businesses, have cisterns—large concrete storage tanks—below their floor slabs, where rainwater collected on the roof is stored. In times of rain, cisterns can sometimes overflow. In times of drought, every last drop is rationed. Cistern water is generally used for showers, washing, cleaning, and flushing. It should be boiled for drinking.

The other main source of freshwater is seawater desalination plants, which use reverse osmosis technology to make freshwater out of saltwater. Desalinated water is safe to drink and does not taste salty, although it does not necessarily taste good, either.

Desalination is an energy-intensive process and therefore expensive. Water authorities are unable to keep up with growing demand, and water outages are not unknown. Whether water comes from cisterns or a desalination plant, it is precious. Guests should do their part to conserve water by avoiding long showers and reporting leaky faucets and toilets right away.

Sewage

It is a little too tempting to dump one's raw sewage straight into the ocean. After all, it is free and easy to do so, and the ocean is big, so what does it matter, right? When the Virgin Islands were more sparsely populated than they are today, when millions of people did not visit them annually, and when the islands were not already under environmental stress, that view may have been correct. But today, dumping raw sewage into the ocean is an environmental problem, causing beach closures and impacting the health of coral reefs and other underwater habitats.

The U.S. Virgin Islands' wastewater treatment system is old and overwhelmed. Frequent malfunctions cause wastewater to flow, untreated, into the ocean. In the British Virgin Islands, there is no wastewater treatment system at all, except in the community of Cane Garden Bay. Sewage from Road Town is collected and pumped untreated into the sea. In other areas, residents rely on septic tanks.

Energy

While Americans bawl about $3-per-gallon gasoline, residents of the Virgin Islands have become accustomed to paying nearly $5 per gallon. The cost of diesel (used to generate electricity) and cooking gas are also high, and as a result, residents of both territories are left paying extremely high prices for electricity, gasoline, and things such as frozen or refrigerated goods that require a great deal of energy. The average cost per kilowatt hour is between 38 and 42 cents, compared to average costs below 10 cents in most U.S. cities. The high cost of electricity is a major drag on the economy.

There is some movement towards alternative energy. The USVI Water and Power Authority has invested in a mix of alternative energy projects, including solar and waste-to-energy. Federal funds were used in 2011 to install a large solar array at the Cyril E. King Airport on St. Thomas. Residents of the U.S.

Virgin Islands can also take advantage of a federal solar roof initiative. In the BVI, however, policymakers have continued with an utterly incomprehensible policy that not only fails to incentivize alternative energy, but actually forbids residents from setting up their own power-generating systems, such as a solar or wind power system at home, as long as the power grid is available to them. The final insult is that the BVI Electricity Corporation does not have the capacity to meet the BVI's growing power needs, so power outages are frequent.

Since the BVI law only restricts those with access to the power grid, resorts and hotels on the out islands have been trendsetters. Peter Island Resort has two wind turbines that generate about 25 percent of its energy. Cooper Island Beach Club has installed solar panels that generate 70 percent of its power needs. Virgin mogul Sir Richard Branson, owner of Necker and Mosquito Islands, is building an eco-resort on Mosquito Island that he says will be run totally on solar and wind power.

One of the reasons policymakers have failed to act more quickly on alternative energy is that it is not cheap. Even advocates concede that, with the current state of technology, in the short- and medium-terms the cost of solar, wind, and other forms of alternative energy will be even higher than that of energy produced from diesel fuel. At the same time, there is a serious knowledge gap and need for investment in training and education on the maintenance and operation of new energy systems. Another real problem for the Virgin Islands is their small scale. The Water and Power Authority of the U.S. Virgin Islands has proposed an undersea cable to connect the Virgin Islands with Puerto Rico as a means of improving reliability and improving economies of scale.

Visitors should be aware of these issues if only so you can be mindful of the energy that you use. Air-conditioning and the heating of water are the two largest consumers of power at most homes and hotels. Turn off air conditioners, lights, and fans when you're leaving your hotel room for the day and take short showers.

Flora

From gardens to wild forests, the Virgin Islands are host to a rich diversity of plant life, much of it remarkable for its adaptation to the dry, inhospitable climate of the islands.

AT THE SEASIDE

The tree most associated with the beach is the **coconut,** a member of the palm family. Coconut trees are hardy and useful. Their fronds, or leaves, can be used to make thatch roofs and mats. The coconut seed, when green, contains coconut milk, a sweet and somewhat viscous drink. When dried, the nut contains coconut meat, which can be used in cooking, baking, or even industry. Coconut trunks can be used for lumber, and the oil is used in cooking and beauty preparations.

Surprisingly, coconuts are not native to the Caribbean. They originated in the western Pacific and eastern Indian Ocean and were brought to the region by early Portuguese voyagers. Coconut trees are adaptable and can withstand significant periods of drought.

Another common seaside plant is the **sea grape,** or *Coccoloba uvifera,* a member of the buckwheat family. These adaptable trees grow along both protected and windswept shores. Many bathers find shade and shelter tucked beneath sea grape branches at the beach. The sea grape has round leaves, reaching up to about six inches wide. They produce strings of edible grapelike fruits in cluster, turning

© SUSANNA HENIGHAN POTTER

The nondescript leaves and fruit of the manchineel tree are worth knowing: they are highly poisonous, and should be avoided.

from green to purple in fall. The fruits have large pits and range from sour to sweet. They are quite tasty.

Don't try to eat the fruit of the **manchineel** (*Hippomane mancinella*) tree, a plant so toxic that its sap can take the paint off a car. The fruit of these trees can kill, and even brushing against one can lead to uncomfortable rashes. Manchineels have shiny, dark, elliptical leaves that droop on long, yellowish stalks. Look closely at the junction of the leaf and leaf stalk and you will see a tiny raised dot about the size of a pinhead. Manchineels are the only beach trees with this feature.

Manchineels produce shiny, green fruits that look like apples. Don't eat them! Also avoid touching the leaves, scratching yourself on the bark, or using the wood for a fire. It is even a bad idea to take shelter under a manchineel during rain, since the rainwater can wash tiny bits of the sap onto your skin.

AROUND THE HOUSE

Virgin Islanders love to plant colorful gardens around their homes. With the palette of colors and plant types available to these tropical gardeners, it is easy to see why.

One of the favorite decorative trees is the **flamboyant,** or flame tree, which produces a bright red crown of blossoms every June. When it is not in bloom, the flamboyant's wide canopy makes it a great shade tree. Another favorite for color is the **bougainvillea,** a hardy bush that can grow to great heights if allowed. Bougainvillea comes in a dazzling array of colors including red, pink, orange, and white. The "blooms" are actually modified leaves, called bracts, which the bushes produce to attract pollinators to their small, white flowers.

Hibiscus blooms are also bound to catch your eye. These bushes produce brightly colored flowers that can grow as large as seven inches across. Practiced gardeners compete

© SUSANNA HENIGHAN POTTER

A rare tree fern is seen at Sage Mountain National Park on Tortola.

annually at flower shows for the best hibiscus bloom. Locals also use the petals to make a sweet, red drink.

Often used as a natural fence, **oleander** is a plant worth identifying, if only because of its capacity to poison. Oleander puts out five-petaled blossoms of pink, purple, and white. Do not ingest any part of the plant—it is deadly.

One of the most beautiful decorative shrubs in the islands is the **poinsettia.** Once you see one of these growing over your head with dense red bracts brilliant in the sun, you will never think the same about the pitiful potted ones you see every Christmas. **Yellow allamanda** is another favorite among Caribbean gardeners, for its bright yellow flowers and neat, shiny leaves.

IN THE FOREST

Wet tropical forests can be found at Sage Mountain on Tortola and in Caldonia, the hilly, damp forest on St. Croix's northwestern tip. Plant species here thrive in low light and moisture. Instead of building defenses against grazing cattle and drought, plants here have developed bitter-tasting and toxic leaves to defend against insects that thrive in the damp forest.

Bromeliads are members of the epiphyte family that nest among the branches of larger trees, gathering nutrients from the air and storing rainwater in their leaves. Bromeliads look like the leafy top of a pineapple; some produce beautiful flowers.

One especially beautiful forest plant is the **tree fern,** or *Cyathea arborea*. A straight, single stem rises leafless, topped off by delicate fern leaves. These trees look like normal ferns at first; they reach their full diameter on the ground before starting to grow upward.

Dry tropical forests are common; in fact, most of the wooded areas you see around you would fall into this category. In these ecosystems, trees and plants are adapted for long periods of drought.

One of the telltale signs that you are in a dry forest is the presence of the **turpentine tree,** or *Bursera simaruba*. This beautiful tree has dozens of familiar nicknames, including gumbo limbo, West Indian birch, gommier, and tourist tree. It is easily identified by its peeling, red bark and its graceful limbs.

The Virgin Islands have an abundance of cactus types. **Turk's head cacti** are almost perfectly round balls that sit right on the ground, with a reddish "cap" atop. The fuchsia fruits are edible, and a particular favorite of birds. These cacti are said to tilt toward the equator, which earned them the nickname "compass plant."

The **prickly pear cactus** is characterized by flattened oval pads that pile on top of and around one another to form a single plant. The deep, dark red fruits are edible, but be sure to peel them first to get rid of the prickles.

Some of the largest and most majestic trees you will see in the Virgin Islands are **kapok**

© SUSANNA HENIGHAN POTTER

The head of the Turks head cactus is said to point to the equator.

trees, also called **silk cotton trees** *(Ceiba pentandra)*. These trees can grow to magnificent heights—up to 75 feet—with trunks as wide as a car. Kapok trees produce large pods full of short, lustrous fibers. This fiber has been used to stuff pillows, lifejackets, and furniture.

One of the most beautiful tropical flowering trees is the **frangipani,** often seen in gardens as well as in the wild. At first glance you may wonder if the tree is even alive—there are very few leaves. Look again, though, and you will see the lovely white flowers and long, dimpled leaves. In the spring, at the beginning of the dry season, colorful frangipani caterpillars come to munch on the leaves.

Other important features of the dry forest are the **aloe** and **century plants.** Aloe grows wild throughout the dry forest and is a useful plant: The gooey substance that oozes out when you crack a leaf can be useful in treating burns and cuts. Look for aloe's yellow blooms in the spring. Century plants are the flowering stalk of the agave, whose yellow blossoms stand as high as 12 feet. One of the great botanic tragedies of recent years has been the virtual elimination of native century plants from the Virgin Islands due to an invasive insect. You can still find century plants on Anegada, but it is not clear how long they will survive.

ON THE FARM

Fruit trees are hardly limited to the farm; many households plant them around the house for their obvious utilitarian purpose. **Sugarcane** makes a good natural fence, since it grows tall and straight. A member of the grass family, sugarcane takes about a year to mature. Most gardens around the Virgin Islands have a small patch, not for sugar production, but for chewing and eating on its own. Other fixtures in many backyard gardens are **banana** and **plantain** "trees." These fast-growing plants are distinguishable by their long, slatted leaves. After the plant has produced, it is cut down, and a new one will sprout in its place. The whole process takes about nine months.

Magnificent fruit trees are abundant in the Virgin Islands. **Avocado pear** trees are handsome, especially when they droop with the weight of ripe avocados every summer. These tropical avocados are large and bright green but just as tasty as the small, dark fruits familiar in the supermarkets of North America. Another fruit tree sure to catch your eye is the **breadfruit,** which grows to towering heights and has large, lobed, handsome leaves. The fruit grows to be as large as a basketball and ripens during the summer. It tastes like potato and can be seasoned and roasted, boiled, or fried. The fruit is not highly prized, however, and often goes uneaten.

Other common fruit trees are the guava, mango, and papaya. **Guava** trees are bushy and produce small, lemon-size fruits used to make guava candy and preserves. The **mango** is probably the most popular tropical fruit; its sweet, juicy flesh is the perfect finish to any meal. The trees themselves are handsome, with long, droopy leaves that produce dense shade. Few household yards are without a mango tree of their own. **Papayas,** the other favorite tropical fruit, ripen just below the leaves on the fast-growing papaya tree. Pick these out by their tall, slender stalks and round, intricately lobed leaves.

Fauna

CORAL REEFS

There are some 386 square miles of coral reef in the Virgin Islands, more than twice the total landmass of the territories. The Horseshoe Reef around Anegada, in the British Virgin Islands, is one of the largest barrier reefs in the world. Buck Island, near St. Croix, is surrounded by 31 square miles of barrier reef.

The most common type of reef in the Virgin Islands is the fringing reef, which runs parallel to the shore, providing protection for coastal areas. In other places, coral has begun to grow on underwater rocks and other hard surfaces.

Ecology

Home to some two million plant and animal species, coral reefs are the most biologically diverse ecosystem in the ocean and the second most diverse in the world—only the tropical rainforest supports more plant and animal species.

There are almost a thousand different coral species, each with its own growth and reproduction pattern. Each also has its own unique style: Some resemble wrinkled brains and mushrooms, while others look like pillars, tabletops, moose antlers, wire strands, or cabbages.

Coral reefs provide a habitat for a wide range of sea creatures, including mollusks and urchins. Sea fans, anemones, and sponges fasten onto the coral. Small creatures find nourishment and protections amid the coral, and in turn attract large sea species like sea turtles, rays, and sharks.

The building block of the coral reef is the coral polyp, a tiny, soft creature that attaches itself to hard surfaces in shallow sea areas. Polyps can range from the size of a pinhead to that of a football. The polyps have slit-like "mouths" at their top, surrounded by tentacles, which they use to sting and trap food—mainly plankton. Cells on the bottom of the polyps produce calcium carbonate, which builds islands and reefs. When a polyp dies, it hardens into "rock," creating the reefs that we know.

Coral reefs grow slowly. While some reefs can grow as much as two feet per year, most grow only a few inches. The coral reefs that exist in the Virgin Islands have been growing for millions of years.

Small algae called zooxanthellae live

symbiotically within coral polyps. The algae get shelter and food from the polyp, while the polyp gets food from the algae via photosynthesis. Photosynthesis requires sunlight, so coral reefs can only grow where the ocean is shallow and clear. Coral also requires ocean currents, which bring it plankton, the tiny organisms that sustain it, and warm ocean temperatures—between 75 and 85 degrees.

The polyps and algae are a food source for other sea creatures, and the reef's caves and crevices are ideal locations for breeding and protection from large predators. More than one-quarter of all marine life is found in coral reefs.

Life on the Reef

Coral reefs are cities under the sea. Even when the surface of the sea is glassy and there is not a sound except the wind, the underwater reef is teeming with life. It is a joy to float above and observe.

There are two main types of coral: hard coral and soft coral. Hard coral, the bricks and mortar of the coral reef, takes on a fantastic array of shapes and colors. **Elkhorn coral** looks like clusters of antlers reaching out sideways toward the surface of the ocean. **Brain coral** colonies are spheres imprinted with a pattern that makes them look remarkably like brains. **Pillar corals** grow like candelabras reaching to the sea surface, and **staghorn coral** looks like great colonies of orange starfish. Pay particular attention to **fire coral,** yellow stony coral that looks something like giant lichen. A brush against one of these can leave you with painful cuts.

Like hard coral, soft coral is made up of colonies of coral polyps. But unlike hard corals, soft corals have skeletons consisting of needles encased in softer, more flexible material. **Sea fans** are a common kind of soft coral. Others resemble whips and plumes.

A host of other sea creatures live among

Sea urchins live in tidal pools and shallow reefs.

the coral. **Sea anemones** are soft, translucent tentacled creatures often seen anchored in cracks between the reef. The sharp, black barbs of **sea urchins** can easily be seen poking out from under and between rocks. There are many types of **sea sponges**—soft, multicellular animals that act as filters for the ocean. Crustaceans including **lobsters** and **crabs** are also found on the reef, often beneath a dark ledge. It takes a practiced eye to find these reclusive animals.

Fish, of course, are the star of the show on the coral reef. They dart around, nibbling, weaving in and out of the current, showing colors ranging from deep purple to bright yellow and every hue in between. One of the most common reef fish is the **parrot fish,** which comes in colors ranging from red to rainbow to black. Look closely and you will see its distinctive fused teeth, which it uses to scrape chunks of coral into its mouth. Using a mill at the back of its throat, the parrot fish grinds the coral into a powder, which is excreted as sand.

The yellowtail **damselfish** begins life a vivid shade of dark blue with bright blue spots before turning to a nondescript brown as an adult. Look for the feelers on the lower lip of the **goatfish.** One of the most common types of reef fish is the **wrasse,** a small fish which often has bright stripes of color near its head. **Triggerfish,** one of many types of fish that can change colors based on its surroundings, are distinguished by their tails, which extend to two long points.

Some fish have very distinctive shapes. **Trunkfish** are easy to spot because of their triangular build. Long and thin, the **trumpet fish** eats by sucking unsuspecting fish into its vacuum-like mouth. You will often encounter them standing on their heads to mimic some part of the underwater landscape. Colorful **angelfish** are flat and can grow to be the size of a dinner plate. They swim elegantly around the reef and will surely catch your eye. **Butterfly**

fish resemble angelfish but are distinguishable by a large black dot near their tails, meant to confuse predators.

Look out for **squid,** easily recognized by their large white eyes, which look almost human. Most reef squid are small—about a foot long—and can be seen swimming around just like a fish. The **octopus,** on the other hand, often hides.

One of the greatest joys of snorkeling on the reef is seeing a school of fish. Near shore, you may find yourself engulfed in a mass of tiny fry. Pop your head above water and you will no doubt see pelicans diving for dinner. On the reef, schooling species include goatfish, grunts (named for a noise they make), and spadefish. You may also encounter schools of jacks and silversides.

You will also see larger sea creatures on the coral reef, attracted by the presence of so much potential food. **Hawksbill turtles,** one of the three kinds of sea turtle in the Virgin Islands, look for food and shelter around the reef. **Green turtles** prefer sea grass beds, and **leatherbacks** are most often seen in the open ocean.

MAMMALS

The only indigenous mammal in the Virgin Islands is the bat. All others were introduced by people who migrated through and eventually settled in the islands. Pre-Columbians introduced dogs, pigs, guinea pigs, and agoutis (although the latter two have not survived in the wild). European settlers introduced a wide range of domesticated animals, including goats, sheep, horses, and white-tail deer.

Europeans are also responsible for two of the islands' worst pests: the rat, which arrived as a stowaway on ships, and the mongoose, introduced to kill rats that had taken up residence in sugarcane fields. The mongoose was a disappointment to rat control; it was active during the day (while rats slept) and could not climb trees in pursuit of the more agile rodents.

Instead, mongooses fed on lizards, birds, turtle eggs, and chickens. They have been responsible for wiping out whole species of lizards on some islands. Today, mongooses remain a problem for conservationists and farmers.

BIRDS

Birds are some of the most delightful animals of the Virgin Islands, and birders will be rewarded by the colors, acrobatics, and songs of the island residents.

Near the sea, there is usually no better show than the one put on by **pelicans,** which glide (look: no wing flapping) far above the ocean surface only to crash down with incredible force, gathering tiny fish and other sea creatures in their pouches. Pelicans have special air chambers on their chest and special film over their eyes to cushion the sea landing.

One of the most easily identifiable shorebirds is the **magnificent frigate bird,** sometimes called a man-o-war. This long-winged black bird with a forked tail and bent wings looks like a holdover from the dinosaur era. Male frigate birds have a strip of bright red skin on their throats, which they blow up like a balloon to attract females during mating season. Frigate birds catch fish at the surface of the sea, but their biggest food source is in the air; they chase other seabirds fiercely until they drop their catch. Then the frigatebird glides down to catch it.

Look out as well for **brown boobies, laughing gulls, royal terns,** and **tropic birds.** Boobies, now endangered, got their name from the Spanish word *bobo,* meaning "dunce." They are large and excellent divers. Caribbean gulls are smaller than the seagulls many are used to; listen to their song, "ha, ha, ha, ha." Tropic birds are elegant and beautiful. Look for the long streamers that extend from their tails.

Inland, birds are smaller and much more difficult to watch. Flower gardens tend to attract **doctor birds** and **green-throated caribs.**

One of the favorite birds of the island **bananaquit,** a ubiquitous and cheerful tures you will see in flower gardens and forest. They have a wheezy, squeaky call and build untidy nests of grass and leaves. They often have bright yellow bellies, set off by black around the head.

Many open-air restaurants suffer an abundance of **Carib grackles,** medium-size birds that make sport of eating crumbs, leftovers, and even whole meals from diners' plates. There are two kinds of doves on the islands: the **common ground dove** and the **zenaida dove,** also called turtledove.

The mascot of the Charlotte Amalie High School athletics department is the **chickenhawk.** These common hawks can be seen soaring high above farms, fields, and woodland. They keep an eye out for favorite food sources: snakes, lizards, frogs, and rats.

Another bird that is easy to see is the **cattle egret,** a long-legged white heron that follows cattle, sometimes on their backs. These birds are natives of Africa and were first reported in the Caribbean in 1933.

REPTILES AND AMPHIBIANS

Many travelers are taken aback by the pulsing, almost deafening, song of the bo-peeps, or **coquis,** at night. The call of these small frogs is often at first mistaken for the sound of crickets or cicadas. In the rainforest, they sing all day; in drier habitats, they sing only at night. Listen closely, and you will hear that they are saying their name: "ko-kee, ko-kee."

Less melodious is the song of the **giant toad,** a brown, blotchy creature that can grow as large as a softball. These toads hide out during the day but often sing the praises of the rain at night.

One of the most delightful animals in the Virgin Islands is the lizard. Newcomers never fail to delight in their omnipresence, agile movement, and—in some cases—impressive shows. The most common kind of lizard is the **ground**

wn lizard that munches
rds change colors to suit
nd males have rounded
ts. When they want to
males will inflate their
do "push-ups" in place. The third
common type of lizard is the **house gecko,** or
wood slave. These helpful creatures are used to
people and are often found inside. House geckos
have Velcro-like feet that allow them to climb
on just about any surface. They feed on insects
(they are great for killing mosquitoes that make
it inside) and are active at night.

CRABS

It is easier to see the zigzagging tracks of the
ghost crab than to spot the animal itself,
which can scurry sideways so quickly it seems
to disappear. Ghost crabs live on the beach,
burrowing into the sand for protection and
safety. Farther inland, it is the **land crab,**
or white crab, that dominates. These large,
whitish crabs have one claw larger than the
other and are sometimes eaten. Another very
common crab is the **hermit crab.** Although
associated with the sea, these crabs are found
miles away from the shore and high up on
mountainsides. Many take up residence in
the shells of West Indian top snails. When
hermit crabs outgrow their shells, they have
to find new ones. Hermit crabs will eat just
about anything, including rat poison, car-
rion, and feces. Their flesh is a traditional
fish bait.

History

The Virgin Islands have been defined by their
history. The islands possess a rich legacy of pre-
Columbian settlement, and the physical, cultural, and economic footprint of the plantation
era—its contradictions, cruelties, and extravagance—remains. In more modern times, waves
of immigrants have enriched the islands' culture, and economic and natural challenges have
defined the Virgin Islander's resilient character.

EARLY PEOPLES

Four waves of pre-Columbian settlers found
homes in the Virgin Islands: the Ciboney,
Igneri, Taino, and Kalinago peoples. Each
group arrived in the Virgin Islands from South
America, and each brought new advances in
crop cultivation, social structure, and tools.

Ciboney

The first humans are thought to have been
present in the Virgin Islands as early as
2200 B.C. These earliest islanders, called
Ciboney by the Spanish and Ortoiroid by
today's archaeologists, were fisher-foragers who
did not make pottery or cultivate plants. They
lived nomadically and used crude stone tools to
prepare food. Shellfish was probably an important part of their diet.

The Ciboney lived in crude shelters, fash-
ioned out of palm fronds and other material
at hand. Social organization was primitive;
families who lived and traveled together con-
stituted a single band, without organized leadership. Archaeological evidence of these Stone
Age people has been discovered at Krum Bay,
St. Thomas, and Brewer's Bay, Tortola.

Igneri

The next wave was the Igneri, or Saladoid, people, who migrated from South America around
400 B.C. and lived undisturbed in the Virgin
Islands for almost 1,000 years. They cultivated
crops, including yucca and cassava. In addition
to fish, the flesh of the agouti, a ratlike animal
they raised, was their primary source of protein.

The Igneri knew how to make pottery and

© SUSANNA HENIGHAN POTTER

Archaeology interns excavate at Cinnamon Bay, once the site of a large Taino settlement.

produced thin griddles on which they cooked cassava. They lived in communal round houses.

Taino

Much more is known about the third and most sophisticated group of pre-Columbians to live in the Virgin Islands. These people, defined by a different style of pottery and more advanced cultivation and social systems, have become known as Taino (the Arawaks of popular legend). Tainos lived throughout the Virgin Islands beginning around A.D. 100; archaeologists have found evidence of Taino settlement at some 32 sites on Tortola alone. The Salt River Bay area of St. Croix is widely believed to be an important Taino settlement and has been studied extensively. Digs at Cinnamon Bay, St. John, and Hull Bay, St. Thomas, have unearthed evidence of Taino settlements at those locations.

Tainos traveled between islands in large canoes. Their caciques (chiefs) arbitrated disputes, oversaw cultivation and hunting, and made decisions about the future of the village. Cacique was a hereditary position.

Ornamentation was important to the Tainos, for it was linked to their religious beliefs. In their worship they used zemis—idols made of wood, stone, bone, shell, and clay—through which they worshipped the gods and sought to exert control over them. The Taino god of wind and water, Jurakan, is the namesake of today's hurricanes. Some zemis were believed to influence the weather, crops, hunting, wealth, and childbirth. Religious leaders called *behiques* communicated with the gods and healed the sick and injured.

Taino villages were typically a ring of circular huts. The cacique lived in a large rectangular house with his wives; commoners lived in round thatched-roof huts with dirt floors and one door. They slept in hammocks.

Tainos enjoyed parties. They created castanets out of stone and used them to make music. Both men and women played a ball game using a rubber ball. Evidence of ball courts has been found at Belmont, Tortola, and Salt River Bay, St. Croix.

Kalinago

The final wave of pre-Columbian people arrived in the Virgin Islands shortly before Christopher Columbus's "discovery" of the islands. The Kalinago (popularly known as Caribs) were a martial society that had made its way northward from South America, conquering the more peaceful Tainos along the way. Defeated Taino males were killed or taken as slaves, while Taino women were absorbed into the Kalinago society.

It was a Kalinago village that Columbus and his men set upon on November 1493, when they sailed into Salt River Bay, St. Croix, but archaeologists do not know whether the Kalinago had reached St. Thomas, St. John, or the other islands at that time. No archaeological evidence has been unearthed that they had, and since Columbus and his fleet did not stop at any of the other Virgin Islands, no documentary evidence exists either.

The myth that the Kalinago were cannibals has never been substantiated, and, if they did eat human flesh, it is almost certain they did so for ceremonial purposes only. More likely, the myth came from the Kalinago's fierce nature and the fact that their way of honoring the dead was to hang their bones in pots from the rafters of their homes—a practice misinterpreted by the Spanish who came into contact with them. The Spanish, who originated the myth of the cannibalistic Carib, benefited from its spread because it justified their ruthless extermination of the islands' native populations.

Like Taino marriages, Kalinago marriages were polygamous, although not every man could afford to have more than one wife. For Tainos, it was the caciques who were most likely to have multiple wives; for the Kalinago it was the warriors. Believing that it made them more

beautiful, the Kalinago flattened the front and back of their children's heads.

The Kalinago social organization was looser than that of the Taino; Kalinago culture emphasized physical prowess and individualism. While settlements had a leader, his authority was limited. War chiefs were chosen from among villagers based on their skill in battle. The Kalinago lived separated by gender; the men lived together in a large building called a *carbet,* while the women lived in smaller houses. Tobacco was the standard of exchange.

Kalinago military dominance was due to the culture's focus on training and their development of more deadly weapons than the Taino had. Young Kalinago men were trained as children to be warriors, and the values of courage and endurance were highly valued. The bow and arrow was the most common Kalinago weapon; poison from deadly plants was used on the tip of the arrow to increase the chance of death. The Kalinago depended on the element of surprise in achieving military victories.

Demise

Within 100 years of Spanish arrival in the Caribbean, there were no more indigenous people living in the Virgin Islands. Some were captured as slaves to work in Spanish gold mines, and others fled southward to islands farther away from the Spanish strongholds of Puerto Rico and Hispaniola. The Caribbean island of Dominica still has a "Carib" community—descendants of these people.

Others stayed put and fought their new Spanish neighbors. St. Croix's Caribs, as the Spanish called them, violently opposed Spanish settlement of the region; the new Spanish settlement on Puerto Rico was the target of numerous raids and attacks between 1510 and 1530. On one raid, the Caribs killed the newly appointed governor of the colony. In response to the aggression, the Spanish crown formally gave its settlers in the region license to hunt and kill Caribs in 1512, a move that marked the beginning of the end for the remaining Virgin Islands native people. Although they continued to raid and attack Puerto Rico between 1520 and 1530, they were ultimately no match for the Spanish. By 1590, and probably well before that on most of the islands, indigenous people had disappeared from the Virgin Islands.

Today, there are no native people in the Virgin Islands. Only a few of their words—such as hurricane, hammock, and barbecue—remain.

EXPLORATION

Christopher Columbus (or Cristóbal Colón, as the Spanish knew him) sailed through the Virgin Islands in November 1493, during his second voyage to the New World. The admiral's first voyage in 1492 had taken him to the Bahamas, Cuba, and Hispaniola. On Christmas Eve 1492, his flagship, the Santa Maria, grounded on a reef and sank off Hispaniola. Columbus and his men salvaged what they could from the ship to build a settlement for the 40 men he would have to leave behind at what he called La Navidad.

The aim of Columbus's second voyage was settlement. Seventeen ships and more than 1,000 men departed the Canary Islands on October 13, 1493. The fleet made good time across the Atlantic and spotted the island of Dominica on November 3, 1493. They sailed northward along the northern Leeward Islands until November 13, when they reached a large, fertile, and well-populated island that Columbus decided to name Santa Cruz (the Holy Cross).

Columbus sent some of his men ashore at Salt River Bay for freshwater and, some reports claim, to capture natives who could tell him where he was. When the advance party was returning to the fleet, it encountered a canoe carrying four Carib men, two Carib women, and two Taino slaves. A fight between the two parties ensued; Columbus's men overturned the canoe while the Caribs peppered the Europeans with poison arrows. Columbus's party was impressed by the Caribs' prowess as warriors. Columbus's son, Don Fernando, wrote later about one Carib who kept shooting after the canoe was upset "as if he had been on dry land."

Columbus named the area in front of Salt River Bay the Cape of Arrows after the skirmish. In the end, one member of Columbus's party died, and one Carib was killed. The rest of the native party was taken as prisoners and eventually transported to Spain. It was, no doubt, a terrible fate for these captured people. A glimpse of their treatment is given by Columbus's crewman Michele de Cuneo, who recorded matter-of-factly the details of his sexual assault on "a very beautiful Carib woman whom the Lord Admiral gave to me."

After the skirmish at St. Croix, Columbus divided his fleet; the small caravels, including the one in which he rode, sailed northward through what is now Drake's Channel. As he sailed, Columbus was impressed by the number of small islands before him and named them Las Virgenes, after the then-popular myth of St. Ursula and her 11,000 virgin martyrs killed by the Huns. St. Ursula remains on the official seal of the British Virgin Islands. The second half of Columbus's fleet remained south and sailed straight for the eastern end of Puerto Rico, where the two parties met up and continued on their way to Hispaniola.

Although Columbus did not stop to explore these islands, he did name many of them. During the passage he labeled Virgin Gorda (Fat Virgin) and gave Tortola the name Santa Ana, which did not stick.

Other early explorers passed through the islands but did not settle. Ponce de Leon led voyages in the area in the early 16th century and Sir Sebastian Cabot and Sir Thomas Pert passed through in 1517 after exploring Brazilian waters. Sir John Hawkins sailed through in 1563 with his first cargo of African slaves for Hispaniola. On a third voyage, Hawkins sailed with young Francis Drake. After being knighted, Drake returned to the Virgin Islands in 1585, where he mustered his fleet in North Sound, Virgin Gorda, for what would be a disastrous attack on the Spanish settlement on Puerto Rico. The main passage through the island group now bears Drake's name. Eleven years later, the Earl of Cumberland used the same North Sound as a staging area for a more successful attack on Puerto Rico.

Piracy

The stories of pirates in the Virgin Islands are long on legend and short on fact, but that has not stopped many of these tales from remaining popular today. St. Thomas's Bluebeard and Blackbeard's Castles really have nothing to do with piracy—they were fortifications built to protect Charlotte Amalie Harbor from enemy attack. History knows nothing about a pirate called Bluebeard. Blackbeard is the pirate Edward Teach, who plundered Caribbean trading ships from 1716 to 1718. Whether he had any special affiliation with St. Thomas is unknown, but he did travel through the Virgin Islands.

The true history of piracy in the Virgin Islands is relatively short. From 1680 to 1684, under the leadership of brothers Adolph and Nicolaj Esmit, St. Thomas developed a reputation for tolerating and even indulging piracy. In 1683, Adolph Esmit was accused of offering safe harbor to *La Trompeuse,* a pirate ship captained by Jean Hamlin. The British ship *HMS Francis,* captained by Charles Carlile and sent to hunt the pirate ship, sailed into St. Thomas's harbor and found *La Trompeuse* alongside five other known pirate vessels. While Carlile made plans to burn the pirate ship, Esmit sheltered the pirates, including Hamlin himself, who reportedly found accommodation at Fort

Christian, the official residence. Esmit flouted English threats by not only refusing to hand Hamlin over to them, but also by selling him a new ship.

The Esmits lost power in 1684, and subsequent governors of St. Thomas were not so tolerant of the illegal trade. In 1698, pirate Bartholomew Sharp was imprisoned for life and his property confiscated; a year later St. Thomas governor Johan Lorentz forbade Captain Kidd from entering St. Thomas's harbor.

Tales of piracy abound in the British Virgin Islands, too, fueled by the legend of treasure found on Norman Island.

COLONIZATION

Early European settlements in the islands were tenuous. The Virgin Islands, like the rest of the Caribbean, were the stage for European battles for supremacy. Alliances and enemies changed quickly; depending on your perspective, marauding ships were either pirate or patriot. Disease, war, and economic uncertainty made life difficult and unpredictable.

From 1493 until the late 1500s, settlements in the Virgin Islands were actively discouraged by the Spanish, who had established a colony on nearby Puerto Rico. Some historians say that the Spanish established a small mining outpost on Virgin Gorda in the first half of the 16th century, further discouraging other European powers.

By the beginning of the 17th century, Spanish supremacy was fading, and other European powers grew intent on settling the islands. There is evidence of Dutch and English settlements on St. Croix as early as 1625. In the British Virgin Islands, there are records of English settlements in 1640 and 1646, and a French settlement in 1648. Early settlers were a hardy bunch, drawn by the lure of adventure, the possibility of profits, and, in some cases, desperation.

British Virgin Islands

The earliest European settlement on Tortola dates back to 1649, when Dutch settlers arrived. They lived in relative peace until war broke out between the Dutch and the English in 1665. During that war the English attacked Tortola, destroyed the Dutch settlements, and took 67 enslaved African they found there. This is the first record of the presence of slaves in the British Virgin Islands.

The Dutch returned after the 1665 attack, and three years later a report describes the population of Tortola as "80 Irish, English, and Welsh under the Dutch." The English and Dutch did not remain at peace, however, and during another war in 1672 the Dutch settlement was again attacked by the English. This time, the Dutch surrendered before a drop of blood could be shed. The islands became British, and they remain so today.

The future remained uncertain for settlers of the British Virgin Islands even after the Dutch surrender in 1672. During peace negotiations after the war between England and the Netherlands, it was agreed that the Virgin Islands would eventually be handed back over to the Dutch. This never happened, but the uncertainty over the islands' future discouraged large-scale settlement and investment. The islands became home to people who could not get land on other, more prosperous, islands.

U.S. Virgin Islands

Meanwhile, the Danes grew interested in establishing a Caribbean colony. **St. Thomas,** still unsettled and possessing a good natural harbor, caught their eye. Their first attempt at colonizing St. Thomas came in 1665, under the leadership of Captain Erik Nielson Smith. Settlers of a number of different nationalities were recruited and began to establish trading facilities and clear the land for plantations. The colony weathered attacks from English privateers,

sickness, and even a hurricane before it was abandoned 19 months later.

The Danes' second attempt at colonization took place in 1672, when the *Faero* set sail for the West Indies with 190 people on board. The Danes had recruited a diverse bunch of settlers for St. Thomas. The 128 Danish West India Company employees were indentured servants, contracted to work for the company for between three and five years. The remaining 62 people were recruited from prisons and poorhouses in Denmark.

When the *Faero* arrived on St. Thomas in May 1672, their numbers had declined to just 104—9 had escaped and 77 died. During the first seven months of the colony's life, another 75 people died, leaving a bare 29 people in the nascent colony. Dutch, German, English, French, Norwegian, Swedish, Scottish, Irish, Flemish, and Jewish settlers arrived and grew the colony. By 1680 there were 156 Whites and 175 slaves on the island.

An eight-year tax holiday announced in 1688 drew even more settlers, including French Huguenots and many more Dutch. By 1715 the island's population had increased to 547 Whites and more than 3,000 slaves. St. Thomas's plantation economy grew in tandem with its population. In 1688 there were 90 surveyed plantations on the island; by 1720 there were 164. Cultivation on the island peaked in 1725, with 177 plantations.

St. Croix's early years were a time of shifting alliances and uncertainty. Although Columbus claimed St. Croix for the Spanish when he sailed by in 1493, the Spaniards made no attempt to colonize the island, probably because of the continued presence of hostile indigenous people there. Early European settlers on St. Croix were English, French, and Dutch adventurers who established tentative settlements under constant threat of attack. By 1650, the French had the upper hand on the island and developed a small-scale plantation

Slaves were transported to the Virgin Islands on overcrowded slave ships. Many did not survive this horrific Middle Passage.

St. John was the last of the Virgin Islands to be substantially settled by Europeans. Danish attempts to settle the island in 1675 and again in 1684 failed, in part because of disturbances by the English, who had claimed nearby Tortola in 1672, and in part because the Danes were preoccupied with establishing their colony on St. Thomas. By the early 1700s, St. Thomas was thriving and its harbor was one of the busiest in the Caribbean. Agriculture had taken a backseat to commerce, and planters were looking for an island that could provide space for plantations. St. John fit the bill.

In 1718, the Danish West India Company sent 20 planters, 5 soldiers, and 16 slaves to St. John to begin dividing, settling, and cultivating the island. To lure settlers, the Danes offered a seven-year tax hiatus and welcomed all nationalities. The deal attracted a number of established St. Thomas planters, who remained on St. Thomas but hired overseers to manage their St. John plantations. The opportunity also drew a number of poor settlers who started by cultivating cotton, indigo, and tobacco in the hopes of raising the capital required to set up a sugar plantation.

PLANTATION ERA

Political stability and the availability of capital led to growth of the Virgin Islands' plantation economy. On the flat, fertile plain of St. Croix, plantations were set neatly next to each other, windmills dotting the landscape. On the other, more hilly islands, slaves cleared whole hillsides of native forest and terraced the slopes for the cultivation of sugar. The plantation era was one of contradictions and great cruelty. For planters, it was often a gamble; fortunes were won and lost in a single growing season. For the enslaved Africans who produced the wealth, it was brutal and dehumanizing.

Africans who survived the devastating Middle Passage from Africa's west coast were auctioned in markets at Charlotte Amalie,

colony, where they produced indigo, cotton, and sugar.

The French abandoned St. Croix in 1696 in favor of Haiti, and the island was virtually unoccupied until 1733, when it was sold to the Danes. It was the first time title to a West Indian island had been exchanged by means other than warfare. Denmark sent its first shipment of materials and men to St. Croix in August 1734, under the command of Frederik Moth, who had been named governor of the island. About 150 British people, who were living on the island with about 450 slaves, were allowed to stay if they pledged allegiance to the king of Denmark. The island was promptly surveyed and subdivided into 400 estates, which were sold to aspiring planters from Europe and the surrounding Caribbean colonies. The opportunity attracted Danes, Scots, English, Dutch, Irish, and Sephardic Jews.

Christiansted, and Road Town and worked, some to death, on the plantations. Those who endured performed the grueling work of clearing land and planting and harvesting sugarcane.

Danish West Indies

By the end of the 18th century, St. Croix was second only to Jamaica in sugar production per acre. In 1800, the island had the fourth largest sugar product in the Caribbean. The colony's success meant planters and their families could afford to lead lives of opulence. Many of the island's elaborate estate houses date back to the period from 1760 to 1820, the heyday of the plantation period.

On St. John, the plantation era began with Danish settlement. A 1733 slave rebellion caused some planters to pull out of the island, but others remained. Many St. John plantations were owned by absentee planters.

While St. Croix and St. John grew in importance as sugar islands, St. Thomas turned its focus away from agriculture and toward trade. Delegations from the colony to Denmark in the early 18th century led to easing of trade restrictions, which allowed ships of all nations to trade in St. Thomas on payment of fixed import and export duties. Over the coming decades, trade restrictions were further eased, until St. Thomas became a free port in 1764. Denmark's declared neutrality allowed St. Thomas to flourish even in times of war.

British Virgin Islands

The British islands got off to a slow start with the plantation industry. Uncertainty about the islands' ownership discouraged investment, so while the Danish West Indies were being cultivated with sugar (which required major capital investment), plantations on the British islands continued to produce cotton, indigo, ginger, and coffee—all of which required little investment but yielded much more modest profits.

The plantation era began in earnest in the British Virgin Islands in 1747, when an Englishman named James Purcell was appointed lieutenant governor of the territory. Purcell lobbied for local government and traveled to Liverpool, England, to seek financing for Tortola's planters. Purcell's efforts bore fruit. Financing was provided, and plantations all around the island turned to sugar cultivation.

It is during this time that whole hillsides of native timber were cut down to make space for sugar fields and many of the fortifications now in ruin around the island were built. James Purcell died in 1759 and was succeeded by his brother, John Purcell, who continued to govern over peace and prosperity. In 1774, the same year that sugar production reached its peak on Tortola, representative government was established for the first time—another sign of the colony's development.

SLAVERY

Prosperity for planters meant something entirely different for the enslaved Africans brought to the islands to provide the labor that fueled the plantation economy. During the most prosperous years of plantation life here, slave ships sailed to St. Thomas, St. Croix, and Tortola with cargo directly from Africa. Newly arrived Africans were given one week of "seasoning" to recuperate from the horrific Middle Passage from Africa before being put to work; mortality rates among newly arrived slaves were as high as 30 percent.

Slave Life

Most slaves lived in mud and thatch huts on their plantations, except for the slave driver, or *bomba,* who often lived in a wooden house. Field slaves worked from sunup to sundown, with longer hours during the arduous sugar harvest period. Slaves were often given small patches of land on which they were expected to

MAKING SUGAR

© SUSANNA HENIGHAN POTTER

Bowls called coppers were used in the manufacture of sugar in the Virgin Islands. Here, an intact copper is visible at Annaberg Plantation on St. John.

A lot of work went into producing sugar on a 17th- or 18th-century sugar plantation in the Virgin Islands.

The process began with the clearing of huge swaths of land on which cane would be planted. Slaves would use machetes to clear the brush, let the cut brush dry out, and then burn the dried brush. Heavy rocks also had to be cleared from the land, and on hilly islands like St. John and Tortola, terraces were cut into the hills to provide space to grow the cane.

Once the land was cleared, cane was planted. Sugarcane takes between 12 and 15 months to mature, and during this time slaves were put to work weeding and fertilizing the crops and building the sugarworks.

When the time came for harvest and production, the plantation worked 24 hours a day. The cane was cut and carried to the sugar factory, where it had to be crushed within 24 hours of its cutting. The long canes were run through wheels that crushed the cane and extracted juice, which ran into a reservoir beneath the wheels. Cane crushers were powered either by wind or animal. On flat islands like St. Croix, windmills were common, but on hilly islands, where you were less assured of a good, steady breeze, animals were relied upon.

Once the cane juice was gathered, it was poured into a series of "coppers"—large round bowls placed over fires. The fires were carefully regulated so the cane juice never boiled but stayed hot enough to slowly evaporate until a thick syrup was all that was left. A skilled slave, called the boilerman, kept close watch over the pot. When he declared it was time to "strike" the sugar, the liquid was quickly removed from the heat and placed in a cooling pan, where it would stay until crystals began to form.

At this stage the sugar was transferred to pyramid-shaped bags that hung from the ceiling of the curing house. Any remaining liquid ran out, leaving a pure block of sugar.

produce food for themselves and their families, which was augmented by meager provisions from their owner. Each slave was supposed to receive one new piece of clothing each year but on some occasions got none.

Slaves in the British Virgin Islands were subject to unfettered brutality, in part because of a Slave Code now noted as one of the most repressive in the entire Caribbean region. One report from Tortola tells of a planter stabbing a slave through the heart because he did not like the meal she prepared. In another case, slaves who executed a rebellion on Josiah's Bay Plantation in 1790 were tortured for days and then put to death in a public execution. In the Danish islands, authorities responded to the 1733 St. John rebellion by instituting repressive rules against slave gatherings.

The miracle of slavery is that the slaves not only survived but developed a rich culture and strong character despite oppression and brutality. Most plantations allowed slaves one and a half days off each week. On Saturday afternoons they were expected to cultivate their own crops, on which they depended for food, and on Sundays they rested.

Many slaves found ways to earn money, some developing skills that allowed them to buy their freedom and the freedom of their families. A market was held on Sunday mornings in Charlotte Amalie, Christiansted, Frederiksted, Road Town, and other villages, where slaves would bring produce and other goods to sell. Slaves also depended on their religious beliefs. Before missionaries began Christianizing slaves in the late 1700s, many slaves practiced the religions of Africa, labeled obeah today. These religions involved belief in various gods, and also knowledge of bush medicine and other healing methods. Recognizing the threat of the slaves' religious gatherings and beliefs, authorities passed laws making obeah illegal. It remains illegal in the British Virgin Islands today.

EMANCIPATION

By the turn of the 19th century, doubts were increasing about slavery. Abolitionists in the United States and Europe were gaining strength, and social changes were bringing about a greater awareness of human rights and freedoms. The Haitian revolution of 1804 had forced the issue of slavery and freedom to the forefront. Between 1834 and 1886, slavery would be abolished in the Caribbean.

The end of slavery did not automatically address the social and economic oppression experienced by Africans in the islands, but it was the first in a long series of steps toward equality and empowerment, a process that continues today.

British Virgin Islands

As the plantation industry in the British Virgin Islands grew, doubts about slavery were developing in England. Abolitionists fought for decades against the slave trade and slavery itself, eventually prevailing in 1807 when Parliament ended the transatlantic slave trade. The act meant no more Africans could be brought to the New World as slaves but did not necessarily improve the lives of slaves already in the region. Nor did it end the slave trade within the Caribbean, and many slaves from small, declining territories like the British Virgin Islands were sent to colonies still experiencing growth.

In 1811, the trial and hanging of Tortola planter Arthur Hodge for the murder of his slave, Prosper, further fueled concern over the treatment of slaves in the British West Indian colonies. The case received attention in England and throughout the West Indies, and testimony about Hodge's brutal treatment of Prosper and other slaves further turned public opinion against slavery.

Also, the slaves themselves were changing. Methodist missionaries arrived on the island in 1789 and were the first Christians to minister directly to the slaves. The Methodists soon had a following of more than 2,000 slaves, and

QUELBE MUSIC

A panel from the Fahie Hill Mural in the British Virgin Islands depicts men and women dancing to traditional fungi music.

The traditional music of the Virgin Islands is quelbe, also called scratch or fungi. A quelbe band consists of a banjo, a conga drum, a squash, and a triangle. Other instruments sometimes included are guitar, bass, saxophone, and flute. Quelbe musicians use objects close at hand to construct their instruments, although today some have adopted more modern instruments. The banjo was often made out of an old sardine can. The squash was a dried local gourd, serrated and then scratched with a comb or wire-pronged stick. The bass line was usually provided by someone blowing into the discarded tailpipe of a car.

Quelbe music developed on sugar plantations, where slaves used materials at hand to provide a rhythm and melody to which they could tell stories, share jokes, and spread gossip. The music was influenced by African rhythms and the sound of Danish and British military bands. Quelbe music grew in popularity as the restrictions of slavery ended and the music form could spread freely. Many older Virgin Islanders have sweet memories of nights spent dancing to the sound of the village quelbe band.

Quelbe music still tells stories and jokes, often with a risqué undertone. Quelbe is especially popular at Christmastime, providing a new and refreshing take on Christmas music.

Traditionally, quelbe bands would go serenading in the wee hours of Christmas morning, wishing their neighbors a merry Christmas.

Today, quelbe music is being preserved by a handful of bands. In the British Virgin Islands, the Lashing Dogs and Loverboys perform fungi music (as it is called there) at bars and festivals. In the U.S. Virgin Islands, Jamesie and the Allstars, Stanley and the Ten Sleepless Nights, Bully and the Kafooners, and Blinky and the Roadmasters carry on the tradition. Jamesie Brewster, the leader of Jamesie and the Allstars, was the subject of a documentary. You can hear a snippet of his music at www.jamesieproject.com.

The British Virgin Islands host Fungi Fest, a two-day fungi music festival, in November.

The traditional accompaniment to quelbe music is the quadrille, a kind of square dancing introduced to the Virgin Islands from the French Caribbean and influenced by English and Irish planters. Quadrille or not, it is impossible to stand still listening to quelbe music. St. Croix culture bearer and writer Richard Schrader wrote in his book *Maufe, Quelbe, and t'ing* that when Jamesie Brewster performs, "trees shake their branches and grass bends down low." That just about sums it up.

in 1823 the Methodist church opened the first Sunday school on the island, a small but important step toward education.

In 1790 and 1821, slaves at Josiah's Bay rioted in response to rumors that their owner was withholding freedom from them and that he was going to send them to Trinidad. While both riots were ultimately put down, planters were frightened.

Economic forces also caused planters to lose interest in their plantations. Sugar prices fell during the first half of the 19th century, after the discovery of a way to extract sugar from the sugar beet, which could grow in Europe. At the same time, the cost of maintaining slaves was higher since they could no longer be worked to death and then replaced. Finally, a major hurricane hit the islands on September 22, 1819, destroying 100 of the 104 plantations in cultivation. Many planters decided not to rebuild after the storm.

These factors and others led to the end of slavery in the British West Indian colonies, including the British Virgin Islands, on August 1, 1832. Historians disagree on how the emancipation proclamation was communicated in the British Virgin Islands. Some say it was read aloud at the Sunday Morning Well in Road Town, where a plaque now hangs. Others say it was more likely announced in churches around the territory.

Today, Tortola celebrates its annual Emancipation Festival on the first Monday in August in commemoration of the slaves' first days of freedom.

Danish West Indies

Slavery persisted in the Danish colonies for 16 years longer than in the British islands. After the British ended slavery in 1832, Denmark knew it had to plan for emancipation in its colonies. In 1840, the Danish king proposed a scheme where slaves would be given an extra day off per week, during which they could work for their owner for wages and eventually buy their freedom. While some planters agreed to giving slaves an additional free day, few agreed to pay them, and the proposal was not accepted.

In 1847 another proposal was made, this one accepted by both Danish officials and planters. Under the plan all babies born to slaves would be free from that date on, but adult slaves would have to wait 12 years before freedom would be granted. While the Danes had consulted extensively with planters on the plan, no one had thought it necessary to consider the opinion of the slaves themselves, a decision that proved to be shortsighted. On July 3, 1848, thousands of slaves on St. Croix rose up, led by a young slave named Buddhoe, to demand their freedom. The disturbance moved through the countryside to Fort Frederik, where the slaves lay down their single demand: freedom. A deadline of noon came and went with no sign of freedom or the governor, Peter von Scholten, who had the authority to grant it. In response, the slaves wrested the hated "justice post," where many slaves had been beaten and killed, from its position near the fort and threw it in the water. Buddhoe uttered an ultimatum: "Freedom by four o'clock or we burn the town."

Von Scholten arrived in Frederiksted before 4 P.M. and went into the fort, where he consulted with planters and officials. Von Scholten, faced with a crowd of some 8,000 slaves, rejected their counsel, instead uttering the words that soon became famous: "From this day forward, all unfree in the Danish West Indies shall be free."

AFTER EMANCIPATION

The end of slavery marked the beginning of a long economic decline in the Virgin Islands. The Danes and British did very little to support the newly freed slaves, and many of the planters pulled out. Left virtually alone, the former slaves turned to subsistence farming, fishing, and small-scale trade to survive. St. Croix was the only island that maintained a sugar industry significantly beyond the end of slavery; its last sugar mill closed in the 1960s.

British Virgin Islands

In the British colonies, slavery was followed by a period of apprenticeship, a stepping stone between slavery and freedom. Under apprenticeship former slaves were no longer subject to the brutality they knew under slavery and were free to move about the island as they wished. But they were required to remain on the plantations where they once were slaves, where they worked for a small salary.

Apprenticeship ended around 1840, and by then the sugar industry was close to its death. In 1839, five years after the end of slavery, Tortola produced 423 hogsheads of sugar. In 1852, it produced just one. During this time, most English planters left.

The freed slaves became yeoman farmers, merchants, and seamen. Farmers kept cattle, raised fruits and vegetables, fished, and cleared timber to make charcoal, most of which was sold to St. Thomas. In fact, aside from small-scale production for local use and the brief burst of rum production during American Prohibition, the islands said goodbye to sugar for good.

What few Whites remained on the island fled after riots broke out in 1853. Angered by the government's decision to double the cattle tax overnight, islanders gathered in Road Town to protest the tax and demand the release of two men arrested because of their refusal to pay it. Eventually, the rioters broke into the prison where the men were being held, took the firearms, and spent two days burning and destroying Road Town and what plantations remained throughout the island. Only one Road Town building survived the fire; it is still known as the "fireproof building."

The second half of the 19th century was quiet in the British Virgin Islands. Some islanders persevered by hard work, while some migrated to the United States and other places that promised more opportunity. The British government neglected the islands. The only schools were operated by the Methodist and Anglican churches, and health care was primitive. The Legislative Assembly, still a White-only establishment, disbanded in 1902, and responsibility for the islands fell to a British governor stationed in Antigua, where it remained for 50 years.

Danish West Indies

While emancipation was achieved in 1848, Black laborers in the Danish West Indies were still forced to work under slave-like conditions. Immediately after slavery was abolished, the Danish administration enacted rules designed to prevent newly freed slaves from leaving their plantations. Rules required laborers to enter into one-year contracts with their employer at terms set out by law: a five-day work week, and wages of 5, 10, or 15 cents a day, depending on whether the slave was skilled or unskilled. Laborers were told they could apply to change employers only once a year. In addition, passport requirements were designed to limit the number of people who could leave the islands altogether.

Rules or no, many Blacks did not remain on the plantations. On St. John, where the sugar industry collapsed almost immediately after the end of slavery, the population of the island fell from 2,228 to 994 between 1850 and 1880. Those people who remained turned to subsistence farming, fishing, and trade to survive.

On St. Croix, while many former slaves were restricted from leaving the island, they did leave the plantations to live in town, where they sought employment as servants, port hands, or artisans. To fill a shortfall of agricultural labor, St. Croix was opened to immigrants from the nearby British islands, Barbados, and St. Eustatius.

FIREBURN

Discontent with working conditions and restrictions on free movement came to a head on St. Croix in October 1878, when a riot broke out in Frederiksted, fueled by rumors that the Danes had stopped issuing passports and that police had killed a laborer. A crowd in Frederiksted stormed the fort but was unable to scale the internal gate. They turned instead on the town and nearby plantations, setting fire to townhouses, businesses, great houses, sugar mills, and crops. Crowds of laborers roamed the island for days, armed with sticks and fire. Leaders included three Crucian women: Mary Thomas ("Queen Mary"), Rebecca Frederik, and Axelline Saloman.

It took the Danes two weeks to put down the Fireburn, as the riots have come to be known. In the final analysis, nearly 900 acres of agricultural land were destroyed, 60 laborers were killed, and 3 soldiers perished. More than 400 laborers were arrested; 75 of these were sentenced to jail. Mary, Rebecca, and Axelline, the "Queens of the Fireburn," were sent to Denmark to serve their sentences. They returned to St. Croix and worked as street vendors until their deaths.

THE MERCHANT ISLAND

St. Thomas did not fare much better than its sister islands. Cholera outbreaks there in 1853 and 1866 killed an estimated 3,200 people. A devastating hurricane in 1867, followed by an earthquake and tidal wave in the same year, destroyed the island's reputation as a safe harbor.

The beginning of the steam age and advances in communications contributed to the island's decline. St. Thomas's harbor was too small for the large steam ships of the late 19th century, and the advent of telegraphic connections allowed merchants to acquire market information without making the journey in person. The number of steamships calling on St. Thomas peaked in 1880 and declined after.

Meanwhile, the island saw an influx of people. Former slaves left plantations on St. Croix and St. John in high numbers, many of them heading to Charlotte Amalie, where they sought work on the docks and in subsidiary trade businesses.

THE 20TH CENTURY

A few attempts were made in the early 20th century to diversify and strengthen the economies of the then-Danish West Indies and the British Virgin Islands. On St. Thomas, the National Bank of the Danish West Indies was established in 1904 after the St. Thomas Bank ceased operations in 1898. A new shipping authority was created in 1904 to encourage trade. In 1912, the Danish West Indian Company was founded, and in 1915 its headquarters were moved to St. Thomas. (Its offspring, the West India Company, is still the largest cruise ship agent on the island.)

On St. Croix, plantations turned to other crops, such as citrus, coconuts, and tomatoes. Cattle also began to be an important part of the island economy. On St. John, the Danish Plantation Company opened experimental bay rum factories in 1903 in hopes of providing some economic stimulus for the island. Bay rum proved to be a successful export, and several former sugar factories were converted to bay rum plants. One of the largest was at Cinnamon Bay.

On the British islands, authorities established an agriculture station in 1902, which was supposed to introduce new crops and agricultural skills to the islanders.

World War I and the Transfer

Despite feeble attempts to the contrary, the Danish West Indies' economy worsened at the outbreak of World War I. Shipping ground to a near halt, and living conditions were poor. In 1916, inspired by a successful strike by sugarcane workers on St. Croix, St. Thomas coal

THIRD TIME'S THE CHARM

The islands of St. Thomas, St. John, and St. Croix became U.S. possessions in 1917, but America flirted with the idea of buying the islands as far back as 1865.

At a dinner party in Washington, D.C., in January 1865, U.S. Secretary of State William Seward approached the Danish minister in Washington, Waldenmar Raasloff, with a proposal to buy the islands. But discussion on the proposal was delayed by a number of circumstances.

In January 1866, Seward visited the islands and was impressed, but he did nothing for more than a year. Negotiations finally began in May 1867, and an agreement was made in October of that year. The treaty provided for U.S. acquisition of St. Thomas and St. John for $7.5 million, with the understanding that inhabitants of the island would first be allowed to voice their support or opposition through a referendum. Following that, ratification would be needed by the Danish Rigsdag and the U.S. Senate.

The vote was carried out on January 9 and 10, 1868. A total of 1,244 people voted in favor of the sale; 22 against. Islanders were hopeful that affiliation with the United States would lead to more economic opportunities.

But the 1867 treaty languished in the U.S. Senate. Post-Civil War America was not interested in expansion overseas, and many believed that Seward, unpopular over his purchase of Alaska, had overstepped his authority in negotiating the treaty, despite the fact that Presidents Lincoln and Johnson had approved of the purchase. The devastating hurricanes and earthquake of 1867 did not help matters. One observer put it this way: "Immediately everyone began to make fun of the treaty, as one for the annexation of hurricanes and earthquakes, and the subject was fairly laughed out of court."

The parties tried again in 1900, and another treaty was negotiated in 1902. This time, the treaty was drafted in Washington and was placed first before the U.S. Senate. The sum agreed on was $5 million for all three islands: St. Croix, St. Thomas, and St. John. No vote was required in the islands, where many residents were still smarting over the U.S.'s rejection of the previous sale.

This time, however, it was the Danes who stood in the way of the sale's completion. The upper house of the Danish parliament found itself in a 32-32 tie on the treaty, and so it was vetoed.

Negotiations began again in 1915, between Dr. Maurice Egan, the U.S. minister to Copenhagen, and the Danish foreign minister. This time, talks went smoothly. The U.S. public was behind the sale, and Danish interest in the islands was waning. In January 1916, the parties agreed to a sale price of $25 million. The treaty was approved by the U.S. Senate on September 7, 1916. In Denmark, the matter went to a national referendum before being approved by both houses of the legislature.

In the Virgin Islands, public opinion was in favor of the sale. Formal transfer ceremonies were held on St. Thomas and St. Croix on March 31, 1917. The Danish Dannebrog was taken down, and the U.S. Stars and Stripes was raised.

© U.S. VIRGIN ISLANDS DEPARTMENT OF TOURISM

The U.S. Virgin Islands and United States flags fly high.

carriers struck. Led by George A. Moorhead, the strike was successful and led to a doubling of the wage, from $0.01 to $0.02 per basket.

While St. Thomas and the other Danish West Indies were an increasing financial liability for Denmark, the United States saw them as islands of potentially strategic importance. The United States needed to protect approaches to the Panama Canal and also wanted to prevent the islands from winding up in the hands of a foreign nation hostile to America. U.S. interest in the islands also coincided with a growing imperialist attitude in the country.

The sale was negotiated between 1915 and 1916, and the official transfer took place on March 31, 1917. The last day of March is still observed as Transfer Day in the territory. The United States paid $25 million for the three islands.

From 1917 until 1931, the islands were administered by the U.S. Navy, and little emphasis was placed on developing democratic institutions or meaningful economic growth. However, some accomplishments were made. Naval officials reorganized hospitals, vaccination programs were put in place, and a sanitary code passed. Concrete water catchments were built on St. Thomas following a 1924 drought, and schools were built and opened.

On St. Croix, thousands of Puerto Ricans were encouraged to migrate to the island to provide agricultural labor. New Deal–era homesteading programs provided some economic opportunity for Crucians and served to subdivide several of the largest plantations. The 1934 program saw the subdivision of about 5,000 acres at estates Whim, LaGrande Princess, Northside, and Bethlehem. Under the scheme, settlers could buy six acres of land for about $18 a year, paid over 20 years.

Economic Growth

World War II contributed to a minor economic boom for the islands. Construction of military installations on St. Thomas drew more laborers away from the farm, and when the building boom was over, they did not go back. In 1952, the U.S. Virgin Islands Tourist Development Board was formed, and travelers began to discover St. Thomas.

While St. Thomas and St. John were focusing solely on tourism, St. Croix was opening its doors to industry. Tax incentives approved in the 1960s encouraged the development of the island's industrial economy. In 1966 Hess Oil and Harvey Alumina established industrial centers on the island. Some of the early hotels—Carambola and the Buccaneer—date from this period, too.

One of the early visitors to the islands was Laurance Rockefeller, the grandson of John D. Rockefeller. Rockefeller visited the islands during the early 1950s on a Caribbean cruise and immediately saw their potential as national parks and tourist destinations. He and his agents quickly began negotiating with landowners to buy up large tracts of St. John.

Rockefeller spent an estimated $2 million to buy more than 5,000 acres of land on St. John, which was handed over to the government when the Virgin Islands National Park was declared at a ceremony on December 1, 1956. The same day, Rockefeller reopened Caneel Bay Plantation, a luxury resort completely surrounded by park land. St. John's nature-based tourism industry was born.

Having made his mark on the U.S. Virgin Islands, Rockefeller moved on to the British islands, where he bought large expanses of land on Tortola and Virgin Gorda to form national parks and developed Little Dix Bay Hotel, which opened its doors in 1964, on Virgin Gorda.

The Cuban Revolution in 1959 proved to be the launchpad for the Virgin Islands' tourism industry: There was a seven-fold increase in the number of tourists between 1959 and 1969.

Hurricanes

Hurricanes Hugo in 1989 and Marilyn in 1995 dealt a terrible blow to the islands—St. Croix and St. Thomas in particular—razing whole homes and destroying hundreds of hotel rooms.

Hugo killed three people and left an estimated one-third of St. Croix's residents homeless. The island's hillsides were totally denuded, and damage to buildings was widespread. Even today, island residents who lived through that storm speak of two segments of their lives: before Hugo and after Hugo.

Marilyn struck the Virgin Islands on September 15–16, 1995, and St. Thomas bore the worst of the storm. There was an estimated $2.1 billion in direct damage, eight people died, and 21,000 homes were damaged or destroyed. The Charlotte Amalie waterfront was dotted with boats that had been carried ashore by the storm surge, including a U.S. Coast Guard cutter.

Despite the terrible damage, many island residents say that media coverage of both hurricanes, which focused on isolated incidents of looting and overstated the destruction, was responsible for compounding the islands' post-hurricane woes.

Subsequent hurricanes have largely spared the Virgin Islands.

Government and Economy

U.S. VIRGIN ISLANDS

The U.S. Virgin Islands are an unincorporated territory of the United States, subject to U.S. laws. Virgin Islanders are U.S. citizens and the U.S. president is the head of state, although Virgin Islanders do not vote in presidential elections (but they do vote in presidential primaries).

Since 1970, the governor of the U.S. Virgin Islands has been chosen by popular election. Before that, the governor was appointed by the U.S. president. As the head of the executive branch, the governor chooses commissioners to oversee departments, proposes the territory's annual budget, and signs (or vetoes) legislation. The governor is assisted by a lieutenant governor, elected as part of a gubernatorial ticket, like the U.S. president and vice president.

John deJongh Jr., a Democrat and former businessman, began his second four-year term as governor in 2011 with promises to focus on education, public safety, and economic growth.

The 15-member unicameral legislature is elected every two years. The Senate passes laws and can petition the U.S. Congress to make changes to the Organic Act, the territory's constitution. Seven of the 15 senators are elected from the St. Croix district and seven are elected from the St. Thomas–St. John district. The final member is chosen at large but must be a resident of St. John.

Virgin Islanders also choose a nonvoting delegate to the House of Representatives, who can take part in debates and serve on committees but does not have a vote on the floor. Donna Christensen, a Democrat, has held this post since 1996.

Elections

Elections for governor are held every four years; elections for Senate and delegate to Congress every two. The vast majority of Virgin Islanders align themselves with the Democratic Party, so much so that political parties are largely irrelevant in local elections. Personality and political alliances are much more important; party affiliation is easily shrugged off when found inconvenient.

Election season is marked by spirited debates, lots of political banners and signs, and a seemingly endless sequence of open-air political rallies.

Judicial and Penal Systems

There are both local and federal courts in the U.S. Virgin Islands. Territorial court judges are

Government House on St. Thomas houses the governor's offices and those of his cabinet.

appointed for 10-year terms by the governor and hear civil and criminal cases based on local laws. U.S. District Courts in St. Thomas and St. Croix are part of the Third U.S. Circuit, the same as Pennsylvania, New Jersey, and Delaware. The Third Circuit Court of Appeals is the territory's appeals court; cases from the Virgin Islands can be appealed all the way to the U.S. Supreme Court.

Crime

The Virgin Islands have a higher crime rate than many U.S. cities of similar population. In 2010 the islands counted 50 homicides, some 10 times the national average when considered alongside population. The overwhelming majority of victims are young men, and police say that poverty, gangs, and drugs are the cause of most of the violence. A myriad of community organizations work to combat violence through intervention, police-community outreach, and rehabilitation. It is an uphill battle, however.

Tourists are generally not the targets of violent crime, but they have been affected. In 2010 a 15-year-old cruise ship visitor was killed when she was caught in the cross fire during a gang shooting incident at Coki Point Beach. The incident led to an aggressive clean-up of the area, with increased police presence and the construction of visitor facilities. To avoid getting mixed up in anything, it's best for visitors to steer clear of dodgy areas at night, including the back streets of Charlotte Amalie.

To avoid theft exercise the same caution you would in a U.S. city: don't flash your jewelry or leave valuables out in plain sight.

Economy

The U.S. Virgin Islands' economy is highly dependent on tourism—80 percent of the $1.5 billion GDP comes from that industry. Some 2.5 million people visit the U.S. Virgin Islands every year, most of them aboard cruise ships. In 2010 1.9 million cruise ship passengers and

The HOVENSA oil refinery on St. Croix closed in 2012 after more than 40 years in business, laying off some 2,000 workers and putting the economic future of the island in jeopardy.

664,000 overnight guests visited. There are small agriculture, manufacturing, and industrial sectors, too.

Despite the large number of visitors, the U.S. Virgin Islands economy is struggling. The government is bloated and inefficient, providing poor services at high prices. Tourism slumped following Hurricane Hugo in 1989, Hurricane Marilyn in 1995, the terrorist attacks of 2001, and during the global recession of 2008 and beyond. In 2011 government workers in the U.S. Virgin Islands took an 8 percent pay cut, but that was not enough to stop widespread layoffs that began in early 2012 with over 500 workers laid off. Also in 2012, the HOVENSA oil refinery on St. closed, delivering a body blow to that island's economy. Some 2,000 refinery workers lost their jobs.

One-third of the government's annual revenue comes from individual income tax ($334 million); other major sources of revenue are business taxes ($61 million) and the rum excise tax ($111 million). The U.S. federal government spent $821 million in the U.S. Virgin Islands in 2010.

One-third of households in the Virgin Islands have incomes below the federal poverty line, and more than 40 percent of children grow up in poverty. Unemployment is 6 percent. Some 68.5 percent of births are to unmarried mothers, and nearly half of all households are headed by a single mother.

BRITISH VIRGIN ISLANDS

The British Virgin Islands are an overseas territory of the United Kingdom, one of five remaining U.K. colonies in the West Indies. Power is shared between a locally elected government and the British governor, who is appointed by the queen. The local government is responsible for most areas of administration, including finance. The British governor administers the courts, the police, and the public service and is responsible for external affairs. In 2007 a new constitution was enacted that enhanced the authority of the local government and introduced a bill of rights for the first time.

Since 1978, the territory has paid for itself. British aid is minimal and is used for areas of special interest to the British government. In the early 1990s the U.K. government paid for a new prison; in 2001 it contributed to the building of a new residence for the governor. Smaller sums of money from the United Kingdom go to support environmental and good-government projects.

The BVI has a ministerial government, modeled after the Westminster system. Ministers, who are the chief policymakers in the government, are chosen from among members of the majority in the legislature. Together, the ministers form the cabinet, which meets weekly to make policy decisions. The premier is the most senior minister; together with the governor, he or she guides the cabinet and leads the government.

The public service is nonpartisan. Ministers are supported by permanent secretaries and other officials who do not change when a new party comes to power. They are obligated to serve the government of the day, whether they voted for it or not.

Laws are proposed and passed in the 13-member House of Assembly. House meetings, which take place about every four to six weeks, are broadcast live on television and radio and can be interesting to listen to. Debate is decorous, but in between the references to "honorable members" you will pick up carefully worded barbs. Most meetings include a question-and-answer segment not unlike the British question time.

While the BVI government is not especially modern, and while it sometimes reacts very slowly, it is generally effective, transparent, and accountable.

Elections

Elections must be held at least every four years, or sooner if the ruling party requests, or if the ruling party or coalition seems to have lost its ability to control the government.

The last elections were held in 2011, when the National Democratic Party led by physician-statesman Dr. Orlando Smith won a 9–4 seat majority with promises to focus on economic development. Former Premier Ralph T. O'Neal of the Virgin Islands Party, who has represented the district of Virgin Gorda and Anegada for 40 years, won re-election and is Leader of the Opposition.

There are about 12,000 registered voters in the BVI— about half of the population. Immigrants who have settled in the territory must obtain citizenship—called belonger status—before they can register to vote.

Judicial and Penal Systems

The BVI is part of the Eastern Caribbean Supreme Court, which administers courts in eight different eastern Caribbean jurisdictions. Judges are rotated among the jurisdictions. Rarely will a judge or magistrate from the Virgin Islands preside over court there. The law is based on English common law, and courtroom practices follow those used in England. Appeals are heard by the three-judge Eastern Caribbean Court of Appeals. The final court of appeal is the privy council in the United Kingdom.

In 2009 the BVI opened a new courthouse dedicated to commercial matters, an offshoot of the territory's financial services industry.

Lawyers and judges wear black robes with high white collars in court, but no wigs. In magistrate's court, the attire is business suits.

Prisoners serve their sentences in a hilltop prison on the northeastern corner of Tortola. A prison farm provides produce, eggs, chicken, and other goods for use at the prison; look for Her Majesty's Prison eggs in local grocery stores.

Few people remember when the last person

was executed in the BVI, but that did not stop a loud public outcry in 1999 when the United Kingdom required all its territories to remove capital punishment from the law books.

Crime

Not long ago, violent crime was virtually unheard of in the British Virgin Islands. In the past decade, however, serious crime has become a fact of life. Homicide figures are still relatively low—there were three homicides in 2011—but the upward trend is unmistakable and troubling to this peace-loving community.

The most common crime against tourists is theft, so be sure to lock your hotel room, car, or villa and avoid bringing valuables with you in the first place. There have also been occasional incidents of muggings in Road Town at night, typically after victims have been drinking. If you are walking in town after dark, do so in a group, stick to well-lit areas, and keep your wits about you. Better yet, take a taxi to your destination, especially if you've had too much to drink.

Economy

Tourism and financial services fuel the British Virgin Islands economy. **Tourism** accounts for the lion's share of employment, while financial services bring in more than half of the government's annual revenue. The recession of 2008 and onwards has impacted the BVI: there were layoffs in both tourism and financial services and a number of small businesses closed or consolidated. But on the whole the territory fared better than many of its neighbors, though the protracted nature of the recession is taking a toll.

GDP is estimated at $850 million, or just over $38,000 per capita, one of the highest in the Caribbean. At the same time, the BVI continues to import labor to meet demand: More than half of the workforce is on work permits. Though 217th in the world by population, the BVI has the 14th fastest rate of inward migration in the world.

But there is more to the picture than meets the eye. The minimum wage is a staggeringly low $4 per hour, and the cost of living is among the highest in the Caribbean. A recent study found that almost 25 percent of people in the BVI live below the poverty line. Many of the poorest workers are immigrants from other Caribbean islands who are employed in the construction and tourism industries.

At the same time there is a growing segment of unemployed young people—especially young men. While foreigners obtain work permits to take high-paying jobs in the finance sector, young people from the Virgin Islands often struggle to find work for myriad educational, social, and economic reasons. Unemployment leads to increased crime and other social problems that tax public resources. The government in 2011 launched an outreach program for unemployed youth, but a comprehensive strategy to improve education and training and understand the needs of the private sector will be needed to truly address this problem.

The BVI's **financial services** industry is built upon its companies legislation. More than 800,000 companies have been incorporated in the BVI since the early 1980s, attracted by low incorporation fees, no taxes, a creditor-friendly regime, and the BVI's political and economic stability. Since 1990, the territory has sought to diversify its offshore sector, with the addition of legislation for mutual fund administration, captive insurance, insolvency, and special trusts.

So far, the BVI has escaped inclusion on so-called offshore blacklists. Neither has it ever been named in any high-profile money laundering or terrorist financing case. BVI companies are used for commercial purposes around the world, from financing films in Hollywood to joint venture projects in China. Thousands of mostly European professionals work in the BVI's financial services industry, which is centered in Road Town.

People and Culture

The Virgin Islands are diverse—residents hail from nearly every Caribbean island, plus Asia, Africa, Europe, and North America. Although both Virgin Island territories have administrative links with western countries—the United Kingdom and the United States—these islands and their people are distinctly Caribbean.

Three-quarters of the people in the U.S. Virgin Islands and some 83 percent in the British islands are Black, descended from African slaves brought to Caribbean islands during the plantation era. In both territories there are Indian, Middle Eastern, and White minorities.

Both territories are made up of highly mobile people. In the U.S. Virgin Islands, about one-third of the population is foreign born, with most of the foreign immigrants coming from other Caribbean islands. The British Virgin Islands are highly dependent on immigrant labor in both tourism and financial service fields—the latest figures suggest that more than 60 percent of the labor force in the BVI is foreign.

The presence of such a large number of immigrants has led to some degree of xenophobia in both the British and U.S. Virgin Islands, although it is stronger in the BVI. There are distinct "rungs" of the local society, beginning at the bottom with newly arrived immigrants and ending at the top with prominent local families whose ancestry is traceable in the Virgin Islands all the way to emancipation. Virgin Islanders are astute catalogers of people: They know, seemingly by instinct, who is "from here," who is "born here," who is "come here," and who is just passing through. Don't think for a moment that you can just blend in.

Virgin Islanders in both territories have strong ties with the United States, due largely to widespread outward migration that took place during the first 75 years of the 20th century. Many Virgin Islanders still travel to the United States to attend college—some do not return home. When you talk to Virgin Islanders, do not be surprised to learn that they are far more familiar with your country than you are with theirs. Although British Virgin Islanders are U.K. citizens, with the right to live and work in the United Kingdom and entire European Union, the destination of choice for British Virgin Islanders seeking opportunity abroad remains the United States.

DAILY LIFE

The tropical climate makes early morning a good time to get things done, and many households are up before sunrise. Many women rise early to prepare breakfast and lunch for their families. Early morning is also a popular time of day to exercise or work outside. By 8 A.M. the sun is on full bore, and there is a general bustle toward school and work. Traditionally, children and working men and women returned home for lunch, and some still do. Increasingly, however, lunch is eaten out. For those unrestrained by rigid work or school commitments, midday makes the perfect time for a nap.

After-work time is golden. Between four and six, the heat of the day begins to subside, and the pressures of the day are past. This is the time when men stop "under the tree" to catch up with friends or when neighbors linger to talk over the fence. Schoolchildren, no longer concerned with keeping their uniforms clean, run around and play.

Darkness signifies the time to come home and settle in for the night. Virgin Islanders' belief in jumbies, evil spirits of the night, may have subsided in recent generations, but it has not gone completely. Evenings not spent at home may be spent playing sports or attending church group meetings or social events.

Saturdays are the traditional day for cleaning, cooking, washing, shopping, and general chores around the house. Most households try to get these things done in time for the Sunday Sabbath, when they go to church and spend the afternoon at home. Many families adhere to the tradition of Sunday dinner at home. Sunday afternoon is also the traditional time for family outings to the beach, playground, or ice-cream shop. Many shops are closed on Sundays.

MEN AND WOMEN

On one hand, women in the Virgin Islands are ahead of their sisters in more "developed" countries. Because racist laws limited the rights of Black men and women for centuries, women were never banned from voting, owning property, or obtaining an education because of their sex. During slavery, Black women were expected to carry the same load as a man, and they did. After the end of slavery, women continued to work—and not just around the house. Women were farmers, laborers, fishers, and more.

When secondary education was introduced, girls were just as likely to go to school as boys. As a result, the first generation of educated local leaders included both men and women. Today, women are legislators, ministers, commissioners, judges, teachers, principals, and religious leaders. Although women have been elected to both territories' legislatures, a woman has not yet achieved the highest elected office of governor or premier.

In recent years, women and girls have outachieved boys in secondary and tertiary education in the Virgin Islands, leading to concern that the education system unfairly favors girls. Indeed, boys are much more likely to drop out of school, fail, or be unemployed than girls. These trends have led some—men and women—to believe that women have actually gained the "upper hand" in Virgin Island society.

Despite the trappings of gender equality that abound in the public sphere, women still face inequality, particularly in their private lives. In the home, men and women often follow traditional male-female roles. Indeed, most men and women would probably agree that the man is the head of the household. Many men have not embraced the notion of shared housework or, to a large extent, coparenting. Neither have some men adopted the concept of monogamy.

Many couples live together and have children but do not marry. Having children out of wedlock is widespread and widely accepted (statistics in both territories show that between 60 and 65 percent of births occur out of marriage). Indeed, many married men have "inside children," born to their wife, and "outside children," born to their girlfriends.

Inequality between men and women is about more than heartache or jealousy, however. Campaigns against domestic violence are only starting to gain traction in the islands—women who choose to leave abusive relationships still face an uphill battle for acceptance and support. The spread of HIV also makes marital infidelity a serious health issue for many women, who find it difficult to insist on condom use by their husbands.

CHILDREN

Virgin Islanders like and welcome children. Very few households do not know the presence of at least one child, grandchild, niece, or nephew. Traditionally children were raised by the whole community—neighbors freely disciplined other people's children, and children knew they could get food, shelter, or help from any adult if they needed it. There is still a good deal of communal child-rearing, although in many cases the community circle has shrunk to one's immediate and extended family and friends. "The family circle" is a phrase in common parlance.

Corporal punishment at home is common, although it is practiced in moderation and probably much less than it once was. Often the threat of the belt is enough to get misbehaving children to do as they are told. In Virgin Islands culture, children are supposed to obey their parents at all times. In traditional families asking questions, talking back, or sharing one's own opinion is considered undesirable, cheeky behavior. Children who are coaxed into conversations about their experiences, thoughts, and feelings are being spoiled.

Virgin Islanders are particularly aware of their children's behavior in public or with company and cannot understand why American and European parents are so unconcerned about their own rambunctious little ones.

PERCEPTIONS OF TIME

Island time is well known and well appreciated in the Virgin Islands. Very few things here start on time. Meetings start anywhere from 10 to 30 minutes late. Many offices and shops open later than their posted hours. Nighttime concerts or pageants are notorious, sometimes starting hours late.

If someone says they are coming "now," that means they are coming soon. If someone says they are coming "soon," look for them in a few minutes (or even hours). If someone says, "I'm coming to you," it means "hold on, and I will take care of you in a few minutes." Impatience is an undesirable trait associated with Americans and Europeans.

Service in restaurants and shops runs on island time, too. Unless you want to be perpetually annoyed during your vacation, just go with the flow. Maybe you will even start to appreciate the fact that just as no one else hurries, neither should you. Even if you can't adopt the island-time mentality, don't try to fight it. Getting frustrated or angry does absolutely no good. If you are really in a hurry, politely inform the waitstaff right away and they will surely do what they can to speed things up.

There are some exceptions to the island time rule. Ferries and airplanes run generally on time. There are also individuals who are perpetually on time. If you have made arrangements with someone, try to find out if he or she is an on-time person or an island-time person.

CLOTHING

Virgin Islanders put considerable stock in their appearance. It is disrespectful, not to mention embarrassing, to show up in professional or religious environments without proper attire or without being properly groomed. Virgin Islanders wear their clothes well pressed and their shoes well shined.

Office attire tends to be conservative; the general trend toward casual office wear has not been accepted here. Church clothing is even more formal; many men wear suits and women don colorful and elaborate hats, with matching dresses and shoes. Casual functions, such as afternoon picnics and outdoor concerts, call for casual clothing: blue jeans and T-shirts, for example. Whenever you leave the house, however, you should look neat and clean. Many Virgin Islanders reserve shorts for the beach or sports field only.

Few things offend a Virgin Islander more than seeing someone who is dressed inappropriately. They will let a slightly wrinkled shirt or scuffed shoes slide (but don't think they don't notice), but instances of gross fashion miscalculation are not forgiven easily. Bathing suits are not acceptable attire for town, for example. Shorts and a T-shirt are not appropriate for church.

RELIGION

Virgin Islanders are highly religious and churchgoing. Christian churches of nearly every persuasion exist in the Virgin Islands, although the Methodist, Moravian, Catholic, and Anglican have been here for the longest period of time. Statistics from the British Virgin Islands demonstrate this: Of 20,000 churchgoers, 97 percent are Christian. Of those, 37 percent are Methodist, 19 percent are Anglican, and 12 percent are Catholic.

There is no attempt at separating church and state in the British Virgin Islands. Prayers open House of Assembly meetings; school days begin with prayer; and references to God are common in political discourse.

In the U.S. Virgin Islands, which are governed by U.S. laws, including the separation of church and state, religion plays a less obvious but no less influential role in daily life.

There are small groups of non-Christians in both territories. Arab immigrants from Palestine and Syria form an Islamic society, while immigrants from Guyana and Trinidad practice Hinduism. There are also some Rastafarians. These groups do not suffer outright religious discrimination, although they are rendered nearly invisible by the sheer size and influence of the Christian community.

FOOD

The food of the islands is influenced by the diverse cultures that have settled there, as well as the meats, fruits, and vegetables that are widely available. But do seek out traditional Virgin Islands dishes while you visit.

Seafood

No food group is as traditional in the islands as seafood. **Pot fish,** the reef fish caught in fish pots, is ubiquitous in local restaurants and is served grilled, boiled, or fried. Common species are yellowtail, trigger fish, snapper, red hind, and blue runner. Pot fish are typically served whole, sometimes with the head; larger fish are cut into steaks, locally called "junk." **Grilled fish** is cooked over a fire with onions, peppers, and other seasonings wrapped in aluminum foil. **Fried fish** (everyone's favorite) is cooked in hot fat over a charcoal fire. **Boiled fish** is topped with a sauce made of cooked onion, pepper, and mayonnaise thinned with the fish-cooking water.

Locally caught pelagic species will be found on the menus of more upscale restaurants. Mahimahi (also called dolphin fish), tuna, grouper, swordfish, and wahoo are some of the most common.

Saltfish is another island favorite, and its history dates back to the days when it was given to slaves as food. Made from imported salt cod, which stores forever without refrigeration, saltfish is a pungent hash of flaked fish seasoned with onions and peppers. It is often served for breakfast, or cooked inside **patés**—fried, meat-stuffed bread eaten for breakfast or a snack.

Whelk and **conch** are species of shellfish served stewed, wrapped in rotis, or stuffed in patés. Naturally tough, conch and whelk are tenderized in a pressure cooker before being served. Conch soup, made with dumplings and vegetables, is also well-liked and every restaurant in the islands has a recipe for **conch fritters,** fried morsels of batter and conch meat similar to the hush puppies of the north.

The Caribbean spiny **lobster** is smaller than northern species but equally prized on the dinner plate. Anegada serves the best and freshest lobsters, cut in half, doused with garlic butter, and grilled over a wood fire. Lobster meat also finds its way into rotis and patés.

Meat

Goat meat, called mutton, is the most traditional red meat. **Stewed mutton** is flavorful, filling, and tender. **Goat water** is goat soup, often served late at night. Curried goat is a traditional Jamaican dish now popular in the Virgin Islands.

Pork is a favorite; many locals swear by **souse,** made of pig's head and tail. Roasted, spicy pork will be found on the menu at restaurants with a Latino slant. In the holiday season, no home misses the opportunity to serve a ham.

Chicken, the most ubiquitous of meats, is consumed in many forms, including stewed, barbecued, fried, and curried. **Chicken palau** is chicken cooked with seasonings and rice.

Often served whole, fried fish comes with sides like rice and peas, fried plantains, and coleslaw.

Vegetables

Nowadays you can find any vegetable under the sun at island supermarkets, which import produce from around the world. But before container ships made weekly stops in the islands, residents grew their own produce, most commonly tomatoes, eggplant, cucumber, okra, cabbage, and peppers—sweet, hot, and "seasoning." **Pumpkin** finds its way into rice, bread, soup, and stews. Wild and cultivated greens are picked and used in **kallaloo,** a vegetable stew seasoned with pork and well worth trying if you encounter it on a the menu of a local restaurant.

Without rice, wheat, or widespread corn cultivation, starchy vegetables, called ground provisions, served as carbohydrates on the traditional dinner plate. Local **sweet potatoes** are white, starchy, and mildly sweet when boiled. **Breadfruit,** a distinctive-looking fruit the size of a basketball, can be served boiled, fried, or roasted. The flesh is not unlike potato.

Bananas and **plantains** serve as fruit or vegetable: green bananas are boiled and served as a starchy side. Ripe plantains can be boiled, fried, or mashed to provide a touch of starchy sweetness to the plate.

Fruits

Everyone loves tropical fruits. **Mangoes** ripen in summer and are eaten in hand, outside where the juicy, sticky mess can be hosed off. **Papaya,** also called paw-paw, are sweet, yellow- and red-fleshed fruits cut up and eaten as a snack. Local **bananas** come in a number of varieties, but try to find the tiny sweet fig bananas, also called man-toasters.

Local fruits are used to make drinks, including **guavaberry,** a sweet, alcoholic Christmas drink; **sorrel,** made from the red flowers of the sorrel bush; **soursop,** often made with milk and a popular flavor of ice cream; **hibiscus,** made from the petals of hibiscus flowers; and

maubi, made from the bark of a local tree. In addition, fruit punch made from guava, mango, passion fruit, pineapple, orange, and other fruits is popular.

Grains and Bread

The most common grain is rice, and it is often cooked with pigeon peas, beans, or seasonings. In the British Virgin Islands, **peas and rice** are cooked with a little bit of sugar. **Fungi,** a side dish made from cornmeal and not unlike polenta, is another traditional accompaniment to fish, although its popularity is waning.

Johnnycakes are discs of fried, hot bread, served alongside fish or chicken or just eaten as a snack. **Coconut bread** is a round, flat, mildly sweet loaf made with grated coconut, delicious and filling when eaten warm with egg and cheese in the morning. Flat, dry discs of **cassava bread** were once a staple but are now hard to find.

Bread was baked in brick ovens, which you can still see here and there, especially in the British Virgin Islands. Taste brick-oven-baked **"dumb bread"** at Annaberg on St. John, where docents act the part of traditional bakers three days a week. Dumb bread, baked without yeast, is a bit like a heavy biscuit. Local yeast bread is white, light, and bland. **Tittle bread** has been shaped into a long, narrow loaf with small round points on each end.

Desserts

Tarts are the most celebrated of island desserts. Homemade pastry a bit like shortbread is stuffed with fruit fillings (coconut, pineapple, and guava are the most common) and baked. **Vienna cake,** especially well-known on St. Croix, is a seven-layer cake with a variety of fruit fillings. **Black cake** is a rum-soaked fruit cake traditionally served at Christmas.

LANGUAGE

English is the predominant language of the islands, but some islanders speak Spanish. The Virgin Islands English dialect is at first very difficult for many visitors to understand, particularly when it is being spoken between Virgin Islanders. Listen carefully and you will pick up more and more words. Many Virgin Islanders, especially those whose work brings them into contact with visitors, will slow down for your benefit.

Listen for dialects of other Caribbean islands as well. Once your ear becomes accustomed, you will be able to pick up the difference between, say, a Jamaican and a Barbadian dialect.

One of the most beautiful things about the language of the Virgin Islands is the colorful metaphors and sayings. Virgin Islanders are excellent orators and storytellers, skilled at metaphor and suggestion. They often use proverbs to communicate subtle and straightforward advice. Here's a sample of some classic proverbs:

- *God Almighty never shut he eye.* (God is always watching.)
- *When rat see cat he never laugh.* (Don't take those who can cause you injury lightly.)
- *Every fool got he own sense.* (To each his own.)
- *Empty bag can't stand up.* (A weak or virtueless person is but an empty sack.)
- *If wind don't blow, you won't see the fowl's bottom.* (An ill wind can do good.)
- *Time longer than twine.* (Time will tell.)
- *Bush have ears; long grass carry news.* (Gossip and scandal spread in mysterious ways.)
- *If you play with a dog, he'll lick your mouth.* (Familiarity breeds contempt.)
- *Trial make mention.* (Merit comes to he who overcomes adversity.)
- *Sleep steal me.* (I overslept.)

ESSENTIALS

Getting There and Around

GETTING THERE

Although the Virgin Islands are surrounded by sea, most travelers will get to them by air. With the exception of cruise ships and a twice-monthly passenger ferry from Puerto Rico, no passenger ships sail regularly to the islands.

By Air

Travelers from North America have the option of flying directly to St. Thomas, directly to St. Croix, or indirectly through San Juan, Puerto Rico. Keep in mind that many flights are seasonal, with the greatest number from January through March.

TO THE U.S. VIRGIN ISLANDS

At the time of research, major airlines providing nonstop service to St. Thomas's **Cyril E. King Airport** (STT) are **American Airlines** (800/433-7300, www.aa.com), with service from Miami, New York, Boston, and San Juan; **Delta Airlines** (800/221-1212, www.dclta.com), with service from Atlanta and New York; **U.S. Airways** (800/428-4322, www.us-airways.com), with service from Charlotte and

© SUSANNA HENIGHAN POTTER

The Cyril E. King Airport on St. Thomas, built almost entirely on landfill, is the largest international airport in the Virgin Islands.

Philadelphia; **United Airlines** (800/241-6522, www.united.com), with service from Chicago; **Jet Blue** (800/538-2583, www.jetblue.com), with service from Boston, via San Juan; **Air Canada** (888/247-2262, www.aircanada.com), with service from Toronto; **Spirit** (800/772-7117, www.spiritair.com), with service from Fort Lauderdale; and **Continental Airlines** (800/525-0280, www.continental.com), with service from Newark.

There are fewer direct flights to St. Croix's **Henry E. Rohlson Airport** (STX). During the winter tourist season, **American Airlines** (800/433-7300, www.aa.com) flies there from Miami and San Juan; **Delta Airlines** (800/221-1212, www.delta.com) flies from Atlanta; **Jet Blue** (800/538-2583, www.jetblue.com) flies from Boston, via San Juan; and **U.S. Airways** (800/428-4322, www.usairways.com) flies from Charlotte.

If your final destination is St. Croix, you can also fly to St. Thomas or San Juan and take a commuter plane to St. Croix.

TO THE BRITISH VIRGIN ISLANDS

The **Terrence B. Lettsome International Airport** (EIS) is not large enough to accommodate large aircraft. Commercial service into the BVI is limited to short-haul flights from San Juan, Antigua, and other nearby places. **Cape Air** (800/352-0714, www.flycapeair.com) and **American Eagle** (800/433-7300, www.aa.com) are the primary airlines connecting Tortola with San Juan. For service down island to the Caribbean, contact LIAT Airlines (866/549-5428, www.liatairline.com).

VIA SAN JUAN

San Juan, Puerto Rico's **Luis Munoz Marin International Airport** (SJU) is a major transportation hub for the Caribbean. American and international airlines provide service here from cities around the world, including Montreal, Toronto, London, Frankfurt, Madrid, and Panama City, plus a host of major U.S. cities.

From San Juan, you can fly on commuter airlines including **Cape Air** (800/352-0714, www.flycapeair.com) and **American Eagle** (800/433-7300, www.aa.com) to get to your final destination, including St. Thomas, St. Croix, and Tortola.

VIA ANTIGUA AND BARBADOS

Travelers from Europe can reach the Virgin Islands on flights routed through Caribbean hubs. **British Airways** (800/247-9297 or 0844/493-0787, www.ba.com) flies to V.C. Bird International Airport (ANU) in Antigua, and **Virgin Atlantic** (800/744-7477 or 0870/380-2007, www.virgin-atlantic.com) flies to Grantley Adams International Airport (BGI) in Barbados. LIAT Airlines (866/549-5428, www.liatairline.com) and **BVI Airways** (www.gobvi.com) provide regional service from these islands to Tortola and St. Thomas.

VIA SINT MAARTEN

The **Princess Juliana International Airport** (SXM, www.pjiae.com) in Sint Maarten is another gateway to the Virgin Islands, especially if you are traveling from Europe. Corsair, Air Caraibes, and Air France fly to Sint Maarten from Paris; KLM flies from Amsterdam; WestJet and Air Canada fly from Toronto. Once in Sint Maarten you can fly to Tortola or St. Thomas on **LIAT** (866/549-5428, www.liatairline.com) or **BVI Airways** (www.gobvi.com).

COSTS

Airfares vary considerably by season; average round-trip fares from major American cities to St. Thomas, St. Croix, or Tortola (Beef Island) range from $300 to $800. A fare below $400 round-trip is a good deal. Fares from Europe can easily top $1,000 round-trip. The best way to find cheap fares is to start at the online search engines like www.cheaptickets.com and www.orbitz.com. Check the low-fare carriers, too. Fare sales are common during the summer and shoulder season (March–October). Expect to pay premium fares to travel around Christmas or the new year.

By Ferry

There is occasional ferry service between the U.S. Virgin Islands and Fajardo, Puerto Rico. **Transportation Services of St. John** (340/776-6282, $125 round-trip) schedules trips to coincide with holiday weekends and peak shopping dates.

Cruises

St. Thomas is one of the most popular cruise ship ports of call in the world. Nearly every cruise that passes through the eastern Caribbean stops at Charlotte Amalie. Major cruise lines also call on Road Town, Tortola, but with considerably less volume. The megaships of **Carnival, Disney, Celebrity, Holland America, Royal Caribbean, Norwegian, P&O Cruises** and **Costa** are among the most frequent visitors.

Several smaller ships also call in the Virgin Islands. **Arabella** (800/395-1343, www.cruisearabella.com) cruises around St. Thomas, St. John, and the British Virgin Islands every winter with no more than 42 people. **Seabourn Cruise Line** (800/929-9391, www.seabourn.com), noted for luxury and intimacy, departs Fort Lauderdale and stops at Jost Van Dyke, Virgin Gorda, St. John, and St. Croix. **Star Clippers** (305/442-0550, www.starclippers.com) offers a "Treasure Islands" cruise that visits many of the Virgin Islands.

The cost of cruises varies considerably depending on the type of cruise, the length, and the season. Three-day cruises on major cruise lines can cost as little as $300 per person, while 7-day cruises can range from $700 to $2,000. Upscale cruises on small ships can cost upwards of $3,500 per outing per person.

Seaplanes shuttle between Charlotte Amalie Harbor and Christiansted Harbor hourly.

GETTING AROUND
By Air

Flying is a fun, fast, but expensive way to get around the Virgin Islands. There are airports on St. Thomas, St. Croix, Tortola (Beef Island), Virgin Gorda, and Anegada. In addition, seaplanes fly between San Juan, St. Thomas, St. Croix, and Virgin Gorda, and helicopters can fly to many more of the islands, including the private island retreats. In addition to being fast and efficient, flying around the islands is beautiful. A standard sightseeing tour costs about $100 per person for 45 minutes flying time.

Charter airline companies include **Bohlke International Airlines** (340/7789177, www.bohlke.com) and **Capitol Air** (340/998-8654) operating out of the U.S. Virgin Islands and **Fly BVI** (284/495-1747), **Island Helicopters** (284/499-2663), **Caribbean Wings** (284/495-6000), **Air Culebra** (284/496-8962 or 787/268-6951), and **Island Birds** (284/495-2002) operating out of the BVI.

By Boat

Boats are the most popular and most natural way to get around the Virgin Islands. There is nothing quite so pleasant as striking out over the water to a new destination. Whether you travel by ferry, sail, or power, time spent on the water is almost always pleasant. Visitors can build their whole vacation around a boat by chartering a sailboat. Land-based visitors can take day sails to out islands, rent a powerboat for the day, or catch an interisland ferry or water taxi to reach their destination.

Ferries operating in the Virgin Islands range from large catamarans with a capacity of several hundred to smaller monohulls built for 40 or fewer. While ferries are generally reliable, it is always wise to call ahead on the day of your trip to confirm the schedule. Engine problems sometimes cause cancellations. When planning to cross between the U.S. and British Virgin Islands, plan on spending anywhere from 15–45 minutes clearing customs.

Ferries, such as this one traveling from Tortola to Virgin Gorda, connect many of the major islands.

Specific information about ferry routes and prices is dispersed throughout this book, in the relevant chapters. Popular routes include St. Thomas–St. John (16 trips daily), Tortola–St. Thomas (10 trips daily), and Tortola–Virgin Gorda (10 trips daily). Ferries also serve Anegada, Jost Van Dyke, St. Croix, and many of the smaller islands.

By Taxi

Taxis are widely available on all the islands and can be a good way to get around if you are nervous about driving on the left or if you don't want to move around too much. There are cars, but most taxis are large multipassenger vans. It is common to share a taxi with strangers when arriving at any of the major airports or ferry terminals. If you call for a taxi from your hotel or elsewhere, it will be a private charter. Large open-air buses locally called "safaris" are geared more towards cruise ship visitors and island sightseeing tours.

Taxis do tend to be expensive and rates are by person, not by trip. So if you want to do a lot of exploring you would be better off renting a car and driving yourself.

Rental Cars and Motorcycles

Rental cars are available on all the islands. For the greatest comfort, rent a four-wheel-drive vehicle, which will be handy for negotiating hills and unpaved mountain roads, especially on St. John, Tortola, and Virgin Gorda.

Driving on the islands can be intimidating. Traffic flows on the left, so that's an adjustment for visitors from North America. Other challenges include steep hills, poor road signs, narrow streets, impediments like goats and donkeys, and other drivers who seem to treat the road like a NASCAR racetrack. But there are no freeways and local drivers are used to tottering rentals slowly making their way along the roads. If you're up for a challenge, have a reliable navigator, and take safety seriously, there is no reason not to drive yourself.

For the best rates, and to be sure that you'll have a car at all, reserve your rental car early, especially on small islands like Anegada, Jost

FINDING YOUR WAY

Many visitors from North America or Europe are used to neat addressing systems in their home countries, where streets have names and buildings have numbers. This makes it easy to find your way around with the aid of a good map or, in these modern times, a GPS device.

Do not expect such luxury in the Virgin Islands. In all but a few urban areas, most buildings do not have assigned numbers, and those that do often do not post them outside. Street signs are equally scarce outside of urban areas. In remote parts, residents cannot even agree on the names of the roads.

Instead, directions are often given in a roundabout manner describing a building's proximity to landmarks, such as supermarkets, government offices, or trees. If you are invited to someone's home, don't be surprised when the directions include things like, "turn left at the big tamarind tree and then right at the road past the pink house." That is just how these things work in the islands. Throughout this book, exact addresses have been given where they are available. In other cases, the general location has been given and described.

One of the reasons the addressing system is less extensive in the Virgin Islands is that there is no home delivery of mail. (Or, perhaps, one of the reasons there is no home delivery is because the addressing system is such a mess.) Most people rent a post office box at central post offices.

There are movements afoot to improve addressing systems in both territories, largely for the benefit of emergency services, who must sometimes find houses and buildings on nothing but guesswork.

Van Dyke, and Virgin Gorda, which have relatively small rental fleets. Well-known U.S. car rental companies, including Avis and Hertz, have shops throughout the U.S. and British Virgin Islands. Budget and Thrifty have shops in the U.S. Virgin Islands.

Hitchhiking

Many residents catch rides in the Virgin Islands, but few tourists do. Hitchhiking is safer, and more widespread, in the British islands. It is not safe on St. Thomas or St. Croix. Hitchhikers do not stick their thumbs out in the Virgin Islands. Instead, they simply stand on the side of the road and wait. Sometimes they raise an arm out in front of them and make a flagging motion.

Visas and Officialdom

U.S. VIRGIN ISLANDS
Visas

Travelers who do not qualify for visa-free entry to the United States will need a nonimmigrant visa to visit the United States. Check with the nearest U.S. embassy to find out if you need a visa, or check the U.S. State Department website at http://travel.state.gov/.

Travelers from most European countries, Canada, and Australia do not need a nonimmigrant visa, although they must obtain prior authorization to land under the United States Electronic System for Travel Authorization (ESTA) program. ESTA applications can be made on the U.S. Customs and Border Protection Service website (www.cbp.gov) and should be made at least 72 hours prior to your trip to the United States. There is a $14 processing fee for each ESTA application; once obtained, an ESTA is valid for two years.

An ESTA is required even if you are merely in transit through the United States.

Taxes

There is no sales tax in the U.S. Virgin Islands, but hotels and guesthouses levy a 10 percent hotel tax on rooms. There is also a $3.75 per day charge on car rentals. Residents of the islands fill out a federal tax return but pay the bill to the local tax bureau, which uses the income to finance local government.

Customs

The U.S. Customs and Border Protection Agency considers the U.S. Virgin Islands outside the customs territory of the United States mainland. This means that you will have to clear customs before you board your aircraft in St. Thomas or St. Croix. Fill your customs declaration form in completely and accurately and you should have no trouble.

U.S. residents, including children, can bring back up to $1,200 in goods duty-free from the U.S. Virgin Islands. Additionally, $1,000 in goods can be imported at a flat rate of 5 percent, and you can mail an unlimited number of gifts up to $100 in value, excluding perfume, liquor, and tobacco products. U.S. residents over 21 can bring five bottles of liquor home, or six if one is locally produced in the Virgin Islands.

If you arrive via private boat from an international destination (including the British Virgin Islands), you must proceed directly to a port of entry to clear U.S. Customs and Border Protection. Ports of entry are at Charlotte Amalie, St. Thomas; Gallow Bay, St. Croix; and Cruz Bay, St. John. Hours are 8 A.M.–noon and 1–4:30 P.M. daily. Telephone 340/774-6755 for more information. If you arrive after hours, raise your quarantine flag, stay aboard, and report to customs as soon as it opens the next day.

Permits and Licenses

There are no special work permit requirements in the U.S. Virgin Islands. As long as you can legally live and work in the United States, you can do so in the U.S. Virgin Islands. No cruising permit is required for boats in the Virgin Islands for less than six months. If you plan to stay longer, you will need to register your boat with the Department of Planning and Natural Resources (340/774-3320).

Bribes

Don't embarrass yourself by trying to bribe officials in the U.S. Virgin Islands. It is insulting to the officers, and you may well find yourself in serious trouble for doing it.

BRITISH VIRGIN ISLANDS

All visitors except Americans and Canadians must have a passport to enter the BVI. U.S. and Canadian citizens can enter using a birth certificate and government-issued ID. However, all travelers, including U.S. citizens, need a passport to re-enter the United States from the Caribbean. This means that American visitors to the British Virgin Islands are not required to have a passport to get in, but they need one to get back home. Canadians who have to go through the United States to get home also need a passport.

Visas

Visitors are allowed to stay in the BVI for up to one month in the first instance. Further tourist visas must be applied for once you are here. All visitors must have a return ticket home and prearranged accommodations. Nationals of 91 different countries, including Jamaica, China, Cuba, Guyana, Haiti, Russia, and Suriname need to apply for a visa at the local British Embassy before traveling to the territory. Americans, Canadians, Mexicans, and Western Europeans do not need a visa. Call the BVI Passport Office (284/468-3701, ext. 3038) for complete visa information.

Belonger Status

You may encounter the term "belonger" during your visit. It is a legal category first introduced by the British during the colonial period. Belonger status does not depend on one's citizenship or nationality. Instead it confers that, regardless of nationality, the holder has permanent family ties to the British Virgin Islands. Most belongers obtain their status by being born to a belonger. But belonger status can also be obtained by application (there is a twenty-year minimum residency requirement) and by marriage (there is a five-year waiting period). Belongers are free to work and buy land without a special permit, they may vote, they pay lower property taxes, and they will find it easier to obtain a business license. Other UK overseas territories utilize the term belonger to describe a category of people as well, but being a BVI belonger does not give you belonger status in another overseas territory, say, Anguilla, or the Turks and Caicos Islands.

Work Permits

All foreign citizens must have a work permit to work in the BVI. British citizens are not exempt from this requirement. Work permits must be applied for by your employer while you are outside of the territory. In other words, it is not OK to come to the BVI, look for work, and apply for a work permit while you are supposedly on vacation. If you make the mistake of telling an immigration officer that you are looking for a job, you might very well be on the next plane home.

If you are interested in working in the BVI, find a job first. Vacancies are listed in the local papers. Once you are hired, you and your employer will have to navigate the formidable maze of labor and immigration rules to get a work permit and entry permit. Work permits are issued for one-year periods and must be renewed. While you are on a work permit, you cannot work for anyone else.

Taxes

There is no income tax in the BVI, although a payroll tax functions much like a flat income tax would. Employees' annual salaries over $10,000 are taxed at 8 percent. At the same time, employers pay 2–6 percent of their total payroll in taxes, depending on the size of the business. There is

no sales tax, but the government charges a 7 percent hotel tax, which is added to hotel bills, often along with a service charge. Most hotels do not include the tax in their published rates. There is also a departure tax of $5 by sea, $20 by air, and $7 for cruise ship passengers.

Customs

Customs duties are one of the reasons why goods and services are so expensive in the BVI. Duties range from zero to 20 percent, depending on the good and the purpose for which it is being imported. Most goods are charged a 10 percent customs duty. Everything coming into the country is subject to customs duty, including mail-order items and gifts. Residents returning to the BVI after more than 72 hours away are allowed the paltry sum of $50 duty-free. A retailer bringing items in for resale will pay the same customs duty as people bringing the same item in for themselves.

Permits and Licenses

Charter boats pay a special charter boat permit fee to the Customs Department. The fee is $4 per person per day for boats based outside of the BVI and $2 per person per day for BVI-based boats December–April. The rate for BVI-based boats goes down to $0.75 per person per day during the summer.

You must obtain a fishing license before you can fish in the BVI. Fishing licenses are obtained from the Ministry of Natural Resources and Labour (284/468-3701, ext. 2147). Many crewed charter boats, plus all fishing charters, have the necessary license already. If you want to fish, your best bet is to sign up with one of these operators or take part in a fishing tournament.

Bribes

Offering a bribe is a highly disrespectful move that will backfire on you. Police, customs, and immigration officers do not accept bribes and will not welcome your suggestion that they do.

Conduct and Customs

Yes, you are in the islands, but you should still follow basic common sense and etiquette.

ETIQUETTE

Good manners are an essential feature of daily interactions in the Virgin Islands. The only way to begin a conversation with someone is to first wish him or her a "good morning," "good afternoon," or "good night." Indeed, these should be the first words out of your mouth when you enter a room with others already inside or walk up to a group of people. Of course, if the roles are reversed, the only correct way to reply to someone else's "good morning" is to echo the words. Only then can you begin to talk of something else.

In some situations, it is also good manners to ask how the person is or offer an observation about the weather before delving directly into the business at hand. This may not be appreciated by the immigration officer who has a whole line of people to deal with, but in slightly less congested situations, it is the right thing to do.

Very mannerly people will look you in the eye when they meet you on the street and wish you a good day, regardless of whether they know you or not. This is a delightful practice, and if you do it consistently you may get a few odd looks now and again, but your heart will soon be overflowing with love for the world.

Asking a lot of questions is considered rude. A few general queries about someone's family and background are all right, but know when to stop. Virgin Islanders cherish their privacy and resent your intrusion into things that do not concern you. If you really cannot bear not to know, learn the very Virgin Islandish art of careful observation and listening.

STYLES OF COMMUNICATION

Virgin Islanders like to joke with each other and have developed very thick skins for this very purpose. Friends who meet each other on the street will immediately start giving each other a hard time about whatever comes to mind. If a barb is thrown your way, you are expected to respond with an equally stinging barb. This kind of exchange has nothing to do with embarrassing or insulting your friends, but is merely the way people interact. Even business conversations usually begin with a few moments of lightheartedness.

BODY LANGUAGE

Acknowledge people when you come into contact with them, with a handshake, nod, or eye contact. A smile is appreciated, but don't take it too far. Virgin Islanders appreciate sincere friendliness, not pretense. Stand at least a few feet away from the person you are speaking to.

TERMS OF ADDRESS

In keeping with the generally conservative and mannerly culture of the Virgin Islands, courtesy titles are used frequently and extensively. Until you are told otherwise, it is best to call people Mr. or Mrs. so-and-so. Police, immigration, and customs officials are often Officer so-and-so. Lawyers are Attorney so-and-so, and the list goes on.

On the opposite end of the spectrum from courtesy titles, nicknames are commonly used and generally lots of fun. Some people are better known by their nicknames than their given names. The sports field, the ocean, and the playground are places especially conducive to nicknames, although those that are particularly evocative seem to find a foothold in every setting.

TABLE MANNERS

Virgin Islanders are not hung up on table manners. You would no doubt feel awkward slurping your food at a fine restaurant, but that has more to do with the restaurant itself than the country in which it is set.

While Virgin Islanders do not employ strictures about knives, forks, and elbows on the table, they are sensitive about cleanliness and the potential contamination of their food. This arises in part from superstitions and fears of obeah; food and drink are one vehicle by which practitioners of obeah are believed to reach their victims.

DRUGS

Both the U.S. and British Virgin Islands have stiff drug laws. Marijuana, cocaine, and other drugs are illegal here. The islands are also a major drug transshipment point—for your own safety and health, don't get mixed up with drugs while you are in the islands.

Tips for Travelers

ACCESS FOR TRAVELERS WITH DISABILITIES

The U.S. Virgin Islands, which are governed by the Americans with Disabilities Act, are much better equipped for disabled travelers than the British Virgin Islands. Even so, getting around the islands will not be easy for those with physical disabilities. Many shops, restaurants, and hotels are not designed for wheelchairs, and even those hotels that claim to be accessible may not meet your needs. Always call the hotel directly and explain your exact requirements before booking a room. Once you arrive on-island, do not be shy about speaking up for whatever you need; hotel, restaurant, and shop staff members are normally very accommodating and will help to overcome whatever accessibility challenges exist.

The Cyril E. King Airport on St. Thomas uses a lift to transport wheelchairs from the plane to the tarmac. Accessible and affordable transportation is available through **Dial-A-Ride** (340/776-1277, fax 340/777-5383), but call at least a week ahead to arrange for an airport pickup (don't expect taxis to accommodate a wheelchair).

St. John's **Concordia Eco-Resort** (www.concordiaeco-resort.com) has pioneered accessible design through a partnership with the Rhode Island School of Design, which designed four accessible units at this eco-camp. Concordia Eco-Resort owner Stanley Selengut and the design experts are now working with the local government to improve accessibility around the island.

You can reach the TTY/TDD call relay operator in the U.S. Virgin Islands by dialing 800/440-8477. Gimp on the Go has a detailed review of St. John its the website (www.gimponthego.com), and www.allabilities.com includes links to other disabled travel resources. **Connie George Travel Agency** (Glenolden, PA, 610/532-0998 or 800/532-0998, www.cgta.com) specializes in planning trips in the islands for disabled visitors.

Cruises

A good option for disabled travelers is a cruise. A 2005 Supreme Court ruling requires all cruise lines that operate in the United States, including those that are registered in other jurisdictions, to adhere to the Americans with Disabilities Act. Some cruise lines were already catering to disabled passengers; **Princess Cruises** (800/774-6237, www.princess.com) and **Royal Caribbean Cruise Line** (866/562-7625, www.royalcaribbean.com) have received good marks from disabled travelers.

Charter cruises aimed at passengers with specific accessibility needs are also available. **Dialysis at Sea** (www.dialysisatsea.com) organizes cruises for travelers who need kidney dialysis. **Passages Deaf Travel** (http://passagesdeaftravel.com) organizes charter cruises for cruisers with hearing impairments, and **Accessible Journeys** (http://disabilitytravel.com) offers cruises for guests who are in wheelchairs or who are slow walkers. Mind's Eye Travel (http://mindseyetravel.com) occasionally offers cruises for blind or visually impaired travelers.

TRAVELING WITH CHILDREN

The Virgin Islands provide a whole range of appealing activities for children: swimming, snorkeling, hiking, and water sports are especially suitable. However, a few hotels, especially in the British Virgin Islands, don't allow children under a certain age, so be sure to check first. For parents who want a little time out from the kids, many larger hotels offer child-care service (be sure to check it out before leaving your child there).

TRAVELING WITH PETS

Unless you are moving to the Virgin Islands, leave your pets at home. You will have to overcome serious administrative hurdles to bring your animal to the British Virgin Islands, and it is not much easier to get a pet into the U.S. Virgin Islands. It will also not be easy to find a hotel that will let Fido stay with you.

WOMEN TRAVELING ALONE

Women are sometimes the target of harassment in the Virgin Islands, and women traveling alone should always be aware of their surroundings. Don't walk alone at night in town, and certainly don't try to catch a ride alone at any time. Catcalls, often in the form of a hiss, are common.

Women dining or drinking alone are a prime target for harassment. Bring a book and develop a very cold demeanor if you really want to be left alone. Likewise, a woman alone on the dance floor is a magnet for men. Often, it seems like it does not matter how many times you tell a man you do not want to dance with him. This can easily spoil a evening. Some men consider all female visitors to be in the market for a steamy West Indian vacation romance. If you're not, don't let anyone think you are.

SENIOR TRAVELERS

Seniors can and do travel to the Virgin Islands in great numbers. Don't expect senior discounts, however: They are virtually unheard of. **Elderhostel** (877/426-8056, www.elderhostel.org) organizes occasional trips in both the British and U.S. Virgin Islands, often focusing on historical preservation. The **American Association of Retired Persons** (www.aarp.org) publishes travel advice for destinations around the world, including the Virgin Islands.

GAY AND LESBIAN TRAVELERS

Homosexuality is not widely accepted in the Virgin Islands, and many islanders are extremely homophobic. But where gay Virgin Islanders face an uphill battle for acceptance, gay and lesbian travelers are tolerated. For the warmest welcome and greatest freedom, gay and lesbian travelers should first consider St. Croix, which has several openly gay-friendly hotels and nightspots.

Gay travelers are particularly welcome at Sandcastle on the Beach (www.sandcastle-onthebeach.com) and Palms at Pelican Cove (www.palmspelicancove.com) on St. Croix, Fort Recovery on Tortola (www.fortrecovery-tortola.com), and VIVA Vacations (www.vivacations.com) on St. John.

Virgin Islanders everywhere will turn a blind eye to your sexuality as long as you let them, so it is best to avoid open demonstrations of affection and obvious indications of your sexuality. Don't ask, don't tell is the unspoken and unwritten social contract for gays and lesbians in the islands.

OPPORTUNITIES FOR EMPLOYMENT
U.S. Virgin Islands

The tourism industry generates opportunities for employment in the U.S. Virgin Islands. Food service, retail sales, hotel management, and the marine industry are the areas where you will find the greatest number of jobs available. Salaries are not always generous, particularly in the service industry, and the cost of living in the islands can be quite high.

British Virgin Islands

In addition to tourism, job opportunities exist in the financial services industry. Accountants, lawyers, and those with special knowledge of offshore finance will find it quite easy to land a job in the islands. In tourism, opportunities exist particularly in the marine fields: sailors, diving professionals, and those with experience servicing boats are in demand.

Remember that you will have to apply for and receive a work permit (via your employer) before you can start work in the BVI. The application must take place while you are off-island. Work permits are issued only when the employer can demonstrate that there are no belongers qualified or interested in the job.

OPPORTUNITIES FOR STUDY
U.S. Virgin Islands

The University of the Virgin Islands (www. uvi.edu) is a four-year, accredited university with campuses on St. Thomas and St. Croix. Founded in 1963 as the College of the Virgin Islands, UVI offers both bachelor's and master's degree opportunities.

British Virgin Islands

H. Lavity Stoutt Community College (www. hlscc.edu.vg) is a two-year college founded in 1990. The New England Culinary Institute (www.necibvi.com) has a satellite school attached to HLSCC, and students enroll in a two-year course leading to an associate's degree in the culinary arts.

Health and Safety

The most common health problem experienced by travelers to the Virgin Islands is sunburn. Nevertheless, the possibility exists for more serious problems, especially if you take risks swimming, diving, boating, driving, or with sexual behavior. Health care in the islands is generally good, although specialist services are limited, and ambulance service may be very slow, especially in remote or outer islands.

The U.S. Centers for Disease Control and Prevention (877/FYI-TRIP, www.cdc.gov) maintains up-to-date health information for travel destinations around the world, including the Virgin Islands. This is a good resource for travelers.

Before traveling make sure you are up to date on all routine immunizations, including hepatitis A and B, tetanus, diphtheria, and measles. There is no risk of malaria or yellow fever in the Virgin Islands.

DENGUE

While mosquitoes in the Virgin Islands do not spread malaria or yellow fever, there have been cases of dengue and dengue hemorrhagic fever. Dengue is a virus characterized by fever, headaches, and joint and muscle pain, sometimes accompanied by nausea, vomiting, and rash. Symptoms usually appear 4–7 days after the person is bitten by a dengue-carrying mosquito. There is no cure or vaccine for dengue. Treatment is available for the symptoms. In rare cases, dengue can be fatal, especially in cases of small children or older adults.

The only way to avoid dengue is to avoid mosquito bites. Use a mosquito repellent containing DEET, and stay within screened-in or air-conditioned rooms. Avoid being outside during the early morning and late afternoon hours favored by mosquitoes.

© SUSANNA HENIGHAN POTTER

In the BVI, beach safety warnings are communicated through colored flags. Yellow means caution and red means it is unsafe to enter the water.

THE SUN

Take precautions against the powerful tropical sun. Apply **reef-safe sunscreen** 15–20 minutes before you go out, and reapply regularly. The chemical **oxybenzone**, commonly used in many sunscreens, has been proven to negatively affect coral reefs, already under stress from disease, rising sea temperatures, pollution, and careless snorkelers and boaters. When you're stocking up on sunscreen, carefully check the label and look for formulas whose active ingredients are zinc oxide or titanium dioxide instead.

Be especially careful when you are swimming or sailing, since the coolness of the water and breeze may make you forget how strong the sun is. Wear a T-shirt when snorkeling for long periods to protect your back, and be sure to apply sunscreen to the back of your legs.

On land, wear hats and long-sleeved loose clothing to protect your skin. Avoid direct sunlight altogether between 10 A.M. and 2 P.M.

THE OCEAN

Do not overestimate your swimming, snorkeling, diving, or sailing abilities. The ocean can be powerful, unpredictable, and deadly. Pay attention to weather forecasts. Yes, you are on vacation, but terrible things can still happen.

Swimming-related deaths occur annually in the Virgin Islands, usually when someone overestimates their ability or underestimates the physical challenge involved. If you have had heart trouble or are at risk for a heart attack, be especially careful. The only beaches with lifeguards are Magen's Bay on St. Thomas and Trunk Bay on St. John. All the rest are swim at your own risk.

If you are susceptible to motion sickness and plan to sail or ride in a boat, bring Sea-Bands, the wristbands that help prevent motion sickness. Ginger is also a proven remedy. You could also pack over-the-counter motion sickness medicine like Dramamine.

Sharks live in Virgin Islands waters, but they mostly stay in deep water well offshore. It is unlikely you will encounter a shark at all. You will, however, see barracudas if you snorkel. Barracudas tend to stay still in the water; do not bother them and they will not bother you. Moray eels live inside dark caves and crevices—don't reach into one of these unless you have checked it out with your light first. Learn to recognize sea urchins—their long, black spines are a giveaway. Step on one and you will be in a lot of pain.

TROPICAL FISH POISONING

One of the most mysterious and worst tropical maladies is fish poisoning, a severe illness caused when you eat a fish containing ciguatera toxins. Symptoms of fish poisoning are severe nausea, diarrhea, vomiting, and weakness. In addition, there are neurological symptoms such as tingling feet and hands, itchiness, and the sensation of hot things feeling cold and cold things feeling hot. Muscle weakness and pain in the bones and joints are also symptoms.

Depending on the severity of the case, symptoms can range from mild to completely debilitating. If you experience any of the symptoms, think of whether you have eaten fish in the last 24 hours. In many cases, hospitalization is required to prevent dehydration.

Unless you swear off tropical fish all together, there is no sure way to avoid fish poisoning. Restaurants, groceries, and reputable fishermen use testing kits to determine if fish contain poison. The best way to avoid fish poisoning is to buy fish from people, restaurants, or stores that you trust.

BEACH POLLUTION

Pollution caused by the discharge of untreated sewage from aging sewerage systems on St. Thomas and St. Croix causes beach closures on those islands from time to time. The U.S. Virgin Islands Department of Planning and Natural Resources is responsible for testing the water quality of beaches and for alerting the public if pollution reaches dangerous levels. Beach closures are announced in the local newspapers, and you will be alerted by notices posted around the beach. You can also contact the DPNR at 340/773-1082 on St. Croix or 340/774-3320 on St. Thomas.

In the British Virgin Islands, the authorities are not as fastidious about testing water quality, so use common sense. Popular anchorages, such as Road Harbour, Cane Garden Bay, and Trellis Bay, are probably not the cleanest places to swim.

BOTHERSOME INSECTS AND ANIMALS

Mosquitoes tend to come out at dusk and dawn. They are worst in urban and suburban areas where trash, flowerpots, cisterns, and other containers serve as breeding grounds. They are also common around ponds. Mosquitoes are most prevalent in the rainy season and are easily tempered by breeze.

Bring insect repellent, especially if you will be camping or staying in rustic accommodations. Always keep screen doors closed. Mosquito coils, which are burned like incense, work well, but the fumes bother some people.

Another pesky bug is the biting midge, known locally as the sandfly. These annoying bugs live in sand and come out during dusk and dawn. They resemble a gnat and deliver uncomfortable bites. Bug repellent works against them. Be careful not to track too much sand into your room, villa, or boat, or sand flies will follow.

There are no dangerous wild animals or snakes in the Virgin Islands. Many islands have large populations of feral cats and dogs, which can be problematic. Dog packs are known to attack livestock, especially at night. In the British Virgin Islands, look out for goats, cows, and chickens while driving.

PRESCRIPTIONS

There are good, well-stocked pharmacies in St. Thomas, St. Croix, and in Road Town, Tortola, but to avoid hassle, bring any prescription medicine you need (in its original container) with you to the islands. It is also a good idea to bring the prescriptions themselves in case you need a refill.

BIRTH CONTROL
Condoms are available at drugstores and grocery stores around the islands, and birth control prescriptions can be filled at pharmacies. The brands that you are used to may not be available in the British Virgin Islands, however. Abortion is illegal in the British Virgin Islands but legal in the U.S. Virgin Islands.

SEXUALLY TRANSMITTED DISEASES
The Caribbean has the second highest prevalence rate for HIV/AIDS in the world, behind sub-Saharan Africa. In 2009 there were 17,000 new infections in the region and 12,000 people died from AIDS-related causes. Infection rates in the region are between 1 and 3 percent.

The Virgin Islands have relatively low rates of infection, although AIDS advocates say that much more needs to be done to arrest the spread of the disease. They emphasize that, due to the tight-knit society, many persons choose not to disclose their status, causing official statistics to be misleading.

Unsafe sex is dangerous in any country, including the Virgin Islands. If you plan to have promiscuous sex (or even if you don't), pack condoms and use them.

Information and Services

MONEY
Both the U.S. and British Virgin Islands use United States currency. Travelers from Europe, Canada, and other parts of the world can exchange money at banks throughout the islands. Banking hours are generally 9 A.M.–3 P.M., although some banks have longer hours. There are no independent money changers.

Hotels, car rental agencies, charter boat companies, retail shops, and large restaurants almost always accept credit cards and travelers checks. In fact, many hotels and car rental companies require a credit card. Some smaller establishments do not accept these forms of payment, however, and others require a minimum purchase amount to process a credit card payment. Always ask first.

Tipping
Tipping follows the same general pattern as in the United States: Tip between 10 and 20 percent for restaurant service and a few dollars for someone who helps you with your bags. Taxi drivers can be tipped if you are especially impressed with their service, but a tip is generally not expected.

Many hotels tack a 10 percent service charge on their bills. Many restaurants follow suit, tacking a 10 or even 20 percent service charge onto bills. Be sure to look closely at your restaurant bill before adding an additional tip.

MAPS AND TOURIST INFORMATION
Free, pocket-size road maps are widely available throughout the Virgin Islands. These are handy and reliable and will meet the needs of most travelers. Maps are also printed in the free tourist-oriented magazines that are widely available.

Specialized hiking maps of St. John are available from the National Park Service headquarters in Cruz Bay. The NPS shops in Cruz Bay and Christiansted, St. Croix, have the best selection of maps in the islands.

If you want a good, detailed map of the entire Virgin Islands, you should buy it before you come. Map publishers Berndtson and International Travel Maps have high-quality maps available at major online map stores and booksellers, including Barnes and Noble and Amazon. You can also find them at www.vitrader.com. The National Geographic Society has an excellent map of the Virgin Islands National Park on St. John.

Detailed government survey maps of the British Virgin Islands are on sale at the Survey Department (284/494-3459). This office also sells what it calls a "tourist map" for $12, which is a detailed, large-format, foldout map of the BVI.

Nautical Charts

It is best to obtain nautical charts before you arrive in the Virgin Islands. This will allow you to plan your cruise ahead of time and avoid the frustration of looking for charts in the islands, where availability is often limited. While most charter companies provide a chart with the boat, you may find it is not as detailed as you want. Chart series published by Caribbean Yacht Charts, Imray, the U.S. National Ocean Service (NOAA), the U.S. National Imagery and Mapping Agency, and British Admiralty are all fine for navigating in the Virgin Islands. The NOAA, Caribbean Yachting Charts, and Imray products are probably the easiest to find. A good source for nautical charts is www.nauticalcharts.com. The National Oceanic and Atmospheric Agency (www.nauticalcharts.noaa.gov) lists official NOAA chart retailers throughout the United States.

The U.S. National Ocean Service chart no. 25640 is the only chart that encompasses the entire U.S. and British Virgin Islands. Other charts, however, show greater detail. Single charts range $20–30; a complete, detailed set of charts for the Virgin Islands can cost several hundred dollars.

Electronic charts are the latest thing in sailing, but they can be very hard to obtain in the islands. Electronic charts produced by C-Map, Navionics, Garmin, and BSB/NOAA are good for cruising the Virgin Islands.

Tourist Offices

You will find tourist offices and information desks in Road Town, Tortola; Spanish Town, Virgin Gorda; Charlotte Amalie, St. Thomas; and Christiansted, St. Croix. The National Park Service office on St. John doubles as an information desk. Both the U.S. and British Virgin Islands have tourist offices in the mainland United States and Europe, plus useful websites.

The **British Virgin Islands Tourist Board** (www.bvitourism.com) has offices in Road Town, Tortola (284/494-3134); Virgin Gorda (284/495-5181); San Juan, Puerto Rico (787/721-2525); New York (212/563-3117 or 800/835-8530); London (44/207-355-9585); Milano, Italy (39/02-667-14374); and Düsseldorf, Germany (49/2104-286671).

The **U.S. Virgin Islands Department of Tourism** (800/372-8784, www.usvitourism.com) has a stateside sales team as well as offices in St. Thomas (340/774-8784), St. Croix (340/773-0495), and St. John (340/776-6450).

Public Libraries

There are public libraries on St. Thomas, St. John, St. Croix, Tortola, Virgin Gorda, Anegada, and Jost Van Dyke. The larger libraries have Internet access.

FILM AND PHOTOGRAPHY
Photo Tips

The Virgin Islands' endless summer is a photographer's best friend and worst enemy. The sunshine and blue sky make it nearly impossible to take ugly photos. For the best shots of the crystal blue water, choose an absolutely sunny day and seek out the highest elevation you can find. While a sunny day almost guarantees good scenery photos, it makes photographing people difficult. If it is very bright, you may need to use a flash to fill in the shadows of a person's face. Remember the old rule to always put the camera's back to the sun, but watch out as well for squinty eyes.

It is well worth picking up a cheap, disposable underwater camera to bring with you. You can also buy them at shops throughout the islands, and just about every dive shop stocks them. Don't bother taking underwater shots on a cloudy day; you really need sunlight to boost the colors. Also try to avoid windy or rough days, when waves have churned up clouds of sediment. The built-in flash on many of the point-and-shoot disposable cameras is quite weak; don't try to take photos of things more than six feet away if you're depending on the flash.

The disposable waterproof cameras are handy even if you're not planning on underwater photography. Seawater and sun can damage your camera; if you anticipate lots of beach, boat, or surf photography, protect your camera by leaving it at home. If you insist on taking a regular camera to the beach or on a boat, pack it in a plastic bag. Better yet, use a "dry bag." Remember that even a mild saltwater spray can damage your camera.

Photo Etiquette
In the Virgin Islands, it is rude to take photographs of strangers without their permission. On some islands, St. Thomas in particular, there are a few outgoing entrepreneurs who make a living by posing in colorful Caribbean garb astride a donkey. If you want something a little more authentic than that, you will have to do some legwork of your own. The only exception to this is at local fairs or cultural events, where it is OK to photograph performers or participants. However, it is still a good idea to ask first.

COMMUNICATIONS AND MEDIA
Postal Services
Postal service in both the U.S. and British Virgin Islands is reliable. The U.S. Virgin Islands are served by the U.S. Postal Service, and the same products and services available on the mainland are available at post offices in the islands, including overnight, registered, and priority mail. Zip codes for the U.S. Virgin Islands are 00801–00809. There is one post office on St. John, five on St. Thomas, and six on St. Croix. Postal rates are the same as in the mainland United States.

While not as sophisticated or fast as the mail service in the U.S. Virgin Islands, the BVI Post Office is just as reliable. You can mail letters and packages, buy stamps, and purchase money orders. There is no overnight or priority mail service, however.

It costs 50 cents to mail a letter from the BVI to the United States, Canada, and Europe, and 35 cents to mail a postcard. It takes 7–10 days (and sometimes longer) for a letter mailed in the BVI to reach the United States or Canada. Many a traveler has had the experience of already being home when their postcards start to turn up in friends' mailboxes.

In the British Virgin Islands, an alternative to using the local postal service is to send mail through one of the mailbox service companies. These businesses rent post office boxes to residents who want to be able to receive mail at a U.S. address. They also take your letters and packages and mail them at U.S. Virgin Islands post offices. While expensive, this can be the best way to send mail if you are in a hurry or need the added security of insurance or a return receipt.

Try Inland Messenger Service (Lower Main St., 284/494-6440) or Khoy's Mailing Service (R. G. Hodge Plaza, 284/494-4539), both in Road Town. International couriers FedEx, DHL, and UPS also have offices in both territories.

Neither the U.S. or British Virgin Islands have a system of postal addresses. With the exception of downtown Christiansted in St. Croix, all customers use post office boxes to receive their mail. This is one reason why giving directions is so challenging in both territories.

Shipping Packages
In both territories, the most affordable way to

ship a package back home is through the post office. This method is also quite reliable. In the U.S. Virgin Islands, you can bring your package to any post office. Rates depend on the destination but can be as low as $6 for a five-pound package to the United States and $17 for air parcel post to the United Kingdom.

In the British Virgin Islands, bring your package to the parcel post desk at the Road Town Post Office in the Qwomar Building, where you will have to fill out a customs declaration form. It costs $14 to mail a five-pound package to the U.S. and $17 to mail it to the United Kingdom.

Telephone and Fax Services
U.S. VIRGIN ISLANDS
Placing calls to and from the U.S. Virgin Islands is easy and relatively affordable. As part of the United States, the territory is usually not considered an international call, although you should check your long-distance plan before making any calls. The area code is 340, and calls can be made on pay phones, using calling cards, or on cellular phones. Major U.S. cellular phone companies provide service in the U.S. Virgin Islands. Check your wireless plan for information on roaming charges.

BRITISH VIRGIN ISLANDS
Things are more complicated in the British Virgin Islands. Historically, telecommunication rates in the BVI have been high; Cable & Wireless West Indies Ltd. and CCT Global Communications had a monopoly on landlines and cellular service respectively for many years. Between 2005 and 2007 the market was liberalized and rates have fallen considerably, although not to the level that many travelers are used to paying at home.

International roaming rates in the BVI can be hefty; always contact your home cellular provider before you leave to find out what type of coverage they have in the BVI, what the rates will be, and if they have a preferred roaming partner.

For information on telecommunication services in the BVI, contact LIME (284/494-4444, www.time4lime.com); CCT Global Communications (284/444-4444); or Digicel (284/300-1000, www.digicelbvi.com).

Internet Access
Internet service is generally reliable in both the U.S. Virgin Islands and British Virgin Islands. Wireless Internet access or a dedicated Internet workstation are common features at most hotels and villas; inquire when you make your reservation if this is especially important to you.

The demand among travelers for Internet access has spawned a few cybercafés around the islands and a number of wireless hotspots. Check marinas, restaurants, and hotels to find a wireless connection.

Two-Way Radio
Radio is the best and most reliable way for mariners to communicate. All boats should be equipped with a VHF radio, and boat captains should make sure that not only they, but all members of the party, know how to use it. Channel 16 is used for standby and for emergency calls. Virgin Islands Radio, which can facilitate ship-to-shore calls, monitors channels 24, 85, and 87. Register and pay ahead of time with Virgin Islands Radio, and you will be able to make and receive local and international phone calls with their assistance. Channels 3, 4, and 6 are used for weather updates.

Be sure to review proper radio use before casting off. For example, channel 16 should only be used to establish contact with another party and not for conversations. In the case of a real emergency, use channel 16 and call "Mayday, mayday, mayday"; state the name of the vessel; and then say "over" until someone responds. It is important to remain calm and speak clearly so you can be understood.

Local Newspapers and Magazines

The *Virgin Islands Daily News* is the best and most reliable newspaper in the Virgin Islands. It covers happenings in the U.S. Virgin Islands in great detail and often includes stories about the British Virgin Islands as well. It reports regional and international news and includes comics, TV listings, crosswords, weather, and more. The *Daily News* is published every day except Sunday and costs $1.

The *St. Croix Avis* is a daily focusing on St. Croix news, widely available on that island. *St. Thomas-St. John This Week* and *St. Croix This Week* are monthly (yes, there's a contradiction there) magazines geared toward tourists. Both contain calendars of events, useful phone numbers, and lots of advertising.

The British Virgin Islands are served by three different national weekly newspapers. *The BVI Beacon,* published on Thursdays, is the best. Others are the *The Virgin Islands StandPoint,* which comes out on Wednesdays, and *The Island Sun,* published on Fridays. For entertainment news, pick up the free entertainment guide the *Limin' Times,* a small glossy publication.

The *BVI Welcome* is a free bimonthly glossy magazine for tourists with thoughtful articles, lots of useful information, and advertising. It is widely available at hotels, restaurants, and other tourist-oriented places.

Local Radio and Television

There is an abundance of local radio stations in the Virgin Islands. Listening to local radio is a great way to soak up the local culture, pick up on Caribbean music, and find out where the big party is on the weekend.

Some good bets on the radio dial are: **Mongoose 104** (104.9 FM; oldies and classics); **Isle 95** (95.1 FM; reggae and urban); **Magic 97** (970 AM; news, talk, and Caribbean music); **WRRA** (1290 AM; blues, jazz, calypso); **ZVCR** (106.9 FM; Caribbean); **ZBVI** (780 AM; news, Caribbean, oldies); **KISS 101.3** (urban); **105 JAMZ** (Caribbean, reggae); and **WVGN** (107.3 FM; NPR news). Not all radio stations can be picked up on every island.

WEIGHTS, MEASURES, AND TIME

Despite being British, the British Virgin Islands use imperial measures: Miles, feet, and pounds are the common parlance. Speed limits are posted in miles, gas is sold by the gallon, and groceries are weighed in pounds and ounces. The same is true for the U.S. Virgin Islands.

Electricity is 110 volts, 60 cycles, the same as in the United States. No transformers or plug adapters are required. Both the U.S. and British Virgin Islands experience occasional power outages, but many hotels and guesthouses have backup generators, so you may not notice.

The Virgin Islands are on Atlantic standard time, one hour earlier than eastern standard time and four hours later than Greenwich mean time. There is no daylight saving time.

RESOURCES

Suggested Reading

HISTORY

Anderson, John L. *Night of the Silent Drums.* Rome: Mapes Monde, 1992. John Anderson conducted exhaustive research into the 1733 slave rebellion on St. John and brought what he learned to life in this story, told through the eyes of a Danish plantation doctor who is sympathetic to the Africans' cause. Although fictional, the book is the best retelling of the events of 1733 around. The story was first published by Charles Scribner and Sons in 1975; the 1992 edition is beautifully illustrated with rare West Indian hand drawings and prints.

Andrew, John. *The Hanging of Arthur Hodge.* Philadelphia: Xlibris, 2000. This self-published thesis is a comprehensive account of the 1811 trial of Tortola planter Arthur Hodge, who was hanged for the murder of one of his slaves. The event was an antislavery milestone in the Caribbean, and Andrew's telling is both informative and entertaining.

Armstrong, Douglas. *Creole Transformation from Slavery to Freedom: Historical Archaeology of the East End Community, St. John, Virgin Islands.* Gainesville, Florida: University Press of Florida, 2003. This academic work looks closely at the social transformation that took place at the end of slavery in the Caribbean, through a close examination of the St. John east end community, which gained freedom 40 years before the 1848 emancipation in the Danish West Indies.

Bastian, Jeannette Allis. *Owning Memory: How a Caribbean Community Lost Its Archives and Found Its History.* Westport, Connecticut: Greenwood Publishing Group, 2003. A former librarian and archivist in the U.S. Virgin Islands, Jeannette Bastian writes how the community was forced to develop its own history because the historical record was stored in Copenhagen and Washington, D.C., the seats of the two colonial powers.

Chernow, Ron. *Alexander Hamilton.* New York: Penguin Press, 2004. The definitive biography of St. Croix's most famous native son.

Cohen, Judah. *Through the Sands of Time: A History of the Jewish Community of St. Thomas, U.S. Virgin Islands.* Waltham, Massachusetts: Brandeis University Press, 2012. This hefty work records the long and colorful history of St. Thomas's Jewish community, from its early roots in the 17th century to today.

Dookhan, Isaac. *A History of the Virgin Islands of the United States.* Jamaica: Canoe Press, 1994. First published in 1974, this was one of the first comprehensive histories of the U.S. Virgin Islands and it remains a good introduction to the history of the islands. Dookhan, a Guyanese scholar, also wrote a history of the British Virgin Islands, but it is out of print and extremely difficult to find.

Gill, Patricia. *Buddhoe*. 1976. This self-published work is a fictional account of the 1848 slave uprising on St. Croix and its charismatic leader.

Lewisohn, Florence. *St. Croix Under Seven Flags*. Hollywood, Florida: The Dukane Press, 1970. Well written and engaging, this hefty history of St. Croix is one of the best-told stories of the island. Although it is dated in some respects, students of history will still appreciate Lewisohn's research and the numerous illustrations.

Low, Ruth Hull, and Rafael Valls. *St. John Backtime: Eyewitness Accounts from 1718 to 1956*. St. John: Eden Hill Press, 1985. This attractive, slim volume contains excerpts of firsthand accounts of St. John, from the earliest days of Danish settlement to the 1950s. While some were authored by native St. Johnians, most provide an outsider's view of the island. It is also nicely illustrated.

O'Neal, Eugenia. *From the Field to the Legislature: A History of Women in the Virgin Islands*. Westport, Connecticut: Greenwood Publishing Group, 2001. The former head of the BVI Government's women's affairs desk wrote the first history of the women of the Virgin Islands in 2001. This academic work provides a valuable and rare picture of the role of women in Virgin Islands society and history.

St. John Historical Society. *St. John: Life in Five Quarters*. St. John, 2010. Selected readings, maps, photographs, and drawings from the St. John Historical Society, ideal for a history lover who also loves St. John.

CHRONICLES

Benjamin, Guy H. *Me and My Beloved Virgin*. New York: Benjamin's Publishing Co., 1981. St. Johnian Guy Benjamin tells of growing up in Coral Bay, St. John, in the early part of the 20th century.

Flax, Andria D. *The Way We Were*. Road Town, Tortola: Andria D. Flax, 2010. An utterly charming memoir of life on Peter Island and in Road Town during the author's childhood in the 1960s, this book offers a portrait of an island now lost to time.

Melchior, Ariel, Sr. *Thoughts Along the Way: Virgin Islands Reflections*. St. Thomas: Ariel Melchior Inc., 1981. One of the founders of the *Virgin Islands Daily News*, Ariel Melchior has compiled some of the best editorials from that newspaper, from its founding in the 1930s until the 1970s. The result is a fascinating picture of the U.S. Virgin Islands' struggle for self-government and a greater sense of identity.

Seaman, George. *Ay-Ay: An Island Almanac*. London: Macmillan Publishers, 1989. A St. Croix native, George Seaman grew up to be one of the island's greatest fans. In this memoir he shares his delight in the annual rhythm of seasons, animals, weather, and human events. Woven in are descriptions of the Crucian lifestyle, history, and a boyhood on a quiet Caribbean island.

Svalesen, Leif, Selena A. Winsnes (translator), and Pat Shaw (translator). *The Slave Ship Fredensborg*. Bloomington: Indiana University Press, 2000. Underwater archaeologist Leif Svalesen recounts the journey of the slave ship *Fredensborg*, which sank off the coast of Norway in 1768 on its way back from the Danish West Indies. The wreck was discovered in 1974, and Svalesen uses artifacts from the wreck, including the captain's log, to tell the detailed story of its journey. The book forms the basis of an exhibit at the Fort Frederik Museum in Frederiksted, St. Croix.

FLORA AND FAUNA

Barlow, Virginia. *The Nature of the Islands.* Dunedin, Florida: Chris Doyle Publishing, 1993. Exhaustively researched, beautifully written, and charmingly illustrated, this is the best and most accessible guide to the nature of the islands. This book is well-organized and makes it easy to learn more about the plants, trees, and animals around the islands.

Lazell, James. *Island: Fact and Theory in Nature.* Berkeley: University of California Press, 2005. Scientist James "Skip" Lazell has lived on and studied Guana Island for decades, and this work examines the remarkable diversity of life on this tiny British Virgin Island. His analysis raises questions about prevailing scientific wisdom and evolves into an argument about the critical importance of biodiversity for life on earth.

Kirk, T. Kent. *Tropical Trees of Florida and the Virgin Islands.* Sarasota, Florida: Pineapple Press, 2009. Color photographs of common native and naturalized trees make this a handy reference for residents and visitors.

Nellis, David W. *Puerto Rico and Virgin Islands Wildlife Viewing Guide.* Helena, Montana: Falcon Publishing, 1999. This guide includes descriptions and information about the major natural attractions in the Virgin Islands and Puerto Rico, as well as full-color photos of common birds, lizards, and other animals.

Raffaele, Herbert A., Cindy J. House, and John Wiessinger. *Guide to the Birds of Puerto Rico and the Virgin Islands.* Princeton, New Jersey:

Princeton University Press, 1989. This is the definitive and best guide to the birds of the Virgin Islands, with detailed descriptions of 284 species, 273 of which are illustrated. In addition, there are practical tips for birders visiting the area.

Rogers, Caroline. *The Mysterious, Magical Mangroves of St. John, U.S. Virgin Islands.* St. John: Caroline Rogers, 2011. Travel through the underwater world of the mangroves with marine biologist Dr. Caroline Rogers in this beautifully illustrated book.

Stokes, F. Joseph. *Handguide to the Coral Reef Fishes of the Caribbean.* New York: Lippencott and Cromwell, 1980. This illustrated guide includes descriptions of hundreds of reef fish, plus tips on how to identify mystery fish.

Thomas, Toni. *Traditional Medicinal Plants of St. Croix, St. Thomas, and St. John.* St. Thomas: University of the Virgin Islands, 1997. This informative field guide contains detailed information about traditional uses of hundreds of plants, including appropriate warnings. Its information is applicable to the British Virgin Islands, too.

FOOD AND DRINK

Clarke, Clarice C., ed. *Native Recipes.* St. Thomas: University of the Virgin Islands Cooperative Extension Service, 1998. Produced by the University of the Virgin Islands, this is a good resource for traditional Virgin Islands cooking and recipes, including dishes that are hard to find in other Caribbean cookbooks. Nutritional analysis of the recipes is included.

Morgan, Jinx, and Jefferson Morgan. *The Sugar Mill Caribbean Cookbook.* Boston: The Harvard Common Press, 1996. Owners of the Sugar Mill Hotel and Restaurant on Tortola's north shore, Jinx and Jefferson Morgan offer an engaging Caribbean-inspired cookbook designed for cooks in North America and Europe, where Caribbean ingredients may be hard to find. Many of the recipes take an authentic Caribbean dish and add an elegant twist—often with superb results.

Watkins, Jane. *St. Croix Food & Wine Experience.* Florida: JWatkins Publishing, 2011. Lavishly illustrated, this cookbook is inspired by St. Croix's annual culinary extravaganza and features favorite recipes from top island and continental chefs.

GUIDES

Gaffin, Pam. *St. John: Feet, Fins, and Four-Wheel Drive.* St. John: American Paradise Publishing, 2009. St. John resident Pam Gaffin provides practical and insightful advice about visiting St. John. The book outlines dozens of different driving tours, hikes, and "scrambles" on St. John.

Lensfestey, Thompson, and Thompson Lensfestey, Jr. *The Sailor's Illustrated Dictionary.* New York: Lyon's Press, 2004. A reference book like no other. Entries include types of knots, clouds, equipment, and much more.

Scott, Nancy, and Simon Scott. *The Cruising Guide to the Virgin Islands, 15th edition.* Dunedin, Florida: Cruising Guide Publications, 2011. Veteran Virgin Islands sailors Nancy and Simon Scott publish the definitive guide for cruisers A sturdy cover and spiral binding make it as practical as it is useful. It is updated annually.

Singer, Gerald. *St. John Off the Beaten Track.* St. John: Sombrero Publishing, 2011. Regularly updated guide by a St. John resident for those wishing to discover lesser-known nooks and crannies of St. John.

THE REGION

Columbus, Christopher, and J. M. Cohen (editor). *The Four Voyages.* New York: Penguin Group, 1992. A new edition of Christopher Columbus's own account of his "discovery" of the Caribbean, including passages describing his encounter with Kalinago people on St. Croix in 1493.

Ferguson, James. *The Story of the Caribbean People.* Kingston, Jamaica: Ian Randle Publishers, 1999. This textbook is a useful resource on Caribbean history, from pre-Columbians to the modern issues of drug trafficking, money laundering, and tourism. While the Virgin Islands play only a minor role in Ferguson's telling, his history provides valuable context for students of the islands.

Kincaid, Jamaica. *A Small Place.* New York: Farrar, Straus and Giroux, 1988. The best portrait of the peculiar history and culture of a small Caribbean island ever written. Although based on Kincaid's native Antigua, *A Small Place* paints a true picture of the entire region. Students of the region turn to this thin tome time and time again.

Las Casas, Bartolomé de. *A Short Account of the Destruction of the Indies.* New York: Penguin Group, 1992. The 1542 account of Spanish settlement of Puerto Rico and Hispaniola by a Spanish priest was an urgent indictment of the treatment of the Igneri and Kalinago people that were found in the region. The description is still as powerful and troubling today as it was then.

BEACH READS

Bramble, Alison Knights. *The Eye of the Storm.* Sea Cows Bay, British Virgin Islands: alookingglass, 2011. Written by a sailing instructor and longtime resident of the British Virgin Islands, this coming-of-age novel chronicles 13-year-old Ben Johnston's adventurous summer vacation on a fictional island uncannily like Tortola. Though it's written for teenagers, adults will also enjoy this story.

Brandt, Kathy. *Dark Water Dive.* New York: Penguin Group, 2004. An underwater murder mystery set in the British Virgin Islands. Homicide detective Hannah Sampson explores the (fictional) underbelly of paradise.

O'Neal, Eugenia. *Just an Affair.* Columbus, Missouri: Genesis Press, 2003. A classic romance set in the British Virgin Islands. Charter boat captain Caryl Walker falls for a smooth-talking music CEO but loses her memory before she can tell her former lover to take a hike.

Wouk, Herman. *Don't Stop the Carnival.* Boston: Little, Brown and Co., 1965. The Caribbean classic, this is the story of an optimistic hotel manager who sets up shop on what is widely believed to be Water Island near St. Thomas in the 1960s. Nothing goes as planned, but there is plenty of laughter and entertainment.

CULTURE

Schrader, Richard A., Sr. *Maufe, Quelbe and t'ing.* St. Croix: 2001. The reminiscences of St. Croix culture bearer, poet, and lecturer Richard Schrader. The stories depict in loving detail the ways of life of Crucians who came of age during the middle part of the 20th century. Richard Schrader is the author of more than a dozen books of poetry, literature, and history, all centered on the rich culture of his native St. Croix.

Sterns, Robin. *Say It in Crucian!* Christiansted, St. Croix: Antilles Press, 2008. A delightful little tome that catalogues the grammar, syntax, usage, and sayings of Crucians, and in fact all Virgin Islanders. A useful resource for anyone wishing to blend in as quickly as possible.

PHOTOGRAPHY

Danish West Indian Society. *St. Croix Historic Photos.* Denmark: Danish West Indian Society, 2011. This handsome hardback volume features more than 100 photographs of St. Croix taken from the 1860s until 1917, when the islands were transferred to the United States. Captions are well-researched and detailed.

Handler, Mauricio. *British Virgin Islands: A Photographic Portrait.* Newton, Massachusetts: Twin Lights Publishers, 2001. Veteran Virgin Islands photographer Mauricio Handler captures the natural beauty of the British Virgin Islands in this high-gloss coffee-table hardback, widely available at bookstores around the islands.

Moll, Verna Penn, ed. *Snapshots of the Past.* Road Town, Tortola: Virgin Islands National Archives, 2010. The catalogue of the first-ever historical photo exhibition to be hosted in the British Virgin Islands includes portraits and photographs of scenery, community life, commerce, architecture, and culture.

Simonsen, Steve, and Peter Mullenburg. *The U.S. Virgin Islands.* Newton, Massachusetts: Twin Lights Publishers, 2003. This book transports you right back to the beautiful islands with color photographs of St. Thomas, St. Croix, and St. John.

ARCHITECTURE

Gjessing, Frederik C., and William P. MacLean. *Historic Buildings of St Thomas and St John.* London: MacMillan, 1987. A detailed discussion of the historical buildings of St. John and St. Thomas.

LITERATURE

Moll, Verna Penn. *Johnny-Cake Country.* Colchester, Essex: Mount Sage Press, 1990. In this slim fictional account of life in the British Virgin Islands, the former chief librarian of the British Virgin Islands describes the contradictions and choices intrinsic in "development."

O'Dell, Scott. *My Name Is Not Angelica* New York: Yearling, 1989. A fictional account of the 1733 slave uprising on St. John, this book for young adults is great for grown-ups too. O'Dell's other works include Newbery winner *Island of the Blue Dolphins.*

Vanterpool, Hugo F. *Dusk to Dawn: Herald of the Virgin Islands.* Kingston, Jamaica: Kingston Publishers Ltd., 1995. Adults and teens will enjoy this story of young Allan Todman.

White, Robb. *Two on the Isle: A Memory of Marina Cay.* New York: W.W. Norton & Co., 1985. This book was originally published in the 1960s as *Our Virgin Island.* In it Robb White remembers three years spent living on Marina Cay in the British Virgin Islands in the late 1930s. The story was later turned into a movie starring Sidney Poitier and John Cassavetes, shot in the islands.

Internet Resources

TRAVEL INFORMATION
British Virgin Islands Tourist Board
www.bvitourism.com
The official tourist board website for the British Virgin Islands.

BVI Welcome
www.bviwelcome.com
An online edition of the glossy visitor magazine, BVI Welcome has feature articles on the BVI; a searchable index of hotels, restaurants, businesses, and services; and ferry schedules. You can also access the online edition of the weekly *Limin' Times,* with information on the local bandstands, upcoming events, and parties.

U.S. Virgin Islands Department of Tourism
www.visitusvi.com
The official tourism department website for the U.S. Virgin Islands. You can download marriage applications, hotel rate sheets, and press releases.

VI Now
www.vinow.com
This up-to-date website is designed to help travelers to the U.S. Virgin Islands plan their trips. There are restaurant, beach, and hotel reviews; calendars of upcoming events; a message board; ferry and cruise ship schedules; and a

marketplace where you can buy books, maps, and Virgin Islands souvenirs. Although advertising-driven, the content here is reliable and substantial.

Go to St. Croix
www.gotostcroix.com
Written by those who live on and love St. Croix, this is the best go-to resource for planning a trip to the Big Island. The events calendar is the best on the island, and the hotel, restaurant, and activities directory is reliable.

Virgin Islands Traveller
www.vitraveller.com
The blog home of *Moon Virgin Islands* author Susanna Henighan Potter, this website features stories and photographs that focus on nature, history, culture, and food, with lots of links to recent writing about Virgin Islands destinations.

NEWS
Virgin Islands Daily News
www.virginislandsdailynews.com
The website for the leading newspaper in the U.S. Virgin Islands. There is a searchable index of recent articles, tourist information, government guides, and a dining guide.

BVI Beacon
www.bvibeacon.com
The leading newspaper in the British Virgin Islands publishes synopses of the major stories of the week.

BVI Platinum
www.bviplatinum.com
An online news site with extensive coverage of the British Virgin Islands.

ZBVI Radio
www.zbviradio.com
The website of the oldest radio station in the British Virgin Islands. You can listen live through online streaming.

VI Source
www.visource.com
An online rival of the *Virgin Islands Daily News,* the VI Source posts news daily, as well as a local calendar and dining guide.

SAILING
Caribbean Weather
www.weathercarib.com
This site maintains up-to-the-minute weather information for the Virgin Islands and the entire eastern Caribbean, including official National Weather Service forecasts, tropical storm bulletins, and radar images. Ideal for mariners.

Windguru
www.windguru.com
A weather site with a cult following in the islands, this website aggregates weather models to predict wind, waves, rainfall, and cloud cover up to two weeks in advance.

National Weather Service San Juan
www.srh.noaa.gov/sju/
The National Weather Service San Juan broadcasts live radar images, weather forecasts, and tropical weather updates on this website.

U.S. Office of Coast Survey
www.nauticalcharts.noaa.gov
The National Oceanic and Atmospheric Agency is the official publisher of nautical charts in the United States, including charts covering the U.S. and British Virgin Islands. Its website has information about the most recent chart updates, the location of chart agents all over the United States, and instructions on how to order charts directly from the government. You can also download electronic nautical charts for free.

TELEPHONE DIRECTORIES
British Virgin Islands Yellow Pages
www.britishvirginislandsyp.com
A fully searchable online edition of the official phone book of the British Virgin Islands, including white pages, blue pages, and yellow pages.

U.S. Virgin Islands Phone Book
www.viphonebook.coms
The fully searchable online edition of the most widely used phone book in the U.S. Virgin Islands.

HISTORY
Danish Archives
www.virgin-islands-history.dk
An English-language website maintained by the Danish Archives, this site contains information about the history of the Danish West Indies, plus access to many of the archives related to their history.

Index

List of Maps

www.moon.com

MOON.COM is ready to help plan your next trip! Filled with fresh trip ideas and strategies, author interviews, informative travel blogs, a detailed map library, and descriptions of all the Moon guidebooks, Moon.com is all you need to get out and explore the world—or even places in your own backyard. While at Moon.com, sign up for our monthly e-newsletter for updates on new releases, travel tips, and expert advice from our on-the-go Moon authors. As always, when you travel with Moon, expect an experience that is uncommon and truly unique.

MAP SYMBOLS

▦ Expressway		🄲 Highlight		✕ Airfield		⚲ Golf Course
▤ Primary Road		○ City/Town		✖ Airport		🅿 Parking Area
▥ Secondary Road		◉ State Capital		▲ Mountain		▤ Archaeological Site
░ Unpaved Road		⊛ National Capital		✛ Unique Natural Feature		⌖ Church
- - - Trail		★ Point of Interest				⌑ Gas Station
···· Ferry		• Accommodation		⤳ Waterfall		◌ Glacier
┅ Railroad		▼ Restaurant/Bar		▲ Park		▦ Mangrove
▬ Pedestrian Walkway		▪ Other Location		⊤ Trailhead		▦ Reef
▨ Stairs		∆ Campground		⤼ Skiing Area		▦ Swamp

CONVERSION TABLES

°C = (°F - 32) / 1.8
°F = (°C x 1.8) + 32
1 inch = 2.54 centimeters (cm)
1 foot = 0.304 meters (m)
1 yard = 0.914 meters
1 mile = 1.6093 kilometers (km)
1 km = 0.6214 miles
1 fathom = 1.8288 m
1 chain = 20.1168 m
1 furlong = 201.168 m
1 acre = 0.4047 hectares
1 sq km = 100 hectares
1 sq mile = 2.59 square km
1 ounce = 28.35 grams
1 pound = 0.4536 kilograms
1 short ton = 0.90718 metric ton
1 short ton = 2,000 pounds
1 long ton = 1.016 metric tons
1 long ton = 2,240 pounds
1 metric ton = 1,000 kilograms
1 quart = 0.94635 liters
1 US gallon = 3.7854 liters
1 Imperial gallon = 4.5459 liters
1 nautical mile = 1.852 km

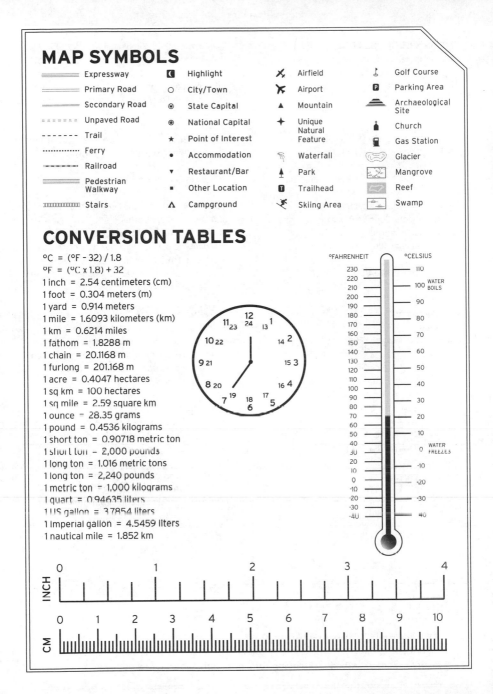

°FAHRENHEIT / °CELSIUS

WATER BOILS
WATER FREEZES

MOON VIRGIN ISLANDS

Avalon Travel
a member of the Perseus Books Group
1700 Fourth Street
Berkeley, CA 94710, USA
www.moon.com

Editor: Kevin McLain
Series Manager: Kathryn Ettinger
Copy Editor: Teresa Elsey
Graphics and Production Coordinator: Darren Alessi
Cover Designer: Darren Alessi
Map Editor: Mike Morgenfeld
Cartographers: June Thammasnong, Claire Sarraillé
Proofreader: Sabrina Young
Indexer: Rachel Kuhn

ISBN: 978-1-61238-340-8
ISSN: 1092-3357

Printing History
1st Edition – 1997
5th Edition – October 2012
5 4 3 2 1

Text © 2012 by Susanna Henighan Potter.
Maps © 2012 by Avalon Travel.
All rights reserved.

Some photos and illustrations are used by permission and are the property of the original copyright owners.

Front cover photo: Sandy Spit near Jost Van Dyke
© Belinda Images / SuperStock
Title page photo: © Susanna Henighan Potter
Interior color photos: All photos © Susanna Henighan Potter except page 7 (top and bottom right) © British Virgin Islands Tourist Board; page 12 © Carlos Villoch; page 17 © U.S. Virgin Islands Department of Tourism; page 20 (both photos) © British Virgin Islands Tourist Board

Printed in Canada by Friesens

KEEPING CURRENT

If you have a favorite gem you'd like to see included in the next edition, or see anything that needs updating, clarification, or correction, please drop us a line. Send your comments via email to feedback@moon.com, or use the address above.